# Applications of CALL Theory in ESL and EFL Environments

James Perren
*Alliant International University, USA*

Ken Kelch
*Alliant International University, USA*

Jin-suk Byun
*Alliant International University, USA*

Seth Cervantes
*Alliant International University, USA*

Setareh Safavi
*Alliant International University, USA*

A volume in the Advances in Educational Technologies and Instructional Design (AETID) Book Series

IGI Global
DISSEMINATOR OF KNOWLEDGE

Published in the United States of America by
IGI Global
Information Science Reference (an imprint of IGI Global)
701 E. Chocolate Avenue
Hershey PA, USA 17033
Tel: 717-533-8845
Fax: 717-533-8661
E-mail: cust@igi-global.com
Web site: http://www.igi-global.com



Library of Congress Cataloging-in-Publication Data

Names: Perren, James M., editor. | Kelch, Ken, 1959- editor. | Byun, Jin-suk, 1964- editor. | Cervantes, Seth, editor. | Safavi, Setareh, editor.
Title: Applications of CALL theory in ESL and EFL environments / James Perren, Ken Kelch, Jin-suk Byun, Seth Cervantes, and Setareh Safavi, Editors.
Description: Hershey : Information Science Reference, PA [2017]
Identifiers: LCCN 2017012045| ISBN 9781522529330 (hardcover) | ISBN 9781522529347 (ebook)
Subjects: LCSH: English language--Study and teaching--Computer-assisted instruction for foreign speakers. | English language--Study and teaching--Foreign speakers--Technological innovations. | English language--Study and teaching--Data processing. | Language and languages--Computer-assisted instruction. | Language and languages--Study and teaching--Technological innovations. | Language and languages--Study and teaching--Data processing. | Second language acquisition--Technological innovations. | Second language acquisition--Interactive media. | Interlanguage (language learning)--Interactive media. | Online data processing.
Classification: LCC PE1128.3 .A66 2017 | DDC 428.0078/5--dc23 LC record available at https://lccn.loc.gov/2017012045

This book is published in the IGI Global book series Advances in Educational Technologies and Instructional Design (AE-TID) (ISSN: 2326-8905; eISSN: 2326-8913)

British Cataloguing in Publication Data
A Cataloguing in Publication record for this book is available from the British Library.



For electronic access to this publication, please contact: eresources@igi-global.com.

# Advances in Educational Technologies and Instructional Design (AETID) Book Series

Lawrence A. Tomei
Robert Morris University, USA

ISSN:2326-8905
EISSN:2326-8913

## Mission

Education has undergone, and continues to undergo, immense changes in the way it is enacted and distributed to both child and adult learners. From distance education, Massive-Open-Online-Courses (MOOCs), and electronic tablets in the classroom, technology is now an integral part of the educational experience and is also affecting the way educators communicate information to students.

The **Advances in Educational Technologies & Instructional Design (AETID) Book Series** is a resource where researchers, students, administrators, and educators alike can find the most updated research and theories regarding technology's integration within education and its effect on teaching as a practice.

## Coverage

- Game-Based Learning
- Hybrid Learning
- Curriculum Development
- Instructional Design Models
- Digital Divide in Education
- Bring-Your-Own-Device
- Instructional Design
- Adaptive Learning
- K-12 Educational Technologies
- Collaboration Tools

IGI Global is currently accepting manuscripts for publication within this series. To submit a proposal for a volume in this series, please contact our Acquisition Editors at Acquisitions@igi-global.com or visit: http://www.igi-global.com/publish/.

The Advances in Educational Technologies and Instructional Design (AETID) Book Series (ISSN 2326-8905) is published by IGI Global, 701 E. Chocolate Avenue, Hershey, PA 17033-1240, USA, www.igi-global.com. This series is composed of titles available for purchase individually; each title is edited to be contextually exclusive from any other title within the series. For pricing and ordering information please visit http://www.igi-global.com/book-series/advances-educational-technologies-instructional-design/73678. Postmaster: Send all address changes to above address. 

## Titles in this Series

*For a list of additional titles in this series, please visit: www.igi-global.com/book-series*

*Handbook of Research on Instructional Systems and Educational Technology*
Terry Kidd (University of Houston-Downtown, USA) and Lonnie R. Morris, Jr. (The Chicago School of Professional Psychology, USA)
Information Science Reference • copyright 2017 • 493pp • H/C (ISBN: 9781522523994) • US $265.00 (our price)

*Applying the Flipped Classroom Model to English Language Arts Education*
Carl A. Young (North Carolina State University, USA) and Clarice M. Moran (Kennesaw State University, USA)
Information Science Reference • copyright 2017 • 277pp • H/C (ISBN: 9781522522423) • US $185.00 (our price)

*Digital Tools and Solutions for Inquiry-Based STEM Learning*
Ilya Levin (Tel Aviv University, Israel) and Dina Tsybulsky (Tel Aviv University, Israel)
Information Science Reference • copyright 2017 • 371pp • H/C (ISBN: 9781522525257) • US $180.00 (our price)

*Exploration of Textual Interactions in CALL Learning Communities Emerging Research and Opportunities*
Jonathan R. White (Högskolan Dalarna, Sweden)
Information Science Reference • copyright 2017 • 195pp • H/C (ISBN: 9781522521426) • US $120.00 (our price)

*Mobile Technologies and Augmented Reality in Open Education*
Gulsun Kurubacak (Anadolu University, Turkey) and Hakan Altinpulluk (Anadolu University, Turkey)
Information Science Reference • copyright 2017 • 366pp • H/C (ISBN: 9781522521105) • US $185.00 (our price)

*Cases on STEAM Education in Practice*
Judith Bazler (Monmouth University, USA) and Meta Van Sickle (College of Charleston, USA)
Information Science Reference • copyright 2017 • 375pp • H/C (ISBN: 9781522523345) • US $195.00 (our price)

*Handbook of Research on Driving STEM Learning With Educational Technologies*
María-Soledad Ramírez-Montoya (Tecnologico de Monterrey, Mexico)
Information Science Reference • copyright 2017 • 590pp • H/C (ISBN: 9781522520269) • US $300.00 (our price)

*Integrating an Awareness of Selfhood and Society into Virtual Learning*
Andrew Stricker (The Air University, USA) Cynthia Calongne (Colorado Technical University, USA) Barbara Truman (University of Central Florida, USA) and Fil Arenas (The Air University, USA)
Information Science Reference • copyright 2017 • 363pp • H/C (ISBN: 9781522521822) • US $200.00 (our price)

IGI Global
DISSEMINATOR OF KNOWLEDGE

701 East Chocolate Avenue, Hershey, PA 17033, USA
Tel: 717-533-8845 x100 • Fax: 717-533-8661
E-Mail: cust@igi-global.com • www.igi-global.com

# Dedication

*The editors would like to dedicate this book to the educators we have met over the years who actively and enthusiastically share their expertise with technology, such as Dr. Elton Robertson (Temple University, Philadelphia, Pennsylvania). He will be remembered as a professor of technology who diligently prioritized teaching teacher candidates to use technology to accomplish learning objectives rather than for the sake of simply using technology. Dr. Robertson left his students with smiles on their faces by using humor to teach a difficult subject. Dr. Robertson was the master of the CITE Department computer/technology lab for educators and he will be missed.*

# Editorial Advisory Board



# List of Reviewers

Steve Pryzmus, *Texas Christian University, USA*
Patrick T. Randolph, *The University of Nebraska – Lincoln, USA*
Victoria Russell, *Valdosta State University, USA*
Andre Scholze, *Eastern Michigan University, USA*
Claire (Hee Eun) Yang, *Alliant International University, USA*

# Table of Contents

# Detailed Table of Contents



This chapter examines the need for a theoretically-informed approach to collaborative English for Academic Purpose (EAP) pedagogy and research. It discusses the relevance of online collaborative learning in EAP and the call for a theoretically-informed facilitative framework to guide the use of online collaborative writing tools to sustain learning communities and language learning. It establishes the importance of virtual learning communities as catalysts for online collaboration and discusses the need to examine technological affordances, adopting an ecological perspective to inform curricular design. The chapter examines the relevance of the Community of Inquiry model and its three presences: cognitive, social and teaching, as a theoretical basis to inform a facilitative framework to design online collaborative EAP writing tasks. The chapter concludes with a discussion of the interactions of these three presences, details on how they can inform online EAP collaborative writing practices and the need for future research in this area.



The primary goal of this chapter is to review two dominant theories of technology and propose a new direction of theory and practice for teaching and learning of English as an additional language. I describe this new direction as a cultural theory of technological mediation. The chapter is divided into three sections. In the first section, I review some dominant theoretical approaches in the literature on CALL. In the second section, I discuss two theories of technology: technological determinism and technological instrumentalism. In the third section, I argue that both determinism and instrumentalism have remained as dominant theoretical approaches in the field of CALL. I discuss why both of these approaches are problematic. Then I propose an alternative to these theoretical approaches. I conclude the chapter by providing three pedagogical principles and a set of heuristic questions that may be helpful for language teachers and language-education researchers.

The primary aim of this chapter is to investigate the effectiveness of Computer Assisted Language Learning (CALL) technologies, tools, and resources for figurative language in general and idiom learning in particular. The secondary aim is to explore the CALL training practices affecting the attainment of idiomaticity in English as a second or foreign language. Idiomaticity training is anchored in an online methodology of idiomaticity teaching that takes into account learners' interests and active involvement. Such focus is particularly useful for the purposes of diagnosis and achievement, and the research to date is a promising start to further work on idiomaticity. The chapter provides recommendations for idiomaticity training-and-teaching as well as time-tested practices for further theorizing and research. It is hoped that the practices and recommendations explored here will spur on more research in this vein. Pedagogical and research implications are also discussed.



The field of computer-assisted language learning (CALL) has grown in terms of second language acquisition (SLA) theory. Researchers have linked sociocultural theories to CALL, noting that technologies can create communities of practice. Although many L2 learners and language teachers are proficient in the use of technology, this does not mean they can use it systematically to learn or teach. The aim of this chapter is to connect current sociocultural perspectives with CALL-based technologies. The first part discusses interactionist and sociocultural theories of SLA and shows how technology can build communities of practice, encourage reflection, and ultimately promote autonomous learning. The second section describes three CALL-based practices: (1) wikis, (2) role-playing games, and (3) online record-keeping. Each description, links these practices to sociocultural perspectives of SLA theory and TESOL Technology Standards (TTS).



The chapter introduces a case study of online language teacher education in a TESOL master's course. Drawing on sociocultural theories, it aims to investigate the patterns of interactions among students and the instructor in online teacher training, and factors that shape the efficacy of quality online language teacher education. Various domains of data were collected and analyzed using analytical codes such as employed tools, participation patterns, rules of interactions, divisions of labor among participants, and goals. The findings suggest that the teacher trainee participants increased active participation among themselves, promoting mutually supportive relationships. The students' participation and learning outcomes were shaped by the learning communities they built, along with diverse pedagogical interests and different perceptions of collaborative work.

This empirical research study inquires as to whether teachers of English as a Second Language and teachers of English as a Foreign Language apply the technological tool–YouTube videos–into their English teaching with the same purposes and approaches. This chapter addresses a variety of activities that teachers in two different ESL and EFL contexts utilize to integrate YouTube videos into their English teaching. Ten teachers from a university in the USA (ESL context) and a university in Vietnam (EFL context) were recruited for this study. The results demonstrate similarities and the differences in the use of YouTube videos and how both ESL and EFL students agree with the potential applications of YouTube videos to maintain students' attention and make them feel motivated in the lesson content. Also reported in this chapter is that ESL teachers believe YouTube videos are a great tool for reflection activities and dealing with challenging content issues, whereas EFL teachers mainly use them as a native-speaking modeling in class for doing language drills and grammatical practice.



This chapter discusses the pitfalls and promises of electronic portfolio assessment for English language learners in high school classrooms in the United States. In a three-year federally funded program designed to improve academic performance among culturally and linguistically diverse students at an urban high school in Honolulu, Hawaii, the author implemented electronic portfolio assessment (EPA) into academic English and heritage language classrooms. This chapter delineates how EPA was developed to enhance academic and linguistic abilities of adolescent ELLs while embracing their multifaceted and hybrid identities. It also presents both challenges and benefits that teachers and students experienced in the process of EPA. It concludes with suggestions for developing and implementing EPA for English language learners in similar contexts.



Among the many facets of Computer Assisted Language Learning (CALL), studies using computer language corpora have risen to considerable prominence in research agendas. The author argues that corpora are useful tools for practicing teachers. However, the myth that corpus-based research is too complicated to be useful for teachers in pedagogical contexts. This chapter strives to dispel that myth by synthesizing a wealth of research and their accompanying pedagogical applications. Secondly, it shares specific pedagogical activities to implement corpus data in classroom teaching. These corpus-informed classroom strategies provide concrete examples that will assist TESOL/TEFL teachers in making their coursework authentic and therefore more meaningful to students learning language.

Researchers and practitioners' interest in finding more effective ways to provide instructional feedback in order to help second language learners in online environments has increased. The majority of studies found evidence about effectiveness of written and oral feedback to improve student's writing in a target language when they enroll in online courses taught in English. However, some studies also found limitations of both types of feedback when they provided for second language learners. Therefore, researchers and practitioners investigated benefits of other types of feedback and among them is audio feedback. The purpose of this chapter is to overview instructional capabilities of written, oral and audio feedback and how they can support ESL and EFL students in asynchronous online courses. This chapter also discusses when and how to provide different types of feedback when ESL and EFL students are enrolled in online courses taught in English.



Flipped learning is an innovative educational model in which content that is traditionally presented in class is completed at home, and in class, students work on applying what they have learned at home to engage in interactive and collaborative activities. Over the past five years, flipped learning has found a strong voice within the field of the field of Teaching English to Speakers of Other Languages (TESOL), as evidenced by the rapid increase in conference presentations, research, and publications noting its implementation. In this chapter, the authors provide an overview of the flipped learning approach within English language instruction. Included is a discussion of flipped learning's evolution and an analysis of current research that identifies areas of consensus, issues, and controversies. Finally, the authors offer six recommendations for implementing flipped learning in English language classrooms and conclude with future directions for inquiry into flipped learning in TESOL.



The purpose of this chapter is twofold (1) to review the benefits of online videogames for promoting second language acquisition (SLA), specifically massive multiplayer online role-playing games (MMORPGs) and (2) to present new research that seeks to explain why and how MMORPGs may be beneficial. The findings from the research indicate that MMORPGs are beneficial to SLA primarily because they provide opportunities for interaction in the target language through participation in collaborative problem solving tasks. The results of the research presented in this chapter show (1) that the requirements of input and output for successful gaming allow for a type of interaction in which the focus on language form leads to modified-output, (2) that players have opportunities to negotiate input as a means of completing in-game tasks, and (3) that in-game tasks are similar to instructional tasks that are believed to be beneficial for SLA in the context of a classroom.

This chapter sheds light on the potential impact of CALL theory and practice on the language and identity socialization of transnational children when educators imagine and promote interaction beyond the classroom. The authors focus specifically on the educational trajectories of 1) children returnees, who were born in Mexico, at some point in their lives moved to the U.S., and then returned to Mexico and 2) international migrants, born and many attended school in the U.S., and then moved to Mexico as a result of repatriation and/or deportation. The authors advocate creating blended affinity spaces at schools where youth can meet and play digital role-playing games, discuss game-ecology literacy development within these spaces, detail the implementation of such spaces in schools, and share game screen shots, blog posts, and the perspectives of transnational students that support this kind of learning within the EFL environment.



Rapid advancement in technology has altered the way language education is conceptualized and practiced. Technological tools, when effectively integrated with appropriate pedagogical foundations, can enhance the quality of teaching and learning experiences. Augmented reality (AR) has emerged as one of the latest technologies offering a new way to bridge virtual and reality worlds. Due to the widespread proliferation of digital technology, the implementation of AR on mobile devices such as smartphones and tablets has become a growing trend in educational settings. Regardless of the advantages that AR technology brings to language classrooms, there have been very few studies exploring the design, evaluation, and applications of AR for educational purposes. Therefore, this chapter aims to (a) introduce AR technology in learning environments, (b) embrace its potentials and foreseeable hindrances to language education, (c) discuss practical and applicable ways to use this merging technology effectively in the classroom, and (d) propose some issues for future research.

# Foreword

It would have been impossible in the 1980s when our ESL/TESOL faculty at a private U.S. university first introduced microcomputers into their academic ESL writing classes to predict where computer-assisted language learning (CALL) would take us three decades later. We did not foresee that we would be using hybrid and online platforms to train TESOL teachers, nor did we visualize that our TESOL graduate programs would feature CALL courses that explored the use of Web 2.0 tools, virtual worlds, or social media for language teaching. Rather, our previous CALL experience had been limited to experimenting with early ESL grammar courseware that served primarily as a tutor and drillmaster. I personally could not have imagined that I would become a passionate researcher and practitioner of CALL and certainly never envisioned authoring articles and books on that topic, but that is the path my TESOL career took.

Looking back, it is fascinating to observe how the developments and paradigm shifts in technology and second language acquisition (SLA) theory and pedagogy were so frequently intertwined. The evolution of these dual fields was never linear, but rather each era drew upon previous technologies and teaching practices as TESOL educators adapted to the latest technological and pedagogical breakthroughs. In the 1950s and 1960s, the behaviorists and structural linguistic theories of the Audio-Lingual Method (ALM) easily meshed with program instruction in which the computer was viewed as a task-master that allowed students to learn linguistic patterns. In the 1970s and 1980s, one of the most pivotal changes in language teaching occurred with the emergence of the Communicative Language Teaching (CLT) approaches. Language teaching focused on the authentic use of language that required language learners to negotiate meaning in real world situations that extended beyond the classroom. It was against the CLT backdrop demanding increased interaction and expanded communication opportunities that the invention of the microchip led to the widespread introduction of the personal computer into language classrooms in the 1980s and 1990s. The computer became a vehicle that allowed students to interact via email, provided multimedia tools and experiences that increased student engagement, and offered powerful applications such as the word processor that were aligned with the TESOL pedagogy of that time. The expansion of the Web and access to the Internet in the 1990s permitted the computer to play a more integrative role in support of new directions in second language teaching including the expansion of the CLT umbrella to include task-based language teaching (TBLT) and the global adoption of content-based English for specific disciplines.

With the turn of the century came the second generation of web-based tools (Web 2.0) including blogs, podcasts, wikis, Google Docs, and web-based videos combined with the expansion of social networks, digital games and virtual worlds. These new resources perfectly supported interaction and social constructivist theories and vastly expanded the integrative and social nature of CALL by affording students the ability to participate in collaborative learning communities and share knowledge in more creative and personal ways. Students could engage in synchronous oral communication instead of relying solely on text to establish a social as well as cognitive presence online. The massive multiplayer online roleplaying games (MMORPGs) extended games-based language learning far beyond the physical classroom to virtual worlds. As digital devices including smartphones and tablets became more mobile and accessible, teachers began to recognize their potential to harness the interest and engagement of students for language learning purposes. With these devices, students were also able to take advantage of short durations of time and limited spaces for mobile-assisted language practice outside of the classroom. We are now witnessing the normalization of digital and social media that have rapidly become an integral part of our students' daily lives. This trend will only increase as the next generation of "digital natives" comes of age and continues to forge new paths with the technologies of the future.

Another transformational phenomenon in the CALL context has been the rapid adoption of online teaching in ESL, EFL and TESOL teacher training. Today's computer-mediated communication tools and platforms can provide both synchronous and asynchronous delivery modes with varying components of online experience ranging from instruction delivered exclusively online to a hybrid format that utilizes both classroom and online instruction, to use solely as supplementary resources in support of classroom instruction. With the dramatic proliferation of TESOL degree and certificate programs offered online globally, it is imperative that the TESOL community prepares both teachers of English learners and teacher trainers to understand the contextual aspects of online teaching. The international TESOL professional organization has provided guidelines to meet this challenge with the publication of the TESOL technology standards. It is important to note that for online TESOL-CALL courses, technology is both content and the delivery medium compelling us to address a wide array of related issues and research questions. As we move forward, it will be increasingly crucial that we draw upon a multitude of fields including linguistics, education, psychology, sociology, information and communication technology, and artificial intelligence to develop a CALL theoretical framework that will facilitate fruitful research and support innovative practices for the future.

This call to action brings me back to my narrative recalling early CALL in our ESL classrooms and the purpose of this book. Just as our TESOL faculty in the 1980s and 1990s navigated the advances in technology and paradigm shifts in language teaching, the current faculty of that same TESOL program have encountered exponential technological changes as they both utilize technology in their own teaching and prepare the next generation of TESOL teachers to be effective CALL users. Though I have recently retired from their university, I have had the privilege of observing the extraordinary enthusiasm of these experts as they compiled a comprehensive volume of state-of-the-art articles that tackles the most pressing theoretical and pedagogical issues of today's CALL. This editorial team was uniquely qualified for this task. Over their distinguished careers, the editors of this book have successfully developed and taught ESL, EFL, TESOL and CALL courses in numerous countries and have conducted research, authored scholarly works, and presented internationally on critical TESOL, CALL, and teacher education topics. As director, faculty, and program developers of a regionally accredited online TESOL master's program and a state approved online k-12 teacher certificate program, they have navigated first-hand the complicated administrative, curricular, contextual, and pedagogical considerations that such programs entail.

Whether the reader is a novice teacher or an experienced CALL teacher trainer, this collection of articles, written by TESOL and CALL experts from a variety of countries and cultures, provides an extraordinary resource for TESOL professionals seeking to exploit the power of contemporary CALL. The articles provide important insights through a balance of both qualitative and quantitative research into the theories and practices that inform CALL. Throughout the book, the authors make connections between new perspectives and CALL practices and suggest innovative models and theories like the "Community of Inquiry Model" or the "Cultural Theory of Technological Mediation" to help construct a contemporary theoretical framework for CALL. They also explore creative ways for forging new directions of existing CALL practices as they, for example, reconsider the role of corpora in the digital classroom or compare the integration of web-based videos in ESL and EFL contexts. The book examines the utilization of CALL-mediated, online and hybrid platforms for specific goals such as encouraging stronger engagement of EFL pre-service teachers or providing feedback in ESL and EFL asynchronous contexts. It also focuses on cutting-edge CALL applications and instructional practices such as the use of augmented reality (AR) or massive multiplayer online role playing games (MMORPGs) for language teaching, or the efficacy of the flipped instructional approach for the TESOL context.

My hope is that this book, with its compelling research studies, insightful theoretical and pedagogical discussions, and detailed presentations of highly practical CALL applications, will inspire its readers to become the CALL-using teachers, researchers, program designers, and teacher trainers who will lead the TESOL field into the next era of computer-assisted language learning and teaching.

*Mary Ellen Butler-Pascoe*
*Alliant International University, USA*

# Preface

## INTRODUCTION TO CALL THEORY AND ONLINE TESOL PEDAGOGY

By 2019, roughly half of all college courses will be delivered online. This statement reflects an important interpretation of the changing delivery options for education as described in recent research in higher education (Selingo, 2015). How will TESOL educators be trained and prepare themselves to meet this demand? What theories will guide global TESOL educators to maintain principled teaching practice? What academic disciplines offer suitable theories to support our developing interpretations, planning, implementation, and evaluation of successful use of technology for English as a second language pedagogy? What specific skills, knowledge, attitudes, and dispositions are needed to meet this online teaching demand in ESL and EFL contexts? Selingo (2015) surveyed approximately 400 presidents at four-year colleges regarding their attitudes concerning financial sustainability, college rankings, and student outcomes. One key finding from the survey is that one of the top two strategies college presidents are using to generate revenue is through offering online courses to their students (Selingo, 2015, p. 11). In this Chronicle of Higher Education Special Presidents' Report, the rapidly changing reality of online pedagogy in American higher education is startling.

This growing demand implies a sense of urgency specifically for online TESOL teacher training, and by extension, necessitates contributing to the discussion of what theories to utilize to better meet these pedagogical demands. Given that the difficulties inherent in implementing TESOL teacher training with CALL have been well documented (Kessler, 2006, 2007; Healey et al., 2011; Hubbard, 2008) and specifically the challenges with online TESOL teacher training as well as teaching for online English learning (England, 2012, Kouritzin, 2002; Norton & Nunan, 2002; Pawan, Wiechart, Warren, & Park, 2016), how is this training to be conducted efficiently? How can CALL theory reinforce the teacher training process and provide guidance for quality training and instruction for this demand placed on the profession? Part of this discussion acknowledges that a definition of CALL theory is needed since CALL in ESL and EFL environments is one component in an applied field. CALL theory, according to Hubbard (2008), is:

*The set of perspectives, models, frameworks, and specific theories that offer generalizations to account for phenomena related to the use of computers in all their forms in the pursuit of language learning and teaching objectives, to ground relevant research agendas, and to inform effective CALL practice. (p. 2)*

One aim of this edited collection is to add to the expanding conversation about how CALL and CALL theory are developing even though disagreement is expressed concerning whether CALL theory is needed (Egbert & Hanson Smith, 2007; Hubbard, 2016). Part of this focus was learning more about interdisciplinary conceptual combinations that shed light on the complex and dynamic intersection of online TESOL pedagogy and CALL theory application and development.

The terms, practices, and principles associated with online learning have developed over its history, with practitioners and scholars offering multiple ways in which to define and interpret this facet of the educational field (Goertler, 2011). For example, blended learning, due in part to its popularity with students and administrators alike, appears to be in a position of permanence and is likely to increase in demand (Allen & Seaman, 2010; Goertler, 2011). The benefits of online teaching and learning for the provider and the recipient confirm an equality of focus for both a specified institutional convenience and for learning (Allen & Seaman, 2010; Goertler, 2011). Nevertheless, it is also documented that lack of information, training, and experience with online education has led to frustration among both learners and teachers (Allen, Seaman, & Garrett, 2007).

In response to a systematic review of online TESOL pedagogy, the successes and challenges of online language teaching programs have been documented for at least two decades (Egbert & Hanson-Smith, 1999; England, 2012; Kouritzin, 2002; Levy & Stockwell, 2006; Norton & Nunan, 2002; Pawan, et al., 2016). Some of this research centers on the development of ESL programs delivered fully online or in a particular configuration of blended learning (Banados, 2006). Equally relevant is the argument that "certain elements take on added importance" for online teaching and learning, which is based on TESOL technology standards (Healey et al., 2011, p. 163). Within this framework, the following areas are prioritized for online instruction: technology infrastructure, appropriate learning environment, time management, and participant presence.

## HOW DOES THE CALL LITERATURE ADDRESS THE CHALLENGES OF ONLINE TESOL PEDAGOGY?

Current online TESOL pedagogy research is expanding with a variety of contributions focusing on topics such as teacher training (Douglas & Paton, 2013; England, 2012; Pawan et al., 2016; Peachey, 2013), general English learning (Bilgin, 2013), and English for Specific Purposes (Kern, 2013; Whittaker, 2013). These scholarly resources reflect a growing body of research in CALL and TESOL that integrate context-specific solutions to online ESL and EFL pedagogy constraints as well as answering key questions about TESOL teacher training which incorporate technology. Several example publications with a focus on second language education serve as a useful backdrop to explain where the current book is situated and how it provides intersecting interpretations.

The text, "TESOL Technology Standards: Description, Implementation, Integration," (Healey et al., 2011), was one of the first publications on the market to focus exclusively on technology standards in the field of TESOL directed to both learners and teachers. The authors provide a solid description of the contexts in which the *technology standards* have been developed, but leaves room for specific guidance that practicing online TESOL educators can use regarding real-world pedagogical challenges and effective classroom procedures. Nicolson, Murphy, and Southgate (2011) offer a comprehensive overview of the key issues with blended instruction and developmental issues that may arise for teachers. Their text examines the impact of different learning environments (such as online, face-to-face, and telephone) on pedagogic practice and language learner support, and recognizes the particular sociocultural, psycholinguistic, and cognitive issues that must be taken into account when working with diverse adult language learners in blended settings. Although some of the research presented from this text informs practice in the CALL field, an increased emphasis on systematic and rigorous empiricism would strengthen our understanding of this area. Similarly, Sharma and Barrett (2007) provide language teachers with a practical overview of the technology available at the time, but does not focus specifically on ESL-related issues with online and blended pedagogy. More directly related to CALL theory application is the work of Arnold and Ducate (2011), which provides a collection of interpretations of CALL theory and research.

## JOINING THE ACADEMIC DISCUSSION IN ONLINE TESOL PEDAGOGY AND RESEARCH

In this section, examples are given to show how the content of the current book overlaps with the expanding online TESOL pedagogy literature. Two recent publications relevant to online TESOL pedagogy are edited collections with a TESOL focus (England, 2012; Pawan et al., 2016). England (2012) advanced the discussion of online TESOL pedagogy and emphasized that an increasing number of employers require ESL/EFL teachers to hold a master's degree in TESOL with a substantial and growing number of these teachers developing the necessary professionalization through online instruction (England, 2012). One strength of the England (2012) publication is its inclusion of primary research and case studies of various programs, which provides the reader with reports on the ways in which online programming is changing. England also relates the application of theory to online TESOL pedagogy, including sociocultural theory and communities of practice. A second relevant publication about online TESOL pedagogy prioritizes pedagogy over technology in order to determine characteristics of quality online instruction (Pawan et al., 2016). This publication offers relevant interpretations for applying foundational teaching theories to online pedagogy for both language teacher education and language teaching.

The current edited collection extends this dialogue by highlighting practical responses to context-related technology issues. Several chapters in this book develop concrete connections between CALL theory and online instructional challenges that go beyond *atheoretical* first generation CALL research (Hubbard, 2016), research with "happy" conclusions (Anwaruddin, this volume) and cursory pedagogical implication based on limited to no data collection and analysis (cf. Perren & Wurr, 2015 and *teacher testimonial* research). In addition, various chapters advance our understanding of key concepts such as teaching presence in online learning (England, 2012; Healey et al., 2011; Johnston & Lawrence, this volume; Olesova & de Oliveira, this volume). Another topic of interest is the promotion of active learning and the connection to flipped learning (Kostka & Marshall, this volume). *Third spaces* is an additional concept addressed in Pawan et al. (2016) that suggests ways the online medium provides a safe environment and a shared reality for students (see also Romo Smith & Pryzmus, this volume). Assessment is also a topic presented in the current book that continues the refinement of quality testing and evaluation concepts and practices in CALL and online TESOL pedagogy (see chapters by Monfared, et al., and Cho, both in this volume).

It is equally important to note that England (2012) and Pawan et al. (2016) both represent CALL theory (in relation to online pedagogy) progressing along a CALL theory development continuum. This edited collection contains chapters aligning theoretical interpretations of *theory borrowing* and "more interesting" *theory adaptations* for accommodating differences inherent in the computer-mediated context (Hubbard, 2016, p. 2). Furthermore, the chapters in the current collection contribute further to the online TESOL pedagogy research with evidence of (1) CALL theory synthesis and theory creation, and

(2) providing possibilities for exploration of CALL theory instantiation and CALL ensembles (Hubbard, 2009a, 2016; Hubbard & Levy, 2016). This current book strengthens online CALL theory by building on previous scholarship in online TESOL pedagogy and research in order to promote pedagogical best practices. The impetus for this decision stems from that CALL scholarship which argues that instead of researching CALL vs. non-CALL related language learning activities, which has not yielded significant research results (Hubbard, 2016), that a more productive empirical route is to examine online TESOL contexts and settings for their own value, as in the chapter on different uses of YouTube in TESOL (Dinh, this volume). Moreover, with the increased use of and interest in online teaching and CALL in TESOL, this collection offers an array of innovative online CALL projects that respond to, extend, or critique earlier works, and which apply a variety of established and emerging theoretical frameworks to systematic and rigorous data collection and analysis. The goal of this current publication is to contribute to the next generation of online TESOL pedagogy and CALL scholarship.

## PURPOSE, AUDIENCE, AND INSPIRATION

This book is intended to inform the reader of international applications of CALL theory and in particular, for online delivery of TESOL related content. This publication also explores the thought processes, guiding theoretical frameworks, and practical steps international scholars have initiated in specific global settings. Another purpose of the current text is to provide an update on rapidly evolving TESOL teacher education issues. We hope that through this book the reader can extract approaches to successfully integrating technology for ESL/EFL learning and for teacher training programs based on pedagogical principles informed by theoretical foundations.

This volume includes chapters that focus on blended learning in a variety of configurations, from fully online contexts to face-to-face learning situations with an online component. Additionally, this collection offers a balance of empirical research projects combined with numerous survey reports on a variety of CALL topics in TESOL. The primary audience for this publication are TESOL educators worldwide, as well as educators in other disciplines and contexts who may have English language learners. Readers are encouraged to explore the book's content as a point of departure for ways to scrutinize a number of relevant CALL themes.

The inspiration for this current text is the normalized use of technology in language teaching and language teacher education. That is, both increasing our understanding of how to improve our own online instruction and contributing to the academic discussion, were sources of inspiration to the editors. Discovering solutions for training TESOL educators to more effectively address the needs of the growing number of digital native students is based on raising awareness about how quality use of technology is grounded in a sufficient understanding of the skills, history, trends, and standards emanating from CALL research and teacher training *for* technology (Healey et al., 2011; Hubbard, 2016; Smaldino, Lowther, Mims, & Russell, 2015). Finally, the genesis of this text also came from the five co-editors' interest in and experience with online delivery of TESOL instructional content. It is our belief that early adopters likely experience a considerable amount of trial and error as they refine their instructional delivery based on planning, implementation, and evaluation. It is also important to point out that technology use in various contexts around the globe will vary considerably depending on in which of the three domains (circles) of Kachru's Concentric Circles Model the instruction is situated (Kachru, 1992). It was our goal to know more about these features and contexts and to share this knowledge with others.

## ORGANIZATION OF THE BOOK

The book is organized into 16 chapters outlined in the section that follows, with a brief overview highlighting salient points of each chapter. We recognize that our arrangement of the chapters is but one of numerous ways in which the collected chapters communicate with each other. We encourage readers to explore alternate readings and arrangements that best suit their individual purposes.

Chapter 1 examines the need for a more theoretically-informed approach to collaborative English for Academic Purposes (EAP) pedagogy and research. The authors discuss the relevance of online collaborative learning and the use of writing tools to sustain virtual learning communities as catalysts for online collaboration.

Chapter 2 compares two dominant theories of technology to a new direction of theory and practice for teaching and learning of English described as Cultural Theory of Technological Mediation. Dominant theoretical approaches in the CALL literature are reviewed followed by discussion of the alternative theory aligned with three pedagogical principles.

Chapter 3 investigates the effectiveness of Computer Assisted Language Learning technologies, tools, and resources for figurative language in general and idiom learning in particular. The chapter provides recommendations for idiomaticity training and teaching, as well as time-tested practices for further theorizing and research.

Chapter 4 connects current second language acquisition theory with CALL-based teaching and classroom practices. The authors indicate that sociocultural and constructivist theories linked to CALL potentially create digital communities of practice while strengthening existing ones.

Chapter 5 introduces a case study of online language teacher education in a TESOL graduate course that draws on sociocultural theories to investigate interaction patterns among participants in online teacher training.

Chapter 6 addresses a variety of YouTube video activities used by teachers in two different contexts: ESL in the USA and EFL in Vietnam. The results demonstrate the similarities and differences in the use of YouTube videos and teacher beliefs concerning the technology.

Chapter 7 discusses the pitfalls and promises of electronic portfolio assessment (EPA) for English language learners in high school classrooms in the United States. The author delineates how EPA was developed to enhance academic and linguistic abilities of adolescent ELLs while embracing their multifaceted and hybrid identities. This chapter also presents both challenges and benefits that teachers and students experienced in the process of implementing EPA.

Chapter 8 attempts to dispel that myth of corpora being too complex for classroom use. The author synthesizes the rich tradition of research in corpora focusing on pedagogical implications and insights. The author then offers workable techniques to implement corpus data in the CALL classroom.

Chapter 9 investigates whether hybrid instruction has a positive effect on the development of students' knowledge of English grammar and editing skills, as well as whether learners have positive perceptions of the hybrid design. The authors conducted a study with two sections of an English grammar and editing skills class: one hybrid course and the other face-to-face.

Chapter 10 describes the implementation of an online learning management system, Edmodo, and the activities that were used in an EFL class to improve student engagement. The primary influencing factors of student engagement are highlighted by the authors as teacher instructions, Internet connection quality, and specific Edmodo features.

Chapter 11 situates the current state of teaching and assessing English for Specific Purposes (ESP) at the University of Bucharest, Romania. The author discusses ways in which technology-integrated teaching methods have begun to shape both the content and the delivery format of the specialized English class and to renew the task-based framework on which the course is developed.

Chapter 12 provides an overview of instructional capabilities of written, oral and audio feedback and how they can support ESL and EFL students in asynchronous online courses. The author discusses when and how to provide different types of feedback for ESL and EFL students enrolled in online courses taught in English.

Chapter 13 offers an overview of flipped learning as an educational approach and its early emergence in TESOL. The authors review and discuss present research on its application to language learning, examining issues, addressing controversies, and offering recommendations for pedagogy.

Chapter 14 reviews the benefits of online video games for promoting L2 acquisition, specifically massive multiplayer online role-playing games (MMORPGs), and presents new research that seeks to explain why and how MMORPGs may be beneficial. The authors indicate that MMORPGs are beneficial to L2 acquisition primarily because they provide opportunities for interaction in the target language through participation in collaborative problem-solving tasks.

Chapter 15 describes the potential impact of CALL theory and practice on the language and identity socialization of transnational children in Mexico when educators imagine and promote interaction beyond the classroom. The authors advocate creating blended affinity spaces at schools for digital role-playing games, discuss game-ecology literacy development, and detail the implementation of such spaces in schools.

Chapter 16 introduces Augmented Reality (AR) technology in learning environments by embracing its potentials and foreseeable hindrances to language education. The authors discuss practical uses for this emerging technology effectively in the classroom and propose issues for future research.

This preface closes with the quote, “Computer assisted language learning (CALL) is both exciting and frustrating as a field of research and practice. It is exciting because it is complex, dynamic and quickly changing – and it is frustrating for the same reasons” (Hubbard, 2009b, p. 1). The aim here is to promote the idea that what is presented in this publication is of little value if not considered in concert with previous and future empiricism examining CALL, CALL theory, and online TESOL pedagogy. Utilizing multiple perspectives for how to guide online TESOL educators to theorize from their CALL practice, and to practice what they CALL theorize (Kumaravadivelu, 2006), will likely be further strengthened by embracing a combination of established CALL foundations with online TESOL pedagogy innovations as they emerge. This will hopefully allow global TESOL educators to devote themselves to the growing demand of online pedagogy indicated earlier in the Chronicle of Higher Education special report (Selingo, 2015) regardless of the complexities. We hope that by reading this book TESOL educators can stay informed of the ‘quick changes’ and replace the potential frustrations of CALL implementation with the confidence and joy of fulfilling their students’ learning needs *in* technology and *with* technology.

*James Perren*
*Alliant International University, USA*

*Ken Kelch*
*Alliant International University, USA*

## REFERENCES

Allen, I. E., & Seaman, J. (2010). *Learning on demand: Online education in the United States, 2009.* Babson Research Group. Retrieved from http://files.eric.ed.gov/fulltext/ED529931.pdf

Allen, I. E., Seaman, J., & Garret, R. (2007). *Blending in: The extent and promise of blended education in the United States.* Retrieved from https://www.onlinelearningsurvey.com/reports/blending-in.pdf

Banados, E. (2006). A blended-learning pedagogical model for teaching and learning EFL successfully through an online interactive multimedia environment. *CALICO Journal*, *23*(3), 533–550.

Bilgin, H. (2013). Students' CALLing: Blended learning for students. In B. Tomlinson & C. Whittaker (Eds.), *Blended learning in English language teaching: Course design and implementation* (pp. 207–211). London: British Council.

Douglas, J., & Paton, C. (2013). The Cambridge CELTA course online. In B. Tomlinson & C. Whittaker (Eds.), *Blended learning in English language teaching: Course design and implementation* (pp. 111–123). London: British Council.

Egbert, J., & Hanson-Smith, E. (Eds.). (1999). Computers and pedagogy: CALL environments (Research, practice, and critical issues). Alexandria, VA: TESOL.

England, L. (2012). *Online language teacher education: TESOL perspectives.* New York, NY: Routledge.

Goertler, S. (2011). Blended and open/online learning: Adapting to a changing world of language teaching. In N. Arnold & L. Ducate (Eds.), *Present and future promises of CALL: From theory and research to new directions in language teaching* (pp. 471–502). San Marcos, TX: CALICO.

Healey, D., Hanson-Smith, D., Hubbard, P., Ioannou-Georgiou, S., Kessler, G., & Ware, P. (2011). *TESOL technology standards: Description, implementation, integration.* Alexandria, VA: TESOL.

Hubbard, P. (2008). Twenty-five years of theory in the CALICO Journal. *CALICO Journal 25*(3), 387-399. Retrieved from https://www.calico.org/html/article_707.pdf

Hubbard, P. (2009a). Developing CALL theory: A new frontier. *Proceedings of the JALTCALL Conference*, 1-6.

Hubbard, P. (Ed.). (2009b). Computer assisted language learning: Vol. 1. *Critical concepts in linguistics.* London: Routledge.

Hubbard, P. (2016). *An invitation to CALL: Foundations in computer-assisted language learning.* Retrieved from: http://www.stanford.edu/~efs/callcourse2/CALL6.htm

Hubbard, P., & Levy, M. (2016). Theory in computer-assisted language learning research and practice. In F. Farr & L. Murray (Eds.), *The Routledge handbook of language learning and technology* (pp. 24–38). New York, NY: Routledge.

Kachru, B. (1992). *The other tongue: English across cultures* (2nd ed.). Urbana, IL: University of Illinois Press.

Kern, N. (2013). Blended learning: Podcasts for taxi drivers. In B. Tomlinson & C. Whittaker (Eds.), *Blended learning in English language teaching: Course design and implementation* (pp. 131–139). London: British Council.

Kessler, G. (2006). Assessing CALL teacher training: What are we doing and what could we do better? In P. Hubbard & M. Levy (Eds.), *Teacher education in CALL* (pp. 23–42). Amsterdam: John Benjamins. doi:10.1075/lllt.14.05kes

Kessler, G. (2007). Formal and informal CALL preparation and teacher attitude toward technology. *Computer Assisted Language Learning, 21*(3), 173–188. doi:10.1080/09588220701331394

Kouritzin, S. G. (2002). The personal, practical, and professional rewards of teaching MA-TESOL courses online. *TESOL Quarterly, 36*(4), 621–624. doi:10.2307/3588244

Kumaravadivelu, B. (2006). *Understanding language teaching: From method to postmethod.* Mahwah, NJ: Lawrence Erlbaum.

Levy, M., & Stockwell, G. (2006). *CALL dimensions: Options and issues in computer-assisted language learning*. Mahwah, NJ: Lawrence Erlbaum.

Nicolson, M., Murphy, L., & Southgate, M. (Eds.). (2011). *Language teaching in blended contexts.* Edinburgh, UK: Dunedin Academic Press.

Norton, B., & Nunan, D. (2002). Teaching MA-TESOL courses online: Challenges and rewards. *TESOL Quarterly, 36*(4), 617–621. doi:10.2307/3588243

Pawan, K. A., Wiechart, A., Warren, N., & Park, J. (Eds.). (2016). *Pedagogy and practice for online English language teacher education.* Alexandria, VA: TESOL.

Peachey, N. (2013). A blended learning teacher development course for the development of blended learning in English language teaching. In B. Tomlinson & C. Whittaker (Eds.), *Blended learning in English language teaching: Course design and implementation* (pp. 65–73). London: British Council.

Perren, J., & Wurr, A. J. (2015). *Learning the language of global citizenship: Strengthening service-learning in TESOL.* Champaign, IL: Common Ground Publishing.

Selingo, J. J. (2015). *The view from the top: What presidents think about financial sustainability, student outcomes, and the future of higher education.* Washington, DC: The Chronicle of Higher Education, Inc.

Smaldino, S. E., Lowther, D. L., Mims, C., & Russell, J. D. (2015). *Instructional technology and media for learning*. Upper Saddle River, NJ: Pearson Education.

Whittaker, C. (2013). A military blend. In B. Tomlinson & C. Whittaker (Eds.), *Blended learning in English language teaching: Course design and implementation* (pp. 175–183). London: British Council.

# Acknowledgment

The editors would like to acknowledge the assistance of the people involved in this project and, without whom, it could not have come to fruition. In particular, we would like to thank the contributing authors for their efforts in writing, revising, and re-writing their chapters. Their considerable breadth and depth of knowledge with the important areas of CALL, online TESOL pedagogy, and second language acquisition is a credit to our profession, and we thank them for making their work public.

We wish to acknowledge the valuable commitment of the editorial advisors for their pledge of assistance: Carla Chamberlin-Quinlisk and Elizabeth Hanson-Smith. We are also grateful for the valuable contributions of Camilla Vásquez by providing so many CALL chapter reviewers. We also have a special acknowledgement to Mary Ellen Butler-Pascoe for contributing her author expertise with the foreword.

We would also like to thank the reviewers and editorial assistants for their feedback and insights on the quality and presentation of chapters: Dinah Ouano Perren, Palomar College; Soo Min Lee, Alliant International University; Carmen (Jiamin) Rong, Alliant International University; and Carol (Jialu) Sun, Alliant International University.

We are indebted to the IGI Global Editorial Staff who guided us along the way: Jordan Tepper, Mariah Gilbert, Janine Haughton, and Jan Travers.

Finally, we acknowledge the encouragement of our peers, colleagues, and students throughout the development of this project.

*James Perren*
*Alliant International University, USA*

*Ken Kelch*
*Alliant International University, USA*

*Jin-suk Byun*
*Alliant International University, USA*

*Seth Cervantes*
*Alliant International University, USA*

*Setareh Safavi*
*Alliant International University, USA*

# Chapter 1
# A Theoretically Informed Approach to Collaborative Writing in EAP Contexts Using Web-Based Technologies

**Kris Pierre Johnston**
*York University, Canada*

**Geoff Lawrence**
*York University, Canada*

## ABSTRACT

*This chapter examines the need for a theoretically-informed approach to collaborative English for Academic Purpose (EAP) pedagogy and research. It discusses the relevance of online collaborative learning in EAP and the call for a theoretically-informed facilitative framework to guide the use of online collaborative writing tools to sustain learning communities and language learning. It establishes the importance of virtual learning communities as catalysts for online collaboration and discusses the need to examine technological affordances, adopting an ecological perspective to inform curricular design. The chapter examines the relevance of the Community of Inquiry model and its three presences: cognitive, social and teaching, as a theoretical basis to inform a facilitative framework to design online collaborative EAP writing tasks. The chapter concludes with a discussion of the interactions of these three presences, details on how they can inform online EAP collaborative writing practices and the need for future research in this area.*

## INTRODUCTION

Notions of literacy, writing and communication have dramatically been transformed through the use of Web 2.0 technologies that are inherently interactive, social, and at times, intensely collaborative. Writing in the 21st century has been redefined through our technologies and now requires “new social practices, skills, strategies and dispositions” (Coiro, Knobel, Lankshear, & Leu, 2008, p. 14) that are

DOI: 10.4018/978-1-5225-2933-0.ch001

increasingly digital in nature. Wikis, Google Docs, blogs and social networking demand a participatory, interdependent and interactive approach to writing (Lankshear & Knobel, 2011; Tour, 2015) and have been shown to facilitate a sense of community, discourse and collaboration among English language learners (Kessler, 2009; Lawrence, Young, Owen, & Compton, 2009). Such interactive collaboration has the power to engage learners in meaning-focused tasks while drawing attention to linguistic form along with building autonomy and awareness of learning needs and strategies (Aydin & Yildiz, 2014; Kessler, 2009; Kessler, Bikowski, & Boggs, 2012). The affordances of these emerging online tools hold great potential to facilitate a range of academic and writing skills, learning strategies and transferable digital literacies relevant to learners in today's English for Academic Purpose (EAP) contexts.

Technologies like Google Docs and wikis enable EAP learners to revise each other's content through open editing where learners continuously refine, co-edit and build on each other's thoughts. Writing tasks in these intensely collaborative online environments can initiate and sustain interactions between students of various language proficiencies, while students compare their writing with peers, thus attending to various levels of form and meaning (Li & Zhu, 2013). Such collaboration affords learners a variety of roles such as tutor, coauthor, sounding board or editor (Storch, 2011). This multifaceted interaction enables a high degree of interdependence, autonomy, and can lead to the development of collective scaffolding where members of a learning community are both experts and novices, pooling knowledge and strategies, helping each other solve problems through the use of the English language (Li & Zhu, 2013; Storch, 2011; Stoddart, Chan, & Liu, 2016). Such intensely interactive writing can establish a process of continual collaboration in online and offline contexts that occurs during problem-solving and ongoing negotiation and has the potential to build classroom community. This heightened interaction enhancing linguistic input and output, combined with an enhanced sense of audience, can support a number of language learning benefits but can also present pedagogical challenges. Interactive writing technologies can enhance the importance of revision, reduce the stress of writing, build confidence and change the nature of writing itself (Ware & Kessler, 2013; Yu & Lee, 2016).

Studies in web-based collaborative language learning have aimed to understand the dynamics of the teacher, learner and task as they interact and change over time during interactive and collaborative activity (Garrison, Anderson, & Archer, 2000, 2001, 2010). In this case, the Community of Inquiry model[1] was developed to examine interactions and identify relationships between social, teaching and cognitive presence in online learning (Garrison et al., 2001). The currency of the Community of Inquiry model for online language learning and teaching lies in its ability to describe and anticipate the collaborative learning process as it is mediated through Web 2.0 technologies. This model's application to language teaching and learning will be discussed in detail below.

## ONLINE COLLABORATION LANGUAGE LEARNING BENEFITS

Collaborative learning, especially in the EAP classroom, is increasingly seen as a beneficial approach to learning, whether in the classroom or using web-based technologies (Aydin & Yildiz, 2014; Chao & Lo, 2009; Kessler et al., 2012; Stoddart et al., 2016). In collaborative online environments, second language (L2) writers have been found to spend more time planning and on revising writing when using interactive web-based tools than on paper (Chao & Lo, 2009; Li & Zhu, 2013). Research suggests this may be a result of the extended sense of audience that can fuel a focus on linguistic form to impress this audience and communicate a clear message (Lawrence et al., 2009). This is highly relevant to writing and to academic writing that sees writing as a relationship between the writer and a targeted audience. However, teachers often have difficulty getting their learners to fully understand this connection. Collaborative writing tasks that utilize collaborative technologies can be used to demonstrate the interdependent relationships between the writer and reader by showing how writing is a social activity within a social context (Kuteeva, 2011). In other words, "writing is a cyclical process in which writers simultaneously shape their discourse to involve the reader and are influenced by the reader's expectations resulting from a community practices" (Hyland, 2005, pp. 37-38). Thus, collaborative writing leads to reflective thinking as well as awareness of audience (Storch, 2011).

In a 2009 study on language learners and wiki writing, Chao and Lo found that students found the wiki useful as a platform for collaborative writing and observed that students spent more time on their revisions online than in class. They noted that revisions were also more frequent and anxiety levels lower (Chao & Lo, 2009). However, a number of studies have identified that the benefits of these online interactive writing environments depend greatly on learners' group cohesiveness, engagement with the task, clear expectations around communication protocols and investment with members within these learning environment (Bin, Hu Xiang, & Jeaco, 2012; Kessler, 2009; Lawrence et al., 2009; Lee & Wang, 2013; Storch, 2011).

Open editing actively involves peer feedback and benefits from an immediate sense of audience that can in turn engage investment in writing processes and a focus on linguistic form to clearly convey meaning (Lawrence et al., 2009; Storch, 2011). This pursuit of more accurate and reader-centred texts can promote collective scaffolding and the noticing of gaps and strengths in language proficiency that can help learners consolidate and validate what they know while building awareness of their learning needs (Storch, 2011; Swain, 2000). The use of peer feedback by participants in this collaboration can be a valuable tool in idea development and the mechanics of writing (Ware & Warschauer, 2006). For example, research has found that online interactive writing can expand the quantity of writing practice, focusing attention on linguistic, communicative and interactive features that scaffold writing projects and can act as a bridge to academic writing (Ware & Kessler, 2013). When a learner's attention is directed to problematic areas of knowledge or production, noticing occurs that can foster learning to address this linguistic gap (Gass & Mackey, 2015). Another benefit of collaborative online writing is that this intensely mediated linguistic production can encourage languaging (Swain, 2006) where learners work to make sense of a problem in a language-related episode. The key benefit of languaging in this type of online interaction is that it can prompt reflection on a problem area, raising learner awareness and acting as a cognitive tool to mediate thinking (Swain & Deters, 2007) that can become an ongoing learning strategy.

## Factors Essential for Successful Collaboration

In spite of these potential benefits, the research on the linguistic benefits from interactive online interaction reveals mixed results. In a study with EFL teachers in Mexico, Kessler (2009) found that student teachers did attend to linguistic form, but only when such form impeded meaning, concluding that there may be an "acceptable level of tolerance for errors" (p. 91). On the other hand, studies have also found that groups engaged in corrective and blog-based feedback showed better performance in revised drafts and achieved better test score results than in the control groups (AbuSeileek & Abualsha'r, 2014; Ciftci & Kocoglu, 2012). These differing outcomes suggest that language learning successes often depend on the pedagogy and proactive scaffolding used by the instructor to effectively mediate peer feedback in these interactive online spaces. Writing instructors have an essential role to play when facilitating feedback and scaffolding interaction within these online learning environments (Yu & Lee, 2016).

Lee and Wang's 2013 study on the use of wikis in English language learning identified factors involved in learner participation and lack of involvement. They concluded that if learners can perceive the value in working together and the gains to be made, participation levels would increase. Related research found that collaborative groups with a high degree of mutuality, level of engagement, equality and a degree of control over the task learn more (Li & Zhu, 2013; Storch, 2002). In other words, when members of the group engaged with and responded to other's contributions consistently and were able to have a say in the direction of the writing, they were able to learn more than other groups that had divergent interaction patterns (Li, 2013; Storch, 2002). Research also notes that feelings concerning collaborative learning activities can be related to previous experiences of collaboration (Bin et al., 2012; Watanabe, 2008). As a result, positive perceptions of collaboration are contingent on previous positive experiences of collaboration.

Studies have also suggested that the mode of communication affects learners' awareness of both form and meaning in the language they are producing. Some research has found that peers tend to provide more robust written feedback in online interactions at the mechanical level but that verbal feedback in a face-to-face or video format tends to be the preferred modality for guidance on more global changes (Ware & Kessler, 2013). Studies have shown that collaboration in a face-to-face setting led to more engagement in fellow contributors' work compared to activity seen in a wiki task completed by the same learners (Tan, Wigglesworth, & Storch, 2010). In addition, online collaborative writing, using wikis, has been found to be more cooperative where students contribute equally to the whole text but tend to focus on their respective parts, giving limited feedback to their peers (Storch, 2011; Tan et al., 2010). However, researchers note that true collaborative activity online has a better chance of developing over a longer period of time as trust, group cohesion and identity investment are vital to the success of a collaborative task (Dörnyei, 2007; Kessler & Bikowski, 2010; Lawrence, 2013; Storch, 2011). This includes the development of trust and personal relationships between individual group members (Storch, 2011).

It is clear that collaborative writing tasks, if mediated through technology, must be conducted differently than within face-to-face contexts. Online collaborative interactions that facilitate attention to form and meaning do not happen spontaneously and require a longer period of time to develop. For tasks to succeed, learners need to be fully oriented to online collaboration and be fully supported in these interactions. As a result, instructors must design, structure and scaffold engaging tasks, orient learners to specific roles and responsibilities, define online communication protocols and they must encourage collective ownership of the writing process, which is often a novel concept in teaching and learning environments (Ducate, Anderson, & Moreno, 2011; Storch, 2011). Ultimately, instructors can benefit from adopting a theoretically-informed pedagogical approach that facilitates an empowering, supportive learning community that fosters identity investment, facilitates multimodal interactions and develops supportive social, teaching and cognitive presence.

Although there has been much research into the benefits of collaborative writing tools in computer-assisted language learning (CALL), a 2012 study by Wang and Vásquez investigating research into Web 2.0 technologies found the majority of the research and related teaching practices were ungrounded in theory. This is problematic as research informing teaching practice should be guided by "clearly-stated, clearly-identifiable, theoretical frameworks" (Wang & Vásquez, 2012, p. 420) in order to establish a coherent disciplinary knowledge base in emerging technology-mediated language learning. This chapter will examine this need for a more theoretically-informed approach to collaborative EAP pedagogy and research. By exploring concepts outlined by postmodern theoretical frameworks informing CALL, this chapter will argue that theoretically informed technology-mediated language learning approaches using inherently collaborative writing tools can lead to the formation of sustained learning communities needed in higher education EAP contexts.

This chapter will first discuss the relevance of online collaborative learning in EAP contexts and the call for a theoretically-informed facilitative framework to guide online collaborative EAP writing. It will then establish the importance of virtual learning communities as catalysts for online collaboration and discuss the need to examine the affordances of technologies and learning environments, adopting an ecological perspective that can inform curricular design. The chapter will then examine the relevance of the Community of Inquiry model (COI) (Garrison et al., 2000), and its three presences: cognitive, social, and teaching, as a theoretical model to inform a facilitative framework to guide the design of online collaborative EAP writing. The chapter will conclude with a discussion of the dynamic interactions of these three presences, details on how they can inform online EAP collaborative writing practices and the need for future research in this area.

## THE CALL FOR A THEORETICALLY-INFORMED PEDAGOGICAL FRAMEWORK

Collaborative writing tasks are becoming increasingly common in higher education as this type of team writing reflects collaborative work in employment and in academic research (Storch, 2011). Project work using technology has become common in educational institutions worldwide recognizing the social constructivist benefits of this type of learning that can enhance the learning experience and develop transferable skills (Ducate et al., 2011; Lambert & Fisher, 2013; Stoddart et al., 2016; Storch, 2011). In today's 21st century classrooms, students in higher education are expected to be able to form partnerships among classmates for sustained collaborative work and to utilize a rapidly developing array of collaborative web-based technologies to achieve this aim (Stoddart et al., 2016). Students are expected to have a certain degree of digital literacy and social skills for academic success, prompting the call for a paradigm shift in EAP education (Kuteeva, 2011). This shift includes the need to develop new literacies and skills in learners that focus on effective communication in a variety of academic, social, professional and technologically mediated contexts (Kuteeva, 2011).

In CALL, the use of collaborative and interactive software for language learning is loosely referred to as 'social computing' or social CALL, and usually takes the form of collaborative task-based activities completed with other L2 learners or native speakers using web-based tools or platforms (Garrett, 2009). Collaborative technologies, like wikis and Google Docs, are increasingly used in these efforts to support and scaffold collaborative and digitally relevant learning (Kuteeva, 2011; Lund, 2008). Collaborative learning tasks, such as collaborative writing, can help EAP learners develop the knowledge and skills that lead to successful integration into discourse communities and focused communities of practice (Kuteeva, 2011; Wenger, 2006). Collaboration, thus, creates a level of involvement during the writing process that is essential for academic writing, like argumentative or persuasive essays (Kuteeva, 2011). This is in line with Vygotskian and Bakhtinian views on the dialogic nature of language use and the importance of social interaction in learning (Vygotsky, 1978). This notion of discourse community has led to the development of effective process-oriented writing pedagogies (Kuteeva, 2011) which can be greatly supported through the use of collaborative technologies. These technologies if paired appropriately with a collaborative writing task developed using theoretically-informed pedagogy can lead to a highly rewarding and productive virtual learning community among learners.

As CALL research moves away from the cause-effect relationship between the learner and computer, it is now beginning to focus on the complex relationships that form between learners, instructors, content and technology within particular social and cultural contexts that shape the learning environment (Kern, 2006). As technology diversifies so do the social and cultural contexts of this technology and the resulting goals, content and structure of CALL pedagogy (Kern, 2006). In CALL, some have credited technological developments with already transforming L2 pedagogy, curriculum design, as well as how language learning is conceptualized and researched (Wang & Vásquez, 2012). However, others caution against such a simplistic, technocentric belief (Chapelle, 2009; Garrett, 2009). With the adoption of sociocultural and constructivist perspectives in L2 teaching and learning, much EAP research is now focusing on the skills, discourse, literacies and learning environments needed by learners in diverse higher education contexts, recognizing the complexity of theoretical frameworks that inform learning (Kuteeva, 2011).

Although second language acquisition (SLA) theories have shaped and justified many developments in CALL research and pedagogy, Garrett (2009) warned, we cannot simply 'computerize' what is already practiced in current pedagogy. She states that "for those outside of the field of computer-assisted language learning (CALL) research, CALL is not shorthand for the use of technology, but designates a dynamic complex in which technology, theory and pedagogy are inseparably interwoven" (Garrett, 2009, p.719). Chapelle (2009) points out that SLA theory has moved beyond the "simple, pragmatic needs of communicative CALL" to include an expanded theoretical palette (Chapelle, 2009, p. 742). So, for social CALL research and practice to grow we must adopt multiple theoretical perspectives (Kern, 2006). This also means that we cannot simply apply what is already known in SLA and CALL research, but need to look beyond to new synergies of theory and practice. When developing pedagogical practice in the EAP classroom using web-based technologies, we must be able to adopt perspectives and approaches that help us understand how collaborative learning can be facilitated in EAP and how it can exploit the affordances of intensely collaborative web-based technologies. This exploration needs to include perspectives of social learning and technology-mediated communication that can inform a guiding framework to help educators and researchers develop this emerging area of CALL. One key to this framework is the facilitation of virtual learning communities.

## VIRTUAL LEARNING COMMUNITIES

English language educators have always understood the need to create an engaging, supportive learning environment that encourages interaction and language learning. In online language teaching, the creation of such communities is crucial (Lawrence, 2014). Social interaction and social presence must be methodically cultivated in online EAP learning to connect learners and to increase opportunities for interaction, learning and feedback (Blake, 2011; Lehman & Conceição, 2010). While most EAP learners and many instructors in today's contexts are familiar with social interaction and collaboration using a range of social media platforms they may be quite unfamiliar with the role changes and communication protocols to work with others on specific online projects or tasks. For example, Twitter and Facebook facilitate social group formation, discussion, sharing and group planning. Youtube and Snapchat allow users to collect followers for their original content, and then within these communities, users can facilitate interactive, sustained interactive exchanges. In this way, social media offers online spaces where people interact, publish, collaborate and communicate with others in virtual communities. However, social communities simply founded on social media are very different than virtual learning communities. Social media users congregate around shared interests and thinking, while virtual learning communities are composed of individuals who share a common inquiry or task goals. As a result, virtual learning community members are most likely made up of individuals with distinct personality traits, interests, and goals which can impede community formation and interaction among group members (Lambert & Fisher, 2013).

Virtual learning community members must demonstrate a strong commitment to their community, understand and follow the conditions of membership based on socially constructed behavior, and their success or failure is dependent on their ability to move from being an outsider to become a fully inducted member of the online community (Swan & Shea, 2005). Therefore, the formation of a learning community is both the means and ends to the web-based collaborative learning (Swan & Shea, 2005). Such community formation must often be scaffolded through modeling, guidelines and interactions informed by the instructor's pedagogical approach.

The concept of virtual learning communities is rooted in language socialization theory (Swain & Deters, 2007), Social Presence Theory (Short, Williams, & Christie, 1976), and Community of Practice (Wenger, 2006). Wenger's (2006) ideas situate learning in practice, arguing that practice is social in nature, and in practice, knowledge is co-constructed by community members. In this way, language learning can be informed by a participation metaphor where learning is becoming an active member of a community through language, identity, agency and accepted community behavior (Swain & Deters, 2007, p. 823). From a sociocultural perspective, learning is not an internalized process but happens during interaction; learners, in fact, co-construct the communicative activity they participate in (Hampel, 2006). Lund (2008) states that learning is less about the process within minds, but rather that which occurs between minds (Lund, 2008). In online collaborative tasks using web-conferencing, employing a task that situates the learner as an active participant is a creative and socially interactive process (Hampel, 2003). According to Swan and Shea (2005), "the notion of learning communities is rooted in the observation that knowledge and learning are a natural part of the life of communities that share values, beliefs, languages and always of doing things. Knowledge in this view is inseparable from practice and practice is inseparable from the communities in which it occurs" (Swan & Shea, 2005, p. 245). Consequently, understanding human mental processing is inseparable from the setting in which individuals or groups operate (Hampel, 2006). In terms of collaborative online language learning, the learning environment and the transformation of this environment to a 'community' is a crucial factor when designing EAP collaborative interaction with Web 2.0 technologies.

## ESTABLISHING THE FRAMEWORK: EXAMINING AFFORDANCES AND AN ECOLOGICAL APPROACH

When attempting to design a collaborative writing task using web-based technologies, there are issues to take into consideration. Specifically, all media are unique whereby each medium emphasizes, amplifies or inhibits particular kinds of experience (Swan & Shea, 2005). Where a given tool can enhance a particular learning experience, it can also diminish it. In other words, each medium affords certain interaction but can also constrain it (Swan & Shea, 2005). The way individuals interact in a physical space and a virtual one is different. This is due to the differences in ecology, or rather the difference in affordances each environment imposes upon the individual.

In an ecological sense, van Lier (2004) defines an affordance as "the fit between an animal's capabilities and the environmental supports and opportunities (both good and bad) that make possible a given activity" (p. 90). Affordances are emerging perceptions of the [language learning] benefits a tool can provide learners within a specific context. A key aspect of an affordance is that it is situated in the relationship between the user, the tool and the context (Haines, 2015). For example, asynchronous tools can constrain communication by limiting communication to typical text-based messages. In this case, interaction is delayed, which affects the spontaneity and free-flow of communication, but also gives users time to reflect and plan their responses which can be beneficial for language learning. On the other hand, if the users employ asynchronous video recordings, users can get a sense of the person behind the message conveyed by facial expressions and nonverbal cues. Similarly, synchronous videoconferencing allows for same-time face-to-face communication replete with visual, verbal, text messaging and nonverbal cues in real-time. These latter forms of communication afford learners a multimodal form of communication, potentially enabling learners to relate to the individuals expressing specific identities along with these ideas, building a form of identity investment and deeper connection with each other (Lawrence, 2013).

The ecological perspective helps us understand how interactions can be facilitated with specific tools within a specific online environment or context. This helps us understand how we relate to others within these surroundings, and how this affects the learning process (van Lier, 2004). Adopting an ecological perspective means taking stock of the affordances and constraints of the tools within the learning environment and designing tasks in accordance with this knowledge (Ornberg Berglund, 2009). Tasks therefore need to take into account the functionality of different modes of technologically-mediated communication, which have inherent affordances and constraints associated with them. As affordances are emergent and refined through experience, it is important to re-assess affordances and constraints as instructors and learners become more familiar with online tools and environments.

During a collaborative web-based task, it is important to also understand the effect of one's perception of the role of a peer collaborator or groupmate on learning. The positive psychological effect of perceiving someone at the 'other end' of a communication exchange in a virtual space devoid of an actual physical presence is known as social presence (Ko, 2012; Short et al., 1976). Social presence can be defined as "an individual's ability to demonstrate his/her state of being in a virtual environment and so signal his/her availability for interpersonal interactions" (Kehrwald, 2008 as cited in Lehman & Conceição, 2010, p. 5). Thought, emotion and behavior work together to create social presence. Lehman (2006) emphasizes the perceptual nature of online language learners noting how learners are active perceivers and bring their individual knowledge, skills, attitudes, preferences and diverse backgrounds to the online interactive experience. The degree to which learners display these interrelated aspects builds social presence.

Social presence research has looked at differences between face-to-face classrooms and virtual ones, examining issues related to 'immediacy,' which concerns the psychological distance between the teacher and students in either environment (Swan & Shea, 2005). Studies into social presence and immediacy look at the effect this psychological distance has on learning (Swan & Shea, 2005). For example, Caspi and Blau (2008) examined the self-projection of participants onto the group and their identification with the group and found a positive co-relationship with each other. In this case, social presence created a positive learning environment that facilitated learning. Studies have also confirmed a link between teacher presence and an increase in learners' affective learning and a resulting effect on their cognitive learning (Swan & Shea, 2005). An increase in social presence makes interaction seem real, more personal, and less technologically-mediated, establishing a sense of community and belongingness (Kear et al., 2012). This 'human feel' can reduce the communicative limitations inherent in technology-mediated communication (Lawrence, 2013; Kear et al., 2012). However, student perceptions of satisfaction and learning depend on interaction with a range of factors that include course content, the instructor, peer collaborators and this learning needs to be supported through social and teacher presence (Swan, 2002). For these reasons, structure, leadership, and social presence must be designed into the task itself for virtual learning communities to develop and sustain (Lambert & Fisher, 2013). When EAP instructors initiate a collaborative writing task, they need to keep in mind the ecology and affordances of the collaborative environment, its suitability for the task and how this affects interactions and learning. Instructors must continually assess the perceived distance between learners, their peers and the instructor, and the impact this has on interaction and the formation of a virtual learning community. If the ecology of the task and learning environment affords learners the ability to interact and feel connected, the collaborative writing task will likely sustain collaboration, create a sense of community, and increase the potential of a valuable learning experience.

### The Need for a Facilitation Framework

Collaborative online writing tasks remain constrained by a lack of pedagogical understanding of how teachers can design and implement these types of tasks in the EAP classroom (Colpaert, 2006; Lawrence, 2013; Lawrence et al., 2009; Yu & Lee, 2016). Teachers wishing to facilitate collaborative writing activities using technology face a daunting challenge of initiating, facilitating, and sustaining truly collaborative activity and building social presence among their learners although many learners may be accustomed to interactive features of mobile apps and social media. However, as noted earlier, familiarity with social media does not spontaneously lead to increased "productivity, motivation and enjoyment" (Stoddart et al., 2016, p. 143).

The success of a collaborative task is dependent on the use of a facilitation framework that is used to introduce, initiate, and monitor collaborative activity over the course of the task (Bradley, Lindström, Rystedt, & Vigmo, 2010; Lin & Kelsey, 2009; Kessler & Bikowski, 2010; Stoddart et al., 2016). However, research into effective facilitation frameworks is limited (Stoddart et al., 2016). Thus, there is a need for a theoretically informed framework, especially one that is guided by theory. The Community of Inquiry model outlined below can be used as a foundation to inform such a facilitative framework to guide online collaborative EAP learning.

## THE COMMUNITY OF INQUIRY MODEL

As introduced earlier, the Community of Inquiry model was developed by Garrison, Anderson, and Archer in 2001 to facilitate collaborative online learning communities in higher education using interactive and multimodal Web 2.0 technologies. It was developed with the goal to leverage the potential of computer conferencing with the goals of formal education: the creation and sustainability of a community of inquiry. These researchers aimed to provide a comprehensive framework to guide research and practice of online learning and research (Garrison & Arbaugh, 2007).

The Community of Inquiry (COI) model takes a collaborative constructivist approach framed by sociocultural theory. However, Lund (2008) states that "while sociocultural theory in many ways has become synonymous with the theoretical work of Vygotsky, Valsiner and van der Veer (2000) show that similar perspectives can be traced throughout the 19th century in Europe as well as in American pragmatism" (p. 39). One of the founders of American Pragmatism was John Dewey who held unique views on education, specifically experiential and democratic forms of learning. The COI model is underpinned by John Dewey's (1959) notions of practical inquiry and the role of community in learning. He believed that the educational experience should fuse both the individual and society. In this way, individual development is dependent upon community (Dewey, 1959; Swan, Garrison, & Richardson, 2009). Dewey believed that community was a fusion of both private and public worlds and saw inquiry as being at the heart of education, involving a simplified version of the scientific method that links problem-solving to meaningful learning (Dewey, 1959; Swan et al., 2009). By collaborating, students would be compelled to take responsibility for their own learning experience, construct meaning and confirm it through interaction with peers (Swan et al., 2009).

This is in line with the concept of the Zone of Proximal Development (ZPD) as both Vygotsky and Dewey argued for a social, scaffolded view of learning. Since this time there has a been a huge advance in social learning theories and follow three main themes: cognition as being situated in the social context, knowledge as being distributed across groups, and the notion of learning taking place in communities (Swan & Shea, 2005). Much of the Community of Inquiry model theoretical grounding is derived from social learning theory, based on sociocultural tenets and constructivist thinking (Swan & Shea, 2005). This marks an important overlap between the social turn in SLA and CALL approaches and theory, and in collaborative online language learning in particular. They state that social learning approaches view learning as being essentially social in nature and that learning involves social interaction between peers (same level, grade or status), either direct, mediated or remembered (Swan & Shea, 2005). This is the foundation of language socialization theory that informs many current approaches to language teaching and learning, examining how novices are socialized into communities through the use of language (Swain & Deters, 2007).

The Community of Inquiry is a process model of online learning (Swan et al., 2009). It is concerned with the importance of community and collaborative social knowledge construction in a higher education context. It views learning as the process of meaning-making during learner interaction in a socio-cultural context (Kozan & Richardson, 2014). Thus, the Community of Inquiry model is essentially a constructivist approach to learning. However, though higher education often draws on these approaches, the notion of collaborative construction of knowledge within a learning community is only a point of departure (Swan et al., 2009). Though knowledge is seen as being socially constructed through discourse and reflection, meaning-making and confirmation of this meaning is believed to require collaboration and community (Swan et al., 2009). At the heart of the Community of Inquiry (COI) model is the emphasis on how a community facilitates meaningful learning over time (Garrison et al., 2000).

However, if this ongoing collaboration is mediated through technology, issues can emerge that affect authentic community formation. In an online environment, community formation and collaborative inquiry cannot be taken for granted, but must be actively facilitated and sustained. For this to occur, Garrison et al. (2000) argue that there must be the presence of three overlapping elements: cognitive, social and teaching presence. These three core elements are multidimensional and interdependent. Community and inquiry, together, form a "pragmatic organizing framework of sustainable principles and processes for the purpose of guiding online educational practices" (Swan et al., 2009, p. 45). This is fundamental to creating and maintaining online learning communities during collaborative learning tasks.

## Cognitive Presence

In terms of the COI, Garrison et al. (2000) define cognitive presence as pertaining to learners' ability to make meaning through communication (p. 93). They state that this is either hampered or enhanced by the medium of communication, and requires a high degree of socio-emotional support from its participants. Cognitive presence is the primary construct in the COI model as it is the primary focus of higher education in general. Cognitive presence is facilitated by the embedded outcomes of a task, its fit with the ecological affordances and constraints of the web-based tool being used, and its ability to facilitate the collaborative effort and participant meaning-making to reach these outcomes (Garrison et al., 2000).

Cognitive presence is based on John Dewey's practical inquiry model which consists of four iterative and cyclical stages: a triggering event, exploration of possible problem-solving strategies, integration of solutions, and resolution of the problem by choosing the best solution and its subsequent application (Garrison et al., 2000). Cognitive presence is vital for critical thinking (Garrison et al., 2000, p. 93). Kozan and Richardson (2014) note that "cognitive presence means being cognitively active, in that learners seek the most effective and efficient ways of solving a learning problem, and apply these solutions at the end (p. 68)." In the classroom, activities that develop cognitive presence tend to be well structured tasks where clear roles and responsibilities are defined and learners are encouraged to explicitly work with different opinions and resources to develop critical thinking skills (Kanuka, Liam, & Laflamme, 2007). For example, having EAP learners work in small groups to negotiate and present a unified analysis to a complex reading task based on a class theme can hook learners into meaningful communication. Such a task can then have learners actively negotiate divergent opinions, facilitating cognitive presence through critical thinking and social interaction.

## Social Presence

Social presence is usually described in terms of social interaction. Specifically, it relates to the ability of a task or environment to facilitate social interaction, either in one mode or in multiple modes, synchronously or asynchronously, and the learners' sense of being able to perceive their interlocutor (Ko, 2012). Garrison et al. (2000) define social presence as "the ability of participants in a community of inquiry to project themselves socially and emotionally, as 'real' people (i.e., their full personality), through the medium of communication being used" (p. 94).

When technologically-mediated, interaction and collaboration is complexified, social presence needs to be explicitly scaffolded. In physical classrooms, there is a strong sense of immediacy between the learner and their peers, and learners and their teachers. When interactions are mediated by technology, a greater psychological distance is perceived, which can have a demotivating and isolating effect. Simply, when interaction occurs in a virtual space devoid of the physical presence of an interlocutor, learners feel dislocated from each other. Being able to perceive others during an online collaborative writing task has a huge impact on learning. It can be said that this notion of social presence was an early impetus for the development of the Community of Inquiry model.

Social presence has been shown to be vital for cognitive presence by building mutual understanding and creating personal and purposeful relationships (Garrison & Arbaugh, 2007). In other words, social interaction underpins cognitive presence by reducing the sense of distance between learners and helping learners form social relationships and thus trust, which then helps to establish a sense of community among learners. We now understand that social interaction cannot be taken for granted as it may not occur nor necessarily lead to collaboration. Collaboration, in order to be sustained and contribute to learning, needs to be first understood by the learners and scaffolded by the teacher.

Social presence in online or blended language learning environments can be facilitated by synchronous communication tools like chat and videoconferencing that are interactive, spontaneous and develop peer-to peer connections (Kramsch & Thorne, 2002). For example, at the beginning of an EAP online writing class, learners could be encouraged to work in pairs, to interview each other using a videoconferencing tool about their EAP class goals, to identify a shared goal, to find out about a unique experience in their background, languages learned, successes and challenges. Then each learner would prepare and present a video podcast, introducing some key aspects of their partner to the rest of the class. Such an activity promotes identity investment where learners actively explore and position each other's identity in a multimodal manner, identifying common goals, experiences and challenges (Lawrence, 2013). Such introductory networking activities are crucial and can help create a 'we' feeling in a group, "a gelling force that keeps the group together" (Dörnyei, 2007, p. 721).

## Teaching Presence

According to Garrison et al. (2000), teaching presence is "the design, facilitation, and direction of cognitive and social presences for the purpose of realizing personally meaningful and educationally worthwhile learning outcomes" (pp. 101-102). Teaching presence helps sustain cognitive and social presence through designing instruction and facilitating learning and aligns all the components of a community of inquiry with the learning outcomes, learner needs, and abilities (Kozan & Richardson, 2014). During online collaborative language tasks, Hampel (2006) states that teaching is made up of the teacher's ability to design and facilitate tasks in accordance with their learners' abilities and proficiencies in mind, as well as understanding of the ecological affordances and constraints of the instructional medium (Hampel, 2006, p. 119).

Garrison and Arbaugh (2007) state that it is not enough for learners to interact while working collaboratively on a task. These interactions must have set parameters and clear objectives. This can be provided by a strong teaching presence whether this is by the online environment, learning management system, task structure or through the teacher, or all four. Teaching presence is also provided by the collective ZPD established and maintained by the learners themselves. For example, peer learners can provide teaching presence during a collaborative activity.

Studies have shown that high levels of teacher interaction are connected to high levels of perceived learning among students (Jiang & Ting, 2000; Swan, Shea, Fredericksen, Pickett, Pelz, & Maher, 2000), and with online learning specifically (Richardson & Swan, 2003). Studies also note a correlation between student perceptions of interaction with instructors and the actual frequency of interaction. The higher the interaction level of the teacher the higher the perceived interaction; this suggests the importance of direct teacher instruction and the development of a community feel in a virtual environment (Swan et al., 2000; Swan & Shea, 2005). Therefore, teaching presence is key to a positive learning experience as it pertains to the development of the sense of community (Garrison & Arbaugh, 2007). Teaching presence is particularly crucial at the beginning of an online task to help facilitate connections between learners, building social presence, and setting guidelines and expectations around tasks and subtasks to facilitate cognitive presence. For example, successful facilitative approaches at mediating online collaborative writing can include orienting learners to collaborative online writing, its benefits, challenges, strategies, breaking an assignment down into manageable chunks, assigning subtask deadlines and establishing feedback procedures to provide both critical and encouraging input (Stoddart et al., 2016). A supportive teaching presence requires educators to pay attention to learners, particularly at the beginning of online activities, to offer guidance, to check in with absent learners, to provide reminders and host informal meeting times - like online office hours that can provide learners with informal opportunities to engage with the instructor (Lawrence, 2014).

### The COI as a Dynamic Model

The COI model is a dynamic model as it is in a constant search of balance among all three presences. Each presence interacts and shifts over time and across courses. The strength of the COI lies within the dynamics of the whole community, within the three overlapping constructs (Swan et al., 2009). In a study by Shea and Bidjerano (2009) to investigate the impacts of teaching and social presence on cognitive presence, it was shown that both teaching and social presence made up 70% of variation in learners' reported level of cognitive presence. Furthermore, it was found that social presence was directly related to the establishment of teaching presence. In other words, social presence did not directly affect cognitive presence but served as a mediating force between teaching and cognitive presence. Shea and Bidjerano (2009) concluded that "teaching and social presence represent the processes needed to create paths to epistemic engagement and cognitive presence for online learners" (p. 550).

In a study conducted by Kozan and Richardson (2014) investigating the interrelationships between all three presences, the researchers concluded that there was a strong inter-relatedness among all constructs. They suggest that efforts to increase cognitive presence may also increase social presence, which in turn will reinforce cognitive presence. This iterative relationship is in line with Garrison and Arbaugh's (2007) idea that both social and cognitive presence are important and that social presence in the form of mere social interaction is not enough to establish a community of inquiry. These scholars state that efforts to increase social presence should not focus on social interaction, but focus on increasing cognitive presence through social interaction. This is what Garrison terms purposeful relationships (Garrison & Arbaugh, 2007).

## A COI-INFORMED FACILITATIVE FRAMEWORK

For a given collaborative task to be launched in an interactive technologically-mediated environment, the task should be initiated by a teaching presence. This could be the teacher, the technological environment, and/or the task structure along with clearly expressed goals and defined procedures. For example, when working on an academic research paper assignment, a teacher should carefully design the work details, outline clear instructions, subtask steps, timelines and scaffold strategies on how learners are to work together using various technologies (Colpaert, 2006; Hampel, 2006; Stoddart et al., 2016). The task design itself should provide a step-by-step process of when and how the writing assignment is to be completed and how the subtasks will be monitored and supported (Lawrence, 2013; Ware & Kessler, 2013). Communication, collaboration and feedback protocols need to be established and should be explored through low stake subtasks to build learner familiarity and confidence (Lin & Kelsey, 2009; Stoddart et al., 2016). Such methodical thinking through frontloaded design helps facilitate both social and cognitive presence that can sustain learning throughout a writing assignment.

Once the learning community is established, social interaction can be facilitated through the task design and then monitored and supported by the instructor. Subtasks in the assignment can interactively engage learners within the online writing community. These tasks could require small groups of students to provide feedback on individual thesis statements or to provide peer editing for outlines as well as rough and final drafts. Small groups of students could also work together to create a collaborative thesis or even a collaborative paper (Li & Zhu, 2013). These approaches can enhance social and cognitive presence through peer feedback and the perception of audience (Lawrence et al., 2009). This social presence can create and sustain a feeling of shared inquiry, of being part of a learning community as well as a collective ZPD whereby students can pool their strengths and improve weaknesses (Lehman & Conceição, 2010), enhancing cognitive presence.

At this point, the role of the teacher diminishes and the teacher becomes a facilitating presence, offering feedback and supporting the interaction that unfolds. During the writing activity, technology itself can provide teaching presence, such as in Google Docs, several add-ons allow for easy integration with Google Scholar, Wikipedia, Dictionaries, as well as Writing tips and style checks. This allows for expedient language and academic support. Learner communication can also be enhanced through video conferencing apps like Google+ Hangouts, or by sharing work on Google+ Communities that could be established for a class.

When supported through scaffolded teacher and social presence, the community is able to engage with each other on a meaningful level and cognitive presence becomes sustained. This allows for the learning task to progress over time whereby learners work together and independently to achieve task goals. Learners are further supported by the teacher who works to maintain a balanced level of collaboration in service of her/his teaching objectives. However, as the community attains a high level of independence from the teacher, and a strong level of interdependence among community members, the teacher and the task become less of a driving force and more of a mediating presence, resulting in a self-sustaining learning community. At this stage, the learning task ceases to be an assignment per se and instead begins to simulate an actual collective academic inquiry that leads to meaningful learning.

## CONCLUSION AND IMPLICATIONS

The COI model represents a dynamic and mutable model for collaborative learning using web-based technologies over time (Swan et al., 2009). In EAP education, the Community of Inquiry model informs how learners and teachers can collaborate to achieve the aims of a collaborative writing task. This framework can act as a foundation informing a facilitative framework to guide pedagogy in online collaborative EAP writing. The explanatory power of the COI model is in its ability to show iterative and cyclical nature of the three presences and specifically how collaborative activity evolves over time.

Using a COI model facilitative framework, a learning community evolves through the development of a cognitive presence that is mediated through social presence and supported by a teaching presence. More research examining pedagogy-based approaches in CALL is needed to specifically examine how pedagogical approaches can be used to facilitate collaborative writing in EAP, academic and professional contexts (Colpaert, 2006). There needs to be a more detailed examination of how the Community of Inquiry model can help inform collaborative task design and the linguistic development that occurs within a collaborative online EAP learning task. Research could look at how the role of teaching presence could be modified or expanded to understand how it could better mitigate learner interactions with differing linguistic abilities and proficiencies, and how teaching presence could be used to influence the rate of collaboration.

This chapter suggests that educators and researchers consider this theoretically informed facilitative framework to guide future efforts with the use of Web 2.0 technologies for online collaborative language learning and to consider how a COI-informed framework could be modified for diverse uses and contexts. The strength of the COI model lies in its ability to bring a complex array of issues, theories, approaches and practice together, which has been a major challenge in technology-mediated language teaching and learning. Developing such a framework for online collaborative language learning can help operationalize current teaching and learning efforts, and guide future research and theoretical development in CALL.

## REFERENCES

AbuSeileek, A., & Abualsha'r, A. (2014). Using peer computer-mediated corrective feedback to support EFL learners' writing. *Language Learning & Technology, 18*(1), 76-95. Retrieved from http://llt.msu.edu/issues/february2014/abuseileekabualshar.pdf

Aydin, Z., & Yildiz, S. (2014). Using wikis to promote collaborative EFL writing. *Language Learning & Technology*, *18*(1), 160–180. Retrieved from http://llt.msu.edu/issues/february2014/aydinyildiz.html

Bin, Z., Hu Xiang, C., & Jeaco, S. (2012). An investigation of the use of wikis in English language learning. *Canadian Journal of Applied Linguistics*, *35*(1), 99–116. https://doi.org/10.1515/cjal-2012-0008

Blake, R. J. (2011). Current trends in online language learning. *Annual Review of Applied Linguistics*, *31*, 19–35. doi:10.1017/S026719051100002X

Bradley, L., Lindström, B., Rystedt, H., & Vigmo, S. (2010). Rationalities of collaboration for language learning in a wiki. *ReCALL*, *22*(2), 247–265. doi:10.1017/S0958344010000108

Caspi, A., & Blau, I. (2008). Social presence in online discussion groups: Testing three conceptions and their relations to perceived learning. *Social Psychology of Education*, *11*(3), 323–346. doi:10.1007/s11218-008-9054-2

Chao, Y. C. J., & Lo, H. C. (2009). Students perceptions of wiki-based collaborative writing for learners of English as a foreign language. *Interactive Learning Environments*, *19*(4), 395–411. doi:10.1080/10494820903298662

Chapelle, C. A. (2009). The relationship between SLA theory and CALL. *Modern Language Journal*, *93*(4), 742–754. doi:10.1111/j.1540-4781.2009.00970.x

Ciftci, H., & Kocoglu, Z. (2012). Effects of peer e-feedback on Turkish EFL students writing performance. *Journal of Educational Computing Research*, *46*(1), 61–84. doi:10.2190/EC.46.1.c

Coiro, J., Knobel, M., Lankshear, C., & Leu, D. J. (2008). Central issues in new literacies and new literacies research. In J. Coiro, M. Knobel, C. Lankshear, & D. J. Leu (Eds.), *Handbook of research on new literacies* (pp. 1–21). New York, NY: Taylor & Francis Group.

Colpaert, J. (2006). Pedagogy-driven design for online language teaching and learning. *CALICO Journal*, *23*(3), 477–497. Retrieved from http://www.jstor.org/stable/24156348

Dewey, J. (1959). My pedagogic creed. In J. Dewey (Ed.), *Dewey on education* (pp. 19–32). New York, NY: Teachers College, Columbia University. (Original work published 1897)

Dörnyei, Z. (2007). Creating a motivating classroom environment. In J. Cummins & C. Davison (Eds.), *International handbook of English language teaching* (Vol. 2, pp. 719–731). New York, NY: Springer; doi:10.1007/978-0-387-46301-8_47

Ducate, L. C., Anderson, L. L., & Moreno, N. (2011). Wading through the world of wikis: An analysis of three wiki projects. *Foreign Language Annals*, *44*(3), 495–524. doi:10.1111/j.1944-9720.2011.01144.x

Garrett, N. (2009). Computer-assisted language learning trends and issues revisited: Integrating innovation. *Modern Language Journal*, *93*, 719–740. doi:10.1111/j.1540-4781.2009.00969.x

Garrison, D. R., Anderson, T., & Archer, W. (2000). Critical inquiry in a text-based environment: Computer conferencing in higher education. *The Internet and Higher Education*, *2*(2-3), 1–19. doi:10.1016/S1096-7516(00)00016-6

Garrison, D. R., Anderson, T., & Archer, W. (2001). Critical thinking, cognitive presence, and computer conferencing in distance education. *American Journal of Distance Education*, *15*(1), 7–23. doi:10.1080/08923640109527071

Garrison, D. R., Anderson, T., & Archer, W. (2010). The first decade of the community of inquiry framework: A retrospective. *The Internet and Higher Education*, *13*(1–2), 5–9. doi:10.1016/j.iheduc.2009.10.003

Garrison, D. R., & Arbaugh, J. B. (2007). Researching the community of inquiry framework: Review, issues, and future directions. *The Internet and Higher Education*, *10*(3), 157–172. doi:10.1016/j.iheduc.2007.04.001

Gass, S. M., & Mackey, A. (2015). Input, interaction, and output in second language acquisition. In B. VanPatten & J. Williams (Eds.), *Theories in second language acquisition: An introduction* (pp. 180–206). New York, NY: Routledge.

Haines, K. J. (2015). Learning to identify and actualize affordances in a new tool. *Language Learning & Technology*, *19*(1), 165–180. Retrieved from http://llt.msu.edu/issues/february2015/haines.pdf

Hampel, R. (2003). Theoretical perspectives and new practices in audio-graphic conferencing for language learning. *ReCALL*, *15*(01), 21–36. doi:10.1017/S0958344003000314

Hampel, R. (2006). Rethinking task design for the digital age: A framework for language teaching and learning in a synchronous online environment. *ReCALL*, *18*(01), 105–121. doi:10.1017/S0958344006000711

Hyland, K. (2005). Stance and engagement: A model of interaction in academic discourse. *Discourse Studies*, *7*(2), 173–192. doi:10.1177/1461445605050365

Jiang, M., & Ting, E. (2000). A study of factors influencing students' perceived learning in a web-based course environment. *International Journal of Educational Telecommunications*, *6*(4), 317–338.

Kanuka, H., Liam, R., & Laflamme, E. (2007). The influence of instructional methods on the quality of online discussion. *British Journal of Educational Technology*, *38*(2), 260–271. doi:10.1111/j.1467-8535.2006.00620.x

Kear, K., Chetwynd, F., Williams, J., & Donelan, H. (2012). Web conferencing for synchronous online tutorials: Perspectives of tutors using a new medium. *Computers & Education*, *58*(3), 953–963. doi:10.1016/j.compedu.2011.10.015

Kern, R. (2006). Perspectives on technology in learning and teaching languages. *TESOL Quarterly*, *40*(1), 183–210. doi:10.2307/40264516

Kessler, G. (2009). Student-initiated attention to form in wiki-based collaborative writing. *Language Learning & Technology*, *13*(1), 79–95. Retrieved from http://llt.msu.edu/vol13num1/kessler.pdf

Kessler, G., & Bikowski, D. (2010). Developing collaborative autonomous learning abilities in computer mediated language learning: Attention to meaning among students in wiki space. *Computer Assisted Language Learning*, *23*(1), 41–58. doi:10.1080/09588220903467335

Kessler, G., Bikowski, D., & Boggs, J. (2012). Collaborative writing among second language learners in academic web-based projects. *Language Learning & Technology*, *16*(1), 91–109. Retrieved from http://llt.msu.edu/issues/february2012/kesslerbikowskiboggs.pdf

Ko, C. J. (2012). A case study of language learners social presence in synchronous CMC. *ReCALL*, *24*(01), 66–84. doi:10.1017/S0958344011000292

Kozan, K., & Richardson, J. C. (2014). Interrelationships between and among social, teaching, and cognitive presence. *The Internet and Higher Education*, *21*, 68–73. doi:10.1016/j.iheduc.2013.10.007

Kramsch, C., & Thorne, S. (2002). Foreign language learning as global communicative practice. In D. Block & D. Cameron (Eds.), *Language learning and teaching in the age of globalization* (pp. 83–100). London, UK: Routledge.

Kuteeva, M. (2011). Wikis and academic writing: Changing the writer–reader relationship. *English for Specific Purposes*, *30*(1), 44–57. doi:10.1016/j.esp.2010.04.007

Lambert, J., & Fisher, J. (2013). Community of inquiry framework: Establishing community in an online course. *Journal of Interactive Learning Online*, *12*(1), 1–16.

Lankshear, C., & Knobel, M. (2011). *New literacies: Everyday practices and classroom learning* (3rd ed.). Maidenhead, UK: Open University Press.

Lawrence, G. (2013). A working model for intercultural learning and engagement in collaborative online language learning environments. *Intercultural Education*, *24*(4), 303–314. doi:10.1080/14675986.2013.809247

Lawrence, G. (2014). A call for the human feel in today's increasingly blended world. *Contact - Refereed Proceedings of TESL Ontario Research Symposium, 40*(2), 128-141.

Lawrence, G., Young, C., Owen, H., & Compton, C. (2009). Using wikis for collaborative writing and intercultural learning. In M. Dantas-Whitney & S. Rilling (Eds.), *Authenticity in the adult language classroom* (pp. 199–212). Alexandria, VA: TESOL.

Lee, H., & Wang, P. (2013). Discussing the factors contributing to students involvement in an EFL collaborative wiki project. *ReCALL, 25*(2), 233–249. doi:10.1017/S0958344013000025

Lehman, R. (2006). The role of emotion in creating instructor and learner presence in the distance education experience. *Journal of Cognitive Affective Learning*, *2*(2), 12–26.

Lehman, R. M., & Conceição, S. C. O. (2010). *Creating a sense of presence in online teaching*. San Francisco, CA: Jossey-Bass.

Li, M. (2013). Individual novices and collective experts: Collective scaffolding in wiki-based small group writing. *System*, *41*(3), 752–769. doi:10.1016/j.system.2013.07.021

Li, M., & Zhu, W. (2013). Patterns of computer-mediated interaction in small writing groups using wikis. *Computer Assisted Language Learning*, *26*(1), 61–82. doi:10.1080/09588221.2011.631142

Lin, H., & Kelsey, K. (2009). Building a networked environment in wikis: The evolving phases of collaborative learning in a wiki-book project. *Journal of Educational Computing Research*, *40*(2), 145–169. doi:10.2190/EC.40.2.a

Lund, A. (2008). Wikis: A collective approach to language production. *ReCALL*, *20*(1), 35–54. doi:10.1017/S0958344008000414

Ornberg Berglund, T. (2009). Multimodal student interaction online: An ecological perspective. *ReCALL*, *21*(2), 186–205. doi:10.1017/S0958344009000184

Richardson, J., & Swan, K. (2003). An examination of social presence in online learning: Students' perceived learning and satisfaction. *Journal of Asynchronous Learning Networks*, *7*(1), 68–88. Retrieved from http://hdl.handle.net/2142/18713

Shea, P., & Bidjerano, T. (2009). Community of inquiry as a theoretical framework to foster epistemic engagement and cognitive presence in online education. *Computers & Education*, *52*(3), 543–553. doi:10.1016/j.compedu.2008.10.007

Short, J., Williams, E., & Christie, B. (1976). *The social psychology of telecommunications*. London, UK: John Wiley & Sons.

Stoddart, A., Chan, J. Y., & Liu, G. (2016). Enhancing successful outcomes of wiki-based collaborative writing: A state-of-the art review of facilitation frameworks. *Interactive Learning Environments*, *24*(1), 142–157. doi:10.1080/10494820.2013.825810

Storch, N. (2002). Patterns of interaction in ESL pair work. *Language Learning*, *52*(1), 119–158. doi:10.1111/1467-9922.00179

Storch, N. (2011). Collaborative writing in L2 contexts: Processes, outcomes, and future directions. *Annual Review of Applied Linguistics*, *31*, 275–288. doi:10.1017/S0267190511000079

Swain, M. (2000). The output hypothesis and beyond: Mediating acquisition through collaborative dialogue. In J. Lantolf (Ed.), *Sociocultural theory and second language learning* (pp. 97–114). Oxford, UK: Oxford University Press.

Swain, M. (2006). Languaging, agency and collaboration in advanced second language learning. In H. Byrnes (Ed.), *Advanced language learning: The contribution of Halliday and Vygotsky* (pp. 95–108). London, UK: Continuum.

Swain, M., & Deters, P. (2007). New mainstream SLA theory: Expanded and enriched. *Modern Language Journal*, *91*(5), 820–836. doi:10.1111/j.1540-4781.2007.00671.x

Swan, K. (2002). Building learning communities in online courses: The importance of interaction. *Education Communication and Information*, *2*(1), 23–49. doi:10.1080/1463631022000005016

Swan, K., Garrison, D. R., & Richardson, J. C. (2009). A constructivist approach to online learning: The Community of Inquiry framework. In C. R. Payne (Ed.), *Information technology and constructivism in higher education: Progressive learning frameworks* (pp. 43–57). Hershey, PA: IGI Global. doi:10.4018/978-1-60566-654-9.ch004

Swan, K., & Shea, P. (2005). The development of virtual learning communities. In S. R. Hiltz & R. Goldman (Eds.), *Asynchronous Learning Networks: The Research Frontier* (pp. 239–260). New York, NY: Hampton Press.

Swan, K., Shea, P., Fredericksen, E., Pickett, A., Pelz, W., & Maher, G. (2000). Building knowledge building communities: Consistency, contact and communication in the virtual classroom. *Journal of Educational Computing Research*, *23*(4), 389–413. doi:10.2190/W4G6-HY52-57P1-PPNE

Tan, L., Wigglesworth, G., & Storch, N. (2010). Pair interaction and mode of communication: Comparing face-to-face and computer mediated communication. *Australian Review of Applied Linguistics*, *33*(3), 1–27. doi:10.2104/aral1027

Tour, E. (2015). Digital mindsets: Teachers' technology use in personal life and teaching. *Language Learning & Technology*, *19*(3), 124–139. Retrieved from http://llt.msu.edu/issues/october2015/tour.pdf

Valsiner, J., & van der Veer, R. (2000). *The Social Mind. Construction of the Idea*. Cambridge, UK: Cambridge University Press.

van Lier, L. (2004). The semiotics and ecology of language learning: Perception, voice, identity and democracy. *Utbuilding & Demokrati*, *3*, 79–103.

Vygotsky, L. S. (1978). *Mind in society: The development of higher psychological processes*. Cambridge, MA: Harvard University Press.

Wang, S., & Vásquez, C. (2012). Web 2.0 and second language learning: What does the research tell us? *CALICO Journal*, *29*(3), 412–430. doi:10.11139/cj.29.3.412-430

Ware, P., & Kessler, G. (2013). CALL and digital feedback. In M. T. Reinders & M. Warschauer (Eds.), *Computer-assisted language learning* (pp. 323–339). London, UK: Bloomsbury.

Ware, P. D., & Warschauer, M. (2006). Electronic feedback and second language writing. In K. Hyland & F. Hyland (Eds.), *Feedback in second language writing: Contexts and issues* (pp. 105–122). Cambridge, UK: Cambridge University Press. doi:10.1017/CBO9781139524742.008

Watanabe, Y. (2008). Peer-peer interaction between L2 learners of different proficiency levels: Their interactions and reflections. *Canadian Modern Language Review*, *64*(4), 605–663. doi:10.3138/cmlr.64.4.605

Wenger, E. (2006). *Communities of practice: Learning, meaning, and identity*. Cambridge, UK: Cambridge University Press.

Yu, S., & Lee, I. (2016). Peer feedback in second language writing (20052014). *Language Teaching*, *49*(4), 461–493. doi:10.1017/S0261444816000161

## ADDITIONAL READING

American Public University System. (2017). The Community of Inquiry. Retrieved March 14, 2017 from http://www.apus.edu/ctl/faculty/community-of-inquiry/

Davies, R. J. (2011). Second-language acquisition and the information age: How social software has created a new mode of learning. *TESL Canada Journal*, *28*(2), 11–19. doi:10.18806/tesl.v28i2.1069

Dewey, J. (2010). How we think. Boston, MA: D.C. Heath and Company; Retrieved from https://archive.org/details/howwethink000838mbp

Garrison, D. R. (2007). Online community of inquiry review: social, cognitive, and teaching presence issues. *Journal of Asynchronous Learning Networks, 11*(1), 61+. Retrieved fromk http://sloanconsortium.org/jaln/v11n1/online-community-inquiry-review-social-cognitive-and-teaching-presence-issues

Garrison, R., Cleveland-Innes, M., & Vaughn, N. (2017). The Community of Inquiry. Retrieved March 14, 2017 from https://coi.athabascau.ca/

Garrison, R., Cleveland-Innes, M., & Vaughn, N. (2017). The COI Survey. Retrieved March 14, 2017 from https://coi.athabascau.ca/coi-model/coi-survey/

Hauck, M., & Warnecke, S. (2013). Materials design in CALL: Social presence in online environments. In M. Thomas, H. Reinders, & M. Warschauer (Eds.), *Contemporary computer-assisted language learning* (pp. 95–115). New York, NY: Bloomsbury.

Levy, M., & Stockwell, G. (2006). *CALL Dimensions: Options and issues in computer-assisted language learning*. Mahwah, NJ: Lawrence Erlbaum Associates.

Neumeier, P. (2005). A closer look at blended learning: Parameters for designing a blended learning environment for language teaching and research. *ReCALL*, *17*(02), 163–178. doi:10.1017/S0958344005000224

Potts, D. (2005). Pedagogy, purpose, and the second language learner in on-line communities. *Canadian Modern Language Review*, *62*(1), 137–160. doi:10.3138/cmlr.62.1.137

Senior, R. (2010). Connectivity: A framework for understanding effective language teaching in face-to-face and online learning communities. *RELC Journal*, *41*(2), 137–147. doi:10.1177/0033688210375775

Shea, P., & Bidjerano, T. (2010). Learning presence: Towards a theory of self-efficacy, self-regulation, and the development of communities of inquiry in online and blended learning environments. *Computers & Education*, *55*(4), 1721–1731. doi:10.1016/j.compedu.2010.07.017

Shea, P., Chun, S. L., & Pickett, A. (2006). A study of teaching presence and student sense of learning community in fully online and web-enhanced college courses. *The Internet and Higher Education*, *9*(3), 175–190. doi:10.1016/j.iheduc.2006.06.005

Siemens, G. (2005, January). Connectivism: A learning theory for the digital age. *International Journal of Instructional Technology & Distance Learning*. Retrieved from http://www.itdl.org/Journal/Jan_05/article01.htm

Stockwell, G. (2012). *Computer-assisted language learning: Diversity in research and practice*. New York: Cambridge University Press; doi:10.1017/CBO9781139060981

Wang, Y. (2007). Task design in videoconferencing-supported language learning. *CALICO Journal*, *24*(3), 591–630. Retrieved from http://www.jstor.org/stable/24147979

## KEY TERMS AND DEFINITIONS

**Cognitive Presence:** The degree to which learners can build meaning through sustained reflection and communication.

**Collaborative Learning:** Learning conducted collaboratively with others.

**Community of Inquiry Framework:** A theoretical framework that represents learner-centered and meaningful learning through the active engagement of three elements in an online learning environment: cognitive, social and teaching presence.

**Computer-Assisted Language Learning:** Language teaching and learning that is mediated through computer-based tools.

**ESL:** English-as-a-second language, where English is used as a second or additional language.

**English for Academic Purposes:** The study of English language for use in academic, often post-secondary contexts.

**English Language Writing Instruction:** The process of teaching writing to English language learners.

**Online Language Teaching:** Language teaching that is conducted through online tools.

**Social Presence:** The ability of learners to feel connected within a community in a trusted environment where they can project their individual identities to develop meaningful relationships.

**Teaching Presence:** The design and facilitation of cognitive and social processes to realize meaningful learning outcomes.

## ENDNOTE

1 The Community of Inquiry model is often also referred to as the Community of Inquiry framework. Given this paper's focus on developing a theoretically-informed framework, to avoid confusion we have elected to use the term model to describe this theoretical framework.

# Chapter 2
# Beyond Determinism and Instrumentalism:
## Re-Conceptualizing Technology for CALL

**Sardar M. Anwaruddin**
*St. Francis Xavier University, Canada*

## ABSTRACT

*The primary goal of this chapter is to review two dominant theories of technology and propose a new direction of theory and practice for teaching and learning of English as an additional language. I describe this new direction as a cultural theory of technological mediation. The chapter is divided into three sections. In the first section, I review some dominant theoretical approaches in the literature on CALL. In the second section, I discuss two theories of technology: technological determinism and technological instrumentalism. In the third section, I argue that both determinism and instrumentalism have remained as dominant theoretical approaches in the field of CALL. I discuss why both of these approaches are problematic. Then I propose an alternative to these theoretical approaches. I conclude the chapter by providing three pedagogical principles and a set of heuristic questions that may be helpful for language teachers and language-education researchers.*

## INTRODUCTION

The field of Computer Assisted Language Learning (CALL) has attracted criticism for its alleged lack of a robust theoretical foundation (Chapelle, 1997; Wang & Vásquez, 2012). Huh and Hu (2005) claimed that many CALL studies did not "include rich theoretical support" (p. 10). Similarly, Lomicka and Lord (2009) lamented the lack of "a solid base of well-grounded research investigating Web 2.0 tools in language learning from theoretical and empirical perspectives" (p. 5). However, in recent years, we have seen that a growing number of studies have paid greater attention to theory. Yet, they focus exclusively on sociocultural and cognitive theories related to second language acquisition (SLA), and there is an absence of a clear focus on the theories of technology.

DOI: 10.4018/978-1-5225-2933-0.ch002

Among others, Chapelle (1997) was concerned about the lack of a theoretical foundation in the CALL literature. She argued strongly for the need to ground CALL research in the theories of instructed SLA. In a similar vein, Wang and Vásquez (2012) reviewed 43 empirical studies and found that 24 of the studies "either did not clearly state their theoretical framework or did not appear to have an obvious theoretical foundation" (p. 419). However, compared to the research conducted in the 1980s and 1990s, there has been a much more sustained focus on theory in the studies conducted in recent years. This focus on theory is perhaps a response to Chapelle's (1997) call for a theoretically grounded CALL field.

With regard to Wang and Vásquez's (2012) findings, I am interested more in the studies that clearly stated their theoretical frameworks than in those that did not. So, what are the theories that have been taken up in recent CALL studies? Wang and Vásquez found the following theoretical frameworks used in the empirical studies included in their review:

- Sociocultural Approach
- Activity Theory
- Socio-constructivist Approach
- Community of Practice
- Social Cognitive Theory
- A Framework for Autonomy
- Interactionist Model
- Critical Language Learning
- Speech Act
- Self-determination Theory
- Diffusion of Innovation
- Vygotsky's Notion of Double Stimulation

Summarizing their findings, Wang and Vásquez (2012) write that most "research was framed along sociocultural and sociocognitive dimensions such as sociocultural theory, activity theory, socio-constructivism, community of practice, social cognitive theory, etc." (p. 420). While the theoretical base of CALL has certainly enlarged, I argue that the focus has remained disproportionately on various theories of instructed SLA, mainly in the sociocultural and interactionist traditions. However, there has been very little attention to theories of technology that shed light on the nature of technology and on the interconnection between technology and human activity in various contexts of technology use.

The field of SLA is built upon a rich variety of theoretical foundations. Similarly, CALL also needs to embrace the theoretical richness that exists in the broader literature of educational studies. It should not narrow its focus and investigate crucial pedagogical issues only through the sociocultural and psycho-cognitive theories of instructed SLA. As Kern (2006) warns us:

*Given the complexity and diversity of goals, contexts, and problems in CALL research, a one size fits all approach will not work. Rather, on the micro level of the individual study researchers should rigorously work within the SLA paradigm that most adequately suits their particular research questions, and on the macro level they should look to the synergy of multiple perspectives and paradigms to best inform their understanding and future research. (pp. 187-188)*

For such synergy of multiple perspectives and theoretical richness, I argue, the field of CALL needs to evaluate its theoretical base and pay attention to the theories of technology. Such a move is important not only because teachers are increasingly called upon to use technology, but also due to the fact that technology fundamentally affects the learning and use of languages. For example, instant messaging and social media such as Twitter have contributed much to the shortening of written linguistic expressions.

## TECHNOLOGICAL DETERMINISM AND TECHNOLOGICAL INSTRUMENTALISM

In this section, I briefly review two dominant theories of technology now—technological determinism and technological instrumentalism—and discuss how they have informed the CALL research. My claims and conclusions are based on my extensive review of CALL literature. Since the start of my teaching career in 2007, I have remained deeply interested in CALL. I have integrated various information and communication technologies (ICTs) into my curriculum and pedagogy. I have also carried out empirical and theoretical studies on the educational uses of ICTs (e.g., Anwaruddin, 2013, 2015a, 2015b, 2016). For these studies, I have reviewed many journal articles, books, and book chapters both in the field of CALL and in the broader field of educational studies. While this chapter is mainly polemical, I draw examples from various empirical studies to support my claims and recommendations.

### Technological Determinism

The theory of technological determinism maintains that technology is autonomous, that technology has a direct and predetermined impact on the thinking and activities of its users, and that a given society's development and cultural values are shaped by its technologies. In other words, technology determines the structure of social and cultural activities and relationships. As Dusek (2006) writes:

*According to technological determinism, as technology develops and changes, the institutions in the rest of society change, as does the art and religion of the society. For instance, the computer has changed the nature of jobs and work. The telephone led to the decline of letter writing, but the Internet has changed the nature of interpersonal communication again, leaving written records unlike the telephone. (p. 84)*

This theory of technology has had a tremendous impact on the field of CALL. Warschauer (1998) writes that "from a determinist perspective, a computer is an all-powerful machine that in and of itself brings about certain determined results" (p. 757). Proponents of this deterministic view of technology seek to understand the effects of computers on the learning of second/foreign languages. Studies that are based on the deterministic view of technology explore whether computer-based technology makes learning second/foreign language easier and more effective. For example, Dizon (2016) examined the impact of Facebook use on the L2 writing of Japanese EFL students. Comparing the experimental group using Facebook with the control group using paper-and-pencil, the researcher found that "the experimental group made more significant gains in terms of writing fluency" (p. 1249). Another typical example would be the studies that examine "the effects of hypertext gloss use on L2 vocabulary acquisition in computerized reading contexts" (Yun, 2011, p. 39).

The deterministic view of technology use is also dominant in the literature on technology-enhanced teacher development. For example, in 2016, the *Journal of Technology and Teacher Education* published sixteen peer-reviewed articles in four issues. The editors of the journal summarize the articles and discuss their implications (Chenowith & Ferdig, 2016). Below I quote some of their summary statements:

- Wearables can be used to support teacher development;
- Digital tools may best be implemented by further exploring the relationship between practical and conceptual factors;
- Video can support professional development in both cognitive and affective outcomes in areas like classroom management;
- Classroom simulations can positively impact communication self-efficacy as well as self-realization of a need for personal growth;
- Animations can promote the use of noticing as well as assessment of pedagogical content knowledge;
- Mobile technologies enable preservice teachers to make connections between academic learning and everyday settings;
- Twitter can be used as a platform for professional development;
- Preservice teachers may need explicit instruction on what is/is not appropriate to post online (Chenowith and Ferdig, 2016, pp. 374-376).

Despite their brevity, these statements clearly suggest a deterministic approach to technology use for teachers' professional learning and development.

It should be noted that researchers often work under pressure from administrators, research funders, and manufacturers of educational technologies who want to know the causal effects of technology use. Through their studies, researchers are expected to find out the positive impact of technology on teaching and learning. Technology-based teacher development programs carry out their intervention and often employ researchers to find out its impact. In such contexts, researchers tend to use discourses that would make the funders happy. In a previous study, I examined one such teacher development project in Bangladesh. It is a 9-year, nation-wide project known as English in Action (EIA). This £50 million-project (approximately 64 million US dollars) is funded by the United Kingdom's Department for International Development, and supported by the Bangladesh government. The EIA project aims "to contribute to the economic growth of Bangladesh by providing communicative English language as a tool for better access to the world economy" (Walsh, Power, Khatoon, Biswas, Paul, Sarkar, & Griffiths, 2013, p. 189). One of the key goals of this project is to provide professional development to 75,000 teachers by the year of 2017 (EIA, 2015). EIA uses the slogan "trainer in your pocket" to highlight its uses of handheld mobile devices (e.g., iPod, low-cost mobile phones, and portable amplifiers) to provide teachers with professional development (PD) materials. My analysis of discourses used in various EIA publications revealed EIA researchers' enthusiasm for the popular discourses of technology use for educational development. It also showed how discourses of technological determinism muddle our understanding of teachers' lived experiences of learning and teaching in various cultural and material contexts (Anwaruddin, 2016).

A small but growing body of literature shows that the deterministic view of technology is not helpful in the realm of teaching and learning. Education is such a complex enterprise that there is very little scope to "determine" in advance how an individual will learn and act upon his/her learning. As Oliver (2011) argues, "technology should not be understood to operate on a causal model; it does not have straightforward 'impact' in some simple, mechanical way on the practices that it encounters" (p. 381). Yet, a key research goal in the field of educational technology has been "to 'prove' that technology leads to 'effective' learning outcomes" (Selwyn, 2008, p. 83). A dominant tendency in research within this field is "to focus only on the positive aspects of education technology use" (Selwyn, 2008, p. 83). Consequently, there is an increasingly abundant supply of research studies that document what I call "happy-ending stories" of technology use in education.

One of the dangers of an over-reliance on technology is that it ignores human agency, which is always influenced by cultural and materials contexts. Agency is always emergent, arising from multiple factors (Morgan, 2010). Therefore, it is important that we take a look at technology-integrated curricula and examine how teacher agency is conceptualized in such curricula. Here I adopt Priestley, Edwards, Priestley, and Miller's (2012) view that:

*Teacher agency is largely about repertoires for manoeuvre, or the possibilities for different forms of action available to teachers at particular points in time. These are dependent upon temporal aspects—the iterative and projective, as well as the practical evaluative possibilities afforded by the material and social configurations of the present context. (p. 211)*

Unfortunately, we often see that this notion of teacher agency is restricted in the curricula that are based on a deterministic view of technology. In Anwaruddin (2015a), I have analyzed a teaching segment and discussed how a classroom teacher's agency is extremely restricted in a technology-integrated classroom. While carrying out her lesson, the teacher is seen as a mere "tool" for implementing a top-down, pre-packaged curriculum.

A deterministic view of technology use in teaching and learning avoids asking deep questions about "how digital technologies sit alongside pre-existing cultures and structures of schooling" and other important "questions which explore educational technologies from the lived experiences of those using (and those *not* using) them" (Selwyn, 2008, p. 83). Thus, the field of CALL needs to move beyond using technology as a means of control, and to embrace technology as one of the many actors in a complex environment where the teaching and learning of languages take place. Such a move is imperative because "technology shapes how people use language in particular instances, not as an autonomous, deterministic force, but in interaction with a range of factors including individual volition, social conventions, situational context, and material constraints" (Chun, Smith, & Kern, 2016, p. 65). Therefore, the cultural structures within which technology is to be utilized are something that cannot be ignored. (I will return to the topic of culture in the following section.)

## Technological Instrumentalism

There is a growing body of literature that opposes technological determinism. It asks us to recognize that individual users always bring their own experience, knowledge, and understanding to the technology they use. A general line of argument is that technology is neither bad, nor good. What matters is how we use it. Here, the user is viewed as an active and autonomous agent capable of resisting the deterministic tendency of technology (Mason, 2016). Thus, the theory of instrumentalism maintains that "technology is neutral and that it evolves from previous technologies in response to our needs, to make our lives easier and more productive. In this view, technology does not influence society but rather it is used for people for good or bad purposes that they decide by themselves" (Carr, 2013, para. 10). Technology is understood as tools that are used by individuals to meet their own diverse needs and purposes. Instrumentalism is, in many ways, similar to the idea of instrumental rationality, which gained prominence in the twentieth century. Dusek (2006) believes that "instrumental rationality is means–end rationality. It involves the search for the most efficient means to reach a given end" (p. 57). It is based on "the causal sequences or "if–then" connections of science. If one wishes to reach a certain goal, then one must follow a certain procedure" (p. 57).

In the field of CALL, the instrumental view of technology finds its expression when various kinds of technology are conceptualized and used as effective tools. In many studies, ICTs are used as tools to teach the four skills, to keep students on task, or to facilitate students' active learning (for a review of literature, see Golonka, Bowles, Frank, Richardson, & Freynik, 2014). In recent years, much attention has been focused on the advantages of using cell phones, iPad, and various mobile apps as language learning tools (Blake, 2013; Godwin-Jones, 2011; Kiernan & Aizawa, 2004). The technology-as-neutral view is being popularized with the shift from a cognitive approach to a socio-cognitive approach to language education. This shift generally considers "the computer as a tool that mediates interactions between language learners and other humans" (Wang & Vásquez, 2012, p. 420). This view of technology-as-a-neutral-tool has been manifested, among others, in the body of literature focused on learner autonomy. As Kim (2014) writes, "Learners can control their learning processes as much as possible and can become quite independent of teachers when they work with computers" (para. 2). Lee's (2016) study finds that learner autonomy is fostered when students engage in language learning activities through computer-mediated communication using digital tools.

However, this perspective of technological instrumentalism is problematic because we can never become a fully autonomous agent. Our agency is always *co-shaped* not only by the tools we use, but also by the socio-material environment in which we use the tools. We always operate within certain ecology of practice, which binds us—through intricate multilayered relationships—to self and others. These others can be both human and non-human actors. Therefore, technology use is neither completely deterministic, nor fully instrumental. I would like to propose that our agency for using technology for educational purposes is not *fixed*, but rather *fluid*. Drawing from Priestley, Biesta, and Robinson (2015), I suggest that teachers' and students' agency to utilize technologies should not be "understood as individual capacity—as something that individuals have or don't have—but as something that is achieved in and through concrete contexts-for-action" (p. 34). In this light, agency to use technology in appropriate ways is distributed between the technology-user and the broader socio-cultural-material context.

## TOWARD A CULTURAL HERMENEUTICS OF TECHNOLOGY

Both determinism and instrumentalism are unsatisfactory because none of these approaches sufficiently addresses the complexities involved in pedagogy. By pedagogy, I do not mean a simple and linear way of transmitting information from the teacher to the student. My use of the term pedagogy is broad, and it involves a particular kind of thoughtfulness that permeates the interactions and relationships that go on in various settings of education. Here my understanding of pedagogy is influenced by Max van Manen's works. For him (1983), pedagogy involves:

*A thoughtfulness of how we speak and listen to children; a thoughtfulness of the way we are in the world as men and women, mothers and fathers, but also as teachers, friends, lovers, comrades, and so forth;*

*a thoughtfulness about the limits and possibilities of how we speak, of the languages of common sense and of science; a thoughtfulness of how we construct and perpetuate the often repressive institutional and ideological environments in which we live and in which we place our children; a thoughtfulness of how we should conduct and interpret our research activities; and generally, a thoughtfulness of the principle that allows us to be principled actors in the first place. (p. 1)*

This kind of phenomenological thoughtfulness opposes an instrumental view of pedagogy as a method of transmitting knowledge and information.

Pedagogy also involves a cultural politics and a variety of social practices. It is not a value-free technique of knowledge transmission. As Hamilton (2009) writes:

*Pedagogy entails a political orientation towards the good life, towards using a moral compass, and towards following prescribed courses. To characterize pedagogy as relating merely to ways or methods of instruction is, therefore, reductionist. It misses the point that teaching (including self-instruction) is a goal-directed activity where the goals and the means of reaching such goals are defined in terms of social values. (p. 14)*

In this light, pedagogy points to the complexities that characterize the (often unpredictable) relationships between teaching and learning.

Yet, in much of the literature, pedagogy is used as a synonym for teaching. It is conceptualized, in a narrow sense, as a way of transmitting information. In the field of CALL, when technology is used as a means to achieve pre-defined goals, a narrow view of pedagogy is adopted. Commenting on North American educational practices, van Manen (2008) argues that:

*The dominance of technological and calculative thought is so strong and deeply embedded that it seems well-nigh impossible to offer acceptable alternatives to the technocratic ideologies and the inherently instrumental pre-suppositional structures of teaching practice. The roots of this technologizing of curriculum and teaching knowledge have grown deeply into the metaphysical sensibilities of western cultures. (p. 4)*

Although van Manen's writing is not pointed directly to the field of CALL, it bears important implications for it. The technocratic ideologies that van Manen discussed are visible in the literature on CALL. For this reason, I argue that the curriculum and pedagogy of CALL need to move beyond the deterministic and instrumental views of technology.

Such a movement is imperative because three decades of enthusiasm for computer-based technologies has yielded very little change in language education. After years of empirical research, we now have very little reliable evidence that digital technologies have significant impact on the language development of second/foreign language learners. A recent review of studies of technology in L2 learning finds that:

*The evidence that technology has a direct beneficial impact on linguistic outcomes is slight and inconclusive, but it may impact indirectly and positively on learner attitudes and behaviours and may promote collaboration. On the whole, the research reviewed lacked the quality that would reassure practitioners and policy-makers that technological investment is warranted. (Macaro, Handley, & Walter, 2012, p. 1)*

This finding warrants a serious re-thinking of the uses and abuses of new technologies in the curriculum and pedagogy of second/foreign language education.

## A Cultural Theory of Technological Mediation

In order to initiate such a re-thinking and to avoid the deterministic and instrumental tendencies in the CALL literature, I propose an alternative view of technology, which I describe as a cultural theory of technological mediation. My proposal is influenced by the empirical turn of American philosophy of technology (Achterhuis, 2001). This empirical turn rejects the classical and modernist views of technology. It also rejects the dualism between nature and culture that has existed in Western thought for centuries. The empirical turn

*...refuses the nostalgic Heideggerian move of rejecting technology in favor of a purportedly more idyllic and premodern relationship between culture and nature. Instead, though it necessarily assumes a critical stance toward technological practices, American philosophy of technology seeks to understand contemporary technological culture so that more primordial human meanings can be derived from within it. (Koukal, 2003, p. 226)*

Among the American philosophers of technology, I draw particularly upon Don Ihde's works. Ihde (1990) illustrates the role of tools and artifacts in our relationship to the world, the diversity of human-technology relations, and the non-neutrality of technology. A central theme in his philosophy of technology is that technologies are always culturally embedded. In other words, Ihde (1990) is interested in how "cultures *embed* technologies" (p. 124, emphasis original). Ihde's core argument is that

*Human beings have always already left the Garden of Eden for a technically mediated world of some sort. We are homo technologicus by our very nature. Technology is not something added on after the fact.... Technology is as natural to human beings as language and culture; its specific content is historically contingent but it will always be found wherever there are human beings. (Feenberg, 2012, p. 1)*

One of the central tenets of Ihde's works is the notion of technological mediation. It is concerned primarily with "the role of technology in human action (conceived as the ways in which human beings are present in their world) and human experience (conceived as the ways in which their world is present to them)" (Verbeek, 2006, p. 363).

At the heart of the concept of technological mediation is the argument that technologies are always culturally embedded. Elaborating on this argument, Ihde (1990) discusses a number of relationships that we can establish with/through technology. Two of these relationships are pertinent to my purpose in this chapter. The first one is the *embodiment relation*. This happens, for example, when I use a pair of glasses to look at the world. The world is perceived in a different way. In Ihde's (1990) words, "I am aware of the glasses, but the focal phenomenon is the perceptual transparency that the glasses allow" (p. 94). Here, technology (the glasses) becomes an extension of the human body. The second relation is *hermeneutical*. In this relationship, technology provides us with a particular representation of the world, which requires interpretation. For instance, "reading off a thermometer does not result in a direct sensation of heat or cold but gives a value that requires interpretation to tell something about reality"

(Verbeek, 2006, p. 365). This view of technological mediation, I argue, has the potential to resist the CALL field's obsession with technological determinism and instrumentalism.

If the embodiment relation is about perception, the hermeneutical relation is about interpretation. Technology always mediates our experience of the world. It does not simply present the world *to* us. We use our own interpretive lenses to make sense of what is presented to us through technological artifacts. However, the notion of mediation does not suggest that technological artifacts simply mediate the subject and the object in their original states of being. Instead, they shape and re-define the very ideas of the subject and the object. As Verbeek (2001) summarized:

*Mediating artifacts shape not only the way a predefined subject relates to a predefined object or the way a predefined object can appear to a predefined subject. They shape the interrelation itself between subject and object, from which both are constituted. Mediation does not simply take place between a subject and an object, but rather co-shapes subjectivity and objectivity. (p. 131)*

In this light, technology does not provide a simple "access" to a world: both the human and the world are transformed as part of the mediation.

In any form of technological mediation, culture plays very important roles. In Ihde's works, the idea of culture is used in broad terms to encompass artifacts, beliefs, and practices. Technological artifacts are not autonomous tools that work independently of the broader culture. Understanding the role of mediation is complicated not only by the relation of perception, but also by the relation of interpretation. How do I make sense of my sensory perception when I use an artifact? The answer lies in our turn to culture. Our cultural knowledge provides us with certain interpretive frameworks, and we make sense of our perceptions by using these frameworks. As Ihde (1990) summarized:

*Technologies are non-neutral and essentially, but structurally, ambiguous. In the relationship with humans and humans-in-culture, technologies transform experience and its variations....at the complex level of a cultural hermeneutics, technologies may be variantly embedded; the 'same' technology in another cultural context becomes quite a 'different' technology. (p. 144).*

Thus, it is not just technological artifacts that matter. Our cultural knowledge helps us understand how artifacts co-shape our relationship with the world around us.

Technological artifacts gain or lose meaning and significance in relation to specific use-contexts. A good example is how Indian prayer wheels became windmills in the West. In a similar way, a mobile phone can become a tool for foreign language learning. However, the use of this tool and the kind of relation it may foster between the language learner and the object of learning will be significantly influenced by the cultural context of its use. A number of factors such as the learner's prior knowledge, existing culture of technology use, availability of material resources, and a supporting environment of pedagogical practice will enable or restrict the learner's agency to use the phone in beneficial ways. Therefore, teachers, learners, and researchers need to pay close attention to how new technologies interact with existing cultural norms and practices. Too much trust in technology's capacity to support language learning will reinforce a corporatist agenda, which aims for more sale of technological tools and for more monetary profits for the "Silicon Valleys" of the world. On the other hand, too much trust in the agency of individual user will ignore the situated and distributed nature of human agency. It will put undue emphasis on the individual, who is only a part of a bigger whole that makes successful language learning possible.

## FUTURE RESEARCH DIRECTIONS

I have argued that the field of CALL has been heavily influenced by two dominant views of technology: determinism and instrumentalism. I have discussed why both of these views are limiting. In general, there is a tendency in the CALL literature to focus more on technology itself than on the pedagogy. As Huh and Hu (2005) complained, "some studies focus on the technology used in the study rather than on what happens through, with, or around the technology, making the technocentric results of limited use to researchers and practitioners" (p. 10). To move the field of CALL beyond this focus on technology itself, I have proposed a cultural theory of technological mediation.

This concept of technological mediation provides at least three important implications for language teaching and for future research on language education. First, technology co-shapes, but never fully determines, the activity of its users. The moment I begin to use an artifact (e.g., a cell phone to have a conversation with a friend) I enter into a different reality. My subjectivity transforms when the cell phone shrinks the distance between my friend and me. But, the phone does not determine my experience of the conversation (although it provides us with much convenience). Now I do not have to travel 100 miles to have the conversation with my friend. With regard to the phone's agency, it connects two persons, and also facilitates the conversation. But, it does not determine the directions and outcomes of our conversation. A relevant research question to explore this implication is: How does technology interact with the existing culture in which language learning takes place?

However, the first implication does not mean that the cell phone is neutral. This leads us to the second implication that technological artifacts—when in use—become a part of a complex web of actors that are interdependent. For example, without the cell phone I would not be able to have the conversation with my friend today. Thus, technology enhances my agency, which is also influenced by other factors such as the availability of a network signal and my friends' ability to pick up the phone at the right time. Thus, artifacts do not simply enable humans to do something and then cease to remain part of the human activity. They remain intertwined with the activity itself in complex ways. A research question that may be helpful to understand this implication is: What is the nature of human agency as manifested in the activities of language learners and teachers?

The third implication is that technological artifacts help us enter into a relation of perception with the external world. But, they require us to use interpretive frameworks to understand the sensory perceptions. Thus, it becomes a moral choice for us to make sense of what artifacts do to us. Our cultural knowledge is a major resource in this interpretive work. Both the ideology and materiality of our culture influence our decision to choose one particular interpretation of the perception over other possibilities. Therefore, any de-contextualized understanding of technology use in language education is partial and incomplete. A relevant research question to explore this implication may be: How do the participants in a CALL environment make sense of their activity, and what kinds of interpretive resource do they use for such sense-making? These questions, I hope, will be helpful to respond to Stickler and Shi's (2016) call for moving the CALL field from positivist methodologies toward interpretivist approaches. Such a movement will not only make "the human element eminently valuable," but also provide the CALL field with "innovative approaches and surprising outcomes" (Stickler & Shi, 2016, p. 125).

## CONCLUSION

These implications of a cultural theory of technological mediation and the heuristic questions invite us to view students of second/foreign languages as situated in a complex network of actors comprising people (e.g., students, teachers, and parents), technological artifacts, linguistic knowledge and skills, and various forces of ideological and material cultures. Learning languages is a complex and unpredictable enterprise; so, it is erroneous to assume a simple one-way delivery of information and knowledge from the teacher to the learner. Yet, much work on the integration of technology in the curriculum and pedagogy of second/foreign language education is based on an unwarranted enthusiasm for technology. Like any other content areas, language education is investing heavily in technology use in the classroom. However, we have very slim evidence that the use of new technologies significantly improves students' learning outcomes (Macaro, Handley, & Walter, 2012). Therefore, it is important to develop a critical awareness of the over-optimistic rhetoric of the technology enthusiasts. Such awareness is crucial because nowadays the "education technology research is overpopulated by in-depth case studies of 'model' schools and classrooms, with enthusiastic teachers and well-resourced students basking in the glow of the 'Hawthorne effect' of research attention" (Buckingham, 2007 as cited in Selwyn, 2008, p. 83). It is my hope that the cultural approach to technological mediation presented in this chapter will be helpful to develop such an awareness among the teachers and researchers of second/foreign language education.

## REFERENCES

Achterhuis, H. (Ed.). (2001). American philosophy of technology: The empirical turn. Bloomington, IN: Indiana University Press.

Anwaruddin, S. M. (2013). Web 2.0 and language learners' motivation: An action research study. *Canadian Journal of Action Research*, *14*(1), 51–68.

Anwaruddin, S. M. (2015a). ICTs in language and literacy education in Bangladesh: A critical review. *Current Issues in Education*, *18*(1), 1–13.

Anwaruddin, S. M. (2015b). Teacher professional learning in online communities: Toward existentially reflective practice. *Reflective Practice: International and Multidisciplinary Perspectives*, *16*(6), 806–820. doi:10.1080/14623943.2015.1095730

Anwaruddin, S. M. (2016). ICT and language teacher development in the global south: A new materialist discourse analysis. *Educational Studies*, *52*(3), 260–278. doi:10.1080/00131946.2016.1169183

Blake, R. J. (2013). *Brave new digital classroom: Technology and foreign language learning*. Washington, DC: Georgetown University Press.

Carr, P. (2013). *What makes technology change?*. Retrieved from https://impactofinformationsystemsonsociety.wordpress.com/2013/01/21/what-makes-technology-change/

Chapelle, C. (1997). CALL in the year 2000: Still in search of research paradigms? *Language Learning & Technology*, *1*, 19–43.

Chenowith, N., & Ferdig, R. (2016). Editorial: What we learned about technology and teacher education in 2016. *Journal of Technology and Teacher Education*, *24*(4), 373–382.

Chun, D., Smith, B., & Kern, R. (2016). Technology in language use, language teaching, and language learning. *Modern Language Journal*, *100*(1), 64–80. doi:10.1111/modl.12302

Dizon, G. (2016). A comparative study of Facebook vs. paper-and-pencil writing to improve L2 writing skills. *Computer Assisted Language Learning*, *29*(8), 1249–1258. doi:10.1080/09588221.2016.1266369

Dusek, V. (2006). *Philosophy of technology: An introduction*. Malden, MA: Blackwell.

English in Action. (2015). *English in Action Teaching and Learning Materials*. Retrieved from http://www.eiabd.com/eia/

Feenberg, A. (2012). *Making the gestalt switch*. Paper presented at the Society for Phenomenology and Existential Philosophy Conference, Rochester, NY. Retrieved from https://www.sfu.ca/~andrewf/Don_Ihde.pdf

Godwin-Jones, R. (2011). Emerging technologies: Mobile apps for language learning. *Language Learning & Technology*, *15*(2), 2–11.

Golonka, E. M., Bowles, A. R., Frank, V. M., Richardson, D. L., & Freynik, S. (2014). Technologies for foreign language learning: A review of technology types and their effectiveness. *Computer Assisted Language Learning*, *27*(1), 70–105. doi:10.1080/09588221.2012.700315

Hamilton, D. (2009). Blurred in translation: Reflections on pedagogy in public education. *Pedagogy, Culture & Society*, *17*(1), 5–16. doi:10.1080/14681360902742829

Huh, K., & Hu, W.-C. (2005). Criteria for effective CALL research. In J. L. Egbert & G. M. Petrie (Eds.), *CALL research perspectives* (pp. 9–21). Mahwah, NJ: Lawrence Erlbaum.

Ihde, D. (1990). *Technology and the lifeworld*. Bloomington, IN: Indiana University Press.

Kern, R. (2006). Perspectives on technology in learning and teaching languages. *TESOL Quarterly*, *40*(1), 183–210. doi:10.2307/40264516

Kiernan, P. J., & Aizawa, K. (2004). Cell phones in task based learning: Are cell phones useful language learning tools? *ReCALL*, *16*(01), 71–84. doi:10.1017/S0958344004000618

Kim, H.-J. (2014). The use of technology for learner autonomy in language classrooms. *ITBE Link*, *42*(3). Retrieved from http://www.itbe.org/v_newsletters/article_23358209.htm

Koukal, D. R. (2003). Review of the book American philosophy of technology: The empirical turn, edited by H. Achterhuis. Technology and Culture, 44(1), 225-226.

Lee, L. (2016). Autonomous learning through task-based instruction in fully online language courses. *Language Learning & Technology*, *20*(2), 81–97. Retrieved from http://llt.msu.edu/issues/june2016/lee.pdf

Lomicka, L., & Lord, G. (2009). Introduction to social networking, collaboration, and Web 2.0 tools. In L. Lomicka & G. Lord (Eds.), *The next generation: Social networking and online collaboration in foreign language learning* (pp. 1–11). San Marcos, TX: CALICO.

Macaro, E., Handley, Z., & Walter, C. (2012). A systematic review of CALL in English as a second language: Focus on primary and secondary education. *Language Teaching, 45*(1), 1-43. https://doi.org/10.1017/S0261444811000395

Mason, L. (2016). McLuhans challenge to critical media literacy: The City as Classroom textbook. *Curriculum Inquiry*, *46*(1), 79–97. doi:10.1080/03626784.2015.1113511

Morgan, B. (2010). Fostering conceptual roles for change: Identity and agency in ESEA teacher preparation. *Kritika Kultura*, *15*, 34–55.

Oliver, M. (2011). Technological determinism in educational technology research: Some alternative ways of thinking about the relationship between learning and technology. *Journal of Computer Assisted Learning*, *27*(5), 373–384. doi:10.1111/j.1365-2729.2011.00406.x

Priestley, M., Biesta, G., & Robinson, S. (2015). *Teacher agency: An ecological approach.* London: Bloomsbury.

Priestley, M., Edwards, R., Priestley, A., & Miller, K. (2012). Teacher agency in curriculum making: Agents of change and spaces for manoeuvre. *Curriculum Inquiry*, *42*(2), 191–214. doi:10.1111/j.1467-873X.2012.00588.x

Selwyn, N. (2008). From state-of-the-art to state-of-the-actual? Introduction to a special issue. *Technology, Pedagogy and Education*, *17*(2), 83–87. doi:10.1080/14759390802098573

Stickler, U., & Shi, L. (2016). TELL us about CALL: An introduction to the Virtual Special Issue (VSI) on the development of technology enhanced and computer assisted language learning published in the System Journal. *System*, *56*, 119–126. doi:10.1016/j.system.2015.12.004

van Manen, M. (1983). Editorial. Invitation to Phenomenology + Pedagogy. *Phenomenology + Pedagogy, 1*(1), i–ii.

van Manen, M. (2008). Pedagogical sensitivity and teachers practical knowing-in-action. *Peking University Educational Review*, *6*(1), 1–23.

Verbeek, P.-P. (2001). Don Ihde: The technological lifeworld. In H. Achterhuis (Ed.), *American philosophy of technology: The empirical turn* (pp. 119–146). Bloomington, IN: Indiana University Press.

Verbeek, P.-P. (2006). Materializing morality: Design ethics and technological mediation. *Science, Technology & Human Values*, *31*(3), 361–380. doi:10.1177/0162243905285847

Walsh, C., Power, T., Khatoon, M., Biswas, S., Paul, A., Sarkar, B., & Griffiths, M. (2013). The trainer in your pocket: Mobile phones within a teacher continuing professional development program in Bangladesh. *Professional Development in Education*, *39*(2), 186–200. doi:10.1080/19415257.2013.766232

Wang, S., & Vásquez, C. (2012). Web 2.0 and second language learning: What does the research tell us. *CALICO Journal*, *29*(3), 412–430. doi:10.11139/cj.29.3.412-430

Warschauer, M. (1998). Researching technology in TESOL: Determinist, instrumental, and critical approaches. *TESOL Quarterly*, *32*(4), 757–761. doi:10.2307/3588010

Yun, J. (2011). The effects of hypertext glosses on L2 vocabulary acquisition: A meta-analysis. *Computer Assisted Language Learning*, *24*(1), 39–58. doi:10.1080/09588221.2010.523285

## ADDITIONAL READING

Chapelle, C. (2003). *English language learning and technology: Lectures on applied linguistics in the age of information and communication technology*. Amsterdam: John Benjamins Publishing. doi:10.1075/lllt.7

Feenberg, A. (1991). *Critical theory of technology*. New York, NY: Oxford University Press.

Feenberg, A. (2002). *Transforming technology: A critical theory revisited*. New York, NY: Oxford University Press.

Schmid, E. C. (2006). Investigating the use of interactive whiteboard technology in the English language classroom through the lens of a critical theory of technology. *Computer Assisted Language Learning*, *19*(1), 47–62. doi:10.1080/09588220600804012

Sproat, R. (2010). *Language, technology, and society*. New York, NY: Oxford University Press.

## KEY TERMS AND DEFINITIONS

**Culture:** Ideas, practices, and behaviors that are shared by a group of people in a given historical period.

**Determinism:** A doctrine that human activities are determined by external forces such as material tools or social norms.

**Empiricism:** A theory that all knowledge derives from sense experiences.

**Hermeneutics:** The branch of philosophy that deals with the interpretation of texts and phenomena.

**Instrumentalism:** A doctrine of pragmatic philosophy, which maintains that human activities are directed towards achieving pre-defined goals. It views technology as tools for solving practical problems.

**Sociocultural:** Related to the interface of social and cultural factors.

**Technological Mediation:** Intervention of technologies in the relations between human beings and the world.

## ENDNOTE

1 During the formative period of the CALL literature in the 1990s, the computer was at the center of attention. But, today our lives are marked by the pervasive use of various media technologies. For this reason, Kern (2006) asks an interesting question: "Should CALL still be called CALL?" Kern (2006) believes that "the rapid convergence of functionality across digital devices, and our growing reliance on such devices for communication, means we may soon need to refer broadly to information and communication technologies rather than specifically to computers in our research" (p. 185). Following Kern's suggestion, I believe that we need to re-name the field of research that we have been calling CALL. Yet, in keeping with the title of this book, I use the term CALL. However, by using the acronym CALL, I intend to mean the teaching and learning of languages by utilizing a variety of information and communication technologies.

# Chapter 3
# Understanding Idiomaticity in CALL

**John I. Liontas**
*University of South Florida, USA*

## ABSTRACT

*The primary aim of this chapter is to investigate the effectiveness of Computer Assisted Language Learning (CALL) technologies, tools, and resources for figurative language in general and idiom learning in particular. The secondary aim is to explore the CALL training practices affecting the attainment of idiomaticity in English as a second or foreign language. Idiomaticity training is anchored in an online methodology of idiomaticity teaching that takes into account learners' interests and active involvement. Such focus is particularly useful for the purposes of diagnosis and achievement, and the research to date is a promising start to further work on idiomaticity. The chapter provides recommendations for idiomaticity training-and-teaching as well as time-tested practices for further theorizing and research. It is hoped that the practices and recommendations explored here will spur on more research in this vein. Pedagogical and research implications are also discussed.*

## INTRODUCTION

The rising importance of online pedagogy in American higher education is fast becoming a topic of intense research interest for online teacher training. Many Computer Assisted Language Learning (CALL) practitioners in teaching English as a second language (ESL) or foreign language (EFL), including general English, adult workplace English, intensive English programs (IEP), and English for Specific Purposes (ESP), remain interested in the ways the English language and culture is impacted by online education in their teaching and research (Adair-Hauck, Willingham-McLain, & Youngs, 2000; Arnold & Ducate, 2011). Even so, only a small number of online (or hybrid) ESL/EFL programs attempt to include in their curricula, for example, idiom, metaphor, simile, metonymy, hyperbole, proverb, slang, cliché, collocation, colloquialism, or various tropes of figurative language (henceforth *idiomaticity*) as a viable area of exploration for their PreK-12 teachers and teacher educators working with linguistically and culturally diverse learners in local or international settings. Lack of information, training, and experience with online education emphasizing idiomaticity has led to marginal results at best.

DOI: 10.4018/978-1-5225-2933-0.ch003

*Understanding Idiomaticity in CALL* addresses this gap in an effort to foster a new kind of CALL knowledge concerning the reconstructive nature of idiomatic understanding and production in English. The argument presented here for *idiomaticity training* is anchored in an online methodology of *idiomaticity teaching* that takes into account learners' interests and active involvement, with special attention paid to how such training can be best utilized in online instructional contexts reflecting authentic language use. To this end, the chapter begins with a brief discussion of some of the most significant themes and concepts spanning the CALL literature to date before highlighting critical notions of idiomaticity research and praxis. It then prioritizes the challenges and the opportunities present in today's interactive digital tools and resources while advocating for authentic intercultural communication practices through CALL, mobile learning, electronic learning, and Web 2.0 technologies.

A considerable amount of discussion is devoted to how best ensure successful technology integration in pedagogic constructs promoting language learning in general and idiomaticity in particular. Both the advantages and disadvantages derived from such purposeful technology integration are emphasized amid digital and multimedia environments known to support diverse conditions for learning across various educational and cultural contexts. This is followed by a detailed exposition of what CALL practitioners and language teachers need to know and do to take full advantage of the emerging technologies, applications, or tools available for attaining idiomaticity in CALL. For ease of presentation, the account termed here *idiomaticity training-and-teaching*—from inception through development to application and integration—encompasses key theoretical considerations and pedagogical constructs worthy of critical reflection. An array of solutions and recommendations in applying idiomaticity resourcefully in CALL *with a purpose* and *for a purpose* follows. The discussion concludes with a brief summary of time-tested, task-based projects that make a significant contribution to the next generation of CALL scholarship on idiomaticity. Throughout, pedagogical and research implications for technology integration with proven teaching practices supporting the needs of language teachers and their students through sustainable CALL initiatives are also discussed.

## BACKGROUND

No discussion of CALL training practices affecting the attainment of idiomaticity in English as a second or foreign language can be complete without first exploring what is meant by using CALL technologies, electronic tools, and digital resources in online English education. To "see how the CALL land lies," we begin with the term itself: Computer Assisted Language Learning (CALL) or Information Communication Technology (ICT), as it is called in Europe. Levy (1997) succinctly but broadly defined CALL as "the search for and study of applications of the computer in language teaching and learning" (p. 1). It follows that computer applications 'searched for' and 'studied' are designed to promote and enhance language teaching and learning in specific areas of language use (listening, speaking, reading, writing), including vocabulary, grammar, pragmatics, and culture.

What started as relatively naïve drill-and-practice software with limited language practice in the 1960s and 1970s, today CALL is widely associated with and characterized by web-based distance learning, virtual learning environments, interactive whiteboards, computer-mediated communication, and mobile-assisted language learning, to name but five of the most important developments in recent years. Throughout the decades, scores of studies investigated the efficacy of a variety of approaches and technologies for language learning (e.g., Burston, 2003; de Quincey, 1986; Higgins & Johns, 1984; Stoks, 1993; Zhao,

2003). From Traditional CALL and Explorative CALL to Multimedia CALL and Web-based CALL, CALL practitioners, technology educators, applied linguists, and language teachers in general sought to define, expand, and evaluate the integration of technology in second/foreign language learning and beyond (e.g., Alatis, 1983; Daud, 1992; Hubbard, 2008; Rilling, Dahlman, Dodson, Boyles, & Pazvant, 2005; Wildner, 2000). The experimental evidence concerning the expanding field of idiomaticity saw an equally impressive record of research activity and epistemological knowledge discovery (e.g., Arnaud & Savignon, 1997; Boers, Eyckmans, & Stengers, 2007; Bortfeld, 2003; Chen & Lai, 2014; Dong, 2004; Hatami, 2015; Martinez & Murphy, 2011; Omidian, Shahriari, & Ghonsooly, 2016).

Yet despite all this research activity, few empirical studies to date have sought to investigate matters of idiomaticity via technological constructs. Barring a handful of exceptions, the lack of applicable research is particularly glaring here. Nevertheless, in a study examining the attitudes of Hong Kong students and teachers to learning Chinese idioms it was found that computers can assist students in learning Chinese idioms more effectively than idiom dictionaries (Lewis, Luk, & Ng, 1998). Similarly, the use of iPads during the teaching of abstract and concrete Chinese idioms to heritage learners showed that learners enjoy learning via mobile devices (Yang & Xie, 2013). Learner-created content in learning English prepositions and Chinese idioms, when primary school students employ mobile devices to take photos in real-life contexts, has the potential to transform language learning into an authentic seamless learning experience (Wong & Looi, 2010).

Strong positive attitudes toward the use of mobile technology in language learning was also found in Amer's (2014) study in which 45 participants used a mobile software application for learning idiomatic expressions and collocations. Findings suggest that participants' usage of the app correlated with their average scores on the quizzes in the app and, furthermore, that app usage can be predicted by factors such as language proficiency, average daily usage of mobile devices, and motivation and learning goals. Indeed, learners' involvement in knowledge sharing in a contextualized mode appears to have a discernible impact on idiom learning and learner autonomy. More specifically, Foomani and Hedayati (2016) asked 24 Iranian students to use their mobile devices to take photos and create artifacts to represent English idioms learnt and share them on Padlets with their peers for further discussion and feedback. Post-study reflections and interview results obtained from students and the teacher at the end of the 6-week long study lend strong support to the claim that the 4-week in-classroom and 2-week independent out-of-classroom learning can be bridged successfully by contextualized learner-generated content favoring a seamless learning approach to idiom teaching and learning (see also Hayati, Jalilifar, & Mashhadi, 2013; Wong, Chin, Tan, & Liu, 2010).

Additionally, the integration of a game-based learning strategy and a tangible user interface device both facilitates meaningful learning and improves the learning achievement of fifth-grade students in studying Chinese idioms (Ku, Huang, & Hus, 2015). The systematic integration of CALL technologies with ever-expanding notions of idiomaticity appears to positively impact learners' performance attitudes toward figurative and metaphoric learning, especially when CALL is used as an effective tool to improve students' learning of English idioms (Liontas, 2002f, 2006, 2015b; Tabatabaei, 2012). To be sure, the extent to which such CALL or MALL (Mobile Assisted Language Learning) integration can be validated experimentally remains open to future investigations just as the challenges and opportunities in employing emerging digital technologies (i.e., electronics, networking, interfaces) will continue to define our understanding of idiomaticity in CALL in the years ahead. Taking stock of such technologies appears a necessary first step.

## TAKING STOCK OF CALL TECHNOLOGIES: CHALLENGES AND OPPORTUNITIES

Since the mid 1980s, the world has seen an explosion of computer-based information systems, particularly software applications and computer hardware, devices, peripherals, and tools too numerous to name all in a single paragraph. Suffice it to say that with each new advancement and innovation in concepts, methods, and applications, our collective understanding of technology grew as exponentially as the ever-expanding typology used to describe and situate the new technology within the scores of other research-based and pedagogical constructs (Johnson, 1987; Kornum, 1993; Luke & Britten, 2007; Magrath, 2001). Some of those constructs now include the internet, enterprise software/authoring tools, blackboards, distance learning, electronic dictionaries/books, hypertext annotations, graphical animations, corpus linguistics, digital storage, operating systems, middleware, streaming media, discussion lists, and email. Add to those constructs human language technologies, speech technology, machine translation, Web 2.0 applications, AI systems, virtual worlds, MUDs, MOOs, MUVEs, AR/VR, chat rooms, wikis, blogs, social networking, and podcasting/vodcasting and the list is still far from complete (see also *Key Terms and Definitions* at the end of this chapter for additional information).

The integration of these constructs in teaching and learning also gave rise to a new nomenclature to better characterize and clarify the theoretical underpinnings surrounding CALL applications and its components. Notwithstanding the critical paradigm shifts in the underlying pedagogies witnessed along the way—*Structural CALL* (1970s to 1980s), *Communicative CALL* (1980s to 1990s), and *Integrative CALL* (2000 onwards) (see Blake, 2013; Chapelle, 2005; Chapelle & Jamieson, 2008; Egbert, 2005; Smith, 2016; Warschauer & Healey, 1998)—the term CALL (Computer-Assisted Language Learning) will henceforth be exclusively used as the single unified phrase in this chapter to stress the critical role it plays in assisting with the teaching and learning of language and idiomaticity. Where appropriate, the CALL umbrella term will also include other nomenclature or variations of the phrase to emphasize the distinct nature of a particular technology, tool, or resource involved in idiomaticity training, including those involving a/synchronous m-learning (i.e., mobile learning that uses personal handheld-based electronic devices and applications in learning across multiple contexts and through diverse social and content interactions to extend the educational processes of self-paced electronic learning and deliver content to a large and geographically diverse student body in all kinds of formats) and e-learning (i.e., electronic learning that employs software or online web services to assist users to design courses, simulations, or other educational experiences) delivery modes and Web 2.0 technologies (e.g., Web 2.0 internet-based applications, text-based chat programs, audio/video podcasts, SNS/SM sites, web-based social networking services, and wikis and blog sites).

### First Steps

Given the ever-expanding, at times even confusing, assortment of terms and software tools CALL practitioners and language professionals need to be aware of in today's fast-changing technical landscape, it is perhaps best that they first compile a working list of the technologies available for use before becoming consumed with *which* particular technology, electronic tool, or digital resource to use *when, where,* and for *what* purpose to enhance a specific language skill or facet of idiomaticity. Just as it is wise in a face-to-face (F2F) classroom to first make an inventory of the available classroom technology, an online or hybrid (blended) learning environment could easily profit from such an exercise.

Naturally, the presentational organization of the list could and would vary depending on course, program, or curricular goals envisaged just as the scope of the technologies available in many classrooms today would vary in availability and quantity. Organized in columns and rows, the *Tech Inventory List* (TIL) proposed here could easily include types of information and communication technology organized in media to record information, technology for broadcasting information, technology for communicating through voice and sound or images, computing and general tech hardware, personal hardware, and internet access —an encouraging list for sure with many promising elements and types (see *Key Terms and Definitions* at the end of this chapter for additional TIL information).

And just as it is not wise to 'throw the baby out with the bathwater,' CALL practitioners and language professionals would be equally wise to curtail their desire to eliminate from the list those so-called "aging" technologies, hardware, or peripherals still found in storage in many classrooms today that have long lost their shine in the eyes of many. Similarly, the newest class of technologies, hardware, and peripherals, including software applications and apps on nearly every facet of life imaginable (recall Apple's renowned ad, "There's an app for that!"), should not be given primary consideration just because they are widely available today, because everyone else is using them, or because it is politically expedient to 'go along' with the latest trend just to 'get along' and 'be cool' with those that are already doing so. 'Keeping up with the Joneses' is one sure way to miss out on taking full advantage of a particular technology, both aging and emerging, for the benefit of our students.

The decision to *use* or *not use* a particular technology, tool, or resource should never rest on what others say or do, but on the promise the targeted technology holds for language teaching and learning. Only because everyone seems to have a *Facebook* page nowadays should not in and of itself compel us to do the same. Similarly, we should not take to *Twitter* just to match someone else's 140-character post with an equally 'short burst of inconsequential information' in an effort to 'join the club.' Instead, regardless of pervasive appeal or institutional pressures, both aging and budding technologies need to be chosen on the basis of what learners will actually do with those technologies, the skills those technologies uniquely address, and the direct benefits derived from using those technologies to meet students' diverse linguistic needs and interests that would otherwise be hard to realize. Time, effort, and cost considerations notwithstanding, adding those astute decisions to the list next to each technology column not only expands and enriches the list in significant new ways, more importantly, it adds a much needed pedagogical value to the entire enterprise of cataloguing and selecting the right technology for the right language and cultural learning outcome (e.g., listening, speaking, reading, writing, vocabulary, grammar, pragmatics, and culture) targeted.

## Making Wise Selections: M-Learning, E-Learning, and Beyond

To begin, CALL decisions should not be focused on technology per se but on language learning goals pursued and the distinct ways in which each technology (hardware, software, network, etc.) can enhance, assist, or facilitate the language learning process (e.g., Bickerton, 1999; Bickerton, Stenton, & Temmermann, 2001; Davies, 1991; Gillions, 1987; Schneider & Bennion, 1984). Said another way, what drives instruction is not technology, but language learning through technology. As such, it occurs in varied contexts (child, student, adult, adult workplace English, EFL, ESL, IEP, ESP, etc.), with learners of all ages (young learners, teens, adults) and levels of language proficiency, and in classes (one-computer classroom, class-lab, fully online or hybrid) and communities around the world. Both CALL practitioners and language teachers in general must be prepared to meet a variety of learner needs across contexts both inside and outside of the classroom. It is only prudent that they do so as effectively and efficiently as possible. To this end, practitioners and teachers alike are counseled to articulate and define the principles of using technology in support of second/foreign language learning and idiomaticity. Five questions merit particular consideration here:

1. Which technologies are best positioned to support language learning in general and idiomaticity in particular?
2. What are the conditions that will help create the most optimal learning environment regardless of the technology, tool, or resource used?
3. What are the specific teaching and learning contexts under which language learning and idiomaticity are best supported?
4. What are the expected benefits of using CALL (or MALL) for language and idiom learning?
5. What are the value statements or propositions in favor of mLearning, eLearning, or Web 2.0 learning for understanding idiomaticity in CALL?

Using a computer (or any other electronic technology) from virtually anywhere in the world, mobile learning, or mLearning for short, embraces a wide set of electronic applications to conduct webinars, communicate with users via chat and message forums, share material, and deliver content to a large and geographically diverse student body in all kinds of formats. Videos, slideshows, word documents and PDFs via network (internet, intranet, extranet), audio and video recordings, satellite broadcast, interactive TV, and CD-ROM, as well as many others not listed here, are some of the formats mLearning employs to extend the educational processes of electronic learning, or eLearning for short, such as computer-based learning, web-based learning, blended learning, distance learning, flexible learning situations, virtual classrooms, and digital collaboration forms. mLearning is primarily characterized by the use of personal handheld-based electronic devices (e.g., portable computers, MP3 players, notebooks, smartphones, and tablets) in learning across multiple contexts and through diverse social and content interactions.

In contrast to traditional F2F language learning approaches and methods, including many eLearning formats, mLearning is flexible, self-paced, and easily modified. It can occur anytime, anywhere via the internet or network, and be delivered on any platform at the time of need through mobile apps, socially authentic interactions, and online educational hubs. As such, it redefines how information is received or manipulated on virtually any subject. Engaging in a form of distance education and informal learning, m-learners use mobile device educational technology to learn at their own pace and at times that are convenient for their schedule. From virtually anywhere in the world, they retrieve, consume, create, and share learning content and products, potentially making language learning a more readily available and rewarding a/synchronous learning experience. The mobility of the learner and his or her interacting with portable technologies form the nucleus of learning in the acquisition and development of knowledge and understanding.

Both in the classroom or in fully online or hybrid settings, mobile devices with integrated Wi-Fi capabilities can be used to enhance student-centered learning and group collaboration among students through communication applications, interactive displays, and video features. Prudent use of mobile tools can easily replace cumbersome resources such as textbooks, notes, visual learning aids, and presentation technology with tailored learning contents and feedback that is almost instantaneous among m-learners who are dispersed globally and who use and share the same content. *Portability*, *accessibility*, and *convenience*, three undeniable value statements in favor of mLearning, not only provide a viable continuum for interactive, multimode learning inside and outside of the classroom, more importantly, mLearning both supports the learning process for on-demand access to information on the one hand and differentiates the types of learning activities students partake in online social groups to complete specific language tasks on the other.

mLearning apps and eLearning authoring tools typically support conventional, presentation-like courses, multimodal interactivity, screen recordings, multimedia, quizzes, and non-linear or adaptive approaches. *Adobe Captivate* (www.adobe.com) is one such example of a rapid responsive eLearning authoring tool used for building electronic content such as branched scenarios, randomized quizzes in dynamic HTML5 formats or Small Web Formats (.swf), and software simulations and demonstrations. In contrast, *Canvas* (www.canvas.net), *Blackboard,* (www.blackboard.com), and *Moodle* (www.moodle.org) are all internet-based learning management systems (LMS) software used for delivering, tracking and managing training and education online.

Regardless of educational level addressed or curricular goals pursued, CALL practitioners and language professionals are counseled to learn about these technologies, tools, and resources first, prior to implementing them blindly across their curricula in pursuit of idiomaticity knowledge on the account that they are the 'latest and the greatest since sliced bread.' And since technology, in any iteration or configuration, singly or in combination with other instructional technologies, is not the be-all and end-all of the educational enterprise we so aim to advance, let alone with unwarranted words and deeds devoid of rational reflection or pragmatic understanding of how idiomaticity in CALL is yet to be realized, generally speaking, those tasked with making the selection should have a good grasp of all that is involved in the effective integration of such technology for language and idiom learning.

As the need arises, professional development training for pre-service and in-service teachers at the tertiary level and CALL practitioners at the college and university level should also be offered where such knowledge may still be lacking. Without exception, using technology for the sake of technology will fail to capture the advertising prowess of the technology being eulogized today or those emerging digital and communication technologies being envisioned for the future in electronics (e.g., digital currencies, botsourcing, smart dust sensors, printed electronics, meristors), networking (MOOCs, 5G telecommunications, WiGig, high-altitude stratospheric platforms) or interfaces (context-aware computing, annotated-reality glasses, tileable, interactive wall-sized and wrap-around screens, telepresence via telerobotics, immersive multi-user VR), if Policy Horizons Canada, a predictive planning organization within the Canadian federal government, is to be believed (see the diagram on digital and communications technologies at http://www.horizons.gc.ca/sites/default/files/Publication-alt-format/pdf_version138_367kb-1p.pdf; see also Oliver, Osa, & Walker, 2012).

## What CALL Practitioners and Language Teachers Need to Know, What They Need to Do

*Understanding idiomaticity in CALL* calls for a careful reexamination of the role of technology in developing knowledge of figurative language. This includes new pedagogical as well as technical and management skills that need to be developed in parallel with the expansion of teachers' overall language professional skills in online or blended environments (e.g., Arnold, 2013; Blake, 2011). To begin, CALL practitioners and language teachers need to become aware of what CALL can and cannot accomplish inside and outside of the learning environment, and then adjust and fine-tune these concepts and expectations (knowledge) to their teaching of idiomaticity. However, they cannot be expected to reach such awareness unless they are first willing to engage in reflective practice that drives them to explore and articulate their personal teacher beliefs and classroom practices. To gain a deeper understanding of their classroom practices through reflective practice, they will need to become cognizant of the ways their own beliefs impact the overall culture of idiomatic learning and the meaning these beliefs hold for attaining success beyond formal instruction. Armed with such deep-seeded awareness, they can then focus on the technology, tools, and resources believed to support the development and refinement of idiomaticity in CALL. Upon such distinct practices, a more solid foundation for effective idiomaticity training can be anchored and more fully exploited on the basis of sound principles of learning, not unconfirmed anecdotes and tall tales of a bygone era. Critical to note here is the recognition that while some technology-based productivity or research tools can aid particular language skills in specific ways some of the time (e.g., gamification tools, tools for brainstorming and creating graphic organizers, spell-checkers, electronic thesauri, translators, and quiz- and puzzle-making applications), all digital technologies cannot equally accommodate all language skills all the time.

What is essential for effective CALL thus becomes the driving force behind the decisions made. In turn, the decisions reached through critical reflective practice become the training principle around which idiomaticity is carefully organized and systematized at each subsequent grade and language proficiency level while also acknowledging potential limitations in achieving some curricular goals via certain technologies, tools, or resources. It is important to underscore here that the limitations professed, both real and fictitious, are not the direct result of using a particular technology, tool or resource per se, but the inherent nature of said technology, tool or resource to deliver upon the benefits advertised and the means by which language and academic content may be accessed naturally for purposes of idiomatic learning.

Equally important, the settings in which idiomaticity training is actualized must be purposeful to the extent possible and must involve authentic audiences where desirable. Having access to authentic input and feedback is key to developing real-world communicative skills and knowledge in the target language. Concepts prevalent in educational technology, or EduTech for short, can provide a much-needed support and guidance in meeting particular goals in language comprehension and production. From facilitating language learning to improving performance in knowledge of idiomaticity, EduTech can significantly impact the planning, organization, leading, and controlling of teaching. When designing instruction for CALL-based contexts emphasizing language and cultural learning outcomes, teachers must also consider how to use technology so that it supports both effective learning practices and the curricular goals of the class. Such designs must take into account students' types of intelligence and styles of learning to better address the needs and interests of diverse learners (Liontas, 2001a, 2002a, 2006). Cognizant of such learner variability, instructional designs using EduTech practices and approaches must also be useful for a variety of instructional purposes highlighting distinct idiom-learning activities and task-based projects in diverse ways. Above all, such designs must employ technology effectively and efficiently in socially and culturally appropriate, legal, and ethical ways and must complement students' grade level and language proficiency level. Simply said, they must contribute directly to achieving the stated curricular goals in ways that non-technology language learning and teaching approaches to idiomaticity can ever hope to match with book, paper, and pencil alone.

It goes without saying that teachers need to cogently integrate digital technology into their pedagogical approaches to support language learning and communication. Mindful of the theoretical considerations worth considering, and consistent with the curricular goals and objectives pursued, they are counseled to repurpose relevant research findings to inform the planning of idiom-learning activities and tasks that embody pragmatic constructs befitting natural language use. It is not enough to claim that pragmatics is included in the curriculum or lesson plan. Sprinkling some student-led role plays here and there does not make a curriculum focused on real-life pragmatic communication. Norms and practices of social appropriateness or pragmatic violations abound in authentic materials (e.g., Bardovi-Harlig & Dörnyei, 1998; Schauer, 2006). Collectively, they underscore the fact that while knowledge of idiomaticity comprises a large part of the lexicon, expressions displaying idiomatic value do not appear one after another as if they were going out of style nor do they appear at the end of a sentence each and every time. Far from it! They are used sporadically and only as there is need to communicate specific pragmatic intents within the parameters of natural conversations. Pedagogically prepared materials, websites, and resources displaying unnatural use of idiomatic language should be avoided or used only as "inauthentic samples" of how *not to* use language for real purposes. If authentic idiom use is the goal of instruction, students should be guided to seek only those behaviors and resources that exemplify naturalness of language use. Anything less would indeed be a grave disservice to the language and culture study itself regardless of the technology being employed.

Instead, those tasked with exploring idiomaticity in CALL, including learners, should collect samples that truly exemplify the naturalness of language. Audio and video clips, for example, targeting specific idioms or tropes of figurative language should be selected for language practice and idiomaticity training. Students could be asked, for example, to watch or listen for paralanguage features that epitomize natural communicative and metacommunicative behavior. As they begin to selectively notice these features in the samples selected, they will soon realize that the interplay between linguistic and paralinguistic features is not as mysterious as first believed. Native speakers do not use one idiom after another to showcase their vast idiomatic repertoire. Instead, they employ idioms when the communicative need arises and when it befits the situation at hand. Replaying particular segments of audio or video helps learners notice authentic idiom use in native speech for specific functional or pragmatic purposes. They get to hear the "melody" of the expression as uttered by native speakers or see the body language accompanying the expression in question. Embedded in authentic language constructs, students could see how context permeates and dictates linguistic behavior that refrains from employing a half a dozen or more idioms in less than one paragraph. In noticing the text that precedes and follows an expression, students will also begin to notice how an aural (or written) text provides the support that makes the very use of an expression desirable in the context in which it is fully exploited by the speaker(s) *with a purpose* and *for a purpose*. Similar adaptations in selection and evaluation should also be made with respect to written texts.

Regardless of modality targeted, only those materials that embody purposeful CALL integration need be utilized for language instruction and learning. Purposeful integration of technology is as crucial as the activities students are asked to partake in. Students should not be asked to collaborate on task-based projects that lack specific guidelines or product expectations. While student behavior is expected to follow authentic communication whenever and wherever possible, it must be said, students should be afforded targeted opportunities to first manipulate language in structured idiom-learning contexts before they are expected to begin creating with the target language for real purposes. During the manipulation phase of instruction, teachers should make sure that students are provided with ample exposure to language and idiomatic input that is both varied and challenging befitting their interests and levels of language proficiency. The roles students assume during this idiom-learning phase should also provide for a variety of native and nonnative speaker interactions that are conducive to learning the targeted material while also permitting them to notice their errors and learn from them in a supportive learning environment. A variety of proven strategies and techniques can then be employed to promote sustained collaboration and creativity between and among students and groups (e.g., Arnold & Ducate, 2006; Arnold, Ducate,

& Kost, 2012; Arnold & Paulus, 2010; Sykes & Reinhardt, 2012). For optimal results, teachers are encouraged to ask several important questions including, but not limited to:

1. Are students capable of exploiting profitably the value of available technology-based language skill-building applications and productivity tools for electronically mediated communication and collaboration?
2. Can selected digital technologies, tools, or resources be easily accessed and are they adaptable to the needs and values of diverse learners?
3. How much time and training in how to use digital production or editing tools and related input and output devices will be required prior to having students demonstrate competent use of these tools and devices?
4. Is the idiomatic content students are asked to produce pedagogically sound and instructionally viable?
5. Is the idiomatic context in which students will employ selected technology applications or tools authentic and naturalistic and does it comply with accepted communication conventions across cultures and communities?
6. Are the idiom-learning activities and task-based projects resulting from the application of certain digital technologies interactive in nature, purposeful and creative in design, and suitable to students' level of language proficiency and interests?
7. Is the idiomaticity knowledge base and skill students are expected to develop, either collaboratively or individually, firmly grounded on accepted practices of cognitive development and language acquisition theories and/or methodologies?
8. Are the learning environments in which students are asked to produce idiom-relevant products and artifacts communicative in nature and learner-centered?
9. Are the conditions of idiomaticity learning optimized to support students' personal pursuits of self-directing creativity and imagination, reflective cognition and metacognition, and purposeful collaborative productivity and lifelong learning?
10. How can understanding idiomaticity in CALL be further systematized in language education curricula and programs, thoughtfully anchored in carefully planned opportunities for learners to experience idioms in natural settings revealing authentic language use, and made still more robust and relevant to the real world of human communication?

Many more questions could be posed here but the point remains: if teachers have difficulty answering these questions in the affirmative, then perhaps it is best that the chosen technology, tool, or resource not be given further consideration. The use of a digital technology (tool, resource) for the sake of a digital technology (tool, resource) is, to put it in figurative pictorial terms, as futile as *putting the cart before the horse while chasing red herrings in shallow waters.* Consequently, to further work on idiomaticity, it is best that CALL practitioners and language teachers engage learners in multimodal environments that resemble to the extent possible authentic language use behaviors in both reception/perception and production. Such behaviors are best exemplified in authentic constructs for which language is creatively and productively used by native speakers and with native and non-native speakers (readers, writers, or listeners) alike. Lesson plans and curricular units targeting natural use of idioms should thus be embedded in idiom training sequences addressing distinct instructional goals of learning at different intervals. With preparation and extension/expansion forming the beginning and end of the lesson plan cycle, care should be taken with the remaining presentation, interactive practice, and authentic evaluation structure of idiomaticity training and learning. (For a detailed methodological framework for developing idiomatic competence, see Liontas, 2008, 2015a).

The two sections—*Solutions and Recommendations* and *Future Research Directions*—that follow next build upon the questions professed here and provide specific answers and extensive discussion of delivery modes to extend the use of available technologies CALL practitioners and language teachers may want to experiment with and repurpose in their own online/offline classrooms and beyond for the purposes of idiomatic diagnosis and achievement. Collectively, these two sections seek to offer an easy-to-follow road map that helps practitioners and teachers alike to choose and integrate selected technologies across the curriculum to develop more effective and creative idiomaticity-driven lessons by purposefully exploiting flexible mobile delivery or online delivery modes—teaching at any time and from any place to ensure optimal idiomatic learning. Time-tested practices affecting the attainment of idiomaticity in English as a second or foreign language, including those involving further theorizing and research, are also offered and are discussed next.

## SOLUTIONS AND RECOMMENDATIONS

In contrast to the first generation of the Web 1.0-era websites where content with text often unlinked was limited to passive viewing, the Web 2.0-era has brought an important shift in the ways digital information is now created, shared, stored, retrieved, distributed, and manipulated. Users of Web 2.0 websites can often "click on" or "hover over" words in the text to access additional content on the website (e.g., definition, audio, video, image) or be linked to an external website via a hyperlink (see Liontas, 2001a; 2002a). They can exploit interactive Web 2.0 internet-based applications to create and promote user-generated idiom content (UGIC). Using *Google Docs,* for example, students can interact and collaborate contemporaneously on the same document without downloading any additional software. If desired, students can access and publish on a regular basis their own newsletter on idiomaticity. Following some software training, students can use dictation software such as *Dragon Naturally Speaking* to speak into a microphone and watch the software type their speech onto a page. Integrated learning systems such as *Rosetta Stone* model native speaker pronunciation aurally that learners can listen to and repeat as desired. Using automatic voice recognition tools, students can emulate the sound, word, or phrase provided in the model by recording their own voice. A visual representation of their speech is often provided in the form of a spectrogram which, in turn, can be played back to compare it to that of the model.

Students can compose asynchronous messages in email list management software applications for automatic redistribution of email transmission to subscribers on an electronic mailing list of people who share a common interest (listservs) to exchange ideas and information on particular idiom-learning issue or topic or use a synchronous voice chat application tool such as *Audio-Tips* (www.audio-tips.com) or *Yahoo Messenger* (www.messenger.yahoo.com) to instantaneously discuss with their peers (both native and non-native English-speaking) authentic uses of figurative or idiomatic language. Alongside trendy Short Message Service (SMS, commonly referred to as "text messaging") and Multimedia Messaging Service (MMS) providers, students can also use Apple's built-in instant messaging (IM) service, called *iMessage* (www.support.apple.com/explore/messages), to send text, pictures, videos, sound, and location, including bubble and screen effects, emoji tapbacks and full-on emojification, digital touch and handwriting—right from their iPhone, iPad, Mac, or Apple Watch—quickly and easily to anyone else using *iMessage*.

Popular text-based chat programs for desktops, notebooks, and smartphones include *Google Talk* (integrated with Google's *Gmail*) and *WhatsApp* (with some 800 million users worldwide and counting) for mobile devices. Similarly, *Skype, FaceTime*, and *Hangouts*, for example, offer learners the ability to meet with native speakers face-to-face via HD video, voice or text and even host "Hangouts" for up to 25 people within or outside of one's organization. If multi-user web conferencing and file/screen sharing features is desired, subscription services such as *Adobe Connect* (www.adobe.com) can deliver such immersive online meeting experiences for collaboration, virtual classrooms, and large scale webinars. With software such as *Wimba Create* (www.wimba.com/index.php) both teachers and students can create voice discussion boards where instead of posting text, they record their message orally. Tech-savvy users can convert *Microsoft Word* documents into interactive content and generate a set of webpages featuring flashcards, HTML, Java, and other code, hyperlinks, popups, definitions, Windows media, flash, and *QuickTime* movies, streaming audio and video, and Information Management System (IMS) metadata. Similar to blogging, students can individually or collaboratively create and publish their own idiom-based content on topics of interest for a real audience as an audio or video podcast (or vodcasts) on a variety of hosting sites. For example, *Audacity*, available for Windows, Mac, GNU/Linux, and other operating systems (www.audacityteam.org), is a free, open source, cross-platform audio software for multi-track recording and editing. Featuring spectrogram view of tracks, resulting podcasts or vodcasts can be revised as desired based on peer or teacher feedback received. The constructive nature of the feedback received in itself can further help students plan, attend to, and self-evaluate formal aspects of language, including prosodic features, stress, rate, pronunciation, and intonation of targeted idiomatic strings and phrases.

Because Web 2.0 is primarily social in nature, teachers and students are encouraged to rethink and repurpose the very nature of the application of social media for idiomaticity training and learning. Social Networking Services (SNS) and Social Media (SM) sites are primarily used by people to build social networks or social relations with other people who share similar personal or career interests, activities, backgrounds or real-life connections across political, economic, and geographic borders, ranging from across a city to across the world. Web-based social networking services (e.g., *Facebook, Pinterest, Instagram*), career and employment-oriented social networking services (e.g., *LinkedIn, Monster.com*), and social navigation social network services (e.g., *Goodreads, LibraryThing, BookLikes, Bookish, The Reading Room,* and *ThirdScribe* for books) facilitate the development of online social networks and professional "connections" to each other by connecting or linking a user's public profile with those of other individuals and/or groups to share text, images, and video with others.

Analogously, students can exploit quite profitably SNS and SM sites to create service-specific public/semi-public profiles and UGIC for the site or app that is designed and maintained by the SNS organization. They can view their list of connections or links within the system, share ideas, digital photos/videos, and lists of contacts, post blog entries, and inform others about online or real-world activities and events with people in their network in online forums or via email and instant messaging covering a wide range of UGIC and its applications in real-life. More specifically, using *Pinterest*—a photo sharing website where users can upload, save, sort, and manage images (known as *pins*) and other media content (e.g., quotes, travel, videos) through unique, personalized collections known as *pinboards*—students can (re-) post or (re-)pin their own *figpins* or *idiopins* (i.e., content displaying figurative or idiomatic language) on pinboards organized by a central figurative/idiom type, theme, or function. Using *Pinterest* as a personalized media platform, students can personalize their experience by pinning items, creating public and "secret" figboards and idioboards, and interacting with other class members (or followers) in their pin feed. Displaying the chronological activity from the Pinterest boards that a user follows, students can browse, comment, and like other *figpins* or *idiopins* that have either been uploaded or linked from a website. An account can also be created and accessed by linking Pinterest to a Facebook or Twitter profile. When students re-post or re-pin a figurative/idiomatic image to their own figboards or idioboards, they have the option of notifying their Facebook and Twitter followers as well.

In similar vein, using *Instagram*—an online mobile photo-sharing site that enables its users to take pictures and videos (up to 60 minutes in 1080p) and share them either publicly or privately on the app, as well as through a variety of other social networking platforms, such as *Facebook, Twitter, Tumblr,* and *Flickr*—students can repurpose the site's Web Profile, featuring a selection of recently shared idiom-based photographs, biographical information, and other personal details, to use their Instagram public or private account like a social media site to share instant messaging posts and profiles from feeds directly to other classmates or users. Within Instagram Direct, students can use the Instagram Stories with Live Video to send photos and videos displaying authentic idiom language use only to a specific user or group of users, rather than having them be viewable by all. Idiom-based photos and videos, which can be tagged with a comment for groups and friends in Instagram Direct, disappear after 24 hours and will not appear on the user's profile grid or in their feed once they are seen by the recipient(s). Followers get a notification of the same against the profile of their contacts. During the "private" broadcast, learners can comment and like as much as they want.

To deliver explicitly short-lived and self-deleting images and videos of up to 10 seconds in length, known as "snaps", in real time, learners can exploit for their idiom learning purposes, *Snapchat,* an image messaging and multimedia mobile application or selfie app. These private message idiom-based photo snaps can be viewed for a user-specified length of time (1 to 10 seconds as determined by the sender) before they become inaccessible. After a single viewing, the UGIC-based image and video disappears by default to encourage playfulness and to emphasize a more natural flow of interaction among users. *Figsnaps* or *idiosnaps* (i.e., content displaying figurative or idiomatic language) can be edited to include filters and effects, text captions, and drawings, and be directed privately to selected contacts, or to a semi-public "Story." The "My Story" feature allows users to compile snaps into chronological storylines, accessible to all of their "friends." Direct messaging features allow users to send ephemeral text messages to classmates (and other users worldwide) while saving any needed information by clicking on it. "IdioFriends" can be added via usernames and phone contacts, using customizable "Snapcodes", or through the "Add Nearby" function. *Spectacles*, a pair of smartglasses with a built-in camera, can record 10 seconds of video at a time. Other features students can exploit profitably here include "Memories" which allows *figsnaps* or *idiosnaps* and story posts to be saved into a private storage area, where they can be viewed alongside other idiom-based photos stored on the device, as well as edited and published as UGIC-based snaps, story posts, or messages. UGIC in *Snapchat* can be searched by date or using a local object recognition system. For example, *figsnaps* or *idiosnaps* accessible within "Memories" can additionally be placed into a "My Eyes Only" area that is locked with a PIN. "Live Idiom Stories" are viewed in chronological order, and each segment is accessible for 24 hours. Users can contribute *figsnaps* or *idiosnaps* to a curated idiom-based story advertised to all users. As a result, multiple contributors could be presenting the same idiom-learning event from varying viewpoints. Users can also use messages to reply to *figsnaps* or *idiosnaps* that are part of an idiom-based story. They can also create UGIC multimedia messages, leave in-the-moment audio or video "idionotes", write text messages, share recent camera photos, communicate via video chat, and participate in audio and video conferencing.

Depending on the language modality targeted and the curricular goals followed, students can create group *IdioWikis*, that is, websites accepting collaborative excision of its content and structure by its users using a simplified markup language. By extension, using any one of the free blog sites (e.g., *Blogger, WordPress, LiveJournal, Tumblr, Weebly, Penzu, Squarespace*) or *Edublogs,* the largest education blogging platform on the web for education related blogs (www.edublogs.org), students can create a discussion or informational *IdioBlog* site published on the world wide web to post discrete ideas, opinions, experiences, videos, text, digital images, and other types of media files and links covering a single figurative language subject, idiomatic topic, or idiomatic/pragmatic function. Regularly updated by the blog owner(s) or author(s), IdioBlog readers will receive automatic updates every time a blog is updated or revised. Displayed in reverse chronological order, readers can post comments on each blog entry, thereby making IdioBlogs highly interactive. Alternatives to IdioBlogs include *IdioVlogs* (or video blogs), music blogs, photoblogs, podcasts, and vodcasts, all of which, along with *Twitter*, are by far the most recognizable microblogging types available to date for students to take full advantage of in pursuit of understanding idiomaticity in CALL and beyond.

Each one of the Web 2.0 technologies, applications, and tools discussed heretofore, irrespective of the delivery mode applied, has the potential to significantly affect learners in different ways. Each medium in its own right can be repurposed and adapted to specifically address students' idiom-learning needs and interests in meaningful new interactive ways. Coupled with sustained access to Web 2.0 technologies and tools, and driven by their systematic use in pursuit of communicative goals, these technology-borne attributes are prone to influence the quantity of the input learners receive and the quality of the output they are likely to produce. To that end, curricular goals, including district-wide, state, and professional standards, may well serve as the foundation upon which these idiomaticity pursuits can be explored advantageously by those involved in education, language programs, or both. As they so do, it is equally imperative that they become cognizant of the various ways in which today's digital technologies may be exploited profitably for the benefit of their students. Having access to websites, mobile apps, or software is less critical than knowing how best to select and evaluate the most appropriate CALL resources for maximum exploitation.

## FUTURE RESEARCH DIRECTIONS

Over the years, language professionals have widely postulated that it is difficult for language teachers and material writers to make principled decisions about which idioms should be taught directly and which should be left open to discovery by students (e.g., Fernando, 1996; Liontas, 2015a; Liu, 2003; Macis & Schmitt, 2016; Vasiljevic, 2015; Wray, 2000). The use of CALL technologies makes such a selection profusely easy in that both teachers and learners can employ without curricular or program constraints their own applications and tools to discover the idioms they believe are important to their own learning based on their own linguicultural research. Having easy and direct access to copious multimedia texts exhibiting multimodal authentic use of idioms and other tropes of figurative language on nearly every topic imaginable can provide fruitful ground upon which future research directions may explore the specific ways by which such knowledge is best encouraged and which technology in particular appears to have the most meaningful impact on understanding idiomaticity in CALL. When combined with authentic feedback, multifarious inputs displaying multiple encounters with the target idiomatic expressions will no doubt influence greatly the conditions of language learning and culture and, ultimately, the level of success achieved.

Equally important, it could be fruitful to carry out studies investigating the effect authentic feedback has on student production of idiomatic output, specifically the gains made from feedback received and from in-class awareness raising and attention-direction activities. Because communication conventions differ across cultures, communities, and contexts, comparing the effectiveness of these types of input as a means of promoting knowledge of idiomaticity could yield some powerful constructs worthy of serious research acumen. Future studies exploring idiomaticity in CALL could be designed in such a way so as to discern English language learners capabilities in disambiguating the multiple semes (senses), or sememes, of polysemous words (units of expression), when such words are presented in contextual constructs supporting more than one monosemous meaning at a time (see Liontas, 2001b, 2002b, 2002c, 2002d, 2002e, 2003, 2007; Verspoor & Lowie, 2003). Within such multimedia environments, game-enhanced environments included, authentic oral and written texts could be selected for learners to identify and explain a range of figures of speech (see Liontas, 2017; Van Lacker Sidtis, 2003). In accessing their library of mental imagery to link the world of literal and figurative language (see Palmer, Shackelford, Miller, & Leclere, 2007), learners could also be asked to employ their predictive mechanisms and intuitions of the transparency of such expressive expressions (see Malt & Eiter, 2004; Vespignani, Canal, Molinaro, Fonda, & Cacciari, 2010). Throughout these investigations, it remains to be seen which CALL or MALL technology is best positioned to support the ongoing development of idiomatic competence. Equally important, it remains to be seen which CALL or MALL conditions are likely to create the most optimal learning environment for understanding idiomaticity regardless of the technology or the interactive digital tools and resources used.

While certain CALL or MALL tasks may predispose learners to use particular strategies to fulfill specific communicative intents, others may be even more conducive in how learners discover which idiomatic expressions serve which functions in discoursal transactions and beyond (Liontas, 2008, p. 23). In itself, this is indeed a noteworthy pursuit (see Gibbs, 2002; Hussey & Katz, 2009; Wray & Perkins, 2000). More to the point, in both second language research and pedagogy on understanding idiomaticity in CALL, it becomes critical to selectively scrutinize the (meta)cognitive and processing path(s) learners take in acquiring idiomatic knowledge. As this knowledge continues to be variously understood and defined by researchers and language practitioners alike, employing different criteria or features of typology in the process, it would be interesting to discover the various contributions such selected expressions, especially those connoting a figurative metaphoric meaning, can make to the fields of idiomaticity and CALL. (For a detailed discussion concerning the anatomy of knowledge systems for idiom learning, see Liontas, 2006).

Against this backdrop, research and pedagogical endeavors aiming to increase students' knowledge of idiomaticity including, but not limited to, idioms, metaphors, similes, metonymies, hyperboles, proverbs, slang, clichés, lexical bundles, phrasal expressions, multiword constructions, collocations, and tropes of figurative language in academic written English and spoken English, can and should be given serious consideration (see, for example, Laufer & Waldman, 2011; Martinez & Schmitt, 2012; Shin & Nation, 2008). Individually, each idiomatic type forms the nucleus of targeted investigations worth pursuing. Collectively, they embody a multipath framework around which understanding idiomaticity in CALL may be systematically organized and profitably exploited for the benefit of all students at all levels. The findings from such studies could then be utilized by CALL practitioners, language professionals, and materials developers to improve instruction of idiomaticity in English language education.

## CONCLUSION

This chapter investigated the effectiveness of Computer Assisted Language Learning (CALL) technologies, tools, and resources for developing idiomaticity within authentic digital environments. In an effort to foster a new kind of CALL knowledge concerning the reconstructive nature of idiomatic understanding and production in English, the discussion focused exclusively on the exploration of CALL training practices known to affect the attainment of idiomaticity in English as a second or foreign language. It then presented arguments in favor of *idiomaticity training*. Such training, it was argued throughout, is best anchored in an online methodology of *idiomaticity teaching* that supports and promotes learners' interests and active involvement. Particular attention was paid to how such training can be best utilized in online instructional contexts reflecting authentic language use. This focus was deemed particularly useful for the purposes of diagnosis and achievement. Research studies were referenced where needed to underscore the promise digital technologies hold for further research work on idiomaticity. In the hope that these results will spur on more research in this vein, much of that work was highlighted amidst pedagogical constructs, recommendations, and implications for idiomaticity training-and-teaching as well as time-tested practices for further theorizing and research.

In closing, while CALL technologies, tools, or resources can support distinct language and cultural learning outcomes to enhance student learning in and of itself, it bears repeating that those tasked with integrating idiomaticity in their teaching and research first assign to each technology medium the affordances and/or constraints associated with each technology selected (i.e., temporality, anonymity, modality, spatiality, telecollaboration), the student-expected learning behavior engendered in the purposeful application of these technologies, the specific language skill(s) addressed separately or in combination, and the discoursal nature of idiomaticity pursued in various synchronous or asynchronous communication events through sustainable CALL, MALL, or Web 2.0 initiatives known to support diverse conditions for learning across various educational and cultural contexts. (For a detailed account of the affordances here discussed, see Smith, 2016.)

Armed with such information, and cognizant of the impact such a diverse array of technologies can have on understanding idiomaticity in CALL, both CALL practitioners and language professionals can then feel confident in knowing that harnessing all these new digital technologies for language learning purposes can indeed positively impact the time, effort, and cost it will take to fully exploit it for attaining idiomatic competence. In the end, CALL, and any iteration of it, and there are many indeed, is only a means to an end, not an end in itself. *Understanding idiomaticity in CALL* can be achieved not because of the computer (or mobile device), but because technology, including those emerging digital and communication technologies being envisioned for the future in electronics, networking or interfaces, can make that which needs to be learned more palatable and viable in a variety of digital and virtual ways, thereby achieving greater effectiveness and efficiency while concomitantly defying conventional modes of language teaching and learning. In the end, *Understanding idiomaticity in CALL* is but a single step in a journey of a thousand miles full of promise and untapped potential.

## REFERENCES


Adair-Hauck, B., Willingham-McLain, L., & Youngs, B. E. (2000). Evaluating the integration of technology and second language learning. *CALICO Journal*, *17*(2), 269–306.

Alatis, J. E. (1983). The application of instructional technology to language learning. *CALICO Journal*, *1*(1), 9–14.

Amer, M. (2014). Language learners usage of a mobile learning application for learning idioms and collocations. *CALICO Journal*, *31*(3), 285–302. doi:10.11139/cj.31.3.285-302

Arnaud, P. J., & Savignon, S. J. (1997). Rare words, complex lexical units and the advanced learner. In J. Coady & T. Huckin (Eds.), *Second language vocabulary acquisition* (pp. 157–173). Cambridge, UK: Cambridge University Press; doi:10.1017/CBO9781139524643.012

Arnold, N. (2013). The role of methods textbooks in providing early training for teaching with technology in the language classroom. *Foreign Language Annals*, *42*(2), 230–245. doi:10.1111/flan.12020

Arnold, N., & Ducate, L. (2006). Future foreign language teachers' social and cognitive collaboration in an online environment. *Language Learning & Technology*, *10*(1), 42–66.

Arnold, N., & Ducate, L. (Eds.). (2011). *Present and future promises of CALL: From theory and research to new directions in language teaching*. San Marcos, TX: CALICO Publications.

Arnold, N., Ducate, L., & Kost, C. (2012). Collaboration or cooperation? Analyzing group dynamics and revision processes in wikis. *CALICO Journal*, *29*(3), 431–448. doi:10.11139/cj.29.3.431-448

Arnold, N., & Paulus, T. (2010). Using a social networking site for experiential learning: Appropriating, lurking, modeling and community building. *The Internet and Higher Education*, *13*(4), 188–196. doi:10.1016/j.iheduc.2010.04.002

Bardovi-Harlig, K., & Dörnyei, Z. (1998). Do language learners recognize pragmatic violations? Pragmatic versus grammatical awareness in instructed L2 learning. *TESOL Quarterly*, *32*(2), 233–259. doi:10.2307/3587583

Bickerton, D. (1999). Authoring and the academic linguist: The challenge of MMCALL. In K. Cameron (Ed.), *CALL: Media, design and applications* (pp. 59–79). Lisse, The Netherlands: Swets & Zeitlinger.

Bickerton, D., Stenton, T., & Temmermann, M. (2001). Criteria for the evaluation of authoring tools in language education. In A. Chambers & G. Davies (Eds.), *ICT and language learning: A European perspective* (pp. 53–66). Lisse, The Netherlands: Swets & Zeitlinger.

Blake, R. (2011). Current trends in online language learning. *Annual Review of Applied Linguistics*, *31*, 19–35. doi:10.1017/S026719051100002X

Blake, R. (2013). *Brave new digital classroom: Technology and foreign language learning* (2nd ed.). Washington, DC: Georgetown University Press.

Boers, F., Eyckmans, J., & Stengers, H. (2007). Presenting figurative idioms with a touch of etymology: More than mere mnemonics? *Language Teaching Research*, *11*(1), 43–62. doi:10.1177/1362168806072460

Bortfeld, H. (2003). Comprehending idioms cross-linguistically. *Experimental Psychology*, *50*(3), 217–230. doi:10.1026//1617-3169.50.3.217 PMID:12874990

Burston, J. (2003). Proving IT works. *CALICO Journal*, *20*(2), 219–226.

Chapelle, C. A. (2005). *Computer applications in second language acquisition: Foundations for teaching, testing, and research* (4th ed.). Cambridge, UK: Cambridge University Press; doi:10.1017/CBO9781139524681

Chapelle, C. A., & Jamieson, J. (2008). *Tips for teaching with CALL: Practical approaches to computer-assisted language learning*. White Plains, NY: Pearson Education.

Chen, Y., & Lai, H. (2014). The influence of cultural universality and specificity on EFL learners comprehension of metaphor and metonymy. *International Journal of Applied Linguistics*, *24*(3), 312–336. doi:10.1111/ijal.12021

Daud, N. M. (1992). Issues in CALL implementation and its implications on teacher training. *CALICO Journal*, *10*(1), 69–78.

Davies, G. D. (1991). Expodisc: An interactive videodisc package for learners of Spanish. In H. Savolainen & J. Telenius (Eds.), *EUROCALL 91: Proceedings* (pp. 133–139). Helsinki, Finland: Helsinki School of Economics.

de Quincey, P. (1986). Stimulating activity: The role of computers in the language classroom. *CALICO Journal*, *4*(1), 55–66.

Dong, Y. R. (2004). Dont keep them in the dark! Teaching metaphors to English language learners. *English Journal*, *93*(4), 29–35. doi:10.2307/4128977

Egbert, J. (2005). *CALL essentials: Principles and practice in CALL classrooms*. Alexandria, VA: TESOL.

Fernando, C. (1996). *Idioms and idiomaticity*. Oxford, UK: Oxford University Press.

Foomani, E. M., & Hedayati, M. (2016). A seamless learning design for mobile assisted language learning: An Iranian context. *English Language Teaching*, *9*(5), 206–213. doi:10.5539/elt.v9n5p206

Gibbs, R. Jr. (2002). A new look at the literal meaning in understanding what is said and implicated. *Journal of Pragmatics*, *34*(4), 457–486. doi:10.1016/S0378-2166(01)00046-7

Gillions, M. (1987). Interactive video in schools: Modern languages project. In E. Brown (Ed.), *CALL Report 5* (pp. 28–30). London: Center for Information on Language Teaching and Research.

Hatami, S. (2015). Teaching formulaic sequences in the ESL classroom. *TESOL Journal*, *6*(1), 112–129. doi:10.1002/tesj.143

Hayati, A., Jalilifar, A., & Mashhadi, A. (2013). Using short message service (SMS) to teach English idioms to EFL students. *British Journal of Educational Technology*, *44*(1), 66–81. doi:10.1111/j.1467-8535.2011.01260.x

Higgins, J., & Johns, T. (1984). *Computers in language learning*. London: Collins.

Hubbard, P. (2008). CALL and the future of language teacher education. *CALICO Journal*, *25*(2), 175–188.

Hussey, K., & Katz, A. (2009). Perception of the use of metaphor by an interlocutor in discourse. *Metaphor and Symbol*, *24*(4), 203–236. doi:10.1080/10926480903310237

Johnson, N. (1987). Current uses of computers in ESOL instruction in the U.S. *CALICO Journal*, *5*(2), 71–77.

Kornum, L. (1993). Foreign language teaching and learning in a multimedia environment. *CALICO Journal*, *10*(3), 65–76.

Ku, D. T., Huang, Y.-H., & Hus, S.-C. (2015). The effects of GBL and learning styles on Chinese idiom by using TUI device. *Journal of Computer Assisted Learning*, *31*(6), 505–515. doi:10.1111/jcal.12085

Laufer, B., & Waldman, T. (2011). Verb-noun collocations in second language writing: A corpus analysis of learners English. *Language Learning*, *61*(2), 647–672. doi:10.1111/j.1467-9922.2010.00621.x

Levy, M. (1997). *CALL: Context and conceptualization*. Oxford, UK: Oxford University Press.

Lewis, R., Luk, R. W. P., & Ng, A. B. Y. (1998). Computer-assisted learning of Chinese idioms. *Journal of Computer Assisted Learning*, *14*(1), 2–18. doi:10.1046/j.1365-2729.1998.1410002.x

Liontas, J. I. (2001a). Reading and multimedia annotations: Going beyond bells and whistles, hot links and pop-up windows. *The IALL Journal of Language Learning Technologies*, *33*(1), 53–78.

Liontas, J. I. (2001b). That's all Greek to me! The comprehension and interpretation of Modern Greek phrasal idioms. *The Reading Matrix: An International Online Journal*, *1*(1), 1–32.

Liontas, J. I. (2002a). CALL media digital technology: Whither in the new millennium? *CALICO Journal*, *19*(2), 315–330.

Liontas, J. I. (2002b). Vivid phrasal idioms and the lexical-image continuum. *Issues in Applied Linguistics*, *13*(1), 71–109.

Liontas, J. I. (2002c). Context and idiom understanding in second languages. In S. H. Foster-Cohen, T. Ruthenberg, & M-L. Poschen (Eds.), *EUROSLA yearbook: Annual conference of the European second language association* (vol. 2, pp. 155-185). Philadelphia, PA: John Benjamins Publishing Company. doi:10.1075/eurosla.2.11lio

Liontas, J. I. (2002d). Reading between the lines: Detecting, decoding, and understanding idioms in second languages. In J. H. Sullivan (Ed.), Literacy and the second language learner: Vol. 1. Research in second language learning (pp. 177-216). Greenwich, CT: Information Age Publishing Inc.

Liontas, J. I. (2002e). Transactional idiom analysis: Theory and practice. *Journal of Language and Linguistics*, *1*(1), 17–53.

Liontas, J. I. (2002f). Exploring second language learners notions of idiomaticity. *System: An International Journal of Educational Technology and Applied Linguistics*, *30*(3), 289–313. doi:10.1016/S0346-251X(02)00016-7

Liontas, J. I. (2003). Killing two birds with one stone: Understanding Spanish VP idioms in and out of context. *Hispania, 86*(2), 289–301. doi:10.2307/20062862

Liontas, J. I. (2006). Artificial intelligence and idiomaticity. *The APAMALL Higher Education Journal: Language Learning & Technology*, *1*(1), 1–33.

Liontas, J. I. (2007). The eye never sees what the brain understands: Making sense of idioms in second languages. *Lingua et Linguistica, 1*(2), 25–44.

Liontas, J. I. (2008). Toward a critical pedagogy of idiomaticity. *Indian Journal of Applied Linguistics, 34*(1-2), 11-30.

Liontas, J. I. (2015a). Developing idiomatic competence in the ESOL classroom: A pragmatic account. *TESOL Journal*, *6*(4), 621–658. doi:10.1002/tesj.230

Liontas, J. I. (2015b). Straight from the horse's mouth: Idiomaticity revisited. In R. R. Heredia & A. B. Cieślicka (Eds.), *Bilingual figurative language processing* (pp. 301–340). New York, NY: Cambridge University Press; doi:10.1017/CBO9781139342100.016

Liontas, J. I. (2017in press). Let the games begin! Harnessing the power of gaming in second language education. In A. Faravani, H. R. Kargozari, M. Zeraatpishe, & M. Azarnoosh (Eds.), *Issues in SLA research: Syllabus designing and curriculum development.* Rotterdam, The Netherlands: SENSE Publishers B.V.

Liu, D. (2003). The most frequently used spoken American English idioms: A corpus analysis and its implications. *TESOL Quarterly*, *37*(4), 671–700. doi:10.2307/3588217

Luke, C. L., & Britten, J. S. (2007). The expanding role of technology in foreign language teacher education programs. *CALICO Journal*, *24*(2), 253–267.

Macis, M., & Schmitt, N. (2016). Not just 'small potatoes': Knowledge of the idiomatic meanings of collocations. *Language Teaching Research*, 1–20. doi:10.1177/1362168816645957

Magrath, W. (2001). A return to interactivity: The third wave in educational uses of information technology. *CALICO Journal*, *18*(2), 283–294.

Malt, B. C., & Eiter, B. (2004). Even with a green card, you can be put out to pasture and still have to work: Non-native intuitions of the transparency of common English idioms. *Journal of Memory and Cognition*, *32*(6), 896–904. doi:10.3758/BF03196868 PMID:15673178

Martinez, R., & Murphy, V. A. (2011). Effect of frequency and idiomaticity on second language reading comprehension. *TESOL Quarterly*, *45*(2), 267–290. doi:10.5054/tq.2011.247708

Martinez, R., & Schmitt, N. (2012). A phrasal expressions list. *Applied Linguistics*, *33*(3), 299–320. doi:10.1093/applin/ams010

Oliver, A., Osa, J. O., & Walker, T. M. (2012). Using instructional technologies to enhance teaching and learning for the 21st century pre K-12 students: The case of a professional education programs unit. *International Journal of Instructional Media*, *39*(4), 283–295.

Omidian, T., Shahriari, H., & Ghonsooly, B. (2016). *Evaluating the pedagogic value of multi-word expressions based on EFL teachers' and advanced learners' value judgments. TESOL Journal.* doi:10.1002/tesj.284

Palmer, B. C., Shackelford, V. S., Miller, S. C., & Leclere, J. T. (2007). Bridging two worlds: Reading comprehension, figurative language instruction, and the English-language learner. *Journal of Adolescent & Adult Literacy*, *50*(4), 258–267. doi:10.1598/JAAL.50.4.2

Rilling, S., Dahlman, A., Dodson, S., Boyles, C., & Pazvant, O. (2005). Connecting CALL theory and practice in preservice teacher education and beyond: Processes and products. *CALICO Journal*, *22*(2), 213–235.

Schauer, G. A. (2006). Pragmatic awareness in ESL and EFL contexts: Contrast and development. *Language Learning*, *56*(2), 269–318. doi:10.1111/j.0023-8333.2006.00348.x

Schneider, E. W., & Bennion, J. L. (1984). Veni, Vidi, Vici, via videodisc: A simulator for instructional courseware. In D. H. Wyatt (Ed.), *Computer assisted language instruction* (pp. 41–46). Oxford, UK: Pergamon Press.

Shin, D., & Nation, P. (2008). Beyond single words: The most frequent collocations in spoken English. *ELT Journal*, *62*(4), 339–348. doi:10.1093/elt/ccm091

Smith, B. (2016). *Technology in language learning: An overview*. New York, NY: Routledge.

Stoks, G. (1993). Integrating new technologies into the modern languages curriculum. *CALICO Journal*, *11*(1), 76–93.

Sykes, J., & Reinhardt, J. (2012). *Language at play: Digital games in second and foreign language teaching and learning*. Boston, MA: Pearson Education.

Tabatabaei, O. (2012). The effect of computer-assisted language learning (CALL) on learning idiomatic expressions: A case of Iranian EFL students. *Language, Culture, and Translation*, *1*(1), 119–137.

Van Lancker Sidtis, D. (2003). Auditory recognition of idioms by native and nonnative speakers of English: It takes one to know one. *Applied Linguistics*, *24*(1), 45–57. doi:10.1017/S0142716403000031

Vasiljevic, Z. (2015). Teaching and learning idioms in L2: From theory to practice. *MEXTESOL Journal*, *39*(4), 1–24.

Verspoor, M., & Lowie, W. (2003). Making sense of polysemous words. *Language Learning*, *53*(3), 547–587. doi:10.1111/1467-9922.00234

Vespignani, F., Canal, P., Molinaro, N., Fonda, S., & Cacciari, C. (2010). Predictive mechanisms in idiom comprehension. *Journal of Cognitive Neuroscience*, *22*(8), 1682–1700. doi:10.1162/jocn.2009.21293 PMID:19580384

Warschauer, M., & Healey, D. (1998). Computers and language learning: An overview. *Language Teaching*, *31*(2), 57–71. doi:10.1017/S0261444800012970

Wildner, S. (2000). Technology integration into preservice foreign language teacher education programs. *CALICO Journal*, *17*(2), 223–250.

Wong, L.-H., Chin, C.-K., Tan, C.-L., & Liu, M. (2010). Students' personal and social meaning making in a Chinese idiom mobile learning environment. *Journal of Educational Technology & Society*, *13*(4), 15–26.

Wong, L.-H., & Looi, C.-K. (2010). Vocabulary learning by mobile-assisted authentic content creation and social meaning-making: Two case studies. *Journal of Computer Assisted Learning*, *26*(5), 421–433. doi:10.1111/j.1365-2729.2010.00357.x

Wray, A. (2000). Formulaic sequences in second language teaching: Principle and practice. *Applied Linguistics*, *21*(4), 463–489. doi:10.1093/applin/21.4.463

Wray, A., & Perkins, M. R. (2000). The functions of formulaic language: An integrated model. *Language & Communication*, *20*(1), 1–28. doi:10.1016/S0271-5309(99)00015-4

Yang, C., & Xie, Y. (2013). Learning Chinese idioms through iPads. *Language Learning & Technology*, *17*(2), 12–23.

Zhao, Y. (2003). Recent developments in technology and language learning: A literature review and meta-analysis. *CALICO Journal*, *21*(1), 7–27.

## ADDITIONAL READING

Idiom Connection. (n.d.) In *Idiom Connection's* online resource. A website designated to idioms. The idioms on this website are organized by keyword. The site gives a brief definition and sentence example for each idiom. Retrieved from http://www.idiomconnection.com/

Kalkstein Fragiadakis, H. (2007). All Clear 2: Listening & Speaking (3rd edition). Boston, MA: Thomson Heinle. All Clear teaches students to recognize and produce the high-frequency idioms, phrases, and contemporary expressions needed in a range of conversational situations.

McPherron, P., & Randolph, P. T. (2014). *Cat got your tongue? Teaching idioms to English learners.* Alexandria, VA: TESOL.

## KEY TERMS AND DEFINITIONS

**AI Systems:** Abbreviation for *Artificial Intelligence* computing systems that make use of high-level, complex-programming techniques simulating human intelligence and cognitive functions in various contexts seeking computer application solutions to learning and problem solving as in Machine Translation (MT), for example, where dynamic computer software is used to translate natural language text or speech from one language to another (see Liontas, 2006).

**Distance Learning:** A form of asynchronous or synchronous learning form transpiring in physically separate locations.

**eLearning:** A form of online learning on the web, *Electronic Learning*, or *eLearning* for short, is an umbrella definition relating to and embracing the use of ICT (an abbreviation for Information and Communications Technology, same as the reverse British term, CIT, Communications and Information Technology) in teaching and learning that widely employs eLearning authoring tools (i.e., software or online services that assist users to design courses, simulations, or other educational experiences).

**Idiomatic Competence:** The ability to understand and use idioms appropriately and accurately in a variety of sociocultural contexts, in a manner similar to that of native speakers, and with the least amount of mental effort. It includes knowledge the speaker-hearer has of what constitutes appropriate and accurate idiomatic language behavior in relation to particular communicative goals as well as linguistic (phonology, morphology, syntax, semantics) and pragmatic (non-linguistic, paralinguistic, sociolinguistic/functional, discourse, personal/world, intra/intercultural) knowledge (see Liontas, 2015).

**MOO:** Deriving from the earlier MUD, MOO stands for *Multi-User-Domain Object Oriented.* It is, as the term states, a multi-user, programmable, interactive system of a persistent object database allowing players from around the world, either synchronously or asynchronously, to build their own landscape and objects within the MOO (or MUVE) environment by using object-oriented techniques and domain-specific programming language (DSL) to author new rooms, objects, or interface operations. *Adventure Games* are a prime example of MOOs. (see Liontas, 2017).

**MUD:** Abbreviation for *Multi User Domain* or *Multi User Dungeon*, MUD is primarily a collaborative text-based multiplayer real-time virtual fantasy world in which players can engage across computer networks in online chat, role-playing adventure games, or reading/viewing descriptions of objects, actions, rooms, players, and other non-player characters, including real-time web environment fictional races and monsters.

**MUVE:** Considered a further development of the MOO and MUD concepts, MUVE is an abbreviation for *Multi User Virtual Environment*, also known as a *Virtual World.* Today, MUVEs are closely associated with Web 2.0 applications. *Second Life* is a prime example of a MUVE that allows hundreds of simultaneous users to interact with other residents through self-created 3D avatars in a virtual reality playground bursting with people, entertainment, experiences, and opportunity. (see Liontas, 2017).

**Online Learning:** Closely associated with the concept of *eLearning, Online Learning* is learning that employs primarily Email and the Internet in following a course online that can result in the award of a course grade, certificate, or degree completion.

**TIL:** Abbreviation for *Tech Inventory List*, TIL includes types of information and communication technology organized in media to record information.

**VLE:** Abbreviation for *Virtual Learning Environment*, VLE is an internet-based learning management software package used to deliver, track, and manage training and education online.

**Web 2.0:** Characterized by the user experience need to stay connected incessantly to and with other people in the form of social media to share user-generated content and knowledge of all sorts in real time, Web 2.0 now includes online social networking service platforms and social media sites (e.g., *Facebook).*

# Chapter 4
# Establishing a Praxis Between SLA Theory and CALL-Based Practices

**Amirhossein Monfared**
*Alliant International University, USA*

**Soo Min Lee**
*Alliant International University, USA*

**Seth Eugene Cervantes**
*Alliant International University, USA*

**Monica Jackson**
*Alliant International University, USA*

## ABSTRACT

*The field of computer-assisted language learning (CALL) has grown in terms of second language acquisition (SLA) theory. Researchers have linked sociocultural theories to CALL (Youngs, Ducate, & Arnold, 2011), noting that technologies can create communities of practice. Although many L2 learners and language teachers are proficient in the use of technology (Prensky, 2001), this does not mean they can use it systematically to learn or teach (Healey et al., 2011). The aim of this chapter is to connect current sociocultural perspectives with CALL-based technologies. The first part discusses interactionist and sociocultural theories of SLA and shows how technology can build communities of practice, encourage reflection, and ultimately promote autonomous learning (Hubbard, 2004). The second section describes three CALL-based practices: (1) wikis, (2) role-playing games, and (3) online record-keeping. Each description, links these practices to sociocultural perspectives of SLA theory and TESOL Technology Standards (TTS).*

## INTRODUCTION

In the field of computer-assisted language learning (CALL), the use of digital technologies to facilitate the teaching and learning of a second language has grown in terms of second language acquisition (SLA) theory development and classrooms applications. Researchers have linked sociocultural and constructivist theories to CALL (Dalgarno, 2001; Levy & Stockwell, 2006; Youngs, Ducate, & Arnold, 2011; Warschauer 2000), noting that digital technologies have the potential to create communities of practices in the digital realm while strengthening existing ones (Abrams, 2011). This sort of community

DOI: 10.4018/978-1-5225-2933-0.ch004

building and strengthening can be viewed in terms of how people use digital devices (e.g., smartphones, smartwatches) to run applications that build digital social spaces (Hubbard & Levy, 2006). Although many L2 learners are digital natives and many language teachers are proficient in the everyday use of digital technology (Prensky, 2001), this is by no means a guarantee that both the learners and teachers can use digital tools in a systematic way that creates a praxis between theory, teaching, and learning (Healey, et al., 2011).

## BACKGROUND

In the field of TESOL, the use of technology for language learning has been guided by the roles of tutor, tool, and medium. From a theoretical perspective, theories of learning and language color and shape the use of technology in the language classroom. As Richards and Rodgers (2001) and Salaberry (1996) note, the audio-lingual method relied heavily on audio-visual playback and recording devices, with the language lab playing a central role in the language learning experience. In this learning environment, technology took on the role of tutor, providing both instruction, feedback, and testing (Ducate & Arnold, 2011; Kern, 2006). When the audio-lingual method fell out of favor, so did language labs. As a tool for language learning, technology provides English language learners (ELLs) with information about the target language and culture. An excellent illustration of the role of technology as a tool is data-driven learning or DDL (O'Keeffe, McCarthy, & Carter, 2007). With the help and guidance of an instructor, ELLs can employ corpora, such as the Michigan Corpus of Spoken Academic English (MICASE) or Corpus of Contemporary American English (COCA), to examine concordance lines to view how specific node words (i.e., a specific vocabulary item or structure) collocate or colligate (Lin & Lee, 2015). Finally, technology can play the role of medium in which ELLs use computer-mediated technology to interact, collaborate, and form identities (Kern, 2006).

In his corpus-based study, Hubbard (2008) examined the words that collocated with the word *theory* in over 244 journal articles in 25 volumes of the *CALICO Journal*. One of the questions Hubbard asked was what specific theories were mentioned. He discovered that 113 distinct theories were mentioned, suggesting that that CALL theory is an "amalgam" of theories extended to and adapted for CALL environments (Hubbard, 2008, p. 393). In an early analysis, Kern (2006) noted the controversies surrounding which theory to apply to CALL. As was found in Hubbard (2008), CALL (not unlike the field of second language acquisition) is informed by a hodgepodge of theories and approaches. Ducate and Arnold (2011) identified four approaches to past CALL research: technological, psycholinguistic, sociocultural, and ecological approaches. For this chapter, we have adopted social and sociocultural perspectives of learning (Zuengler & Miller, 2006) to CALL, while, at the same time, acknowledging that other perspectives and orientations have their place in CALL. Thus, we focus our attention on the role of technology as a medium for interaction.

The aim of this chapter is to explore how theory—in particular, sociocultural theory—informs CALL practices. It follows then, that the authors of the current chapter identify with Vygotsky's (1997) view that theory and practice share an interdependent relation in which each acts as a guide for the other (Lantolf & Poehner, 2014). To accomplish this, three CALL applications are examined related to writing (wikis), interaction (online gaming), and evaluation/feedback (online record keeping). For technology to be implemented and evaluated successfully, the TESOL Technology Standards (Healey, et al., 2011) were used as a guide for each of the three CALL applications described in the sections that follow.

Prior to examining the CALL applications, the next section explores SLA theory and its relevance to CALL. As the aim of this chapter is to demonstrate how theory and practice in CALL form a praxis, the sociocultural perspectives of SLA covered in the section are as follows: (1) constructivism, (2) interactionist perspectives, and (3) sociocultural theory.

## SLA THEORY AND CALL

### Constructivism

One theory related to CALL is constructivism. There are various interpretations and definitions of constructivism. Constructivism has three general principles, (a) everyone forms his/her representation of knowledge, (b) individuals learn through active exploration, and (c) learning takes place in a social context and interaction among learners is essential in learning (Dalgarno, 2001, p. 184). Regarding the relationship between constructivism and CALL, Dalgarno (2001) suggested that general exploration in CALL is within a virtual environment. Instead of or in addition to classroom interaction, a computer supported collaborative system is a tool for mediating interaction. Overall, in the use of technology in collaborative tasks, learners play a central role, and are actively constructing the knowledge they need to achieve tasks.

### CALL and Interactionist Perspectives of SLA

There is a body of research that relates interactionist theory and CALL. Chapelle (2009) has labeled interactionist theory as a psycholinguistic approach. Interaction can be linguistic or nonlinguistic, and involve everyday social actions, such as sending an instant message to a colleague or responding to a friend's post on a social network site. In these instances, the learner has the goal of performing social functions and is involved in constructing meaning in such exchanges. From an interactionist perspective, as Chapelle (2009) suggests, social interaction is the locus of language development. Chapelle (2005) also noted that Gass (1997) has explained the specific psycholinguistic processes involved in acquisition, and Ellis (1999) described the perspective of interactionist SLA for applying the concepts of interactionist theory to CALL.

CALL is also related to SLA interaction classifications; however, interaction in CALL occurs electronically and it can differ from face-to-face interaction (Cervantes & Olson, 2012). It includes interaction mediated between the learner and the computer. Interactionist theory argues that interaction provides a trigger for acquisition (Chapelle, 2005, 2008). Even though the benefits of interaction types are similar, Chapelle (2005), citing Gass (1997), noted that there are three distinct kinds of benefits from interaction: opportunities for negotiating meaning, gaining enhanced input, and directing attention to linguistic forms. Also, negotiations including learner-computer interaction benefit conversational adjustments that help learners connect form and meaning that promote acquisition (Long, 1996). For example, research on CALL has shown that learner-computer interactions are useful in vocabulary acquisition (Plass, Chun, Mayer & Leutner, 1998). Moreover, intrapersonal interaction involves internal mental processing that can promote acquisition, and such interactions can be observed indirectly within everyday social interactions. Thus, opportunities for interaction mediated through CALL-based activities has the potential to shift the learners' attention to linguistic input, thus promoting noticing (Chapelle, 2005).

Chapelle (1998) has linked aspects of interactionist theory of SLA and CALL pedagogy, and has drawn up guidelines for integrating an interactionist perspective into CALL instructional design. Chapelle's (1998) guidelines include: (a) instruction must make key linguistic characteristics salient, (b) offer modifications of linguistic input, (c) provide opportunities for comprehensible output, (d) provide opportunities for learners to notice their errors, (e) provide opportunities for learners to correct their linguistic output, (f) support modified interaction between the learner and the computer, and (h) provide opportunities for the learner to act as a participant in L2 tasks (pp. 26-28).

Different elements (i.e., computer, task, language, the learner, etc.) cannot be studied in isolation and their interaction cannot be explained by adding up the results. That is, different elements should be regarded on their own. Moreover, Doughty and Long (2003) presented CALL related task-based language learning guidelines for distance learning relevant to the collaborative/interactive nature of CALL. These guidelines include: (a) the use of tasks, not texts, as the unit of analysis, (b) access to rich input, (c) the promotion of cooperative/collaborative learning, and (d) the individualization of instruction. Interactionist theory has served in research hypotheses formulation for the investigation of CALL as indicated in the literature (Chapelle, 2005). For instance, Chapelle mentioned interactional theory can test the necessity of negative feedback in an activity for some learners or evaluate features of negotiation in learner-language relationship between requests for modifications and comprehension of those forms in CALL-based activities. In an ESL listening task, Kon (2002) studied incidental vocabulary acquisition in a CALL-based academic listening activity. In addition to listening to a lecture, the learners watched a video, viewed overhead transparency/picture slides, and completed a multiple-choice test. Also, the researcher identified the acquired vocabulary during the listening activity and tested if acquisition had occurred as a result of CALL-based input and interaction. In addition to the overall positive findings on incidental vocabulary acquisition, the mode in which input was presented proved to be vital.

These studies highlight the growth of interactionist-based research on CALL, and as Chapelle (2005, 2008) contends, interactionist theoretical research and its application to CALL practice can contribute to and inform applied linguistics.

## Sociocultural Theory

A central theory to sociocultural perspectives on language learning is the notion that knowledge is socially constructed in interaction. As Vygotsky (1978) illustrated, cognitive development appears first at the psychological level and then becomes available for use by the individual. Cultural development appears first at the social level—*interpsychological*, and then at the individual level—*intrapsychological* (Vygotsky, 1978). In the classroom, this development is a collaborative effort between teachers and learners and between learners and learners; through these processes, ELLs develop their ZPD, that is, the distance between what they can achieve themselves and what they can achieve when assisted. This concept of social learning is important for CALL as learners and teachers socialize through technology during collaborative learning and assessment tasks, such as the ones later described in this chapter. Other scholars who value sociocultural theory note an equally important element in SLA is that social interaction enables internalization and language use through a dynamic process (Ohta, 2000).

Sociocultural perspectives have been influential in informing the design and classroom use of CALL technology and applications for collaborative learning environments (Youngs et al., 2011). According to Donato (2000), instruction is one of the most important issues in sociocultural perspectives in relation to classroom instruction and learning. Instruction is a collaborative activity in which zones of proximal development (ZPD) are co-constructed by teachers and ELLs. Donato (2000) also stated that in relation to CALL, sociocultural theory has three aspects: (a) social learning, (b) mediation, and (c) genetic analysis. One important aspect of Vygotskian and sociocultural theory is *mediation*—that is, people use signs and tools to mediate social actions. These tools are not seen as abstract but rather as medium to alter human behavior. The utilization of tools is the process of behavior rather than simply a necessity for facilitating an action. In relation to CALL, this concept highlights the transformative potential of modern technologies to remake previous forms of human activity anew.

From a Vygotskian perspective, to understand many aspects of mental functioning and their origins, the developmental process needs to be understood first. For instance, we need to understand the unfolding of events, the development of the individual, sociocultural history, and even the development of the species (Vygotsky, 1978). This suggests that we need to put CALL in a larger perspective and in its broader social, cultural, and historical contexts. For example, we cannot understand our students' motivations as they use new technological applications unless we realize their social and cultural significance within a specific context (Warschauer, 2000).

### Language Teachers, Learners, and ZPD

Teachers play an important role in the application of sociocultural theory. Teachers like learners are participants in the communication and learning process. To be more precise, teachers scaffold learning until the learners can be independent. Thus, teachers help learners overcome the distance between what they can do with the help of others and what they will be able to do alone. Previous studies have shown that computers like teachers are mediators (Levy & Stockwell, 2006). In general, Levy and Stockwell (2006) claim that Vygotsky's work in relation to CALL supports cooperative and collaborative learning and learning in social groups and communities of practice.

## CALL APPLICATION: LINKING PRACTICE WITH THEORY

The CALL applications covered in this section demonstrate how interactionist and sociocultural SLA theories inform how these applications are implemented to promote language teaching and learning. Moreover, the TESOL Technology Standards (Healey et al., 2011) were used as a guide to direct and evaluate the design and implementation of the three CALL applications described below. The three CALL technology applications are wikis, role-playing games, and online record keeping.

### Using a Wiki as a Collaborative Writing Tool

Wikis have received significant attention from SLA researchers as part of the Web 2.0 technologies integration (Du, Chu, Chan, & He, 2016; Stoddart, Chan, & Liu, 2016; Woo, Chu, & Li, 2013) since they facilitate group-writing tasks (Hadjerrouit, 2013, 2014; Stoddart et al., 2016). Research by Wiseman and Belknap (2013) suggested that wikis are a form of technology that not only promotes communication, collaboration, and efficiency in language teaching, but also assists language learning. However, Stoddart et al. (2016) pointed out that the outcomes of collaborative writing via wikis have not sufficiently been presented in the literature. In addition, collaborative writing on wikis still has much room for further investigation into the processes and activities involved in student interaction and learning (Du et al., 2016).

This section attempts to make a connection between research on wikis as a collaborative learning tool and teaching second language (L2) writing, and investigates the following points: (1) The role of wikis in SLA, (2) benefits and challenges of using wikis as a collaborative writing platform, and (3) pedagogical implications of implementing collaborative writing tasks through wikis in SLA.

## Wikis and Wiki Technology

Research with wikis presents several important features that wikis offer. Wikis, from a sociocultural perspective, provide an environment in which learners meaningfully exchange ideas and negotiate meaning to accomplish a common goal (Wang, 2014; Wiseman & Belknap, 2013). Wikis, from a SLA perspective, are a writing platform where L2 learners can practice multimodal, hyperlinked text, and hypertext activities in groups (Nakamaru, 2012; Rott & Weber, 2013). Although the literature discusses different types of wikis available, such as Wikispaces, PBWorks, and MediaWiki, researchers have shown that wikis provide an ease-of-use environment (Hadjerrouit, 2013; Wang, 2015). With the application of Web 2.0 technologies, wikis allow multiple users for online collaborative writing by recording all the fundamental activities, which include page edits, page view, and page comments made to the document (Hadjerrouit, 2014; Nakamaru, 2012). Among those features, because of the built-in tracking feature, each edit is recorded in the history log and allows both the teacher and students to track down all the changes being made. Additionally, there are areas where users can communicate on their shared task such as page comments or discussion function.

## Collaborative Writing With Wikis

This section identifies two essential components in collaborative writing with wikis: (1) collaboration versus cooperation and (2) collaborative writing. In terms of collaboration versus cooperation, since a growing body of literature describes wiki-based collaborative writing, there is a need to define collaboration and cooperation. Operationalized definitions of the two terms by Arnold, Ducate, and Kost (2012) follow: collaboration is defined as "Learners [taking] responsibility for the text as a whole and [editing] their own as well as their group mates' contributions"; and cooperation is "Learners divide the work and focus their revisions mostly on their own contributions to the text" (p. 433). It appears that collaboration distributes more ownership of a wiki project among group peers.

In discussing collaborative writing, students in a composition course typically go through various steps before they have a final draft. Writing is a complex process that generally involves planning, writing, revising, and editing (Lai, Lei, & Liu, 2016; Ortiz Navarrete & Ferreira Cabrera, 2014). The ability to write a quality product in the L2 is developed through social interaction, which is associated with "functional, relevant, and meaningful" uses of the target language, and collaboration among students (Wiseman & Belknap, 2013, p. 362). When students are to do a writing task in a group, they complete the assignment by communicating, coordinating, and discussing with group members during writing phases (Ortiz Navarrete & Ferreira Cabrera, 2014). The social and interactive nature of a collaborative writing task is rooted in sociocultural perspectives that have been influential in informing the design and classroom use of CALL technology and applications for collaborative learning environments (Youngs et al., 2011).

## Wiki-Based Collaborative Writing Outcomes

The literature on wiki-based collaborative writing suggests that equal opportunities to access the wiki project and mutual engagement among group peers both result in positive learning experiences and quality final drafts. Through a learner perception study with second-year university EFL students in China majoring in international business English, Lai et al. (2016) stated that many of the students failed to demonstrate collaborative work even though group collaboration comprised 20% of the final grade. Recruited from two sections of introductory university writing course, the researchers trained students to be competent users of wikis. Interestingly, student groups' various collaboration styles led them to have differing learning experiences via wikis. For instance, group members being highly equal and highly mutual in their composition process resulted in mainly "more positive perception of enjoyment of the projects, enhanced writing confidence and skills and attitudes toward collaborative writing" (Lai et al., 2016, p. 92). Likewise, Li (2013) reports a similar finding that all the three students of a group that had equal contributions and mutual engagement more actively contributed to the group discussion and to revising both global and local issues of the collaborative writing tasks. Indeed, all the group members' active participation and mutual engagement assisted them to produce quality final drafts that were rich in content and coherent.

Collaborative writing via wikis in L2 classrooms has also been shown to integrate students' research skills, communicative competence, and cultural competence into a research project that peers work on. Rott and Weber (2013) implemented wikis for intermediate learners of German at a college. These participants constructed wiki sites on German popular music of the 20th and 21st centuries not only to promote students' writing skills, but also to raise their cultural awareness. The researchers elaborated that creating wiki sites within a group of L2 learners can play an impressive role in language learning skills and development of writing skills. Due to the nature of the project, students' engagement generated a meaningful as well as communicative environment. For learners to have successful and collaborative outcomes using wikis, the researchers suggest that teachers provide learners with various knowledge skills, which include knowledge of technology, awareness of differing genres within one assignment, and the ability to take notes for each wiki task.

The level of student engagement and contribution toward a wiki writing task is likely to lead to positive outcomes. For instance, Wang (2015) showed that a great deal of student involvement and collaboration on wiki writing tasks enabled students to search for a topic more extensively, and consider the target language more carefully. In addition, leaners can benefit from wikis as a collaborative learning tool in language classrooms. Arnold et al. (2012) shared some obvious benefits of collaborative writing via wikis: wikis encouraged the majority of students to share their tasks; the level of each student's contribution was high; and each student completed the project in a timely manner without much teacher intervention. Hubbard (2016) commented that less teacher intervention is closely related to institutional efficiency. As these studies demonstrate, wikis as a collaborative learning tool play a role in L2 learning, help learners become autonomous, and make language learning more efficient.

In terms of learner engagement in wiki projects, researchers do not coincide. Nakamaru (2012), for instance, elaborated that students who engaged more in wikis apparently had more passing scores on final exams than the ones who did not, but the overall student engagement was very low. Nakamura adds that existing studies on wikis do not explicitly discuss students' engagement. In a study on the level of collaboration, Hadjerrouit (2014) argued that wikis might provide learning opportunities, but they do not promise automatic and straightforward effects of collaboration without evaluating and fine-tuning the learners' needs and previous knowledge, classroom environment, and teachers' pedagogy. These studies indicate that learners cannot benefit from wikis' collaborative feature unless classroom teachers plan appropriately to promote engagement.

### Pedagogical Implications

Collaborative learning and collaborative writing through wikis have become important areas of focus in CALL research. Arnold et al. (2012), despite the benefits, suggest that since research studies on collaborative writing in a digital environment is still in an early stage, there might be more venues for qualitative research to explore learners' collaborative writing processes, such as learners' decision-making processes, think-aloud protocols, and interviews. In contrast, there seem to be negative viewpoints on the effects of collaborative writing via wikis that wikis are not a promised land where both instructors and learners can have immediate, positive results of increased motivation, engagement, and collaboration (Hadjerrouit, 2014; Nakamaru, 2012). For instance, previous research suggests that when implementing wikis for collaborative writing projects, educators should make certain that students' knowledge of technology is adequate (Hubbard, 2016; Rott & Weber, 2013). It is worth noting that without an extensive understanding of how technology affects the learning environment, it seems that what technology-based tools bring to a learning environment would be limited (Hubbard, 2016). In a more positive light, Nakamaru (2012) makes suggestions for wiki implementation that L2 teachers might find relevant and beneficial. First, students should create most of the wiki content and instructors should let learners structure their own content. She pointed out that this is in accordance with a constructivist perspective because wikis facilitate creating content in a digital environment. Second, learners' activities on wikis, such as in- and out-of-class edits, over time can lead learners to successful academic outcomes.

Although it was not necessarily long ago since its debut in the field of education, implementing wikis especially in language classrooms made an impact on how L2 writing is developed among students in a group. It might be too early to draw a big picture of wikis and collaborative L2 writing in the theory of CALL, but wikis have potential that could make L2 learning and writing more efficient and effective. L2 educators should implement technology to make language teaching and learning more efficient and effective—reflecting the link to TESOL Technology Standards for Language Teachers, Goal 2 (Healey et al., 2011). Moreover, wiki technology provides a digital space where learners can integrate their research skills, communicative competence, and creativity while working on a project collaboratively. Wikis, as a technology tool, serve multiple functions in L2 classrooms: they facilitate learner communication, promote learner become autonomy, and facilitate working together toward one goal. The pedagogical implications discussed in previous wiki research suggest that, when appropriately researched and documented in the literature, collaborative L2 writing via wikis would have a more solid theoretical foundation as well as a stronger, positive influence on L2 education.

## Role-Playing Games

Role-playing games (RPGs) have become very popular in the world of digital gaming. RPGs involve detailed story lines that require players to read parts of the story to complete tasks. This unique feature of these games provides a method for introducing technology into reading classes, particularly English as a Second Language (ESL) courses. ELLs can acquire the different elements of storytelling and plot sequence. This can lead to classroom activities such as discussion groups and writing short essays. ELLs can also bring RPGs to life by performing skits based on these games. RPGs are beneficial to ELLs because they can incorporate the four main skill areas of reading, writing, listening and speaking. Overall, the RPGs act as mediation—as a physical artifact—through the use of technology. Interactionist theory holds that interaction provides a trigger for acquisition. Despite the fact that benefits of interaction types are similar, the three distinct benefits are opportunities for negotiating meaning, gaining enhanced input, and directing attention to linguistic forms (Gass, 1997).

Although it has been somewhat difficult to create a concrete definition of what role play is, it has been an ongoing method in teaching language learners (Shapiro & Leopold, 2012). This is because role play exposes students to language that can be used for different purposes. The improvisational nature of role playing provides a source for more authentic language use (Shapiro & Leopold, 2012). Students can create their own dialogue in response to scene prompts. Depending on the genres of the scene prompts, role playing can encourage dialogue related to academics or everyday activities. This allows teachers to present different formats of language use to their students. Role-playing typically involves acting out a scene and students are usually able to complete this task physically. However, one growing trend of technology use in the classroom is creating ways to develop role-play activities through digital games. This presents a motivational factor for students as video games are often categorized as being a form of entertainment. Games that encourage reading and critical thinking are beneficial to teachers because they support language practice in the classroom. As video games become a more common part of everyday life, teachers should take advantage of video games as an educational resource (Cruz, 2007).

The use of RPGs is a simple way of incorporating technology into the ESL classroom, while also meeting learner needs. RPGs keep the students focused on target skill areas such as reading and listening. The students are required to read or listen to parts of the story in an RPG for the game to continue. In an analysis of the game *Dungeons & Dragons*, Adams (2013) examined how players are responsible for the creativity of the storyline. This means that the development of characters, dialogue, interactions, and setting is dependent upon the player. In addition, the game requires players to work together in small groups to complete missions. This encourages speaking and writing practice and support modified interaction between the learner and the computer as well as opportunities for the learner to act as a participant in L2 tasks (Chapelle, 1997).

Additionally, Adams (2013) explains how RPGs are beneficial for cognitive development. By encouraging the player to act as a certain fictional character, the player becomes relieved from the social anxiety, which is often found in ESL settings. Many ESL students tend to shy away from speaking practice for fear of making mistakes. They usually worry about judgment from others. Through RPGs, the students would not be face-to-face, but rather online, which gives them more freedom to explore how language is used. "As shown, players are more likely to feel estrangement and alienation. Therefore, it stands within reason to expect that RPG players may have different social needs which may not be fulfilled during everyday interactions; rather, these needs are achieved to some degree through fantasy game-play" (Adams, 2013, p. 72).

Not only do RPGs support learner needs, they also introduce students to the gaming industry which is continuing to be globalized. With digital games becoming increasingly popular worldwide, it is important for students to know about this type of technology. This is because they will most likely encounter digital gaming at some point and they can benefit from knowing how to use it. The goal of many language teachers is to help students develop skills they can use in real-life situations. Digital games have become an increasing part of everyday life as anyone with a smartphone has access to them. Therefore, an understanding of how to play games while interacting with others at the same time is useful for ELLs.

Although there are many more questions to be considered, we asked the following questions to evaluate the effectiveness of RPGs inside the ESL environment. These questions were formulated using the TESOL Technology Standards as a guide to better establish a praxis between practice and theory. Are the ELLs familiar with the type of technology being used?—TTS, Learner Standards, Goal 1; Does the technology improve and promote communication in English?—TTS, Teacher Standards, Goal 4); Does the technology develop knowledge and skills to enhance language teaching and learning?—TTS, Teacher Standards, Goal 2 (Healey et al. 2011, p. vii).

## Student Familiarity With Digital Gaming

Mobile phones have become lifestyle products for people all over the world. This is because they can be used for a variety of purposes including communication, scheduling, and entertainment. Digital gaming falls into the entertainment category. Mobile phone companies have noticed the popularity of digital games and have started marketing their products with the inclusion of gaming features. Penttinen, Rossi, and Tuunainen (2010) state, "The growth of the smartphone market creates a more fruitful basis for the diffusion of mobile games as the games played on smartphones are more sophisticated and more interesting" (p. 2). Many ESL students have smartphones which make them part of a larger target audience for digital games. This includes RPGs such as *The Sorcery Trilogy* and *Dragon Quest*. As a part of the target audience, many ESL students are familiar with digital gaming to some degree.

## English Inside and Outside of the Classroom

The use of RPGs as a learning tool in ESL classrooms can encourage students to practice using the target language. Digital games are a motivational tool because they are a source of entertainment. This means that students will be more likely to participate in classroom activities that involve some form of digital gaming. Additionally, with the games loaded onto mobile devices, students can transport them anywhere. This encourages game play even after class is over. Reinhardt and Sykes (2014) examined how game-enhanced L2 learning could benefit students by requiring the use of the target language. In gaming communities, players can interact with each other from different parts of the world. This intercultural context requires the use of a common language of communication among players. Communication is an important part of RPGs because players are not able to advance to different levels unless they complete missions, which mostly involve working within groups. Therefore, RPGs can afford ELLs opportunities to engage in speaking practice with others in a real-life context. ELLs develop a need to use the target language to participate in an everyday task, namely, *digital gaming*.

## A Useful Tool for Enhancing Knowledge and Skills in the L2

RPGs require players to use different skills to complete tasks and move to higher levels. These games always involve reading and listening to passages so that the players are part of a story. This format allows ESL students to practice reading and listening in the target language. In some cases, these games also encourage note-taking. For example, in the Nancy Drew series of RPGs, players are expected to find clues to solve mysteries. To prevent constant backtracking, many players opt to write down notes so that the game can keep moving forward. This promotes writing in the target language. Finally, when students work with other players, they can communicate through writing, but also in some cases, by speaking through headsets. This allows the students to participate in meaningful speaking practice.

RPGs have many benefits for ESL students. While promoting growth in the four developmental skill areas (reading, writing, speaking, and listening), they also provide a source of entertainment within an academic environment. This creates a correlation between language learning and amusement. When students enjoy the learning process, they become motivated to participate. This type of intrinsic motivation is a leading factor in how successful a student will become in learning a language. Bernard (2010) found that students in various age groups performed better on classroom tasks when they were intrinsically motived. That is, when students have a desire to participate in classroom activities, they are more likely to learn the different processes behind their own learning. This keeps them actively engaged, which leads to continued practice in using the target language. Through the use of RPGs, interaction occurs electronically over a computer network and it differs from face-to-face interaction. It includes interaction between the learners and the computer that can provides a trigger for acquisition. For example, socially constructed knowledge through interaction can determine if feedback is necessary following a task.

## Moodle's 3.1 Gradebook: Online Record Keeping

The issue of assessment in second language teaching and learning has long held importance in the field of applied linguistics (Bachman & Palmer, 2010). One aspect of the assessment process often overlooked is the accurate record keeping needed to make effective assessments and feedback (Black & Wiliam, 1998). The importance of record keeping has even been recognized by the TESOL Technology Standards (TTS)—Teacher Standards, Goal 3, "Language teachers apply technology in record keeping, feedback, and assessment" (Healey et al., 2011). In the age of Web 2.0, a variety of applications are available to assist teachers in keeping accurate assessment records. These applications are available mostly free of cost, and provide functionality for summative and formative assessments. Some popular applications include engrade.com and thinkwave.com; however, these are proprietary applications whose free versions have limited functionality. Another option is the Gradebook, which is available on Moodle 3.1, a free and open-source learning management system. To explore Moodle 3.1's Gradebook assessment functions and its relation to interactionist and sociocultural SLA theories, the following questions are addressed: (1) What has research revealed about formative assessment? and (2) How can Gradebook be used to meet TTS for Teachers, Goal 3? The answers to (1) and (2) should show how SLA theory (i.e., interactionist and sociocultural theories) informs the use of online record keeping.

### What Has Research Revealed About Formative Assessment?

Starting from the assumption that formative assessment is the means through which teachers can assess student needs to create more meaningful learning outcomes, Black and Wiliam (1998) conducted an extensive literature review that included 160 journals. They found that enhanced formative assessments do improve standards, especially for low-achieving students; to be effective, formative assessments must result in teacher and student adjustments. They also found considerable room to improve assessments, suggesting that teachers often failed to strike a balance between giving grades for evaluation and providing advice for improvement. Another area for development, and one most relevant to Moodle 3.1's Gradebook, is the management of assessment results. That is, the teachers in the reviewed literature marked grades but often failed to analyze them. To improve formative assessments, Black and Wiliam (1998) suggested that teachers adopt an interactive approach to formative assessment.

Rea-Dickins (2001) noted that the assessment cycle that teachers go through to do formative assessments needed further exploration. Following a qualitative research design, Rea-Dickins (2001) conducted classroom observations, audio and video recorded classes, and interviewed both teachers and supporting staff; data collection lasted a whole school year. An analysis of the data provided rich details of the assessment cycle, which involved a (1) planning stage (i.e., deciding the purpose of the assessment), an (2) implementation phase (i.e., introducing assessments, self- and peer-monitoring, immediate feedback), an (3) appraising and monitoring phase (i.e., recording evidence of achievement and adjusting assessment, teaching, and learning plans), and a (4) recording and reporting phase (Rea-Dickins, 2001, p. 435). Rea-Dickins (2001) discovered that many of these phases, apart from the recording and reporting stage, have the potential to help students develop a greater awareness of objectives and potential for student-student and teacher-student collaborations.

With the advantages and necessity of self- and peer-assessment becoming more apparent in research (Alderson & Banerjee, 2001; Brown & Lee, 2015), Saito (2008) investigated the effects of training on the quantity and quality of peer-assessment. All 81 participants in Saito's study had no experience with peer-assessment; these participants were placed in either a control or treatment groups. Each group received instruction in skill aspects but only the treatment group received rater training. Analysis of the assessment comments found that the treatment group gave more substantive and relevant feedback. These findings align with Rian, Hinkelman, and McGarty's (2012) study in that both suggest that students require training and guidance for peer- and self-assessments to be meaningful and successful when using online peer- and self-evaluation with technology.

The above research findings provide useful suggestions on how to conduct formative assessments using Web 2.0 technologies (e.g., Rian, Hinkelman, & McGarty, 2012) and how to improve the quality of formative assessments through training (e.g., Saito, 2008). Moreover, Rea-Dickins (2001) found that throughout the process of assessment, both learners and teachers have opportunities to collaborate and become aware of language content and learning objectives. Thus, it is no wonder why the use of technology for record keeping was included in the TESOL Technology Standards (Goal 3). Moreover, it is clear from the studies cited above that interaction and sociocultural factors play a vital role in assessment, including online assessment tools.

## How Can Gradebook Be Used to Meet TTS (Goal 1)?

The Gradebook is an application in Moodle, an open-source virtual learning environment. According to recent statistics on Moodle users, there are almost 88 million users worldwide and used in over 234 countries (Moodle Statistics, n.d.). One of the key components of Moodle is its record keeping capabilities; not only does it allow for detailed feedback, it also permits teachers to design evaluation scales related specifically to language achievement (Barrington, 2014; Stanford, 2009). The next section provides examples of Gradebook's functionality, and shows how this functionality is related to TTS for Teachers, Goal 3.

## Gradebook Functionality

The first function of Gradebook is the ability to create online assignments with a scale or number grade. Prior to assigning an assignment, an instructor creates a scale (e.g., poor, fair, good, etc.) that can include descriptive texts. Gradebook also has the functionality to add notes if specific feedback is required. From a practical perspective, scales are simple formative assessments that can encourage students reflect on their level of participation. These scales allow teachers to take note of students whose level of participation is high or low. The second functionality is the ability to design, create, and implement alternative grading methods. Marking guides give teachers the ability to add criteria for both the student and instructions for the grader. Another function of marking guides is the ability to add frequently used comments. Once the marking guides are created, they can be saved as templates for later use.

Along with rubrics, scales, outcomes, and marking guides make it possible to match a task with an assessment. Some tasks, such as those that are not graded, such as daily participation, may only require a scale. This relates to the TTS for Teachers, Goal 3, Standard 1, "Language teachers evaluate and implement relevant technology to aid in effective learner assessment" (Healey et al., 2011, p. vii). These Moodle functions allow teachers to meet this standard. Additionally, the types of feedback the students receive act as learning devices for the learner and the instructor, and, according to Brown and Lee (2015), enhances learner autonomy and self-confidence.

The third functionality is Calculations. Calculations differs from the other three functions mentioned in that it relates to how grades are aggregated and calculated. Once an assignment is graded and feedback provided, a score is recorded. Each learning task or activity is assigned to a category, such as participation, attendance, homework, exams, papers, and projects. These categories are weighted and given a specific percentage of the course. In a conversation course, for example, attendance could be worth 5%; participation worth 20%; quizzes worth 25%; and exams worth 50%. Within these categories assignments can be assigned a category and a point value. In this way, points for one category are not counted in other categories. Another useful addition to the Calculator function is the ability to add the category of extra credit.

Once students receive initial training and guidance on how to use the Gradebook, they can track their grade and view comments. If students do not quite understand the feedback, they can send messages to the teacher to ask for clarification. This sort of (authentic) social interaction that Moodle allows for helps make the Gradebook a useful tool to ensure that feedback is effective and that learners take a more active role in the assessment process. When students have a clearer understanding of the assessment process, they are better positioned to make self-assessments of their current proficiency level and what they need to do to improve. Because the student can access this information without contacting the instructor, the Gradebook can also promote learner autonomy. The potential for developing autonomy is a key part of the TESOL Technology Standards for Learners (Goal 3, Standard 5); With proper training (see Saito, 2008), Reinders and Hubbard (2013) argued that access to information, such as feedback, and giving learners a say in the assessment process empower learners. They are empowered in part because they are more reflective and have greater agency of their learning (Brown & Lee, 2015).

The Gradebook application in Moodle 3.1 could be used to keep accurate records for analysis and provide meaningful feedback for positive washback through the scales, marking guides, and the Calculator functions. The use of these functions not only help teachers meet TTS for Teachers, Goal 3, but also afford learners the chance to meet TTS for Learners, Goal 3, Standard 5. Moreover, there are additional benefits to the effective use of the Gradebook, such as teachers becoming more reflective of their teaching and students being more reflective of their learning. For teachers, this relates to TTS for Teachers, Goal 4, Standard 2, "Language teachers regularly reflect on the intersection of professional practice and technological developments so that they can make informed decisions regarding the use of technology to support language learning and communication (Healey et al., 2011, p. vii)"

Assessment is a key component of language curriculum development and teaching (Richards, 2001). The functions of the Gradebook give teachers the necessary tools to develop and create assessments that match language achievement objectives (Stanford, 2009). For instance, a language teacher can have a group of students record a conversation, submit it on Moodle, and use the marking guides functions to create an alternative assessment designed for assessing conversation. The feedback provided from this assessment could be used to give them counseling in face-to-face meetings. At the end of the year, information can be used to inform feedback and comments about final grades for students, learners, and the school. Their assignment's prompt and rubric are great guidelines for them, too. Through the use of Gradebook technology (mediation), they can narrow the gap between what they can do and what they are supposed to do.

## CONCLUSION

This chapter discussed SLA theories relevant to CALL through sociocultural perspectives. Regarding sociocultural theory, theory and practice are not (and should not be) separate. To look at praxis more closely, we examined three CALL applications using the TESOL Technology Standards as a guide for evaluation. Instruction enhances ZPD and CALL also co-constructs ZPD thorough social learning and mediation. Furthermore, constructivism suggests that through technologically enhanced collaborative and interactive tasks, learners can actively construct the knowledge they need. Also discussed was interactionist theory and some of its application in CALL. Interactionist theory in general is interpersonal activity; however, in relation to CALL it usually involves interactions between computer and the learners or it is the medium between the teacher and the leaners. In general, like face-to-face interaction, computer learner interactions in CALL tasks have their distinct benefits. For example, these benefits include making a linguistic feature salient or supporting modified interaction between the learner and the computer.

More importantly, the collaborative use of digital technology in CALL has been investigated from SLA theory to its application and has been guided from its application to theorizing. Although many language learners and teachers are proficient in the use of technology, they are not using the available technology in a systematic way. We suggest that teachers, hoping to create a praxis between SLA theory and CALL-enhanced classroom practices, use the TTS to evaluate and improve upon how technology applications are applied to language learning and teaching. Further, we encourage teacher educators to use the TTS to help students consider how SLA theory relates to implanting and evaluating CALL.

The use of CALL in general might have its challenges. The limitations range from the hardware and software utilized, to the availability of high-speed internet connection. Once the technology is available, teachers need to be informed about both SLA theories and TESOL Technology Standards. Moreover, students need to be trained and motivated to use the relevant technology based on their needs. English language instructors need to provide sufficient training and practice in the class and discuss in detail the benefits of incorporating CALL-based practices appropriately. For instance, teachers need to emphasize to their students the benefits of technology by explicitly describing the benefits of wikis for collaborative writing and learning, RPGs (digital gaming) for social interaction, and online record keeping for assessment and feedback. Sociocultural perspectives including sociocultural theory and interactionist theory provide the theoretical underpinnings for the dynamic social and interaction demands of second language classroom. Ultimate attainment is not limited to actual face-to-face communication. CALL-based practices provide a wealth of opportunity to employ social and interactive tasks and provide students with effective feedback.

## REFERENCES

Abrams, Z. (2011). Interpersonal communication in intercultural CMC. In N. Arnold & L. Ducate (Eds.), *Present and future promises of CALL: From theory and research to new directions in language teaching* (pp. 61–92). San Marcos, TX: CALICO.

Adams, S. (2013). Needs met through role-playing games: A fantasy theme analysis of dungeons & dragons. *Kaleidoscope*, *16*, 69–86.

Alderson, J. C., & Banerjee, J. (2001). Language testing and assessment (Part I). *Language Teaching*, *34*(4), 213–236. doi:10.1017/S0261444800014464

Arnold, N., Ducate, L., & Kost, C. (2012). Collaboration or cooperation? Analyzing group dynamics and revision processes in wikis. *CALICO Journal*, *29*(3), 431–448. doi:10.11139/cj.29.3.431-448

Bachman, L., & Palmer, A. (2010). *Language assessment in practice.* Oxford, UK: Oxford University Press.

Barrington, R. (2014). *Moodle Gradebook.* Birmingham, UK: Packt Publishing Ltd.

Bernard, J. (2010). Motivation in foreign language learning: The relationship between classroom activities, motivation, and outcomes in a university language-learning environment (Honors Thesis). Pittsburgh, PA: Carnegie Mellon University. Retrieved from http://repository.cmu.edu/cgi/viewcontent.cgi?article=1077&context=hsshonors

Black, P., & Wiliam, D. (1998). Assessment and classroom learning. *Assessment in Education: Principles, Policy & Practice*, *5*(1), 7–74. doi:10.1080/0969595980050102

Brown, H. D., & Lee, H. (2015). *Teaching by principles: An interactive approach to language pedagogy.* White Plains, NY: Pearson Education.

Cervantes, S. E., & Olson, R. C. (2012). Face-to-face communication and instant messaging: Similarities and difference. In R. Chartrand, S. Crofts, & G. Brooks (Eds.), *The 2012 Pan-SIG Conference Proceedings* (pp. 43-48). Hiroshima, Japan: JALT.

Chapelle, C. (1998). Multimedia CALL: Lessons to be learned from research on instructed SLA. *Language Learning & Technology*, *2*(1), 22–34. Retrieved from http://llt.msu.edu/vol1num1/chapelle/default.html

Chapelle, C. (2003). *English language learning and technology: Lectures on teaching and research in the age of information and communication.* Amsterdam, The Netherlands: John Benjamins Publishing; doi:10.1075/lllt.7

Chapelle, C. (2008). Interactionist theory in CALL research. In M. Warschauer & R. Kern (Eds.), *Network-based language teaching: Concept adpractice* (pp. 53–64). Cambridge, UK: Cambridge University Press.

Chapelle, C. A. (1997). CALL in the year 2000: Still in search of research paradigms? *Language Learning & Technology, 1*(1), 19–43. Retrieved from http://llt.msu.edu/vol1num1/chapelle/default.html

Chapelle, C. A. (2005). Interactionist SLA theory in CALL research. In J. Egbert & G. Petrie (Eds.), *CALL research perspectives* (pp. 53–64). London: LEA Publication.

Chapelle, C. A. (2009). The relationship between second language acquisition theory and computer-assisted language learning. *Modern Language Journal*, 93741–93753. doi:10.1111/j.1540-4781.2009.00970.x

Cruz, J. Q. (2007). Video games and the ESL classroom. *The Internet TESL Journal, 13.* Retrieved from http://iteslj.org/Articles/Quijano-VideoGames.html

Dalgarno, B. (2001). Interpretations of constructivism and consequences for computer assisted learning. *British Journal of Educational Technology, 32*(2), 193–194. doi:10.1111/1467-8535.00189

Donato, R. (2000). Sociocultural contributions to understanding the foreign and second language classroom. In J. P. Lantolf (Ed.), *Sociocultural theory and second language learning* (pp. 27–50). Oxford, UK: Oxford University Press.

Doughty, C. J., & Long, M. H. (2003). Optimal psycholinguistic environments for distance foreign language learning. *Forum for International Studies, 23*, 35–73.

Du, H. S., Chu, S. K. W., Chan, R. C. H., & He, W. (2016). Collaborative writing with wikis: An empirical investigation. *Online Information Review, 40*(3), 380–399. doi:10.1108/OIR-06-2015-0173

Ducate, L., & Arnold, N. (2011). Technology, CALL, and the net generation: Where are we headed from here? In N. Arnold & L. Ducate (Eds.), *Present and future promises of CALL: From theory and research to new directions in language teaching* (pp. 1–22). San Marcos, TX: CALICO.

Ellis, R. (1999). Theoretical perspective on interaction and language learning. In R. Ellis (Ed.), *Learning a second language through interaction* (pp. 3–32). Philadelphia, PA: John Benjamin; doi:10.1075/sibil.17.04ell

Gass, S. (1997). *Input, interaction, and the second language learner.* Mahwah, NJ: Lawrence Erlbaum Associates. doi:10.4324/9780203053560

Hadjerrouit, S. (2013). A framework for assessing the pedagogical effectiveness of wiki-based collaborative writing: Results and implications. In E. Cohen & E. Boyd (Eds.), Proceedings of the Informing Science and Information Technology Education Conference 2013 (pp. 29–49). Informing Science Institute. Retrieved from https://www.learntechlib.org/p/114617

Hadjerrouit, S. (2014). Wiki as a collaborative writing tool in teacher education: Evaluation and suggestions for effective use. *Computers in Human Behavior, 32*, 301–312. doi:10.1016/j.chb.2013.07.004

Healey, D., Hanson-Smith, E., Hubbard, P., Ioannou-Georgiou, S., Kessler, G., & Ware, P. (2011). *TESOL technology standards: Description, implementation, integration*. Alexandria, VA: TESOL.

Hubbard, P. (2004). Learner training for effective use of CALL. In S. Fotos & C. Browne (Eds.), *New perspectives on CALL for second language classrooms* (pp. 45–67). Mahwah, NJ: Lawrence Erlbaum.

Hubbard, P. (2008). Twenty-five years of theory in the CALICO Journal. *CALICO Journal*, *25*(3), 387–399. doi:10.1007/978-94-009-8831-6

Hubbard, P. (2016). Unit 6-CALL theory and research. In *An invitation to CALL*. Retrieved from http://web.stanford.edu/~efs/callcourse2/CALL6.htm

Hubbard, P., & Levy, M. (2006). The scope of CALL education. In P. Hubbard & M. Levy (Eds.), *Teacher education in CALL* (pp. 3–20). Amsterdam, The Netherlands: John Benjamins. doi:10.1075/lllt.14.04hub

Kern, R. (2006). Perspectives on technology in learning and teaching languages. *TESOL Quarterly*, *40*(1), 183–210. doi:10.2307/40264516

Kon, C. K. (2002). *The influence on outcomes of ESL students' performance strategies on a CALL listening comprehension activity* (Unpublished master's thesis). Iowa State University, Ames, IA.

Lai, C., Lei, C., & Liu, Y. (2016). The nature of collaboration and perceived learning in wiki-based collaborative writing. *Australasian Journal of Educational Technology*, *32*(3), 80–95. doi:10.14742/ajet.2586

Lantolf, J., & Poehner, J. P. (2014). *Sociocultural theory and the pedagogical imperative in L2 education*. New York, NY: Routledge. doi:10.4324/9780203813850

Levy, M., & Stockwell, G. (2006). *Call dimensions: Options and issued in computer assisted language learning*. New York, NY: Lawrence Erlbaum Associates. doi:10.4324/9780203708200

Li, M. (2013). Individual novices and collective experts: Collective scaffolding in wiki-based small group writing. *System*, *41*(3), 752–769. doi:10.1016/j.system.2013.07.021

Lin, M. H., & Lee, J. (2015). Data-driven learning: Changing the teaching of grammar in EFL classes. *ELT Journal*, *69*(3), 264–274. doi:10.1093/elt/ccv010

Long, M. H. (1996). The role of linguistic environment in second language acquisition. In W. C. Ritchie & T. K. Bhatia (Eds.), *Handbook of second language acquisition* (pp. 413–468). San Diego, CA: Academic Press. doi:10.1016/B978-012589042-7/50015-3

Moodle Statistics. (n.d.). Retrieved from https://moodle.net/stats/

Nakamaru, S. (2012). Investment and return: Wiki engagement in a remedial ESL writing course. *Journal of Research on Technology in Education*, *44*(4), 273–291. doi:10.1080/15391523.2012.10782591

O'Keeffe, A., McCarthy, M., & Carter, R. (2007). *From corpus to classroom: Language use and language teaching*. Cambridge, UK: Cambridge University Press. doi:10.1017/CBO9780511497650

Ohta, A. S. (2000). Re-thinking interaction in SLA: Developmentally appropriate assistance in the zone of proximal development and the acquisition of L2 grammar. In J. P. Lantolf (Ed.), *Sociocultural theory and second language learning* (pp. 51–78). Oxford, UK: Oxford University Press.

Ortiz Navarrete, M., & Ferreira Cabrera, A. (2014). Proposing a wiki-based technique for collaborative essay writing. *Profile Issues in Teachers' Professional Development*, *16*(2), 185–198. doi:10.15446/profile.v16n2.38877

Penttinen, E., Rossi, M., & Tuunainen, V. K. (2010). Mobile games: Analyzing the needs and values of the consumers. *Journal of Information Technology Theory and Application*, *11*(1), 2.

Plass, J. L., Chun, D. M., Mayer, R. E., & Leutner, D. (1998). Supporting visual and verbal learning in a second-language multimedia learning environment. *Journal of Educational Psychology*, *90*(1), 25–36. doi:10.1037/0022-0663.90.1.25

Prensky, M. (2001). Digital natives, digital immigrants (Part 1). *On the Horizon*, *9*(5), 1–6. doi:10.1108/10748120110424816

Rea-Dickins, P. (2001). Mirror, mirror on the wall: Identifying processes of classroom assessment. *Language Testing*, *18*(4), 429–462. doi:10.1191/026553201682430120

Reinders, H., & Hubbard, P. (2013). CALL and learner autonomy: Affordances and constraints. In M. Thomas, H. Reinders, & M. Warschauer (Eds.), *Contemporary computer assisted language learning* (pp. 359–375). London: Bloomsbury.

Reinhardt, J., & Sykes, J. M. (2014). Special issue commentary: Digital game activity in L2 teaching and learning. *Language Learning & Technology*, *18*(2), 2–8. Retrieved from http://llt.msu.edu/issues/june2014/commentary.pdf

Rian, J. P., Hinkelman, D., & McGarty, G. (2012). Integrating video assessment into an oral presentation course. In A. Stewart & N. Sonda (Eds.), *JALT 2011 Conference Proceedings* (pp. 416-425). Tokyo, Japan: JALT.

Richards, J. C. (2001). *Curriculum Development in Language Teaching*. Cambridge, UK: Cambridge University Press; doi:10.1017/CBO9780511667220

Richards, J. C., & Rodgers, T. S. (2001). *Approaches and methods in language teaching* (2nd ed.). Cambridge, UK: Cambridge University Press. doi:10.1017/CBO9780511667305

Rott, S., & Weber, E. D. (2013). Preparing students to use wiki software as a collaborative learning tool. *CALICO Journal*, *30*(2), 179–203. doi:10.11139/cj.30.2.179-203

Saito, H. (2008). EFL classroom peer assessment: Training effects on rating and commenting. *Language Testing*, *25*(4), 553–581. doi:10.1177/0265532208094276

Salaberry, M. R. (1996). A theoretical foundation for the development of pedagogical tasks in computer mediated communication. *CALICO Journal*, *14*(1), 5–34.

Shapiro, S., & Leopold, L. (2012). A critical role for role-playing pedagogy. *TESL Canada Journal*, *29*(2), 120. doi:10.18806/tesl.v29i2.1104

Stanford, J. (2009). *Moodle 1.9 for second language teaching*. Birmingham, UK: Packt Publishing Ltd.

Stoddart, A., Chan, J. Y., & Liu, G. (2016). Enhancing successful outcomes of wiki-based collaborative writing: A state-of-the-art review of facilitation frameworks. *Interactive Learning Environments*, *24*(1), 142–157. doi:10.1080/10494820.2013.825810

Vygotsky, L. S. (1978). *Mind in society*. Cambridge, MA: Harvard University Press.

Vygotsky, L. S. (1997). The collected works of L.S. Vygotsky: Vol. 3. *Problems of the theory and history of psychology*. New York, NY: Plenum.

Wang, Y. (2014). Using wikis to facilitate interaction and collaboration among EFL learners: A social constructivist approach to language teaching. *System*, *42*, 383–390. doi:10.1016/j.system.2014.01.007

Wang, Y. (2015). Promoting collaborative writing through wikis: A new approach for advancing innovative and active learning in an ESP context. *Computer Assisted Language Learning*, *28*(6), 499–512. doi:10.1080/09588221.2014.881386

Warschauer, M. (2000). Online learnings in a second language classroom. An ethnographic study. In M. Warschauer & R. Kern (Eds.), *Network-based language teaching: Concept ad practice* (pp. 41–58). Cambridge, UK: Cambridge University Press. doi:10.1017/CBO9781139524735.005

Wiseman, C. S., & Belknap, J. P. (2013). Wikis: A knowledge platform for collaborative learning in ESL reading. *TESOL Journal*, *4*(2), 360–369. doi:10.1002/tesj.83

Woo, M. M., Chu, S. K. W., & Li, X. (2013). Peer-feedback and revision process in a wiki mediated collaborative writing. *Educational Technology Research and Development*, *61*(2), 279–309. doi:10.1007/s11423-012-9285-y

Youngs, B., Ducate, L., & Arnold, N. (2011). Linking second language acquisition, CALL, and language pedagogy. In N. Arnold & L. Ducate (Eds.), *Present and future promises of CALL: From theory and research to new directions in language teaching* (pp. 23–60). San Marcos, TX: CALICO.

Zuengler, J., & Miller, E. R. (2006). Cognitive and sociocultural perspectives: Two parallel SLA worlds? *TESOL Quarterly*, *40*(1), 35–58. doi:10.2307/40264510

## ADDITIONAL READING

Beatty, K. (2013). *Teaching and Researching: Computer-assisted Language Learning*. New York, NY: Routledge.

Chun, D. M. (2011). Developing intercultural communicative competence through online exchanges. *CALICO Journal*, *28*(2), 392–419. doi:10.11139/cj.28.2.392-419

Crystal, D. (2008). *Txtng: The Gr8 Db8*. Oxford, United Kingdom: Oxford University Press.

Darhower, M. (2002). Interactional features of synchronous computer-mediated communication in the intermediate L2 class: A sociocultural case study. *CALICO Journal*, *19*(2), 249–277.

Garrett, N. (2009). Computer-assisted language learning trends and issues revisited: Integrating innovation. *Modern Language Journal, 93*(1), 719–740. doi:10.1111/j.1540-4781.2009.00969.x

Holton, D. L. (2010). Using Moodle to teach constructivist learning design skills to adult learners. In T. T. Kidd & J. Keengwa (Eds.), *Adult learning in the digital age: Perspectives on online technologies and outcomes* (pp. 40–51). Hershey, PA: IGI Global. doi:10.4018/978-1-60566-828-4.ch005

Karlström, P., & Lundin, E. (2013). CALL in the zone of proximal development: Novelty effects and teacher guidance. *Computer Assisted Language Learning, 26*(5), 412–429. doi:10.1080/09588221.2012.663760

Kessler, G. (2013). Collaborative language learning in co-constructed participatory culture. *CALICO Journal, 30*(3), 307–322. doi:10.11139/cj.30.3.307-322

Mroz, A. (2015). The development of second language critical thinking in a virtual language learning environment: A process-oriented mixed-method study. *CALICO Journal, 32*(3), 528–553. doi:10.1558/cj.v32i3.26386

Ockey, G. J. (2009). Developments and challenges in the use of computer-based testing for assessing second language ability. *Modern Language Journal, 93*(s1), 836–847. doi:10.1111/j.1540-4781.2009.00976.x

Overby, A., & Jones, B. L. (2015). Virtual LEGOs: Incorporating Minecraft into the art education curriculum. *Art Education, 68*(1), 21–27.

Peterson, M. (2012). Learner interaction in a massively multiplayer online role playing game (MMORPG): A sociocultural discourse analysis. *ReCALL, 24*(3), 361–380. doi:10.1017/S0958344012000195

Pifarré, M., & Fisher, R. (2011). Breaking up the writing process: How wikis can support understanding the composition and revision strategies of young writers. *Language and Education, 25*(5), 451–466. doi:10.1080/09500782.2011.585240

Thorne, S. L., & Smith, B. (2011). Second language development theories and technology-mediated language learning. *CALICO Journal, 28*(2), 268–277. doi:10.11139/cj.28.2.268-277

Turkle, S. (2012). *Alone together: Why we expect more from technology and less from each other*. New York, NY: Basic books.

Yates, N. (2008). Wikis and constructivism: Exploring the links. *The JALT CALL Journal, 4*(3), 15–28.

## KEY TERMS AND DEFINITIONS

**CALL:** The abbreviation for computer assisted language learning. The use of computer in teaching or learning of a second or foreign language.

**Communities of Practice:** A term used to refer to a group of individuals' participation in a communal activity that involve collaboration to achieve a goal.

**Praxis:** The interconnectedness of theory and practice in which each informs and guides the other.

**Record Keeping:** (In language program) the maintenance of the file of data on student performance.

**Role-Playing Games (RPG):** RPGs involve detailed story lines that require players to read parts of the story to complete tasks.

**Sociocultural Perspectives:** Perspectives of learning that focus on the roles of social and cultural factors in learning. These perspectives are informed by the work of Vygotsky.

**TESOL Technology Standards (TTS):** Technology standards that focus on how English language teachers, teacher educators, and administrators can and should use technology in and out of the classroom.

**Wikis:** The Hawaiian word for *quick*, used to refer to a website with pages that the users can contribute and edit, often including photos, videos and texts.

**Zone of Proximal Development (ZPD):** ZPD is the difference between what a learner can do without help and what he or she can do with help. It is a concept introduced, yet not fully developed, by Soviet psychologist Lev Vygotsky (1896–1934) during the last ten years of his life.

# Chapter 5
# Contextual Factors of Online Teacher Education in TESOL:
## An Activity Theory Perspective

**Dong-shin Shin**
*University of Cincinnati, USA*

## ABSTRACT

*The chapter introduces a case study of online language teacher education in a TESOL master's course. Drawing on sociocultural theories, it aims to investigate the patterns of interactions among students and the instructor in online teacher training, and factors that shape the efficacy of quality online language teacher education. Various domains of data were collected and analyzed using analytical codes such as employed tools, participation patterns, rules of interactions, divisions of labor among participants, and goals. The findings suggest that the teacher trainee participants increased active participation among themselves, promoting mutually supportive relationships. The students' participation and learning outcomes were shaped by the learning communities they built, along with diverse pedagogical interests and different perceptions of collaborative work.*

## INTRODUCTION

Along with the ever-growing use of computer technologies in education, a significant number of online programs are offering academic degrees and professional development credentials in foreign and second language teacher education (England, 2012; Murray, 2013; Pawan, Wiechart, Warren, & Park, 2016; White, 2014). The proliferation of online language teacher education programs reflects the benefits that distance education via computer-related technologies offers in terms of delivery mode. In particular, the increased accessibility allows not only students to afford education beyond time and place constraints, but also language teacher education programs to recruit students widely around the globe in a relatively economical way. The increased accessibility of online education has brought about an expanded diversity in the pedagogical context of online language teacher education, given that more students are enrolled in such programs from various parts of the world (Pawan et al., 2016). Students bring diverse cultural and

DOI: 10.4018/978-1-5225-2933-0.ch005

educational backgrounds into computer-mediated class interactions, in addition to providing a variety of professional experiences and aspirations.

Research has yet to show, however, how the contextual factors of online second language teacher education influence interactions among all class participants, including students and the instructor, as well as class activities and tasks. There are few studies that investigate online second language teacher education, compared to a plethora of studies of computer-assisted language learning (CALL) and computer-mediated communication (CMC). The lack of research on online programs is due to concerns regarding copyright, intellectual property, and competition in recruiting students among institutions (Hall & Knox, 2009). Even the small number of existing studies tends to focus primarily on how to manage an online course using computer technologies (Murray, 2013; White, 2014). Therefore, there is a need for more studies that critically examine curriculum and instruction of online language teacher education and learner participation in course activities.

This chapter introduces a case study of the effectiveness of learning activities, modules, and tools of online language teacher education in order to identify ways in which online language teacher education can successfully be implemented. Focusing on students' learning experience and agency, it investigated the patterns of interactions among students and the instructor in online teacher training, and it explored the contextual factors that shape the quality of online language teacher education. This investigation addresses the following questions:

1. How do teacher trainees interact with each other and participate in learning activities of an online TESOL course?
2. What kinds of contextual factors shape their learning activities?
3. What kinds of constraints and benefits do the teacher trainees configure regarding an online learning environment?

Drawing on social and cultural perspectives of language and learning, this chapter first reviews studies of online language learning and teaching by referencing relevant studies of Computer Assisted Language Learning (CALL) and Computer Mediated Communication (CMC) due to the lack of studies on online language teacher education in the field of second language teacher education. Next, it presents the methodology used in the current study. After presenting findings based on qualitative data analysis, it concludes with a discussion of issues and suggestions for promoting quality online teacher education in teaching English as a second language.

## LITERATURE REVIEW

Grounded in sociocultural theories of learning (Engeström, 1987, 2001; Leonti'ev, 1978; Vygotsky, 1978; Wertsch, 1998), this study understands online language teacher education as comprised of human activities in social and cultural contexts. From this perspective, online mediums of instruction have brought pedagogical, social, and cognitive changes to language teacher education. Those changes are related to affordances of online education, "the possibilities for action which people identify in relation to specific recourses" (Barton & Potts, 2013, pp.186-187). The foremost change is associated with accessibility unhampered by constraints on a user's location, technology mediation, and learner agency. Online teacher education programs allow those who would normally be unable to obtain higher education due to busy schedules or distant locations to earn degrees or professional certificates. Open accessibility has brought students from diverse backgrounds and contexts around the globe into virtual classrooms, and this has encouraged language teacher educators to address cultural and intercultural issues as much as linguistic and pedagogical knowledge (Blake, 2007; Ware, 2005). Provided that the pedagogical, social, and cognitive changes of online second language teacher education involve computer-mediated and computer-assisted education, a few concerns and issues that relate to medium, interaction, and role come to light. The following section presents a discussion of affordances of instructional mediums, cultural and intercultural issues regarding computer-mediated interactions, and teachers' roles in online language teacher education through references to relevant studies of CALL and CMC.

## Pedagogical Change: Affordances of Online Instructional Mediums

The combination of synchronous and asynchronous delivery and communication methods provides various ways for learners to design their learning with increased agency. That is, learners can make decisions about which learning activities and materials they engage with, in addition to governing when and how long they will engage with them. Asynchronous activities include use of technologies such as e-mail, discussion forums, PDFs, document files, presentation slides, video lectures, and websites. Synchronous communication methods utilize chat rooms and webcam conversations (Hockly, 2015; Liu, Liu, Lee, & Magjuka, 2010; Osman, 2005; Pawan et al., 2016). It is reported that asynchronous online course activities in which students are unable to ask teachers questions and receive immediate feedback could lead them to be dependent on each other and more collaborative among themselves (Kamhi-Stein, 2000). In light of the notion of constructivism, this kind of online environment is conducive to enhanced learning. For instance, studies of TESOL teacher education courses show that the use of asynchronous communication allows students to compose and post messages without pressure, to retrieve the messages for reflection (Kamhi-Stein, 2000), and to have student-centered interactions with opportunities for students to express their voices as often as in face-to-face classrooms (Nunan, 1999). More recently, studies have demonstrated that online courses provide pre- and in-service teachers with a forum for "reflection-in-action" and learning communities throughout their professional careers (Grant & Lee, 2014).

In investigating uses of synchronous and asynchronous communication tools in language teaching education, researchers have reported that synchronous CMC tools provide a good environment for negotiating meaning (Blake, 2000). Learners are able to negotiate meanings when they encounter new ideas, and decision-making tasks are a form of supported negotiation (Smith, 2003). Other researchers (Davis & Thiede, 2000; Schultz, 2000) have examined how asynchronous CMC as a pedagogical tool support second language development. Looking into the effectiveness of CMC as a feedback tool, Schultz (2000) studied the relationship between second language writing development and CMC activity in more complex ways. These studies collectively show that the interrelationship between CMC and language education is not a simple matter of claiming that CMC is a medium that is either superior or inferior to face-to-face communication for second language education. It is apparent, rather, that students' language proficiency level, types of activity, and medium are all interconnected dynamically.

## Interactional Change: Cultural Differences and Challenges of Online Instruction

Computer-mediated communication is complicated, and the choice of medium contributes to a reexamination of the current notion of learner agency in online language teacher education courses. Studies show that CMC tools have social and cultural values, and its practices should be understood as social and cultural practices (Belz, 2002; Crawford-Ferre & Wiest, 2012). For instance, Zhao and McDougall (2008) challenged the widespread notion that students who do not have native proficiency in a target language can participate in online discussions without language barriers, unlike interactions in face-to-face settings, while highlighting cultural differences that students bring to online courses. They showed that Chinese students were uncomfortable about disagreeing with instructors and unwilling to post messages that would show disagreements. Hence, equal participation among students is not guaranteed considering the detracted affordances for discussion. Similarly, Liu et al. (2010) reported that students from China, Russia, and India had difficulties participating in class discussions online due to their common prior experiences with reading, attending lectures passively, focusing on passing exams, and figuring out when to cite references in online writing.

Additional studies that examined cultural discourses that shape computer-mediated communication, researchers (Kramsch & Thorne, 2002; Thorne, 2003) argued that social and cultural discourses surrounding Internet communication tools (e.g., e-mail, chat rooms, and instant messaging) are varied across social, generational, institutional, and national groups. In this vein, CMC should be understood as existing against a backdrop of social discourses from the viewpoint of different communicative genres of CMC, linguistic styles, academic cultures, and cultural characteristics. To give a specific example, Kramsch and Thorne (2002) studied e-mail exchanges between French students of English and American students of French to investigate what it means to be a competent communicator in intercultural CMC. They found that what disturbed students' cross-cultural understanding were differences in cultural frames and communicative genres of CMC, and not linguistic misunderstanding. They contended that what needed to be negotiated in CMC were stylistic conventions of the genre–e.g., formal versus informal, edited versus unedited, literate versus orate.

Drawing on a comprehensive and critical perspective, Ware (2005) investigated a telecollaborative intercultural project between German university students who studied English to become EFL teachers and American university students who majored or minored in German. She defined "moments of missed communication" as moments of disengagement, miscommunication, or missed opportunities for intercultural learning, and studied how different genres and discourses of CMC were operating as causes for these moments of missed communication in a telecollaboration project between these two groups of students. She found that CMC featured in many forms with different styles of genre and discourse, which led to difficulties and disconnects in intercultural learning. She contended that online communication discourse normally tended to be brief rather than sustained, and that it lacked the social consequences of dropping topics. These discourse features hindered the participants from engaging deeply in intercultural inquiry.

These studies have demonstrated that online language learning is a complicated fabric with multilayered contexts of pedagogical, institutional, social, and cultural materials, as well as nationality-based factors and discourse styles, a conclusion which challenges a simplistic, reductive view of CMC as a matter of *typing skill* for online education. The studies also maintained that the attention to communicating with *native speakers* in CMC and quantity of interactions obscured different genres and discourse rules shaped by the cultural values and generic expectations of its participants, which in turn reflected different social, generational, and national groups (Hanna & de Nooy, 2003). As such, computer-mediated interactions in online courses involve cultural and intercultural tasks that allow students to negotiate and develop class interactional norms, in reflection of what they bring to virtual learning contexts.

## Changes of Teacher's Role in Online Education

Online language teacher education is mediated by various communication technologies as well. Researchers have reported that a curriculum based on CMC tools brought changes in the teacher's role, from "authoritative figure" to "facilitative coach" (England, 2012; Murray, 2013; Pawan et al., 2016; White, 2014). This revised teacher's role is built around structuring, juxtaposing, interpreting, and reflecting on intercultural experiences. Additionally, the students took on new roles of their own that involved questioning, contradicting, and confirming their assumptions and hypotheses regarding others' cultures with materials from the CMC electronic discussion forum.

On the other hand, studies of intercultural collaborative CMC projects caution against widespread misconceptions of the teacher's role in online teaching (Balkin, Buckner, Swartz, & Rao, 2005; Crawford-Ferre & Wiest, 2012; Doman & Webb, 2016). That is, since the early days of online teaching, the fact that students are connected with native speakers or are able to interact with each other in an asynchronous manner with more time for processing language has led many language educators to have a reductive view of their own involvement in online teaching practices. These studies emphasize that successful online education courses requires active teacher involvement in identifying, explaining, and reflecting upon culturally contingent patterns of interaction in electronic discourse, away from the common image of an instructor as *a guide on the side* in online classrooms.

# METHODS

## Context

The current study was conducted in an online TESOL master's program at a university in the United States. The program offers a certificate and a master's degree in TESOL primarily through a course management tool, Blackboard. The course that was the focus of the study was titled Content-Based Language Teaching, and it was designed to help pre-and in-service teachers to develop knowledge about a range of approaches and methods for teaching L2 so that they can make informed pedagogical decisions in supporting ESL students' academic language and literacy development. The course materials, content, and activities were based on eclectic perspectives of L2 education and adopted pedagogical strategies, materials, and methods from a range of paradigms, from behavioral to psycholinguistic to sociocultural perspectives. The course had student-centered instruction as its principal orientation, and it promoted students' ownership of the newly learned knowledge and information through their application into the students' own teaching.

The course included assignments and tasks such as weekly reading/discussion, textbook reviews, unit plans, and classroom discourse analyses. It involved various activities, including class and group discussions, individual postings, collaborative group work, and teacher conferences. The activities were carried out through mediation of Internet-related tools such as a discussion forum, iMovie, Kaltura and Audacity audio recording software, video chat, and YouTube. The course assignments, activities, and content were offered both synchronously and asynchronously, depending on the nature of each assignment and task.

## Participants

Fifteen pre-and in-service teacher trainees residing in different parts of the US, China, and South Korea were enrolled in the class; those who were living in China and Korea were US born and educated EFL teachers. Their teaching contexts were diverse, from rural area schools in which the number of English learners is growing, to urban schools in which most students are from linguistically and culturally diverse backgrounds. They were teaching English as a second or foreign language to learners ranging from young children to adults in public school settings or private institutes. In terms of teaching experiences, they also showed diverse backgrounds, from beginner teachers who are new to ESL teaching, to experienced teachers working toward master's degrees as certified ESL teachers. The course participants were experienced with the instructional technologies utilized and could participate in various class activities without difficulty.

## Data Collection and Analysis

Drawing on the principles of ethnographic case studies (Merriam, 2009), as the course instructor, the author collected various domains of data (e. g., student work samples, course instructional materials, class interactions, interview data, observation notes) over the course of a semester. The researcher was an active participant and the course instructor. The collected data were analyzed using analytical codes such as tools employed, participation patterns, divisions of labor among the students and the instructor, goals, and course policies. These codes were developed based on activity theory to explore the tool-mediated and goal-oriented online learning as social and cultural processes (Engeström, 1987, 2001; Leont'ev, 1978; Vygotsky, 1978; Wertsch, 1998).

# FINDINGS

## How Do Teacher Trainees Interact With Each Other and Participate in an Online TESOL Course, and What Kinds of Contextual Factors Shape Their Learning Activities?

Students' participation varied across course activities. Their participation was categorized as either individual work or collaboration. Collaborative interactions occurred specifically when students posted answers to questions in weekly reading discussion activities. In the discussion forum, the most common participation pattern was *acknowledgment* of the opinions of other classmates with whom they shared similar experiences and cases. The second most common participation pattern was *extending* the shared ideas and opinions. The third was *questioning* the information that was presented in the classmates' postings, and the fourth was *disagreeing* with the presented ideas by offering alternative cases. The following comment excerpts, which are from the third week's discussion forum activity on the efficacy and applicability of the sheltered instruction observation protocol (SIOP) model of teaching, show examples of these interactional patterns. The names of all participants are pseudonyms:

*Cara,*

*I liked your idea about giving more focus to the objectives at the beginning of the lesson. I usually write down the objectives before the students come class and read them right after I greet them....I also agree with you about the importance of the review. I usually summarize the main points of the lesson at the end of each class in order to highlight the main ideas that we worked on....*

*Susan*

*Hi, Ryan,*

*When speaking about your planned use of some of the strategies, I like how you've emphasized the affective dimension/benefit. When students are empowered to face new material with various strategies -- like tools in their toolbelts -- it seems that they're much more likely to succeed rather than succumb to discouragement or frustration.*

*Christine*

*I previously taught in an adult program as well, so I understand the inability to differentiate formal assessments....How do you decide what topics to teach? Does your program have a focused curriculum? If not do you find that incorporating the SIOP model is difficult?*

*Sarah*

*Hi Sandra*

*I do not think that one method is necessarily superior to the other or that they need be seen as mutually exclusive. I suppose the objectives of instruction might serve as guide as to which tools from each approach could be used.*

The four excerpts above demonstrate the typical pattern of student interactions. Excerpts one and two represent acknowledgment and expansion of peers' ideas; excerpt three represents an example of questioning, and excerpt four shows an example of disagreement. A majority of the interactions relate to acknowledging and expanding peers' ideas. For example, out of the 47 postings regarding the SIOP model of teaching, only two postings are examples of questioning and only one posting is an example of disagreement.

The factors that shape the different participation relate to tools, rules, and divisions of labor. Clearly, the foremost mediating factor was the tools that stimulated different interactional patterns and engagements among students, given that specific tools trigger specific patterns of action (e.g., individual work, collaborative work). For example, the discussion board is more suitable for collaborative discussion than the dropbox in Blackboard. However, the various tools for delivering different assignments were utilized in compliance with different rules, and the cultural norms of uses of mediating tools shaped students' participation in social practices of achieving goals in the course work. In light of this, the tool mediation in the activity of online learning should be explained by not only the actual tools, but also by other interconnected social and cultural factors. The contextual factors shaping student participation could be explained with key components of the activity system of this course, as seen here:

- **Tool:** Computer, Internet, Blackboard, Skype, email, Word
- **Subject:** The instructor and students
- **Rule:** Participation rules such as contributing to collaborative knowledge construction in a respectful manner.
- **Community:** Instructor, students, staff members of IT support office, e-learning board committee
- **Object:** Managing the quality of online language teacher development
- **Outcome:** Offering a successful course through online delivery

These six components were interactively linked to each other as a process-as-a-whole in the activity system, in which the instructor and students were engaged in achieving the goal of the quality of online language teacher development. As such, the participant students' engagements were tool-mediated actions that complied with the course principles for student-centered reflective learning and the course policies for managing respectful collaboration among class members.

The division of labor among the students was another factor shaping their participation. That is, every student was equally responsible for managing productive discussions for joint knowledge construction. For example, they were required to post their answers to the reading discussion questions and three responses to peers' postings. This mandate was a main driving force for ensuring active participation from all the students and distributed attention across the students, as seen in the fact that the number of comment postings each student made was nearly the same as those received over the course of the semester. Each of the students exchanged, on average, 82 postings with the other participants in the discussion forum and the same number of feedback responses from the instructor—two rounds of feedback for assignments and weekly feedback on the unit plan for five weeks.

Beyond looking at the contextual factor that contributed to the quantity of student participation, the quality of interactions is worth investigating. It is necessary to investigate what caused different participation patterns among the six components of the activity system. The patterns of students' interactions were shaped by the course policy for discussion activities that required students to share their own answers to questions before commenting on their peers' answers. These multiple steps provided a variety of choices for them to respond to, and enough time for them to respond. In doing so, the students responded to the postings that introduced issues directly relevant to their own teaching contexts. For example, during week five, Ryan, who taught a community-based adult ESL course to immigrants, posted his idea about designing a content-based language-learning lesson using documents about immigrants and green cards. All adult ESL teachers shared their opinions about his text choices and lesson plan as seen below:

*Hi Ryan,*

*I really love the idea of the green card research. This is the perfect example of an authentic assignment for adult learners.*

*Susan*

*Hi Ryan,*

*I really like your immigration essay idea. I can see how it can truly be relevant to the students that you are working with. Dealing with the familiar topic would help them formulate their supporting details as they practice writing in the argument essay genre.*

*Mary*

*I think that you can choose to use one of your own paper excerpts as an example including nominalization. Given their countries of origin, the stipulations of their stay, and the possibility of them obtaining green cards....Your idea is a wonderful and extremely relevant one that would no doubt engage those students! I'm sure that they would have much to say toward the betterment of the system:o).*

*Courtney*

The similar teaching contexts and experiences allowed the students to express their point of view regarding the discussed issue and to jointly construct knowledge. As seen in the second and third comments responding to the posting that introduced new pedagogical issues to them, the students expressed not only acknowledgement of the shared ideas but also suggested pedagogical ideas.

## What Kinds of Constraints and Affordances Do the Teacher Trainees Configure Regarding an Online Learning Environment?

The affordances that students reported regarding online language education were focused on the accessibility to the course materials beyond the constraints of time and place. This increased accessibility made students' learning more autonomous in terms of scheduling, class interactions, and construction of knowledge. First, students made postings for discussion activities and assignments at times that were convenient to them. In fact, postings were often made late at night and during weekends when the students had more time, free of their daytime teaching responsibilities. In addition, students who had not participated in class activities due to emergency situations could complete the missed course activities later by reading saved class discussions on the Blackboard. Similarly, students reviewed and utilized the previous postings and received responses for follow-up conferences with the instructor.

In interactions with class participants, students could choose interesting and relevant postings from among those made by their peers. The posts that students made allowed the course instructor/author to provide students with more individualized feedback and guidance. In addition, the saved interactions allowed students to review their performances of how they contributed ideas and supported peers in joint construction of knowledge. As such, the students took an active role in the process of constructing knowledge by not only identifying and researching inquiries, but also by reflecting on their collaboration with others.

Despite these affordances, online learning mediated by computer technologies constrained students' learning. The constraints that the students reported concern the aspect of building communities among all of the course participants. In particular, students reported a desire for building a stronger sense of learning community with the entire group of students. The class had a range of meetings that included weekly virtual office hours, conferences between the instructor and students, and group meetings through a video chat program. The students reported that these meetings allowed them to feel connected to the members of the course. Specifically, group work was reported to be an opportunity for them to collaborate for a task in mutually supportive relationships with group members. However, when the instructor had conferences with students, they often stated that what was missing in online courses was the sense of full engagement with peers that was available only in face-to-face meetings. The following excerpt from a group-meeting transcript shows to this end:

*I can talk about ELLs all day long. I love this kind of meeting. This is what is missing in an online class.*

As seen in this excerpt, students expressed a lack of opportunities to meet in groups and build a learning community compared to a face-to-face course. They also expressed a wish for meeting as an entire class at least once without the constraints of technology.

## IMPLICATIONS FOR PEDAGOGY AND FUTURE RESEARCH

The findings suggest that the students actively participated in the course interactions by acknowledging, expanding, questioning, and challenging the shared ideas, while co-constructing knowledge in mutually supportive relationships (Wigglesworth & Storch, 2012). The main factor that shaped students' participation patterns were their teaching interests and the course principles regarding participation. The affordances that they reported regarding online language teacher education were closely related to the accessibility of the course beyond time and place constraints. The online delivery mode mediated by computer technologies increased student's autonomy in schedule, interaction, and knowledge construction. The main reported constraint was the inability to have a whole-class virtual meeting. The students expressed this constraint in comparison to a face-to-face class meeting in which they could meet each other altogether at once. These findings provide implications for future pedagogy and research on the quality online language teacher education.

Given that pedagogical interests shaped the students' participation, course tasks and activities need to address diverse pedagogical contexts and issues that are meaningful to students. This principle is more critical to a course that serves teachers from diverse educational settings. Reflecting the international nature of TESOL, for example, students in the current course are involved in teaching English in both US and international contexts, K-12 and adult education settings, and formal and informal institutes (England, 2012; Murray, 2013). The diverse backgrounds that students bring to the online course should be reflected in the curriculum and instruction of online language teacher education and utilized as pedagogical resources throughout instruction, so that students could have personalized learning experiences even without face-to-face interactions.

The students' diverse backgrounds shaped perceptions of participation and collaborative work. The students in this study, contrary to their diverse teaching contexts, had the same linguistic and educational backgrounds; they used English as their first language and were educated in US schools. These same backgrounds allowed them to interact with each other without cultural conflicts on interactional norms among themselves. In doing so, their participation tended to acknowledge and expand classmates' ideas, based on their interpretations of respectful, collaborative knowledge construction. This shows that there is a need for students to practice various ways to offer dynamic constructive feedback and to construct knowledge with explicit guidelines for mutual collaboration (Wigglesworth & Storch, 2012). Having this stated, future research studies can also examine how students with different L1 backgrounds participate in class interactions.

## CONCLUSION

The reported constraint of online teacher education is its limited ability to develop interpersonal relationships and to build communities. To mitigate the sense of isolation and ensure a strong sense of community among all participants, it is suggested that the instructor of online courses can manage synchronous group work and virtual face-time office hours through social networking. In pursuing these community-building strategies, it is critical for the instructor to take on the role of a facilitative collaborator, with empathy toward students' pedagogical situations (White, 2014). In addition, given that sustaining quality interactions is contingent upon securing access to appropriate mediating technologies, it is necessary to examine not only what kinds of computer technologies are available to the students, but also how they use those technologies, before engaging in specific pedagogical tasks.

In conclusion, to secure the quality online language teacher education, the study suggests that research should be undertaken to examine the activity of online language teacher education within its social, cultural, material, and pedagogical contexts (Engeström, 1987, 2001; Leont'ev, 1978; Vygotsky, 1978; Wertsch, 1998). In doing so, the dynamics of online learning activities between the instructor and students and among students need to be investigated as a social cultural practice. That is, the outcomes of online language teacher education are shaped by mediating tools, rules for social practice, and divisions of labor among the participants. The current study suggests reexamining interaction, access, and community building in the activity system as core tasks and research areas. This will examine the quality of online language teacher education as a whole in terms of its instructional tasks and related learning outcomes, beyond the effectiveness of one or two particular pedagogical tasks or tools.

## REFERENCES

Balkin, R. S., Buckner, D., Swartz, J., & Rao, S. (2005). Issues in classroom management in an interactive distance education course. *International Journal of Instructional Media*, *32*(4), 363–372.

Barton, D., & Potts, D. (2013). Language learning online as a social practice. *TESOL Quarterly*, *47*(4), 815–820. doi:10.1002/tesq.130

Belz, J. (2002). Social dimensions of telecollaborative foreign language study. *Language Learning & Technology*, *6*(1), 60–81.

Blake, R. (2000). Computer mediated communication: A window on L2 Spanish interlanguage. *Language Learning & Technology*, *4*(1), 120–136.

Blake, R. (2007). New trends in using technology in the language curriculum. *Annual Review of Applied Linguistics*, *27*, 76–97. doi:10.1017/S0267190508070049

Crawford-Ferre, H., & Wiest, L. (2012). Effective online instruction in higher education. *The Quarterly Review of Distance Education*, *13*(1), 11–14.

Davis, B., & Thiede, R. (2000). Writing into change: Style-shifting in asynchronous electronic discourses. In M. Warshauer & R. Kern (Eds.), *Netwok-based language teaching: concepts and practice* (pp. 87–120). Cambridge, UK: Cambridge University Press. doi:10.1017/CBO9781139524735.007

Doman, E., & Webb, M. (2016). The flipped experience for Chinese university students studying English as a foreign language. *TESOL Journal*, *8*(1), 102–141. doi:10.1002/tesj.264

Engeström, Y. (1987). *Learning by expanding: An activity-theoretical approach to developmental research*. Helsinki, Finland: Orienta-Konsultit Oy.

Engeström, Y. (2001). Expansive learning at work: Toward an activity-theoretical perspective. *Journal of Education and Work*, *14*(1), 133–156. doi:10.1080/13639080020028747

England, L. (Ed.). (2012). *Online language teacher education: TESOL perspectives*. New York, NY: Routledge.

Grant, K., & Lee, V. (2014). Wrestling with issues of diversity in online courses. *Qualitative Report*, *19*(12), 1–25.

Hall, D., & Knox, J. (2009). Issues in the education of TESOL teachers by distance education. *Distance Education*, *30*(1), 63–85. doi:10.1080/01587910902845964

Hanna, B., & de Nooy, J. (2003). A funny thing happened on the way to the forum: Electronic discussion and foreign language learning. *Language Learning & Technology*, *7*(1), 71–85.

Hockly, N. (2015). Developments in online language learning. *ELT Journal*, *69*(3), 308–313. doi:10.1093/elt/ccv020

Kamhi-Stein, L. (2000). Looking to the future of TESOL teacher education: Web-based bulletin board discussions in a method course. *TESOL Quarterly*, *34*(3), 423–455. doi:10.2307/3587738

Kramsch, C., & Thorne, S. (2002). Foreign language learning as a global communicative practice. In D. Block & D. Cameron (Eds.), *Globalization and language teaching* (pp. 83–100). London, UK: Routledge.

Leont'ev, A. N. (1978). *Activity, consciousness, and personality*. Englewood Cliffs, NJ: Prentice-Hall.

Liu, X., Liu, S., Lee, S., & Magjuka, R. J. (2010). Cultural differences in online learning: Interna- tional student perceptions. *Journal of Educational Technology & Society*, *13*(3), 177–188.

Merriam, S. B. (2009). *Qualitative research and case study applications in education*. San Francisco, CA: Jossey-Bass Publishers.

Meskill, C., & Ranglova, K. (2000). Curriculum innovation in TEFL: A study of technologies supporting socio-collaborative language learning in Bulgaria. In M. Warschauer & R. Kern (Eds.), *Network-based language teaching: Concepts and practice* (pp. 20–40). Cambridge, UK: Cambridge University press. doi:10.1017/CBO9781139524735.004

Murray, D. (2013). A case for online English language teacher education. Monterey, CA: Trustees of the International Research Foundation.

Nunan, D. (1999). A foot in the world of ideas: Graduate study through the Internet. *Language Learning & Technology*, *3*(1), 52–74.

Osman, M. E. (2005). Students' reaction to WebCT: Implications for designing online learning environments. *International Journal of Instructional Media*, *32*(4), 353–362.

Pawan, F., Wiechart, K., Warren, A., & Park, J. (2016). *Pedagogy and practice for online English language teacher education.* Alexanderia, VA: TESOL Press.

Schultz, J. M. (2000). Computers and collaborative writing in the foreign language curriculum. In M. Warschauer & R. Kern (Eds.), *Network-based language teaching: Concepts and practice* (pp. 20–40). Cambridge, UK: Cambridge University press. doi:10.1017/CBO9781139524735.008

Smith, B. (2003). Computer-mediated negotiated interaction: An expended model. *Modern Language Journal*, *87*(1), 38–57. doi:10.1111/1540-4781.00177

Thorne, S. L. (2003). Artifacts and culture-of-use in intercultural communication. *Language Learning & Technology*, *7*(2), 38–67.

Vygotsky, L. (1978). *Mind in society: The development of higher psychological processes.* Cambridge, MA: Harvard University Press.

Ware, P. (2005). "Missed" communication in online communication: Tensions in a German-American telecollaboration. *Language Learning & Technology*, *9*(2), 64–89.

Wertsch, J. V. (1998). *Mind as action.* New York, NY: Oxford University Press.

White, C. (2014). The distance learning of foreign languages: A research agenda. *Language Teaching*, *47*(4), 538–553. doi:10.1017/S0261444814000196

Wigglesworth, G., & Storch, N. (2012). What role for collaboration in writing and writing feedback. *Journal of Second Language Writing*, *21*(4), 364–374. doi:10.1016/j.jslw.2012.09.005

Zhao, N., & McDougall, D. (2008). Cultural influences on Chinese students' asynchronous online learning in a Canadian university. *Journal of Distance Education*, *22*(2), 59–80.

## ADDITIONAL READING

Banegas, D. L., & Busleimán, G. I. M. (2014). Motivating factors in online language teacher education in southern Argentina. *Computers & Education*, *76*, 131–142. doi:10.1016/j.compedu.2014.03.014

Gibson, J. J. (1979). *An ecological approach to visual perception.* Boston, MA: Houghton Mifflin.

Hampel, R., & Stickler, U. (Eds.). (2015). *New language learning & teaching environments. Developing online language teaching: Research-based pedagogies and reflective practices.* London, UK: Palgrave Macmillan. doi:10.1057/9781137412263

Lantolf, J. (2000). Introducing sociocultural theory. In J. Lantolf (Ed.), *Sociocultural theory and second language learning.* New York, NY: Oxford University Press.

Lantolf, J. (2000). Second language learning as a mediated process. *Language Learning*, *33*(2), 79–96.

Lektorsky, V. A. (2009). Mediation as a means of collective activity. In Sannino, A., Daniels, H., & Gutierrez, K. D. (Eds.). Learning and expanding with activity theory. (75-87). New York, NY: Cambridge University Press. doi:10.1017/CBO9780511809989.006

Phan, H. P. (2011). A cognitive multimedia environment and its importance: A conceptual model for effective e-learning and development. *International Journal on E-Learning*, *10*(2), 199–221.

Ruckriem, G. (2009). Digital technology and mediation: A challenge to activity theory. In A. Sannino, H. Daniels, & K. Gutierrez (Eds.). Learning and expanding with activity theory (88-111). New York, NY: Cambridge University Press. doi:10.1017/CBO9780511809989.007

Shin, D. (2006). ESL students' computer-mediated communication practices: Context configuration. *Language Learning & Technology*, *10*(3), 65–84.

Smith, S. U. (2014). Frameworks shaping an online professional development program for K-12 teachers of ELLs: Toward supporting the sharing of ideas for empowering classroom teachers online. *TESOL Journal*, *5*(3), 444–464. doi:10.1002/tesj.154

van Lier, L. (2000). From input to affordances: Social interactive learning from an ecological perspective. In J. Lantolf (Ed.), *Sociocultural theory and second language learning* (pp. 133–153). New York, NY: Oxford University Press.

van Lier, L. (2002). *Ecology and Semiotics of Language Learning: A Sociocultural Perspective*. Norwell, MA: Kluwer Academic Publishers.

## KEY TERMS AND DEFINITIONS

**Activity Theory:** Is an umbrella term for a line of eclectic social sciences theories and research with its roots in the Soviet psychological activity theory pioneered by Lev Vygotsky, Alexei Leont'ev and Sergei Rubinstein.

**Affordances:** Possibilities for action which people identify in relation to specific recourses.

**Constraints:** Something that limits or restricts someone or something.

**Context:** The circumstances that form the setting for an event, statement, or idea, and in terms of which it can be fully understood and assessed.

**Interaction:** A kind of action that occurs as two or more objects have an effect upon one another.

**Online Language Teacher Education:** The education of pre-school, primary, lower and upper secondary school teachers of languages conducted through fully or partially online instructional delivery.

**Participation:** The action or state of taking part in something: as a: association with others in a relationship (as a partnership) or an enterprise usually on a formal basis with specified rights and obligations.

**TESOL:** TESOL refers to both teaching English to speakers of other languages, the teaching of English as a second or foreign language and also as TESOL International Association, a professional organization for teachers of English as a second or foreign language.

# Chapter 6
# Teachers' Uses and Beliefs in the Integration of YouTube Videos Into English Language Teaching:
## A Comparison Between ESL and EFL Contexts

**Hanh Dinh**
*Murray State University, USA*

## ABSTRACT

*This empirical research study inquires as to whether teachers of English as a Second Language and teachers of English as a Foreign Language apply the technological tool–YouTube videos–into their English teaching with the same purposes and approaches. This chapter addresses a variety of activities that teachers in two different ESL and EFL contexts utilize to integrate YouTube videos into their English teaching. Ten teachers from a university in the USA (ESL context) and a university in Vietnam (EFL context) were recruited for this study. The results demonstrate similarities and the differences in the use of YouTube videos and how both ESL and EFL students agree with the potential applications of YouTube videos to maintain students' attention and make them feel motivated in the lesson content. Also reported in this chapter is that ESL teachers believe YouTube videos are a great tool for reflection activities and dealing with challenging content issues, whereas EFL teachers mainly use them as a native-speaking modeling in class for doing language drills and grammatical practice.*

DOI: 10.4018/978-1-5225-2933-0.ch006

## BACKGROUND

Since February 2005, YouTube has been hosting videos that are viewed more than 2 billion times each day with numerous channels highly suitable for English teaching such as TED Talks, TED Edu, Crash course, and other channels designed exclusively for teaching English such as BBClearningenglish, etc. YouTube estimates that such media channels can be a promising resource for educators and language teachers in the era when their students are born surrounded by technology (Cardine, 2008). In ESL learning settings such as in the USA, the use of YouTube videos in English teaching have proven to generate numerous cognitive benefits, increase students' attention, and develop language skills (Berk, 2009; Brook, 2011; Buzzetto-More, 2014; Chun, 2012; Desmet, 2009; Eick & King, 2012; Greenberg & Zanetis, 2012; Jaffar, 2012; Logan, 2012; Mayora, 2009; Tan & Pearce, 2011).

Not only ESL contexts, but also in EFL contexts in other countries, using Youtube videos in English teaching is also becoming increasingly popular (Alimemaj, 2010; Alwehaibi, 2015; Chen, 2013; Hsu, Hwang, Chang & Chang, 2013; Kuo, 2009; Tamim, 2013; Wang, 2005). Particularly in Vietnam, it has been sixteen years since the parameters for the English Program were revised by the National Education Department, highlighting the importance of incorporating technology tools such as YouTube videos into teaching and learning for 21st-century language learners with the emphasis on higher order thinking skills.

Though a great deal of research has been completed with analysis of the potentials and benefits of using YouTube videos as a resource in teaching, there has been limited research into the beliefs of English teachers in those two contexts (ESL and EFL) whether they truly support YouTube videos in English teaching or not. This current chapter addresses the belief that a study needed to be conducted to highlight teachers' opinions on the advantages and disadvantages of using YouTube in 21st-century real-life classroom settings. The research project examined different teaching conditions and YouTube availability in both the ESL and EFL environments. Furthermore, from ESL and EFL teachers' beliefs, a comparative perspective can be seen concerning the activities they design in their class with YouTube videos. From that, pedagogical implications are made available from the comparison about how to overcome various current implementation constraints; meaningful suggestions for effective YouTube video use in the future from both contexts are extracted. The research questions guiding this study are:

1. What is the rationale of teachers in ESL and EFL teaching contexts when they integrate YouTube videos into their lessons?
2. How do teachers in those two teaching contexts integrate YouTube videos? Which specific activities do they organize in class?

## THE INTEGRATION OF YOUTUBE VIDEOS IN ESL CONTEXTS

YouTube videos have demonstrated their value and usefulness as a pedagogical tool. With the emphasis on the international undergraduate students, Tan and Pearce (2011) conducted a case study of the incorporation of YouTube videos in learning and teaching a ten- week introductory sociology course at Durham University, United Kingdom. The results of this research indicated that the use of YouTube videos in education could promote students' deep understanding on the subject by providing alternative viewpoints and stimulate interactions amongst them. One of students expressed his belief that YouTube videos were particularly effective in generating more intriguing opinions (besides the lecturer) on the discussed topic, and then he could exchange ideas with his peers and collaboratively work out something innovative.

Explaining more about the reasons why content-based YouTube video segments engage students and enhance their understanding about lessons, Berk (2009) and Logan (2012) pointed out the same conclusion that a YouTube video could tap into the characteristics of multiple learning styles, intelligences, and a wide range of students' proficiency levels, making learning more personalized. YouTube videos stimulated both hemispheres of the brain, including the areas related to verbal/linguistic, musical, and visual information. Such stimulation in those areas created ideal conditions for learning and memory. Students' emotions were affected when teachers used YouTube videos, so students felt that the learning experience became more authentic and related to them. When students learned new information with the emotional relations, their attention span and anticipation were extended and they even felt inspired to give more feedback and even regarded learning as an autonomous opportunity to create responsive video projects of their own (Berk, 2009). In another study by Eick and King (2012), written survey responses showed that YouTube videos played a role with memory cues and visual connections while students conceptualized new knowledge.

Buzzetto-More (2014) presented a similar perspective. She carried out a survey research investigation at a Mid-Atlantic institution on the effects of YouTube videos used in classrooms. The research focused on the students' perceptions and predilections regarding the integration of YouTube in the teaching and learning process. The survey results indicated that students preferred the use of YouTube videos in the classroom instruction because they made the lessons more interesting and engaging. In addition, research participants reported that YouTube videos assisted their learning process and supported the teachers when they delivered the course content. Interestingly, when looking specifically at the ideal video length, the researcher claimed that students preferred to watch videos less than 3 minutes. This is similar to what Greenberg and Zanetis (2012) has stated about the relationship between the length of YouTube videos and the influence on students' attention. They concluded that short segments would appeal to the students as they retain students' attention and interest more than long segments, which exceeded 15 minutes in length. Besides the length of the clips, YouTube videos became effective for students' learning if their content was relevant to the course objectives, was diversified and was examined carefully by the teachers (Jaffar, 2012).

Furthermore, by looking at how teachers incorporate YouTube videos into the course instruction, researchers found that teachers used YouTube videos in many different ways. For example, Mayora (2009) described that teachers encouraged ESL students to practice leaving comments under the YouTube videos they were required to watch. The word limit feature of YouTube, the chances to read other comments as authentic language input, and the teacher's writing instruction helped students to produce more grammatical and expressive feedback. Similarly, the teachers who participated in the Desmet (2009) study used YouTube videos as an assignment for students to produce a parody such as Hamlet and Romeo and Juliet to enhance their comprehension of Shakespeare literature.

In another interesting YouTube study in an ESL context, Brook (2011) proposed some ways for ESL teachers to use YouTube videos in teaching writing. Teachers could make students edit a part in the YouTube clip and relate its topic with a local interest to write about it. In a case study of an Intensive English Program (IEP) instructor at a large North American public university located in an urban area for "post-advanced-level" ESL students, Chun (2012) described the observed instructor that she showed her students the YouTube videos, let them take notes, then read the transcript. Next, she asked them elicitation questions, and let them discuss related issues. The YouTube videos acted as a discourse prompt and their topics focused on controversial issues that happened in business settings in different cultures, through which the teacher initiated conversational exchanges with the students. The observed teacher stated that by using YouTube videos, she could approach the matters related to cultural difference in a flexible and polite way. According to the studied teacher, YouTube videos reflected the globalization in ESL classrooms for students coming from diverse cultural backgrounds.

## THE INTEGRATION OF YOUTUBE VIDEOS IN EFL CONTEXTS

Due to the imminent arrival of multimedia, many EFL teachers have become interested in applying YouTube videos into their classrooms, particularly in listening comprehension enhancement curricula (Beare, 2008; Harmer, 2007; O'Dowd, 2007). In the EFL teaching contexts, YouTube videos as an emerging technology in English Language Teaching can provide language learners with language immersion opportunities. In other words, students have more chances to be exposed to English language input and interactional patterns in a natural setting (Godwin-Jones, 2007). To be specific, English language used in YouTube videos is considered a source of voices from native-speakers. The native speakers from YouTube videos demonstrate actual interactions in the culture of the target language. Thus, studying with YouTube videos engage students in acquiring language naturally through voices and visual illustrations. They can teach students about metalinguistic skills, such as language noticing and interactional patterns, and even cultural awareness.

Kuo (2009) carried out an experiment to demonstrate the effects of integrating YouTube videos into teaching listening comprehension at the Applied Foreign Language Department at one university in central Taiwan. The control group was taught by traditional teacher-centered teaching methods, which followed the procedure of using a CD and going through all the tasks designed in the chosen course book without extensive interactional activities. The experimental groups were assigned different numbers of YouTube videos as extra practice material. Teachers in those groups designed additional worksheets to assist students in understanding the material's meaning and noticing the new language patterns used in the YouTube clip as a way to enhance their listening comprehension attainment. As a result of the quantitative data analysis, groups taught by the use of YouTube video segments performed better on a final standardized listening comprehension test than the control group. At the same time, listening comprehension attitude surveys for the Taiwanese EFL learners were also collected to examine their responses to the application of YouTube videos. Students who were taught with the employment of YouTube videos showed higher levels of positive attitudes toward English learning instruction.

Even with the positive reports that can be found in this literature, contrasting findings are also part of the discussion of using YouTube videos. For example, an interview study conducted by Alimemaj (2010) with a group of EFL learners at the University of Vlora in Albania pointed out that the proliferation of YouTube videos in listening instruction may benefit students as well as present new challenges for them. The students reported in the study that although the YouTube videos were a great source of authentic materials, containing daily spoken English by native speakers and demonstrating different styles of English in target culture settings, they found inconsistent sound quality, local pronunciation, and slang featured in those videos difficult to understand. The longer they were exposed to this type of input, the more confused they were. Thus, Alimemaj emphasized the role of teachers in using YouTube videos; this could serve as a model to encourage students to watch them continuously outside classroom.

This was suggested to develop learning autonomy, which was very necessary for EFL learners who have limited chances to practice English after class time. Chen (2013) also states that YouTube videos could serve as a catalyst for the development of learning autonomy among students in EFL classrooms.

Not only should EFL teachers apply YouTube videos into teaching listening for better listening comprehension performance with the conditions that (1) they need to consider how long the clips are, and (2) their quality and their assisted learning activities, but they also have to consider the effects of the caption modes. Captioning modes are options for the viewers to choose whether they want to turn on the subtitles when they listen to the video or not. The extended study by Hsu et al. (2013) conducted in an EFL program in Taiwan was about YouTube videos with English and Chinese subtitles and their effects on listening comprehension and vocabulary acquisition. In the experiment, the teacher gave students chances to complete a vocabulary task by listening to twenty-second YouTube videos with English and Chinese captions of only the target words on their individual mobile phones, compared with groups with no captions and full English and Chinese captions. On one hand, the results showed that teaching YouTube videos with captions had better effects on vocabulary acquisition and listening comprehension than videos with no captions. On the other hand, amongst YouTube videos with captions, the only target-word caption strategies proved better effects than full caption videos. In the interview, students claimed that the YouTube videos with target-word captions made them more motivated to listen and stay more focused.

Besides using YouTube videos in teaching English skills, EFL teachers have also integrated YouTube videos in their teaching for other purposes related to the informational content of the lessons. Tamim (2013) investigated the United Arab Emirates teachers' perceptions about the advantages of YouTube in the classroom, their current practices and perceived challenges. The findings revealed that the majority of teachers were using YouTube videos to illustrate complex concepts for presentation purposes. This study was then extended by Alwehaibi (2015) by stating that teachers use YouTube videos in explaining conceptually complex topics for EFL college students. Two groups of second year EFL college students at the Department of Curriculum and Instruction in Riyadh, Saudi Arabia, were randomly assigned to two groups. In the experimental group, teachers showed students a YouTube video first, made them orally recite what they had watched and then let them discuss in groups what they thought about that concept. The statistical procedures and major findings between the two groups yielded favorable results for the use of YouTube videos in assisting EFL students in understanding the given content and even more importantly, motivating them think critically about it. Students would have a better chance to observe the concept in the target language discourse, from that they could deduce pragmatic underlying patterns of the discussed topic and construct the new information based on their background knowledge. Students even might contemplate questions related to the topic and negotiate the meaning to find out the answers to such questions. That was also how YouTube videos could be used to teach students about problem-solving skills (Wang, 2005).

However, though there are many encouraging empirical findings of research on the effectiveness of YouTube videos embedded in classroom instruction from the students' perspectives, there is limited research how the YouTube videos are actually used in classrooms by the teachers and what is their rationale behind such uses. Their YouTube employment in specific teaching stages and activities and their perceptions for such applications are important because they will affect their teaching practices and their students' learning process.

## THE CURRENT STUDY

The study took place during the spring semester of 2016 after the IRB application was processed. There were ten teacher participants. Five of them were ESL teachers in an ESL Programs for pre-college students at a four-year public university in far western Kentucky, USA. All of them were teaching English for international students in level 6, the highest level in the ESL program available at that university. Thus, the students were supposed to be pre-advanced English language learners. Meanwhile, the other five teachers came from the Department of English also in a four-year public university in Ho Chi Minh City, Vietnam. All of them were teaching English for first-year college Vietnamese students who study English as a foreign language (EFL learners) as a compulsory subject. The requirement for first-year college students in that university was also pre-advanced English level. The teachers participated in the study taught different English language skills. Table 1 shows research participant demographic information.

In order to have an overview on the research topic, weekly observation sessions were implemented in one ESL class and on EFL class. Two teachers who usually integrate YouTube videos in the same skill (Pronunciation) were selected, and it was suggested that the researcher/author could come and observe them once every week. The class was attended by the researcher through video conferencing for the EFL class in Vietnam. Notes were taken during the observation sessions in these two classes and used for further interview question design.

Next, each recruited teacher was interviewed for approximately 40 to 60 minutes after the systematic classroom observations. All the interviews were conducted in English, recorded and transcribed for data analysis. There were 12 questions used to ask 10 teachers about their rationale for YouTube video use (See Appendix). The first two questions were lead-in questions, asking about teachers' general ideas on YouTube integration into English Language Teaching (ELT) while the ten following questions particularly emphasized their uses of YouTube videos and their beliefs about why they thought such uses were beneficial in their teaching as well as their reflections on students' attitudes and learning responses.

For the five ESL teachers, the interviews were conducted in their offices, while the five EFL teachers, the interviews took place via Facebook through video calls. All the interviews were recorded. After that,

*Table 1. Research Participant Demographic Information*

| ID | Gender | ESL/EFL | Teaching Experience | Skill(s) or Language Aspects Currently Teaching with YouTube Videos |
|---|---|---|---|---|
| 1 | Female | ESL | 25 | Oral Skills: Pronunciation |
| 2 | Male | ESL | 15 | Listening: Speaking |
| 3 | Female | ESL | 2 | Reading |
| 4 | Male | ESL | 6 | Listening |
| 5 | Male | ESL | 3 | Writing |
| 6 | Male | EFL | 3 | Speaking: Pronunciation |
| 7 | Male | EFL | 10 | Speaking: Grammar |
| 8 | Male | EFL | 5 | Public Speaking |
| 9 | Male | EFL | 15 | College Essay Writing |
| 10 | Female | EFL | 4 | Writing |

the audio data was transcribed and read several times to search for recurring themes relevant to teacher uses and beliefs in integrating YouTube videos in their classes. Any implicit themes on how they selected a particular YouTube video for their lesson, based on their beliefs, was also reviewed.

## RESULTS AND DISCUSSION

### Theme 1: Teachers' Integration of YouTube Videos Into English Language Teaching

#### Observations From an ESL Class and an EFL Class

Both the ESL and EFL class observed covered a Pronunciation lesson called "Contraction and Reduction." Both the teachers integrated a YouTube video into their lesson though the clips they chose were different. In addition, they conducted different steps and activities revolving around the video clips as they taught. In the ESL class, the teacher started by introducing the topic of the lesson and then she summarized what she would show them in the clip. She stated that they would see two people role play a conversation in two different scenarios. The first one was pronouncing every single word in the conversation, which she said was *unnatural*. The second one was the same conversation, but the two people talking in a *natural* way with the American English style. Then, the teacher gave students a worksheet, which was the content of the conversation. She asked them to underline which words would be contracted and reduced in the clip when the two speakers conversed in the natural style. In the clip, there were English subtitles as the people were talking. The words contracted and reduced were highlighted and students noted these down on their worksheets.

During the video clip, students had some questions. The teacher paused the clip and replayed the part that students asked about. The whole class would engage in a discussion to find out the answer until student who asked the question was satisfied. The teacher did directly provide the answer. In some cases, when the students could not hear the reduction sounds because the fast clip speed, the teacher would model the sound again with a lower speed until the students got it. After the clip, the teacher divided the class into small groups and with the script they had been highlighted, they practiced the conversation with their friends. Then, she called some pairs of students demonstrated the conversation again. The teacher complimented on students' speaking and the lesson ended there.

In the EFL class, the teacher wrote some sentences on the board and invited some students to speak the sentences. He then explained that as Vietnamese learners, one of the most common mistakes in pronunciation that makes them sound unnatural was their lack of contraction and reduction. Then, he also briefly explained what they would see in the clip. The clip he chose was not about the two people talking in two different scenarios. The clip was an American person reading the sentences he had written on the board with contractions and reductions. He let the students watch the clip for the first time and asked them to note down which sounds were contracted in the clip. The clip was played without any pauses and all the questions the students had to be written down in their notebook.

After the clip stopped, the teacher asked students to show him which linking sounds were mentioned in the clip and he demonstrated them on the board. The teacher wrote down the rules of contractions and reductions on the board. The students then noted these items down in their notebook. Then, the teacher demonstrated the pronunciation again by himself. Students repeated after him. He pointed out some mistakes Vietnamese learners could improve on. He used himself as an example explaining how he could improve his pronunciation skills. The clip was played again. After the second time, students were asked to repeat again. The teacher encouraged students to sound like the speaker in the clip. He invited some individual students to say the sentences. Before the end of the lesson, the teacher divided students into different mixed groups, appointed a group leader, and gave that student the permission to help and monitor his members to practice the pronunciation.

## The Use of YouTube Videos in ESL and EFL Contexts: Similarities and Differences

The observations were integrated to determine whether the teachers in those two contexts would apply YouTube videos into their classroom with a consistent procedure or not. Thus, the two teachers (mentioned earlier) and the remaining participants were interviewed. Table 2 provides information about common (similar) and unique (different) YouTube videos use in two ESL and EFL contexts.

Generally, both ESL and EFL teachers stated that they use YouTube videos as a warm up activity for students to guess the topic of the lesson. One EFL teacher stated that instead of introducing the lesson verbally, teachers could let students watch a short video clip because, "YouTube videos set the context and indirectly introduce the topic" (T9). That was similar to an ESL teacher who shared the activity he usually used at the beginning of a lesson: "Mute the sound of the clip (which introduce the topic of the lesson) and let students discuss what they are going to learn." Another activity frequently used in both contexts is "Watch the clip. Notice what is mentioned. Reconstruct the content of the clip." For this activity, teachers usually require students to watch the clip and write down its organization by filling in the blanks or answering guiding questions. These are some comments from teachers in both contexts about how they carried out this type of activity:

*...always prepare questions to ask them to do something while they are watching... I always gave them a very basic outline of bullets on different levels and there were about noticing supporting details. (T3)*

*Write down 2 things you notice that what they are good at and what they can improve on...' (T1)*

*I ask them 3 questions from the video: What was the failure? What lesson did you learn from it? Brainstorm and reflect on your own experience. (T9)*

*Table 2. A Comparison of Integrated Activities With YouTube Videos Between ESL and EFL Teachers*

<table>
<tr><td>Common Features</td><td colspan="2">• Warm up activity: Guess the topic of the lesson<br>• Watch the clip. Notice what is mentioned. Reconstruct the content of the clip<br>• Illustrate what is being said</td></tr>
<tr><td rowspan="2">Unique Features</td><td>ESL Context</td><td>EFL Context</td></tr>
<tr><td>Discuss with personal viewpoints on the content of the clip</td><td>Point out the gap between native speakers and language learners and practice to improve on the language point</td></tr>
</table>

The last common activity both ESL and EFL teachers use is letting students watch YouTube videos as an illustration for what the teacher is explaining or lecturing. Then, students will demonstrate their understanding by answering the teacher's questions or completing an assigned exercise. One teacher showed me an example of this activity: "There is one time I chose a story from Pakistan about a man's friend died from mice and he invented a "mice coffin". Then, after watching the clip, I asked students to describe it" (T2). In this case, students have difficulty transferring the word "mice coffin" into a vivid tangible image in their mind. The YouTube video, with a clear visual model of the object described, assists the cognitive recognition of the stated object. Thus, this allows the students to remember the word with a visual cue.

However, there are also some key differences in the integration of YouTube videos in these two specific ESL and EFL environments. In the ESL contexts in this study, teachers prioritize activities that foster students exchanging ideas; thus, they use YouTube videos as a discussion prompt. Students will watch the video clip and respond to the clip by voicing their opinion on the discussed matter or even produce another video clip to respond to it (T2, T3, and T4). This use of YouTube videos is demonstrated through the ESL class observation when the teacher allowed students to raise questions and the whole class expressed their opinions until they reached a mutual agreement on an answer. This ESL use is in contrast to some EFL teachers using YouTube videos as an activity asking students to point out their struggles in learning a foreign language so they can improve and become closer to the standard American English. For example, teachers suggest students watch a YouTube video as an error analysis activity. Teachers then ask students to compare it with the mistakes Vietnamese learners can make while learning English, discuss ways to overcome the problems, and practice how to improve (T6, T7, T8, T9). This use of YouTube videos can be seen through the observation in the EFL Pronunciation class when the teacher highlighted the common pronunciation mistakes EFL learners made and pointed out ways to correct them.

## Theme 2: Teachers' Beliefs in the Integration of YouTube Videos Into English Language Teaching

### Some Similar Beliefs in Both Contexts

Teachers agreed that YouTube videos would motivate and engaged students effectively. They also believed that those videos generated positive learning attitudes and responses from the students. Table 3 outlines findings about the beliefs of ESL and EFL teachers regarding the integration of YouTube videos into English teaching.

*Table 3. ESL and EFL Teachers' Beliefs Regarding the Integration of YouTube Videos Into English Teaching*

| **Similar Beliefs** | • Motivate and engage students<br>• Assist student learning | |
|---|---|---|
| **Different Beliefs** | **ESL Context** | **EFL Context** |
| | • Help students think critically in English<br>• Help students to discuss aspects of cultural and social topics | • Help students master the target language point<br>• Help students to self-study at home to be closer to native-speakers' linguistic abilities |
| **Teacher Roles** | • A facilitator, an observer | • A knowledge deliverer, a corrector |

As ESL teachers expressed their beliefs, "YouTube videos are something to wake them up" (T2) and made them "...come back to the engagement" (T4). One EFL teacher described, "Class starts at 6:30 am, so the audio makes them feel sleepy but the videos make them engage and concentrate better. I can see their eyes wide open." Second, they believed that by using YouTube videos in their teaching, students would learn better as they provided them more non-verbal and visual cues, which assisted their memory and their visual conceptualization of new concepts. One teacher, for instance, stated, "They seem to learn more and understand the main ideas better rather than just hear the audio files. They can "see" the organization, the structure of the talk in a more effective way..." Another teacher clarified more about the convenience and the effectiveness of YouTube videos: "...in the video, it can capture things that I cannot capture simply by me standing in the classroom. It will be able to show more images or examples that I wouldn't be able to do." (T1)

## ESL Teachers' Beliefs: YouTube Videos as a Reflective Tool

For ESL teachers, they claimed their beliefs that YouTube videos are a great tool to teach students how to think critically in English, build rapport amongst the class with interactions, overcome cultural differences and openly discuss the mentioned topics. ESL teachers expressed their concerns that the course books they are using may not suit the needs and the interests of their students who come to study in the USA from different cultural backgrounds and different learning styles. One teacher described the struggle his international students were facing:

*Several students when they come here, they can write well and speak well. That is not enough. They still feel like struggling with the classroom in the American culture setting. In the United States, teachers want students to use English to express their ideas. Some students are not familiar with that style. They prefer sitting quietly and taking in anything the teacher says. They do not question what they are taught or voice their opinions. There is nothing wrong with it, but the American classroom reflects the American culture. If they want to succeed in studying here, they must make some changes. They even find it hard to communicate with American people because they do not understand the cultural customs. (T3)*

These challenges in American academic and social settings have been mentioned in the literature (Trice, 2001). Here, the teacher confirmed their focus on teaching English for ESL students. Not only do the students need their linguistic abilities and their academic English, but they also need to upgrade their cultural awareness and their target culture's learning style. It is very important for students because they need to use English in their daily interactions in and outside of their ESL class. In order to help students succeed in the English environment, ESL teachers think that YouTube videos (with a wide variety of well-discussed topics and updated news) are beneficial and effective. One teacher explained his belief in using YouTube videos along with his chosen course book in his Listening class. He emphasized that YouTube videos equipped students with knowledge on various aspects of the topic, which is essential for the enhancement of social and communication skills:

*I want them to think critically in English. Even the books for advanced level students are still simple compared to what the real life requires. YouTube videos help students to talk about ideas on biology, science, politics... They can communicate these topics in English. That is important in real life. Small talks on different topics are very common in real life. (T2)*

While another ESL teacher said:

*Earthquake in local area is a piece of English news I chose to keep them updated. We can have really nice discussion about this disaster and in nearby local areas and it can be a very interesting lesson. Thus, they have their own ideas, the opinions of the speakers in the clip and they have me as part of the opinion. A lot of participation. That's nice! I allow them to stop/pause the video if they have questions and want to discuss even when we are watching it. I will stop and let them say what is still fresh in their mind. I want to adapt to what the students' needs. (T4)*

The ESL teachers are aware of the cultural differences in their classroom and they respect such diversities. The evidence is that teachers choose video clips with diverse accents and it does not matter whether the speakers are native or non-native language speakers (T2, T4, and T5) in order to give students varied experience with English accents spoken in the US. One caveat is that teachers do not want to lecture about American cultural customs and impose on students to talk if the students do not want to. However, at the same time, ESL teachers seek activities that promote students' participation and that foster the exchanging of ideas more in the American English classroom. In other words, they want to encourage students to play an active role in a student-centered class. YouTube videos are their choice. Integrating them into their class lets the teacher step back and act as a facilitator, motivates students to reflect on what they have seen, and speak up with their opinions. The ESL teachers beliefs give credence to use of YouTube videos in such a way that within a short length of time, the videos can demonstrate enough intriguing and informative content to lead students in a natural and comfortable discussion (T1, T2, T3, T4, and T5). Teachers also take advantage of conveying messages and choosing videos that reflect American cultural values or news in the local area, so that students can become more familiar with the culture they are experiencing. With this in mind, the ESL teachers believe that students would be more open-minded, responsive and contemplative.

## EFL Teachers' Beliefs: YouTube Videos as a Modeling Tool

EFL teachers hold the opinions that YouTube videos are a good source for bringing authentic materials into classroom settings. It is very beneficial to EFL students because after the English classes finish, students do not have many opportunities to use English in their daily life. Teachers make use of the class time to immerse students in English input and through the integration of YouTube videos; teachers introduce good resources for students to practice at home. They emphasized the importance of practicing English correctly in class, with the help of YouTube videos as a modeling tool, and promoting students' learning autonomy. Those are the critical factors to help students succeed in English learning:

*My philosophy in teaching is not just about the practice but to let the students understand the value of the learning resources the students have. I try to encourage them. (T8)*

They chose YouTube videos as a tool that challenged students' current English abilities and urged them to put their effort in practicing the language point discussed in the clips and upgrade their knowledge. When they integrate YouTube videos into their teaching, teachers play the key role in explaining and delivering the theory of the language point mentioned in the clip. They make sure students can produce similar language outcomes. They believe students can master English knowledge and its use, especially its linguistic structures and sharpen their skills more when they are exposed to English sources from YouTube. Students were believed to use English more accurately and closer to the native speakers:

*I share my learning experience that even I am an English teacher, I still watch English clips every day and practice every day. Sometimes in the future, when I talk to native speakers, I use a phrase or I use the accent that I have seen in the episode and that will surprise me because I did not think that I could say that without thinking. It is just like my reflection that I have improved. I used the results to motivate my students. I push them to always like looking forward.... (T6)*

## CONCLUSION AND PEDAGOGICAL IMPLICATIONS

From the data analysis, the research questions raised in the chapter introduction can be answered. Regarding the first question about the rationale of ESL and EFL teachers when they integrate YouTube videos into their lessons, both ESL and EFL teachers agree that the integration of YouTube videos motivate students and maintain their engagement in the lesson. In addition, students can learn more effectively with the effects of both audio and video features of the clip. Besides, ESL teachers believe that YouTube videos can upgrade students' cultural knowledge, their critical thinking and their abilities to talk about varied topics in the native-speaking culture where they are studying. They hold the opinion that with YouTube videos integrated into the lesson, students from different cultural backgrounds can involve more actively in the class activities. Whereas in EFL contexts, teachers believe that YouTube videos are a standard language-modeling tool for students to practice under the guidance of the teachers. EFL teachers claim that YouTube videos make students more confident in speaking English and more motivated to self-study outside the classroom.

In response to the second research question concerning *how* teachers in the two teaching contexts integrate YouTube videos and specific activities organized in class, this study found common and unique features. Both ESL and EFL teachers provide opportunities for students to watch the YouTube videos with a set of well-prepared questions to answer or tasks to complete, in which students focus on the topic, structure and content mentioned the clips. Teachers also use YouTube videos along with their explanation or knowledge delivery as an illustration and ask students to describe the visual displays they have seen in verbal or written forms. The most noticeable difference in the uses of YouTube videos is that ESL teachers let students watch the clip and regard it as a discussion prompt to encourage students to reflect on what they have seen whereas EFL teachers let students watch the clip, recite the theory implied in it and practice the language point covered in it under the guidance and the control of teachers. Thus, YouTube videos can be an essential complementary tool for teachers to employ in their teaching, which confirmed their benefits like the previous studies have highlighted.

Such differences in the teachers' beliefs and uses come from the differences in the aims of studying English. ESL students learn English to communicate and live in the local culture while EFL students learn English to pass English proficiency tests or work with foreign companies in their home country. Thus, the focus of the ESL teachers is to help students blend in the cultural context and get familiar with the American classroom culture. On the contrary, the focus of EFL teachers is to help students imitate the accents of the native speakers and master the linguistic structures in order to pass tests and work with native-speaking partners in Vietnam. Consequently, from their beliefs, they have different focuses on the types of activities they use with YouTube videos. As a pedagogical implication, it can be noted that EFL teachers may consider other uses of YouTube videos in some less controlled practice while ESL teachers, knowing that students from other countries may want to speak English accurately, can consider YouTube videos as a way to help students speak more accurately.

## LIMITATIONS AND FUTURE RESEARCH DIRECTIONS

A major limitation of this study is that the data collected was on a small scale. More interviews or more participants should be considered for generalization. For the observations, it could be more critical to examine the language use, the frequency of the activities with YouTube videos, the procedures of the tasks, and the interactional patterns between the teacher and the students. In terms of the data analysis, further studies can use classroom video recordings and study the screenshots as strong evidence to argue the diversity in classroom activities; this alternative research design method may enhance the quality of the research. Additionally, the length of the study is limited to one semester, which may not represent consistency in the video use by the teachers. Longitudinal case studies can also be a good way to examine future findings of this type of research. Furthermore, the teachers who participated in this study teach several skills, so their beliefs and uses of YouTube videos cannot be specific to a particular aspect of English teaching. With such subjective perspectives when the participants answer the interview questions, it may be difficult to generalize the findings on a large scale. It is impossible to argue whether the differences in learning activities design presented in this paper are because of the teaching beliefs in general or because of the nature of teaching that particular skill. For example, teachers who teach Speaking skills are more likely to organize discussion and debate activities when teaching with YouTube videos, compared with those who teach other skills and also use the videos. With this in mind, future research can perhaps include researchers choosing to focus on one single skill or one particular group of students with different proficiency levels besides pre-advanced students. It may be argued that for other levels, the differences in learning activities integrating with YouTube videos are not significant.

## REFERENCES

Alimemaj, Z. (2010). YouTube, language learning, and teaching techniques. *AngloHigher Journal*, *2*(3), 10–12.

Alwehaibi, H. O. (2015). The impact of using YouTube in EFL classroom on enhancing EFL students content learning. *Journal of College Teaching & Learning*, *12*(2), 121–126. doi:10.19030/tlc.v12i2.9182

Beare, K. (2008). *YouTube in the classroom*. Retrieved from http://esl.about.eom/od/listeninglessonplans/a/youtube.html

Berk, R. A. (2009). Multimedia teaching with video clips: TV, movies, YouTube, and mtvU in the college classroom. *International Journal of Technology in Teaching and Learning*, *5*(1), 1–21.

Brook, J. (2011). The affordances of YouTube for language learning and teaching. *Hawaii Pacific University TESOL Working Paper Series, 9*(1-2), 37-56.

Buzzetto-More, N. A. (2014). An examination of undergraduate student's perceptions and predilections of the use of YouTube in the teaching and learning process. *Interdisciplinary Journal of E-Learning and Learning Objects*, *10*, 17–32.

Cardine, S. (2008). *Is Education Ready for YouTube?*. Retrieved from http://www.centerdigitaled.com/edtech/Is-Education-Ready-For-YouTube.html

Chen, Y. (2013). The possibility of applying YouTube to motivate learning autonomy. *Journal of International Education Research*, *9*(3), 207–216.

Chun, C. W. (2012). The multimodalities of globalization: Teaching a YouTube video in an EAP classroom. *Research in the Teaching of English*, *47*(2), 145–170.

Desmet, C. (2009). Teaching Shakespeare with YouTube. *English Journal*, *99*(1), 65–70.

Eick, C. J., & King, D. T. Jr. (2012). Nonscience majors' perceptions on the use of YouTube video to support learning in an integrated science lecture. *Journal of College Science Teaching*, *42*(1), 26–30.

Godwin-Jones, R. (2007). Emerging technologies. Digital video update: YouTube, Flash, High-Definition. *Language Learning & Technology*, *11*(1), 16–21. Retrieved from http://llt.msu.edu/vol11num1/emerging/

Greenberg, A., & Zanetis, J. (2012). *The impact of broadcast and streaming video in education*. Report Commissioned by Cisco Systems Inc. to Wainhouse Research LLC. Retrieved from http://www.cisco.com/web/strategy/docs/education/ciscovideowp.pdf

Harmer, J. (2007). *How to teach English*. London, UK: Longman.

Hsu, C. K., Hwang, G. J., Chang, Y. T., & Chang, C. K. (2013). Effects of video caption modes on English listening comprehension and vocabulary acquisition using handheld devices. *Journal of Educational Technology & Society*, *16*(1), 403–414.

Jaffar, A. A. (2012). YouTube: An emerging tool in anatomy education. *Anatomical Sciences Education*, *5*(3), 158–164. doi:10.1002/ase.1268 PMID:22383096

Kuo, L. (2009). *The effects of YouTube listening/viewing activities on Taiwanese EFL learners' listening comprehension* (Doctoral dissertation). Available from ERIC Document Reproduction Service. (ED 535284)

Logan, R. (2012). Using YouTube in perioperative nursing education. *AORN*, *95*(4), 474–481. doi:10.1016/j.aorn.2012.01.023 PMID:22464620

Mayora, C. A. (2009). Using YouTube to encourage authentic writing in EFL classrooms. *TESL Reporter*, *42*(1), 1–12.

O'Dowd, R. (2007). *Online intercultural exchange: An introduction for language teachers*. Clevedon, UK: Multilingual Matters.

Tamim, R. M. (2013). Teachers use of YouTube in the United Arab Emirates: An exploratory study. *Computers in the Schools*, *30*(4), 329–345. doi:10.1080/07380569.2013.844641

Tan, E., & Pearce, N. (2011). Open education videos in the classroom: Exploring the opportunities and barriers to the use of YouTube in teaching introductory sociology. *Research in Learning Technology*, *19*(sup1), 128–137. doi:10.3402/rlt.v19s1/7783

Trice, A. G. (2001). *Faculty perceptions of graduate international students: The benefits and challenges.* Paper presented at the 26th Annual Meeting of the Association for the Study of Higher Education, Richmond, VA. (ERIC Document Reproduction Service No. ED 457 816)

Wang, L. (2005). The advantages of using technology in second language education: Technology integration in foreign language teaching demonstrates the shift from a behavioral to a constructivist learning approach. *Technological Horizons in Education Journal*, *32*(10), 39–42.

## ADDITIONAL READING

Arcario, P. (1992). Criteria for selecting video materials. In S. Stempleski & P. Arcario (Eds.), *Video in second language teaching: Using, selecting and producing video for the classroom* (pp. 109–121). Alexandria, VA: TESOL.

Bax, S. (2011). Normalisation revisited: The effective use of technology in language education. *International Journal of Computer-Assisted Language Learning and Teaching*, *1*(2), 1–15. doi:10.4018/ijcallt.2011040101

Bouman, L. (1990). Veni, video, vici: Video in language teaching. *Journal of English Teaching Forum*, *18*(2), 1–8.

Galbraith, J. (2004). *Active viewing: An oxymoron in video-based instruction?* Society for Applied Learning Technologies Conference.

Hemei, J. (1997). Teaching with Video in an English Class. *Journal of English Teaching Forum*, *35*(2), 45–47.

Jin, D. (2005). Video captions and foreign language teaching. *Computer-Assisted Foreign Language Education*, *6*, 18–22.

Kern, R., & Warschauer, M. (2000). *Network-based language teaching: concepts and practice*. Cambridge, UK: Cambridge University Press.

Laurillard, D. (2002). *Rethinking university teaching: A framework for the effective use of educational technology* (2nd ed.). London, UK: RoutledgeFalmer. doi:10.4324/9780203304846

Mayer, R., & Gallini, J. (1990). When is an illustration worth ten thousand words? *Journal of Educational Psychology*, *82*(6), 715–726. doi:10.1037/0022-0663.82.4.715

Motteram, G., Slaouti, D., & Onat-Stelma, Z. (2013). Second language teacher education for CALL: An alignment of theory and practice. In M. Thomas, H. Reinders, & M. Warschauer (Eds.), *Contemporary Computer-Assisted Language Learning*. London, UK: Bloomsbury Academic.

Omaggio, A. (1979). Pictures and Second Language Comprehension: Do They Help? Foreign Language Annals, 12, 107-116. Özkan, B. (2002). The Use of Video Cases in Teacher Education. *Turkish Online Journal of English Teaching*, *1*(1), 12–18.

Willis, J. (1983). 101 Ways to Use Video. In *McGovern, J., Video Applications in English Language Teaching. English Language Teaching Documents*. Oxford, UK: Pergamon Press.

Willmot, P., Bramhall, M., & Radley, K. (2012). *Using digital video reporting to inspire and engage students.* Retrieved from http://www.raeng.org.uk/education/hestem/heip/pdf/Using_digital_video_reporting.pdf

## KEY TERMS AND DEFINITIONS

**CALL:** *Computer Assisted Language Learning* is the use of computer applications and technology in the teaching and learning of language.

**Communicative Approach:** A way of teaching a second or foreign language that is based on meaningful communication and interaction as both the means and the ultimate goal of language learning.

**Cultural Awareness:** An understanding of the differences (and similarities) between one's culture and people from other countries or other backgrounds, particularly in relation to cultural values, beliefs, attitudes and perceptions.

**ESL:** *English as a Second Language* refers to the field of teaching the English language to people who speak a different language and live in an English speaking country.

**EFL:** *English as a Foreign Language* refers to the field of teaching the English language to people who speak a different language yet are learning English in their native country.

**Sociocultural Language Learning:** An awareness of language learners' circumstances or surroundings and how their mental/physical/emotional/psychological behaviors and processes are influenced by social and cultural factors.

**YouTube Videos:** Videos available for free from an American video-sharing website (YouTube.com) created in 2005.

## APPENDIX

### Interview Questions

Lead-In questions:

1. What do you think about the development of technology nowadays?
2. Do you subscribe to any educational YouTube channels?

### Questions About Teacher's Uses and Beliefs in Integrating YouTube Videos Into English Language Teaching

1. What do you think about the idea of using YouTube videos in teaching English?
   (**Follow up Questions:** Do you think they are beneficial for ESL/EFL learners? Why? Why not?)
2. What are some activities you can use with YouTube videos?
   (**Follow up Questions:** Can you describe those activities in details? For the same activity, for example…., why do you use YouTube videos instead of …….?)
3. How do you feel when you deliver a lesson with the integration of YouTube videos?
   (**Follow up Questions:** What do you think about the difference between you delivering the knowledge for students and you letting them watch a YouTube video to withdraw the knowledge themselves? Do you think it is easier to let the YouTube video deliver the knowledge?)
4. Is there any variety in students' reactions when they see you use YouTube videos in the lesson? Can you describe them in specific detail?
5. What do you think about students' feelings when you integrate YouTube videos in your lesson?
6. Is there any variety in students' learning outcomes when you use YouTube videos in the lesson compared to lessons without them? Can you describe them in specific detail?
   (**Follow up Question:** How do you assess the students' learning outcomes?)
7. What is the role of YouTube videos in developing students' language skills?
   (**Follow up Question:** Can you clarify their impact on students' Listening/Speaking/Writing/Reading?)
8. Besides language skills, what are other benefits you think students can gain from a lesson with YouTube videos?
9. What challenges do you think the students may have when they have lessons with YouTube videos?
10. From such challenges you think students may have, which criteria do you take into consideration before you use a YouTube video in your class?

# Chapter 7
# The Pitfalls and Promises of Electronic Portfolio Assessment With Secondary English Language Learners

**Hyesun Cho**
*University of Kansas, USA*

## ABSTRACT

*This chapter discusses the pitfalls and promises of electronic portfolio assessment for English language learners in high school classrooms in the United States. In a three-year federally funded program designed to improve academic performance among culturally and linguistically diverse students at an urban high school in Honolulu, Hawaii, the author implemented electronic portfolio assessment (EPA) into academic English and heritage language classrooms. This chapter delineates how EPA was developed to enhance academic and linguistic abilities of adolescent ELLs while embracing their multifaceted and hybrid identities. It also presents both challenges and benefits that teachers and students experienced in the process of EPA. It concludes with suggestions for developing and implementing EPA for English language learners in similar contexts.*

## INTRODUCTION

Portfolio assessment has been used as an important means of capturing a dynamic picture of academic and language development among English language learners (ELLs) (Baturay & Daloğlu, 2010; Chang, Tseng, Liang, & Liao, 2013; Davison & Leung, 2009; Holmes, 2016; Lam & Lee, 2010; Romova & Andrew, 2011). As a viable alternative to standardized tests, portfolio assessment has been increasingly implemented at local and state levels (e.g., Ward & Bennett, 2012; Zubizarreta, 2009).

Despite the potential of portfolio assessment, however, how to store and manage portfolio materials has been a concern shared by many educators. Teachers have been reluctant to employ portfolio assessment because traditional paper-based portfolios require a large amount of room to store. Also, manage-

DOI: 10.4018/978-1-5225-2933-0.ch007

ment problems (e.g., how to update students' portfolios, how to transport records of student work) have been raised among teachers who otherwise would be interested in using portfolios in their classrooms. A likely solution to these problems is the creation and storage of portfolios using computer technology.

Electronic portfolio assessment (EPA) has emerged to maximize the benefits of portfolio assessment, using a variety of computer-assisted language learning (CALL) technology. Not only do electronic portfolios solve storage and management problems of a traditional paper-based portfolio, but they support an expanded notion of literacy that incorporates multimedia, including text, graphics, sound and video (Kress, 2011). In other words, EPA provides an opportunity for ELLs to embrace multiliteracies (Cope & Kalantzis, 2000; Knobel & Lankshear, 2014; New London Group, 1996) and recognize new ways of capturing the complex ways people read, write, and understand text in the technology-driven global community.

Further, EPA can encourage students to become responsible for their products as electronic portfolios are shared with a wider audience when compared to the teacher and classmates who are the usual audience for paper-based portfolios (Barrot, 2016). The result of this transfer of responsibility to students is that they are often more motivated to engage in the process of reflection and revision that deepens their understanding of curriculum content. As a consequence, EPA can demonstrate student achievement and the growing capabilities in utilizing CALL technology to support lifelong learning (Baturay & Daloğlu, 2010).

This chapter describes an exploratory case of a program for English language learners (ELLs) employing electronic portfolio assessment. The *Studies of Heritage and Academic Languages and Literacies* (SHALL) Program was designed to improve academic performance among culturally and linguistically diverse high school students in the United States by capitalizing on heritage language and cultural resources (Davis, 2009). This three-year federally funded program was implemented in collaboration with the University of Hawaii at Manoa (UHM) and Harrison High School (pseudonym) located in Honolulu, Hawaii. To assess and facilitate student progress, SHALL incorporated alternative assessments that were congruent with its approach to teaching ELLs who were also speakers of heritage languages such as Samoan and Ilokano. Specifically, SHALL teachers and curriculum specialists employed EPA as an alternative to traditional student evaluation (i.e., standardized testing).

This chapter presents a conceptual framework for electronic portfolio assessment, followed by a sociolinguistic context unique to the state of Hawaii. The research site and the student population, along with research methods employed for the study, are discussed. Also, the process, the pitfalls, and the promises of EPA in the SHALL program are presented. The chapter concludes with implications for developing and implementing EPA in similar contexts.

## BACKGROUND

This study derives a framework for electronic portfolio assessment from two bodies of literature: portfolio assessment as alternative assessment in language minority student education[1] and a multimedia design process for the development of electronic portfolios. These complimentary processes are both essential for effective EPA (Barrett, 2007). Understanding how these processes fit together may contribute to the development of electronic portfolios.

## Portfolio Assessment

Portfolio assessment is one kind of authentic assessment in which portfolios are used as an assessment tool (Little, 2005). It is an assessment procedure that is systematically planned, implemented, and evaluated to capture student growth over time. In other words, portfolio assessment is a longitudinal and reflective collection of student work created in response to specific instructional objectives and evaluated in relation to the same criteria.

The rationale for using portfolio assessment of ELLs' academic and language development derives from two considerations: (1) limitations of standardized tests and (2) criticism about a single language developmental model. One of the primary reasons for increasing discussion about portfolio assessment involves problems with standardized tests. As Au (2010) points out, the biggest misuse of standardized tests is their overuse. In an era of high-stakes accountability in the U.S., many school districts now administer such tests at every grade level and define success or failure of schools based on student test scores (Darling-Hammond, 2004). Low content validity is claimed to be another drawback of standardized tests (Menken, 2008; Shohamy, 2011) because standardized tests tend to contain test items that reflect the language, culture, and learning styles of the middle class, European-Americans (Kohn, 2000; Neill & Medina, 1989). Accordingly, low content validity in standardized tests results in consistently low scores for ELLs in all skill areas (Shohamy, 2011).

Second, the multifaceted nature of language proficiency makes it difficult for any single measure to represent a student's linguistic competence (Little, 2005). Many language educators acknowledge that no single measure is capable of estimating the diversity of knowledge, skills, processes, and strategies that combine to determine a student's language development (Menken, 2008; Valdés & Figueroa, 1994). Developmental models "assume a linear progression for learning in which earlier stages will not normally be repeated, and behavior characteristics of later stages will not precede or appear in the place of those behaviors judged as simpler or more fundamental than others" (Heath, 1983, p.150). Yet, the developmental models have been widely argued for by cognitive linguists who do not take social, cultural, historical, and political factors into consideration in the process of language development (Shohamy, 2011). Instead, portfolio assessment negates the single language developmental model. It reflects an important conception that language proficiency is multifaceted and varies depending on the context in which the learner is situated. As assessment is viewed as a culturally and socially selective practice, it becomes problematic for evaluators (i.e., teachers, administrators, and policy makers) to recognize the progress of students who are not members of their cultural and linguistic community (Davison & Leung, 2009; Freiberg, 2001).

Portfolio assessment offers opportunities to make assessment more equitable and authentic than standardized tests (Cummins & Davesne, 2009). The abbreviated time frame in standardized tests is likely to negatively affect the performance of students whose level of language proficiency is not advanced enough to complete the task within a short period (Menken, 2008).

Portfolio assessment is also aligned with the goals of the curriculum of a language course, as well as with projects done by students in the classroom. It can inform teaching and learning practices, which in turn reconstructs the assessment practices. Accordingly, portfolios bring teaching, learning, and assessment together as mutually supportive tasks. Further, the greater degree of student choice afforded by portfolio assessment—such as topics to write on or projects to conduct—may motivate students to take cultural differences into account (Clark, Chow-Hoy, Herter, & Moss, 2001).

## Electronic Portfolio Assessment

An electronic portfolio is a form of combining the use of technologies and portfolios. The electronic portfolio differs from its paper counterpart primarily in that portfolio materials are created and stored in a digitized form, such as on a computer network (Hawisher & Selfe, 1997; Yancey, 2009). It utilizes electronic technologies that allow the portfolio developer to collect and organize portfolio artifacts in multimedia types, including audio, video, graphics, and text. However, an electronic portfolio is not a random collection of digitized artifacts; rather, it is a purposeful and reflective tool that demonstrates growth over time (Jafari & Kaufman, 2006). In other words, what differentiates an electronic portfolio from a digital scrapbook is the organization of the portfolio around the set of learning goals, in addition to learner reflections and the rationale for selecting specific artifacts (Barrett, 2007).

Electronic portfolio assessment (EPA) has several potential benefits. First of all, EPA offers an opportunity to expand a notion of literacy (Blair & Takayoshi, 1997; Early, Kendrick, & Potts, 2015; Goodson, 2007). It shifts conceptions of literacy as new ways of capturing the complex ways people read, write, and understand the text. That is, electronic portfolios can serve as a tool for students to expand their knowledge of the rhetoric of digital environments. Multimodal practices in EPA enable ELLs to develop multiliteracy skills (Early et al., 2015; Vinogradova, Linville, & Bickel, 2011). Also, EPA can make students more responsible for their products than they are when developing paper-based portfolios. This results from the fact that electronic portfolios can be shared with a wider range of audience than merely the teacher or classmates. For example, web-based electronic portfolios can be viewed to anyone who has Internet access. Thus, students have to decide how far to go regarding releasing their ownership of their products and deciding what (not) to include in their portfolio.

The motivational impact of utilizing technology in the classroom has been well- documented in the literature (e.g., Beckers, Dolmans, & van Merrienboer, 2016; Erhel & Jamet, 2013; Papastergiou, 2009). Having students construct a multimedia presentation provides a great responsibility for their projects. This transfer of responsibility for learning results in an increased level of motivation among students. Moreover, students who develop multimedia presentations for outside audiences are rarely satisfied with their initial designs. As a result, students readily engage in the process of reflection and revision that deepens their understanding of curriculum content.

EPA can also showcase student achievement and their growing capabilities in utilizing technology to support lifelong development. In the electronic portfolio development process, each stage of the process can contribute to student learning, including self-reflection as well as multimedia technology skills (Early et al., 2015). The practice of multimedia design has been considered as a form of reflection-in-action (Schön, 1983). It cultivates a variety of cognitive skills that are crucial to students' academic success, such as understanding curriculum content, communicating ideas to external audiences, and organizing thoughts in a logical manner. Research has shown the potential of multimedia development to support the development of these design skills and the emergence of self-reflection among learners in the construction of electronic portfolios (Yancey, 2009).

## THE RESEARCH CONTEXT

Hawaii is unique in many ways. Its culture, history, geography, and demographics are vastly different from those of the continental Unites States. According to the recent U.S. Census (2016), 73% of the population in the state of Hawaii is Asian-Pacific Islander, or mixed race, with only 24% reporting as Caucasian. That is, racial minority and majority are inverted in Hawaii (along with three other states: New Mexico, California, and Texas). Ongoing immigration to the Hawaiian Islands contributes to a diverse cultural and linguistic landscape in Hawaii. The recent U.S. Census indicates that 130 languages are spoken in homes across a total Hawaiian population of less than 1.2 million. Approximately 25.4% of Hawaii's residents speak a non-English language at home (The State of Hawaii, 2016). Along with Hawaii Creole English (HCE), or Pidgin English, as a local language, there is a broad repertoire of heritage languages, including Ilokano, Samoan, Cantonese, Mandarin, Japanese, Vietnamese, Korean, Thai, and Laotian. On the surface, Hawaii seems to be a rich multicultural/multilingual community.

However, in terms of language planning and policy, Hawaii's situation is not entirely different from other urban areas on the U.S. mainland. Although Hawaii offers a wide array of necessary responses to the academic, linguistic, and social needs of language minority students, schools in Hawaii have been unable to respond fully to those needs. In general, teachers do not capitalize on cultural and linguistic resources from diverse ethnic communities to help students reach their full potential. This is because Hawaii historically views language diversity as a problem rather than a resource (Przymus, 2016; Ruiz, 1984; Talmy, 2008).

Harrison High School is one of the largest public schools in Hawaii. Among the approximately 2,500 students enrolled in Harrison, most students are first-or second-generation immigrants. The student population of Harrison represents a typical ethnically diverse working-class community in Hawaii. The largest single student ethnic group is Filipino, who makes up 58.4% of the total student population, followed by Samoan (13.3%) and Part-Hawaiian (10. 2%). The school is located in a low-income area in Honolulu where many families are challenged by poverty and unemployment. Harrison is also a Title I school, meaning that more than 50 percent of its students qualify for the free and reduced lunch program.

## METHOD

In this study, I used an interpretive qualitative approach (Hatch, 2002). Based on the ideas of naturalistic inquiry (Lincoln & Guba, 1985), the investigative mode of choice was a case study (Yin, 2013). The case study design allowed me to gather in-depth descriptions of the SHALL program. The findings of a case study cannot be easily generalized beyond the particular case; rather, they provide a highly contextualized understanding of complex interactions of organizational and individual variables in the given context. By providing 'thick description' (Geertz, 1973) necessary for judgments of transferability, hopefully these insights can, in turn, lead to a deeper understanding of the potential benefits of EPA in similar contexts.

### Participants

#### Students

Given the demographics of the student population at Harrison, the SHALL project team members decided to serve Filipino and Samoan students. The students registered to participate in the SHALL program were divided into two classes according to their heritage language, Ilokano or Samoan. Twenty students were enrolled in the Ilokano class and 15 in the Samoan class. All students were freshmen, and their ages ranged from 14 to 15 years.

Of the 20 students of Ilokano heritage, ten were born in the Philippines and 10 in the United States. Among the students who arrived in the U.S. after birth, the average age of arrival was seven years old. Five students used Ilokano to communicate with their parents, grandparents, and relatives at home. On the other hand, one student in Samoan class was born in American Samoa, one in New Zealand, and 13 in the U.S. Five out of 15 students used Samoan (more than 50% or more of the time) at home.

## SHALL Team

The SHALL project team consisted of teaching staff, a curriculum development team, and an on-site coordinator between the site and the university. One Ilokano and two Samoan teachers led one Ilokano and one Samoan class, respectively. The curriculum planning team comprised of a university professor as primary investigator, a curriculum director, a program evaluator, a technology consultant, and an administrative assistant. My role in the SHALL team was to coordinate EPA while helping teachers with the development of the SHALL curriculum. I also co-taught a computer class every Friday with the technology consultant. All SHALL staff members worked collaboratively for the development and implementation of the curriculum. To capture the intended objectives of the curriculum, the curriculum team members participated in a weekly three-hour professional development seminar and discussed a theoretical framework for the curriculum. Also, they attended a two-hour meeting to adjust the curriculum based on ongoing analyses of student development and corresponding curriculum effectiveness.

### SHALL Curriculum

It should be noted that SHALL was not an after-school or an add-on program. As a result of the negotiation between the SHALL team and the high school administrators, it was offered as a part of the existing curriculum for students who were in a "consortium" for language, literacy, and culture at the high school. In lieu of foreign language courses offered on campus, such as Spanish, French or German, interested students were able to take either Ilokano or Samoan classes offered by the SHALL team. Technology classes were also offered in conjunction with the language classes and the Academic English class as a part of the SHALL curriculum. That is, EPA was integrated into all aspects of the SHALL curriculum that encompassed Academic English, Heritage Languages, and Technology.

My goal as a teacher-researcher was to illuminate the complexities of evaluating student progress in their academic abilities through EPA. Specifically, I focused on addressing the following questions:

1. How does EPA evolve to enhance academic abilities of secondary English language learners?
2. What are the challenges that teachers and students encounter in EPA?
3. What perceived benefits by students and teachers have emerged from the procedure of implementing EPA?

## Data Collection and Analysis

Before the data collection process, the SHALL team obtained approvals from the University's Human Subject Committee and the local school district. The consent forms for parents and students were translated into either Ilokano or Samoan so that participants had options to choose either the English version or their home languge one. To address the aforementioned research questions, triangulation was accomplished through the use of various data collection methods as follows: (1) participant observation of the computer classes and SHALL team meetings; (2) analysis of students' personal reflections on their electronic portfolios; (3) informal interviews with students and teachers; and (4) gathering of documents and materials related to SHALL.

Data analysis took place throughout the data collection procedure through an iterative process: cycling between refining strategies for data collection and thinking about the data I had already collected. Data were entered into a word processor, and artifacts were filed. The first stage of data analysis involved careful coding of all interview data and my field notes. The coding categories were developed initially before and during the study, and then were refined for the purposes of the study.

Comprehensive analysis involved a recursive process of reducing, displaying, explaining, and verifying the data (Miles & Huberman, 1994). With the strategy of analytic induction (Bogdan & Biklen, 1998), I repeatedly read through students' reflections, my field notes, and SHALL-related documents during and after data collection. I then created a visual representation that highlighted relationships among the codes. This draft of a conceptual map enabled me to identify and note recurrent, salient themes with respect to the process, pitfalls, and promises of EPA in the SHALL program. I conducted member checks throughout the program with students, teachers, and SHALL team members on a monthly basis.

## FINDINGS

### The Process

The initial step in the development of EPA was the estimation of students' technological experiences and skills. To gauge the level of students' computer skills and prior experience working with computers, we distributed survey questionnaires on the first day of the computer class. Consistent with the findings of some research on the availability of computers among minority students (e.g., Servon, 2008), the survey results indicated that only 5 out of 15 Samoan students (33%) had a computer at home. On the contrary, in the Ilokano class, more than 88% of the students (16 out of 18 respondents) had computer access at home.

For nine weeks, students worked on their electronic portfolios during a one-and-half-hour block class period on Friday mornings. The technology consultant and I co-taught the class while other teachers (one Ilokano and two Samoan teachers) were helping individual students at the lab. To accomplish goals of EPA, students learned how to do word processing, scan and edit pictures, search the Internet, and work with a presentation software program. Anticipating a lack of familiarity with Microsoft PowerPoint®, we assigned three class hours to teach PowerPoint. We provided students with handouts and demonstrated how to make a presentation. Later, their files were saved in a school network drive. The final week of the quarter was given over to completing the students' electronic portfolios and presenting their project to parents. Students and teachers invited parents over to a celebration event (i.e., Parent Night) to showcase students' work and celebrate the end of the quarter. The students and parents expressed their pleasure with the creativity of visual designs and contents of each project.

## Assessment for Electronic Portfolios: Rubrics

Teachers employed rubrics to assist students in the production and evaluation of their own work. Rubrics translate teachers' expectations for students' work in ways that students can independently utilize. We adapted rubrics from the Internet for the purpose of EPA and discussed them with students on a regular basis to ensure that the students could fully understand the goals and rationales for EPA. At the final stage of the development of EPA, we provided a checklist to facilitate students' revision of their electronic portfolios. Although we encouraged the creativity of students, there were required elements for electronic portfolios. These components included such items as a personal profile, reflections on the EPA project, and a description of their portfolio entries. As EPA supported the connections between process and product, students were required to submit their process work (e.g., their interview transcripts, references, visual representations) as well as a final research paper. As I was working closely with the students regularly during the quarter, the final assessment of the portfolio was relatively less time-consuming. During the final week, I read the portfolio to respond to the work as a whole and wrote a narrative comment at the bottom of the evaluation sheet (see Appendix 1 for the rubric).

## THE PITFALLS

Based on the findings, I identify three challenges that we encountered in the development of EPA: (1) technology overshadowing curricular goals, (2) lack of teacher professional development opportunities, and (3) lack of appropriate technology.

### Technology Overshadowing Curricular Goals

Given the participatory and interactive nature of the SHALL curriculum, teachers created a classroom environment where students would assume responsibility for their learning. At the heart of this task was a desire to encourage students to understand the application of technology not as learning every facet of individual software programs, but rather, as a tool for demonstrating their progress and achievement in SHALL classes. To support this learning attitude toward technology as a useful vehicle for their academic and career pursuits, we encouraged the students to be responsible for their learning processes and products.

Nevertheless, my observations of the computer classes revealed that students concentrated more on the quality of their multimedia design elements than the quality of their content. Students began to engage in computer work enthusiastically without having careful consideration of their choice of portfolio artifacts. For example, a few Ilokano male students downloaded pictures of sports cars from a car company's website. When I asked them to write down their explanation of the use of those pictures, they hastily answered without any thought, "Why not? It's cool!" "I don't know. I just like them." Often, some students spent too much time on what to download from the Internet and how to design their pages. This resulted in the lack of time for some students to complete their electronic portfolios although teachers constantly reminded students of the computer class schedules and due dates.

The data I collected through students' reflections on their electronic portfolios also indicated that their lack of understanding of EPA presented an obstacle to some students' effort toward building a reflective electronic portfolio. In sum, the technology seemed to overshadow the curricular goals that the electronic portfolios were designed to serve.

### Lack of Teacher Development Opportunities

New educational practices utilizing technology demand a high level of computer literacy for all teachers, not merely for technology teachers. One of the challenges faced by content area teachers in the SHALL program was a lack of technological skills to effectively implement multimodal practices into instruction (e.g., Shanahan, 2013). In implementing EPA into the SHALL curriculum, some content area teachers expressed their concern about being 'computer illiterate' during computer classes. An issue that emerged repeatedly was the need for more time for content area teachers to engage in professional development involving technological skills necessary for EPA. The difficulty in finding the time in teachers' already overcrowded schedules for training in technology was a challenge. It seemed fairly clear that if teachers were fully equipped with technological knowledge and skills they could adapt for their instruction, the implementation of technology-integrated instruction, such as EPA, would be a less daunting process than it was in SHALL.

### Lack of Appropriate Resources

Lack of adequate resources for developing electronic portfolios was a major obstacle for both teachers and students. The computer lab at a community center nearby Harrison had only eight personal computers with no Internet connection. As the room was too small for all students to work with computers simultaneously, teachers divided the class into small groups and made students wait until others finished their work. Students were often frustrated when they had to wait for their turn. In addition, we experienced the usual technological glitches. Students frequently lost their computer files because the computers were too obsolete to contain large-sized files. Most computers were not installed with even the basic software programs that were necessary for creating electronic portfolios. Even in a computer lab at Harrison, which was a better facility than the community computer lab, the server computer often froze during class time. This inevitably caused the delay of saving student work because all students had to wait until the technology consultant finished troubleshooting. Without the provision of appropriate technological support and access, it was extremely challenging for teachers and students to accomplish the goals we envisioned in EPA.

## THE PROMISES

Despite the pitfalls of using technology in language education, an increasing number of studies have indicated that learners are often much more motivated to learn with technology (e.g., Hafner, 2015; Morrell, Duenas, Garcia, & Lopez, 2013; Vasudevan, 2006). This is because students take a greater ownership over their learning when they work with technology. The following section describes several promises of EPA observed in the SHALL program: (1) Increased student motivation, (2) integration of heritage language and culture into the curriculum, and (3) promotion of student-centered learning.

### Increasing Student Motivation to Learn

The most profound benefit of EPA that I observed was an increase in student motivation. Consistent with numerous studies on student motivation and engagement in technology (e.g., Cole, 2009; Morrell et al., 2013; Turner, 2011), the data I collected throughout EPA pointed to the enhancement of student motivation. I found students enthusiastically engaging themselves in learning with the use of technology. Students often asked, "Can we have the computer class more often?" "Can we come here [to the computer lab] other days, too?" "Can I stay here and work on my stuff during the next period?" "Can I work on my portfolio with my computer at home?" "I have a flash drive that has files of my journal entries and a research proposal. Can I bring it in and put the documents in my electronic portfolio?" A number of instances in the lab demonstrated that many students took the initiative to make their electronic portfolios better in content and more visually appealing.

Students considered their EPA experiences to be valuable and meaningful as they had an opportunity to utilize a variety of technologies. They expressed strong interest in using technology in reflective journals on their electronic portfolios:

*It was fun because I learned a lot of computer skills that I had never known before. In this class, we learned how to do PowerPoint presentations, scan pictures and edit them. Learning how to change slides with sound effects and make buttons on each slide that connect to one another were so much fun (reflection journal, Samoan male student).*

One student from the Ilokano class reflected on her experience with EPA in comparison with her English portfolio:

*It was really fun making my electronic portfolio because it was a great learning experience. I have never learned a number of computer skills before. I learned how to do PowerPoint presentation, scan pictures, and edit them. Also, I learned to design my electronic portfolio with word art and clip art. I know that I can use the electronic portfolio for my college application or my job application. I have done a portfolio project in my English class before, but I have never done an electronic portfolio working with computers. Both English and Electronic Portfolios are process-oriented, which means I had to revise my work over and over again until I had a final product. They are also different in a sense that I could put digital pictures and images on my electronic portfolio, in addition to written texts. For the English portfolio, I collected my writing examples I had done the whole semester in school: for the electronic portfolio, I was able to include my personal stuff as well as the things I had done in Freshmen Exploration class. I want to thank the people who have encouraged me to complete this project. This was the best class I had ever had!*

It is noted that she recognized the nature of EPA as a process rather than a product as it involved a series of revisions throughout the program. By comparing her experiences creating a portfolio both in the English classroom and the SHALL class, she appreciated the acceptance of personal stories ("I was able to include my personal stuff") as well as the inclusion of multimodal means of communication ("digital pictures and images") in her electronic portfolio whereas in her English portfolio, she collected her academic, non-personal, written texts from the English class. Even the students who were distracted easily in other classes kept themselves busy working on their individual electronic portfolio at the lab. One Samoan female student, who rarely attended school, showed up one Friday and wrote her reaction to EPA in her journal entry:

*If you really know me, you will know that I don't get along with school. My punishment for this is not being able to get the opportunity to work with this project as well as I could have. Fortunately, I am here today and right now I think that this project is really neat. I really wish that I chose to come class more often because then I would have a lot more to say about this portfolio. I guess I could just say that I really like this portfolio and I really regret not coming to class.*

As Beckers et al. (2016) have shown in their review of EPA, it was evident that EPA in SHALL helped students reflect on their learning and becoming self-directed in schoolwork, thereby giving them an opportunity to take their ownership over learning.

## Linking Heritage Resources and Academic Learning

One of the positive changes in student attitude was that students began to incorporate their heritage language and culture into their electronic portfolios. Through EPA, students seemed to change their perspectives on their heritage language and culture. At the beginning of the SHALL curriculum implementation, students were reluctant to use their heritage language in the classroom. Although teachers constantly encouraged the students to capitalize on their heritage linguistic and cultural resources, students were skeptical and unreceptive. However, at the later stage of EPA, I found out that most students incorporated their heritage language and culture into their electronic portfolios to some extent, if not fully. For example, some students used their heritage language for greetings on their cover page (e.g., *Talofa* in Samoan). Others searched research topics related to their culture (e.g., *Tatau,* or Samoan tattoo, Filipino folklore, songs, and food) and wrote a research paper on their topic. Also, others downloaded some beautiful scenic pictures of their home country for their personal profiles. One Hawaiian student expressed her appreciation for the heritage language and culture encouraged throughout the process of EPA:

*It was so cool that we could include our cultural stuff here in our portfolios. I really like the opportunity to use my Hawaiian knowledge in my portfolio, which I never did before this class.*

Overall, students were proud of their achievement when they demonstrated the integration of their heritage knowledge into their electronic portfolio.

## Promoting Student-Centered Learning

The need for students to develop an internal locus of control in their learning is critical as students must become their own monitors of comprehension, production, and behavior. EPA in SHALL attempted to help students to set goals for learning, review their goals periodically, and assume responsibility for their projects. It also encouraged students to engage in self-reflection, a critical component of learning.

Furthermore, the integration of technology into the SHALL curriculum provided a flexible instructional environment in which students were able to be given individualized instruction depending on the level and progress of their project. The use of technology seemed to create a shift in the classroom where students had considerable control over the direction their learning took (e.g., Beckers et al., 2016). A high level of interactions among students was observed in the computer lab while students were working on their electronic portfolios. Some students who were more technologically advanced than others were able to share their expertise for the learning of their peers. Students who tended to be reticent in other classes seemed to feel less intimidated by the technology class. One content area teacher also confirmed the advantages of individualized computer lessons that were responsive to individual student interest and ability: "It is very good to see those students [who tended to be behind and unmotivated] on track in this class. Since they are getting individual attention from you guys, they can easily catch up with other kids." Not only the individual attention that students received from their teachers, but hands-on classroom activities utilizing technology seemed to contribute to a student-centered classroom environment where students took a great deal of responsibility for their learning (e.g., Chang et al., 2013).

## RECOMMENDATIONS

Based on these findings, there are several suggestions for teachers and administrators in the development and implementation of electronic portfolio assessment for English language learners:

1. To develop and maintain interactive electronic portfolios, the provision of appropriate resources should be discussed among stakeholders before the implementation of EPA. Easy access to web-based portfolios will enable students to share their work consistently with their instructors and to revise assignments online throughout the school year. The provision of technical support is a necessary, although not sufficient, condition to maximize the benefits of electronic portfolios.
2. Teachers need to create a classroom environment in which students can co-construct the procedure of EPA. More specifically, teachers can negotiate the scoring criteria with students rather than imposing them into the curriculum. Through negotiation, students will have an opportunity to discuss the rationale for their portfolio artifacts and consequently will be able to structure the EPA to support curriculum and instructional goals. Engaging students in the development of an electronic portfolio requires students to have a conscious conception of portfolio artifacts. They also should be able to justify their portfolio entries based on the goals and objectives of EPA. This will, in turn, allow students to transform the classroom into an environment where they can play a role as active agents in their learning.
3. Teacher professional development is pivotal to the success of any technology-rich project. The critical role of professional development in improving teachers' technological knowledge and skills should be recognized to carry out new approaches to instruction. Judgments about appropriate technologies require both knowledge about technology and content knowledge. Thus, one of the prerequisites for effective use of technology is a professional development program that encompasses a range of activities with technology. Effective professional development should provide authentic tasks in collaborative settings. For example, creating CALL projects as a team and developing assessment tools can be powerful ways for teachers to develop their technological and pedagogical expertise. Offering ample opportunities for teachers to develop technological knowledge and skills necessary for implementing EPA will enable teachers to feel comfortable with technology and consequently will allow teachers to transform their teaching practices.

## CONCLUSION

This chapter has elucidated the intricacies of implementing EPA in the curriculum for secondary English language learners in the United States. For SHALL students, it was not just the learning of technology, but the affordances of the social practices that surrounded their multimodal narratives, which served as a new form of mediational means for them (Cho & Gomabon, 2017). In other words, the EPA project provided an opportunity to reposition students' narratives in relation not to a monolithic discourse, but to a range of competing discourses that otherwise may be rejected or ignored in the classroom. In this regard, students' multiple, hybrid identities and literacies were recognized not only in instruction but in the curriculum and assessment using electronic portfolios. That is, EPA in this study afforded student multimodal displays of content knowledge and identity construction, as argued in the works of Kress (2011), Rogers (2011), and especially Blommaert (2010).

EPA utilizing CALL technology has been shown to be a potentially useful tool for structuring project-based work to engage student learning. As an essential component of EPA, student reflections on what they have learned and produced throughout the course enable students to assume responsibility for ongoing examination of their progress and achievement throughout the development of an electronic portfolio. Of course, technology in and of itself is not a remedy for solving all educational problems. Nonetheless, it is a tool which, if used successfully, can help to address educational issues faced by teachers and students. Efficient use of EPA requires sustained attention to curricular and instructional goals, as well as technology solidly grounded in theories of action. Without careful, long-range planning on how EPA can be interwoven to further curricular goals, the likelihood that EPA will be used successfully is considerably reduced. Furthermore, implementing technology into a curriculum geared toward English language learners requires collaboration among teachers, students, and school administrators. Combined with the best efforts from all stakeholders, EPA can play a significant role in the education of English language learners.

## REFERENCES

Au, W. (2010). *Unequal by design: High-stakes testing and the standardization of inequality*. New York, NY: Routledge.

Barootchi, N., & Keshavarz, M. H. (2002). Assessment of achievement through portfolios and teacher-made tests. *Educational Research*, *44*(3), 279–288. doi:10.1080/00131880210135313

Barrett, H. C. (2007). Researching electronic portfolios and learner engagement: The REFLECT Initiative. *Journal of Adolescent & Adult Literacy*, *50*(6), 436–449. doi:10.1598/JAAL.50.6.2

Barrot, J. S. (2016). Using Facebook-based e-portfolio in ESL writing classrooms: Impact and challenges. *Language, Culture and Curriculum*, *29*(3), 286–301. doi:10.1080/07908318.2016.1143481

Baturay, M. H., & Daloğlu, A. (2010). E-portfolio assessment in an online English language course. *Computer Assisted Language Learning*, *23*(5), 413–428. doi:10.1080/09588221.2010.520671

Beckers, J., Dolmans, D., & van Merrienboer, J. (2016). e-Portfolios enhancing students' self-directed learning: A systematic review of influencing factors. *Australasian Journal of Educational Technology*, *32*(2).

Blair, K. L., & Takayoshi, P. (1997). Reflections on reading and evaluating electronic portfolios. In K. B. Yancey & T. Weiser (Eds.), *Situating portfolios: Four perspectives* (pp. 357–369). Logan, UT: Utah State University Press.

Blommaert, J. (2010). *The sociolinguistics of globalization*. Cambridge, UK: Cambridge University Press. doi:10.1017/CBO9780511845307

Bogdan, R., & Biklen, S. K. (1998). *Qualitative research for education: An introduction to theory and methods* (3rd ed.). London: Allyn & Bacon.

Chang, C. C., Tseng, K. H., Liang, C. Y., & Liao, Y. M. (2013). Constructing and evaluating online goalsetting mechanisms in web-based portfolio assessment system for facilitating self-regulated learning. *Computers & Education*, *69*, 237–249. doi:10.1016/j.compedu.2013.07.016

Cho, H., & Gomabon, R. (2017). Engaging urban youth in critical media literacy. In R. Gordon (Ed.), *Challenges associated with cross-cultural and at-risk student engagement* (pp. 149–170). Hershey, PA: IGI Global. doi:10.4018/978-1-5225-1894-5.ch008

Clark, C., Chow-Hoy, T., Herter, R., & Moss, P. (2001). Portfolios as sites of learning: Reconceptualizing the connections to motivation and engagement. *Journal of Literacy Research*, *33*(2), 211–241. doi:10.1080/10862960109548110

Cole, M. (2009). Using Wiki technology to support student engagement: Lessons from the trenches. *Computers & Education*, *52*(1), 141–146. doi:10.1016/j.compedu.2008.07.003

Cope, B., & Kalantzis, M. (Eds.). (2000). *Multiliteracies: Literacy learning and the design of social futures*. New York, NY: Routledge.

Cummins, P. W., & Davesne, C. (2009). Using electronic portfolios for second language assessment. *Modern Language Journal*, *93*(1), 848–867. doi:10.1111/j.1540-4781.2009.00977.x

Darling-Hammond, L. (2004). Standards, accountability, and school reform. *Teachers College Record*, *106*(6), 1047–1085. doi:10.1111/j.1467-9620.2004.00372.x

Davis, K. (2009). Agentive youth research: Towards individual, collective, and policy transformations. In T. G. Wiley, J. S. Lee, & R. Rumberger (Eds.), *The education of language minority immigrants in the USA* (pp. 202–239). London: Multilingual Matters.

Davison, C., & Leung, C. (2009). Current issues in English language teacher-based assessment. *TESOL Quarterly*, *43*(3), 393–415. doi:10.1002/j.1545-7249.2009.tb00242.x

Early, M., Kendrick, M., & Potts, D. (2015). Multimodality: Out from the margins of English language teaching. *TESOL Quarterly*, *49*(3), 447–460. doi:10.1002/tesq.246

Erhel, S., & Jamet, E. (2013). Digital game-based learning: Impact of instructions and feedback on motivation and learning effectiveness. *Computers & Education*, *67*, 156–167. doi:10.1016/j.compedu.2013.02.019

Freiberg, J. (2001). Criteria-based assessment in senior high school English: Transcending the textual in search of the magical. In P. Freebody, S. Muspratt, & B. Dwyer (Eds.), *Difference, silence, and textual practice* (pp. 287–322). Cresskill, NJ: Hampton Press.

García, O., & Sylvan, C. E. (2011). Pedagogies and practices in multilingual classrooms: Singularities in pluralities. *Modern Language Journal*, *95*(3), 385–400. doi:10.1111/j.1540-4781.2011.01208.x

Geertz, C. (1973). *The interpretation of cultures: Selected essays*. New York, NY: Basic Books.

Goodson, F. T. (2007). The electronic portfolio: Shaping an emerging genre. *Journal of Adolescent & Adult Literacy*, *50*(6), 432–434. doi:10.1598/JAAL.50.6.1

Hafner, C. A. (2015). Remix culture and English language teaching: The expression of learner voice in digital multimodal compositions. *TESOL Quarterly*, *49*(3), 486–509. doi:10.1002/tesq.238

Hatch, J. A. (2002). *Doing qualitative research in education settings*. Albany, NY: State University of New York Press.

Hawisher, G. E., & Selfe, C. L. (1997). Wedding the technologies of writing portfolios and computers. In K. B. Yancey & T. Weiser (Eds.), *Situating portfolios: Four perspectives* (pp. 305–321). Logan, UT: Utah State University Press.

Heath, S. B. (1983). *Ways with words: Language, life, and work in communities and classrooms*. New York, NY: Cambridge University Press.

Holmes, T. (2016). PBLA: Moving toward sustainability. *TESL Canada Journal*, *32*(Special issue), 113–123. doi:10.18806/tesl.v32i0.1220

Jafari, A., & Kaufman, C. (Eds.). (2006). *Handbook of research on ePortfolios*. Hershey, PA: Idea Group. doi:10.4018/978-1-59140-890-1

Knobel, M., & Lankshear, C. (2014). Studying new literacies. *Journal of Adolescent & Adult Literacy*, *58*(2), 97–101. doi:10.1002/jaal.314

Kohn, A. (2000). Burnt at the high stakes. *Journal of Teacher Education*, *51*(4), 315–327. doi:10.1177/002248710005100407

Kress, G. (2011). Discourse analysis and education: A multimodal social semiotic approach. In R. Rogers (Ed.), *An introduction to critical discourse analysis in education* (pp. 205–226). New York, NY: Routledge.

Lam, R., & Lee, I. (2010). Balancing the dual functions of portfolio assessment. *ELT Journal*, *64*(1), 54–64. doi:10.1093/elt/ccp024

Lincoln, Y. S., & Guba, E. G. (1985). *Naturalistic inquiry*. Beverly Hills, CA: Sage Publications.

Little, D. (2005). The common European framework and the European language portfolio: Involving learners and their judgements in the assessment process. *Language Testing*, *22*(3), 321–336. doi:10.1191/0265532205lt311oa

Menken, K. (2008). *English learners left behind: Standardized testing as language policy*. Clevedon, UK: Multilingual Matters.

Miles, M. B., & Huberman, A. M. (1994). *Qualitative data analysis* (2nd ed.). Thousand Oaks, CA: Sage Publications.

Morrell, E., Duenas, R., Garcia, V., & Lopez, J. (2013). *Critical media pedagogy: Teaching for achievement in city schools*. New York, NY: Teachers College Press.

Neill, D. M., & Medina, N. J. (1989). Standardized testing: Harmful to educational health. *Phi Delta Kappan*, *70*, 688–697.

New London Group. (1996). A pedagogy of multiliteracies: Designing social futures. *Harvard Educational Review*, *66*(1), 60–92. doi:10.17763/haer.66.1.17370n67v22j160u

Papastergiou, M. (2009). Digital game-based learning in high school computer science education: Impact on educational effectiveness and student motivation. *Computers & Education*, *52*(1), 1–12. doi:10.1016/j.compedu.2008.06.004

Przymus, S. D. (2016). Challenging the monolingual paradigm in secondary dual-language instruction: Reducing language-as-problem with the 2–1-L2 model. *Bilingual Research Journal*, *39*(3-4), 279–295. doi:10.1080/15235882.2016.1220995

Rogers, R. (Ed.). (2011). *An introduction to critical discourse analysis in education*. New York, NY: Routledge.

Romova, Z., & Andrew, M. (2011). Teaching and assessing academic writing via the portfolio: Benefits for learners of English as an additional language. *Assessing Writing*, *16*(2), 111–122. doi:10.1016/j.asw.2011.02.005

Ruiz, R. (1984). Orientations in language planning. *NABE Journal*, *8*(2), 15–34.

Schön, D. (1983). *The reflective practitioner: How professionals think in action*. New York, NY: Basic Books.

Servon, L. J. (2008). *Bridging the digital divide: Technology, community and public policy*. Malden, MA: Blackwell Publishing.

Shanahan, L. E. (2013). Composing kid-friendly multimodal text: When conversations, instruction, and signs come together. *Written Communication*, *30*(2), 194–227. doi:10.1177/0741088313480328

Shohamy, E. (2011). Assessing multilingual competencies: Adopting construct valid assessment policies. *Modern Language Journal*, *95*(3), 418–429. doi:10.1111/j.1540-4781.2011.01210.x

Talmy, S. (2008). The cultural productions of the ESL student at Tradewinds High: Contingency, multidirectionality, and identity in L2 socialization. *Applied Linguistics*, *29*(4), 619–644. doi:10.1093/applin/amn011

The State of Hawaii. (2016). *Detailed languages spoken at home in the state of Hawaii*. Retrieved from http://files.hawaii.gov/dbedt/census/acs/Report/Detailed_Language_March2016.pdf

Turner, K. C. N. (2011). Rap universal: Using multimodal media production to develop ICT literacies. *Journal of Adolescent & Adult Literacy*, *54*(8), 613–623. doi:10.1598/JAAL.54.8.6

U. S. Census. (2016). *Population demographics for Hawaii 2017 and 2016*. Retrieved from https://suburbanstats.org/population/how-many-people-live-in-hawaii

Valdés, G., & Figueroa, R. A. (1994). *Bilingualism and testing: A special case of bias*. Westport, CT: Ablex Publishing.

Vasudevan, L. M. (2006). Looking for angels: Knowing adolescents by engaging with their multimodal literacy practices. *Journal of Adolescent & Adult Literacy*, *50*(4), 252–256. doi:10.1598/JAAL.50.4.1

Vinogradova, P., Linville, H. A., & Bickel, B. (2011). Listen to my story and you will know me: Digital stories as student-centered collaborative projects. *TESOL Journal*, *2*(2), 173–202. doi:10.5054/tj.2011.250380

Ward, W. C., & Bennett, R. E. (Eds.). (2012). *Construction versus choice in cognitive measurement: Issues in constructed response, performance testing, and portfolio assessment*. New York, NY: Routledge.

Yancey, K. (2009). Reflection and electronic portfolios: Inventing the self and reinventing the university. In D. Cambridge, B. Cambridge, & K. Yancey (Eds.), *Electronic portfolios 2.0* (pp. 5–16). Sterling, VA: Stylus.

Yin, R. K. (2013). *Case study research: Design and methods* (5th ed.). Thousand Oaks, CA: Sage Publications.

Zubizarreta, J. (2009). *The learning portfolio: Reflective practice for improving student learning*. San Francisco, CA: Jossey-Bass.

## ADDITIONAL READING

Acosta, T., & Liu, Y. (2006). ePortfolios: Beyond assessment. Handbook of research on ePortfolios, 15-23.

Cambridge, D. (2010). *Eportfolios for lifelong learning and assessment*. London, United Kingdom: John Wiley & Sons.

Davis, V. (2015). 11 essentials for excellent e-portfolios. Retrieved from https://www.edutopia.org/blog/11-essentials-for-excellent-eportfolios-vicki-davis

E-portfolio Webinar Series: Exploring Assessment and Evidence. (2015). Retrieved from https://youtu.be/srsdb1u2Fq8

Examples of Student e-Portfolios. Centre for Teaching Excellence. Retrieved from https://uwaterloo.ca/centre-for-teaching-excellence/resources/integrative-learning/eportfolios/examples-student-eportfolios

Lorenzo, G., & Ittelson, J. (2005). An overview of e-portfolios. Retrieved from https://net.educause.edu/ir/library/pdf/eli3001.pdf

Luchoomun, D., McLuckie, J., & van Wesel, M. (2010). Collaborative e-Learning: e-Portfolios for Assessment, Teaching and Learning. *Electronic Journal of e-Learning, 8*(1), 21-30.

Morton, M. (2012). An example of an excellent e-portfolio. Retrieved from https://youtu.be/3_FmRH6Lj5c

Moya, S.S., & O'Malley, M. (1994). A portfolio assessment model for ESL. *The Journal of Educational Issues of Language Minority Students*, v13 p. 13-36, Spring 1994.

Novak, L. (2012). Using E-portfolios to assess student learning. Retrieved from https://youtu.be/ji9xI-NssQk

Principles and Practices in Electronic Portfolios: Conference on College Composition and Communication Position Statement. Retrieved from http://www.ncte.org/cccc/resources/positions/electronicportfolios

Ring, G., & Ramirez, B. (2012). Implementing ePortfolios for the Assessment of General Education Competencies. *International Journal of ePortfolio, 2*(1), 87-97.

Singh, S., Samad, A. A., Hussin, H., & Sulaiman, T. (2015). Developing a portfolio assessment model for the teaching and learning of English in Malaysian L2 classroom. *English Language Teaching*, *8*(7), 2015. doi:10.5539/elt.v8n7p164

Stevenson, H. J. (2006). Using ePortfolios to foster peer assessment, critical thinking, and collaboration. Handbook of Research on ePortfolios, 112-124.

## KEY TERMS AND DEFINITIONS

**Authentic Assessment:** A form of assessment in which students are asked to perform real-life tasks that demonstrate the application of knowledge and skills.

**Critical Language Awareness:** An approach to language learning and teaching through the understanding of power and discourse embedded in society.

**Electronic Portfolio:** Electronic materials, such as text, image, audio, video that are purposefully assembled and managed by a user (usually online).

**Heritage Language:** A language other than English spoken at home in the United States.

**Multimodality:** A practice in which multiple modes (e.g., visual, textual, spatial, aural) are used for communication.

**Portfolio Assessment:** An assessment of student performance with the use of student-generated artifacts over a period of time.

## ENDNOTE

1 As one of the reviewers pointed out, I recognize that the term *language minority students* often presumes limited competence of these students, not recognizing their bilingualism and full semiotic repertoire that they bring to the classroom. As a result, the term, "emergent bilinguals" (García & Sylvan, 2011) has emerged in the literature. However, I use 'language minority students' in this chapter to indicate the power differential and inequity that inevitably exist between mainstream students and language minority counterparts regarding access to resources for success in academia. Drawing upon Spivak's (1993) notion of "strategic use of essentialism," Pennycook argues that "it allows us to consider when we want to question identities, realities, rights, or language and when we need to operationalize more fixed and concrete notions for strategic purposes" (p. 172). Yet, it should be noted that the analysis of the focal students' academic experiences shows that they are multidimensional, dynamic, and complex social beings.

## APPENDIX: EPA RUBRIC

Your electronic portfolios will be evaluated according to the following rubric (Table 1). The third column in the rubric below, "Right on Target" shows what is expected of each student.

*Table 1.*

| Electronic Portfolio Scoring Rubric | | | | |
|---|---|---|---|---|
| | **Missed the Mark!** 5 pts. | **Getting Close!** 10 pts. | **Right On Target!** 15 pts. | **Bulls Eye!!!** 17 pts. |
| **Title Card** | Design is inappropriate. | Design could be neater or might be inappropriate. | Design is attractive and colorful. | Design is attractive, colorful, and shows creativity. |
| **Mechanics** | Spelling and punctuation errors are distracting. | Spelling and punctuation errors are evident. | Errors in spelling and punctuation are minor and few. | There are NO errors in spelling or punctuation. |
| **Pages** | The student project contains 3 or fewer pages. | The student project contains 4 pages. | The student project contains 5 pages. | The student project contains 6 or more pages. |
| **Contents** | Few reflections include: the program used and the main skills learned. | Some reflections include: the program used and the main skills learned. | All reflections include: the program used and the main skills learned. | All reflections include: the program used and a detailed account of all skills learned. |
| **Personal reactions to projects** | Few reflections include personal reactions. Reactions are vague or repetitive. | Some reflections include personal reactions. Reactions may be vague or repetitive. | Reflections include personal reactions that clearly reflect the student's feelings. | All reflections include personal reactions that are descriptive and insightful. |
| **Comments** | | | | |

# Chapter 8
# Embracing Computer Corpora in the Language Learning Classroom and Using It in Your Classroom

**Sally Durand**
*University of Illinois at Chicago, USA*

## ABSTRACT

*Among the many facets of Computer Assisted Language Learning (CALL), studies using computer language corpora have risen to considerable prominence in research agendas. The author argues that corpora are useful tools for practicing teachers. However, the myth that "corpus-based research is too complicated to be useful for teachers" (Conrad, 2009) prevails in pedagogical contexts. This chapter strives to dispel that myth by synthesizing a wealth of research and their accompanying pedagogical applications. Secondly, it shares specific pedagogical activities to implement corpus data in classroom teaching. These corpus-informed classroom strategies provide concrete examples that will assist TESOL/TEFL teachers in making their coursework authentic and therefore more meaningful to students learning language.*

## INTRODUCTION

What is a corpus? What is corpus-based research? When I gave my first presentation on the topic of using corpora in the classroom at Illinois' TESOL conference in early 2014, two attendees answered my opening question, *"What do corpora in the classroom mean?"* with: "*Our bodies, using the body in the classroom?"* While my presentation title and topic may have misled those two guests, the word *corpus,* in fact, does mean body in Latin. A corpus is a collection of texts and speech (written) comprised for the purpose of linguistic analysis. Corpus linguistics has roots in theology. Religious scribes scoured their bibles, coding certain words or themes, making lists of their locations together in a kind of index, in other words, collecting a corpus. Imagine how those early scholars would have benefitted from our

DOI: 10.4018/978-1-5225-2933-0.ch008

modern technology. In his book, *An Introduction to Corpus Linguistics*, Kennedy (1998) attributes the modern field of corpus linguistics to the capabilities offered by computerized databases. As we will see shortly, interest in corpus data has spread beyond linguists to pedagogical researchers and teachers. While linguists study language corpus data to better understand the language, corpus-informed/based language learning researchers examine corpus data to understand how language is learned and taught. This pedagogically-oriented area of inquiry, made possible by computers, is the epitome of Computer Assisted Language Learning.

The creation of computer technology has made corpus research possible, as the computer is able to store, code, categorize, and retrieve massive amounts of information. The field began with just a small group of dedicated enthusiasts, but by the end of the century, it had become a major research strand in both the fields of linguistics and language learning. Over the last two decades, educators have been finding ways to exploit the potential of corpora (the plural of corpus), channeling research data into pedagogical applications for language instruction. Research using corpus data in English language learning has become a broad field drawing from a wealth of corpora. This abundance and breadth of corpora and corpus-based research studies may contribute to the myth that it is all just too complicated for teachers (Conrad, 2009). Some teachers believe that the technology is too advanced or that the data are incomprehensible. These may be common sentiments and they are easily understandable. The sheer mass of a given database alone can be overwhelming. In my experience discussing corpora use in the classroom with peers, I have found that a few teachers are unaware of the existence of corpora. Many are vaguely to somewhat familiar with the concept of corpora and generally aware of the growing interest and research in corpus-informed language learning. Most have limited to no hands-on experience working with corpora. It is noted in the field that academic preparation programs lack any training in corpus linguistics (Granger, 2009; Hasko, 2013).

Many research studies use prominent corpora such as the British National Corpus (BNC), and the Corpus of Contemporary American English, usually referred to as COCA (Davies, 2008). These immensely huge corpora contain hundreds of millions of words from sources of news broadcasts to literary fiction. These resources allow for the analysis of language features and use such as medium and register by searches for spoken versus written language use, for example. Corpora also consist of professional and academic content, facilitating research in academic disciplines or subfields, and enabling comparisons on aspects of general English use versus English for specialized or specific purposes. Learner corpora provide insights into the language use of language learners as they collect actual learners' work. One prominent corpus of this kind is the Michigan Corpus of Upper level Student Papers (MICUSP), from the University of Michigan. Another is the International Corpus of Learner English (ICLE). Learner corpora provide insight into learners' needs and actual habits of learners' language use. The features of corpora seem limitless as does the pedagogical potential. For example, along with generating millions of words in frequency lists, certain corpora are capable of charting changes in usage patterns over time, or the geographical status of varied world Englishes.

It is not necessary for teachers to become extensively familiar with the range and navigation of extant corpora, or even one corpus, in order to benefit from this technology and area of research. Therefore, the goal of this chapter is to address the following two questions: How have corpora been used for pedagogical purposes by researchers and teachers? How can teachers use corpus data in their language learning classrooms?

## RESEARCH TO PEDAGOGY

This brief history and review of the literature highlights the major contributions of corpus research to language learning pedagogy. Table 1, *Corpus contributions to language learning pedagogy at a glance,* is an overview of scholarly articles dating from 2000 to 2014 with an emphasis on their value added to language learning pedagogy. These demonstrate the expansion and evolution of corpus linguistics to corpus-informed instruction and the pedagogical potential of corpus data.

To compile this review of the literature, I searched in major journals such as *Modern Language Journal* and *TESOL Quarterly*. I did not include the more technical linguistics journals such as the *Journal of Corpus Linguistics*. Likewise, I did not include research articles that are statistics-heavy, highly esoteric, or those which rely on field jargon. This decision was made in order to focus on more teacher-friendly publications. The search also included international journals in order to include EFL research studies. Throughout the process of search and selection, I continually considered the knowledge and needs of the intended audience, practicing teachers. At the forefront of my selection process was a pedagogical implication of teachers. Databases of major journals were searched by keywords such as corpus and pedagogy, data-driven, corpus-based, and corpus-informed instruction. I filtered articles by those pertaining to ESL academic English instruction and those which I considered seminal in the field, or representative of a turning point or innovation in the field. I chose literature with specific links to the pedagogical activities that I have developed for my classroom use. This collection is in no way comprehensive, but I hope it will provide enough background knowledge and a clear view of the path of teachers embracing corpora as language learning resources.

Research studies using corpus data hold rich implications for pedagogical practices in language learning classrooms. Over the last two decades, scholars, researchers, and researcher-practitioners have been finding ways to exploit the potential of corpus data and in turn channel the data into improving pedagogical practices for language instruction. These articles all contribute to debunking the myth that corpus is too complicated for the average teacher to utilize. While some argue that "description is not prescription" (Leech, 1998), there is abundant evidence to support the claim that corpora are useful tools for language instruction. Table 1 provides a quick overview and salient points of corpus contributions. A more detailed discussion of the research articles follows.

This chart depicts the evolution of the field from corpus linguistics to corpus-informed instruction. Corpus linguistics uses corpora as a research method of analysis seeking to uncover patterns in usage, and may or may not concern phenomenon of teaching/learning language. Pedagogical implications are implicit in most studies although they are more inherent in learner corpora studies. Corpus-informed or corpus-based instruction or language learning is a research area that sees corpora not as tools for linguistic analysis, but seeks to tap the wealth of rich and varied data for pedagogical purposes. This means using the computer tool to assist language learning, not simply describe language usage patterns or features.

This body of literature connects research to the development of pedagogical practices in English language learning, primarily academic English. This is demonstrated in one of the first practical uses of corpus data, the Academic Word List, abbreviated AWL (Coxhead, 2000). By putting forth a frequency-driven list, this corpus data provides an authentic authority on language use. The AWL provides a concrete list of basic lexical items, which are essential to academic English competence which is an obvious attribute to teachers. Without this data, lexical items would be included in curricula based on

*Table 1. Corpus Contributions to Language Learning Pedagogy at a Glance*

| Author, Year | Article Title | Research Focus | Pedagogical Implication(s) |
|---|---|---|---|
| | | **Linguistic Inquiry** | |
| Coxhead, 2000 | A new academic wordlist | Uses corpus data focused on considerations such as type of corpus, size and kinds of texts included to produce the most useful word list | Provides a concrete list of basic lexical items which are essential to academic writing guiding instruction and curricular choices |
| Biber & Conrad, 2001a | Multi-dimensional analysis and the study of register variation | Examines relationships between particular verbs and particular aspects; certain grammar structures and lexical items used inAcademic English | Advocates using corpus data to inform pedagogical practice by considering three main functions: common lexical verbs across registers, aspect across registers and co-occurrence |
| Flowerdew, 2003 | A Combined Corpus and Systemic Functional Analysis of the Problem-Solution Pattern in a Student and Professional Corpus of Technical Writing | Compares an undergraduate student corpus (STUCORP), the corpus of professional, technical reports (PROCORP), and the British National Corpus (BNC) along with systemic functional analysis to discover how student writers treat problem/solution patterns in writing compared to professional writers | Results imply that students lack an awareness of causative verbs as well as the appropriate register of verbs; suggests that teachers implement concordancing exercises with causative verbs such as *arise from, pose, present, minimize, alleviate* etc. to help students learn cause/reason and result/effect patterns |
| Biber, Conrad & Cortes, 2004 | If you look at it…: Lexical bundles in university teaching and textbooks | Investigates spoken and written academic language: textbooks, classroom teaching, conversation and academic prose; lexical bundles of across register in the academic setting | Reveals the register of academic written prose to have less variation and more limitations; textbooks contain relatively few bundles, while classroom instruction is awash with them; examines the lexical bundles by categorizing them by function |
| Gardener & Davies, 2007 | Pointing Out Frequent Phrasal Verbs: A Corpus-Based Analysis | Targets phrasal verbs and their constituent parts: using the British National Corpus to identify which phrasal verbs are the most frequent | Targets one feature of immense difficulty for learners; helps materials writers and instructors prioritize teaching of phrasal verbs by identifying the most common, therefore most useful, phrasal verbs |

a writer/teacher's intuition. Coxhead (2000) urges teachers and materials designers to utilize the lists in the classroom by focusing on smaller sub lists, through direct instruction, and through meaning-based exercises. Beyond generating word lists, corpus research has progressed to guiding and encouraging teachers on how to examine and exploit corpus data in the classroom (Coxhead, 2000), as well as how to narrow the focus to discipline-specific lists (Römer & Wulff, 2010). There are now dozens of word lists including the subject-specific BEL (Basic Engineering List) and multi-word lists of formulaic expressions (Lessard-Clouston, 2012).

Another development in corpus linguistics research which offers pedagogical applications is the inclusion of register considerations (Biber & Conrad, 2001a; Biber, Conrad, & Cortes, 2004). While AWLs tell teachers and learners which words to know, the remaining questions of how, by whom, and in which contexts they are used are of equal importance. Examination of which lexical items appear in a given register, in which tense or aspect, and in which surroundings provides more information to guide educational choices. The language used in academic writing is very different from everyday language (Conrad, 2009). Moreover, data on lexical *bundles* offer insights on collocations and the bigger building blocks necessary to produce language output. Teaching students the top bundles for a particular function will give them the language expected in academic writing (Biber et. al., 2004).

With the development of learner corpora, researchers are able to understand more about what learners lack (Flowerdew, 2003; Granger, 2003; Hinkel, 2001) or habits unique to nonnative-speaking learners (Chen & Baker, 2010). These studies present an argument for utilizing corpora in a different method. Rather than focusing on what to teach based on frequency driven data, learner data provides patterns and linguistic variations which provide insight for teachers as well. For example, learners may have acquired "stock phrases" which are appropriate and frequent in spoken communication, but inappropriate in the realm of academic writing (Gardner & Davies, 2007). Likewise, this data can reveal how learners over- or underutilize an important element, such as hedging devices (Chen & Baker, 2010). Finally, it can demonstrate that learners are lacking the language for specific linguistic functions such as describing causation (Flowerdew, 2003). This data offers educators with a form of needs analysis otherwise unattainable. As Coxhead (2000) points out, learner data may not show incorrect language use, but that the language needed is missing. Therefore, not only can materials/curriculum be corpus-driven, or informed by native use or frequency, they can also be designed based on the absence of use by learners or learners' non-target-like patterns. Learner data can demonstrate lacks in awareness of genre, register, and rhetorical modes which are necessary in academic writing. As seen in the Chen and Baker's (2010) study, learners were unfamiliar with noun phrase constructions typical in academic writing.

The more recent articles signal a shift away from linguistic inquiry toward instructional dynamics. While the earlier corpus research noted pedagogical implication, recent work is empirically testing pedagogical applications of corpus data as indicated in Table 1. Smart's (2014) study focused on the instructional dynamic of an ESL classroom engaged in grammar learning with data-driven, or corpus-informed, materials. This study compares the effectiveness of corpus-informed materials with traditional, non-corpus informed materials. Two important conclusions could be drawn from the study. Firstly, Smart's findings showed corpus-informed instruction to be more effective in teaching grammar. Second, in comparing instructional techniques with the corpus-informed materials, Smart found that an inductive instructional approach is more effective than a deductive one.

Liu and Jiang's (2009) large-scale international study, which included three sites: two US universities and one EFL site in China, examined corpus-informed instruction in lexicogrammar. Their analysis of both learner and teacher reflections supports the use of context rich concordance data as a means to illuminate usage patterns. Their evidence shows grammar and vocabulary learning to be more effective when learned inductively in corpus contexts, which corroborates Smart's findings. Liu and Jiang assert: "In terms of inductive learning, language learners observe grammar and vocabulary usages in concordance data, and then they discover and generalize findings about usage patterns and rules" (p. 62).

Another recent EFL research study examined corpus-based instruction of lexical collocation (Ashouri, Arjmandi & Rahimi, 2014). In providing background for their current study, the authors first make a case for lexical collocation in language learning, citing a dearth in collocation knowledge among their students in Iran. Likewise, the authors note that common vocabulary teaching practices often entail single items irreverent to collocates. This Iranian study found that an experimental corpus-informed collocation instructional treatment yielded greater knowledge of collocations than did the non-corpus informed "traditional" collocation instruction of the control group. In discussing their findings, the authors note additional benefits of the corpus-based teaching beyond item learning extending to the social realm. The authors claim: "teaching corpus-based collocations had a positive effect on collocation learning and awareness...also help learners get familiar with the language socioliguistically and pragmatically" (p. 478). Findings also indicate that the instructional treatment influenced students' own study habits and increased motivation to search out collocate data on their own.

An optimistic and encouraging sentiment is present in this body of literature. Motivations for research are driven by curiosities less in theory and more in practical applications. As Granger (2003), the founder of the International Corpus of Learner English, states: "On a practical level, the ICLE can help produce more learner-aware pedagogical material designed for advanced EFL learners in general or focused on the needs of one national learner population" (Granger, 2003). Likewise, Hasko's (2013) introduction to a special volume of *Modern Language Journal* devoted to learner corpora and language development touts the array of benefits from investigating learner corpora. Learner corpus data can provide profound insights on multiple facets of the language learning phenomenon. While theory may indeed be aided by corpus data, the argument for the pedagogical potential and new ways to extract pedagogical practices is paramount for teachers. This strand of research has led to improvements in curriculum and materials as publishers now select content based on corpus-generated data (Read, 2004). Target vocabulary items are chosen from word lists, and grammatical content is selected and sequenced based on corpus-based needs analysis. Textbook writers can tailor their content, register, and style to reflect linguistic variations in authentic language use. These improvements represent research to pedagogy actualization.

In review of these research studies, teachers can use corpora in a variety of ways to enrich their TESOL pedagogical practices. In short, teachers can use corpora in the classroom:

1. To generate vocabulary word lists.
2. To generate discipline specific word lists.
3. To extract vocabulary words from authentic texts.
4. To generate collocation lists.
5. To create collocation activities based on parts of speech and word order.
6. To create activities to promote register awareness of written vs. spoken forms.
7. To extract concordance lines to encourage inductive learning.
8. To identify lexical bundles associated with language functions.
9. To identify learner lacks or non-target-like patterns.
10. To make decisions about course and/or materials design.
11. To make decisions about text selection.

## PRACTICAL IMPLEMENTATION

Exploring corpora from a purely practical standpoint, this section discusses and demonstrates how teachers can effectively extract and implement corpus data in their teaching. While much of the featured research in this chapter is complex and conducted by scholars with extensive experience in corpus linguistics, there are several ways in which a novice in the user of corpora can extract valuable data to use in shaping classroom curricula, materials, and lessons. This section illustrates how one burgeoning area of CALL, corpus-informed instruction, can provide unlimited resources not only to researchers, but also to teachers themselves. This includes the creation of classroom materials and activities from corpus data such as vocabulary and collocation activities and games, inductive grammar exercises, and the creation of activities to promote register awareness.

Corpus data can be extremely useful for teachers as course and materials designers. On the larger scale, creating curricular content and making decisions can be based on evidence. For example, let's imagine that an experienced teacher is assigned a new special course for a new undergraduate exchange program at her university. The course will focus on academic writing skills and the incoming students are all biology majors. A few searches on the learner corpus MICUSP can provide a graphic representation of the distribution of writing genres across disciplines, allowing the teacher to identify which genres of writing will be most beneficial and therefore should be prioritized in her syllabus. Corpus data serve as a mode of needs analysis even before the students have arrived to class.

On a more daily scale, corpus data can help teachers improve their classroom instruction and activities. Perhaps, you are not designing the course. It is set, and complete with a textbook. And perhaps in that text there is one section that you want to skip over, which can be confusing. The examples may be unclear, the expected answer may be ambiguous, or something about the wording seems unnatural to you. This presents an opportunity to augment the text with authentic data. For example, several years ago I was teaching abroad using a British English text. One worksheet in the students' workbook made me feel incompetent every time we came around to it. It was an exercise on using the verbs *make* and *do* in set phrases. My students' L1, Italian, uses the same verb for *make* and *do* so the topic was valid. The worksheet consisted of a long list of expressions that began with *make* or *do*. Students had to choose and write the correct verb before each expression, e.g., "____ *your bed*" and "____ *the dishes.*" The problem for me was that the sheet was rather long and many of the later expressions seemed ambiguous to me and/or not common enough to merit inclusion on the list. Had I known about the existence of corpora at that time, I could have easily done a few quick frequency checks to provide data-driven alternatives on my own original, and more authentic, worksheet. In the years since, through courses and professional development conferences and workshops, I have been learning about the power and potential of corpora and attempting to bring it into my teaching with corpus-informed content.

One prominent corpus, the Corpus of Contemporary American English abbreviated and usually referred to as "COCA" (Davies, 2008), has a very user-friendly interface. COCA is accessible online at: http://corpus.byu.edu/coca/. Users can conduct hundreds of searches with a guest login. COCA has resources such as tutorials and charts of search commands such as the parts of speech tags legend, so novice users can easily run searches. Additionally, there are hundreds of YouTube video tutorials on every kind of search and feature (see this chapter's Additional Resources for suggested video links). While it is beyond the scope of this paper to demonstrate how to run certain searches, readers can look online for tutorials. The classroom activities which are explained in the following section are based on the teachers' corpus searches and data. Another great resource for teachers is the Vocabulary Profiler (Cobb, 2002; Heatley, Nation, & Coxhead, 2002), available at http://www.lextutor.ca/vp/eng/. It is an extremely useful and simple tool for dissecting authentic texts into frequency-driven word lists. Finding word frequencies, collocations, and using concordance lines are three ways in which teachers implement corpus data into their classroom activities.

## Finding Word Frequencies

The simplest way to use a corpus is in the word frequency finder application. One can create vocabulary lists from authentic texts. After inputting a text such as a local daily newspaper article, the corpus provides frequency results identifying words on the academic word list, words belonging to the most common word lists, and options to generate synonyms for certain words. These results help instructors choose which words to bold and gloss or eliminate for a cloze exercise, for example. This kind of resource allows teachers to move beyond their own intuition and make evidence-based choices when presenting a new authentic text. Both The Vocabulary Profiler (Cobb, 2002; Heatley et. al., 2002), and the COCA (Davies, 2008) have tools for this analysis.

### Using Collocation Searches

Identifying collocates is another very simple feature of a corpus. As supported in research, collocation learning may be enhanced by instruction using corpus data (Ashouri, Arjmandi, & Rahimi, 2014). Additionally, Flowerdew's (2003) research demonstrated that learners may be unfamiliar with preferred collocations, and their use may be limited in range. Collocation searches in COCA, for example, can generate collocations with any part of speech and up to four places before or after a selected word. Collocations can be displayed by frequency and within a given register. Collocation search results provide excellent data for creating classroom materials and games.

### Using Concordance Lines

Concordance lines are a display of authentic examples of a searched word or phrase generated by a search in a corpus. Each line shows the keyword in context along with the source. In the COCA, if you click on one concordance line, it will open the original example to display more context showing the text before and after the keyword as well as its source. Searches can be tailored to include all examples of a particular keyword in the database, or within a particular genre such as academic writing, or fiction, or spoken language. Concordance lines offer extensive examples of words in context. This encourages noticing of syntax features such as the use of a preposition following a verb, verb pattern variations, and register awareness of spoken versus written usage patterns. As noted in regard to lexicogrammatical learning in Liu and Jiang's (2009) study, finding patterns and rules becomes more evident to learners through the use of corpus-based materials. The rationale for inductive grammar exercises originates in the 1995 research of McCarthy and Carter with the concept of the three *I*s. The first *I* stands for illustration, which prompts consciousness raising through the examination of authentic data. The second *I* is for interaction, meaning learners' discuss their observations and share opinions. The third *I* represents induction, which involves "encouraging learners to draw conclusions" or making one's own rule for a particular feature (McCarthy & Carter, 1995). Skeptics have criticized corpus-based learning for its association with an inductive approach, which they argue may not appropriate for all learners (Flowerdew, 2009). This criticism serves to point out the vital importance of the teacher to know her/his learners, select material and scaffold activities appropriately.

## ACTIVITIES FOR YOUR CLASSROOM

The following sections showcase classroom activities designed from COCA corpus data. Each activity below includes steps to implement corpus data into pedagogy. They also include research-based rationale for their use.

### Inductive Grammar Exercise for Beginners: *Hear* vs. *Listen To*

Inspired by the work and empirical evidence supporting inductive approaches to learning grammar (Smart, 2014), this first activity uses concordance lines in an inductive grammar activity (see Appendix 1, Inductive Grammar Activity, for the handout of concordance lines for this exercise). To start this activity, conduct a search for the word, *hear* and another for the word, *listen*. As we know, these two synonymous words have distinctive syntactic features, which often cause errors for early learners. Each search will generate one page of concordance lines for each verb. Present the two pages to the students who then use the concordance lines for the verb *hear* juxtaposed with concordance lines for the verb *listen*. First, ask students to read the lines and share their insights, any observations and/or comments. Steer students toward noticing the word *to* following the verb *listen* to identify the pattern and induce the rule.

## For Intermediate Level Students

You can follow the same procedure as above: conduct searches and extract exemplary concordance lines to illustrate semantic differences in verb patterns, for example. Concordances highlight differences in verb patterns, e.g., *stop* plus a gerund versus *stop* plus the infinitive form of the verb. The concordance lines can help students induce verb patterns which change meaning, e.g., *stop smoking* versus *stop to smoke*. This will also work with the oft-confused adjectives ending in *-ing* and *-ed* such as *interesting* vs. *interested* or *bored vs. boring.*

## For Advanced Learners

Concordance lines can provide an opportunity to raise awareness of register, rhetorical mode, genre, and socio-cultural nuances. Concordance lines also offer an opportunity for learners to make inductive insights about register considerations. Here is one example activity designed to increase register awareness. When introducing new idioms, for example, concordance lines allow increased awareness of idioms' authentic use in context. For example, the idiom *in the long run,* which was mentioned in Chen and Baker's (2010) research. In that study, corpus analysis revealed a learner's repeated use of the spoken idiom in academic writing. Conduct a few searches for idiomatic phrases such as *in the long run* or phrases that are distinctive to a particular register. For this activity, it is important to hide or remove the source column from your handouts of concordance lines. After collecting several concordance lines for each idiom and/or phrase, cut the lines apart and give them to the students one at a time. Ask students to guess or discuss as a class, or in groups, the potential sources of each and to justify each answer. After some discussion and thoughtful engagement, ask students if this idiomatic phrase generally occurs in spoken or written form. Lead students in a discussion about register, asking if each phrase is appropriate in spoken or written registers. Finally, provide the frequency statistics for each to demonstrate the disparity of use between registers. This activity could also be used to raise awareness of genre or discipline specific features of academic writing. (See Appendix 2, Register Awareness Activity, for an example worksheet).

The activities above are just a few examples of concordance line use in classroom activity/materials creation. Research demonstrates that there are numerous ways to use concordances in the classroom. In sum, concordance lines offer:

- Extensive authentic examples of words and phrases in context.
- Ready made cloze (by deleting keyword).
- Opportunities for semantic and syntax induction.
- Noticing of differences across register and genre.

### Collocation Game for Multiple Levels: Family Feud

Flowerdew's (2003) study revealed that student writers used (and overused) the verbs *make, create,* and *be* while professional writers employed a wider range of verbs including causal verbs such as *arise, attribute,* and *derive.* This research finding inspired the creation of a "Family Feud" style game in which the instructor extracts a collocation list of verbs (in base form) which occur before the noun *problem.* For this activity, run a collocation search to determine which verbs most frequently collocate with the noun *problem* in academic writing (select the additional parameter of academic writing) and select frequency list for the data display. The corpus provides an ordered list of verbs. This search produces the following ordered list of the top ten verbs: *solve, face, address, experience, identify, see, pose, cause, create* and *discuss.*

This list of the top ten verb collocations is all you need to create the game. Using the board or projection screen, write the list of collocations horizontally starting with the most frequently occurring verb at the top. Then, cover each of the words with a paper box (or digital one) with a point value displayed. The highest frequency collocation is worth the highest point value, say 1000, and so on until the 10th, *discuss,* is worth only 100 points. The direction to the students states: Which verbs collocate with the noun *problem* in academic writing? Two teams of students take turns submitting one answer with the instructor revealing the word hidden beneath the point value as they choose correctly.

As a follow-up exercise, have the students use the uncovered boarded list to complete an evaluation exercise such as grouping the words semantically as positive, negative, or neutral. Also, it will be helpful to offer the full concordance lines for each verb as a model prior to asking students to produce their own sentences with each collocation. This type of game can be used for any collocations and/or parts of speech, e.g., the noun *reader* preceded by an adjective. An instructor can tailor his/her choices of collocations to those which are problematic to his/her class or are featured in the lesson/book, as an extension or review activity. Another game which is easily created from collocation lists is "One of these things does not belong." In this game, students identify one of the four words provided that is not a collocation of a given word.

The above activities are corpus-informed, or data-driven, based on research described in the literature review (Ashouri, Arjmandi, & Rahimi, 2014; Flowerdew, 2003; Smart, 2014). As a critical and practical consumer of research studies, I noted the issues and findings which echoed and addressed my own students' needs. With these activities, you can use corpora in your classroom in the following ways:

1. To generate a vocabulary word list from an authentic text.
2. To create a collocation activity based on parts of speech and word order.
3. To create an activity to promote register awareness of written vs. spoken forms.
4. To extract concordance lines to encourage inductive learning.

## CRITICISMS OF CORPORA

While the above research shows that corpus can be useful in pedagogy, why do teachers shy away? Despite a wealth of research showing the benefits of corpus data, criticisms and hesitations persist. In addition to doubts about complexity and coherence, opponents charge issues of decontextualization, lack of meaningfulness, size limitations, hindered accessibility, and the weaknesses of the computer technology itself. Much criticism is rooted in unfamiliarity with corpora and what this technology is capable of revealing. Teachers need not understand every aspect of this research nor utilize even a fraction of a corpus' capabilities in order to profit from corpora.

## Incomprehensible Data

Some opponents contend that it is not clear what to do with the data. While some early criticisms of corpus linguistics deemed the quantitative analysis of corpus data as "bean counting," casting doubt on its applications to much more than lists, prominent scholars in the field, such as Biber and Conrad (2001b), argue otherwise, asserting that corpus collected data provides educators with indispensable tools to counter the "unreliable intuition" of the text or test writer. Furthermore, pedagogical applications are made explicit in research focused on how to interpret corpus findings to make practical applications (Coxhead & Byrd, 2007). Numerous studies demonstrated that the language presented in textbooks prior to corpus research findings was often based on faulty intuition (Holmes, 1988). As a result of corpus-based research, "faulty intuition" has been replaced with authentic language and language usage patterns leading to major changes in materials creation. Top text publishers tout their corpus-informed vocabulary content (Folse, 2011) and grammatical sequencing choices (Liu & Jiang, 2009). Corpus linguistics has reshaped the practices of materials' developers and publishers. It is now common for text books to use corpus data to select key text vocabulary words, such as in the celebrated Cambridge series *Grammar & Beyond* which prominently advertises their corpus-driven content (Reppen & Gordon, 2011).

## Accessibility Issues

There are also drawbacks and limitations of corpora. These include difficulties in accessing or navigating learner corpora (Hinkel, 2001). As Römer and Wulff (2010) point out, the MICUSP exists as one of the few corpora of native speaker student writing. Additionally, corpora are limited in technical and specific areas. The Chen and Baker's (2010) study exemplifies a drawback of integrating corpora and L2 writing instruction, citing limited learner data in existence. Because learner corpora are still rather limited, comparing a learner corpus to a larger one can be problematic. The disparity in size may affect research results (Flowerdew, 2003). While these may be drawbacks to researchers, the ability to access, create, or conduct research in learner corpora is not an obstacle for instructors. Teachers may access authentic and extensive language input gleaned from a mega corpus. Gaining access to the University of Michigan's corpora, for example, is relatively easy for teachers. It requires only email registration for the creation of a free account.

## Questioning Meaningfulness

Other critics point out that computer corpora are still computers and do not represent the whole picture or possibility of language use (Xiao, 2008). They argue that corpus data, concordance lines specifically, are decontextualized, which means they may not be transferable or meaningful to learners in communicative settings (Flowerdew, 2009). To counter this, Coxhead and Byrd (2007) advocate for teacher mediation in teaching lexical items and bundles alongside lexical functions to increase meaningful learning. In their pedagogically-centered article, they argue that collocation and lexical bundle should be part of learning a new word, as well as contextualization within a specific language function. Also, some critics point to an oversimplification of word frequencies as computers are unable to mark meaning frequencies or polysemy. However, Liu and Jiang's data (2009) demonstrate that learners experience heightened awareness of synonymy from the context of concordance lines. Participants also reported increased awareness of "connection between form, meaning, and pragmatics and the importance of context" (Liu & Jiang, 2009, p. 68).

Finally, we face the limits of computer technology. First, the inability to identify non-contiguous word patterns may result in missed data. Furthermore, there are limits on concordances across genres. For example, Flowerdew (2003) points out that the phrase "get rid of" would not be appropriate in technical writing, but it would be frequently found in concordances in writing of other types. A similar observation from Gardner and Davies (2007) concedes that corpus data does not provide everything. The semantic analysis conducted on the phrasal verbs to determine meaning is beyond the capabilities of computer corpora, requiring human analysis. "Subsequent semantic analyses show that these 100 high-frequency phrasal verb forms have potentially 559 variant- meaning senses" (Gardner & Davies, p. 353). The researchers suggest that a sort of semantic tag is necessary in order for corpus data to provide a complete picture. This criticism points to potential improvements to corpus technology along with re-emphasizing the vital role of the teacher. Flowerdew (2009) tackles many of the above criticisms, arguing that for these very reasons, this work requires "pedagogic mediation" (Flowerdew, 2009, p. 403). If publishers have embraced corpora, can't educators too? Like any pedagogical tool, the teacher is central to making the materials meaningful and the learning experience context rich.

While some of the criticisms may hold merit, corpora as a pedagogical tool has profound benefits for teaching in the language classroom. It is not too complicated for teachers for three reasons: First, TESOL/TEFL teachers do not have to familiarize themselves with the extensive body of research. Second, TESOL/TEFL teachers do not have to gain knowledge of the extent of its capabilities or its navigational tools. Finally, TESOL/TEFL teachers need not be corpus experts to use corpus to enhance their teaching. Language corpora can be a useful resource for teachers and learners as well as material writers and text publishers.

## CONCLUSION

The link between corpus-based research and teaching is based on the idea that corpus evidence suggests "which language items and processes are most likely to be encountered by language users, and which therefore may deserve more investment of time in instruction" (Kennedy, 1998, p. 281). Research in this area has expansive pedagogical potential. With future research and teacher education/professional development in this area of CALL and the continued progress of computer technology, corpora will make an even bigger contribution to teaching theory and pedagogy. Corpora are neither too complex nor too decontextualized to use in the TESOL classroom. Teachers just need training. There is an urgent need for professional development and a call for focus in academic preparation programs. Training in using corpora is especially relevant as availability and accessibility of corpus data to practicing teachers increases. Corpus-informed classroom activities offer ESL/EFL teachers multiple ways to make their coursework authentic and therefore more meaningful to students learning language. The specific pedagogical activities outlined in this chapter are just a starting point for strategies and techniques to implement corpus data in your classroom.

## REFERENCES


Ashouri, S., Arjmandi, M., & Rahimi, R. (2014). The impact of corpus-based collocation instruction on Iranian EFL learners' collocation learning. *Universal Journal of Educational Research*, *2*(6), 470–479.

Biber, D., & Conrad, S. (2001a). Multi-dimensional analysis and the study of register variation. In S. Conrad & D. Biber (Eds.), *Variation in English: Multidimensional Studies* (pp. 3–12). London: Longman.

Biber, D., & Conrad, S. (2001b). Quantitative corpus-based research: Much more than bean counting. *TESOL Quarterly*, *35*(2), 331–336. doi:10.2307/3587653

Biber, D., Conrad, S., & Cortes, V. (2004). If you look at…: Lexical bundles in university teaching and textbooks. *Applied Linguistics*, *25*(3), 371–405. doi:10.1093/applin/25.3.371

Chen, Y. H., & Baker, P. (2010). Lexical bundles in L1 and L2 academic writing. *Language Learning & Technology*, *14*(2), 30–49.

Cobb, T. (2002). *Web Vocabprofile* [An adaptation of Heatley, Nation & Coxhead's (2002) *Range*]. Retrieved from http://www.lextutor.ca/vp/

Conrad, S. (2009). Corpus-based research is too complicated to be useful for writing teachers. In J. Reid (Ed.), *Writing myths: Applying second language research to classroom teaching* (pp. 115–139). Ann Arbor, MI: University of Michigan Press.

Coxhead, A. (2000). A new academic word list. *TESOL Quarterly*, *3*(4), 213–238. doi:10.2307/3587951

Coxhead, A., & Byrd, P. (2007). Preparing writing teachers to teach the vocabulary and grammar of academic prose. *Journal of Second Language Writing*, *16*(3), 129–147. doi:10.1016/j.jslw.2007.07.002

Davies, M. (2008) *The Corpus of Contemporary American English: 520 million words, 1990-present*. Retrieved from http://corpus.byu.edu/coca/

Flowerdew, L. (2003). A combined corpus and systemic-functional analysis of the problem-solution pattern in a student and professional corpus of technical writing. *TESOL Quarterly*, *37*(3), 489–511. doi:10.2307/3588401

Flowerdew, L. (2009). Applying corpus linguistics to pedagogy: A critical evaluation. *International Journal of Corpus Linguistics*, *14*(3), 393–417. doi:10.1075/ijcl.14.3.05flo

Folse, K. (2011). Applying L2 lexical research findings in ESL teaching. *TESOL Quarterly*, *45*(2), 362–369. doi:10.5054/tq.2010.254529

Gardner, D., & Davies, M. (2007). Pointing out frequent phrasal verbs: A corpus-based analysis. *TESOL Quarterly*, *41*(2), 339–359. doi:10.1002/j.1545-7249.2007.tb00062.x

Granger, S. (2003). The international corpus of learner English: A new resource for foreign language learning and teaching and second language acquisition. *TESOL Quarterly*, *37*(3), 538–546. doi:10.2307/3588404

Granger, S. (2009). The contribution of learner corpora to second language acquisition and foreign language teaching. *Corpora and Language Teaching*, *33*, 13–32. doi:10.1075/scl.33.04gra

Hasko, V. (2013). Capturing the dynamics of second language development via learner corpus research: A very long engagement. *Modern Language Journal, 97*(S1), 1–10. doi:10.1111/j.1540-4781.2012.01425.x

Heatley, A., Nation, I. S. P., & Coxhead, A. (2002). *Range and frequency programs.* Retrieved from http://www.victoria.ac.nz/lals/staff/paul-nation.aspx

Hinkel, E. (2001). Matters of cohesion in L2 academic texts. *Applied Language Learning, 12*(2), Ill-132.

Holmes, J. (1988). Doubt and certainty in ESL textbooks. *Applied Linguistics, 9*(1), 21–44. doi:10.1093/applin/9.1.21

Kennedy, G. (1998). *An introduction to corpus linguistics.* London: Longman.

Leech, G. (1998). Preface. In S. Granger (Ed.), *Learner English on computer.* London: Longman.

Lessard-Clouston, M. (2012). Word Lists for vocabulary learning and teaching. *CATESOL Journal, 24*(1), 287–304.

Liu, D., & Jiang, P. (2009). Using a corpus-Based lexicogrammatical approach to grammar instruction in EFL and ESL contexts. *Modern Language Journal, 93*(1), 61–78. doi:10.1111/j.1540-4781.2009.00828.x

McCarthy, M., & Carter, R. (1995). Spoken grammar: What is it and how can we teach it? *ELT Journal, 49*(3), 207–218. doi:10.1093/elt/49.3.207

Read, J. (2004). Research in teaching vocabulary. *Annual Review of Applied Linguistics, 24*, 146–161. doi:10.1017/S0267190504000078

Reppen, R., & Gordon, D. (2011). *Grammar and Beyond Level 2 Student's Book.* Cambridge, UK: Cambridge University Press.

Römer, U., & Wulff, S. (2010). Applying corpus methods to written academic texts: Explorations of MICUSP. *Journal of Writing Research, 2*(2), 99–127. doi:10.17239/jowr-2010.02.02.2

Smart, J. (2014). The role of guided induction in paper-based data-driven learning. *ReCALL, 26*(2), 184–201. doi:10.1017/S0958344014000081

Xiao, R. Z. (2008). Theory-driven corpus research: Using corpora to inform aspect theory. In Corpus linguistics: An international handbook. Berlin, Germany: Mouton de Gruyter.

## ADDITIONAL READING

Aston, G., Bernardini, S., & Stewart, D. (Eds.). (2004). *Corpora and Language Learners.* Amsterdam, The Netherlands & Philadelphia, PA: Johns Benjamins. doi:10.1075/scl.17

Barker, F. (2004). Using corpora in language testing. *Modern English Teacher, 13*(2), 63–67.

Biber, D. (1988). *Variations across speech and writing.* Cambridge, United Kingdom: Cambridge University Press. doi:10.1017/CBO9780511621024

Biber, D., Conrad, S., & Reppen, R. (1998). *Corpus linguistics: Investigating language structure and use*. Cambridge, United Kingdom: Cambridge University Press. doi:10.1017/CBO9780511804489

Biber, D., Johansson, S., Leech, G., Conrad, S., & Finegan, E. (1999). *The Longman grammar of spoken and written English*. Harlow, United Kingdom: Pearson Education.

Boulton, A., & Landure, C. (2016). *Using corpora in language teaching, learning and use*. Retrieved from http://apliut.revues.org/5433. DOI: 10.4000/apliut.5433

Conrad, S. (2000). Will corpus linguistics revolutionize grammar teaching in the 21st century? *TESOL Quarterly*, *34*(3), 548–560. doi:10.2307/3587743

Conrad, S. (2002). Corpus linguistic approaches for discourse analysis. *Annual Review of Applied Linguistics*, *22*, 75–95. doi:10.1017/S0267190502000041

Fan, M. &, Xu, F. (2006). Enhancing the learning of business English using corpora: A case study. *IATEFL/BESIG Business Issues, 1,* 6-8.

Granger, S. (2003). The international corpus of learner English: A new resource for foreign language learning and teaching and second language acquisition research. *TESOL Quarterly*, *37*(3), 538–546. doi:10.2307/3588404

Granger, S. (2012). Learner corpora. In C. A. Chapelle (Ed.), *The encyclopedia of applied linguistics* (pp. 3235–3242). Oxford, United Kingdom: Wiley-Blackwell.

Granger, S., Hung, J., & Petch-Tyson, S. (Eds.). (2002). *Computer learner corpora, second language acquisition, and foreign language teaching* (Vol. 6). Amsterdam, The Netherlands & Philadelphia, PA: John Benjamins Publishing. doi:10.1075/lllt.6

Higgins, J., & Johns, T. (1984). *Computers in Language Learning*. London, England: Collins ELT.

Johns, T. (1997). Contexts: The background, development and trialling of a concordance-based CALL program. In A. Wichmann, S. Fligelstone, T. McEnery, & G. Knowles (Eds.), *Teaching and language corpora* (pp. 100–115). New York, NY: Addison Wesley Longman.

OKeeffe, A., & Farr, F. (2003). Using language corpora in initial teacher education: Pedagogic issues and practical applications. *TESOL Quarterly*, *37*(3), 389–418. doi:10.2307/3588397

Sinclair, J. M. (Ed.). (2004). *How to use corpora in language teaching* (Vol. 12). Amsterdam, The Netherlands & Philadelphia, PA: John Benjamins Publishing. doi:10.1075/scl.12

*The British National Corpus*, version 3 (BNC XML Edition). (2007). Distributed by Oxford University Computing Services on behalf of the BNC Consortium. Retrieved from: http://www.natcorp.ox.ac.uk/

Tognini-Bonelli, E. (2001). *Corpus linguistics at work* (Vol. 6). Amsterdam, The Netherlands & Philadelphia, PA: John Benjamins Publishing. doi:10.1075/scl.6

## KEY TERMS AND DEFINITIONS

**Collocation:** Two words that frequently occur together or near each other in natural language use.
**Concordance Line:** A line of text displaying a keyword in context within a corpus.
**Corpora:** The plural of corpus.
**Corpus:** A digital collection of language in use; includes written texts and spoken utterances.
**Corpus Linguistics:** The analysis of language using corpus data.
**Lexical Bundles:** Multi-word units which serve particular language functions.
**Polysemy:** Multiple meanings for one word; the meaning depends on context and use.
**Semantics:** The study of word meanings in context.

## APPENDIX 1

## Inductive Grammar Activity

Read the lines below (Figures 1 and 2). What do you notice about the words *hear* and *listen*. Talk to your group about your ideas.

Examples extracted from COCA. Davies, Mark. (2008-) *The Corpus of Contemporary American English: 520 million words, 1990-present*. Available online at http://corpus.byu.edu/coca/.

*Figure 1. Examples Using "Hear"*

sign on the floor that opened our door to the belowground world. I could **hear** the far-off music already, flute, harp, fiddle, and drum, and

from one of his wars, " he says and he makes sure everyone can **hear** him, and I guess I'm thinking about the stupid joke because I mess

traitorous, will unmask the subtle undersounds of existence one is not ordinarily supposed to **hear**: breath, heartbeat, the purr of the CPU-processing, of course, very

, Tom. He's a good boy. Thanks... " # He could **hear** himself breathing in the telephone and his voice sounded spurious and thick. # "

" Tell me, MacAdam, " he said loudly enough for the onlookers to **hear**, " do they even play the sport where ye're from? " #

sat on the sagging couch and read. RabiA lesson was slow going-I could barely **hear** her whispered words. At one point, I noticed her gazing at the photo

! " And they look at each other and can't grasp it. They **hear** steps. That is the hunter. Little Red Ridinghood runs to meet him outside

anyone's shoulders. " // " I agree, but I'm glad to **hear** you verbalize it just the same. " // " Well, that's how

helper, out in the bays, began running the compressor. " Can't **hear** you, " said Alva. " Where's Homer? " " Not here

... # HELEN # What's that music. It's Abba. I can **hear** it. It's Abba. # RUBEN # What's Abba? M.J. Bunch of

hug. " Monique, your friend will be fine. " # I can **hear** a mob coming, but my parents are more interested in Hine. Papa climbs

STREET. # ACE (V.O.) #... thing is, they go and **hear** all this stuff about Las Vegas and the casinos and the suitcases, and that

LaVerne and her mother shouted more and more lies about me. No one would **hear** my pleas of innocence. My fears were confirmed when the tough policeman ordered me

like nothing he had ever seen before. And he wanted to hear it; **hear** the loud roar of the car engines, the soft, tinkling laughter of the

n't kill yourself. It's a mortal sin. " # She smiled to **hear** religious terms on my lips. # " You'll have your house here at

the trigger; he couldn't use it even if he tried. Suddenly we **hear** a metallic CLICK, which registers with unnatural amplification, as - Clarice reacts,

you there, gentlemen-anytime. " Matthews bowed curtly and strode away. Rokey could **hear** him whistling happily to himself, an irritating sound. Ray asked if the message

the bathroom. Finch, still restraining, listens for a moment... only to **hear** the CLICK-CLICK-CLICK of heels. INT. EAST GREAT FALLS HIGH - MAIN HALL -

in her window every morning. It's shining in now, and she can **hear** him let himself out the door and set down his lunch bucket on the step

other bad, locked in eternal combat. " You go south to death! **Hear** me, Father Sun! I, Crow Caller, have your Dream. Feel

has sagged in the firestorm. Small skulls look accusingly from the ash-drifts. WE **HEAR** the distant echo of children's voices... playing and laughing in the sun.

animals upstairs. Nearly two hours passed. Jeremy was starving, and he could **hear** Molly's stomach grumbling. He was ready to end the spying mission when a

Evidently Clayton's North Shore wedding was progressing. Fred hadn't been happy to **hear** of the police detectives' concentration on Smykal's missing painting, but there was

*Figure 2. Examples Using "Listen"*

superior to the one she played at home. And Selina asked if she might **listen** to the music rather than playing whist, being an indifferent card player at best

, halt a star in its wandering. But you render me powerless. Now **listen**. Only I can bring you through my father's trials alive. What will

Vi was only nine, and not handy. # " We'll manage. **Listen** up, Nell -- if you don't want Jack, I'll tell #

# Zavitz, what? You want your old job back? # ZAVITZ # **Listen** to me -- # ALFONSO # Tired of chasing squirrels around the park? #

she is half-raised on her knees while Esther stands over her and says, " **Listen** to me, Shena Lena. Today you will shop for me. Tonight we

crowded together on the highway to watch me pass by. I have had to **listen** to all classes of commentary. But now (it has already been five good

I'd never heard her voice before. Contralto, soothing, very pleasant to **listen** to. The sort of voice that makes you turn around to find the source

" I'll see who's about, " replied Daine. " Oh, **listen** -- the pack's coming. "? We must take your word for that

now. I wonder what became of her. In English that I have to **listen** to closely to understand, Dinh talks for a while about the Khanh Hoa Hospital

became too much for me to take. I'd make the effort to go **listen** to gramophone records, but after only the first two or three phrases I'd

under the cover of night. More than once, Suzie had been forced to **listen** to sounds a mother should not have to, her own daughter writhing in some

to cry, but I made myself breathe hard. " Violet, honey. **Listen**. We have to. I wouldn't do it other-wise. Her voice sounded

the damn neighborhood is comin'. MURPHY All right, love ya ma. **Listen**, before ya go just give us the goods, eh? # CONNOR #

walk into Spanish III, coolly note the first boy to mock you, and **listen** for his name at roll call. Ben Robinson. You turn in your seat

done, " I assured her. " They're AFOSI.They didn't have to **listen**. Still, wasn't very polite. " Once she left, I did

. " # " I miss you, too, Jake. " # " **Listen**, I've got to go. " # " I love you. "

ceremony; another time they witness people handling snakes and talking in tongues. They **listen** to stories, true and folk, and keep to the back roads. They

her view. Sidney moves to the center of the jeep, trying hard to **listen** over her own RAPID BREATHING, every sound AMPLIFIED. Then she hears it,

world of objection swam in Nella's troubled eyes. " Will you not even **listen** to the dangers? " " I ken the perils... and their consequences.

bait, and after a moment she adds: " My children will learn to **listen** to God, and I don't want them taught evil. " I do

coming in first thing. # CRAIG # Enjoy. # LOTTE # Craig, **listen**, honey, I've been thinking... maybe you'd feel better if you

" she said. " There's no wrong way to move certain parts. **Listen** to mama. " Van Morrison's lovely burred baritone filled the air. Everybody

he was listening to on his Walkman. Then she added, " Could I **listen** for a minute? " As soon as she put on the earphones, she

at the end of a gentle rain, waiting for the storm to come. **Listen** to the air, as the trembling of events gets closer and closer. Let

## APPENDIX 2

### Register Awareness Activity

Work with a neighbor to decide if each line below is from a written academic text (W) or spoken (S). Discuss how you decided.

1. What he'd actually said was he was thinking they should *get rid of* that chair - it was an old kitchen table-style chair and had a rip in it.
2. The proportion increased to 68% by 2004. *Moreover*, when considering advanced mathematics courses (defined as " more challenging than algebra II...
3. Based on the *foregoing* conclusions, the following recommendations are made: # Teachers do not make sufficient use..
4. Costs exceed more than $300 billion annually *as a result* of medical care and lost productivity related to disabilities.
5. Stu's secret was only going to hurt everyone more *in the long run*. Of course, she'd assumed he'd be there in the morning
6. And I think it's very important that we *look into* climate change in our own planet right now. Don't get me wrong.

Examples extracted from COCA. Davies, Mark. (2008-) *The Corpus of Contemporary American English: 520 million words, 1990-present*. Available online at http://corpus.byu.edu/coca/.

# Chapter 9
# Teaching English Grammar in a Hybrid Academic ESL Course

**Tülay Dixon**
*University of Utah Asia Campus, South Korea*

**MaryAnn Christison**
*University of Utah, USA*

## ABSTRACT

*This study investigates whether hybrid instruction has a positive effect on the development of students' knowledge of English grammar and editing skills, as well as whether learners have positive perceptions of the hybrid design. The study was conducted in two sections of an English grammar and editing skills class. One section was designed as a hybrid course, while the other was a traditional face-to-face (f2f) class. To determine the effectiveness of hybrid instruction, a quasi-experimental design with a pre- and posttest was employed. To investigate learner perceptions of the hybrid design, learners completed a questionnaire and participated in a focus group. The results indicate that there was no significant difference between the two groups in terms of their knowledge of English grammar and editing skills after the treatment. The learners had positive perceptions of the hybrid design and also offered some suggestions for improving course effectiveness.*

## INTRODUCTION

According to the Institute for International Education (IIE), there are currently 1,043,839 international students studying in institutions of higher education (IHE) in the United States, and this number represents an increase of almost 100% from the 554,766 students from a decade ago in Academic Year 2005-06 (IIE, 2015). The trend is not unique to the United States but is consistent with other BANA countries (i.e., Britain, Australasia, and North America). The presence of an increasing number of second language (L2) users of English has impacted IHE in significant ways. Because most international students are second language (L2) academic English users, IHEs have found it necessary to develop specific courses to assist them in improving their academic English skills. The ability to use English effectively in academic settings demands advanced language proficiency (Hinkel, 2011, 2013; Weigle,

DOI: 10.4018/978-1-5225-2933-0.ch009

2002), and achieving this level of proficiency requires "focused instruction and concerted effort from both teachers and learners" (Hinkel, 2013, p. 4). Research has established strong positive correlations between students' abilities to perform well in academic environments and their proficiencies in grammar and writing (Byrd & Reid, 1998; Johns, 1997; Zhou, 2009). Furthermore, Celce-Murcia (1991) states that grammar instruction is essential for academic learners if they are to achieve their educational and professional goals in academic contexts. A high frequency of grammatical errors in L2 student writing makes the writing unacceptable to most university faculty, so it is critical that L2 English users develop effective skills in editing their academic writing.

Most English language teaching programs in IHE include courses in grammar and academic writing to help English learners achieve their professional goals; however, there are a number of different ways in which grammar courses are conceptualized and included in the curriculum. Grammar courses can be conceptualized as stand-alone courses very much like the four skills (i.e., reading, writing, speaking, and listening). In this type of approach to teaching grammar, there is a focus-on-forms or the deliberate teaching of grammar to produce an understanding of grammatical forms with the hope that it will lead L2 learners to use the forms correctly (Doughty, 2003). Another approach to teaching grammar is conceptualized as deriving from specific content, such as chemistry or engineering, as in content-based instruction (CBI) or content and language-integrated learning (CLIL). In such an approach the focus on grammatical structures is based on their use in written texts that are discipline specific. Another approach is called an integrated approach, as grammar is integrated into one of the four skills, such as writing. In the latter, the focus for grammar instruction is on the development of editing skills (i.e., the ability to correct grammatical errors in the context of one's own academic writing). The approach for teaching grammar that is the focus of the research in this chapter is the integrated approach.

The focus for the delivery of academic English courses has been the traditional face-to-face (f2f) model of teaching; however, with the increasing number of individuals worldwide who are interested in studying academic English at the tertiary level, English language teaching programs and other units that oversee academic English requirements in IHE are looking for more effective and efficient course delivery options, such as exploring the uses of computer technology. Computer technology has been used in education for more than two decades in language learning. The overarching term for talking about the use of computer technology to promote language learning is CALL (computer-assisted language learning). The term was defined by Levy (1997) as "the search for and study of applications of the computer in language teaching and learning" (p. 1). It embraces a wide-range of applications and approaches to teaching and learning foreign language (see Dudeney & Hockly, 2012 for a brief history of CALL). A combination of f2f teaching and CALL is most often referred to as blended learning, and the courses that result from this blending are called hybrid courses. In hybrid courses the f2f teaching time is reduced and replaced by online learning. Hybrid courses have been reported to be as effective as f2f language courses (Rubio & Thoms, 2012); however, little research is available to date that specifically focuses on academic English as a second language (ESL) hybrid courses, especially ESL hybrid courses for teaching English grammar using an integrated approach.

In addition to the scant research on hybrid courses in academic ESL contexts, there is a dearth of research on academic English learners' perceptions of hybrid courses in general and specifically relative to teaching English grammar using an integrated approach. Gage and Berliner (1992) refer to all the ways in which people think as cognition. As can be inferred from this definition, cognition includes a broad range of constructs that can affect learning, and in particular language learning (Borg, 2003). The term learner cognition is used to refer to the unobservable and cognitive dimensions of language learning—what language learners know, believe, and think about language learning and the relationships of the mental constructs to what learners do as learners in language classrooms. In other words, the thoughts and beliefs that learners have about language and language learning affect the process of second language acquisition. Therefore, it is important to investigate not only the effectiveness of the inclusion of online technologies on learning outcomes but also to determine what learners think about new models for learning.

## BACKGROUND

The use of computer technologies in education has grown at a remarkable pace in recent years, including in the area of foreign and second language (L2) learning (Reinders & White, 2011; The Sloan Consortium, 2005; Thomas, Reinders, & Warschauer, 2013). There is a range of delivery options available for L2 instructors who wish to make use of online technologies in their second and foreign language courses from the inclusion of supplemental online readings and media files that can be accessed through an external URL to the use of learning managements systems (LMSs) in which the administration, tracking, reporting, and the delivery of content are all available within the same software application. The use of these delivery options varies greatly among course designers and instructors. Perhaps the most significant difference is in the extent to which online technologies are used for providing support for primarily face-to-face (f2f) courses (i.e., web-facilitated courses or enhanced courses) or for the delivery of totally online courses with no f2f meetings (Murray & Christison, 2017; The Sloan Consortium, 2005).

Murray and Christison (forthcoming) propose five different course design formats: (1) web-facilitated or enhanced, (2) blended or hybrid, (3) flipped, (4) online with a synchronous component, and (5) asynchronous online. Enhanced or web-facilitated courses are primarily f2f courses that are supported by some course activity online. In hybrid (or blended) courses the key content is delivered in f2f classes; however, the online activities are substantially increased over the enhanced courses and the number of f2f meeting times is reduced. Picciano (2009) outlines characteristics of a blended course to include the integration of traditional f2f activities with online activities in a planned and pedagogically valuable manner. In addition, a portion of f2f time is replaced by the online activity. In a flipped course design, the key content is delivered online, while f2f time is devoted to discussion and problem solving, or in the case of L2 learning to interaction and practice of specific language features introduced online. There are two different course design options for totally online courses. One option requires that students meet regularly online at the same time. It is referred to as a totally online course with a synchronous option. The other option is called asynchronous because learners do not meet online at the same time. For the purposes of this chapter, we will use the term hybrid to include blended courses.

In recent years, the number of hybrid foreign language courses has been increasing, and the increase is due to a number of factors, such as budget cuts in foreign language programs together with the increase of enrollments in higher education, foreign language textbooks' that have readily available online components, access to technology, and the growing number of research studies that indicate hybrid language courses can be as effective as f2f courses (see Thoms, 2012). Key among those factors must be the "any time, any place affordance" (Murray & Christison, forthcoming) that the use of online technologies allows, thereby giving a greater number of learners access to foreign language classes and offering more flexibility in access and opportunities for autonomous and independent learning. At the same time, hybrid courses provide learners with the advantages traditionally associated with f2f classes, such as target language input from the teacher and opportunities for interaction and communication with peers.

The research study reported on in this chapter is designed to facilitate our understanding of hybrid English grammar courses, a largely understudied area in the field of CALL. To this end, it employs mixed methods in the design of the research to answer the following research questions.

1. Does hybrid/blended instruction have a positive effect on students' development of English grammar and editing skills?
2. What are the ESL students' perceptions of the hybrid/blended course design?

The study provides quantitative data to determine the effectiveness of a hybrid course in terms of students' gains in their knowledge of English grammar and qualitative data to explore the perceptions of students relative to the effectiveness of the course. By focusing the research questions on the apparent gap in the existing literature, the researchers hope to improve the use of online technologies in teaching academic ESL courses, specifically those courses that are focused on teaching English grammar using an integrated skills approach. As part of the University's requirements for the protection of human subjects, the study was reviewed and approved by the IRB and identified as a minimal risk study with a waiver of documentation of informed consent.

## METHODOLOGY

To answer the first research question, a quasi-experimental research design was employed as in Figure 1. The research was conducted in two sections of an academic ESL course that was devoted to teaching English grammar and editing skills at a university in the United States. One section of the course was designated as the control group. It met face-to-face (f2f) three times a week for 50 minutes. The other section was a hybrid course and was designated as the experimental group. It met f2f only once a week for 50 minutes, while rest of the time was spent participating in online activities through the University's LMS.

Data were collected from pre-and posttests. The pretest was used to determine if both groups (i.e., hybrid and f2f) were statistically equal in terms of their knowledge of English grammar and editing skills before instruction, while the posttest was used to determine if hybrid instruction had a positive effect on students' knowledge of English grammar and editing skills. The pre- and posttests were the same. The researchers did not believe that using the same test would pose a problem regarding practice effect (i.e., gains in scores that result when a learner is retested using the same instrument) because the time between the two tests was 15 weeks, and students had no knowledge that the test used for the pretest would also be used as the posttest.

The constructs that were being measured (i.e., knowledge of English grammar and editing skills) need to be defined within the parameter of this study. For the purposes of this study, knowledge of English grammar refers to one's knowledge of structures considered to be problematic for advanced academic English writers (see Folse, 2009). These structures include nouns, articles, verb tenses, prepositions, passive voice, participial adjectives, subject verb agreement, modals, gerunds, infinitives, adjective clauses, adverb clauses, noun clauses, conditionals, run-on sentences, sentence fragments, and sentences with comma splices. Collectively these structures, as they presented issues in learners' writing, comprise the

*Figure 1. Quasi-Experimental Research Design*

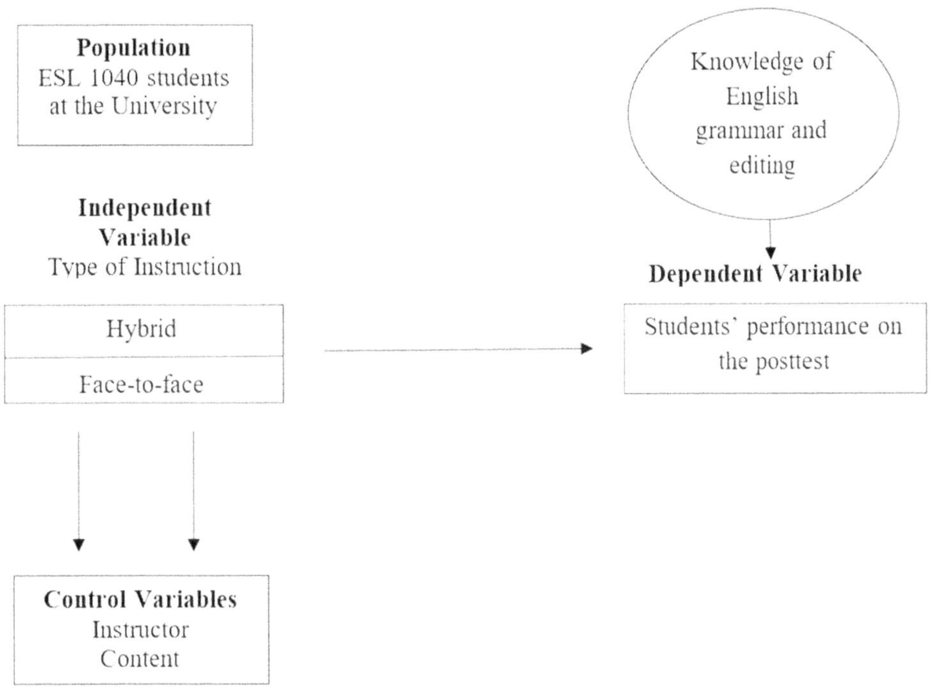


focus of instruction in the course for both the control and experimental groups. Editing skills can be defined as the ability to repair grammatical errors at the sentence and discourse levels. The ability to repair grammatical errors in this study was limited to the structures deemed problematic for advanced academic English writers as outlined in the course syllabus.

Controlled variables in the study were the instructor and content taught in both groups. Although the same instructor taught both sections and covered the same content in both groups, the teaching methods employed were different due to the differences between hybrid and f2f instruction. For example, the control group used the learning management system (LMS) only to submit homework and access the syllabus, while the hybrid group used it for learning course content through online activities and video lectures. A complete discussion of the curricular differences between the hybrid and f2f sections of course is beyond the scope of the chapter. The amount of time that learners in the hybrid course would have spent completing the online tasks and activities was intended to be equivalent to the time students would have spent learning the content in class (i.e., approximately 100 minutes per week). However, the amount of time students spent learning and practicing concepts outside of class was a variable for which we could not control.

To answer the second research question related to investigating student perceptions of their learning experiences in the hybrid course, students completed an online questionnaire (see Appendix 1) and joined a focus group (see Appendix 2), which was led by a professional facilitator at the University who had experience with focus groups. Using an external person to facilitate the focus group was important because the presence of the instructor could unduly influence the results. The focus group discussion was completed on the last day of class and lasted 40 minutes. On the same day, the questionnaire was given to students in the hybrid section. The students took the questionnaire with them and brought it back on the day of the final exam when the posttest was given.

The participants in the study were international students at the University who did not speak English as a mother-tongue and who had enrolled through the normal registration process in one of the two sections for this course. On the first day of class, students in the hybrid group were given information about what hybrid instruction was and were given the option of changing sections. In total, there were 17 students enrolled in the hybrid section and 25 in the f2f section; however, some students were absent on the day the pretest was given; only posttest data from the students who took the pretest were used. There were 13 students in the hybrid section and 19 in the f2f section who took both the pre- and posttests. The questionnaire data came from the 12 students who volunteered to complete it. All of the students in the hybrid group who participated in the questionnaire were male, and 91.7% were between the ages of 18-22 while 8.3% were between the ages of 22-24. The majority of the students were from China with 91.7% speaking Chinese as their mother tongue and 8.3% speaking Korean. Students with no experience taking hybrid or online courses made up 83.3% of the class, while 16.7% had previous experiences with either hybrid or online courses.

## RESULTS AND DISCUSSION

### Learner Pre- and Post-Test Data

The results of the pretest data show that there was no significant difference between the control and experimental groups (i.e., hybrid and f2f groups) in terms of their knowledge of English grammar and editing skills before treatment (see Table 1). A simple t-test was used to determine whether the difference between the mean scores was significant. The alpha decision level for this study was set to .05. There was no significant difference between the two groups as measured by the pretest; $t(30) = .392$, $p = .698$.

Because the pretest showed that the two groups were not significantly different in terms of their knowledge of English grammar and editing skills prior to treatment, the posttest data were also analyzed using a t-test. However, because of the difference between standard deviations (see Table 2), equal variances were not assumed, and t-test results were interpreted accordingly. The results showed that there was no significant difference between the two groups after the treatment; $t(30) = .628$, $p = .535$.

*Table 1. Pretest descriptive statistics*

| Groups | Number of Students | Mean Scores | Standard Deviation |
|---|---|---|---|
| Hybrid | 13 | 41.6154 | 10.59511 |
| F2F | 19 | 40.1053 | 10.79040 |

*Table 2. Posttest Descriptive Statistics*

| Groups | Number of Students | Mean Scores | Standard Deviation |
|---|---|---|---|
| Hybrid | 13 | 49.5385 | 6.66603 |
| F2F | 19 | 47.5789 | 9.77705 |

The results provide support for previous studies showing that hybrid courses for L2 and foreign language (FL) learning can be at least as effective as a traditional f2f class (Rubio & Thoms, 2012). Compared to the f2f course, the hybrid course seems to be a very promising format for teaching English grammar using an integrated model. In other words, the hybrid course was just as effective as the f2f course and allowed the L2 language users to take advantage of additional affordances offered through online learning, such as increased flexibility and ongoing access to learning materials.

## Learner Perceptual Data

To understand students' perceptions of the hybrid format, they completed a questionnaire and participated in a focus group. The questionnaire included three sections. Section A gathered data related to students' age, language background, hybrid or online course experience, and gender. Sections B and C used Likert-scale questions for gathering quantitative data about how students perceived the hybrid format and how they interacted with the online exercises set up on the LMS used at the University. The qualitative portion of the questionnaire included two open-ended questions, and the focus group was asked six primary questions (see Appendix 2). The categories or themes for analyzing the data were not set in advance; rather, categories or themes emerged from the data. In reporting the results, the categorical data resulting from an analysis of the open-ended questions and data from the focus group were considered against the backdrop of the data collected using Likert-scale questions in Sections B and C. In other words, the two sources of qualitative data were used to provide additional support for the perceptions that had already been identified in the Likert-scale questions.

Table 3 shows how students perceived the hybrid format in general and whether they were satisfied with the course or not. Students either "strongly agreed" or "agreed" with the three statements given in Table 3, which indicated that they were satisfied with the hybrid format, wanted to take another hybrid course, and found the hybrid format as effective as f2f courses.

Table 4 presents data related to students' perceptions of the online component in general. Once again, they "strongly agreed" or "agreed" with all four statements related to the organization of the online exercises, the ease of following the exercises, whether the video lectures were helpful, and whether the online experience gave them sufficient opportunities to practice English grammar and editing skills.

All the statements in Table 5 are deeply rooted in the concept of learner autonomy. Although learner autonomy has been defined differently over the years (Benson, 2013; Dickinson, 1987; Little, 1991), at the heart of all these definitions is the idea of students' taking charge of their own learning. Littlewood's (1999) distinction between proactive and reactive autonomy is useful in understanding learner autonomy in this study. According to Littlewood (1999), when students are proactively autonomous, they have

*Table 3. Perception of the Hybrid Format in General*

| Statements / Levels of Agreement | Strongly Agree | Agree | Disagree | Strongly Disagree |
|---|---|---|---|---|
| I am very satisfied with this hybrid course. | 41.7% | 58.3% | 0 | 0 |
| I would like to take another hybrid course. | 58.3% | 41.7% | 0 | 0 |
| I believe hybrid courses are as effective as face-to-face courses. | 33.3% | 66.7% | 0 | 0 |

*Table 4. Students' Perceptions of the Online Component*

| Statements / Levels of Agreement | Strongly Agree | Agree | Disagree | Strongly Disagree |
|---|---|---|---|---|
| The modules online were easy to follow. | 58.3% | 41.7% | 0 | 0 |
| The online video lectures helped me with English grammar and editing. | 50% | 50% | 0 | 0 |
| The online exercises helped me practice English grammar and editing skills. | 75% | 25% | 0 | 0 |
| I had enough opportunities to practice English grammar and editing. | 41.7% | 58.3% | 0 | 0 |

greater flexibility in that they determine their objectives, and method of study and evaluation; however, when students have reactive autonomy, they work independently to achieve the objectives the teachers set for them. The ultimate goal for the students would be to move from reactive to proactive autonomy and to become life-long learners.

In CALL, there is an emphasis on student-centered activities that require students to work independently and autonomously and take responsibility for their own learning; consequently, hybrid courses are conducive to promoting autonomy, especially reactive autonomy, as they allow students flexibility, while at the same time guiding them through the learning process using an LMS. Table 5 offers data on students' perceptions of the features that promote learner autonomy and distinguish hybrid course design from f2f courses, such as whether the flexible schedule that online instruction affords was perceived to be helpful, whether ongoing access to video lectures was useful, and whether working individually at their own pace was important. The majority of the responses given by the students were "strongly agree" and "agree."

The decrease in the f2f time was perceived to be a positive characteristic of the hybrid design. Analyses of data from the questionnaire and the focus group showed that students in the hybrid group appreciated having more autonomy and flexibility, stating that they could study wherever and whenever they desired and could spend as much time as they needed completing the online exercises or reviewing the video lectures. In the focus group, one student expressed that he liked the freedom that the hybrid course af-

*Table 5. Students' Perceptions of the Distinguishing Features of Hybrid Course Design*

| Statements / Levels of Agreement | Strongly Agree | Agree | Disagree | Strongly Disagree |
|---|---|---|---|---|
| I enjoyed having control over my schedule. (Being able to study online whenever and wherever I wanted.) | 75% | 25% | 0 | 0 |
| It was helpful to have access to the video lectures all the time so that I could watch them whenever I needed. | 50% | 41.7% | 8.3% | 0 |
| It was good to be able to work individually at my own speed. | 50% | 50% | 0 | 0 |
| I spent more time thinking about English grammar during the online discussions, assignments, and exercises than I would have in a face-to-face class environment. | 50% | 41.7% | 8.3% | 0 |

forded, "we just have one day per week for class. I can study home . . . and I like that." Another student from the focus group added that learning online did not interfere with his understanding of the material because "[they] can meet with the instructor if [they] have any questions. So, that doesn't interfere." The flexibility that the hybrid course allowed was a theme running through the data from the focus group, which supports previous research showing that learner autonomy is the most salient feature of the learners' experiences (Murray, 1999).

It should also be acknowledged that 8.3% of the students did not spend more time thinking about English grammar during the online discussions, assignments, and exercises than they would have in a face-to-face class environment. This result is surprising because the time to think about the concepts during the online activities was one of the affordances of the hybrid design for helping students develop and improve their knowledge of English grammar and then incorporate this knowledge into their own writing. Because the online activities provided explicit instruction and also allowed students to determine the amount of time they felt they needed to focus on the structures, it was assumed that students would spend more time thinking about English grammar.

The decrease in f2f time, which was perceived to be positive, also meant that there would be fewer opportunities for f2f interaction. The limited f2f interaction could possibly lead to difficulties in creating a sense of community in the classroom. To this end, the questionnaire included a statement designed to help the researchers understand students' perceptions of community in hybrid courses. Responses to the question, "The course created a sense of community among students that was comparable to a regular face-to-face classroom," showed that 75% agreed with the statement and 8.3% strongly agreed. Nevertheless, 16.7% strongly disagreed with the statement. Data from the open-ended questions may provide some insight into students' negative perceptions. For example, one student stated that he could not make friends in the class. In addition some students in the focus group commented on the fact that they did not interact with their peers outside of the class. Failure to create a sense of community in the hybrid course for these students could be attributed to the fact that there were not sufficient opportunities for students to work together f2f to create a community, as the class met f2f only once a week for 50 minutes. If creating a sense of community is considered an important factor in promoting student learning in hybrid courses, then course designers and instructors need to consider ways of developing community among L2 learners that do not rely solely on f2f interaction, such as online activities that ask students to work together to complete semester long projects or activities that create opportunities for students to learn more about one another.

Qualitative data from the open-ended questions and from the focus group supported the perceptions of students from the questionnaire data in Table 5. The communication between the students and the instructor, as well as the communication among the students, were asynchronous during the online days. Because there was no synchronous communication on-line, the students indicated that they could study without worrying about time limitations, which are usually set by teachers in f2f courses. The online portion of a hybrid course is similar to an individualized learning experience in that the students indicated that they were able to make some of the decisions about learning for themselves instead of having the teacher make the decisions for them. Students in this study also stated that they enjoyed being able to study whenever and wherever they wanted because everything was available through the LMS, and no synchronous communication was needed. The fact that students could work at their own pace also allowed them to spend more time thinking about each online activity in preparation for the f2f class.

Students in this study considered asynchronous form of communication an advantage, especially for L2 learners who have a hard time interacting with others f2f. During the online learning in the hybrid course, students could work online without needing to communicate orally with the teacher or peers. The opportunity to communicate through writing is an important component of the online activities for the hybrid course design and can help students realize their L2 writing potential in a way that f2f classes cannot.

There were also some disadvantages associated with asynchronous communication online. First, during the focus group one student expressed that he did not like the fact that he was never able to ask questions to the teacher immediately when he had a question, and he felt that sending an email to the teacher or waiting for the f2f days to get an answer was tedious. His perception may be related to his individual preferences as a student; however, it is important to point out that when students need help and assistance in learning, there should be mechanisms that allow them to receive the help they need during the learning process. As the focus group data show, hybrid course design may not be appropriate for all learners, and students who typically have needs for f2f feedback from instructors would probably perform better in a f2f traditional classroom where they could work with their peers and the teacher through synchronous communication (Chapelle & Heift, 2009).

Because of the reduced f2f time in the hybrid course, the researchers were interested in whether students were able to receive the individualized attention they needed in a hybrid course design. In response to the statement, "I was able to get individualized attention from the instructor when I needed it," 66.7% responded with "strongly agree" and 33.3% with "agree," and none of the students responded in the "disagree" and "strongly disagree" categories. Providing timely feedback to students on their online assignments is also an important feature of hybrid courses. About two-thirds of the students in this study responded that they strongly agreed with the statement that they received timely feedback on their assignments, while the remaining one-third agreed to this statement.

One of the factors that is considered crucial in L2 acquisition is feedback. Through feedback students notice the differences between their own interlanguage and the target language that is used by more proficient users or native speakers (Goertler, 2012). The hybrid format was perceived as helpful in that it not only allowed students to work on the online exercises at their own pace but also had the potential to provide them with immediate feedback as soon as they submitted their answers.

Students' perceptions of the feedback they received as a result of the online exercises also provided important insight about course design. Some online exercises did not have detailed explanations as to why an answer was correct or incorrect. The reason for this was due to the fact that there was a limited amount of time for the development of online materials. However, it seems that students appreciated the exercises that provided them with explanations and feedback on their answers to the quizzes. In the focus group, Students 5 and 10 stated that they needed and wanted explanations and feedback for all of the online exercises and appreciated the immediacy of the feedback. Student 10 wrote that it was especially frustrating when the ". . . assignment answer is not clear [to me] which means I don't know why to choose this one. And [the LMS] just give[s the] correct answer."

Perceptual data from the questionnaire pertaining to feedback from the online activities were also supported by data from the focus group. Some students indicated that there were no explanations for some of the online exercises. One student stated, "I think [t]hat is not helpful. Hmm . . . There are not explanations after the answer. They are just answers. There are a few explanations why we should choose this answer." That students paid attention to the feedback available in the online exercises and used the explanations and feedback to promote their own learning is itself an important piece of information for instructors of hybrid courses to have.

In a hybrid course design the relationship between online and f2f learning must be a direct one; therefore, the researchers believed that it was important to determine students' perceptions of this relationship. The last statement in Section B of the questionnaire asked students whether the f2f days helped them practice the content they had studied online. About two-thirds of the students marked "strongly agree" and the remaining "agree," indicating that they had noticed the relationship. Some students in the focus group commented on the complementary relationship between the f2f and online days. One student agreed that f2f days complemented the online days when he said, "I like that the activities in class were related to the [online] assignments and the lecture we took before."

The researchers were also interested in gathering information about how students used some of the online components in the LMS, particularly the recorded video lectures, as video lectures are intended to deliver content to the students that they would normally get in the f2f lectures. The lectures that were done via video also allowed students to watch them at their own pace, thereby providing more flexibility. It is important for teachers and course designers to have information about how students perceive online videos of lectures because making recorded videos is a rather labor intensive task for instructors. If students perceive them as helpful and if they were actually using them, it is worth the effort. When asked about the extent to which they watched the videos, 83.3% of the students said they "always" or "usually" watched them; still 16.7% said they only "sometimes" watched them.

An analysis of the qualitative data from the open-ended questions also suggests that students perceived the videos as useful for their learning. Student 7 stated, "I can have time to look for something about the class when I take it. I can stop it anytime." Another student wrote the following:

*Also, the online teaching videos provide us with opportunities of taking detailed notes. In traditional classes, students, especially those who write carefully and slowly like me, often don't have enough time to take detailed notes because the teacher has to finish the content he or she has prepared before the class and they usually don't leave much time for students to take note. (Student 11)*

The same student offered suggestions for the improvement of the video lectures.

*I think you can also divide the videos into some shorter videos, each with a clear topic. Usually, we got a video of 20, or 30 minutes in a module which includes all the contents. That can be difficult to find a specific topic. Also, please don't divide them into too many parts because it will be tedious to keep changing videos. (Student 11)*

In the focus group, students also commented on the video lectures by pointing out that they always had access to the video lectures, so they could watch them as many times as they desired. One student commented on this fact when he said, "I like the online lectures because if we don't understand, we can watch it again and again." In the open-ended questions and in the focus group that they found the video lectures helpful and stated that they were able to stop the video lectures, take notes easily, and watch the videos several times if they needed to. However, we note that 8.3% of the students who filled out the questionnaire did not share the points of view related to the time spent learning online and the helpfulness of the video lectures.

Because the online course format provides students with increased flexibility, it also requires that students must manage their time and take more of the responsibility for their own learning. Many of the online exercises provided students with the correct answers or examples of appropriate responses. These resources were included so that after students had completed the exercises or quizzes they could check their answers, as the purpose was to promote learning. When asked about how honest they were with themselves in responding to the online exercises, 100% of the students said they were "always" or "usually" honest, which indicates to the researchers that the students in their study perceived their behaviors to be consistent with the intended use of the online activities. When asked whether they finished the online module before the f2f class, 92.7% said they "always" or "usually" did; however, when they were asked *when* they finished the module, one-third (33.3%) admitted that they finished the night before the f2f class. These responses indicate that students at this stage in their educational pursuits can benefit from deadlines throughout the course to guide their online learning. The responses also seem to indicate that some of students may not have benefitted from consistent and regular interaction with the content but relied on intensive last minute work.

All of the students in this study indicated that they "always" or "usually" participated fully during the in-class activities, read the instructor's comments on their assignments carefully, and managed their time responsibly. In responding to the statement, "When I didn't understand something, I searched for the answer (e.g., searching online, asking the instructor)," 16.7% responded by stating they only "sometimes" searched for the answers.

Student 11 made the connection between a student's personality (i.e., conscientiousness, motivation) and being successful in the hybrid format by saying the following:

*Human beings are inclined to be lazy. The face-to-face class is a kind of force that pushes students to study. Since the class is online, the only thing that can push a student to study is his or her own self-discipline. But for most students who are not so excellent, this kind of force is very, very weak.*

To take full advantage of the affordances that online technologies provide in terms of flexibility, students in hybrid courses must be conscientious learners and take responsibility for their own learning. When students take responsibility for their own learning, having autonomy in the learning process can foster learning and increase motivation. However, as Student 11 also stated, not every student can stay on top of things, and some tend to postpone completing tasks to the very last minute, which are behaviors that can affect one's learning in a negative way.

Some students were not motivated to work on the online activities because only 30% of their final grade came from the online exercises. During the focus group, one student believed that he would be more motivated to finish the online activities if they were worth more points. Thus, increasing the weight of the online exercises could help motivate students extrinsically during the online days.

Student 11 then recommended a solution that would help students better manage their time during the online days. He recommended that the due dates be scheduled periodically throughout the week instead of allowing students to work on the online activities until the f2f class.

*For deadlines, I think you can separate them, and not make everything due on Wednesday. You can make several homework terms due on every day to keep the students to study every day. If things are accumulated to the only due day, I don't think they will really work hard on understanding things. I think all they want to do is to finish the homework as quickly as they can before the due time instead of really remembering and understanding things.*

Following the Likert-scale questions, there were two open-ended questions. The first question asked students to focus on how the hybrid course compared to a traditional face-to-face class, and the second one asked students to focus on what they might change in the course. In response to the first question, students distinguished the hybrid course from traditional f2f courses in several ways. First, all the students but four commented on hybrid courses' "any time, any place affordance" (Murray & Christison, forthcoming), allowing for much appreciated flexibility. In addition, students also mentioned that hybrid courses were useful in helping students manage anxiety. Third, students commented on the immediate feedback they were able to receive. Student 10 noted, "I can get faster feedback about what I did right or wrong," and Student 11 stated "as all the grades will be put on the [LMS] instantly, we can check them right after we finish the homework or exams and get detailed, personal feedbacks." A fourth way in which hybrid and traditional f2f courses were perceived as different by the students in this study was the increase in opportunities for participation in grammar practice activities and the accessibility of materials. For example, Student 5 stated, "The hybrid course is better than traditional face-to-face class because I can do more practice on [the LMS], and it really improved my grammar," Student 8 wrote, "I can easily review things on [the LMS]. Everything is there. Very convenient."

Responses to the second question, "What would you change in this course? Why?"are included in the recommendations and are combined with recommendations based on the observations and experiences of the researchers.

## RECOMMENDATIONS

Students indicated that the length of the f2f sessions in relationship to online instruction should be carefully considered. For f2f days to be useful, they should be long enough to allow for sufficient interactive practice opportunities relative to the main concepts taught in the module. In the focus group, one student expressed the fact that he wanted to practice everything that he studied online during the f2f sessions; however, he felt that he was able to practice only a small portion of the online information during the f2f class time.

The second recommendation relates to helping students take responsibility for their own learning by providing structure and support for meeting deadlines and submitting materials in a timely fashion. In the hybrid course format in this study, students completed one module (i.e., unit) per week. The f2f classroom was designed so that new material was presented first online and then practiced and expanded on during the f2f sessions. New modules were unlocked immediately after the f2f classes; then, students had access to all materials from the module and were allowed to work on the assignments until the next f2f day. However, some students tended to postpone completing their assignment to the last night, which left them insufficient time to reflect on their learning before the next f2f classes. Student 11 suggested that the instructor include extrinsic motivational components into the course by dividing the modules into several parts and making each part due at a different time, thereby helping learners who are new to online learning understand the importance of completing work in a timely fashion. When implemented, this suggestion could also make a difference in students' study habits and motivate them to finish the assignments before the due dates, helping them become a more autonomous learner.

The third and fourth recommendations relate to designing and managing assessments for learning. Students pointed out that not all online exercises and quizzes included explanations as to why a particular answer was correct or incorrect. Although the online practice exercises that focused on the form of the grammatical structures did not require explanations, the ones that focused on the functions of the grammatical structures required explanations. Some of the students regarded the lack of explanations for the answers for the online exercises as a shortcoming. When the course is taught again, the explanations should be added for all the online exercises.

Data also revealed that some students did not use the quizzes as they were intended, in other words as assessments *for* learning. Rather than searching for the correct answers and seeing the process as an essential part of learning, they could not resist clicking the submit button to determine the correct answers and then using the correct answers when they took the quiz again. Instructors and course designers need to think about ways to encourage students to make learning, rather than simply obtaining correct answers, a priority.

The fifth recommendation is also relevant for course designers. Some students were not motivated to work on the online activities because they were only 30% of their final grade. During the focus group, one student believed that he would be more motivated to finish the online activities if they were worth more points. Thus increasing the weight of the online exercises could provide extrinsic motivation for some students to use the online activities appropriately.

The final recommendation is related to the use of videos and pre-recorded lectures. Data from students suggest that video lectures should be short or annotated to help learners find relevant information quickly. The video lectures in the hybrid course in this study were sometimes up to 30 minutes, which is too long to keep students actively involved. If longer videos are used, they should be annotated so that students can search and easily find information. One student suggested that the instructor divide the video lectures into shorter, more specific topics as another way of making the information in the videos more manageable and accessible.

## DIRECTIONS FOR FUTURE RESEARCH

A review of the literature on the use of the hybrid course design for L2 learners, as well as results of the current research, suggest that hybrid courses can be as effective as traditional f2f courses. In the case of the current study, effectiveness was determined by students' knowledge of English grammar and improvement in editing skills, as well as their perceptions of the learning experiences.

The research on hybrid course design in L2 and FL classes is still quite limited. The current study has contributed to our understanding of the usefulness of the hybrid model for teaching English grammar to L2 learners, but more data are needed. Future studies should include other types of language courses, English and other languages, as well as different approaches to teaching English grammar. The learners in this study were all advanced learners of English who were studying in IHEs. Research that focuses on learners of different proficiency levels and learners in different contexts will also help us in furthering our understanding of the effectiveness of the hybrid model for L2 learning.

Although this research study did not include an in depth presentation of the curriculum design features of hybrid courses, the design is important in considerations of effectiveness. In this study most of the pedagogical considerations were related to helping students manage their time better during the online activities and providing assessments for learning rather than to investigating the types of learning activities that would be most effective in promoting L2 acquisition. Future research needs to also focus on features of hybrid course design that may affect L2 learning.

The allocation time between the f2f and the online component in hybrid courses is a mediating factor in determining learner outcomes. How this allocation of time affects learning is also an important area of investigation for future research. The perceptual data in this study indicate that the ratio of f2f vs. online activities in this study was not as effective as it could have been and that, at least for some students, the time allocated for f2f teaching was insufficient. It is important to note that hybrid course design is constrained in part by scheduling and the allocation of space in IHEs. F2f courses are traditionally scheduled on certain days of the week and for certain amounts of time. These factors are predetermined by the IHE, so designers of hybrid courses must work within this structure. Research that focuses on finding the optimal balance between f2f and online activities and on learning outcomes is a much-needed area of investigation.

There is evidence to indicate that hybrid courses may not be beneficial for all L2 learners. However, more research needs to be done on this topic. Future research should investigate the effectiveness of the hybrid course design as it relates to individual differences among L2 learners, for example students with different learning style preferences. Research is also needed on how to help students with intrinsic motivation by designing online activities that capitalize on factors that learners naturally bring to tasks for which they are intrinsically motivated. Not all students demonstrate a level of individual responsibility that is conducive to online learning. In online learning there is a great deal of flexibility, so learners must be responsible for their own learning and take the initiative to study and learn on their own without extrinsic motivational techniques. Research that focused on the usefulness of online activities for helping learners become aware of themselves as learners and discover their own behaviors prior to enrollment in hybrid courses would be most useful.

## CONCLUSION

This research study examined the effectiveness of a hybrid English grammar and editing skills course at the tertiary level. The participants in the study were international students at the University who were enrolled in the two sections of the course through the normal registration process. One section was taught in the hybrid format (i.e., experimental group) while the other was taught in the traditional f2f format (i.e. control group). Both sections were taught by the same instructor. The researchers collected both qualitative and quantitative data to answer two questions: (1) Does hybrid instruction have a positive effect on students' development of English grammar and editing skills? and (2) What are the students' perceptions of the hybrid course design?, both of which are understudied in the field of CALL. To answer the first research question, a quasi-experimental design was employed with a pre- and posttest. To answer the second question, students answered Likert-scale questions and two open-ended questions as part of a questionnaire and joined a focus group at the end of the semester which was led by an external facilitator to avoid undue influence.

The quantitative data that came from the pre- and posttests that were given at the beginning and end of the semester were used to determine if hybrid instruction had positive effects on students' gains in their knowledge of English grammar and their editing skills. The data were analyzed using a t-test and indicated that after instruction there were no significant differences between the two groups (i.e., hybrid and f2f). This result indicates that the hybrid English grammar course is as effective as the f2f class. The hybrid course design did not jeopardize students' performances in the course; rather, it offered affordances that the f2f courses could not.

The affordances that hybrid courses offer were based on the themes that emerged from the data that came from the questionnaire and the focus group. Overall the students perceived the hybrid format positively, as it allowed them to have more autonomy over their own learning, to have ongoing access to the materials (e.g., online exercises, video lectures, and handouts), and to communicate asynchronously. Asynchronous communication allowed students to study at their own speed, to manage the anxiety that comes from having to speak in an L2 in a classroom setting, and to take better notes as they could stop the video lectures whenever needed.

The data also provided several suggestions for improving the effectiveness of the course. Although students appreciated the immediate feedback they received for the online exercises, they wanted more detailed explanations as to why an answer is correct or incorrect, which can in turn promote better learning. In order to improve their time management skills, students suggested that there be several due dates throughout the week to prevent them from doing intensive last minute work. In addition, students suggested that the weight of online exercise be increased, to motivate them to work in a timely fashion.

## REFERENCES

Benson, P. (2013). Teaching and research autonomy (2nd ed.). New York, NY: Routledge.

Borg, S. (2003). Teacher cognition in language teaching: A review of research on what language teachers think, know, believe, and do. *Language Teaching*, *36*(2), 81–109. doi:10.1017/S0261444803001903

Byrd, P., & Reid, J. (1998). *Grammar in the composition classroom: Essays on teaching ESL for college-bound students*. Portsmouth, NH: Heinle & Heinle.

Celce-Murcia, M. (1991). Discourse analysis and grammar instruction. *Annual Review of Applied Linguistics*, *11*, 135–151. doi:10.1017/S0267190500002002

Chapelle, C. A., & Heift, T. (2009). Individual learner differences in CALL: The field independence/dependence (FID) construct. *CALICO Journal*, *26*(2), 246–266.

Dickinson, L. (1987). *Self-instruction in language learning*. Cambridge, UK: Cambridge University Press.

Doughty, C. (2003). Instructed SLA: Constraints, compensation, enhancement. In C. Doughty & M. Long (Eds.), *The handbook of SLA* (pp. 256–310). London: Wiley Blackwell.

Dudeney, G., & Hockly, N. (2012). ICT in ELT: How did we get here and where are we going? *ELT Journal*, *66*(4), 533–542. doi:10.1093/elt/ccs050

Folse, K. (2009). *Keys to teaching grammar to English language learners: A practical handbook*. Ann Arbor, MI: University of Michigan Press.

Gage, N., & Berliner, D. (1992). *Educational psychology* (5th ed.). Princeton, NJ: Houghton Mifflin Company.

Goertler, S. (2012). Theoretical and empirical foundations for blended language learning. In F. Rubio & J. J. Thoms (Eds.), *Hybrid language teaching and learning: Exploring theoretical, pedagogical and curricular issues* (pp. 27–49). Boston, MA: Heinle/Cengage Learning.

Hinkel, E. (2011). What research on second language writing tells us and what it doesn't. In E. Hinkel (Ed.), *Handbook of research on second language teaching and learning* (Vol. 2, pp. 523–538). New York, NY: Routledge/Taylor & Francis.

Hinkel, E. (2013). Research findings on teaching grammar for academic writing. *English Teaching*, *68*(4), 3–21. doi:10.15858/engtea.68.4.201312.3

Institute for International Education (IIE). (2015). Retrieved from http://www.iie.org/Services/Project-Atlas/United-States/International-Students-In-US#.WErZizvnvdk

Johns, A. (1997). *Text, role, and context: Developing academic literacies*. Cambridge, UK: Cambridge University Press; doi:10.1017/CBO9781139524650

Levy, M. (1997). *CALL: Context and conceptualization*. Oxford, UK: Oxford University Press.

Little, D. (1991). *Learner autonomy 1: Definitions, issues and problems*. Dublin, Ireland: Authentik.

Littlewood, W. (1999). Defining and developing autonomy in East Asian contexts. *Applied Linguistics*, *20*(1), 71–94. doi:10.1093/applin/20.1.71

Murray, D. E., & Christison, M. A. (2017). Going online: Affordances and limitations for teachers and teacher educators. In K. Hyland & L. Wong (Eds.), *Faces of English education: Students, teachers and pedagogy*. London: Continuum.

Murray, D. E., & Christison, M. A. (in press). Online language teacher education (OLTE): Participants' experiences and perspectives. *The International Research Foundation for English Language Education.*

Murray, G. L. (1999). Autonomy and language learning in a simulated environment. *System*, *27*(3), 295–308. doi:10.1016/S0346-251X(99)00026-3

Picciano, A. (2009). Blending with purpose: The multimodal model. *Journal of the Research Center for Educational Technology*, *5*(1), 4–14.

Reinders, H., & White, C. (2011). Learner autonomy and new learning environments. *Language Learning & Technology*, *15*(3), 1–3.

Rubio, F., & Thoms, J. J. (Eds.). (2012). *Hybrid language teaching and learning: Exploring theoretical, pedagogical and curricular issues*. Boston, MA: Heinle/Cengage Learning.

Sloan Consortium. (2005). *Growing by degrees: Online education in the United States, 2005*. Retrieved from http://sloanconsortium.org/sites/default/files/growing_by_degrees_1.pdf

Thomas, M., Reinders, H., & Warschauer, M. (Eds.). (2013). *Contemporary computer assisted language learning*. London: Bloomsbury.

Thoms, J. J. (2012). Analyzing linguistics outcomes of second language learners: Hybrid versus traditional course contexts. In F. Rubio & J. J. Thoms (Eds.), *Hybrid language learning and teaching: Exploring theoretical, pedagogical and curricular issues* (pp. 177–195). Boston, MA: Heinle/Cengage Learning.

Weigle, S. (2002). *Assessing writing*. Cambridge, UK: Cambridge University Press; doi:10.1017/CBO9780511732997

Zhou, A. (2009). What adult ESL learners say about improving grammar and vocabulary in their writing for academic purposes. *Language Awareness*, *18*(1), 31–46. doi:10.1080/09658410802307923

## ADDITIONAL READING

Arispe, K., & Blake, R. J. (2012). Individual factors and successful learning in a hybrid course. *System*, *40*(4), 449–465. doi:10.1016/j.system.2012.10.013

Boyd, P. W. (2008). Analyzing students perceptions of their learning in online and hybrid first-year composition courses. *Computers and Composition*, *25*(2), 224–243. doi:10.1016/j.compcom.2008.01.002

Celce-Murcia, M. (2002). Why it makes sense to teach grammar through context and through discourse. In E. Hinkel & S. Fotos (Eds.), *New perspectives on grammar teaching in second language classrooms* (pp. 119–134). Mahwah, NJ: Lawrence Erlbaum.

Ellis, R. (2006). Current issues in the teaching of grammar: An SLA perspective. *TESOL Quarterly*, *40*(1), 83–107. doi:10.2307/40264512

Sagarra, N., & Zapata, G. C. (2008). Blending classroom instruction with online homework: A study of student perceptions of computer-assisted L2 learning. *ReCALL*, *20*(2), 208–224. doi:10.1017/S0958344008000621

## KEY TERMS AND DEFINITIONS

**Extrinsic Motivation:** Motivation that occurs in performing an action for external gains, such as grades in classes.

**Face-To-Face (f2f):** Refers to interactions that take place in person in the same physical location.

**Integrated Skills:** Integrated skills classes focus on more than one skill (i.e., listening, speaking, writing, and reading) and the components of language that provide support for the acquisition of these skills, such as grammar, vocabulary, discourse, and pronunciation.

**Learner Cognition:** Refers to the unobservable and cognitive dimensions of language learning: what language learners know, believe, and think about language learning and the relationships of the mental constructs to what learners do as learners in language classrooms.

**Learning Management Systems (LMS):** Software that allows educators to administer, track, report, and deliver content in their classes.

**Online Technologies:** Online tools that allow people to communicate and share information orally, visually, or textually.

**Perceptual Data:** Data that focus on how participants interpret their experiences.

## APPENDIX 1

### Part A

### Personal Information

1. Please select the age group to which you belong.
    a. 18-22
    b. 22- 24
    c. Younger than 18
    d. Older than 24
2. Please select your native language.
    a. Chinese
    b. Korean
    c. Arabic
    d. Japanese
    e. Other
3. Please select your gender.
    a. Male
    b. Female
4. Have you taken any hybrid or online courses before?
    a. Yes
    b. No

### Part B

Please indicate how strongly you agree to the following statements (Table 6).

### Part C

Please indicate how often you did the following statements (Table 7).

### Part D

Please answer the following questions.

1. In what ways is a hybrid course better or worse compared to a traditional face-to-face class? Why?
2. What would you change in this course? Why?

*Table 6.*

| Statements | Strongly Agree | Agree | Disagree | Strongly Disagree |
|---|---|---|---|---|
| 1. The modules online were easy to follow. | | | | |
| 2. The online video lectures helped me with English grammar and editing. | | | | |
| 3. It was helpful to have access to the video lectures all the time so that I could watch them whenever I needed. | | | | |
| 4. The online exercises helped me practice English grammar and editing skills. | | | | |
| 5. The readings assigned from the book or outside sources helped me prepare for what we would cover in the module. | | | | |
| 6. I spent more time thinking about English grammar during the online discussions, assignments and exercises than I would have in a face-to-face class environment. | | | | |
| 7. The face-to-face classes provided me with opportunities to practice what I had studied in the modules. | | | | |
| 8. It was good to be able to work individually at my own speed. | | | | |
| 9. I enjoyed having control over my schedule (being able to study online whenever and wherever I wanted). | | | | |
| 10. I received timely feedback (within 24-48 hours) for the assignments my instructor needed to grade. | | | | |
| 11. I was able to get individualized attention from the instructor when I needed it. | | | | |
| 12. Although I only saw the teacher during the face-to-face days of the class, she was active and present online. | | | | |
| 13. This course created a sense of community among students that was comparable to a regular face-to-face class. | | | | |
| 14. I had enough opportunities to practice English grammar and editing. | | | | |
| 15. This hybrid course encouraged students to discuss ideas and concepts with other students. | | | | |
| 16. I think that using computers makes learning more interesting. | | | | |
| 17. This hybrid course met my learning needs. | | | | |
| 18. I believe hybrid courses are as effective as face-to-face courses. | | | | |
| 19. I am very satisfied with this hybrid course. | | | | |
| 20. I would like to take another hybrid course. | | | | |

*Table 7.*

| Statements | Always | Usually | Sometimes | Never |
|---|---|---|---|---|
| 1. I watched the video lectures my instructor recorded for each module. | | | | |
| 2. When I took the online exercises, I was honest. *Honest: I did my best on the first try; I didn't just click on the submit button to get the answers to enter it on my second try.* | | | | |
| 3. I finished the online activities before our face-to-face classes. | | | | |
| 4. I finished the online activities the night before our face-to-face class. | | | | |
| 5. When I didn't understand something, I searched for the answer. (i.e., searching online or asking the instructor or someone else who is knowledgeable). | | | | |
| 6. When my instructor left comments on my assignments, I read them carefully. | | | | |
| 7. I participated in the group activities we had on our face-to-face days. | | | | |
| 8. I found working with computers easy. | | | | |
| 9. I was able to manage my time (i.e., I allowed myself enough time to work on the modules). | | | | |

## APPENDIX 2

### Focus Group Questions

1. What did you like the most about the course?
2. What did you like the least about the course?
3. What do you think about online exercises in terms of their content and organization? Were they helpful?
4. What did you think about the face-to-face days in terms of your own learning?
5. When you compare a hybrid and a traditional face-to-face class, which one do you think is better and why?
6. Did you feel a sense of community with your peers in the class? Do you think your sense of community was influenced by the fact that the class has only met once a week? Why? Do you think your sense of classroom community is different in a f2f class? Why?
7. Do you want to take another hybrid class? Why? Why not?

# Chapter 10
# A CALL-Mediated Course to Enhance EFL Pre-Service Teachers' Engagement

**Sri Rejeki Murtiningsih**
*Universitas Muhammadiyah Yogyakarta, Indonesia*

**Fitria Rahmawati**
*Universitas Muhammadiyah Yogyakarta, Indonesia*

## ABSTRACT

*It is important for students to be engaged in any given course. For EFL pre-service teachers, being engaged in a course is essential because they can benefit linguistically, cognitively, and pedagogically. The present chapter presents a CALL-mediated course that was able to enhance EFL pre-service teachers' engagement by using Edmodo as its learning platform. Also, this study explores the contributing factors that a CALL-mediated course has towards their engagement. Three EFL pre-service teachers agreed to voluntarily participate in this exploratory study. Through in-depth interviews, they described their engagement and factors affecting their participation. The findings reveal that the EFL pre-service teachers were highly encouraged and inspired to utilize Edmodo and adopt the activities designed for the course. Obstacles and challenges encountered by EFL pre-service teachers are also discussed.*

## INTRODUCTION

In light of student-centered learning, engagement is believed to have a significant role to the success of students' learning as it is closely related to students' achievement, attention, retention, motivation, and instructional success (Beer, Clark, & Jones, 2010). When students invest their time, effort, and energy to their own learning, they will likely be more successful in learning than those who do not. For this reason, many university administrators devote a great amount of time and money to design an active, student-centered teaching and learning environment (Laird, Shoup, & Kuh, 2005) that will enhance student engagement by choosing suitable programs, implementing appropriate teaching methods, and providing engaging learning aids.

DOI: 10.4018/978-1-5225-2933-0.ch010

Many EFL teachers struggle to maintain student engagement with their lessons, yet they must continue seeking the best instructional strategies that support student engagement in learning both within and beyond the classroom. Thus, improving student engagement is a significant challenge. The importance of student engagement is addressed by Kuh (2003; 2009) and Taylor and Parsons (2011). They state that student engagement can improve students' learning, lead to student success, and promote life-long learning. It is imperative that student engagement is maintained and improved. One of the examples of these actions is to make use of CALL in the teaching-learning process.

In the development of EFL learning, CALL has not only been referred to as computer-mediated language learning. In addition, this area has also developed to a broader inclusion of technological hardware (Bulger, Mayer, Almeroth, & Blau, 2008), software (Zaini & Mazdayasna, 2015), digital devices, and the Internet (Alabbad, Gitsaki, & White, 2015; Nakamaru, 2012). While many educational institutions around the world have offered fully online courses—including EFL courses—to their students, many others have made efforts to integrate CALL into their face-to-face class meetings. This chapter uses a CALL-mediated course, which utilized an online learning platform to encourage student participation inside and outside the class. Online learning platforms are believed to be able to help EFL teachers enhance their student engagement by reshaping the way they teach (Barkley, 2010; Jarvis, 2005) Not only do online learning platforms help EFL students reinvent themselves, it also enables them to work collaboratively with their friends and solve their problems independently with little help from their teachers (Morgan, 2008).

For EFL pre-service teachers, being able to engage in a CALL-mediated course might be useful for the future when they have to teach EFL students in a similar course. In addition, actively participating in such a course will enable EFL pre-service teachers to make sense of problems that might come up during the teaching learning process and find possible solutions. Using EFL pre-service teachers' voices, the current chapter seeks to answer the following questions: (1) What are the activities in the CALL-mediated course that enhance EFL pre-service teachers' engagement? and (2) What are the contributing factors that affect EFL pre-service teachers' engagement in using Edmodo?

## EFL PRE-SERVICE TEACHERS IN INDONESIAN CONTEXTS

There has been a high demand for EFL teachers in Indonesia because English is the main foreign language that has been taught in Indonesia for decades. Many EFL teachers in Indonesia have started to shift their paradigm from traditional views of English language teaching to the economic value of English (Manara, 2014). By this, Manara (2014) means that Indonesian EFL teachers have thought about the economic benefits that students can obtain from learning English in today's globalized Indonesia. Manara's research implies that integrating CALL in English classes can be one of the solutions to improve the role of English in Indonesia.

EFL pre-service teachers are typically prepared to teach in school contexts, both private and public. A typical EFL class in Indonesia may contain 35-40 students, which is considered quite challenging for many EFL teachers to accommodate. As a result, promoting meaningful interaction among EFL students that can lead to academic engagement is quite a challenge (Brooks & Thurston, 2010). Unfortunately, most EFL pre-service teachers in Indonesia receive minimal exposure to engaging language classroom activities when they were still at school. As Masduqi (2014) asserts, Indonesian students do not generally expect interactive activities in the classroom due to their cultural philosophies "to obey and to follow"

(p. 391). Furthermore, EFL teachers in Indonesia generally take up more teacher talk time than give opportunities to students to be engaged by interacting with their peers and teachers. As a result, many EFL pre-service teachers in Indonesia have very limited examples of activities that they can use to make their students more engaged.

With regard to this particular issue, one way to prepare EFL pre-service teachers to deal with the potential problems they will likely encounter in the future is by providing them with engaging experiences in a CALL-mediated course. Online learning platforms provide opportunities for EFL pre-service teachers to have meaningful interaction with their peers and teachers. At the same time, teachers can distribute equal attention among the students. This study describes the activities that were conducted in an EFL class enhanced student engagement by using Edmodo as an online learning platform in a language class. This chapter also presents EFL pre-service teachers' perspectives on contributing factors that affected their engagement of using an online learning platform in the stated EFL class. With the practical knowledge that EFL pre-service teachers obtained from the class it is expected they would be able to apply it to engage their students.

## THEORETICAL FRAMEWORK

The implementation of CALL-mediated courses to enhance student engagement has been supported by a number of critical learning theories. Educational theory relevant to this investigation includes the Sociocultural theory of learning. In the Sociocultural theory, as advocated by Vygotsky (1978), social interactions play an influential role in the development of engagement constructs. This infers that knowledge is obtained from interacting and communicating with other people. Vygotsky (1978) believes that tools play an important role for students to develop effective correlation between their cognition and their learning environment, which includes peers and other people. In short, a CALL-mediated course is a tool that can facilitate EFL pre-service teachers' engagement by providing opportunities to have meaningful academic interactions with others and their own cognition. In addition, attention, as a form of engagement, is "an essential determinant of the success or failure of any practical operation" (Vygotysky, 1978 p. 35). This statement suggests that enhancing student engagement needs to be done to support students' success in learning.

Based on the framework, Edmodo mediates classroom instructions to engage EFL pre-service teachers. Edmodo is "a free and secure learning platform" specially designed for teachers, students, and parents to communicate and work collaboratively (Majid, 2011, as cited in Al-Khatiri, 2015, p. 189). Edmodo provides familiar navigation and user-friendly features, as well as a safe environment for both teachers and students to interact and collaborate. Edmodo requires a unique code to sign up for every class and school; thus, it prevents outsiders from joining the network. Additionally, Edmodo offers a free application that can be accessed anytime and anywhere through smart phones. Edmodo is believed to facilitate interaction between EFL pre-service teachers with their teachers and their peers both inside and outside the classroom. Edmodo is also effective for engaging students with meaningful activities that will eventually foster students' target language use and communication. The sociocultural theory accommodates the authors by permitting the close and systematic investigation of EFL pre-service teachers' experiences, attitudes, and perspectives on the utilization of online learning platforms to enhance their engagement in language learning.

## EFL PRE-SERVICE TEACHER ENGAGEMENT AND CALL

A number of scholars have defined the concept of *engagement* in general (Barkley, 2010; Bulger et al., 2008; Krause, 2005; Taylor & Parsons, 2011). Chen, Gonyea, and Kuh (2008), for instance, define engagement as a combination of time on task and willingness, effort, and motivation that EFL pre-service teachers dedicate to participate in class activities to achieve desired outcomes, including academic success and personal qualities (e.g., being a lifelong learner). In general, student engagement can typically be seen from their behavior, such as paying full attention to the teacher and actively participating in a class discussion. Although the level of engagement may be different from one student to another, meaningful learning is believed to take place when the students are highly engaged with the lesson.

Kuh (2003) argues that engagement may not take place although they have plenty of resources and/or are involved in meaningful activities. But, more likely than not, students will learn more when they have a carefully designed variety of classroom activities to participate. These activities have to enable students to do active learning (Barkley, 2010), think about their learning in a variety of context (Kuh, 2009), work collaboratively with their peers and teachers (Jarvis, 2005; Taylor & Parsons, 2011), and connect their learning between within the classroom and outside the classroom (Dunleavy & Milton, 2010). However, creating engagement-enhancing activities can be quite challenging. Kuh (2009) asserts these activities should be able to prepare EFL pre-service teachers for life after they graduate and become EFL teachers.

While there has been an increasing number of research studies on engagement and CALL in various contexts, research that correlates EFL pre-service teachers and engagement—in Indonesian contexts specifically—has been extremely scant. In university settings, Alabbad et al. (2015) argue that CALL could enhance student engagement by maintaining their participation in and outside the classroom. The engagement can be seen in students using web-based resources to fulfill the tasks that they typically do outside the class time. In their research, Alabbad et al. (2015) designed a CALL-mediated course in an EFL context, and their study shows that not only had students' motivation improved, but their attitude toward the EFL course had also been positively changed.

Prihatin (2012) conducted research in an Indonesian university and emphasizes the importance of teaching methods in a CALL-mediated class that can encourage student engagement in language learning. Using Communicative Language Teaching, Engagement, and Learner-centered Theories as his research framework, Prihatin (2012) investigated university teachers' perception in integrating technology into EFL classes and the implementation of CALL-mediated course in an EFL university context. After collecting data through in-depth interviews, class observations, and teaching instrument reviews from two EFL university teachers, Prihatin (2012) revealed that teaching strategies which encouraged students to have meaningful interaction with each other using English were essential. The strategies manifested in the CALL-mediated course in that research were role play, grammar practices, games, and other activities that required students to work collaboratively. Despite the similarities between the Prihatin study and the current chapter, for example the research context, Prihatin (2012) does not address students' perception towards the CALL-mediated course.

Other than university contexts in Indonesia, CALL has also evidently been able to improve younger students' motivation in addtional international contexts as shown by Boutonglang and Flores (2011) and Talebinzhad and Abarghoui (2013). Both studies employed computer-assisted activities in school settings to teach English skills and have shown positive influence toward English learning. However, utilizing technology-mediated instruction has not always yielded positive results on student engagement to English language learners. Nakamaru's (2012) study, for instance, indicates that activities designed on CALL-based activities (i.e., web-based activities) in higher education contexts did not necessarily increase student engagement. The low engagement was shown from the minimal student participation to complete required tasks outside the class. Furthermore, improving student engagement using computer-mediated instruction is not without its challenges. Lack of facilities, off-campus computer and Internet availability, as well as teachers' pedagogical knowledge are some of the obstacles that were found (Dashtestani, 2014; Dunleavy & Milton, 2010; Prihatin, 2012).

## CALL IN EFL LEARNING

Student engagement will likely motivate students put more effort into learning, which will result in better academic achievement and important components required to succeed academically. In many EFL contexts, CALL has been used as a means to improve students' English proficiency. CALL has positively influenced students' grammar accuracy (Salmasi, Bonyandi & Alavinia, 2015; Pirahsteh, 2014), writing skills (Shafiee, Koosha, & Afghari, 2015; Zaini & Mazdayasna, 2015), attitude in language learning (Allabbad et al., 2015), and engagement in language learning (Bautonglang & Flores, 2011; Brooks & Thurston, 2010; Bulger et al., 2008; Nakamaru, 2012).

Now that this discussion has specified a number of key issues concerning CALL in general and specifically in Indonesia, it now turns to the key CALL element in the current study, the online learning platform. An increasing number of EFL teachers in Indonesia use an online learning platform to engage their students. Among the numerous learning platforms available online, a Learning Management System (LMS) is the most proliferate and broadly used. Some LMSs that are purposively created for pedagogy are Moodle, Blackboard, WikiSpace, Google Classroom, Schoology, and Edmodo. Many language teachers also incorporate social networks and microblogging such as Twitter, Facebook, and various blogging platforms to support student interaction and open a greater chance to have a more active learning. In the authors' opinion, Edmodo is considered an educational tool that can facilitate the learning needs in CALL-mediated courses in a more private and secure platform. Given contemporary concerns for Internet security regarding the participants' information and identity, both safety and security are critical.

This study differs from other studies on student engagement in many ways. First of all, this study includes participation of EFL pre-service teachers who shared their experiences in a CALL-mediated course with future EFL students. Therefore, their perspectives, feelings, and comments are valuable to explore. In addition, EFL pre-service teachers' opinions can be used as a course evaluation. Moreover, one of the authors was the teacher-observer for this study. Thus, she was aware of each student's level of engagement.

## METHODOLOGY

To explore and deeply understand what activities enhance student engagement and what factors contribute to EFL pre-service teachers' engagement in a CALL-mediated course, the authors employed a descriptive and interpretative qualitative research method. This method allowed the authors to listen to the students' voices, so as to understand their learning experience.

## Setting

This study was conducted at an EFL teacher training institution in Indonesia. The institution strongly encourages the integration of CALL in its teaching learning process. While CALL is implemented to some degree in almost all courses offered, several courses are specifically designed as CALL-mediated in order to fully prepare EFL pre-service teachers with hands-on experiences. The course, from which the study was conducted, provided practical knowledge and skills in using the specific web-based application, Edmodo, and consisted of 16 weeks. The materials for the CALL-mediated course were aligned with the Indonesian high school English materials because at the time of data collection, the EFL pre-service teachers were conducting teaching practicum in high schools during the same semester. Thus, the EFL pre-service teachers could apply materials, pedagogical knowledge, and experiences obtained from the course whenever necessary in different settings. The course was a blend between face-to-face meetings and online sessions, in which Edmodo was used. Throughout the course, EFL pre-service teachers were engaged in various activities such as actively participating in teacher-led discussions, interacting with their peers by giving comments on their posts, and other classroom activities. All activities were conducted in English. Out of the 16 meetings, three meetings were administered in full online mode.

## Participants

In order to obtain a better understanding of the phenomenon, three participants were non-randomly and purposively selected (Creswell, 2012) because they were considered to have actively participated throughout the course, both in and outside the class. These participants were selected through a naturalistic setting (the classroom and Edmodo) since one of the authors was the teacher of the CALL-mediated course. In addition, the participants' involvement in this study was voluntary. The 22 and 23 year-old junior participants verbally agreed to participate and were made aware of their rights as participants and that no benefits were provided for their participation. All participants proceeded with the interviews, which were conducted on campus in fall 2016.

## Data Collection Procedure

The data were collected through in-depth interviews. The interviews were semi-structured with open-ended questions, which allowed the participants to answer follow-up questions (Cohen, Manion, & Morrison, 2011). Each participant principally received eight questions (see Appendix); however, each of them eventually answered a different number of questions depending on their answers. At the time of the data collection, the participants had taught EFL in elementary and middle school since they were freshmen as part of the degree requirement. Since the participants and authors were multilingual, the in-depth interviews used a combination of several languages spoken by both sides.

Member checking was conducted to triangulate the interview data and the data obtained from the classroom and Edmodo, and no participants altered the data. Wiwik, Alia, and Okie—pseudonyms used in the study, were two female and male participants respectively.

## FINDINGS

During the interviews, the EFL pre-service teachers showed that in general, they were highly enthusiastic about using Edmodo. They described the activities and expressed their feelings about the activities. Two major findings emerged from the interview data and each finding had several different themes: (1) engagement enhancing activities, which consists of interaction, self-initiated exploration, and language learning and (2) factors influencing student engagement, which comprises students' and teachers' roles, as well as the institution's role.

## Engagement Enhancing Activities

### Interaction

One of the activities that had encouraged the EFL pre-service teachers to be highly engaged was the collaborative work. This activity allowed them to maintain interactions between their friends and teachers. Alia even mentioned that the interaction could have been set up among her friends, teacher, and parents, although this particular course is exclusively set up for students and teachers. Activities that required them to work as a group also enabled them to share information with their friends, including giving suggestions to the teacher and responding to friends' questions. In short, although they did not always physically meet, they still could interact and discuss the topics under the teacher's supervision. The problem that the participants faced, in the light of maintaining the interaction, was that they were not able to chat privately with the teacher. No features within Edmodo could accommodate this need. So, if a student needed to talk individually with the teacher, they would have to meet the teacher in person or contact the teacher via email or phone.

Okie and Alia were able to maintain their engagement when using Edmodo because they had smartphones that allowed them to download the Edmodo application from the Google Play Store. The application would send them notifications whenever an activity occurred in Edmodo so that they could contribute in the discussion. Wiwik, on the other hand, did not have the application on her smartphone, so she relied on her friends to let her know through other social media which were commonly used among them.

The three participants mentioned that the topics discussed, which were posted mostly by the teachers, were one of the things that made them more engaged. Students were able to relate the topics with their every day life. That was the main reason why they would maintain their interaction. Alia specifically indicated that she sometimes raised a new issue within the discussed topic and was able to engage her friends with a discussion of the new issue. It was also found that Wiwik and Okie used a formal tone when interacting using Edmodo, even when they interacted with their peers. When asked about the reasons for the formality, they said that in their perception, because Edmodo was a learning platform, they were encouraged to use a higher level of formality during the discussions, especially when they were aware that they were monitored by the teacher. Thus, random conversation in English or in their native languages had never taken place in Edmodo.

Several indicators to show that students were engaged were the level of interaction and time invested for the course (Barkley, 2010; Dunleavy & Milton, 2010; Jarvis, 2005; Taylor & Parson, 2011). This study is also in line with Brooks and Thurston (2010) who stated that collaborative learning, especially small group and one-on-one interaction, is a powerful tool to engage students with the course. The participants of this study, unfortunately, did not specify which collaborative learning made them engaged the most and the least. With regard to the Sociocultural theory (Vygotsky, 1978), the EFL pre-service teachers learned how to find and use the appropriate tone—in this case, the formality of the language, when they had to communicate in public. The interaction, to some extent, had developed the EFL pre-service teachers' maturation which can be a bridge for their later individual development (Vygotsky, 1978).

## Self-Initiated Exploration

Evidently, working with Edmodo had raised the participants' excitement, which, in turn, led to their improved engagement. This excitement led the EFL pre-service teachers to do some self-initiated explorations when using Edmodo. The participants explained that they experimented using teacher and student accounts, services that are provided by Edmodo, and that they had found some interesting features about which they were eager to learn. While the student account did not offer as many features as the teacher account, it still provided the EFL pre-service teachers with opportunities to interact with their peers, or in other words, giving comments to each other's posts. Also, student accounts still gave them some privacy in terms of submitting assignments. Okie asserted that, unlike other learning platforms, only the particular individual who submitted an assignment and that student's teacher were able to open the assignment that the student uploaded, although everybody could see the submission. To him, this feature was a new and valuable learning experience.

The teacher account, on the other hand, allowed the EFL pre-service teachers to be creative because it offered a variety of features (e.g., giving badges as rewards, uploading teaching materials in the library, and giving feedback). As a matter of fact, because of Edmodo, Alia was so inspired that she started her business on giving online English lessons, and she had a number of students. She did not use Edmodo in her business because she was concerned that her students might not be familiar with it.

The EFL pre-service teachers also did an exploration on the features provided in Edmodo, such as giving rewards. They were inspired by the activity the teacher designed when she gave away badges to students who did well on assignments. As the participants were future EFL teachers, they stated that the creativity Edmodo offered when they signed in as a teacher was exciting. The participants mentioned several activities that they would do with their students, such as giving rewards, posting some important links, uploading teaching materials, and teaching their students about being disciplined. Okie even compared Edmodo with other learning platforms and stated that he preferred Edmodo. This finding corresponds with Kuh (2003; 2009) and Taylor and Parson (2011) who asserted that student engagement can improve students' learning, lead to student success, and promote life-long learning. Results from this study also demonstrate that the EFL pre-service teachers did some exploration on their own initiative, which means that they continually learned and were more engaged with the course. This finding aligns with Sociocultural learning theory linked to how engagement allows students to apply "not only those objects that lie near at hand" (p. 26), but also other features that can be used to solve problems and plan for the future. The EFL pre-service teachers in this study explored Edmodo on their own initiative for task solutions and future actions, such as planning English courses for their students like Alia.

### Language Learning

The interviews showed that the language skill that was mainly developed was writing, which took place when the students provided comments in response to their friends' posts. Writing comments in English apparently improved the participants' linguistic awareness. This is evident because the EFL pre-service teachers would check their comments, in terms of grammar, lexicon, and spelling.

*I always wrote my comments on a word document first before I posted them online in Edmodo. I also checked my dictionary more often to make sure that everything was okay. I would feel embarrassed if I made mistakes. Now it becomes my habit. So, it is good for me. (Interview data from Alia, 2016)*

For Wiwik, writing her comment, instead of verbally expressing her response, had given her more time to think about what she wanted to comment. This was unlike the traditional class mode that required her to think faster to express her ideas and was usually conveyed in a more casual tone. Not only when writing comments, the EFL pre-service teachers were also required to write assignments in English and post them in Edmodo. In terms of developing other language skills, the participants indicated that the CALL-mediated course had not facilitated development of their speaking skills because they had to interact mainly in writing. Meanwhile, they could, to some extent, develop their reading and listening skills from the articles and videos that the teacher posted in the Edmodo library. This may be due to the fact that video or voice chat was not featured in Edmodo; thus, speaking skills received minimal attention in the CALL-mediated course.

This particular finding suggests that the EFL pre-service teachers invested more time and energy to the course, because they took extra effort to properly contribute in the written discussion. Fredericks, Blumfeld, and Paris (2004) contend that the desire to perform beyond the requirements, to learn more, and to master language skills means that students actually become cognitively engaged. A plethora of research in the area of EFL (Allabbad et al., 2015; Pirahsteh, 2014; Salmasi et al., 2015; Shafiee et al., 2015; Zaini & Mazdayasna, 2015) as stated earlier in the chapter has shown that CALL has positive contributions towards students' linguistic ability. Vygotsky's (1978) Sociocultural learning theory suggests that learning is a social process and that language plays a major role in students' cognitive development. In this study, the EFL pre-service teachers' linguistic ability, especially their writing skills, was developed through the interactions in which they were involved. These linguistic skills can be useful for the EFL pre-service teachers in the future when they have to use them without the supervision from the teacher.

## Factors Influencing Student Engagement

### Students' and Teachers' Roles

One of the important aspects that made the EFL pre-service teachers invest more time and energy when using Edmodo was the fact that they had to be punctual when completing the assignments. Late submission was not tolerable because they had to upload their assignments online, as stated by the three participants. In addition, Wiwik asserted that she did not want to lose face for submitting late because, in her opinion, Edmodo was a public place. Similar to Wiwik, Alia confirmed that the teacher's absence encouraged her to be more independent during the course. For that reason, she had to understand her own way of learning and manage her time wisely so she could meet the class expectations. This particular finding implies that this CALL-mediated course encouraged students to be autonomous by employing metacognitive and reflective strategies towards their own learning. The most important role that the EFL pre-service teachers played in this study was as the decision maker of their own learning.

In this study, the teacher still held a major role to improve engagement. The three participants asserted that although they considered themselves to be active participants, they would not post anything if the teacher did not initiate a discussion. It was the teacher who had to upload the learning materials for students. According to the participants, some students did not give any comments if the teacher had not required them to respond on some posts. In addition, the EFL pre-service teachers were more engaged when the topics discussed were within their area of interest. The data implies that the teacher was responsible for investigating students' interests and meeting students' expectations. In addition to interesting topics, this study also shows that the teacher also need to be able to design activities that can maintain and improve student engagement. Providing rewards to appreciate students evidently had motivated students to maintain their interaction and, in turn, enhance their engagement.

These findings show that although a CALL-based course is able to promote students autonomy (Alabbad et al., 2015), teachers' pedagogical methods also played a significant role toward promoting student engagement (Bulger et al., 2008; Prihatin, 2012). This is especially relevant when the culture in which the EFL environment took place does not encourage students autonomy, in this particular situation, the Indonesian culture (Masduqi, 2014).

## The Institution's Role

With regard to student engagement and CALL-mediated course, institutions also play an even bigger role to the students' success in learning. The equipment, such as computer lab or other equipment that can accomodate students' need to do online learning, is imperative. The three participants pointed out that the major challenge they had to face with regard to the CALL-mediated course was poor internet connection. Not only that students found challenges with this particular problem on campus, they also met this problems off-campus. Alia remarked,

*It needed a good internet connection for us to work on Edmodo, especially if we want to upload videos or other materials with bigger sizes. Before I had my smartphone, I used to go to an internet cafe at least once a week so I could access Edmodo. (Interview data from Alia, 2016)*

Lack of CALL equipment, online facilities, and clear instructions given by the teacher are among the obstacles found in implementing CALL in some EFL environments (Dashtestani, 2014; Sa'd, 2014; Salmasi et al., 2015). CALL equipment may not be a problem in developing countries, but in many EFL contexts, CALL equipment is a massive investment that not all educational institutions can afford. In addition, negative attitude towards the use of CALL can also become problematic in an EFL environment (Sa'd, 2014).

A number of CALL scholars have underscored the need for CALL adoption into pedagogy to enhance student engagement (Kuh, 2009; Laird et al., 2005; Taylor & Parsons, 2011). In accord with these scholars, the current chapter reveals answers to the research questions in support of their assertions. The study shows that a CALL-mediated course can provide a series of engagement enhancing activities through the social process that requires students to have meaningful interaction with each other. Since the

CALL-mediated course was able to improve students' independence and language proficiency, adopting a higher level of CALL integration in more courses might be able to boost these important aspects of learning even faster. The answer to the second research question is related to the degree of teacher guidance as well as students' and institution's initiatives to take the most advantages from a CALL-mediated course. Possibly, institutional policies that encourage the adoption of CALL in all courses would rapidly improve student engagement and independence, which would lead to increased academic success.

The current chapter, however, involved a small number of student-participants, who were considered to be the most active students in the class. This limited selection of research participants might have skewed the results of the study and limit the extent to which the results can be transferrable to other educational settings. Other students might have different perspectives toward the CALL-mediated course. Also, other types of measurements to student engagement, e.g. self-report measures, survey, work sample analysis, time on task, participation rates, student written or verbal self-report reflections, and student self-reporting work (portfolios, products, presentation, student developed projects) can provide different data.

## SOLUTIONS AND RECOMMENDATIONS

A CALL-mediated course that used Edmodo was able to enhance student engagement because of the meaningful interactions in which the EFL pre-service teachers participated. One of the most important notes from this study is that teachers play an important role in CALL-mediated courses. First of all, teachers should be able to create an EFL environment that allows students' sociocultural aspects (Vygotsky, 1978) to flourish and be highly engaged through observation, interaction, and collaboration. When students are cognitively, linguistically, and socially engaged, they will likely invest more time and energy, and active learning will more likely occur (Barkley, 2010; Kuh, 2003).

Teachers' encouragement is another point to ponder. This chapter concludes that motivating students to actively participate in the discussion and other class activities has evidently increased EFL pre-service teachers' participations. Teachers' encouragement can manifest in various forms, such as giving badges to those who do well. This encouragement can be used to maintain student engagement. By being a motivator, a teacher can create a learning environment to encourage students to be more engaged with the lesson (Arkorful & Abaidoo, 2014).

Regarding interaction between participants, in a CALL-mediated course the interaction does not necessarily take place in the physical dimension, for example, face-to-face class meetings. In contrast, a virtual class through Edmodo, was used as a place to *meet* and communicate, so that students would not necessarily be completely disconnected from learning (Dunleavy & Milton, 2010). Most of these students can access Edmodo from their smartphones; thus, disconnectivity can be minimized. Further research needs to be carried out to see whether the types of interaction that students and teachers have online and in traditional classes would be different. If yes, in what ways are they different would be of specific interest.

Apart from interaction, student engagement can be enhanced in a CALL-mediated course with a series of meaningful activities that challenge students to perform well academically (Barkley, 2010; Kuh, 2003). The activities should be within students' ability and, naturally, also related to their interests. This current research and other similar studies that show significant impacts of CALL towards EFL students' linguistic and cognitive competence may be due to the fact that the students were highly engaged with the course.

While the CALL-mediated course described in this chapter was able to improve EFL pre-service teachers' autonomy and engagement, it seemingly did not always reduce students' dependence on teachers' resources. This might be influenced by the cultural aspects related to the geographical location in which the study was conducted. At the same time, teachers who design CALL-mediated courses may need to shift some learning responsibilities to students to foster student independence. This being said, student engagement may not work as well if institutional support is absent. Institutions are responsible for providing the technology by having a steady and reliable internet connection.

## FUTURE RESEARCH DIRECTIONS

The current chapter focuses on the EFL pre-service teachers' engagement with a CALL-mediated course that employed Edmodo. Future research can be directed to explore whether engagement in a CALL-mediated course would be different from that of a non-CALL-mediated course. Additional research can also examine how far Edmodo can improve EFL pre-service teachers' writing ability as indicated in the findings. With regard to institution's roles, a research study can be conducted on the effectiveness of teacher professional development programs held by university administrators for their teachers when incorporating CALL in their classes. In the case of EFL teacher training institutions, investigating how EFL pre-service teachers implement their knowledge and skills they learned and obtained from a CALL-mediated course during their teaching practicum.

## CONCLUSION

One of the strengths of this current chapter is the participants. EFL pre-service teachers are involved in CALL research because they will be able to take away so much from the course. Most importantly, they may apply the skills and knowledge in different settings in the future. The findings of the chapter support findings from previous studies about CALL and EFL environments in which CALL-mediated courses were able to enhance student engagement. However, their engagement is still dependent on the activities designed by the teachers. The implications of the study are that teachers' pedagogical and practical knowledge in CALL-mediated courses have to be strengthened, and educational institutions need to provide training for teachers to utilize online learning and other forms of teaching techniques that involve technology.

## REFERENCES

Al-Khatiri. (2015). Beyond the classroom walls: Edmodo in Saudi secondary school EFL instruction, attitudes and challenges. *English Language Teaching Journal, 8*(1), 189-204. doi:10.5539/elt.v8n1p189

Alabbad, A., Gitsaki, C., & White, P. (2015). CALL course design for second language learning: a case study of Arab EFL learners. In D. L. Pullen, C. Gitsaki, & M. Baguley (Eds.), *Technoliteracy, discourse, and social practice: Frameworks and applications in the digital age* (pp. 88–103). Hershey, PA: Information Science Reference.

Arkorful, V., & Abaidoo, N. (2014). The role of e-Learning, the advantages and disadvantages of its adoption in higher education. *International Journal of Education and Research*, *2*(12), 397–410.

Barkley, E. F. (2010). *Student engagement techniques: A handbook for college faculty*. San Francisco, CA: John Wiley & Sons, Inc.

Beer, C., Clark, K., & Jones, D. (2010). Indicators of engagement. In *Proceedings of ASCILITE - Australian Society for Computers in Learning in Tertiary Education Annual Conference 2010* (pp. 75-86). Australasian Society for Computers in Learning in Tertiary Education.

Boutonglang, D., & Flores, F. (2011). A study on integrating technology to engage 7th grades into an English as a foreign language (EFL) classroom in a rural secondary school, Thailand. *International Journal of Arts & Sciences*, *4*(18), 195–206.

Brooks, K., & Thurston, L. P. (2010). English language learner academic engagement and instructional grouping configurations. *American Secondary Education*, *39*(1), 45–60.

Bulger, M. E., Mayer, R. E., Almeroth, K. C., & Blau, S. D. (2008). Measuring learner engagement in computer equipped college classrooms. *Journal of Educational Multimedia and Hypermedia*, *17*(2), 129–143.

Chen, P. S. D., Gonyea, R., & Kuh, G. (2008). Learning at a distance. *Journal of Online Education*, *4*(3). Retrieved from http://innovateonline.info/index.php?view=article&id=438&action=login

Cohen, L., Manion, L., & Morrison, K. (2011). *Research methods in education* (7th ed.). London: Routledge.

Creswell, J. W. (2012). *Educational research: planning, conducting, evaluating quantitative and qualitative research* (4th ed.). Boston, MA: Pearson.

Dashtestani, R. (2014). English as a foreign language teachers perspectives on implementating online instruction in the Iranian EFL context. *Research in Learning Technology*, *22*(1), 1–15. doi:10.3402/rlt.v22.20142

Dunleavy, J., & Milton, P. (2010). Student engagement for effective teaching and deep learning. *Education Canada*, *48*(5), 4–8.

Fredricks, J. A., Blumfeld, P. C., & Paris, A. H. (2004). School engagement: Potential of the concept, state of the evidence. *Review of Educational Research*, *74*(1), 59–109. doi:10.3102/00346543074001059

Jarvis, H. (2005). Technology and change in English language teaching. *The Asian EFL Journal Quarterly*, *7*(4), 213–227.

Krause, K. L. (2005). *Understanding and promoting student engagement in university learning communities.* Paper presented at the Sharing Scholarship in Learning and Teaching: Engaging Students Conference, James Cook University (Townsville Campus), Queensland, Australia.

Kuh, G. D. (2003). *What we're learning about student engagement from NSSE.* EBSCO Publishing.

Kuh, G. D. (2009). The national survey of student engagement: Conceptual and empirical foundations. *New Directions for Institutional Research*, *2009*(141), 5–20. doi:10.1002/ir.283

Laird, T. F., Shoup, R., & Kuh, G. D. (2005). Measuring deep approaches to learning using the National Survey of Student Engagement. *The Annual Meeting of the Association for Institutional Research*, 1-28.

Majid, N. (2011). The Use of Information Technology in Teaching English: An Attemptto Develop Student-Centered Learning at Telkom Polytechnic. *Prosidingkonferensi Nasional ICT-M Politeknit Telkom (KNIP)*. Retrieved from http://openjournal.politekniktelkom.ac.id/

Manara, C. (2014). "That's what worries me": Tensions in English language education in today's Indonesia. *International Journal of Innovation in English Language Teaching and Research*, *3*(1), 21–35.

Masduqi, H. (2014). EFL reading in Indonesian universities: Perspectives and challenges in cultural contexts. *Journal of Teacher Education*, *3*(03), 385–397.

Morgan, G. L. (2008). *Improving student engagement: Use of the interactive whiteboard as an instructional tool to improve engagement and behavior in the junior high school* (Unpublished doctoral dissertation). Liberty University, Lynchburg, VA.

Nakamaru, S. (2012). Investment and return: Wiki engagement in a remedial ESL writing course. *Journal of Research on Technology in Education*, *44*(4), 273–391. doi:10.1080/15391523.2012.10782591

Pirahsteh, P. (2014). Computer-assisted language learning (CALL) on learning grammar by Iranian EFL learners. *Social and Behavioral Sciences*, *98*, 1422–1427.

Prihatin, P. N. (2012). *The computer integration into EFL instruction in Indonesia: An analysis of two university instructors in integrating computer technology into EFL instruction to encourage students' language learning engagement* (Unpublished doctoral dissertation). Loyola University, Chicago, IL.

Sa'd, S. H. (2014). Implementing Internet-based EFL teaching in Iran: (Dis)advantages, obstacles, and challenges from EFL learners' viewpoint. *Journal of Language and Literature Education*, *10*, 24–40.

Salmasi, M., Bonyadi, A., & Alavinia, P. (2015). CALL-assissted enhancement of gramatical accuracy: Iranian EFL learners studying in rural settings. *Theory and Practice in Language Studies*, *5*(4), 765–772. doi:10.17507/tpls.0504.12

Shafiee, S., Koosha, M., & Afghari, A. (2015). CALL, prewriting strategies, and EFL writing quantity. *English Language Teaching*, *8*(2), 170-177.

Talebinezhad, M. R., & Abarghoui, M. A. (2013). The Iranian high school students attitude toward CALL and the use of CALL for EFL receptive skills. *Theory and Practice in Language Studies*, *3*(2), 329–337. doi:10.4304/tpls.3.2.329-337

Taylor, L., & Parsons, J. (2011). Improving student engagement. *Current Issues in Education*, *14*(1), 1–32.

Vygotsky, L. S. (1978). *Mind in society: The development of higher psychological processes*. Cambridge, MA: Harvard University Press.

Zaini, A., & Mazdayanasna, G. (2015). The impact of computer-based instruction on the development of EFL learners writing skills. *Journal of Computer Assisted Learning*, *31*(6), 516–528. doi:10.1111/jcal.12100

## ADDITIONAL READING


Ally, M. (2008). Foundations of educational theory for online learning. In T. Anderson (Ed.), *The theory and practice of online learning* (2nd ed.). Athabasca, Canada: AU Press, Athabasca University.

Arroyo, G. (2011). *On-Line social networks: Innovative ways towards the boost of collaborative language learning* (4th ed.). ICT for Language Learning.

Cummins, J. C. (2016). *College student engagement patterns in small group learning activities conducted in courses organized using a flipped learning instructional pedagogy* (Doctoral Dissertation, University of Tennessee). Retrieved from http://trace.tennessee.edu/utk_graddiss/3691

Dixson, M. D. (2015). Measuring student engagement in the online course: The online student engagement scale (OSE). *Online Learning, 19*(4).

Fang, Y. (2010). Perceptions of the computer-assisted writing program among EFL college learners. *Journal of Educational Technology & Society*, *13*(3), 246–256.

Hedayati, H., & Marandi, S. S. (2014). Iranian EFL teachers perceptions of the difficulties of implementing CALL. *ReCALL, 26*(3), 298–314. doi:10.1017/S0958344014000172

Hismanoglu, M. (2012). Prospective EFL teachers' perceptions of ICT integration: A study of distance higher education. *Journal of Educational Technology & Society*, *5*(1), 185–196.

Jenkins, E. (2006). The student voice and school science education. *Studies in Science Education*, *42*(1), 49–88. doi:10.1080/03057260608560220

Junco, R., Heiberger, G., & Loken, E. (2011). The effect of Twitter on college student engagement and grades. *Journal of Computer Assisted Learning*, *27*(2), 119–132. doi:10.1111/j.1365-2729.2010.00387.x

Lane, L. M. (2009). Insidious pedagogy: How course management systems affect teaching. *First Monday*, *14*(10). Retrieved from http://firstmonday.org/htbin/cgiwrap/bin/ojs/index.php/fm/article/viewArticle/2530/2303 doi:10.5210/fm.v14i10.2530

Levy, M. (2010). Developing the language skills: Aligning the technological tool to the pedagogical purpose. In C. Ward (Ed.), *The Impact of Technology on Language Learning and Teaching: What, How and Why. Anthology series 51* (pp. 16–27). Singapore: SEAMEO Regional Language Centre.

Liaw, S. C., & Marimuthu, R. A/L., & Idris, M. (2014). Interactive challenges in online student participatory language learning through closed social network. [CPLT]. *Journal of Creative Practice in Language Learning and Teaching*, *2*(2), 27–37.

Ministerial Council on Education. Employment, Training and Youth Affairs (2005). Pedagogy strategy: Learning in an online world. Carlton South, Australia: MCEETYA.

Purnawarman, P., Susilawati, S., & Sundayana, W. (2016). The use of Edmodo in teaching writing in a blended learning setting. *Indonesian Journal of Applied Linguistics.*, *5*(2), 242–252. doi:10.17509/ijal.v5i2.1348

Rubin, C. M. (2013). Teacher stories: Using Edmodo in the classroom. Rubin's online interview series of Global Search for Education. *Education World*. Retrieved July 2016 from http://www.educationworld.com/a_curr/rubin/edmodo-teachers-share-experiences.shtml

Smart, K. L., & Cappel, J. J. (2006). Students' perceptions of online learning: A comparative study. *Journal of Information Technology Education*, *5*, 201–219.

Tanveer, M. (2011). *Integrating e-Learning in classroom-based language teaching: Perceptions, challenges and strategies* (4th ed.). ICT for Language Learning.

West, R. E., Waddoups, G., & Graham, C. R. (2006). Understanding the experiences of instructors as they adopt a course management system. *Educational Technology Research and Development*, *55*(1), 1–26. doi:10.1007/s11423-006-9018-1

Williams, D. L., & Whiting, A. H. (2016). Exploring the relationship between student engagement, Twitter, and a Learning Management System: A study of undergraduate marketing students. *International Journal of Teaching and Learning in Higher Education*, *28*(3), 302–313.

Wolfe, A. M., & College, E. (2007). Students' attitudes towards social networks and modalities. Retrieved from: http://alisonwolfe.com/wordpress/wp-content/uploads/Student_Attitudes_Social_Networks1.pdf

## KEY TERMS AND DEFINITIONS

**CALL-Mediated Course:** A course that uses CALL in the teaching learning process. The class meetings consist of both face-to-face meetings and online.

**Edmodo:** A free online learning platform that can be used by teachers, students, and parents to have meaningful interaction and work collaboratively.

**EFL (English as a Foreign Language) Contexts:** Conditions or environment in which English is not used in daily communication. English is commonly used in the class only.

**EFL Pre-Service Teachers:** College students who are trained to be English teachers in non-English speaking countries. The training is supervised by teacher educators and supervising teachers. They commonly have to do teaching practicum at one point of their degree.

**Engagement Enhancing Activities:** A set of activities that are designed to improve student engagement.

**Online Learning Platform:** An integrated set of interactive *online* services that provide trainers, learners, and others involved in education with information, tools and resources to support and enhance educational delivery and management.

**Sociocultural Theory:** A belief that knowledge is obtained from interacting and communicating with other people in social interactions.

**Student Engagement:** The level of efforts, willingness, time, and attention that students dedicate during a course, which can be seen from the level of participation in class activities.

**Teaching Practicum:** Teaching activities that are conducted by pre-service teachers in school settings. They are generally supervised by university teachers and school teachers.

## APPENDIX

### Interview Questions Used in the Semi-Structured Interviews

1. What activities did you do in this CALL-mediated course?
2. How did you feel about those activities using Edmodo?
3. Can you tell me the features in Edmodo that made you interested in the course?
4. From those activities, which ones did you like most and least? Why?
5. What are the things that encouraged you to participate in this course?
6. What advantages, if any, did you get from this CALL-mediated course?
7. Can you tell me some barriers, if any, that hindered you from participating?
8. How did your participation in this course differ from non CALL-mediated courses?

# Chapter 11
# Technology-Integrated Teaching and Assessment:
## ESP at the University of Bucharest

**Lorena Clara Mihăeş**
*University of Bucharest, Romania*

## ABSTRACT

*The information revolution has enhanced the role of English as the lingua franca of global communication and has dramatically increased the demand for academic English courses which focus on discipline-specific knowledge. The present chapter examines the current state of teaching and assessing English for Specific Purposes at the University of Bucharest, Romania. Against the wider background provided by language education policies and digital initiatives within the European Union, the chapter presents how technology-integrated teaching methods have begun to shape both the content and the delivery format of the specialised English class and to renew the task-based framework on which the course is developed. The assessment, however, is more indebted to the traditional type of evaluation. The undergraduate English for History course will be given as an example in point.*

## INTRODUCTION

A renowned theatre in Bucharest was recently forced to close down because the building was too old and represented a potential threat to the theatre-goers. As it began to organise its performances in various other places, an announcement was placed in the window of the old building: *Our company's headquarters have moved online*. This announcement seems emblematic of the world we inhabit, the virtual merging with, or even replacing the physical. The change is evident everywhere, from the way we communicate daily to the way we work or study. Technology has made the world smaller, work easier, and learning more accessible and affordable. It has also made the acquisition of a second language a more enjoyable experience. As a matter of fact, the study of foreign languages has always been ahead of its time compared to other school subjects, because it has taken advantage of the benefits of technology, in the past and even more so at present. Many people remember, for sure, the heyday of the cassette recorder, which

DOI: 10.4018/978-1-5225-2933-0.ch011

was used for listening activities in the foreign language classes, or the overhead projector and the more appealing VCR, which combined the image with the sounds and brought, for the first time probably, a touch of authenticity to the class. Not to mention the old language laboratory equipped with heavy devices, such as enormous headsets, where several students simultaneously performed listening tasks at their own pace (a real achievement for those times). Those days are gone, as the new technologies have replaced the old equipment with easy-to-manoeuvre computing infrastructure. The compatibility between foreign language teaching and technology, especially in its digital format, can be explained by the former's ceaseless search for authentic immersive experiences that can simulate real-life situations, and by the latter's inexhaustible resources of authentic materials, together with many possibilities of practicing and enhancing practically all language skills. The use of computers in the process of language learning has a name—Computer Assisted Language Learning (CALL)—and has been around us since the 1960s (Warschauer & Healey, 1998).

The present chapter looks at a branch of Language for Specific Purposes - English for Specific Purposes (ESP) in the digital age. With English becoming the lingua franca of education and of research nowadays, there has been an increasing demand for academic courses that support the acquisition of English with a focus on discipline-specific vocabulary. The discussion will be contextualised by referring to the situation of ESP in Romania, in particular at the University of Bucharest, against the larger background provided by post-Bologna European higher education systems and the European Union's language policies and language education in universities. Both teaching and assessment practices will be presented within the task-based framework, with an emphasis on the way the adoption of new technology has begun to shape the once traditionally-taught ESP course. The case of the undergraduate English for History course will be provided as an example in point. The conclusion of this chapter is that, if technology-integrated ESP teaching is a thriving, still not fully exploited area, the assessment procedure is more at ease in a traditional environment, where the computer is used mainly for listening comprehension and searching for appropriate texts on the Internet to devise various reading and speaking tasks.

## BACKGROUND

Specialised literature considers ESP to be part of Language for Specific Purposes, an applied approach to language education, which caters to the linguistic needs of people working or studying in a certain domain. Thus, it is terminologically embedded in a particular domain, but it preserves part of the objectives of general English, such as to improve the learner's ability to communicate effectively, fluently an accurately and to develop and integrate the use of all language skills. ESP is divided into English for Academic Purposes (EAP) and English for Occupational Purposes (EOP) (Dudley-Evans & St John, 1998; Jordan, 1997). EAP is further split up into English for Science and Technology, English for Business and Economics, English for Medical Purposes, and English for Law (Dudley-Evans & St John, 1998). Hutchinson and Waters (1987) contend, however, that there is not a clear-cut distinction between EAP and EOP, as "people can work and study simultaneously and it is also likely that in many cases the language learnt for immediate use in a study environment will be used later when the student takes up, or returns to, a job" (p. 16). This chapter is not so much interested in terminological debates; instead, it will use ESP to refer to the teaching of English to undergraduates enrolled in various non-philological faculties with a view to introducing them to the English terminology of their field of study. It will do so by describing how CALL has made the ESP courses more student-centred and has increased students' overall linguistic performance.

Though it is said that ESP distrusts any underlying theories (Dudley-Evans & St John, 1998; Swales, 1988), there have been several attempts at defining it as a scholarly discipline and classifying it accordingly. Hutchinson and Waters (1987) opine that ESP is not a method, but an approach to language learning based on learner's needs (p. 27). Strevens (1988) considers that ESP is defined by four absolute characteristics (it is need-oriented, it is related to a specific discipline in terms of content, it is focused on language appropriateness for all linguistic levels, and it contrasts with general English) and two variable characteristics (it may focus on the development of one skill only, such as reading, and it does not employ a certain teaching methodology). Unlike general-English classes, the nature of interaction between students and teacher in a ESP course is different, the teacher being more like a language consultant while students are the fledgling experts in their domain (Dudley-Evans & St John, 1998, p. 4). In terms of CALL literature and ESP, Butler-Pascoe (2009) identifies three primary delivery models for the ESP courses: ESP taught by English teachers, English-medium specialised courses taught by field-specific teachers, and a collaborative model, which brings together English teachers and teachers in the disciplines.

If language education in general is compatible with technology, ESP is even more so. More recent trends consider the transformative power of new technologies in the field of ESP teaching. Warschauer (2005) speaks about a change in the context of language learning (communication technologies are, in fact, responsible for the unprecedented growth of ESP through the advent of the Internet) and a change in the way people learn languages as the Internet "provides a vast and valuable repertoire of authentic material and potential interlocutors for language analysis, practice, and learning" (p. xiv). Arnó-Macià (2012) identifies a new dimension that technology has brought to the modern ESP class, which now goes "beyond language learning by focusing on culture and social discourses" (p. 91), via a series of collaboration possibilities with virtual discourse communities. *Skype,* for instance, is a tool which can connect the class with professionals in real-time conversations. It can likewise be employed for synchronous tandem language teaching (Mullen, Appel, & Shanklin, 2009). The teacher can also use *Mixxer*, an educational open-source for language exchanges, to create a group which includes native speakers who share the same interests with the students' and with whom students may engage in conversations on specialised topics. The web is, in fact, a portal to many professional communities and the ESP teachers, too, may connect with peers and field-specific experts around the world to share ideas and good-practice examples. This could make their job easier, especially now that they have to play so many roles, from teacher as such, to materials designer, collaborator, assessor, and researcher (Kern, 2013, p. 99).

In terms of assessment, computer-assisted language testing (CALT) has long been considered to bring certain advantages to the field of evaluation, such as the possibility to measure, control and record task-completion time and test takers' routes through the test (Alderson, 1990). In CALT, computers may perform multiple functions: to assist in constructing the input, to deliver it, to record the responses, to assist rates and scores (Alderson, 1996; Douglas, 2000, p. 270). The computer offers the medium, serves as a repository and as an assessor—a great tool if one thinks about all the above-mentioned tasks that the teacher must undertake. In the narrower field of Language for Specific Purposes, both Alderson (1996) and Douglas (2000) speak about the importance played by computer databases of corpora in selecting relevant test material in accordance with field content, syntax, vocabulary level, etc. Douglas (2013) maintains that currently available software may be used to develop assessment items like multiple-choice and blank-filling, which integrate video, audio and graphics, yet for the field of ESP, "purpose-built software will need to be developed for more sophisticated input and response features" (p. 378).

Technology used for assessment purposes comes with its own drawbacks. A word of caution comes from Douglas (2000), who warns us about the fallacious belief that the technology-enhanced testing environment stands for real life. The problem resides not in the unrealistic testing technique, but in the interpretations based on the test taker's performance on such tests. Though obviously superior to tests in which test takers are simply asked to imagine a situation, the interpretation of the performance in technology-enhanced environments should be cautiously made. Therefore, Douglas (2000) pleads for an analysis of the use of technology prior to implementation, as "Language testing that is driven by technology, rather than technology being employed in the service of language testing, is likely to lead us down a road best not travelled" (p. 275).

## ENGLISH FOR SPECIFIC PURPOSES AT THE UNIVERSITY OF BUCHAREST: ISSUES AND PROSPECTS IN THE DIGITAL AGE

### Language Education Within the European Union in the Digital Era

As early as 1998, the Council of Europe directly strengthened the importance of language education for specific needs and urged member states to take action:

*In the period of transition from full-time education to working life, and at all stages of vocational preparation and training, offer all young people language courses wherever possible and appropriate so as to widen their access to information, equip them to participate in international projects, prepare them for taking up an occupation and increase their vocational mobility. (Council of Europe, 1998, p. 35)*

Probably the most important and useful document released by the European Union concerning language education is the *Common European Framework of Reference for Languages: Learning, Teaching, Assessment* (CEFRL) (Council of Europe, 2001), which "provides a common basis for the elaboration of language syllabuses, curriculum guidelines, examinations, textbooks, etc. across Europe" (p. 1). CEFRL describes the components of communicative language competence (linguistic, sociolinguistic and pragmatic competence), the language activities performed by the learner (reception, production, interaction and mediation), and the domains in which foreign language use may occur (personal, occupational and educational) (pp. 13-15). More importantly, however, the framework settles and describes common reference levels of proficiency.

Another important initiative was the creation of the European Centre for Modern Languages (ECML) in Graz, Austria in 1994. Its mission is to encourage excellence and innovation in language teaching and support its member states (Romania is one of them) in the implementation of effective language education policies. One of the initiatives was the *ICT-REV* project, which developed a *gateway* website with an annotated inventory of free online tools and open educational resources for language teaching and learning (ICT Home, 2017). These tools, such as word cloud creators (*Wordclouds*, *Taxedo*), audio recordings (*Rhinospike*), wiki website creation tools (*PB Works*), or native speakers' correction of writing samples (*Lang-8*), are each described according to pedagogical criteria including interface, time efficiency, multilinguality, respect for privacy, saving work for future use, and tailorability. The project team also created a Moodle workspace (http://moodle.dots.ecml.at/), where teachers can register free of charge and may engage in discussions with other teachers about their own experiences with the use of online technologies in the classroom. The ECML's ongoing programme for 2016-2019 is called *Languages at the heart of learning*. It comprises several development projects, including *Digital literacy for the teaching and learning of languages*. Its purpose is to assist teachers in helping students to build Personal Learning Environments by using relevant resources, software and applications. This aims to increase students' confidence in using the foreign language and aid them to become autonomous learners.

Despite these active policies and measures, a report released by the European Commission (EC) (European Commission, 2014a) has found that, although there has been an increasing demand for language skills on the labour market, the graduates' competence level is below expectations. A similar report has found that, although foreign language learning in school settings is widely available nowadays, it is the quality and the effectiveness of language education that are the source of the problem (European Commission, 2014b). The latter report recommends that a new emphasis should be placed on the quality of language teaching and proposes two methods to reach this goal: CLIL (Content and Language Integrated Learning) and CALL.

The move towards the integration of new technologies in higher education tallies with many initiatives on the digital revolution within the European Higher Education Area (EHEA). EHEA is a common European space created in 2010 to harmonize quality standards for study programmes, as well as qualifications standards across the European Union, thus "making explicit the new commonalities of Europe, be they economic, social or cultural" (Barblan, 2011, p. 573). An early project (1996-1998) was *A Virtual University for Europe* (VirtUE), a feasibility study for the development and implementation of a networked virtual university in cooperation with traditional universities, open universities and technology providers. Under the eLearning initiative, the *Collaborative European Virtual University* (cEVU) was funded from 2001 to 2003 and the outcomes included an inventory of tools and techniques to support virtual mobility actions, including training materials. A more recent initiative from 2013—*Opening up Education: Innovative Teaching and Learning for All through New Technologies and Open Educational Resources*—regards open education as "a way of carrying out education, often using digital technologies. Its aim is to widen access and participation to everyone by removing barriers and making learning accessible, abundant, and customisable for all. It offers multiple ways of teaching and learning, building and sharing knowledge" (Inamorato dos Santos, Punie, & Castaño-Muñoz, 2016, p. 5).

However, there is still talk about the digital divide in higher education across various countries in the European Union and worldwide:

*To the extent that it permits access to higher education for new constituencies of learners who otherwise would be excluded, the digital revolution is a good thing. To the extent that it institutionalises two-tier (elite vs. mass) higher education systems globally, it is less desirable. The digital revolution expresses both of these tendencies at once. (De Wit, Hunter, Howard, & Egron-Polak, 2015, p. 77)*

Fortunately, the gap is closing. In Romania, all universities are provided with computer facilities and Internet access. As contemporary higher education is more and more infused with the new technologies, the European Commission (2013) recommends that higher education institutions adopt a comprehensive internationalisation strategy which also includes "the internationalisation and improvement of curricula and digital learning" (p. 4). Since 1990, Romanian universities have been responding to European trends and policies. The teaching-learning process and research have gained an international dimension, following the increased mobility of students and teaching staff on the one hand, and the international impetus of scholarly activities, such as international conferences and various types of research projects, on the other hand. Most Romanian universities require students to study at least one foreign language, usually English, and, over the past 20 years, many institutions have also offered undergraduates the option of enrolling in a second foreign language course (De Wit et al., 2015, p. 161). To complement the picture, the emergence of English as a medium of instruction for bachelor's and master's study programmes, has turned the inward-looking Romanian universities of the communist regime and of the early 1990s into ones that can now soar as open and competitive institutions.

## The ESP Course at the University of Bucharest: Past and Present Directions

The University of Bucharest (UB) is the second oldest public university in Romania, founded in 1864. The Faculty of Foreign Languages and Literatures first taught Latin and ancient Greek, and then French. Other languages followed. Thirty-three foreign languages are currently taught by the faculty. As part of the international orientation of the university, non-philological faculty members began to introduce courses in foreign languages, mainly English and French and, until the fall of communism, Russian. In order to meet the increasing demand for foreign language courses, the Faculty of Foreign Languages and Literatures established a Department of Modern Languages. As the number of enrolled students shows, English is the language of choice at UB. This is not at all surprising and it is not a local phenomenon only —beginning in 1945, English has started to gain ground as a second or foreign language in more and more schools worldwide. In the European Union, English is now the most studied foreign language in secondary and higher education.

Who has been the audience of the ESP course and how has it been taught? In terms of specialisation, the audience has not changed much. ESP covers a vast area of specialties, from English for sciences to English for business studies, law, political sciences, or history, to mention just a few of them. The method of teaching, however, has changed a lot. A brief look at an English practical course for non-philological faculties published in 1979 and titled *English for Intermediate and Advanced Students* (Retinschi, 1979) reveals that it was mostly grammar-oriented. The same book covered several unrelated domains. As the author professed in the foreword, any foreign language was considered to be a sequence of grammar structures as well as the speaker's linguistic reaction in a variety of situations (Retinschi, 1979). The assessment was based more on the grammar-translation method with a view to checking linguistic accuracy. Learning English was, therefore, static, drill-based, and clearly lacked a practical dimension. Following the restrictions imposed by the communist regime, travelling and studying abroad were forbidden, while specialised literatures were available only in Romanian. Given this confined social context, language education in Romanian universities remained for long indebted to structuralist paradigms and did not get the chance to experience the constructivist revolution of the 1960s-1980s, let alone using computers for language teaching in CALL's early years.

The purpose of learning English, however, has changed over time as a result of societal changes. Since 1989, learning English has gained a more practical outlook. Superior English skills are now acknowledged to boost graduates' employability—44% of Romanian employers consider foreign language skills among top three most important skills and competences when hiring a candidate (Eurobarometer, 2014). English is also essential for graduates who want to apply for English-medium study programmes in Romania or abroad, or who simply want to pursue a career in research and who, therefore, need access to specialised literature mainly available in English. As a consequence, undergraduates are extremely motivated to enhance their knowledge of general English and to learn the terminology of their field of study, and they expect to be able to do so by the end of the ESP course.

Against this backdrop, the mission of the course instructor is not easy. It is made even more difficult by the reduction of the number of English classes following the signing of the Bologna Declaration in 1999, which led to three-year bachelor's degree cycles, one year less than before. As a direct result, English, as well as the other modern languages for that matter, are no longer compulsory for certain specialisations, such as life and natural sciences. The length of the ESP course now varies from two to four semesters, according to the field of study. Faculties such as business administration, history and law still preserve English as a compulsory four-semester course, while chemistry, biology or mathematics offer a two-semester elective ESP course. Besides time constraints, another hindrance is represented by the undergraduates' heterogeneous entry competency level, which usually divides the class into intermediate and advanced students.

The need to engage students in natural language use in order to make them autonomous speakers and masters of the domain-specific vocabulary at the same time has gradually led to a shift from more traditional approaches, which emphasise linguistic accuracy, to content-based and task-based approaches, which favour fluency in simulated professional contexts. Communicative approaches to language learning have been met with some criticism. Nunan (1987), for example, says that the adopters of communicative language learning have failed in recreating real-life communication in their classes, which are largely dominated by non-communicative patterns of interaction. Swan (1985) calls this the "real-life fallacy" (p. 82) and argues against semantic syllabuses which give priority to meaning over structures. However, far from overlooking the importance of grammar, communicative approaches adopt a holistic perspective, which accommodates grammatical structures and knowledge of sociocultural contexts (Canale & Swain, 1980). Practice has confirmed that communicative approaches are one of the best ways of meeting the objectives of the ESP course. Many of today's students will work in international environments where they will most likely use English for professional communication. Moreover, many apply for English-medium master's degrees, in Romania or abroad. In order for the course instructors to help students achieve the course objectives, they have to expose them to a variety of authentic materials and situations, which are meant to turn the artificial environment of the ESP class into one as close as possible to real life. Authenticity is now a major concern and the latest technological advances offer many opportunities to create authentic and immersive learning environments. At this point, modern technologies complement rather than replace the traditional chalk-and-talk methods. The ESP class takes place in a blended learning environment and makes use of technology in various ways, from listening activities to reading based on relevant and up-to-date materials gathered from the World Wide Web.

## Technology-Integrated ESP Teaching: The Task-Based Approach Revisited

The general entry level expected from non-philological students is, according to the *Common European Framework* (Council of Europe, 2001), at least B1 (Threshold Level), although in some cases B1+ (Strong Threshold Level) is desirable in order for them to accomplish certain pedagogical tasks. This means that the student should be able to maintain interaction, manage in a range of contexts, and cope flexibly with problems in everyday life. Students' initial level of general English is assessed by a written diagnostic test and by an interview with the course instructor at the beginning of the course. As it is not possible to divide the class into beginner, intermediate, and advanced levels and work separately with them at different time slots, the teacher's task is not easy from the outset. The traditional grammar and translation-based class usually meant that the less advanced students could catch up with their peers only if they were willing to devote extra time for individual study. They usually scored poorly in the final exams and there was little if any improvement in their skills at the end of the semester.

In the past few years, teachers have reappraised the goals of the ESP course and have reached the conclusion that, as much as they love to teach grammar and find satisfaction when students learn how to use sophisticated linguistic structures, the primary purpose of ESP remains the ability to communicate in professional contexts. The gradual adoption of communicative approaches, which puts fluency and communicative competences at the core of ESP teaching while linguistic accuracy is downplayed (but not overlooked), is part of a larger movement that has been taking place worldwide. A case against the grammatical syllabus is presented by Krashen (1982), who pays special attention to heterogeneous learners' groups and who pleads for the use of natural communicative input over finely-tuned input (i.e., classroom practice aiming to rehearse the structures of the day). This type of communicative approach to language teaching seems particularly fit for the aims of the ESP class, which focuses on developing learners' communicative competences. Alongside grammatical competence, the framework developed by Canale and Swain (1980) adds sociolinguistic competence (the rules of language use), and strategic competence (the ability to compensate for breakdowns in communication by resorting to paraphrasing, role-playing, etc.). Kern and Warschauer (2000) speak about a historical turn in language education from a structural approach to communicative approaches, such as the previously mentioned sociocognitive perspective that helps students to engage in "authentic social discourse situations and discourse communities that they would later encounter outside the classroom" (p. 5). Authenticity has long been acknowledged as being essential for ESP teaching and has been seen as a reaction against the artificiality of previous teaching methods.

The Romanian Ministry of Education does not endorse or make recommendations as to what pedagogical approaches should be used in public universities. The new National Education Law adopted in 2011 (Law No.1/2011) highlights, however, the importance of student-centred learning. The Agency for Quality Assurance in Romania (2006), which sets and checks higher education providers' abidance by national accreditation standards, also states that the main responsibility of the academic staff is to design student-centred learning methods and environments.

In line with these national policies, one of the most frequently used approaches at UB is task-based learning and teaching. The added benefit of this communicative approach is a focus on authentic situations by embedding holistic communicative acts into a specific context (Fisher, Chouissa, Dugovicova, & Virkkunen-Fullenwider, 2011). A pedagogical task is defined in different ways. Nunan (2004), for instance, provides a detailed history of the concept, but the definition of Appel and Gilabert (2006) seems to best capture its essence: "a goal-oriented process, which has a number of steps, that draws on a series of cognitive and communicative procedures and that has a defined outcome" (p. 80). In a typical ESP class taught within this framework, the teacher takes a step back to allow students to take a step forward and make the most of the course time. However, the teacher's role as facilitator (Willis, 1996) remains important, or it becomes even more important than in the traditional approaches because he has to design tasks that are challenging and motivating enough to elicit natural language use. Tasks are chosen according to students' field of study and integrate the five skills: listening, reading, writing, spoken interaction, and spoken production. Gonzalez-Lloret (2016) suggests a new model for technology-integrated task-based approach: starting from the target tasks (what people do in real life outside of class), both pedagogical and technology tasks are derived (what we do in class). Gonzalez-Lloret & Ortega

(2014) identify five features of such a task: primacy of meaning, goal orientation, learner-centeredness, and focus on reflective learning (pp. 5-6).

In what follows, I will present an example from an undergraduate English for History course, which is currently taught in a blended learning environment, that is, traditional and computer-mediated activities are both used during the class. The course favours experiential and collaborative learning strategies.

The English for History is a four-semester long course and introduces students to the terminology of history studies, building upon already acquired grammar and general vocabulary knowledge. First-year students are asked to complete a questionnaire at the beginning of the course (a typical needs analysis). The common reasons they give for enrolling in the English course (they are also given the alternative of German and French) are that they need it to participate in exchange programmes, for their future career, for research and for furthering their studies abroad. Students have very good initial competency levels, usually B+; therefore, the course aims at making them reach proficiency level while becoming masters of the discipline-specific vocabulary. Both receptive skills (listening and reading) and productive skills (speaking and writing) are enhanced during the course, in a holistic manner.

There is no textbook for this course, it is entirely up to the teacher to choose the materials and design the tasks. The Internet is a rich source of authentic materials for reading tasks. Students may be presented with articles or book excerpts on the most recent socio-political international events or discoveries in their domain. As many online specialised magazines offer free (unfortunately limited) views of articles, though sometimes teachers use personal subscriptions to access some of the content (e.g., *The Economist*, *History*, *London Review of Books*), it is up to the teacher to select the ones that appeal the most to the students. The teacher prepares the reading texts and exercises beforehand. The worksheets are distributed to the students via one of the electronic means through which they are permanently in contact: Facebook accounts (more increasingly the students' first choice in terms of social media), WhatsApp Messenger, Yahoo groups or e-mails (for reasons that merit investigation, students seem less and less eager to use e-mail, however). Sometimes, students make paper copies of the texts, but ever more frequently they access them directly from their phone, tablet or laptop. At the beginning of the semester, the teacher posts a list of resources available online, including a list of free-access dictionaries, both general and specialised. The university's computing infrastructure is seldom used for reading activities (students have their own mobile devices), instead the Wi-Fi connection is regularly accessed.

Listening comprehension is now exclusively done on the computer—sometimes the teacher's laptop or the classroom desktop computers. Sources of materials are inexhaustible, like podcasts, multimedia resources or free audio editions offered by specialised magazines and even TED Talks given by native speakers on topics related to history. Web-based materials expose students to a variety of authentic situations similar to those they may encounter in their future profession. In some cases, students are grouped in small teams and work together on a given task. As stated by Nunan (2004), experiential learning is the theoretical blueprint for task-based language teaching. Instead of passively acquiring knowledge from the teacher, the learner is encouraged to actively participate in the transformation of knowledge, sometimes by working in small, collaborative groups. A scenario related to the field of history is set up and various tasks are afterwards embedded into it. The time allotted to task-solving may encompass two courses. The scenarios are usually broad enough and avoid highly specialised topics that might cause difficulties for both undergraduates (who are still in the learning process of their discipline) and the teacher (who is not a specialist in the students' field of study). More often than not, the nature of the scenario is connected to what students study in the specialised disciplines during a particular semester. An example is ancient history, which provided one of the scenarios for the English class.

The ESP class took place in a room equipped with a smartboard and computers connected to the Internet. The overall scenario covered two courses during which all five language skills described earlier were practiced and enhanced. The group consisted of 25 students. The topic was introduced by pre-task activities, which, besides eliciting answers from students regarding background knowledge on the matter, also introduced relevant vocabulary. Brainstorming and mind maps were used for that purpose. The teacher used the interactive whiteboard and a web-based mind map creator, *Cmap* (which she had used before) to visually organise the information around the topic of ancient history (Cmap Home, 2014). This could have also been done as a group activity, but because students had not worked with this tool before, it would have taken too much of the course time and resources.

The reading activity was based on two texts adapted from *The Economist* ("Iconoclasm and Islamic State: Destroying history's treasures" and "Ancient Rome: What a strange lot," a review of Mary Beard's book *A History of Ancient Rome*), and one from *historyextra.com* ("The truth about ancient Egypt"). Reading tasks required students to focus on gist and then on details, to grasp speaker's attitude and opinion, to identify style and language register, etc. Listening comprehension relied on a seven-minute TED lecture on *Hunting for Peru's lost civilisations with satellites* (ted.com/talks) and on a podcast from *historyextra.com* (*Myths of ancient Egypt*). Students answered a set of questions based on the listening excerpt. For both reading and listening activities, students filled out worksheets directly on the computer. The listening activity continued in the second course as well, when students listened to two more podcasts from *historyextra.com—Ancient Egypt through Victorian eyes* and *A history of Istanbul.*

For speaking practice, done as a post-task activity in the second course, each group had to choose a controversial issue related to ancient history, other than the ones in the reading and listening activities, and present it to the class as a *PowerPoint* presentation. Making presentations is a current practice in the ESP class and students are encouraged to pay attention to presentation techniques, because the effective use of visual aids is graded in the end-of-course exam. Groups established their own specific goals and brought arguments to support their ideas. Students were allowed to use whatever Internet resources they found helpful to convey their message. Groups interacted with one another mainly in English (but not exclusively, as sometimes they felt the need to find the Romanian equivalents for certain specialised terms) and activated history-related vocabulary and knowledge to argue for or against a point under discussion. As the author of this chapter noted elsewhere (Mihăeş, 2016), an English-only class is not always the most felicitous choice for ESP. Resorting to mother tongue equivalents when the need arises is an important feature of this new type of technology-integrated ESP class. A challenging task is to find the Romanian corresponding expressions for neologisms that are of English origin, especially for sciences. As the ESP teacher usually does not possess a degree in the field of the students he teaches, and there is a scarcity of specialised bilingual dictionaries, the best solution—though not always the one at hand—is to cooperate with discipline teachers and specialists in the domain and even with English teachers who teach similar ESP classes in other universities. A cooperative (technology-mediated) network of ESP teachers and specialists could bring great progress in the domain of specialised languages. For the time being, nevertheless, students as future specialists are the handiest language consultants.

An important achievement was the fact that students understood how to collaboratively set up a joint framework and then prepare and defend their arguments logically. Thus, instead of focusing on discrete grammar structures, the course contextualised the use of language, giving it a social and a more functional dimension. Less proficient students were encouraged to take the floor too, and present their group's point of view on the matters discussed. Sometimes, the teacher's help was needed to check for correct usage of certain structures, but peer tutoring was prioritized on many occasions (it is true that peer-to-peer support focused less on grammar issues and more on vocabulary and discipline expertise). Though writing within the communicative framework seems to have lost the high ground, several factors have contributed to a renewed focus on writing. One of them is the emergence of English as a medium of instruction, which requires that students produce a whole range of written specialised texts in English, including diploma papers, master and even PhD dissertations, all of them requiring very good writing skills. These skills are also important for those who will work in multinational companies, where most written communication is in English. Writing is usually done as a post-task activity off campus and checked during the class. Students have to write reports, formal letters, opinion essays, book reviews, and so forth. They have to obey the rules and standards of academic writing and employ the terminology of their field of study. They may use, as they often do, Internet resources and do online research, but in a critical and reflective manner. This will help them in the future to prepare diploma papers and to conduct research in their field. Sometimes undergraduates do collaborative written projects using *Google Drive* to collaborate.

## Technology-Integrated ESP Assessment

One of the European Union's language objectives is to improve the relevance and comparability of testing and assessment (European Commission, n.d.). A recent *Study on comparability of language testing in Europe* (European Commission, 2015) found, however, that "language examinations across jurisdictions present a wide variety of features in terms of the constructs tested, the populations of test takers, the interpretations of the results and the measurement characteristics of these examinations" (p. 13).

While it is difficult to ensure full comparability with other language tests, the existence of international language descriptors makes the evaluation bands and rating scales developed by the ESP teachers at UB be compatible and comparable with similar ones. The descriptors for each competency level are provided by CEFRL (Council of Europe, 2001), while the tests are devised and created in accordance with the task-based framework (*Guidelines for task-based university language testing*, henceforth G.U.L.T.) developed by the European Centre for Modern Languages (Fisher et al., 2011). The general targeted level is B2, but, in the past few years, more and more students have been able to reach C1 level. Upon course completion, students receive a certificate of linguistic competency based on final exam scores. The certificate specifies their proficiency level along five skills. They can use the certificate within the university, for English-medium master programmes or to enrol in PhD degree programs where a linguistic certificate is mandatory.

ESP tests are devised to predict the test taker's ability to use English in a specific purpose domain (Douglas, 2000). For that matter, an interactionalist perspective (Bachman, 2007; Chalhoub-Deville, 2003), which focuses on the interaction between the test taker and a real-life situation in a communication context, best fits the objectives of the assessment. During the semester, undergraduates take a series of formative tests, but these are not graded and function more as teaching tools. The end-of-course exam, however, is a summative test. All five language skills are tested separately, not in an integrated way. This allows for a better, more transparent and reliable grading of all skills. Receptive and productive skills are graded according to task-completion success, language competence, pragmatic competence, as well as paralinguistic aspects and presentation techniques. The test is, thusly, criterion-referenced and includes detailed scoring grids. The assessment is performance-based rather than knowledge-based, as it assesses "a relevant performance in a (relatively) authentic and often work or study-related situation" (Council of Europe, 2001, p. 187), yet it sometimes requires test takers to correctly use discipline-specific vocabulary covered during the course. Although some universities in Romania have opted for pass/fail tests for ESP courses, at UB, students are graded on a scale from 1 to 10, with 5 the cut-off point. The immersive linguistic experience provided by the technology-integrated ESP class has dramatically increased the undergraduates' overall competency level. Consequently, in the past years, there has been a visible improvement in students' performance on final exams, so an increasingly smaller number of students do not manage to pass (less than 5%). Speaking is by far the skill that has improved the most. In the not-so-distant past, many students were passive speakers and scored poorly on the speaking section, although many of them had good grammar and writing skills. Most students are now able to talk coherently, logically, and effectively in English about discipline-specific topics.

For the end-of-course exam, the teacher sets up a scenario or a macro-task into which smaller tasks are embedded, each aiming at assessing one of the skills. The scenario is always field-specific and imagines a possible situation in the real world. The materials for reading and listening are usually taken from the Internet, but the exam as such is pen-and-paper based.

For the assessment of the undergraduate English for History course, first-year students were presented with the following scenario: they were to take a summer job as tour guides in Greece. Before going there, they had to read about ancient Greece to refresh and update their knowledge about that period. The scenario was clearly presented on the exam sheets so that students knew what to expect from the outset. The receptive skills were assessed first. This part of the exam spanned 90 minutes. The input for reading was provided by two texts: one taken from *historyextra.com* ("What did the ancient Greeks do for us?") and the other from *National Geographic* ("Tales from the frontier: Out of the chaos"). Both texts contained a total number of approximately 9,000 characters, as suggested for B2 level by the G.U.L.T. framework (Fisher et al., 2011). Reading comprehension included a series of tasks under the form of multiple-choice exercises, open questions, proofreading and error identification. Listening comprehension was computer-mediated and consisted of two podcasts from *historyextra.com*—one on democracy, which explored the Greek roots of mass participation in politics, and the other on ancient cities, namely Athens and Rome. The podcasts were ten minutes long, the maximum recommended by G.U.L.T. for more advanced learners. Before the activity, students were handed the worksheetsand were given instructions. They were allowed one minute to study the requirements and think about the context. The recordings were played twice. The questions on the worksheets came in the same order as the information on the podcasts and referred to main ideas, specific information and speakers' opinions on the discussed matters.

Productive skills were checked during the second part of the exam, which took place on a different day. Students were grouped in pairs and were given 60 minutes to do pair research activities on cultural heritage tourism in Greece. They had to prepare with their partner a list of arguments for and against mass tourism in Greece and to speak about the damages to archaeological sites as opposed to the huge revenues from mass tourism. Students could use the Internet and access whatever e-resources they considered to be reliable and contain relevant information. Exercising how to use resources in a critical and reflective manner is what makes the task-based tests different from most standardised university exams. The use of "the dossier of authentic resources" (Fisher et al., 2011, p. 29) prepare students for situations they are likely to encounter in their profession. Students presented their conclusions in pairs in the speaking section of the exam. The last part of the exam was writing, which lasted 90 minutes. After the discussion about Greek cultural heritage tourism, students were asked to imagine they had a travel blog and were responsible for writing an entry on what was more important: the revenues from cultural tourism or the preservation of archaeological sites by limiting the number of tourists. Papers were marked on style, content and vocabulary. Undergraduates studying social sciences usually score well on the ESP exam, and, unlike many students enrolled in other programmes, have excellent writing skills, most probably because many of the set books for various disciplines are in English. As described above, the digital and Web 2.0-based technologies play a certain role in the ESP assessment. However, language teachers, though more enthusiastic about embracing technology in the teaching activities, are still sceptical about integrating them in the evaluation. Some of the most common reasons are the fear that the computers or the Internet connection might fail precisely at the time of the exam or other technical problems may appear. More importantly, however, many teachers echo Alderson's (1996) fear that many computerised tests promote "test methods of questionable value" (p. 249). Chapelle (2009) states that, in order to minimize threats to test validity, research should be conducted to identify and address these threats.

At this point, we believe that tests that are entirely computer-driven do not dovetail with the type of assessment we carry out for ESP courses. The computer is used neither as a medium for testing nor as an assessor. There has been talk about a revolution in assessment brought about by the use of the new technologies, but some doubt remains due to our limited understanding of the complexity of language learning and use (Alderson, 1990; Chapelle & Douglas, 2006). Douglas (2013) warns that for ESP, computer-delivered tests do not automatically guarantee authenticity and there are cases in which traditional pen-and-paper exams offer the most authentic environments. In their book dedicated to CALT, Chapelle and Douglas (2006) reach the conclusion that "Computer technology may in the future radically change research and practice in language assessment but doing so will require the type of research that engages with the complexity of the issues, crossing the boundaries between assessment, language, and technology for the purpose of developing paths that work toward the goals of applied linguists" (p. 117). While in agreement with their conclusion, this conclusion is drawn including a caveat that, for the time being, while CALL applied to ESP teaching is a thriving area, the assessment is still rightfully indebted to traditional modes of evaluation.

## FUTURE RESEARCH DIRECTIONS

According to findings in the report *Internationalisation of Higher Education,* the English level of the academic staff in Romania could be significantly improved (De Wit et al., 2015). Given the growth of English-medium degrees in Romania and the advent of English as the language of research, there is a stringent need for academic staff to increase their English knowledge. Moreover, it was found that most Romanian universities did not offer language training to academic and non-academic staff (Deca, Egron-Polak, & Fiţ, 2015). Therefore, ESP courses for the academic staff, tailored for particular domains, could be devised and delivered and technology-integrated methods could prove to be a great help. As the target group of these courses are specialists in various fields, some of whom may be conversant with field-specific vocabulary in English but may have insufficient grammar knowledge or speaking fluency to deliver their courses in English, new pedagogical approaches should be used to meet these objectives.

Although technology-enhanced assessment has not entered the mainstream of ESP practice yet, its potential merits closer examination. The exam sheets could be transferred to an open-source blended learning platform such as Moodle so that all students might simultaneously access them. Tests could remain there for future reference, thus ensuring transparency and visibility of testing. The feedback could be instantaneous for those test items originally devised to be checked by computer. Online and computer-based resources for statistics could be used to assist the teacher in calculating scores (Douglas, 2010). Some teachers opt for a "portfolio" approach to examinations, especially for first-year undergraduates whose proficiency level is closer to B1 and who are given more time to reflect upon the ideas they want to express as well as upon the way they use language. In these cases, the end-of-course exam consists of a portfolio in which students present the results of certain tasks they completed during the course, such as various projects or case studies. These portfolios could become e-portfolios, a change which comes with certain advantages, such as traceability of students' work (students would be more aware of the progresses they make, as previous versions of their work may be archived), the inclusion of multimedia features, the possibility of sharing them or collaborating with peers in creating them. E-portfolios can also encourage reflective learning and self-directed critical thinking, and discourage plagiarism.

ESP teaching in Romania lacks specialized bilingual dictionaries and those that are available are outdated. More can be done in this respect with information technology offering the hosting space together with all the facilities that such an enterprise requires. A step forward has already been taken following the decision of the RO+ Excellency Network of Experts, coordinated by the European Commission, General Department of Translations to use the bilingual glossaries compiled by the graduates of Applied Modern Languages as part of their diploma papers as reliable sources for various terminologies (Mihăeş & Ionita, 2016). Plans have already been made by the Department of Modern Languages to launch a virtual platform, which will foster multilingual terminology glossaries.

Now that classrooms are provided with computing infrastructure and Internet connectivity, not to mention the students' own portable devices, we believe that the next step in improving the quality and efficiency of the ESP class is to create and provide digital content that will focus on disciplinary knowledge along both receptive and productive skills.

## CONCLUSION

In 1979, the British Council published a book on how technology could be used in the teaching of English, "The Use of the Media in English Language Teaching." It must have been considered quite revolutionary at the time, although the resources it referred to merely encompassed radio and television. The idea behind the book was a plea for a holistic approach to language learning, one that would reach learners through as many of their senses as possible (Trim, 1979). More than three decades later, the same British Council (Motteram, 2013) published a book on the roles of innovative technologies in language education in the 21st century, "Innovations in Learning Technologies for English Language Teaching." The book reached the conclusion that "Technology is no longer at the periphery of the ELT field, but at its centre, providing teachers with the means to enhance the teaching of languages in classrooms all over the world" (p. 12). Indeed, technology is now the main driver of change in the field of language education, no matter the language, the learners' age, purpose, or interests. The specialised English classes taught in non-philological faculties are no exception to this worldwide trend. After all, we are all digital now, to paraphrase the name of a forthcoming summit on innovation. This chapter has undertaken to describe how teaching and assessing English for specific purposes is done at the University of Bucharest. It has reviewed technology already implemented and what additional technology may be further integrated to make the ESP courses more efficient, enjoyable, and student-centred for digital natives.

Looking ahead to the not-so-very-distant future, it appears that a branch of computer-assisted language learning—mobile-assisted language learning—is gaining more and more ground because, along with the advantages already offered by desktop computers, mobile devices add portability, affordability, and virtually unlimited access on and off campus. How mobile applications can be integrated into the ESP class in a systematic way is the province of further research.

## REFERENCES


Agency for Quality Assurance in Romania. (2006). *External evaluation methodology, standards, reference standards and performance indicators*. Retrieved from http://www.aracis.ro/fileadmin/ARACIS/Proceduri/Methodology_for_External_Evaluation.pdf

Alderson, C. (1996). Do corpora have a role in language assessment? In J. Thomas & M. Short (Eds.), *Using corpora for language research* (pp. 248–259). London: Longman.

Alderson, J. C. (1990). Learner-centered testing through computers: Institutional issues in individual assessment. In J. de Jong & D. K. Stevenson (Eds.), *Individualizing the assessment of language abilities* (pp. 20–27). Clevedon, UK: Multilingual Matters.

Appel, C., & Gilabert, R. (2006). Finding common ground in LSP: A computer-mediated communication project. In E. A. Macia, A. S. Cervera, & C. R. Ramos (Eds.), *Information technology in languages for specific purposes: Issues and prospects* (pp. 75–90). New York, NY: Springer. doi:10.1007/978-0-387-28624-2_5

Arnó-Macià, E. (2012). The role of technology in teaching languages for specific purposes courses. *Modern Language Journal*, *96*, 89–104. doi:10.1111/j.1540-4781.2012.01299.x

Bachman, L. (2007). What is the construct? The dialectic of abilities and contexts in defining constructs in language assessment. In J. Fox, M. Wesche, D. Bayliss, L. Cheng, C. E. Turner, & C. Doe (Eds.), *Language testing reconsidered* (pp. 41–71). Ottawa, Canada: University of Ottawa Press.

Barblan, A. (2011). From the universities in Europe to the universities of Europe. In W. Rüegg (Ed.), A history of the university in Europe: Volume 4. Universities since 1945 (pp. 550-574). Cambridge, UK: Cambridge University Press.

Butler-Pascoe, M. E. (2009). English for specific purposes (ESP), innovation, and technology. In T. Chiang, W. Chuang, & L. Li (Eds.), *English education and ESP* (pp. 1–15). Taipei, Taiwan: Shih Chien University.

Canale, M., & Swain, M. (1980). Theoretical bases of communicative approaches to second language teaching and testing. *Applied Linguistics*, *I*(1), 1–47. doi:10.1093/applin/I.1.1

Chalhoub-Deville, M. (2003). Second language interaction: Current perspectives and future trends. *Language Testing*, *20*(4), 369–383. doi:10.1191/0265532203lt264oa

Chapelle, C. (2009). Computer-assisted teaching and testing. In M. H. Long & C. J. Doughty (Eds.), *The handbook of language teaching* (pp. 628–644). Oxford, UK: Blackwell Publishing. doi:10.1002/9781444315783.ch33

Chapelle, C., & Douglas, D. (2006). *Assessing Language through Computer Technology*. Cambridge, UK: Cambridge University Press. doi:10.1017/CBO9780511733116

Cmap Home. (2014). *Florida institute for human and machine cognition (IHMC) website*. Retrieved April 20, 2017, from http://cmap.ihmc.us/

Council of Europe. (2001). *Common European framework of reference for languages: Learning, teaching, assessment*. Cambridge, UK: Cambridge University Press.

Council of Europe, Committee of Ministers. (1998). *Of the committee of ministers to member states concerning modern languages* (Recommendation No. R (98) 6). Retrieved from http://cm.coe.int/ta/rec/1998/98r6.htm

De Wit, H., Hunter, F., Howard, L., & Egron-Polak, E. (2015). *Internationalisation of higher education*. Prepared for the European Parliament's Committee on Culture and Education. Policy department B: Structural and cohesion policies. doi:10.2861/444393

Deca, L., Egron-Polak, E., & Fiţ, C. R. (2015). Internationalisation of higher education in Romanian national and institutional contexts. In A. Curaj, L. Deca, E. Egron-Polak, & J. Salmi (Eds.), *Higher education reforms in Romania: Between the Bologna process and national challenges* (pp. 127–148). Dordrecht, The Netherlands: Springer International; doi:10.1007/978-3-319-08054-3_7

Douglas, D. (2000). *Assessing language for specific purposes*. Cambridge, UK: Cambridge University Press.

Douglas, D. (2010). *Understanding language testing*. New York, NY: Routledge.

Douglas, D. (2013). ESP and assessment. In B. Paltridge & S. Starfield (Eds.), *The handbook of English for specific purposes* (pp. 367–384). Oxford, UK: Wiley-Blackwell.

Dudley-Evans, T., & St John, M. J. (1998). *Developments in English for specific purposes: A multi-disciplinary approach*. Cambridge, UK: Cambridge University Press.

Eurobarometer. (2014). *EU skills panorama. Analytical highlight. Focus on foreign languages*. Retrieved from http://skillspanorama.cedefop.europa.eu/en/analytical_highlights/focus-foreign-languages

European Commission. (2012). *Key data on teaching languages at school in Europe 2012*. Retrieved from https://webgate.ec.europa.eu/fpfis/mwikis/eurydice/index.php/Publications:Key_Data_on_Teaching_Languages_at_School_in_Europe_2012

European Commission. (2013). *European higher education in the world*. Communication from the Commission to the European Parliament, the Council, the European Economic and Social Committee and the Committee of the Regions. Retrieved from eur-lex.europa.eu/LexUriServ/LexUriServ.do?uri=COM:2013:0499:FIN:en:PDF

European Commission. (2014a). *Languages in Education and Training: Final Country Comparative Analysis*. Prepared by the TWG Languages in Education and Training with support by GHK. Retrieved from http://ec.europa.eu/dgs/education_culture

European Commission. (2014b). *Improving the effectiveness of language learning: CLIL and computer assisted language learning*. Retrieved from http://ec.europa.eu/dgs/education_culture

European Commission. (2015). *Study on comparability of language testing in Europe*. Prepared by Cambridge English Language Assessment. doi:10.2766/082033

European Commission. (n.d.). *Languages in education - Education and training*. Retrieved from http://ec.europa.eu/education/policy/multilingualism/languages-in-education_en

Fisher, J., Chouissa, C., Dugovicova, S., & Virkkunen-Fullenwider, A. (2011). *Guidelines for task-based university language testing*. Graz, Austria: European Centre for Modern Languages.

Gonzalez-Lloret, M. (2016). *A practical guide to integrating technology into task-based language teaching*. Washington, DC: Georgetown University Press.

Gonzalez-Lloret, M., & Ortega, L. (2014). *Technology-mediated TBLT: Researching technology and tasks*. Amsterdam, The Netherlands: John Benjamins Publishing Company. doi:10.1075/tblt.6

Hutchinson, T., & Waters, A. (1987). *English for specific purposes: A learning-centred approach*. Cambridge, UK: Cambridge University Press. doi:10.1017/CBO9780511733031

ICT Home. (2017). *Use of ICT in support of language teaching and learning website*. Retrieved April 20, 2017, from http://ict-rev.ecml.at/

Inamorato dos Santos, A., Punie, Y., & Castaño-Muñoz, J. (2016). *Opening up education: A support framework for higher education institutions*. JRC Science for Policy Report, EUR 27938 EN. doi:10.2791/293408

Jordan, R. R. (1997). *English for academic purposes: A guide and resource book for teachers*. Cambridge, UK: Cambridge University Press. doi:10.1017/CBO9780511733062

Kern, N. (2013). Technology-integrated English for specific purposes lessons: Real-life language, tasks, and tools for professionals. In G. Motteram (Ed.), *Innovations in learning technologies for English language teaching* (pp. 87–115). London: British Council.

Kern, R., & Warschauer, M. (2000). Theory and practice of network-based language teaching. In M. Warschauer & R. Kern (Eds.), *Network-based language teaching – Concepts and practice* (pp. 1–19). Cambridge, UK: Cambridge University Press. doi:10.1017/CBO9781139524735.003

Krashen, S. D. (1982). *Principles and practice in second language acquisition*. Oxford, UK: Pergamon.

Mihăeş, L. (2016). The emergence of English as a medium of instruction and its impact on the English for specific purposes class. *Proceedings of the 8th international conference on education and new learning technologies*, 7169-7176. doi:10.21125/edulearn.2016.0563

Mihăeş, L., & Ionita, D. (2016). Task-based approach revisited: A guide of good practices for university English teaching and assessing (The University of Bucharest). *Proceedings of the 8th international conference on education and new learning technologies*, 6087-6094. doi:10.21125/edulearn.2016.0303

Motteram, G. (2013). Introduction. In G. Motteram (Ed.), *Innovations in learning technologies for English language teaching* (pp. 5–14). London: British Council.

Mullen, T., Appel, C., & Shanklin, T. (2009). Skypebased tandem language learning and web 2.0. In M. Thomas (Ed.), *Handbook of research on web 2.0 and second language learning* (pp. 101–118). Hershey, PA: IGI Global; doi:10.4018/978-1-60566-190-2.ch006

National Education Law no. 1/2011.

Nunan, D. (1987). Communicative language teaching: Making it work. *ELT Journal*, *41*(2), 136–145. doi:10.1093/elt/41.2.136

Nunan, D. (2004). *Task-Based Language Teaching*. Cambridge, UK: Cambridge University Press. doi:10.1017/CBO9780511667336

Retinschi, S. (1979). *English for Intermediate and advanced students.* Bucuresti: Universitatea din Bucuresti.

Strevens, P. (1988). ESP after twenty years: A re-appraisal. In M. Tickoo (Ed.), *ESP: State of the Art* (pp. 1–13). Singapore: SEAMEO Regional Centre.

Swales, J. M. (1988). *Episodes in ESP: A source and reference book on the development of English for Science and Technology*. New York, NY: Prentice-Hall.

Swan, M. (1985). A critical look at the communicative approach. *ELT Journal*, *39*(2), 76–87. doi:10.1093/elt/39.2.76

Trim, J. (1979). The integration of elements in multi-media language learning systems. In *The Use of Media in English Language Teaching* (pp. 8–14). London: The British Council Printing and Publishing Department.

Warschauer, M. (2005). Foreword. In E. A. Macia, A. S. Cervera, & C. R. Ramos (Eds.), *Information technology in languages for specific purposes: Issues and prospects* (pp. xiii–xv). New York, NY: Springer; doi:10.1007/978-0-387-28624-2

Warschauer, M., & Healey, D. (1998). Computers and language learning: An overview. *Language Teaching*, *31*(02), 57–71. doi:10.1017/S0261444800012970

Willis, J. R. (1996). *A framework for task-based learning*. Harlow, UK: Longman Publishing.

## ADDITIONAL READING

Bárcena, E., Read, T., & Arus, J. (Eds.). (2014). *Languages for specific purposes in the digital era*. New York, NY: Springer; doi:10.1007/978-3-319-02222-2

Coniam, D. (2006). Evaluating computer-based and paper-based versions of an English-language listening test. *ReCALL*, *18*(2), 193–211. doi:10.1017/S0958344006000425

Cummins, P., & Davesne, C. (2009). Using electronic portfolios for second language assessment. *Modern Language Journal*, *93*(1), 848–867. doi:10.1111/j.1540-4781.2009.00977.x

Gollin-Kies, S., Hall, D. R., & Moore, S. H. (Eds.). (2015). *Language for Specific Purposes*. London, England: Palgrave Macmillan; doi:10.1057/9781137500762

Ockey, G. J. (2009). Developments and challenges in the use of computer-based testing for assessing second language ability. *Modern Language Journal*, *93*(1), 836–847. doi:10.1111/j.1540-4781.2009.00976.x

Sarré, C. (2013). Technology-mediated tasks in English for specific purposes (ESP): Design, Implementation and Learner Perception. *International Journal of Computer-Assisted Language Learning and Teaching*, *3*(2), 1–16. doi:10.4018/ijcallt.2013040101

Thomas, M., & Reinders, H. (Eds.). (2010). *Task-based language learning and teaching with technology*. London: Continuum International Publishing Group.

Thomas, M., Reinders, H., & Warschauer, M. (Eds.). (2012). *Contemporary computer-assisted language learning*. London, England: Bloomsbury Academic.

Tsai, S. (2011). Courseware integration into task-based learning: A case study of multimedia courseware-supported oral presentations for non-English major students. *ReCALL*, *23*(2), 117–134. doi:10.1017/S0958344011000048

Vetter, A., & Chanier, T. (2006). Supporting oral production for professional purposes in synchronous communication with heterogenous learners. *ReCALL*, *18*(1), 5–23. doi:10.1017/S0958344006000218

## KEY TERMS AND DEFINITIONS

**Authentic Language:** The connotation of authoritative confirmation that things or people are what they are claimed or appear to be.

**Blended Learning:** A method of instruction that combines traditional learning with computer-mediated activities.

**Common European Framework of Reference for Languages- Learning, Teaching, Assessment:** A guide set up by the Council of Europe to provide international standards which describe language ability.

**English For Specific Purposes:** A branch of Language for Specific Purposes, which aims at catering for the linguistic needs of people working or studying in a certain domain.

**European Union:** A political and economic union of 28 European states, with a single market and a single currency (the euro) for many of the member states, and free movement of citizens.

**Performance-Based Testing:** Tests that do not check a definite body of language, but indicate how well the test taker can perform linguistically in a given context.

**Student-Centred Learning:** Methods of instruction which place the students at the centre, aiming at developing their autonomy as learners, so that they may continue to learn on their own even after leaving school.

**Task-Based Language Learning:** A communicative approach to language education which concentrates on students' performance of authentic tasks.

# Chapter 12
# Using Feedback in ESL and EFL Asynchronous Online Environments

**Larisa Olesova**
*George Mason University, USA*

**Luciana de Oliveira**
*University of Miami, USA*

## ABSTRACT

*Researchers and practitioners' interest in finding more effective ways to provide instructional feedback in order to help second language learners in online environments has increased. The majority of studies found evidence about effectiveness of written and oral feedback to improve student's writing in a target language when they enroll in online courses taught in English. However, some studies also found limitations of both types of feedback when they provided for second language learners. Therefore, researchers and practitioners investigated benefits of other types of feedback and among them is audio feedback. The purpose of this chapter is to overview instructional capabilities of written, oral and audio feedback and how they can support ESL and EFL students in asynchronous online courses. This chapter also discusses when and how to provide different types of feedback when ESL and EFL students are enrolled in online courses taught in English.*

## INTRODUCTION

Enrollment trends of international students in U.S. colleges and universities indicate continuous growth (Institute of International Education, 2016). Current 2015/16 data indicate a 7.1% growth over the prior year with 5.2% of the total U.S. higher education population being international (Institute of International Education, 2016). The number of higher education students taking at least one online course in 2015 is up 3.9% from previous years. The steady growth of students taking online courses in U.S. higher education including English as a Second Language (ESL) and English as a Foreign Language (EFL) students has changed instructional strategies and approaches in online courses and programs (Harrison & Shi,

DOI: 10.4018/978-1-5225-2933-0.ch012

2016). It is known that online courses and, specifically, asynchronous online courses with their flexibility, interaction, and open communication at any time and at any place can remove physical barriers and can also initiate meaningful conversation in cross-national settings (Tuzlukova & Hall, 2017). However, asynchronous online courses based on written communication may also bring up some challenges such as miscommunication or difficulties to enhance feelings of connectedness among students and course instructors (Cifuentes & Shih, 2001). These challenges can become a serious disadvantage for students for whom English is not a native language. This disadvantage can impact their participation and success in asynchronous written communication with those for whom English is a first language (Goodfellow, Lea, Gonzales, & Mason, 2001).

To overcome challenges of miscommunication in asynchronous online courses, research has shown the importance of the instructor's role for successful online learning outcomes (Biesenbach-Lucas, 2003). Indeed, the instructor's role in providing guided instruction and giving constructive feedback may help students to overcome difficulties of text-based online communication. Yet, to increase both the verbal and nonverbal cues of asynchronous interactions, studies have proposed using asynchronous audio, specifically, instructional audio feedback (Cavanaugh & Song, 2015; Ice, Curtis, Phillips, & Wells, 2007). In this chapter, following Brown (2006), the term *foreign language* refers to any language that is not a native language in a country. The term *English as a Foreign Language* (EFL) will be used to imply the use of English in a community where it is not the primary means of communication. This chapter will also use the term *English as a Second Language* (ESL) to refer to use of the English language as a medium of education, government, and business in countries where English is not a native language. In addition, we define audio feedback as a recorded instructional comment to enhance feelings of connectedness and to overcome miscommunication challenges in asynchronous online instruction.

## BACKGROUND

Feedback is defined as "information provided by an agent (e.g., teacher, peer, book, parent, self, and experience) regarding aspects of one's performance" (Hattie & Timperley, 2007, p. 81). In teaching practice, feedback has been viewed as one of the core instructional principles in encouraging and consolidating the learning process (Hyland & Hyland, 2006). To encourage learning in asynchronous online environments, feedback has become a required instructional component in building connections between learners and course instructors. In asynchronous online courses, instructors usually provide feedback not only on traditional student writing, such as essays or research papers, but they also have to provide feedback on other student writing assignments, such as online discussions or blogs. However, when non-language instructors need to provide feedback for ESL/EFL students, they usually find it difficult. They provide feedback mostly on ESL/EFL students' language errors by pointing them out in their writing (Stern & Solomon, 2006). It seems that language accuracy has become the main criteria to assess ESL/EFL students' online writing performance. Consideration of language accuracy as the main assessment criteria of online learning performance might impact success in online courses among ESL/EFL students. Therefore, online instructors who work with ESL/EFL students, specifically in non-language courses, need to consider that ESL/EFL students require different treatment than first language students (de Oliveira, Maune, & Klassen, 2014). When providing feedback to ESL/EFL students, it is necessary not only to point out or correct an error, it is also helpful to elicit and explain the correct form for a better learning performance in online courses (Tsutsui, 2004). Instead of correcting language errors, ESL/

EFL students need constructive feedback on the content to produce more accurate writing, including high quality discussion posts or blog entries in the target language (Ashwell, 2000). Thus, a meaningful combination of feedback on language errors and feedback on content is very important to help ESL/EFL students perform successfully in asynchronous online courses.

The combination of different types of feedback is a common practice for language instructors (Stern & Solomon, 2006). This shows how the nature of feedback in ESL/EFL is different compared to the ways in which feedback is provided for first language speakers. It is widely believed that when ESL/EFL students receive constructive corrective feedback in combination with feedback on content, they improve target language accuracy and fluency, or, as Schachter (1983) mentioned, feedback becomes their "nutritional need" (p. 175) and it becomes "knowledge of results" (as cited in Bonnel, 2008, p. 290).

Moreover, taking into consideration that asynchronous online courses are mostly designed around text-based communication, adding other feedback delivery modes in addition to written comments can also help ESL/EFL students succeed in online courses. One of the well-known feedback delivery modes in asynchronous online courses has been recorded instructional comments or so-called *audio feedback*. Audio feedback is usually delivered as an attachment in the form of mp3 files or embedded audio in PDF documents. When students receive audio feedback, they can listen to it and work on writing revisions on their own time. In this way, a combination of written feedback and audio feedback can improve students' writing performance when they revise their research papers, participate in asynchronous online discussions or just simply submit blog entries. The meaningful combination of both written feedback and audio feedback can possibly enhance ESL/EFL students' feelings of connectedness and overcome miscommunication challenges in text-based online environment.

Literature on feedback for ESL/EFL students in asynchronous online courses has discussed mostly the benefits and limitations of written corrective feedback and audio feedback on content to help ESL/EFL students improve their writing performance. Literature has also discussed the use of video or screen-recorded feedback on ESL/EFL writing in online courses. However, this chapter intends to overview two types of feedback, written corrective feedback and audio feedback on content, because of their popularity and ease of use.

## TYPES OF FEEDBACK IN ESL/EFL

### Written Feedback

There are different types of written feedback including direct (explicit) corrective feedback, indirect (implicit) corrective feedback, focused corrective feedback, unfocused corrective feedback, and written feedback on content. Below is a brief overview of each type of feedback to help course instructors provide effective feedback for ESL/EFL students' writing assignments including essays, research papers, discussion posts, or blog entries in asynchronous online courses.

The review of the literature revealed that debates about the effectiveness of *written corrective feedback* in ESL/EFL has been taking place in the field over the years (Bitchener & Knoch, 2009; Saito, 1994). For example, Truscott (1996) claimed that providing corrective feedback on student writing was ineffective and harmful, and, therefore, should be abandoned in the second language writing classroom. However, Truscott (1996) reviewed only a few studies which made generalization of findings problematic. For example, Truscott stated that Cohen and Robbins (1976) did not find significant effects of corrective feedback on students' errors. Another study reviewed by Truscott (1996) was carried out by Robb, Ross, and Shortreed (1986), who also did not find any significant differences in students' writing ability. Finally, Truscott (1996) found positive outcomes of corrective feedback only in the study by Fathman and Whalley (1990). But Truscott argued that even though Fathman and Whalley found positive outcomes in students' final drafts, it was not clear whether students would become better writers in the future. Despite negative findings for the effectiveness of written corrective feedback by Truscott (1996), the majority of studies have stated that using written corrective feedback in ESL/EFL settings is very helpful for learners to improve target language accuracy in their writing (Bitchener & Knoch, 2009; Ferris, 2003).

*Direct (explicit) written corrective feedback* is defined as "the provision of the correct linguistic form by the teacher to the student" (Ferris, 2006, p. 83). Studies on using direct corrective feedback in ESL/EFL writing found that the parameters of specific institutional, classroom, and task contexts should be taken into account when providing direct corrective feedback. Considering specific parameters is very important because sometimes researchers and practitioners try to search for the *best* way to provide direct corrective feedback, which may be fundamentally mistaken. In addition, students' language proficiency level is one of the most important factors to consider when providing effective direct corrective feedback. Ellis (2009) stated that "a sociocultural perspective on [corrective feedback] would emphasize the need to adjust the type of feedback offered to learners to suit their stage of development although how this can be achieved practically remains unclear in the case of written [corrective feedback]" (p. 106). Researchers have examined different types of written corrective feedback to help practitioners find a better way to provide effective feedback based on the learners' stage of development. In this sense, the study conducted by Bitchener and Knoch (2008) seems promising. They found that direct written feedback can be effective if it is provided in combination with other types of feedback, including written and oral meta-linguistic explanation of language structures (Bitchener & Knoch, 2008). The results showed that students who received a combination of direct written corrective feedback and written and oral meta-linguistic explanation, retained the level of writing longer than students who received only written and oral meta-linguistic explanation (Bitchener & Knoch, 2008). Therefore, it seems that a combination of providing correct linguistic form along with meta-linguistic explanation of correction could be an effective way to help ESL/EFL students improve writing in asynchronous online courses.

*Indirect (implicit) written corrective feedback* may be defined as "when the teacher indicates in some way that an error has been made by means of an underline, circle, code, or other mark – but does not provide the correct form, leaving the student to solve the problem" (Ferris, 2006, p. 83). Indirect corrective feedback may be provided in one of four ways: underlining or circling the error; recording in the margin the number of errors in a given line; or using a code to show where the error has occurred and what type of error it is (Ferris & Roberts, 2001). In contrast with direct corrective feedback when the error is corrected by the course instructor, indirect corrective feedback seems more beneficial to engage students in guided learning and problem solving (Lalande, 1982). For example, Li and Lin (2007) reported that receiving teacher feedback with the engagement of revision tasks is very effective in facilitating and promoting accuracy for EFL student writers. These findings show that when students take control over their own learning, they make more progress in writing over time and produce fewer initial errors than when they receive already corrected errors by their course instructor (Rahimi, 2009). Other benefits of indirect corrective feedback include enhancing student reflection, noticing, and attention (Bitchener & Knoch, 2009). These benefits of indirect corrective feedback can help online ESL/EFL students not only in their own writing but also when they participate in peer review activities. For example, Ferris and Roberts (2001) found that indirect corrective feedback can help students' self-editing with success ratios ranging from 47% to 60%. The researchers also did a statistical reanalysis of the data, combining treatable and untreatable errors. Treatable errors include verbs, noun endings and articles. Untreatable errors include word choice and sentence structure (Ferris & Roberts, 2001). The reanalysis showed that there was a statistically significant difference in students' ability to edit treatable and untreatable error types when they received indirect corrective feedback. Successful revision of treatable and untreatable errors as the result of providing indirect corrective feedback may be considered as another benefit of this type of feedback for online instruction.

Other studies examined *focused and unfocused written corrective feedback*. Focused written corrective feedback is usually directed at a single linguistic feature such as prepositions or articles. Unfocused feedback is defined as the traditional feedback approach to correcting all written errors in students' writing (Sheen, Wright, & Moldawa, 2009). Studies found that providing focused corrective feedback on specific linguistic forms can promote increased accuracy in student writing (Sheen, 2007; Sheen et al., 2009). For example, Sheen et al. (2009) examined the impact of focused and unfocused corrective feedback on the acquisition of English articles. The researchers found that focused written error correction directed at indefinite and definite article errors resulted in greater accuracy than unfocused correction directed at a range of grammatical errors. Using focused written corrective feedback in asynchronous online courses could help ESL/EFL students revise and edit a single linguistic form to retain target language accuracy over time.

Since the 1990s, the focus of educators in ESL/EFL has switched to *written feedback on content*, recognizing that ESL/EFL students also need constructive feedback on the content of their writing. In asynchronous non-language online courses, the nature of written feedback on content is usually affected by individual characteristics of the course (Ferris, 2015). Written feedback on content usually focuses on the rhetorical and syntactic levels (macro-level comments) and the sentence level (micro-level). For example, at the rhetoric level, course instructors usually provide feedback to help students develop arguments. At the syntactic level, course instructors usually focus on the key issues connected to the rhetorical level, such as verb tense or vocabulary choice. Feedback on content can also include written comments on developing new ideas and developing the structure and organization of writing (Ferris, 2006).

To reveal the effectiveness of feedback on content for ESL/EFL students, some studies compared written corrective feedback and feedback on content (Fazio, 2001; Yang, 2016) and found positive results for written feedback on content. However, other studies did not find any differences in effects of both types of feedback (Ashwell, 2000; Fathman & Whalley, 1990), stating that both written feedback on grammar and content have positive effects on ESL/EFL students' writing whether given alone or simultaneously. Nevertheless, Zamel (1985) suggested that feedback on content and corrective feedback should be kept separate to avoid confusing students about what they should revise at any particular stages of the process. In consideration of Zamel's assertion, for some ESL/EFL students who may be unprepared for asynchronous online learning or may be at different stages of language proficiency, receiving written feedback on content may pose challenges in the understanding of instructional commentary intent. Difficulties understanding instructional comments are usually based on ESL/EFL students' lack of grammatical and rhetorical knowledge (Hyland & Hyland, 2006). That is why course instructors who provide feedback on content for ESL/EFL students also need to consider the combination of written corrective feedback and feedback on content (Christiansen & Bloch, 2016). Table 1 shows different ways to provide written corrective feedback that might be helpful for online instructors when they provide written feedback for ESL/EFL students.

*Table 1. Types of teacher written corrective feedback (Ellis, 2009)*

| Type of CF | Description | Studies |
|---|---|---|
| 1. Direct CF | The teacher provides the student with the correct form. | e.g., Lalande 1982; Robb et al. 1986. |
| 2. Indirect CF<br>a. Indicating + locating the error<br>b. Indication only | The teacher indicates that an error exists but does not provide the correction.<br>This takes the form of underlining and use of cursors to show omissions in the student's text.<br>This takes the form of an indication in the margin that an error or errors have taken place in a line of text. | Various studies have employed indirect correction of this kind (e.g., Ferris & Roberts 2001)<br>Fewer studies have employed this method (e.g. Robb et al. 1986). |
| 3. Metalinguistic CF<br>a. Use of error code<br>b. Brief grammatical descriptions | The teacher provides some kind of metalinguistic clue as to the nature of the error.<br>Teacher writes codes in the margin (e.g. ww= wrong word; art = article).<br>Teacher numbers errors in text and writes a grammatical description for each numbered error at the bottom of the text. | Mix of direct, indirect (coded & uncoded); notes (marginal & end-of-text); text revision.<br>Various studies have examined the effects of using error codes (e.g., Lalande 1982; Ferris & Roberts 2001).<br>Sheen (2007) compared the effects of direct CF and direct CF + metalinguistic CF. |
| 4. The focus of the feedback<br>a. Unfocused CF<br>b. Focused CF | This concerns whether the teacher attempts to correct all (or most) of the students' errors or selects one or two specific types of errors to correct. This distinction can be applied to each of the above options.<br>Unfocused CF is extensive.<br>Focused CF is intensive. | Most studies have investigated unfocused CF (e.g., Ferris 2006). Sheen (2007), drawing on traditions in SLA studies of CF, investigated focused CF. |
| 5. Electronic feedback | The teacher indicates an error and provides a hyperlink to a concordance file that provides examples of correct usage. | |
| 6 Reformulation | This consists of a native speaker's reworking of the student's entire text to make the language seem as native-like as possible while keeping the content of the original intact. | |

## Oral Feedback

Using oral feedback in the context of ESL/EFL writing is also a common practice. It usually takes the forms of tutoring and teacher-student face-to-face conferences. In typical oral feedback, the student and course instructor communicate and negotiate the text, which they can view, refer to, and mark up in real time. Oral feedback can enhance students' interaction with the course instructor because of opportunities to negotiate meaning and analyze writing (Tuzi, 2004). Oral feedback usually helps ESL/EFL students write based on target audience needs and perceiving their own writing as a process (Ferris & Hedgecock, 1998). Even though oral feedback provides opportunities for real time interactions between the student and course instructor, it also has some limitations for ESL/EFL writers, including ESL/EFL students' comprehension barriers when course instructors use indirect language or when ESL/EFL students are simply not able to take all possible notes on further suggested revisions during oral feedback (Thonus, 2004; Tuzi, 2004). These challenges usually impact the quality of ESL/EFL students' writing revisions. Table 2 below shows the differences between oral feedback and written feedback to help course instructors and other practitioners choose the appropriate type of feedback for ESL/EFL students.

*Table 2. General differences and similarities between oral and written (Tuzi, 2004)*

| Oral Feedback | Written Feedback |
|---|---|
| Face-to-face | Face-to-face/distant |
| Oral | Written |
| Time dependent | Depends whether feedback is given to the writer in class or by the next class |
| Pressure to quickly respond | Pressure to respond by next class |
| Place dependent | Depends whether feedback is given to the writer in class or by the next class |
| Nonverbal components | No nonverbal components |
| More personally intrusive | Depends on whether extended comments are provided or not |
| Oral/cultural barriers | Written/cultural barriers |
| Greater sense of involvement | Greater sense of involvement |
| Negotiation of meaning | Negotiation of meaning |
| Less delivery effort | Greater delivery effort |
| N/A | No cut & paste |

Nevertheless, when the role of technology in society began to increase, course instructors shifted their focus to using technology to provide recorded oral feedback. Technology-based oral feedback, or *audio feedback,* has demonstrated that it can strengthen the benefits of written feedback on content and oral feedback on content and help course instructors provide more effective overall feedback for ESL/EFL students.

## Audio Feedback

Audio feedback is an instructional technique in which the instructors' comments and suggested changes to students' writing are recorded (Nemec & Dintzner, 2016). One of the benefits of audio feedback is that this technique can put listening under student control, allowing for listening at the students' own rate, and for repeated listening (Boswood & Dwyer, 1995).

Recorded instructional comments changed the nature of feedback in the early days of its implementation because it was different in the quantity and quality from instructors' commentary input. Interest in using audio feedback in teaching started in the early 1960s (Tanner, 1964; Moore, 1977). The first empirical studies on the effectiveness of audio feedback were conducted in the field of English composition in high school and revealed that audio feedback was an effective technique to improve students' writing (McGrew, 1969; Coleman, 1972). The first research findings revealed that audio feedback encourages qualitative changes in the content and focus of instructional comments; it allows for the integration of more feedback because "we talk a lot faster than we write" (Patrie, 1989, p. 88). Audio feedback can help course instructors in their effort to provide more detailed corrective feedback both for language accuracy and writing content. This technique is able to provide the correction of specific language errors and it also gives assistance in the correction and improvement of content-related problems, in organization of students' papers, their use of appropriate style in choice of words and phrasing, and their clarity and coherence (Farnsworth, 1974).

Although there were a number of benefits reported in this strand of literature, audio feedback cannot become an effective technique by itself; audio feedback can be more effective when it is used in combination with other types of feedback such as peer review and teacher-student writing conferences. In addition, it is very important that audio feedback be used effectively at all levels of ESL/EFL composition class (Johanson, 1999). When researchers compared the time commitment for providing audio feedback and written feedback, they stated that audio feedback might not allow instructors to save time. On the contrary, audio feedback might require more involvement and effort from course instructors, but the technique allows instructors to provide feedback with more detail, variety, and sophistication that written feedback might not provide (Cavanaugh & Song, 2015). Also, course instructors need time to become comfortable with recording audio feedback, and ESL/EFL students need time to adapt to audio feedback (Johanson, 1999).

Today, due to an increased number of online courses and programs, researchers' and practitioners' interest in using audio feedback in asynchronous online environment has also increased. One of the benefits of providing audio feedback in online courses is its asynchronous component (Ice, 2008). This means that students have more control over their learning because they can listen to instructional audio feedback at their own pace and at their own time. Audio feedback can be provided for different types of online course activities and assignments either individually or group-based. Providing more constructive feedback in asynchronous online courses has become one of the core elements of an instructor's presence. When online students receive audio feedback, their feeling of connectedness is usually increased, which is very important in text-based online communication (Swan, 2003).

## Clarity

Studies on using audio feedback in traditional ESL/EFL classrooms has revealed that audio feedback provides ESL/EFL teachers with an opportunity to critique content (Boswood & Dwyer, 1995, Farnsworth, 1974) and that this technique allows the teacher "to offer more comprehensive and clearer explanations about the function of the text in its social context, the relationship it crystallizes between writer and audience, the effectiveness of its thematic development, and its overall impact on the reader" (Boswood & Dwyer, 1995, p. 54). Providing feedback on content in the field of ESL/EFL has been an important issue widely discussed in the literature. Following the importance of providing instructional feedback on content in the field of ESL/EFL, Syncox (2003) stated that instructional audio feedback on content can build a link between the revision of a draft and the intended meaning of the writing to students. The researcher reported that audio feedback "allows the instructor to expand on the problem of understanding meaning from a variety of different angles in the form of models and prompts" (Syncox, 2003, p. 75). Taking into consideration that audio feedback with its ability to provide content critique can change the way feedback in ESL/EFL is provided, it is necessary to emphasize that ESL/EFL students need to see writing as a means of learning. Farnsworth (1974) was the first to explore the advantages of the use of audio feedback in the correction of ESL compositions at the intermediate to advanced levels. The researcher received positive feedback from ESL/EFL students after the experiment. Even though the researcher was doubtful about the ability of ESL/EFL students to understand the recorded voice, all students in the study preferred audio feedback in combination with the written marks in the margins. Later, Boswood and Dwyer (1995) also confirmed that ESL/EFL students did not have difficulty in understanding instructional audio feedback. The majority of studies on audio feedback in online courses suggest that ESL/EFL students prefer instructional audio comments because they are clearer and more understandable than written comments, which is very important for communication in an asynchronous online environment (Ice et al., 2007). ESL/EFL students preferred audio feedback for better understanding of how to improve their work and for providing greater detail than written comments (Huang, 2000). Findings of other studies also revealed that despite language comprehension problems, ESL/EFL students still perceive that audio feedback could assist in overcoming drawbacks of written feedback on content to provide clarity of meaning, especially for students who are at a lower level of language proficiency (Olesova, 2013; Zhang & Kenny, 2010). The accurate meaning of the message is very important in asynchronous online environments; as Swan (2003) explains, "real-time negotiation of meaning is impossible among instructors and students separated by space and time, clarity of meaning is more important in online classes" (p.7).

## Involvement, Personalization, and Instructor's Care

In the field of online education, research results have showed that students receiving audio feedback described their experience as personal, enjoyable, complete, and clear (Kirschner, van den Brink, & Meester, 2004). A research project funded by the Higher Education Authority (HEA) in the United Kingdom also confirmed students' positive perceptions of receiving audio-recorded feedback in asynchronous online courses (McFarlane, 2009). In an effort to better understand the effectiveness of audio feedback in asynchronous online environment, studies examined the effects of audio feedback on personalization and sense of community (Oomen-Early, Bold, Wiginton, Gallien, & Anderson, 2008; Simonsson, Kupczynski, Ice, & Pankake, 2009). The sense of community or the sense of involvement is very important in asynchronous online environments. Online students usually appreciate emotional support from faculty and their online peers when they provide a sense of belonging to others. To create a safe, fair, and respectful sense of involvement in online courses, course instructors also need to reflect on the meanings and personalization of their responses to students because both the tone and the format of the message are important; both need to be relevant, responsive, accurate, and congruent with the learning task in asynchronous text-based communication (Bonnel, 2008).

Studies also found that audio feedback can increase ESL/EFL students' feelings of instructor's care in asynchronous online courses because students receive more personalized messages from their instructors (Olesova, 2013; Oomen-Early et al., 2008). Students have a preference for receiving audio feedback because it is more personal than written comments. Audio feedback can satisfy online students' needs by bringing emotional support from their instructors and by building a sense of connectedness among learners.

## Motivation and Retention

Earlier studies found that audio feedback positively affected students' motivation and self-confidence (Berner, Boswell, & Kahan, 1996; Jelfs & Whitelock, 2000). Similarly, the majority of studies exploring the use of audio feedback in online courses confirmed that audio feedback increased retention of content and enhanced students' motivation (Ice, Swan, Kupczynski, & Richardson, 2008; Oomen-Early et al., 2008). Audio feedback can also reinforce ESL/EFL students' assignments with an authentic listening exercise, which creates an extra motivating factor (Olesova, 2013). Using audio feedback with ESL/

EFL students in asynchronous online courses can also serve as an extra activity for improving student comprehension of grammar, punctuation, and rhetoric. Moreover, it could be an effective motivating tool to develop students' listening and speaking skills in target language (Hsu, Wang, & Comac, 2008).

## CONCLUSION

Though providing feedback for ESL/EFL students is one of the core principles for successful instruction and learning, ESL/EFL students still struggle to compete adequately in academia when they are enrolled in universities in the United States and other global contexts where English is used as a first language. This may be true because the majority of them face challenges in producing accurate writing in the target language and it becomes more challenging when ESL/EFL students participate in text-based online communication. Since ESL/EFL students require different treatment and different instructional feedback strategies than first language speakers do, and audio feedback has the potential to provide such type of feedback for them, it is reasonable to conclude the review with the still relevant recommendations that Johanson (1999) has provided. Johanson (1999) recommended different treatment for ESL/EFL students because they tend to be concerned about the quality of their English writing and feel like "outsiders" in U.S. universities (p.6). Johanson (1999) gave the following reasons:

- ESL/EFL students often have extremely high expectations of themselves (as most were at the top of the class in their home universities).
- Many professors in U.S. academia tend to view their writing from a deficiency standpoint.
- Although ESL/EFL students rarely have the chance to view their native-speaking colleagues' writing, they often assume that their own is sub-par in comparison.

According to Johanson (1999), ESL/EFL students rarely have the chance to view their native-speaking colleagues' writing. In asynchronous online courses, students are able to see their native-speaking peers' writing, including their discussion posts or blog entries. However, ESL/EFL students still face more challenges and frustration than their native-speaking peers because of language barriers (Zhang & Kenny, 2010). These challenges may prevent ESL/EFL students from active participation as more and more non-language online courses include different types of activities based on interaction among peers, such as peer review activities or pair work.

There are several possible implications and recommendations for those who are interested in providing effective feedback for ESL/EFL students in online courses. One of them is to provide different types of feedback or various combinations of different types of feedback early in the semester to help ESL/EFL students make the necessary adjustment to asynchronous online environments. Providing a combination of written and audio feedback can help build relations with ESL/EFL students, which is very important for successful learning outcomes. In asynchronous online courses where participants are separated by location and time, providing a combination of written and audio feedback can reinforce the feeling of connectedness; students can feel the instructor's care when they hear the voice and the tone of their instructor. When written instructional comments are supported by the tone and other nuances provided by audio feedback, it can increase clear communication between students and their course instructor. However, specific parameters, such as institutional, course, and task contexts, should be taken into account when feedback is provided for ESL/EFL students at different stages of language proficiency. It might be reasonable to use written feedback at the beginning of the course to give students time to adjust to an asynchronous online environment. This approach might help for those students who are at the lower level of language proficiency or new to online learning environments. Adding audio feedback on content in combination with written corrective feedback can enhance ESL/EFL students' motivation and retention of audio comments of what should be revised and why. Further research is needed to investigate other types of feedback (e.g., combination of video feedback and written feedback) to determine the value of feedback for ESL/EFL students in asynchronous online courses (Ice, Swan, Diaz, Kupczynski, & Swan-Dagen, 2010).

## REFERENCES

Ashwell, T. (2000). Patterns of teacher response to student writing in a multiple-draft composition classroom: Is content feedback followed by form feedback the best method? *Journal of Second Language Writing*, *9*(3), 227–257. doi:10.1016/S1060-3743(00)00027-8

Berner, A., Boswell, W., & Kahan, N. (1996). Using the tape recorder to respond to student writing. In G. Rijlaarsdam, H. van der Bergh, & M. Couzijn (Eds.), *Effective Teaching and Learning of Writing* (pp. 339–357). Amsterdam: Amsterdam University Press.

Biesenbach-Lucas, S. (2003). Asynchronous discussion groups in teacher training classes: Perceptions of native and non-native students. *Journal of Asynchronous Learning Networks*, *7*(3), 24–46.

Bitchener, J., & Knoch, U. (2008). The value of written corrective feedback for migrant and international students. *Language Teaching Research*, *12*(3), 409–431. doi:10.1177/1362168808089924

Bitchener, J., & Knoch, U. (2009). The value of a focused approach to written corrective feedback. *ELT Journal*, *63*(3), 204–211. doi:10.1093/elt/ccn043

Bonnel, W. (2008). Improving feedback to students in online courses. *Nursing Education Perspectives*, *29*(5), 290–294. PMID:18834059

Boswood, T., & Dwyer, R. (1995). From marking to feedback: Audio-taped response to student writing. *TESOL Journal*, *5*(2), 20–23.

Brown, E. K. (2006). *Encyclopedia of language and linguistics* (2nd ed.). Boston, MA: Elsevier.

Cavanaugh, A. J., & Song, L. (2015). Audio feedback versus written feedback: Instructors' and students' perspectives. *Journal of Online Learning and Teaching*, *10*(1), 122–138.

Christiansen, M. S., & Bloch, J. (2016). "Papers are never finished, just abandoned": The role of written teacher comments in the revision process. *Journal of Response to Writing*, *2*(1), 6–42.

Cifuentes, L., & Shih, Y.-C. D. (2001). Teaching and learning online: A collaboration between United States and Taiwanese students. *Journal of Research on Technology in Education*, *33*(4), 456–474.

Cohen, A. D., & Robbins, M. (1976). Toward assessing interlanguage performance: The relationship between selected errors, learners characteristics, and learners explanations. *Language Learning*, *26*(1), 45–66. doi:10.1111/j.1467-1770.1976.tb00259.x

Coleman, V. B. (1972). *A comparison between the relative effectiveness of marginal-interlinear-terminal commentary and of audio-taped commentary in responding to English composition* (Unpublished doctoral dissertation). University of Pittsburgh, Pittsburgh, PA.

de Oliveira, L. C., Maune, M., & Klassen, M. (2014). The Common Core State Standards in English language arts in the United States and teaching English language learners: Focus on writing. *L1-Educational Studies in Language and Literature*, *14*, 1–13. doi:10.17239/L1ESLL-2014.01.01

Ellis, R. (2009). A typology of written corrective feedback types. *ELT Journal*, *63*(2), 97–107. doi:10.1093/elt/ccn023

Farnsworth, M. B. (1974). The cassette tape recorder: A bonus or a bother in ESL composition correction. *TESOL Quarterly*, *8*(3), 285–291. doi:10.2307/3586172

Fathman, A. K., & Whalley, E. (1990). Teacher response to student writing: Focus on form versus content. In B. Kroll (Ed.), *Second language writing: Research insights for the classroom* (pp. 178–190). Cambridge, UK: Cambridge University Press. doi:10.1017/CBO9781139524551.016

Fazio, L. L. (2001). The effect of corrections and commentaries on the journal writing accuracy of minority- and majority- language students. *Journal of Second Language Writing*, *10*, 235–249.

Ferris, D. R. (2003). *Response to student writing*. Mahwah, NJ: Lawrence Erlbaum.

Ferris, D. R. (2006). Does error feedback help student writers? New evidence on the short- and long-term effects of written error correction. In K. Hyland & F. Hyland (Eds.), *Feedback in second language writing: Contexts and issues* (pp. 81–104). New York, NY: Cambridge University Press. doi:10.1017/CBO9781139524742.007

Ferris, D. R. (2015). Inclusivity through community: Designing 11 response systems for "Mixed" academic writing courses. In M. Roberge, K. M. Losey, & M. Wald (Eds.), Teaching U.S.-educated multilingual writers: Pedagogical practices from and for the classroom (pp. 11–46). Ann Arbor, MI: The University of Michigan Press.

Ferris, D. R., & Hedgcock, J. S. (1998). *Teaching ESL composition: Purpose, process and practice*. Mahwah, NJ: Lawrence Erlbaum Associates.

Ferris, D. R., & Roberts, B. (2001). Error feedback in L2 writing classes: How explicit does it need to be? *Journal of Second Language Writing*, *10*(3), 161–184. doi:10.1016/S1060-3743(01)00039-X

Goodfellow, R., Lea, M., Gonzales, E., & Mason, R. (2001). Opportunity and e-quality: Intercultural and linguistic issues in global online learning. *Distance Education*, *22*(1), 65–84. doi:10.1080/0158791010220105

Harrison, J., & Shi, H. (2016). English language learners in Higher Education: An exploratory conversation. *Journal of International Students*, *2*, 415–430.

Hattie, J., & Timperley, H. (2007). The power of feedback. *Review of Educational Research*, *77*(1), 81–112. doi:10.3102/003465430298487

Hsu, H., Wang, S., & Comac, L. (2008). Using audioblogs to assist English-language learning: An investigation into student perception. *Computer Assisted Language Learning*, *21*(2), 181–198. doi:10.1080/09588220801943775

Huang, S. (2000). *A quantitative analysis of audiotaped and written feedback produced for students writing and student' perceptions of the two feedback methods.* ERIC Document Reproductive Service. (ED448604)

Hyland, K., & Hyland, F. (Eds.). (2006). *Feedback in second language writing: Contexts and issues.* New York, NY: Cambridge University Press. doi:10.1017/CBO9781139524742

Ice, P. (2008, April). *The impact of asynchronous audio feedback on teaching, social and cognitive presence.* Paper presented at the First International Conference of the Canadian Network for Innovation in Education, Banff, Alberta, Canada.

Ice, P., Curtis, R., Phillips, P., & Wells, J. (2007). Using asynchronous audio feedback to enhance teaching presence and students' sense of community. *Journal of Asynchronous Learning Networks, 11*(2), 3–25.

Ice, P., Swan, K., Diaz, S., Kupczynski, L., & Swan-Dagen, A. (2010). An analysis of students perceptions of the value and efficacy of instructors auditory and text-based feedback modalities across multiple conceptual levels. *Journal of Educational Computing Research, 43*(1), 113–134. doi:10.2190/EC.43.1.g

Ice, P., Swan, K., Kupczynski, L., & Richardson, J. (2008, June). The impact of asynchronous audio feedback on teaching and social presence: A survey of current research. *Proceedings of World Conference on Educational Multimedia, Hypermedia and Telecommunications*, 5646-5649.

Institute of International Education. (2016). *Open Doors 2016 "Fast Facts"*. Retrieved March 14, 2017, from http://www.iie.org/Research-and-Publications/Open-Doors

Jelfs, A., & Whitelock, D. (2000). The notion of presence in virtual environments: What makes the environment real. *British Journal of Educational Technology, 31*(2), 145–153. doi:10.1111/1467-8535.00145

Johanson, R. (1999). *Rethinking the red ink: Audio-feedback in the ESL writing classroom.* ERIC Document Reproductive Service. (ED 467865)

Kirschner, P. A., van den Brink, H., & Meester, M. (1991). Audiotape feedback for essays in distance education. *Innovative Higher Education, 15*(2), 185–195. doi:10.1007/BF00898030

Lalande, J. F. II. (1982). Reducing composition errors: An experiment. *Modern Language Journal, 66*(2), 140–149. doi:10.1111/j.1540-4781.1982.tb06973.x

Li, H., & Lin, Q. (2007). The role of revision and teacher feedback in a Chinese college context. *Asian EFL Journal, 9*(4), 230–239.

McFarlane, K. (2009). *Using audio feedback for summative purposes.* Retrieved March 14, 2017, from http://www.keele.ac.uk/depts/aa/landt/projects/projectreports/talwt/A15-KathrynMcFarlane-TaLwT-portfolio.pdf

McGrew, J. B. (1969). *An experiment to assess the effectiveness of the dictation machine as an aid to teachers in the evaluations and improvement of student compositions.* Report to Lincoln Public Schools, Lincoln, NE. ERIC Document Reproductive Service. (ED 034776)

Moore, G. E. (1977). Providing instructional feedback to students in education classes. West Lafayette, IN: Purdue University. ERIC Document Reproduction Service. (ED 173309)

Nemec, E. C., & Dintzner, M. (2016). Comparison of audio versus written feedback on writing assignments. *Currents in Pharmacy Teaching and Learning*, *8*(2), 155–159. doi:10.1016/j.cptl.2015.12.009

Olesova, L. (2013). *Feedback in Online Course for Non-Native-English-Speaking Students*. Newcastle upon Tyne, UK: Cambridge Scholars Publishing.

Oomen-Early, J., Bold, M., Wiginton, K. L., Gallien, T. L., & Anderson, N. (2008). Using asynchronous audio communication (AAC) in the online classroom: A comparative study. *Journal of Online Learning and Teaching*, *4*(3).

Patrie, K. (1989). The use of the tape recorder in an ESL composition programme. *TESL Canada Journal*, *6*(2), 87–89. doi:10.18806/tesl.v6i2.554

Rahimi, M. (2009). The role of teachers corrective feedback in improving Iranian EFL learners writing accuracy over time: Is learners mother tongue relevant? *Reading and Writing*, *22*(2), 219–243. doi:10.1007/s11145-008-9139-5

Robb, T., Ross, S., & Shortreed, I. (1986). Salience of feedback on error and its effect on EFL writing quality. *TESOL Quarterly*, *20*(1), 83–95. doi:10.2307/3586390

Saito, H. (1994). Teachers' practices and students' preferences for feedback on second language writing: A case study of adult ESL learners. *TESL Canada Journal/Revue TESL du Canada, 11*(2), 46-68.

Schachter, J. (1983). Nutritional needs of language learners. In M. Clarke & J. Handscombe (Eds.), On TESOL '82: Pacific Perspectives on Language Learning and Teaching (pp. 175-189). Washington, DC: TESOL.

Sheen, Y. (2007). The effect of focused written corrective feedback and language aptitude on ESL learners acquisition of articles. *TESOL Quarterly*, *41*(2), 255–283. doi:10.1002/j.1545-7249.2007.tb00059.x

Sheen, Y., Wright, D., & Moldawa, A. (2009). Differential effects of focused and unfocused written correction on the accurate use of grammatical forms by adult ESL learners. *System*, *37*(4), 556–569. doi:10.1016/j.system.2009.09.002

Simonsson, M., Kupczynski, L., Ice, P., & Pankake, A. (2009, April). *The impact of asynchronous audio feedback in the dissertation advising process.* Paper presented at the American Educational Research Association Annual Meeting, San Diego, CA.

Stern, L. A., & Solomon, A. (2006). Effective faculty feedback: The road less traveled. *Assessing Writing*, *11*(1), 22–41. doi:10.1016/j.asw.2005.12.001

Swan, K. (2003). Learning effectiveness: What the research tells us. In J. Bourne & J. C. Moore (Eds.), *Elements of quality online education: Practice and direction* (pp. 13–45). Needham, MA: Sloan Consortium.

Syncox, D. (2003). *The effects of audio-taped feedback on ESL graduate student writing.* Available from ProQuest Digital Dissertations Database. (AAT EC53307)

Tanner, B. (1964). Teacher to disc to student. *English Journal*, *53*(5), 362–363. doi:10.2307/810191

Thonus, T. (2004). What are the differences? Tutor interactions with first- and second-language writers. *Journal of Second Language Writing*, *13*(3), 227–242. doi:10.1016/j.jslw.2004.04.012

Truscott, J. (1996). The case against grammar correction in L2 writing class. *Language Learning*, *46*(2), 327–369. doi:10.1111/j.1467-1770.1996.tb01238.x

Tsutsui, M. (2004). Multimedia as a means to enhance feedback. *Computer Assisted Language Learning*, *17*(3-4), 377–402. doi:10.1080/0958822042000319638

Tuzi, F. (2004). The impact of e-feedback on the revisions of L2 writers in an academic writing course. *Computers and Composition*, *21*(2), 217–235. doi:10.1016/j.compcom.2004.02.003

Tuzlukova, V., & Hall, A. (2017). A virtual professional development model: Bringing innovation to language teaching practice. *Journal of Teaching English for Specific and Academic Purposes*, *4*(3), 603–614.

Yang, S.-H. (2016). Conceptualizing effective feedback practice through an online community of inquiry. *Computers & Education*, *94*, 162–177. doi:10.1016/j.compedu.2015.10.023

Zamel, V. (1985). Responding to student writing. *TESOL Quarterly*, *19*(1), 79–101. doi:10.2307/3586773

Zhang, Z., & Kenny, R. (2010). Learning in an online distance education course: Experiences of three international students. *The International Review of Research in Open and Distance Learning, 11*(1). Retrieved March 14, 2017, from http://www.irrodl.org/index.php/irrodl/rt/printerFriendly/775/1481

## ADDITIONAL READING

Brearley, F. Q., & Cullen, W. R. (2012). Providing students with formative audio feedback. *Bioscience Education*, *20*(1), 22–36. doi:10.11120/beej.2012.20000022

Broadley, T., Pick, D., & Von Konsky, B. R. (2011). Perceptions of audio feedback in higher education assessment. In *EdMedia: World Conference on Educational Media and Technology* (pp. 2668-2673). Association for the Advancement of Computing in Education (AACE).

Cavanaugh, A. J., & Song, L. (2014). Audio feedback versus written feedback: Instructors' and students' perspectives. *Journal of Online Learning and Teaching*, *10*(1), 122–138.

Cuthrell, K., Fogarty, E., & Anderson, P. (2009). 'Is this thing on?' University Student Preferences Regarding Audio Feedback. In I. Gibson et al. (Eds.), Proceedings of Society for Information Technology & Teacher Education International Conference 2009 (pp. 32-35). Chesapeake, VA: AACE

Doehler, K. (2013). Audio explanations to enhance statistical understanding: A case study in Introductory Statistics. *MSOR Connections*, *13*(1), 24–31. doi:10.11120/msor.2013.13010024

Fawcett, H., & Oldfield, J. (2016). Investigating expectations and experiences of audio and written assignment feedback in first-year undergraduate students. *Teaching in Higher Education*, *21*(1), 79–93. doi:10.1080/13562517.2015.1115969

France, D., & Wheeler, A. (2007) Reflections on using podcasting for student feedback. *Planet, 18*. Retrieved March 14, 2017, from http://www.tandfonline.com/doi/full/10.11120/plan.2007.00180009

Khob, M. T., & Rabi, A. (2014). Meaning-focused audiovisual feedback and EFL writing motivation. *Journal of Language and Translation*, *4*(2), 61–70.

McKeown, D., Kimball, K., & Ledford, J. (2015). Effects of asynchronous audio feedback on the story revision practices of students with emotional/behavioral disorders. *Education & Treatment of Children*, *38*(4), 541–564. doi:10.1353/etc.2015.0020

Mellen, C., & Sommers, J. (2003). Audiotaped responses and the 2-year-campus writing classroom: The two-sided desk, the 'guy with the ax,' and the chirping birds. *Teaching English in the Two-Year College*, *31*(1), 25–39.

Nortcliffe, A. L., & Middleton, A. (2007) *Audio feedback for the iPod Generation*. Paper presented at the International Conference on Engineering Education, 3-7 September 2007, Coimbra, Portugal.

Nortcliffe, A. L., & Middleton, A. (2008). A three year case study of using audio to blend the engineers learning environment. *Engineering Education: Journal of the Higher Education Academy Engineering Subject Centre*, *3*(2), 45–57. doi:10.11120/ened.2008.03020045

Olesova, L., Richardson, J., Weasenforth, D., & Meloni, C. (2011). Using asynchronous instructional audio feedback in online environments: A mixed methods study. *Journal of Online Learning and Teaching*, *7*(1), 30–42.

Roberts, S. J. (2008). Podcasting feedback to students: Students' perceptions of effectiveness. *Innovations in Practice*, *44*, 44–47.

Rodway-Dyer, S., Dunne, E., & Newcombe, M. (2009). Audio and screen visual feedback to support student learning. Retrieved March 14, 2017, from http://repository.alt.ac.uk/641/1/ALT-C_09_proceedings_090806_web_0207.pdf

Rotheram, B. (2007). Using an MP3 recorder to give feedback on student assignments. *Educational Developments*, *8*(2), 7–10.

Sipple, S. (2007). Ideas in practice: Developmental writers' attitudes toward audio and written feedback. *Journal of Developmental Education*, *30*(3), 22–31.

Sommers, J. (2002). Spoken response: space, time, and movies of the mind. In P. Belanoff, M. Dickson, S. L. Fontaine, & C. Moran (Eds.), *Writing with Elbow* (pp. 172–186). Logan, UT: Utah State University Press.

Wakeman, C., & McFarlane, K. (2011). Using audio feedback for summative purposes. *Innovative Practice in Higher Education, 1*(1).

Westwater-Wood, S., & Moore, C. (2016). Podcasting of practical summative assessment feedback: An evaluation of practice. *MedEdPublish, 5*(2). Retrieved March 14, 2017, from https://www.mededpublish.org/manuscripts/474/v1

## KEY TERMS AND DEFINITIONS

**Asynchronous Online Courses:** The courses where online communication and interaction between learners and course instructor take place at different time and at different places.

**Audio Feedback:** It is previously recorded instructional comments to be shared with students as an MP3 file or embedded audio file in a PDF document.

**Direct Written Corrective Feedback:** Instructional provision of correct linguistic form in students' writing.

**English as a Foreign Language (EFL):** The use of the English language in countries where it is not the primary means of communication.

**English as a Second Language (ESL):** The use of the English language as a medium of education, government, and business in countries where English is not a native language.

**Feedback on Content:** Instructional comments for rhetoric, syntactic, and sentence organization of students' writing.

**Focused Written Corrective Feedback:** Instructional comments directed at a single linguistic form (e.g., articles or preposition).

**Indirect Written Corrective Feedback:** Instructional indication of an error in students' writing without provision of correct form.

**Oral Feedback:** Instructional comments provided in real time where course instructor negotiates students' writing.

**Unfocused Written Corrective Feedback:** Instructional comments on all errors in students' writing.

# Chapter 13
# Flipped Learning in TESOL:
## Past, Present, and Future

**Ilka Kostka**
*Northeastern University, USA*

**Helaine W. Marshall**
*Long Island University – Hudson, USA*

## ABSTRACT

*Flipped learning is an innovative educational model in which content that is traditionally presented in class is completed at home, and in class, students work on applying what they have learned at home to engage in interactive and collaborative activities. Over the past five years, flipped learning has found a strong voice within the field of the field of Teaching English to Speakers of Other Languages (TESOL), as evidenced by the rapid increase in conference presentations, research, and publications noting its implementation. In this chapter, the authors provide an overview of the flipped learning approach within English language instruction. Included is a discussion of flipped learning's evolution and an analysis of current research that identifies areas of consensus, issues, and controversies. Finally, the authors offer six recommendations for implementing flipped learning in English language classrooms and conclude with future directions for inquiry into flipped learning in TESOL.*

## INTRODUCTION

Applications of Computer-Assisted Language Learning (CALL) in English language instruction have naturally evolved as innovations in technology and pedagogy interact and inform one another, and it is through the interplay between these two areas that a mutual adaptation has occurred. Language teaching and learning has shifted to accommodate digital possibilities, and instructional technology has developed in ways that take into account the unique demands and affordances of language teaching and learning that stand to benefit from such development. As a result, in many contexts and in English as a Second Language (ESL) and English as a Foreign Language (EFL) instruction in particular, the new reality is that CALL, far from its original meaning of *computer-assisted*, has taken on a much more central role.

DOI: 10.4018/978-1-5225-2933-0.ch013

The recent emergence of *flipped learning*, often referred to as the *flipped classroom approach*, is a prime example of the synergy that this mutually adaptive evolution has produced.

Simply defined, flipped learning is an educational approach in which content that is traditionally presented in class is learned at home, and work that is traditionally completed as homework is done in class. What results from this *flip* is a transformation of the classroom into a "dynamic, interactive learning environment where the educator guides the students as they apply concepts and engage creatively in the subject matter" (Flipped Learning Network, 2014). With the assistance of the latest available technological tools and resources, instructors who flip can create a more interactive learning environment in which their role can dramatically shift from being the "sage on the stage" to the "guide on the side" (King, 1993, p. 30). These resources include ready-made materials that can provide authentic English language input, such as YouTube videos, podcasts, and supplemental materials provided by textbooks, among others. Instructors can also create their own content for videos that is specific to their course objectives and students' levels by using tools such as Screencast-o-matic and Adobe Captivate, as well as recording software available in course management programs (e.g., Kaltura in Blackboard). Finally, there are many tools that can help instructors assess students' learning while they are presented with material at home, including Google classroom, EdPuzzle, and PlayPosit. All of these can be leveraged to support learning outside of class.

An important implication of flipped learning is that it can address one of the major challenges of language instruction, which is the substantial amount of time and exposure needed for second language acquisition. In settings where the target language is not the dominant language, exposure to authentic linguistic input and opportunities to interact in English in a classroom setting are limited (Gass, Behney, & Plonsky, 2013). For example, Doman and Webb (2016) state that flipped learning is particularly needed in places like China, where the communicative language teaching (CLT) method is not implemented effectively and students have few opportunities to use English outside of their English classes. In other countries such as Saudi Arabia, teacher-centered language instruction remains prevalent, leaving English language learners with few opportunities to use English both in and out of class (Al-Harbi & Alshumaimeri, 2016). These challenges are not unique to EFL settings, however. In ESL settings, students may also have limited access to the target language if they retreat to enclaves in their local communities where their first language (L1) is the predominant language or if they have few opportunities to use English.

Flipped learning can address another major challenge that language instructors face, which is the wide range of students' language skills in any given classroom. Regardless of whether they are in ESL or EFL settings, students "often come in with mixed language abilities, different goals, and various learning styles that often cannot be addressed in the confines of the classroom" (Webb & Doman, 2016, p. 45). While no single instructional method can effectively address the wide range of students' diverse learning styles and language learning strategies (Oxford, 2001), the flipped learning approach, as the authors demonstrate in this chapter, can make it possible for the instructor to make individual contact with each student in class and thus stay in tune with every learner's needs.

The purpose of this chapter is to present an overview of flipped learning in the field of Teaching English to Speakers of Other Languages (TESOL), tracing its past, present, and future trajectory. The first section of the chapter explains how flipped learning evolved both in other fields and within TESOL and describes how its application to ESL and EFL language teaching may offer substantial rewards for language learning. Following this overview is an examination of research and implementation of flipped learning in TESOL which identifies areas of consensus, highlights implications for pedagogy, and illustrates how flipped learning intersects with blended and online learning. The authors then address the challenges that are inherent to flipping ESL and EFL instruction, focusing on issues and controversies as they relate to more general concerns about flipped learning. In looking to the future, the chapter concludes with recommendations for getting started with this approach and directions for further inquiry into the emerging and exciting field of flipped English language learning.

## BACKGROUND

### How Has Flipped Learning Evolved?

Early approaches to flipped learning can be traced to Mazur's (1997) method of peer instruction, where traditional physics lectures were paused in class to allow time for students to discuss lecture-related questions with each other. A few years later, Lage, Platt, and Treglia (2000) developed the notion of the "inverted classroom," in which students reviewed economics lecture content at home and worked on experiments, review questions, and worksheets together in class. While these two approaches strongly resemble flipped learning as it is known today, flipped learning is widely attributed to the efforts of Jon Bergmann and Aaron Sams, two high school chemistry teachers who founded flipped learning as a grassroots movement in science, technology, engineering, and mathematics (STEM) secondary education. Bergmann and Sams wanted to ensure that students who frequently missed class due to sports and activities did not miss important lecture material, so they began video recording their lectures and posting them online to avoid reteaching what was covered in class. When they found that all students appreciated the opportunity to review lectures at home and watch the lectures as many times as they liked, flipped learning was born (Bergmann & Sams, 2012).

Since its inception in Bergmann and Sams' classrooms, flipped learning has garnered considerable attention in a wide range of educational disciplines for its call to incorporate digital content into out-of-class delivery of instruction (Talbert, 2016). Evidence of flipped learning's rapid emergence on the educational landscape can be found in the growth of the Flipped Learning Network and its Ning, an online professional learning community that included more than 30,000 educators by the end of 2016. In addition, flipped learning has generated widespread international interest. In June 2016, the Flipped Learning Global Initiative (FLGI) was launched to unite flipped learning practitioners, researchers, and professional development providers around the world, coordinate the sharing and disseminating of information, and cultivate partnerships among members of the international flipped learning community (Flipped Learning Global Initiative, n.d.). These initiatives and many others indicate that flipped learning has radically influenced teaching and learning and will continue to gain momentum.

While the flipped learning movement has exploded in STEM and other areas, interest in the approach within the field of TESOL has been more gradual. Webb and Doman (2016) trace the history of flipped learning in ESL and EFL instruction to the development of CALL and blended learning approaches in the early 2000s, where independent e-learning materials were used to supplement instruction in language classrooms. They go on to identify the many types of independent resources that have since developed to support out-of-class language learning, such as course management systems, mobile devices (e.g., smart phones and iPads), social media tools (e.g., Facebook), and online tools (e.g., wikis, blogs, and podcasts, among others). They state that flipped learning can help teachers make use of resources that are already available to support language learning outside of class, echoing an assertion the authors made earlier that flipped learning "provides a digital solution to the lack of time that obstructs us in the classroom" (p. 46).

Despite the growing scholarly interest paid to technology over the past two decades, many TESOL educators have been reluctant to embrace flipped learning in particular.A likely explanation for this reluctance and shortage of empirical work is that flipped learning has historically followed a different path than most other developments in education, as it has focused heavily on practice first and then theory. This nontraditional trajectory has resulted from educators' desire for ways to engage all learners and have more class time for hands-on work to apply concepts, particularly when students were absent and missed important content (Bergmann & Sams, 2012). Because of this reverse direction, there is a dearth of peer-reviewed scholarship, especially in subject areas outside of STEM. Nevertheless, educators in nearly all fields are taking lead in the shift to flipped learning, adopting the approach based on anecdotal evidence and in-class action research projects. Once there is more literature, presuming that it supports the approach and continues to demonstrate its strengths through empirical evidence, flipped learning will likely take hold with a broader range of educators and English language instructors (Marshall & Kostka, 2017). This, in turn, will lead to additional studies of the approach and a refinement of its implementation.

## The Four Pillars of Flipped Learning

The Flipped Learning Network (n.d.) developed the Four Pillars of F-L-I-P™ in an effort to formalize the concepts and principles underlying flipped learning. These pillars align with current blended learning and online pedagogical approaches, especially those which prioritize technology, dynamic learning environments, and active learning, and they serve to guide educators in their implementation of the flipped learning. Each pillar will be described below.

The first is *flexible environment,* where students have multiple ways of accessing course content and language. Because students have greater access to course materials, instructors can extend classroom learning by "shifting the physical location of the classroom to anywhere an Internet or Wi-Fi connection exists, be it a café, a library, a bus, or even a beach" (Webb, Doman, & Pusey, 2014, p. 54). For English language learners, this shift can create a stronger connection between the classroom and the real world and encourage them to use English wherever and whenever they choose. While this extension of the classroom to beyond classroom walls is not a particularly novel idea, what flipped learning offers is an overall openness to flexibility that is leveraged through technology. In many flipped learning environments, there is also no front of the room, and physical configurations of the classroom change regularly. These kinds of fluid arrangements foster spontaneity, interaction, and English language use among students. Students do not stop learning once they leave their English language classrooms.

The second pillar, *learning culture,* emphasizes a learner-centered classroom where students and instructors engage in interactive tasks, and students work on difficult tasks and activities that require analysis, synthesis, and application with their peers and guided by the instructor. These activities parallel theories of learning that emphasize social interaction and the co-construction of knowledge, such as Vygotskian sociocultural theory (Vygotsky, 1978), Lave and Wenger's (1991) notion of communities of practice, and social constructionism (Gergen, 2009). While creating a learner-centered classroom is almost always instructors' primary goal, they may struggle to find the time to go beyond teaching the discrete elements of language listed in their specific syllabus or mandated curriculum, even when they espouse the philosophical view that these approaches can enhance language acquisition. Flipped learning easily allows more time and space for the cultivation of a learning culture among instructors and students, as the authors explain later in the chapter.

The third pillar, *intentional content,* develops students' understandings of major concepts outside of the classroom, allowing for students to work at their own pace and gain control of their learning (Brinks Lockwood, 2014). This is especially beneficial for English language learners who can either find or be directed to material at their precise instructional level and with the online support that can assist them in comprehending material that may be beyond their language level. Today's students routinely access new information digitally (Bergmann & Sams, 2012), instructors can intentionally create and/or curate digital content that is customized to their course objectives and their students' needs. Examples of this content include instructor-created videos and ready-made instructional videos made by their colleagues and other educators, which are increasingly available and easily accessed for any topic and any age group. Curation involves working with any video, often not recorded for teaching purposes, and adding captions, embedded questions, or other enhancements for lesson design. English language learners can also create videos and other materials themselves, which allows them to practice their skills and share them with fellow students, as in peer instruction.

The final pillar is *professional educator,* which emphasizes the role of instructors as the most important resource in a classroom implementing flipped learning. Their role is even more prominent because they are more readily available to provide formative feedback, work with students individually and in groups, and constantly observe the learning process as it occurs. For example, there are many informal language assessments that teachers can conduct as English language learners interact and work in pairs or groups, and the data from these assessments can inform future content delivery. As one student in Marshall's (2014) flipped learning class noted, "Although the instructor is not at the head of the classroom most of the time, she's what I'd call 'leading from behind'—a role I wish more teachers would undertake. If they knew that leading from behind didn't mean a loss of their control or importance, I think more teachers would be willing to try the flipped classroom" (para. 7). As this student correctly stated, instructors remain a crucial participant in the teaching and learning process in flipped learning classrooms. This pillar also encourages professional collaboration as educators connect in their efforts to implement the approach in their teaching contexts and reflect on their successes and challenges to improve their practice.

## Why Should We Flip ESL/EFL Teaching?

Given that flipped learning emphasizes a flexible classroom environment, student-centeredness, active learning, and meaningful communicative interactions among students and instructors, the authors argue that the approach offers tremendous benefits for English language learners. First and foremost, flipped learning allows educators to transform the time students spend learning English both in and out of the classroom. This transformation can result in more time in class for interaction, which "accounts for learning through input (exposure to language), production of language (output), and feedback that comes as a result of interaction" (Gass, Behney, & Plonsky, 2013, p. 348). These processes can occur because the activities taken out of class encompass lower levels of Bloom's taxonomy (Brinks Lockwood, 2014), which may include explanations of grammatical points and teacher talk that gives students procedural information about assignments and rubrics (Webb & Doman, 2016). Once these less communicative and teacher-led tasks are moved out of the classroom, there is more time in class for interaction and communication with peers and the instructor in the target language (Galvez, 2017; Mehring, 2015, 2016).

Bauer-Ramazani, Graney, Marshall, and Sabieh (2016) provide an excellent example of how flipped learning was used for a newscast project conducted by undergraduate students at an intensive English program at a university in the United States. The goal of the project was for student pairs to create a three-minute video recorded newscast, which required them to take on roles of either a reporter or a topic expert. In class, students worked together to discuss the project, analyze elements of newscasts, create storyboards, and edit their work, activities which made effective use of mobile phones and tablets and students' higher-order thinking skills. Outside of class, they researched their topic, viewed sample newscasts, and composed and practiced their recording. As their project illustrates, flipping can provide more time in class for students to work together on more difficult tasks that necessitate collaboration.

A second reason for flipping English language teaching is that the approach has the potential to increase student engagement and the time they spend on learning (Hsieh, Wu, & Marek, 2016; Leis, Tohei, & Cooke, 2015). As the majority of studies on learners' attitudes towards flipped learning have shown, English language learners and educators generally have positive attitudes towards flipping (e.g., Doman & Webb, 2016; Hung, 2017; Webb, Doman, & Pusey, 2014). Therefore, learners may be more inclined to take ownership of their learning, become more engaged, and develop more integrative motivation.

Some work has examined how flipping may affect students' motivation levels specifically. For instance, in a study conducted with post-secondary English language learners in Taiwan, Hung (2015) explored the impact of flipping on English language learners' academic performance, attitudes towards learning, and participation in class. Participants included 75 first-year English majors who were divided into three groups: an experimental group (whose lessons were flipped), a semi-flipped experimental group (who had access to electronic learning materials prior to class), and a control group (who were presented with materials and homework in a conventional way). None of the participants had any prior experience with flipped learning. Results of this study indicated that students in the experimental and semi-flipped experimental groups performed better in their end-of-lesson assessments than participants in the control group in their assessments of the presented lessons. Additionally, students in flipped and semi-flipped classrooms were more satisfied with instruction than students in the control group. Finally, students in flipped and semi-flipped groups spent more time preparing for class and reviewing material before class. Hung's work echoes the assertions of others who have noted that because flipped learning promotes student engagement and collaboration (O'Flaherty & Phillips, 2015), capitalizes on their digital skills (Bergmann & Sams, 2012), and promotes learner autonomy (Han, 2015; Rodriguez-Buitrago, 2016), there is potential to increase students' motivation to improve their language skills.

A third important reason to flip learning is that it can increase the amount of authentic linguistic input that students receive, which is crucial for language development (Gass, Behney, & Plonsky, 2013). In a flipped learning environment, students can be exposed to authentic input out of class and apply what they have learned to produce output in class, working with their peers and instructor on developing both fluency and accuracy. Providing rich authentic input for learners is particularly important in EFL settings, where opportunities to use the target language outside the classroom are more limited than in settings in which English is the dominant language (Doman & Webb, 2016). On the other hand, exposing students to authentic input can also occur in class in a flipped learning model, and the elements needed to prepare students for in-class activities can be flipped. For example, in Fethi and Marshall's (2017) study, advanced intermediate-level English language learners in a secondary school in Morocco watched films together in class; at home, they had engaged in pre-listening activities that helped them prepare for the film-related tasks they would complete together in class. Findings show that students improved their oral and aural English skills and increased their motivation to learn English.

Increasing students' input and output is critical in ESL settings as well. Han (2015) describes how flipped learning was implemented in a five-week English program for 14 adults in the United States and noted:

*Students could digest input at their own pace while spending in-class hours on cooperative activities, which provided meaning-focused output and fluency development. Using this structure, the instructor could create a well-balanced language learning environment outside of class that guaranteed intensive and extensive contact with the target language. (p. 100)*

One of the objectives of flipping was to increase the input received and output that students generated, allowing more opportunities for in-class cooperative activities that encouraged fluency development and encouraged students to apply what they learned at home. Han found that flipping aligned with Nation's (2007) model of Four Strands, which focuses on balancing meaning-focused listening and reading, language-focused instruction, meaning-focused speaking and writing, and fluency development activities. The result of this course format was that instructors were able to use an online space, in this case Google Sites, to explore out-of-class input and Google Voice to produce individual output and then in class focus on the interaction required to develop fluency and deepen understanding.

A fourth reason for flipping ESL and EFL instruction is that flipping a language classroom allows more opportunities for an instructor to provide on-going formative feedback (Bergmann & Sams, 2012; Brinks Lockwood, 2014; Marshall, 2014). In a flipped learning environment, an instructor can observe when a student has difficulty applying a concept and support that student with appropriate pedagogical feedback on the spot, which may not occur if students are first learning concepts in class instead of applying them. As Marshall (2014) asserted, class time revolves around instructors "observing students to ensure on-task attention and equal participation of all learners, assessing how well each student is doing based on their contributions and questions, dealing with confusion or misconceptions about material in the videos, and encouraging higher level thinking" (para. 7). Moreover, instructors can use real-time information to gather data about students' language learning and gain rich insight into how they are progressing. For instance, the instructor could maintain a card for each student indicating areas of difficulty and use that information to inform future lessons and differentiate instruction. All of these elements conducted seamlessly in class reflect the dynamic and flexible nature of the flipped learning environment (Bauer-Ramazani, Graney, Marshall, & Sabieh, 2016).

Finally, flipped learning offers an opportunity for differentiated instruction that meets students' needs (Bergmann & Sams, 2013; Cockrum, 2014), which is often a challenge in English language classrooms (Webb & Doman, 2016). English language learners are often at different developmental stages in terms of their language ability and in the four skill areas of listening, speaking, reading and writing or other aspects of language including pronunciation, grammar, vocabulary, pragmatics, and discourse. Videos that students watch at home can now be customized so that students responding to questions in a video lesson who have an incorrect submission can automatically be redirected to another lesson that reviews a key point needed to master the remainder of the video. Instructors can also assign alternate versions of a video lesson, and in-class activities can naturally be aligned to students' performance on the individual accountability component of the lesson videos viewed prior to class. Although most language learning classrooms contain elements of differentiation, flipped learning renders this aspect of practice easier to implement effectively.

Perhaps the strongest argument for adopting flipped learning in ESL and EFL instruction is that it promotes active learning (Hung, 2017; Jamaludin & Osman, 2014), whereby "the teacher ceases to be the center of attention, and traditionally passive students can assume a larger role in learning and applying most subject matter" (Myers & Jones, 1993, pp. xii). In a flipped learning environment, students are immediately involved in completing the tasks planned for them when they enter class. They take ownership of their learning, control its pace, and receive support and feedback from peers and their instructor when they need and want that type of interaction. Students are also metacognitively engaged and thinking more about their learning, their strategies for learning, and their mastery of the material, and they are deciding when they need more guidance and when they have mastered a given skill. Thus, they may have a sense that they are accomplishing more when their instructors implement flipped learning. Flipped learning can thus be viewed as a means to promote active learning, corresponding to methods of language teaching that emphasize learner-centered instruction, such as communicative language teaching, task-based language teaching, and community language learning (Larsen-Freeman & Anderson, 2011).

## How Does Flipped Learning Intersect With Online Learning?

Most implementations of flipped learning assume an in-class component that is face-to-face. However, flipped learning is generally considered to be a type of blended instruction because some of the material is presented online. In fact, the robust use of out-of-class online elements, combined with in-class activities as extension and follow-up, constitutes a viable model for implementing flipped learning in a language program. This is because blended learning offers instructors the opportunity to use flipped learning as a way to complement class time through additional exposure to the language and to intentionally selected content available through websites, videos, and language games, among others. The flexibility of mixing face-to-face class meetings with online components means that teachers can leverage technology to reach students in between their synchronous meetings. Teachers can create online spaces for asynchronous interaction, such as wikis, discussion boards, blogs, and other individual and group activities that maintain contact among the students and with the teacher throughout the language course.

Flipping entirely online courses is also possible. While online flipped learning can be implemented in a fully asynchronous learning context, the model that is most closely attuned to the spirit of the approach is one that includes synchronous online components. For instance, Marshall (2016) designed a pedagogical grammar course for ESL teachers that met in a virtual classroom each week where students participated in a range of activities. Each class session began with a sign-in activity on a virtual whiteboard where every student would post material based on a prompt related to the video they had worked with prior to class. Students then collaborated on a whole class activity to either practice or analyze some aspect of language guided by the instructor. All the while, the chat was present in the background, and students could post questions, comments, and feedback at any time during class. Then, the students moved into breakout rooms, where they were given an interactive task to work through and later share with the whole class. Breakout room activities also included peer instruction. As an assignment, each student created a mini-lesson video with questions and delivered the lesson live in the breakout room, along with a brief quiz for the other students, which was also downloaded for the instructor to gauge learning. The class ended with a reflection whiteboard activity where students posted a take-away from the lesson. Although this grammar course design, termed the synchronous online flipped learning approach (SOFLA), was developed in a teacher education context, it could be adapted to direct instruction in ESL and EFL classes.

In these online courses, meeting synchronously fostered both the interconnectedness of learners and opportunities to engage with the content. As one student stated, "The webcam and audio are amazing and the breakouts are engaging. It is truly technology at its best for learning" (Marshall, 2016). The classes were also recorded and posted for purposes of review for students who missed classes. In addition to the class sessions in real time, students participated in a range of asynchronous activities. They were assigned interactive video lessons prior to each class. The videos contained questions that students had to respond to at specific points in the recording before moving on to the next lesson. Their responses were then downloaded for the instructor to assess each student's understanding and to prepare for revisiting areas of difficulty in real-time class meetings. Students also participated, as in most online courses, in online discussion forums, blogs, and wikis, and accessed resources posted in the e-learning platform. Bringing flipped learning into an online learning environment goes a long way in addressing the challenges of online learning by creating enriched spaces for students to engage with each other, the instructor, and the material. As one student wrote on a final course evaluation form, "I have taken online courses before but not with as much interaction as this one" (Marshall, 2016).

## ESL/EFL ISSUES AND CONTROVERSIES

As with any innovation, concerns have been raised about flipped learning. In this section, the authors examine the issues around flipped learning in English language teaching and address the controversies that have emerged as this approach is implemented in language classrooms.

### Examining Issues

As noted earlier, flipped learning does not have a long and robust past in the field of TESOL. Nevertheless, the research that has examined the effect of flipped learning on English language learning is generally optimistic. For instance, in a recent study of high-intermediate English language learners at universities in Macau and in the United States, Webb and Doman (2016) examined the effectiveness of flipped and traditional instruction on students' gains in grammar. The researchers divided students into a control group (who received grammar instruction only in class) and an experimental group (who received grammar instruction via flipped learning); both groups took a 32-item pre-test which corresponded to the grammar structures taught in the instructional period that followed. Results showed that after approximately 11 weeks, students in the experimental flipped group made higher gains on a grammar post-test. In addition, data from focus group interviews pointed to three themes: students felt that flipped learning increased their awareness of grammatical structures, flipped learning encouraged them to take more responsibility for the work they needed to do outside of class, and they believed that the out-of-class grammar lessons improved their grammar skills. Their findings align with other studies that have indicated positive learning outcomes for English language learners in flipped classrooms (Al-Harbi & Alshumaimeri, 2016; Hsieh, Wu, & Marek, 2016; Hung, 2017; Leis, Tohei, & Cooke, 2015).

While these findings are promising, what also remains unknown is whether flipped learning is effective given a number of individual variables, such as personality or learning style. It is also unknown whether age, students' first language background, cultural background, and gender affect flipped English language learning. Likewise, research is needed to examine the relative effectiveness of this approach for productive or receptive skills and for the amount of language exposure. Nonetheless, given the complexity of second language acquisition and the importance of individual differences and affective factors (Ortega, 2009), the authors anticipate that the scholars in TESOL who are interested in flipping will address these gaps in the literature, and studies will likely indicate that individual and group differences, as with second language acquisition, also play a role in flipped learning.

There are also concerns about the role of technology and video, with educators asserting either that flipped learning is likely to fade out as other short-lived fads in technology have (Jacot, Noren, & Berge, 2014) or that too many students cannot access technology outside of class and will thus be left out (Bergmann & Sams, 2014). The driving force of flipped learning has been technology; however, Bergmann & Sams (2014) assert that "although video is an important aspect to flipped learning, it is not the most important. Video should be used as an entry point to flipped learning from which deeper and further learning can occur" (p. 16). On a similar note, Brinks Lockwood (2014) emphasizes that English language instruction can be flipped without technology use. For instance, in her college ESL courses, students would read about a new concept or strategy out of class, complete basic exercises, and then return to class to check their responses; in-class time is devoted to practice and application of the relevant concepts and strategies. In terms of limited student access to technology and the internet, Bergmann and Sams (2014) suggest ways that instructors can provide students with the material they need outside of class, such as downloading videos to thumb drives or DVDs that can be watched at home or at a local library. The authors believe that one should think of flipped learning in terms of learning outcomes and see technology as the means by which the outcomes can be reached.

Similarly, flipped educators who do use technology for the out-of-class component may worry that if they are not creating their own content (i.e., videos) that students watch at home, they are not really teaching the class. They may also not even want to create their own videos or be shown on camera (Brinks Lockwood, 2014). Students who are accustomed to teacher-centered instruction may also share this sentiment and have trouble adjusting to this way of presenting material (Webb, Doman, & Pusey, 2014). These are legitimate concerns, as teaching is fundamentally about relationships that are cultivated and nurtured with students (Bergmann & Sams, 2014). In addressing these concerns, the authors argue that in flipped learning, regardless of how content is presented to students, the role of the instructor is not diminished. In fact, by selecting and adapting materials according to the digital content specifically tailored to their students, instructors are even more active in their roles as instructors (Marshall & Kostka, 2017). They can embrace their "guide on the side" role in the classroom and provide more individualized attention to students, placing them in a more consultative and accessible position in the classroom (Brinks Lockwood, 2014, p. 28). Moreover, instructors are providing greater and more convenient access to course materials for students who have to return to their home countries during the semester, have cross-cultural issues, or miss class for visa complications or other personal issues. Under flipped learning, direct instruction is always available at anytime and anyplace, and the instructor is present both in and out of the classroom.

## Addressing Controversies

The first major controversy is the question of which elements of English language teaching could be flipped. In many other fields, a substantial amount of course content is conveyed through teacher-led direct instruction, and lectures can be recorded by instructors for students to watch at home. However, English language instructors often do not teach language by lecturing. While it is true that language classes do include a considerable amount of interaction instead of lecture, several elements of English instruction can still be flipped. For instance, Kvashnina and Martynko (2016) flipped information about the English language (i.e., explanations of grammatical concepts, instructions about writing genres, and vocabulary) using PowerPoint presentations, short videos, and podcasts, and they drew students' attention to the language forms they wanted them to learn by highlighting the forms or placing them in bold font. In addition, teacher talk and teacher-led activity, both of which use valuable class time, can also be flipped (Kostka & Voss, 2016). As Webb and Doman (2016) specify, teacher talk that could be moved out of class includes "descriptions of an upcoming assignment, details of a rubric, or scaffolding of a skill by showing the teacher doing an assignment through a talk-aloud method and recording it" (pp. 41-42). Thus, what is flipped is essentially the lower levels of Bloom's taxonomy, which include understanding and remembering and are referred to as declarative knowledge (Brinks Lockwood, 2014). Finally, samples of authentic language use can be incorporated into the out-of-class materials, such as radio broadcasts, TED talks, and recordings of English speakers using language in natural settings. Zainuddin (2017) describes how undergraduate EFL students at a university in Indonesia watched movie trailers at home and in class participated in listening conversations and storytelling activities based on these trailers. These and many other types of material can be moved to the out-of-class component of the course, freeing up class time for students to use English.

Another concern regarding flipped learning relates to the urgency and desire to cover all the course material (Brinks Lockwood, 2014). Flipped learning necessarily involves collaborative activities, such as project-based learning, yet while they are engaging and dynamic, they may consume a great deal of class time. For example, Webb and Doman (2016) state that grammar is often not taught directly in a communicative language teaching model, as the time and focus of in-class activities is communication, particularly in post-secondary settings. Seen from this perspective, implementing flipped learning addresses a key concern that many instructors share, which is having enough time to cover all of the material in a course syllabus. While meeting the needs of a set curriculum and syllabus is critical, in actuality, flipped learning frees up time in class and reduces the pressure that instructors feel to rush through a syllabus (Brinks Lockwood, 2014). For instance, content related to test preparation, such as practice exercises and test-taking tips for the Test of English as a Foreign Language (TOEFL), can be presented to students out of class, creating additional space in class for students to discuss their answers to practice exercises and help each other solve problems (Kostka & Voss, 2016). Similarly, grammar can be taught explicitly without imposing on class time (Webb & Doman, 2016). By moving direct instruction to the out-of-class component of the course, instructors are less pressured to rush through the syllabus, and students have the time they need to process new content.

Specific to the field of TESOL is the question of whether low proficiency students can comprehend the content outside of class (Milman, 2012). One solution is to include first language (L1) oral and/or written elements in the video lessons as linguistic support, particularly if the focus is on an area such as grammatical explanations. Another solution is to add captions to videos to support comprehension (Leis, Tohei, & Cooke, 2015). On the other hand, if the purpose of video lessons is to increase exposure to authentic input, then use of L1 might be less beneficial, presuming the input is comprehensible to the learners. As with the other controversies, the choice of when and if to use the L1 depends on a multitude of factors related to the instructional context, such as the program type, the age level, and students' proficiency level. Additionally, because language input takes place out of class and students process it at home, students can instantly access L1 support for this instruction as needed without disrupting the flow of class time. If input from the instructor is only provided in class, accessing the L1 is an interruption for the student who may miss further content as a result.

The flipped learning community is also somewhat divided on the matter of whose videos to post for the class and whether videos should be created or curated by the instructor (Cockrum, 2015). Bergmann and Sams (2012, p. 106) assert that "there is certainly value in a student hearing her teacher's voice, reading her teacher's handwriting, and seeing her teacher's face on the instructional video," but they suggest that teachers use videos created by other teachers when beginning to implement flipped learning then gradually create their own materials. Additionally, Milman (2012) noted that instructors may not always produce effective videos even if they are effective instructors in person. One factor to consider is the difference between recording one's own video lessons and finding a lesson that is already made. Instructors are professionals who have their own unique way of teaching coupled with a deep knowledge of their students and their needs, and many lessons that already exist may be designed for a particular population of learners. That said, it is not necessary for instructors to do all the creating because for authentic language samples, videos are already available online as resources for the students to use. A balance of these options allows for flexibility. In addition, with the peer instruction component, students can make their own mini-lesson videos to share with the class. Videos should not, in any case, be the focus of flipped learning (Bergmann & Sams, 2014); instead, the authors stress that instructors should focus on helping their students achieve their learning outcomes.

A final controversy pertains to whether or not to use the webcam in instructor-created videos, and this controversy generally centers on the attention of the viewer. The webcam may distract the viewer from the main portion of the screen where the lesson delivery is concentrated. However, for English language learners, the webcam can display essential non-verbal communication through facial expressions, gestures, eye contact, and lip movements, all of which can increase students' comprehension. The webcam also reinforces the instructor's "presence" in the video lesson for created video materials. Nonetheless, in a study conducted with undergraduate students at University College London Qatar, many of whom were English language learners, Johnston and Karafotias (2016) found that students had varying preferences for the format of video lectures. Some preferred to see the teacher's face because it enhanced the naturalness of the video, and other students preferred to watch videos that only included PowerPoint slides narrated by their instructor because they felt seeing their instructor's face on the screen was distracting. Johnston and Karafotias conclude that although students held varying preferences for how out-of-class content was delivered in videos, flipped learning was useful in reaching students who have a range of learning styles and needs.

For each of these questions, the flipped learning community has presented justifiable yet conflicting arguments. Viewed through the TESOL lens, the search for resolutions to these questions become even more complicated, and instructors will need to address these controversies on a case-by-case basis within their unique teaching contexts.

## RECOMMENDATIONS

Despite the controversies and valid concerns described in the previous section which need to be resolved, the authors suggest six key overarching principles for flipping English language learning.

## 1. Allow Time for Adjustment

As with any educational change, resistance is likely. As Bergmann and Sams (2012) noted, "flipping the classroom is more about a mindset: redirecting attention away from the teacher and putting attention on the learner and the learning" (p. 11). Students might want their instructor to lead the class in traditional ways, particularly if they come from cultures where the instructor primarily leads the class and imparts all knowledge to students. They may also not feel confident enough in the new language to use it extensively in class and feel overwhelmed by new technology. Therefore, the authors recommend that instructors persevere through the initial pushback that may come from students who are used to teacher-centered instruction. They should allow time for students to adapt to this new way of organizing class time and learning yet remain confident in their redefined roles. Students may also need to be reassured that the instructor remains the authority and expert but plays this role in a different way that may seem less obvious, which is by selecting content, providing feedback, and guiding the process of language learning often from the sidelines instead of from the front of the classroom. The gains outweigh the limitations, and the authors are confident that students will learn to see these gains over time.

## 2. Begin at a Measured Pace to Help Ensure Early Success

The authors suggest that instructors, especially those who are new to flipped learning, start flipping in a way that is manageable to them. In other words, they do not have to overhaul their entire courses or make immediate radical changes to their teaching in order to implement flipped learning. They also do not have to purchase expensive state-of-the-art software to create their own content. They can begin by flipping individual lessons or procedural parts of class, and as everyone begins to feel more comfortable with flipping and using technology, instructors can increase the amount of flipping they do (Webb & Doman, 2016). There are also several resources that are available to instructors on the internet to support instructors' efforts as they begin flipping (Kostka & Brinks Lockwood, 2015). As soon as instructors begin reflecting on how they can move less important information to out of class delivery, they are already taking steps towards reconceptualizing their face-to-face time with students.

## 3. Reflect on How Flipping Can Allow for Class Time to be Used More Effectively

All instructors, regardless of which subject area they teach, should constantly ask themselves if they are making the most effective use of their face-to-face class time with students (Bergmann & Sams, 2014). In a flipped learning environment, as the authors have consistently argued throughout the chapter, class time can be used much more effectively for hands-on work that makes excellent use of higher-order cognitive skills. In an English language classroom, class time should be spent on language use and production, rather than on teacher-led discussions of procedures and language. Thus, it is important for instructors to clearly differentiate between information *about* language and language *itself*. One of the most significant benefits of flipped learning is that there is now more time for practice with instructor guidance that is so beneficial for language mastery. Flipped learning allows instructors to reorganize their class time so that valuable face-to-face time with students delivers maximum opportunities for engaged participation by every student in the class.

## 4. Use the Flipped Learning Approach to Maximize Exposure to Authentic Language Out of Class

As noted above, one of the advantages of a flipped learning approach is that moving low-level skills out of the classroom frees up class time for interaction. Thus, instructors should take advantage of the wide variety of authentic language input and modeling of English in its varying registers, discourses, and dialects that students can be exposed to outside of class. For instance, students can watch lectures, find short conversations about a particular topic, listen to the news, or watch lower-level language programs. Students can also research materials online, find samples of the language they are studying in class, and share it with their fellow students. In an ESL setting, students can record natural exchanges, transcribe them, and examine them in class with their fellow students and the instructor. These types of out-of-class activities sharply contrast with the widely used less authentic textbook exercises commonly assigned to language students, and they can help support second language acquisition.

## 5. Connect With Other Flipped Educators to Collaborate

Instructors do not have to work in isolation. They can work with colleagues who may either be flipping or interested in flipping to share ideas, plan lessons, create and/or curate materials, and use each other as a resource. Working in collaboration with others can also help instructors feel less daunted by experimenting with and implementing flipped learning. Additionally, flipped learning communities such as the Flipped Learning Network and the Flipped Learning Global Initiative can give much-needed guidance to instructors seeking support; these organizations also provide information about conferences in varying locations throughout the world where educators can meet either in person or virtually. They can collaborate with each other to design lessons, activities, materials, and projects, as well as keep each other informed on research and pedagogical developments in flipped learning more generally.

## 6. Use the Flipped Learning Network's Four Pillars and 11 Indicators for Guidance

As described previously in this chapter, these four pillars serve as a foundation to guide educators in their implementation of flipped learning. Although there is not yet a set of specific guidelines for English language instructors, the four pillars and its accompanying checklist are useful to all educators who are implementing flipped learning in their classrooms. Within each of the pillars are several statements that instructors can read as they are planning for their classes to ensure they have covered all the elements of flipped learning. To create a flexible environment, flipped educators are flexible in terms of where and when learning takes place, observe and monitor individual progress through a variety of modalities, and offer alternative pathways to mastery. To create a learning culture, they ensure that students are the center of learning activities and that these activities are differentiated for students as appropriate. To distribute intentional content, flipped educators should prioritize concepts to introduce, select or create out-of-class materials for students, and ensure these materials are relevant and accessible to all. As professional flipped educators, instructors are available to students on a regular basis, conduct ongoing individualized informal assessments, and collaborate with colleagues to share ideas and information to enhance learning. Adhering to each of these pillars can ensure that flipped learning is being effectively implemented and chances for success are maximized.

## FUTURE DIRECTIONS AND TRENDS

As we look at the future of flipped learning in TESOL, a few questions remain: Will flipped learning ultimately be considered a passing fad, closely linked as it is to technology and digital tools which are changing constantly (Jacot, Noren, & Berge, 2014)? Will interest and scholarship on flipping English language instruction continue to flourish? When considering further development of this approach and its expansion in a wider range of ESL and EFL settings, future inquiry might take several directions. First, research needs to explore more contexts for language learning and implementation. The authors targeted ESL and EFL instruction very closely in this chapter; however, there are other questions that researchers should consider in the future. For instance, what issues are scholars examining in terms of flipping languages other than English in both second and foreign language classrooms? How are English language practitioners using flipped learning to address the particular needs of their programs? More data is needed to guide educators in making decisions appropriate to their specific context and guide the field of TESOL towards effective practice and implementation. What is also needed is a research framework to examine the effectiveness of flipped learning in English language instruction. Design-based research methods, such as those used in Hung's (2017) study of English language learners in Taiwan and Egbert, Herman, and Lee's (2015) study of an ESL teacher education course, offer a framework for further inquiry into flipped learning.

Next, studies might examine varying models within flipped learning methodology and how they apply to English language teaching. In their efforts, both Bergmann and Sams (2014) and Mazur (1997) were aiming to more actively engage all students in the course material and in their own learning. These processes ultimately lead to an understanding of the material by the entire group. In addition, Flipped Mastery is another approach first implemented by Bergman and Sams (2013) in which students do not proceed through the course at the same pace, but instead access videos and in-class activities when they are ready for them. This can accommodate students who learn more slowly and need more time to process material. Finally, the Explore-Flip-Apply model, favored by Musallam (2011), is consistent with the Freirean approach in which students first examine a problem and then move to solve it through viewing the instructional videos and returning to class to work together on the original problem along with additional ones. All of these related models of flipped learning are promising for English language learning.

Finally, another fruitful area of expanding flipped learning, as discussed earlier, is to develop ways to combine best practices in the intersection of online learning with flipped learning, given that these two approaches have developed separately. Most flipped learning is conducted in face-to-face classrooms. However, given that English language instructors are adopting online language teaching in increasing numbers, there will be an opportunity to examine this emerging trend and to solidify our understanding of the different ways (e.g., SOFLA model) in which flipped learning can find its way into online settings where English is taught as either a second or foreign language. Combining online language learning with flipped learning has great potential to increase the interactivity that takes place in online courses and programs.

## CONCLUSION

A successful shift from a traditional classroom to a flipped learning environment is a major undertaking that constitutes nothing less than both a transformation of practice and a transformation of traditional ways of thinking about the work students do both in and out of class. Because flipped language instruction in language teaching incorporates technology, but does not necessarily depend upon it, and because incorporating changes in both language pedagogy and instructional technology is an on-going process, flipped learning will continue to evolve and take new forms. As a result of this mutual adaptation, it will be changing constantly as technology adapts to the needs of language learners and language teaching in turn adapts to the emerging technology available for educators. Nevertheless, the authors believe that the future of flipped learning is bright, and they encourage educators in the field of TESOL to embrace this innovative approach, mold it to their teaching context, and continue exploring its possibilities for more effective language learning and teaching.

## REFERENCES

Al-Harbi, S. S., & Alshumaimeri, Y. A. (2016). The flipped classroom impact in grammar class on EFL Saudi secondary school students performances and attitudes. *English Language Teaching*, *9*(10), 60–80. doi:10.5539/elt.v9n10p60

Bauer-Ramazani, C., Graney, J. M., Marshall, H. W., & Sabieh, C. (2016). Flipped learning in TESOL: Definitions, approaches, and implementation. *TESOL Journal*, *7*(2), 429–437. doi:10.1002/tesj.250

Bergmann, J., & Sams, A. (2012). *Flip your classroom: Reach every student in every class every day*. Alexandria, VA: ASCD.

Bergmann, J., & Sams, A. (2013). Flipping for mastery. *Educational Leadership*, *71*(4), 24–29.

Bergmann, J., & Sams, A. (2014). *Flipped learning: Gateway to student engagement*. Alexandria, VA: ISTE.

Brinks Lockwood, R. (2014). *Flip it! Strategies for the ESL classroom*. Ann Arbor, MI: University of Michigan Press. doi:10.3998/mpub.7110704

Cockrum, T. (2014). *Flipping your English class to reach all learners: Strategies and lesson plans*. New York, NY: Routledge.

Cockrum, T. (2015, June 11). *Curate or create content in a flipped classroom* [Web log post]. Retrieved from https://flipyourglassroom.com/2015/06/11/curate-or-create-content-in-a-flipped-classroom/

Doman, E., & Webb, M. (2016). The flipped experience for Chinese university students studying English as a foreign language. *TESOL Journal*, *7*(2), 1–40. doi:10.1002/tesj.264

Egbert, J., Herman, D., & Lee, H. (2015). Flipped instruction in English language teacher education: A design-based study in a complex, open-ended learning environment. *The Electronic Journal for English as a Second Language*, *19*(2), 1–23.

Fethi, K., & Marshall, H. W. (2017). Flipping movies for dynamic engagement. In J. Mehring & A. Leis (Eds.), *Innovations in flipped learning in the language classroom: Theories and practice*. New York, NY: Springer.

Flipped Learning Global Initiative. (n.d.). *The Flipped Learning Global Initiative*. Retrieved from http://flglobal.org

Flipped Learning Network. (2014). *The Four Pillars of F-L-I-P*. Retrieved from http://flippedlearning.org/definition-of-flipped-learning/

Galvez, H. (2017). Flipped instruction for language learning. In J. P. Loucky & J. L. Ware (Eds.), *Flipped instruction methods and digital technologies in the language learning classroom* (pp. 91–107). Hershey, PA: IGI Global. doi:10.4018/978-1-5225-0824-3.ch004

Gass, S. M., Behney, J., & Plonsky, L. (2013). *Second language acquisition: An introductory course* (4th ed.). New York, NY: Routledge.

Gergen, K. (2009). *An invitation to social construction* (2nd ed.). London: Sage Publications.

Han, Y. J. (2015). Successfully flipping the ESL classroom for learner autonomy. *NYS TESOL Journal*, *2*(98), 98–109.

Hsieh, J. S. C., Wu, W. V., & Marek, M. W. (2016). Using the flipped classroom to enhance EFL learning. *Computer Assisted Language Learning*, 1–25. doi:10.1080/09588221.2015.1111910

Hung, H. (2015). Flipping the classroom for English language learners to foster active learning. *Computer Assisted Language Learning*, *28*(1), 81–96. doi:10.1080/09588221.2014.967701

Hung, H. (2017). Design-based research: Redesign of an English language course using a flipped classroom approach. *TESOL Quarterly*, *51*(1), 180–192. doi:10.1002/tesq.328

Jacot, M. T., Noren, J., & Berge, Z. L. (2014). The flipped classroom in training and development: Fad or the future? *Performance Improvement*, *53*(9), 23–28. doi:10.1002/pfi.21438

Jamaludin, R., & Osman, S. Z. M. (2014). The use of a flipped classroom to enhance engagement and promote active learning. *Journal of Education and Practice*, *5*(2), 124–131.

Johnston, N., & Karafotias, T. (2016). Flipping the classroom to meet the diverse learning needs of library and information studies (LIS) students. *Journal of Education for Library and Information Science*, *57*(3), 226–238. doi:10.12783/issn.2328-2967/57/3/1

King, A. (1993). From sage on the stage to guide on the side. *College Teaching*, *41*(1), 30–35. doi:10.1080/87567555.1993.9926781

Kostka, I., & Brinks Lockwood, R. (2015). What's on the Internet for flipping English language instruction? *The Electronic Journal for English as a Second Language*, *19*(2), 1–12.

Kostka, I., & Voss, E. (2016). *Flipping the classroom to teach English for Academic Purposes*. Paper presented at the TESOL 2016 International Convention and English Language Expo, Baltimore, MD.

Kvashnina, O. S., & Martynko, E. A. (2016). Analyzing the potential of flipped classroom in ESL teaching. *International Journal of Emerging Technologies in Learning*, *11*(3), 71–73. doi:10.3991/ijet.v11i03.5309

Lage, M. J., Platt, G. J., & Treglia, M. (2000). Inverting the classroom: A gateway to creating an inclusive learning environment. *The Journal of Economic Education*, *31*(1), 30–43. doi:10.1080/00220480009596759

Larsen-Freeman, D., & Anderson, M. (2011). *Techniques and principles in language teaching*. Oxford, UK: Oxford University Press.

Lave, J., & Wenger, E. (1991). *Situated learning: Legitimate peripheral participation*. Cambridge, UK: Cambridge University Press. doi:10.1017/CBO9780511815355

Leis, A., Tohei, A. A., & Cooke, S. (2015). The effects of flipped classrooms on English composition writing in an EFL environment. *International Journal of Computer-Assisted Language Learning and Teaching*, *5*(4), 37–51. doi:10.4018/IJCALLT.2015100103

Marshall, H. W. (2014). *Three reasons to flip your ESL classroom*. Retrieved from http://newsmanager.commpartners.com/tesolc/issues/2014-02-01/2.html

Marshall, H. W. (2016). *Flipping the online learning space*. Paper presented at FlipCon 2016, Allen, TX. Retrieved from http://www.tesl-ej.org/wordpress/issues/volume19/ej74/ej74int/

Marshall, H. W., & Kostka, I. (2017). *Flipped learning in TESOL: The first five years*. Paper presented at the TESOL 2017 International Convention and English Language Expo, Seattle, WA.

Mazur, E. (1997). *Peer instruction*. Upper Saddle River, NJ: Prentice Hall.

Mehring, J. G. (2015). *An exploratory study of the lived experiences of Japanese undergraduate EFL students in the flipped classroom* (Unpublished doctoral dissertation). Pepperdine University, Malibu, CA.

Mehring, J. G. (2016). Present research on the flipped classroom and potential tools for the ESL classroom. *Computers in the Schools*, *33*(1), 1–10. doi:10.1080/07380569.2016.1139912

Milman, N. (2012). The flipped classroom strategy: What is it and how can it be used? *Distance Learning*, *9*(3), 85–87.

Musallam, R. (2011). A pedagogy-first approach to the flipped classroom. *OnCUE*, *35*(1), 6–8.

Myers, C., & Jones, T. B. (1993). *Promoting active learning: Strategies for the college classroom*. San Francisco, CA: Jossey-Bass.

Nation, P. (2007). The four strands. *International Journal of Innovation in Language Learning and Teaching*, *1*(1), 2–13. doi:10.2167/illt039.0

O'Flaherty, J., & Phillips, C. (2015). The use of flipped classrooms in higher education: A scoping review. *The Internet and Higher Education*, *25*, 85–95. doi:10.1016/j.iheduc.2015.02.002

Ortega, L. (2009). *Understanding second language acquisition*. London: Hodder Education.

Oxford, R. L. (2001). Language learning styles and strategies. In M. Celce-Murcia (Ed.), *Teaching English as a second or foreign language* (pp. 359–366). Boston, MA: Heinle & Heinle.

Rodriguez-Buitrago, C. (2016). *Raising EFL teacher-researchers.* Paper presented at the 3rd Symposium on Innovative Pedagogical Project Implementations, Bogotá, Colombia.

Talbert, R. (2016). *How much research has been done on flipped learning?* [Web log post]. Retrieved from http://rtalbert.org/blog/2016/how-much-research

Vygotsky, L. S. (1978). *Mind in society*. Cambridge, MA: Harvard University Press.

Webb, M., & Doman, E. (2016). Does the flipped classroom lead to increased gains on learning outcomes in ESL/EFL contexts? *The CATESOL Journal, 28*(1), 39–59.

Webb, M., Doman, E., & Pusey, K. (2014). Flipping a Chinese university EFL course: What students and teachers think of the model. *The Journal of Asia TEFL, 11*(4), 53–87.

Zainuddin, Z. (2017). First-year college students experiences in the EFL flipped classroom: A case study in Indonesia. *International Journal of Instruction, 10*(1), 133–150. doi:10.12973/iji.2017.1019a

## ADDITIONAL READING

Ahmad, S. Z. (2016). The flipped classroom model to develop Egyptian EFL students listening comprehension. *English Language Teaching, 9*(9), 166–178. doi:10.5539/elt.v9n9p166

DeLozier, S. J., & Rhodes, M. G. (2016). Flipped classrooms: A review of key ideas and recommendations for practice. *Educational Psychology Review*, 1–11. doi:10.1007/s10648-01509356-9

Egbert, J., Herman, D., & Chang, A. (2014). To flip or not to flip? That's not the question: Exploring flipped instruction in technology supported language learning environments. *International Journal of Computer-Assisted Language Learning and Teaching, 4*, 1–10. doi:10.4018/ijcallt.2014040101

Hao, Y., & Lee, K. S. (2016). Teaching in flipped classrooms: Exploring pre-service teachers concerns. *Computers in Human Behavior, 57*, 250–260. doi:10.1016/j.chb.2015.12.022

Hung, H. (2017). The integration of a student response system in flipped classrooms. *Language Learning & Technology, 21*(1), 16–27.

Kang, N. (2015). The comparison between regular and flipped classrooms for EFL Korean adult learners. *Multimedia-Assisted Language Learning, 18*(3), 41–72.

Loucky, J. P., & Ware, J. L. (Eds.). (2016). *Flipped instruction methods and digital technologies in the language learning classroom*. Hershey, PA: IGI Global.

Marshall, H. W. (2017). *Flipped learning in the linguistics classroom: A course redesign.* Retrieved from http://newsmanager.commpartners.com/tesolcallis/issues/2017-02-22/4.html

Marshall, H. W., & Rodriguez-Buitrago, C. (2017). *The synchronous online flipped learning approach - SOFLA*. Retrieved from http://newsmanager.commpartners.com/tesolteis/issues/2017-03-15/6.html

Mehring, J. G., & Leis, A. (Eds.). (2017). *Innovations in flipping the language classroom: Theories and practice*. New York, NY: Springer.

Mori, Y., Omori, M., & Sato, K. (2016). The impact of flipped online Kanji instruction on written vocabulary learning for introductory and intermediate Japanese language students. *Foreign Language Annals*, *49*(4), 729–749. doi:10.1111/flan.12222

Parris, H., Estrada, L., & Honigsfeld, H. (2017). Flipping the classroom for English learners. In *ELL frontiers: Using technology to enhance instruction for English learners* (pp. 51–64). Thousand Oaks, CA: Corwin Press.

Roither, A. (2016). *Classroom assessment techniques (CATs) for flipped learning*. Retrieved from http://newsmanager.commpartners.com/tesolc/issues/2016-11-01/3.html

Silberman, M. L. (1996). *Active learning: 101 strategies to teach any subject*. Boston, MA: Allyn and Bacon.

Wang, Y., Chen, Y., & Chen, N. S. (2014). Is FLIP enough? Or should we use the FLIPPED model instead? *Computers & Education*, *79*, 16–27. doi:10.1016/j.compedu.2014.07.004

Yu, Z., & Wang, G. (2016). Academic achievements and satisfaction of the clicker-aided flipped business English writing class. *Journal of Educational Technology & Society*, *19*(2), 298–312.

## KEY TERMS AND DEFINITIONS

**Active Learning:** An approach to learning in which students are key participants who work with new material. Students take ownership over their learning and are engaged in metacognitive reflection about the learning process.

**Authentic Linguistic Input:** Naturally occurring language use by fluent speakers of the target language that learners receive in their language learning environment.

**Differentiated Instruction:** A teaching approach in which teachers tailor instruction to students' individual needs and abilities. In a flipped learning approach, differentiated instruction is fostered both in and out of class.

**Direct Instruction:** The component of instruction in which the teacher presents and explains new course material to the students. While it may include some interaction, the primary aim is to explicitly provide content intentionally selected by the instructor.

**Flipped Learning:** A pedagogical approach in which direct instruction is moved outside of the classroom and interactive practice and application of content and skills is moved into the classroom, rather than assigned outside of class. This flip allows students to work on more difficult skills in class with their peers and instructor.

**Flipped Learning Global Initiative:** Launched in June 2016, the Flipped Learning Global Initiative brings researchers and educators together from around the world who are interested and actively implementing flipped learning.

**Flipped Learning Network:** The original community website that unites flipped learning educators and provides a forum for members to contribute and share articles and resources. The Networks's four pillars of flipped learning can be found on the Flipped Learning Network's official website.

**Formative Assessment:** On-going assessment that is conducted by teachers during the learning process and used to inform subsequent instruction.

**Inverted Classroom:** A commonly used term that refers to the flipped approach. In this classroom, homework and classwork are inverted to foster more in-class collaboration.

**Learning Culture:** An environment in which learning is cultivated and students are engaged in meaningful activities without the teacher being central, as in student-centered learning.

# Chapter 14
# The Usefulness of Massive Multiplayer Online Role Playing Games (MMORPGs) as Tools for Promoting Second Language Acquisition

**Daniel H. Dixon**
*University of Utah Asia Campus, South Korea*

**MaryAnn Christison**
*University of Utah, USA*

## ABSTRACT

*The purpose of this chapter is twofold (1) to review the benefits of online videogames for promoting second language acquisition (SLA), specifically massive multiplayer online role-playing games (MMORPGs) and (2) to present new research that seeks to explain why and how MMORPGs may be beneficial. The findings from the research indicate that MMORPGs are beneficial to SLA primarily because they provide opportunities for interaction in the target language through participation in collaborative problem solving tasks. The results of the research presented in this chapter show (1) that the requirements of input and output for successful gaming allow for a type of interaction in which the focus on language form leads to modified-output, (2) that players have opportunities to negotiate input as a means of completing in-game tasks, and (3) that in-game tasks are similar to instructional tasks that are believed to be beneficial for SLA in the context of a classroom.*

## INTRODUCTION

Opportunities for target-language interaction and access to rich sources of second language (L2) input have drastically increased over the past several decades as a result of technological advances—Internet bandwidth has grown, processor speeds have accelerated, and access to online technology has increased

DOI: 10.4018/978-1-5225-2933-0.ch014

for both L2 teachers and learners. The development of learning management systems (LMSs), which are software applications for the administration, documentation, tracking, reporting, and delivery of content for online courses, allow teachers to effectively deliver courses completely or partially online, thereby making access to online learning an essential component for educational enterprises in the 21st century. In the past decade, the number of students studying in online courses in U.S. post-secondary contexts has steadily increased. The total number of students studying online in 2012 was 6.7 million, which is 37% of the total number of students in U.S. higher education (Allen & Seamen, 2013). This number is an increase from 25% in 2010 (Blake, 2011) and 11.7% in 2003 (Allen & Seamen, 2013; OECD, 2005).

For almost 20 years second and foreign language teachers have been incorporating online tools such as chat rooms, wiki pages, and discussion boards into course and curriculum design (Dudeney & Hockly, 2012; Rubio & Thoms, 2013). The motivation for this practice has been aimed at providing language learners with increased opportunities to communicate and interact with teachers and other learners. Sykes and Reinhardt (2013) argue for the importance of interaction in language learning. Communicating with other people is the end result of language as a social meaning-making process. These scholars state that this process is essentially enculturation with the fundamental learning that takes place is through activity. The interaction that can take place online is thought to be especially beneficial to L2 acquisition. Blake (2011) argues that online language learning "stimulates students to spend more time engaged with second language (L2) materials, which ultimately promotes greater learning" (p. 21).

Since the early 1980s, second language acquisition (SLA) researchers have recognized the importance of interaction as a key factor in SLA (Gass, 1997; Long, 1983; Pica, Lincoln-Porter, Paninos, & Linneln, 1996; Sykes, & Reinhardt, 2013). The results of interaction between language learners and highly proficient users or native speakers have obvious benefits when it comes to both the amount and type of language to which learners are exposed; however, research also shows that even without the presence of highly proficient users or native speakers, interaction between two or more L2 learners is beneficial and productive for SLA (Beauvois & Eledge, 1995; Lee, 2001; Long, 1996; Pica et al., 1996).

An often-overlooked technological resource for promoting interaction that L2 learners can employ is online games. Recent research on the use of online games as they relate to second language acquisition reports some very positive results, specifically for the genre of massive multiplayer online role-playing games (MMORPGs) (see, for example, Kongmee, Strachan, Montgomery & Pickard, 2011; Peterson, 2016; Scholz & Schulze, 2017; Sylvén & Sundqvist, 2012). MMORPGs allow hundreds of gamers to interact in evolving virtual worlds at the same time via the Internet. L2 learners can cooperate and compete with one another on a large scale and oftentimes interact meaningfully with other L2 learners from around the world. Without the use of the Internet, this type of interaction would otherwise not be available to L2 learners.

In addition to an increase in the number of opportunities to interact with other speakers in the target language, there are additional benefits to L2 learners who participate in MMORPGs. L2 learners who play MMORPGs have opportunities to engage in cooperative problem-solving tasks that share many characteristics with effective language-learning tasks (e.g., language-learning tasks that provide opportunities for the negotiation of meaning). It is important to note that participation in MMORPGs is meant to supplement, not replace, classroom language-learning activity, so learners involved in MMORPGs can also benefit from interaction that occurs in the context of the classroom. In addition, MMORPGs provide opportunities for L2 learners to produce large amounts of output as they work cooperatively to complete in-game tasks. Output produced by one player is a meaningful source of contextual input for other players, thereby eliciting connected interaction between players. Results from the study discussed in this chapter show that participants' implicit focus on form to achieve understanding and communication leads to modified-output (Swain, 2000; Swain & Lapkin, 1995; Varonis & Gass, 1985). Furthermore, players have opportunities to negotiate both player-produced input and environmental input (input that comes from interacting with the game environment rather than another player) as a means to complete game tasks, thereby making the virtual world of MMORPGs a contextually rich social environment.

## BACKGROUND

Over the past several years, researchers have begun to investigate the benefits that online gaming has for language learners. Online gaming provides opportunities for language learners to use the target language in meaningful (i.e., in ways that are important and useful for the learner) and collaborative ways while engaging in tasks in the virtual game world in the target language. Sylvén & Sundqvist (2012) argue that MMORPGs share many instructional features with Content and Language Integrated Learning (CLIL) and Content-based Instruction (CBI) by immersing players in a content-rich environment that fosters authentic language use especially in terms of "input, output, and interaction" (p. 308). Thorne (2008) also supports the claim that MMORPGs share similarities to features of an L2 classroom because the in-game tasks allow for "negotiation of meaning, repair sequences, explicit corrective feedback, and requests for assistance" (p. 322).

It is important to note that the interaction that takes place between players in MMORPGs is facilitated through written communication rather than oral. Therefore, when the researchers cited in this chapter refer to negotiation, feedback, requests, or other types of interaction in their studies, the participants are doing so by sending texts to one another that appear on the users' screens while playing an MMORPG. To date, there is a dearth of published research relative to opportunities for negotiation of meaning using written texts. An examination of L2 data in early studies on negotiation of meaning (see Pica, 1994) necessarily focused on an examination of oral language. Until advances were made in technology, such as the technology used in MMORPGs, written texts could not be examined *in situ*.

More recently, Scholz and Schulze (2017) analyzed data from students playing *World of Warcraft,* an MMORPG, and sought to understand how participants' progression in the game interacted with their second language development (SLD). The researchers argue that SLD occurred when they "detected evidence of a language learner having observed an unfamiliar linguistic construction while playing the game and then being able to produce it in a non-gaming context" (p. 106). They posit that there is ample evidence to demonstrate that these new linguistic constructions stem from gameplay; however, they also caution that these data are not definitive. Nevertheless, they are confident that the language to which participants were exposed in the game is "indeed transferable to non-gaming contexts" (p. 112).

Other research in second language acquisition (SLA) that focuses on the use of MMORPGs has found that the social nature of the games offers opportunities not only for experimenting with an L2, but also for learning new vocabulary (Rankin, McNeal, & Shute, 2008). Peterson (2010, 2011, & 2012) conducted several studies involving MMORPGs and language learning. One of these studies (Peterson, 2011) was a qualitative study conducted in Japan with ESL students, and it revealed that English learners "took the lead in managing their discourse and actively engaged in collaborative social interactions involving dialog in the target language" (Peterson, 2011, p. 56). He writes that the benefits of the in-game interaction "include access to an engaging social context, enjoyment, exposure to new vocabulary, reduced anxiety, and valuable opportunities to practice using a foreign language" (p. 56). The types of interaction and communication strategies used in the MMORPG are also features of productive and engaging English language classroom tasks.

It is important to recognize that the types of interaction and communication strategies used by the learners may not be equally accessible to all learners. Peterson (2011) points out that language proficiency and prior gaming experience are major factors influencing participants' successes and enjoyment of in-game tasks. Additionally, the games may require a rather powerful, and often expensive, computer, which can limit access to the games. Nevertheless, language learners who are new to MMORPGs and willing to put in time can learn to play the game online from more experienced players, while simultaneously learning English. Sylvén and Sundqvist (2012) point out that a context in which novice players are collaborating with experts to achieve a goal provides a perfect example of what Vygotsky (1978) calls the Zone of Proximal Development (ZPD). The ZPD is realized in MMORPGs when English learners work on tasks with players who have more highly developed language skills, thereby moving English learners more quickly from the ZPD to a higher skill level.

MMOPRGs can also benefit English learners because they allow for anonymity and real-time interaction with a large native speaker population, which is not possible in traditional L2 classrooms. L2 speakers can be intimidated by interaction with native speakers. The complexity of face-to-face social relationships and interactions can hinder learners' willingness to engage in the target language in a context in which they feel comfortable (Peirce, 1995). The anonymity in online gaming may lower the affective filter (Krashen, 1982), thereby providing a more relaxed environment for language experimentation. Furthermore, players are able to complete in-game tasks in real time with well- defined rules and goals, which provide important scaffolding for learners. This scaffolding is important for learners as they construct meaning and solve problems (Blake, 2011). As problems are solved, self-confidence increases, as well as the motivation to learn the L2 (Gardner, 1985). This type of learning environment is often unavailable in traditional English language-teaching classrooms or in traditional computer language learning software applications.

## MAIN FOCUS OF THE CHAPTER

### Issues, Controversies, Problems

A number of studies have investigated the potential for MMORPGs as language learning tools and have found positive results (see, for example, Kongmee, Strachan, Montgomery & Pickard, 2011; Peterson, 2016; Scholz & Schulze, 2017; Sylvén & Sundqvist, 2012). Researchers laud participation in MMORPGs as a low-stress activity that L2 learners can use to engage in the target language in an input-rich and authentic language use environment. Additional research is still needed on exactly how and why MMORPGs are beneficial (or are not beneficial). Kongmee, Strachan, Montgomery, and Pickard (2011) state that a deeper analysis of participants' interactions is needed to further understand if these games foster SLA, and if so, how. To investigate how MMORPGs might foster SLA, more hours of recorded data are needed of language learners interacting in a variety of MMORPGs.

Although many researchers cite authentic language use as a major benefit for L2 learners playing MMORPGs, Scholz and Schulze (2017) point out that in most studies the participants are in the same location as, and being watched by, the researchers. They argue that this constant surveillance "potentially detracts from the authentic and common experience of gameplay at the player's leisure and at a preferred location, while at the same time limits the amount of time a player could potentially want to play" (p. 101). This limitation is also noted by Peterson (2012). The study in this chapter seeks to address this limitation by allowing participants to play the game at their desired location, time, and duration. As part of the University's requirements for the protection of human subjects, the study was reviewed and approved by the IRB and identified as a minimal risk study with a waiver of documentation of informed consent.

The purpose of the current study was to investigate whether MMORPGs have the potential to be beneficial tools for promoting SLA. To this end, the current study sought to answer the following research questions:

1. What types of learning strategies are used by learners of English as they play *Guild Wars 2*?
2. How many different types of learning strategies are used?
3. Does *Guild Wars 2* provide opportunities for English learners to negotiate input?
4. What specific strategies do English learners employ in negotiating input?

### Guild Wars 2 and MMORPGs

*Guild Wars 2* is an online video game that falls into the genre of MMORPGs. Like most games in this genre, players create a character by choosing from many customizable options that determine its appearance, abilities, and profession, as well as many other features. These features affect how players progress through the game and the roles they will play when interacting with others in the online game world. In the game world, all players are visually represented by their created character or avatar. The player can see and interact with others who are playing the game at the same time. All interaction is done in real time rather than, for example, sending a message like an email and waiting for a response. At any given time there are literally hundreds of real players with whom one can interact and communicate. Communication is done through texting, and texts can be sent to a specific player, a group of players, or anyone in close proximity in the game world; Figure 1 shows an example of *text dialogue* between players in a game. Players often form groups and cooperate to accomplish tasks. These tasks grant rewards and *experience* that make each player's character stronger, which allows them to progress further in the game. Players are able to progress quicker by forming groups because their strength is greater together. Stronger characters can take on more difficult and rewarding tasks. Thus, there is an incentive to interact with the other players in the game world, a common feature in MMORPGs.

## METHODOLOGY

The three participants in the current study were all undergraduate students in their first or second year of study at a university in the United States. They were all L2 speakers of English and were enrolled in academic English as a second language (ESL) classes during the term in which data were collected. They were all in their early 20s. A copy of the game *Guild Wars 2* was given to each participant at no cost. Participants were also told that they could keep the game after the study, and they could drop out of the study at any time for any reason. These steps were taken to increase the likelihood that participation in the study would be motivated solely by interest in the game.

*Figure 1. Text dialogue between players*

Participants' in-game interactions during *Guild Wars 2* were analyzed and placed into categories associated with two types of strategies—learning and communication. The categories used for analyzing the learning strategies were based on Chamot and O'Malley (1992) and their framework of metacognitive, cognitive, and socio-affective learning strategies. For analyzing the communication strategies, the framework proposed by Lee (2001) was used, which included requesting information, checking information, use of the first language (L1), self-correction, and peer correction. Both types of strategies were adapted to fit a gaming context. Additionally, participants' in-game texts, which were produced in response to previous texts, were tallied so that the degree of connected interaction that took place among participants could be recorded. The quantitative data were used to understand the players' interactions and the potential influence the interactions may have on SLA.

## Data Collection

The three students agreed to play *Guild Wars 2* together at the same time and record their computer screens while doing so. All three students said they had some experience playing games in the MMORPG genre, but none had ever played *Guild Wars 2*. They were told not to play the game unless all other players were able to do so, and they were required to play the game in separate real-world locations so that all communication would be done through the in-game text and communication system. Participants chose to play the game in their campus dorms or apartments. None of the participants were roommates.

Gaming sessions were scheduled in advance to ensure that all participants could commit to the schedule. There was no set time limit on how long a single gaming session could last; however, they were told that they must stop playing if any one player could no longer play. They were required to form an in-game party so that they could always see all other party members on their in-game map. Figure 2 exemplifies the *players-in-party* display. The in-game map shows where other players are located and allows players to easily use the in-game chat function to communicate with one another. The participants

*Figure 2. Players in a party*

were told that they should only use English, which was the L2 for all participants, while playing the game and communicating with one another. The three participants were all native speakers of Chinese. They were asked to complete the in-game tasks together as a group and stay in close proximity to one another in the game world. There was a total of five recorded gaming sessions over the course of about a month. The sessions ranged from about 1.5 to 2.5 hours, totaling about 12 hours over the five sessions. The participants themselves determined the length of each individual session.

Data from the gaming sessions were gathered using a screen-recording program. Participants recorded their screens themselves, and it was the participants' responsibility to remember to run this program before each gaming session. By recording the participants gaming sessions, each participant's chat messages could be analyzed in the context in which they were written. Audio was not recorded, only video. After each session, data were transferred to a hard-drive for analysis. A training session took place before the recorded sessions began in order to familiarize participants with the basic features of the game. Data were not collected during the training session.

There were times when some participants forgot to record their computer screens; however, at least one participant remembered to record for each of the sessions. As long as one participant remembered to record, all text messages sent to and from all participants could be seen because all texts were displayed on all players' screens. Therefore, there was no loss of data even when someone forgot to record their screen.

## Data Analysis

To answer Research Questions 1 and 2 (i.e., What types of learning strategies are used while learners of English play *Guild Wars 2*? How many different types of learning strategies are used?), it was necessary to identify the specific learning strategies that participants used. Chamot and O'Malley's (1992) framework for conceptualizing learning strategies included three different types of learning strategies: metacognitive, cognitive, and socio-affective. In the current research, the focus was on socio-affective learning strategies because the categories that could not be observed through the recorded videos of the participants' gameplay had to be eliminated. For example, cognitive strategies were eliminated because "the learner interacts with the material to be learned by manipulating it mentally" (p. 51), and thus, is unobservable.

Strategies were also adapted to fit an online gaming context. In order to allow for more in-depth analysis of interaction and to understand better what the participants were doing in terms of language use and interaction, subcategories were created. For example, in the framework proposed by Chamot and O'Malley (1992), the category of "cooperation" is defined as "working together with peers to solve a problem, pool information, check a learning task, model a language activity, or get feedback on oral or written performance" (p. 56). Most of the interaction in *Guild Wars 2* could easily fit into this broad category of cooperation because the main purpose of the game is to work cooperatively with other players to complete tasks. To better understand the nature of the cooperation that took place in the game and the way in which the strategies that were being used might further SLA, the concept of cooperation was broken down into subcategories: pooling information, modeling, giving commands, making statements, and making suggestions. To keep data analysis consistent in the study, each individual text was placed in only a single category. For example, a single text such as "look at the map" was only counted as an instance of pooling information and not as a command. Each time one of the strategies occurred in the data, the researchers placed a tally in the appropriate category and the time code was recorded.

## Pooling Information

Whenever a participant produced a text that supplied information directed toward the completion of a game task, the text was tallied as an instance of pooling information. In *Guild Wars 2,* players are incentivized to share task information because cooperation allows a group to move more quickly through tasks and thus receive the task's rewards. Unlike other popular online games, many MMORPGs focus on cooperation rather than competition.

In the interaction shown in Example 1, the three participants are trying to determine which task they should try next. This conversation occurred during the first gaming session. The bolded texts were tallied as instances of pooling information. The names are pseudonyms for the participants' in-game avatars. The texts in the examples are shown exactly as the participants themselves wrote them. For this reason there are spelling, grammar, and punctuation errors that occur in the examples.

Example 1:

**Pine:** Where should we go now
**Thief:** Let me think
**Pine: Look at the map** (Pine circles an area on the game's map.)
**Thief:** I saw ok go
**Mary: We need find the bear trop** (misspelled "troop")
**Pine: Look at the blue point**

In this interaction Pine asks where they should go and then answers his own question by telling the others to look at their maps. Players can circle areas on the map by holding down a button and using their mouse. These actions are necessary so the circles can be seen by all other players in the party. Thus, the text "look at the map," followed by the visual of Pine drawing on the map, was counted as an instance of pooling information. This reason for this categorization is because Pine is giving information related to completing, or in this case, starting a new task. Thief then confirms that he saw the drawing. Both Mary's text and Pine's texts were also counted as instances of pooling information because they were attempts to share information related to the next task.

## Command

A text was counted as an instance of command when a player directly told another player to take an action. Commands were often used to tell players to go to a specific location or tell a player to wait. In the text above, "look at the map" was not counted as a command because the purpose of the text was to share information with the others by circling something on the map. Therefore, a command is telling another party member to take an action that is not clearly related to the task at hand. Example 2 provides an instance of a command.

Example 2:

**Thief:** Follow me
**Pine:** Got it
**Mary:** Look map (Mary circles an area on the game's map)
**Thief: Come here**
**Mary: Wait**
**Mary:** We need finish the work

In the conversation above, two of the six texts were counted as instances of a command, "Come here" and "wait." Thief is telling Mary to come to his location, to which Mary responds with another command, "wait." Both texts are telling the players to take, or not take, some sort of action. Again, "look map" was not counted as a command because the purpose of that text was to pool information by asking other players to see the task information he had marked on the map. "Follow me" was not counted because this was counted as an instance of modeling as described below. Observing the text along with the video of the screen recording, it was clear that "come here" and "wait" were not related to the current task and, therefore, counted as a command rather than an instance of pooling information.

## Statement

A text was counted as a statement when a player's text was very general or unrelated to a specific task or even the game at all. A few examples from the study are when a player said, "This city is big," "I am so hunger," or "My connection is not good." Although statements are not necessarily a form of cooperation, it was included so that texts that were not exactly game-related could be quantified.

## Suggestion

When a player suggests a course of action or implies that another player do something, it was counted as a suggestion. Commands and suggestions are similar, but a suggestion is less direct and includes words such as "should," "maybe," or "I think we need to."

## Modeling

Texts were counted in the category of modeling when the purpose of the text appeared to tell other players to follow the text writer's example. Often players would ask one another what they should do next by texting "follow me" or "talk to this person here." In this sense, they were modeling or showing the other players exactly what they should do in order to progress. The other players did not always follow the example of the writer, but it was still counted as an instance of modeling. Modeling is similar to pooling information, but it had an additional "watch me do this" element to it that can be observed in the context that the text was produced. The recorded screen data provided the additional contextual information that was needed to differentiate pooling information from modeling.

Although modeling indicates that a participant is demonstrating a solution to a problem through action and not necessarily through language, it may seem questionable for it to be deemed a language learning strategy. However, the fact that modeling is initiated through language (e.g., "follow me") makes it both strategically and linguistically interesting because language is being used as a tool for solving a problem.

To answer Research Questions 3 and 4 (i.e., Does *Guild Wars 2* provide opportunities for English learners to negotiate input? What specific strategies do English learners employ in negotiating input?), the ways in which learners negotiated meaning during gaming sessions were analyzed by tallying the number and type of communication strategies that were employed. The tally of communication strategies, similar to the learning strategies tally discussed previously, was based on the participant-produced texts and the context in which they were written.

In the context *of Guild Wars 2*, there are two types of input that can lead to negotiation. The first type is the text messages and visual cues that are received as players communicate during gameplay with one another or other players not in their party. The other source of input is the environment of the game. This type of input can be a task, a player's inventory and abilities, non-player characters (NPCs), enemies, the map, or anything else the players interact with while playing the game. Environmental input is the game's world, and it can be visual, aural, and textual. For the purposes of this study, the communication strategies for both environmental input and player input were analyzed, however, they are not separated in reporting the data because negotiation can only occur between and among humans, although it can originate from either human/player input or from the game environment.

The framework used for analyzing the communication strategies was adapted from Lee (2001): requesting information, checking information, using the L1, self-correction, and peer-correction. Checking information was further broken down into three subcategories, which are clarification checks, confirmation checks, and comprehension checks.

### Requesting Information

Texts were placed into the communication strategy category of requesting information when a participant asked another player for information. This could be a request for information about a player, such as their location or inventory, as well as a request about the game environment, such as how to complete a task or where they should go next.

### Checking Information

Checking information occurred when a player indicated that he did not fully understand a previous text from another player or a writer of a text wanted to confirm that an earlier text was understood. A player's text was counted as a clarification check when a player wrote a text and another player responded with a question asking for more information. Clarification checks were initiated by the receiver of a text and directed to the player who wrote the first message. Thus, players were negotiating meaning as they worked out what the writers of the initial messages were trying to communicate to the other players. A text was counted as a comprehension check when a player wrote two texts, the second of which was to make sure that the receiver of the text understood the initial text. Confirmation checks occurred when a player wrote a text and another player responded to that text by producing a text showing that he understood the initial message.

### Using the L1

When a player typed a message in Chinese (Note: all three participants' were mother tongue speakers of Chinese) the text was categorized as using the L1. The participants were asked to only use English when playing the game, and they followed this request almost perfectly. During the five gaming sessions, only seven of 886 texts showed evidence of L1 use.

### Self-Correction

If a participant typed a message that he felt contained a spelling or grammar error, and, in a subsequent message, corrected himself, this interaction was categorized as a self-correction. For example, when one of the players told the other two players that he was going to take a break and go outside and smoke a cigarette. He first typed, "I am somke." Seconds later he typed another message and wrote "smoke" to correct his earlier message and then added another correction typing, "smoking." These messages would count as two self-corrections.

### Peer-Correction

If one participant typed a message correcting the grammar or spelling of another participant's earlier text this was categorized as a peer-correction.

To better understand the use of learning and communication strategies in the interaction that took place among participants, the number of times that a text was part of a connected interaction was also calculated. In other words, each time a player responded, answered, or reacted to another player's message the interaction was recorded and categorized as an instance of connected interaction.

## RESULTS AND DISCUSSION

An analysis of the language used by the three participants during the 12 hours of gaming provide support for SLA in three general areas: (1) output, input, and connected interaction, (2) form-focused feedback and modified output, and (3) negotiation of meaning.

### Output, Input, and Connected Interaction

As early as the 1980s, researchers argued that output is essential to the process of SLA (see Swain, 1985). If output production is central to SLA, then the massive amount of texts produced by the participants is a strong indicator that MMORPGs have great potential as effective tools for SLA. Output production in the form of text messages while playing *Guild Wars 2* was much higher than what might be typically expected in a traditional language classroom. Ninety minutes of gameplay averaged about 150 texts during the course of the study. It is difficult to imagine a 90-minute ESL class in which students would produce as much target language output. Even though all three participants shared the same native language, 879 of the 886 texts produced were in English. In an L2 classroom, students often resort to their L1 if a majority shares the same native language even when learners are asked to use the target language.

The data that were collected in this study provide evidence for the fact that the participants were not only producing large amounts of output in English, but they were also reading and reacting to one another's texts. Input from fellow participants often elicited additional output from other participants. Half of all texts written during the study were related to a previous message written by another player. Interestingly, the number of connected interactions increased over time, and Sessions 3, 4, and 5 all saw higher rates of connected interaction than the first two sessions. Figure 3 shows data concerning the connected interaction during the 5 gaming sessions of the study. Session 3 had the highest rate, and the possible reasons for this are discussed later in this chapter.

Output in the form of sharing task information, knowledge, or ideas during game sessions was categorized as the learning strategy pooling information. Pooling information had the highest percentage of total texts at 23.4%, as compared to the next highest learning strategy, giving a command, at 9%. Chamot and O'Malley (1992) argue that cooperation or pooling information has positive effects on learners' attitudes toward learning. The participants in this study were very interested in working cooperatively as they pooled information to complete a task cooperatively during the game. They likely saw their combined knowledge as an excellent way to achieve success, which simultaneously had a positive effect on their learning. Experiences with in-game tasks reinforced the idea that they could accomplish more by working together than they could alone as individuals. Not only are enemies in the game defeated more easily through a group effort, but one player may notice something key to completing a task that the others did not notice, thereby contributing to the potential the group will have for success. This cooperation required the participants to produce L2 output in order to coordinate and plan their path to successful task completion. The participants were pushed in terms of their L2 level because cooperation with other

*Figure 3. Connected interaction*

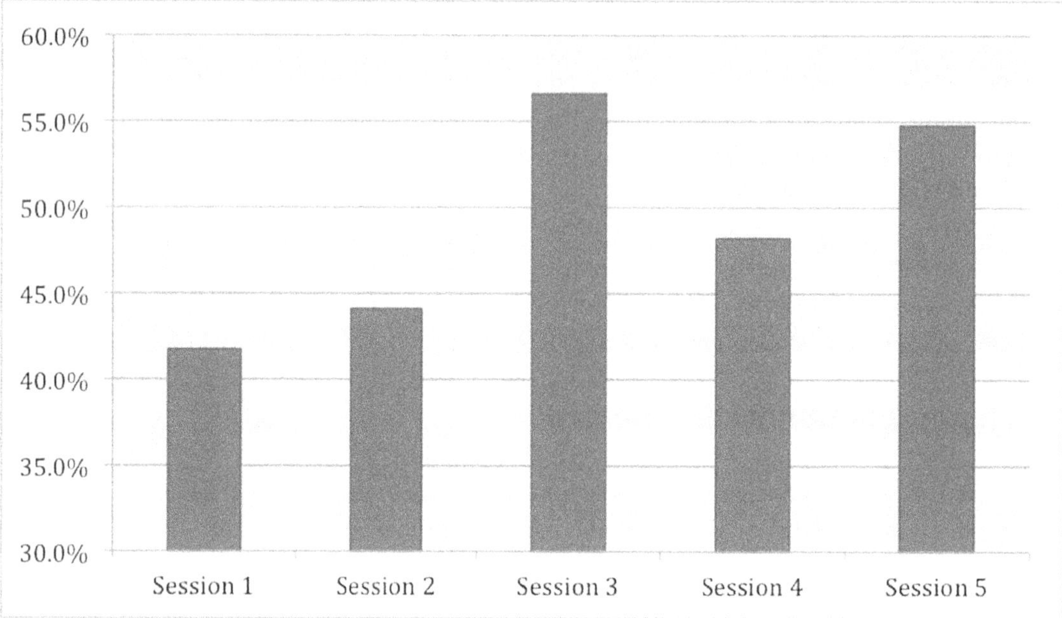


players required that players use language with which they did not have much experience before playing *Guild Wars 2*. In terms of language acquisition, the participants' potential for learning as a group was greater because they were exposed to language forms and vocabulary from one another's output.

An example from the data demonstrates the production of output through the pooling of information. In *Guild Wars 2,* the tasks that players complete come in several different forms. The tasks are marked on a player's map either by a heart-shaped icon or a green star icon. The heart-shaped icons indicate tasks that are specific to an area. Green star icons are particular to the story of a specific player and are based on the race of the character that they have chosen. Figure 4 provides an example of quest objective icons used in the *Guild Wars 2* game interface. The participants' avatars were all the same race and had the same green star tasks for the first two sessions of the study. This means that they could work together on their green star tasks as a group. The heart-shaped tasks could also be done as a group as long as the players were in the same general area.

The conversation in Example 3, which occurred during Session 2, provides an example of pooling information. One of the participants, Thief, had just finished one of the heart-shaped tasks and wanted to know if his fellow players had finished as well. Another player, Pine, did not know how to check to see if he had successfully completed the task. Therefore, Thief explained to Pine where he could find the information. Later, Pine told the others where they should go next and why. Bolded texts were categorized as instances of pooling information.

Example 3:

1. **Thief:** Do you guys finish that?
2. **Thief:** Finish?
3. **Pine:** May be
4. **Pine:** No sure

*Figure 4. Quest objectives*

5. **Thief: You can check heart-shaped is full?**
6. **Thief: Look map (Thief circles the heart on the map)**
7. **Pine:** Yes
8. **Pine:** So let's go another palce

(Some texts omitted.)

9. **Pine:** See the green point?
10. **Pine: That is the main task**
11. **Pine:** We should complete that on
12. **Pine:** One
13. **Thief:** We should come here
14. **Thief:** Finish different work

In Lines 5 and 6, Thief explains that Pine can see if he completed a task by looking at the heart icon on the map. Thief's output is Pine's input, to which he produces additional output, suggesting that they go to a different place as seen in Line 8. Later, Pine pools information telling others what the green icon means, and suggests they go there. Thief reads his text by stating that instead of going to the green icon they should attempt a completely different task.

## Form-Focused Feedback and Modified Output

There are three requirements for L2 learning that takes place through social interaction: (1) comprehensible input, (2) feedback that is focused on form, and (3) modification of output (Pica et al., 1996). For interaction to lead to acquisition, L2 learners need to receive feedback from their interlocutors (i.e., the other participants) and produce modified output. "Interactional input provides a forum for learners to readily detect a discrepancy between their learner language and the target language and that an awareness of the mismatch serves the function of triggering a modification of existing second language knowledge" (Gass & Varonis, 1994, p. 299). A qualitative analysis of the data in this study provided numerous instances of form-focused feedback, which led participants to make modifications in their output (Pica, et al., 1996). In other words, the connected interaction that took place acted as a type of form-focused feedback that could elicit modified output.

Social interaction that facilitates feedback and modified output does not necessarily require a native speaker (Pica et al., 1996). In the Pica et al. (1996) study, L2 learners interacted with other L2 learners, and these interactions provided opportunities for meeting the three needs mentioned above. Even without the presence of a native speaker, L2 learners produced modified output based on feedback from other L2 learners. In this study, participants gave form-focused feedback to one another, albeit often implicitly; however, the feedback led to modified output. An example of modified output from the current study is given in Example 4.

In Session 3, the green-star task of one of the participants was different than the other two participants. At first they did not realize that one of their peer's tasks was different. By asking each other questions and pooling information, they eventually realized this fact. In Example 4, the words "main" and "mainly" are bolded to highlight the discussion of modified input and form-focused feedback.

Example 4:

1. **Mary:** We need to do the **mainly** work
2. **Mary:** Follow the green line
3. **Thief:** I don't know how to do this

(Some texts omitted.)

4. **Mary:** Wait
5. **Mary:** What is your **mainly** task?
6. **Thief:** Did you see daily task?
7. **Pine:** The green one is the **main** task

(Some texts omitted)

8. **Mary:** U need finish the **mainly** task

(Some texts omitted.)

9. **Thief:** I found my **mainly** task.
10. **Thief:** But you guys cannot help me… maybe

(Some texts omitted.)

11. **Mary:** I think we have different **main** task
12. **Thief:** I know

(Several minutes later)

13. **Pine:** So we have to figure what to do later
14. **Thief:** finish
15. **Mary:** I think our **main** task is different
16. **Thief:** Yes
17. **Thief:** Agree

(The following text occurred at the beginning of Session 4.)

18. **Thief:** What's the **main** task?

Both Mary and Thief refer to the green star task as the "mainly" task as seen in Lines 1, 5, 8, and 9. Pine is the only one who uses the correct form of the word "main" in Line 7. Perhaps Pine knew that "mainly" was an incorrect use of the word and in Line 15 he writes, "The green one is the main task." Mary must have noticed that Pine used "main" instead of "mainly." Later, in Lines 11 and 15 he writes, "I think our main task is different." Not only does Mary correct himself, but Thief does as well. (Mary is a pseudonym for a male player who references himself as *he* throughout the game.) In Session 4, Thief wrote, "What's the main task?" In fact, in all the following game sessions all the participants use "main task" instead of "mainly task" when referring to the green star tasks. This is one of several instances in which participants modified output based on implicit form-focused feedback.

Based on the results of this study, it is argued that MMORPGs allow for implicit form-focused feedback leading to modified-output. An analysis of participants' interaction while playing *Guild Wars 2* met the three needs to make interaction beneficial to language acquisition: The participants received comprehensible input, they received implicit form-focused feedback on their output, and they then modified their output according to the feedback received.

## Negotiation of Meaning

The results from the data collected in this study indicate that the two most common communication strategies employed by participants were requesting information and checking information, which accounted for 17.2% and 7.1% of the total texts produced, respectively. The other communication strategies, using the L1, self-correction, and peer-correction, made up less than 2% of the total texts produced during the 12 hours of recorded data. Participants rarely used their native language (i.e., Chinese) as a strategy, and this may be attributable to the fact that they were asked to use only English while playing the game. As for self- and peer corrections, participants were simply told to play the game together and use English. They were focused on understanding and playing the game and may not have noticed errors, or likely ignored them. Although players did modify the form of their output as discussed above, the modifications were not counted as corrections because they were implicit and embedded in the communication. Texts were counted as corrections only when one of the players immediately self-corrected or explicitly corrected a peer.

Requesting information and checking information are communication strategies that the participants used in *Guild Wars 2* to negotiate both environmental input and player-produced input. Researchers have stressed the importance of negotiation of meaning and input as an important part of SLA (Long, 1996; Swain, 1985; Varonis & Gass, 1985). The L2 learners in this study were exposed to environmental input that was above their level of English proficiency. It is impossible to know from the recorded data exactly what they did and did not understand; however, what was clear was that they were putting in a very strong effort to make sense of the virtual world. At times, participants would have difficulties in understanding exactly what another player was asking or trying to tell them. Thus, players would engage in negotiation of meaning in order to reach an understanding of the intended messages. Negotiation of this sort is referred to as human input in this study. If negotiation is key to language acquisition then MMORPGs are beneficial in that they provide numerous opportunities for players to negotiate meaning.

To work out an understanding of the environmental input, participants sent texts to one another and worked out the meaning of the input as a group. They negotiated input that originated from the environment of the game, which is arguably a process that is very similar to the negotiation that takes place in a face-to-face conversation. Obviously, the players could not negotiate with the source of the environ-

*Figure 5. Participants' broken equipment*

mental input because it is a computer program. Instead, they tried to work out the meaning of the input by sending texts to one another.

Negotiation of environmental input most often took place via requests for information. For example, a participant indicated that he did not know what they were supposed to do and wrote, "I have no idea about this task." By writing this, the participant indicated to others that he did not understand what needed to be done to successfully complete the task at hand. Later he requested information from the other players and wrote, "How to finish this?" The players then worked out the details of tasks by requesting specific information from one another and pooling information until they eventually formed a plan and tried it out. Of course, there were times when the task was too difficult, and the players could not figure out what needed to be done; consequently, they simply gave up and moved on to a different task.

An example of negotiation of environmental input that occurred during the game is illustrated in the conversation between participants in Example 5. At this point in the game, the participants were struggling to complete tasks because they continued to get quickly defeated by enemies and could not understand why this kept happening. What they did not realize was that they needed to repair their characters' equipment. The more combat a player engages in, the more their equipment suffers, and players need to go to a town and have it repaired to be at full strength. The participants' equipment had become completely destroyed. When this happens, the broken equipment is automatically unequipped, leaving the players' characters shirtless. Figure 5) illustrates the players' broken equipment.

The interaction in Example 5 takes place as the participants negotiate what needs to be done to remedy their current situation. Bolded texts were categorized as instances of clarification checks and italicized texts were requesting information. Often checks came in the form of a request for specific information, which is why some texts are both bolded and italicized.

Example 5:

1. **Pine:** *What's wrong about our clothes?*

(Some texts omitted)

2. **Thief:** We should fix our equipment
3. **Mary:** We need find somewhere
4. **Mary:** To fix

(Some texts omitted.)

5. **Thief:** Find me

(Some texts omitted.)

6. **Thief:** You should go somewhere to fix your equipment
7. **Pine:** ***How to fix equipment?***
8. **Pine:** How
9. **Thief:** Just talking with NPC
10. **Pine:** ***Where?***
11. **Mary:** See map
12. **Thief:** Look map
13. **Pine:** Ok
14. **Thief:** Follow me

Pine did not understand why his character suddenly appeared shirtless. He indicated his misunderstanding by requesting information from the other two participants as seen in Line 1 above. The other two responded to Pine by telling him that they needed to fix their equipment and that they needed to go "somewhere" to do that, as seen in Lines 2 and 3. Pine still did not understand how to do this and asked for clarification as seen in Line 7. Thief clarified by telling Pine that he needed to speak with an NPC. Pine then asked for further clarification by asking where he would find an NPC. Eventually, they found where they needed to go and successfully fixed their equipment. In Example 5, the input that triggered the negotiation of meaning was environmental (i.e., the loss of clothing to their characters). From that point on in the game, the players knew that they needed to check their equipment and have it repaired. In essence, they modified their future actions based on what they had learned from negotiating environmental input.

The number of times participants' negotiated input was quantified by placing texts into communication strategy categories. During Session 3 checking information accounted for more of the total texts produced than in the other four sessions. Checking information accounted for 11.7% of the total texts produced in Session 3, most of which came in the form of clarification checks. Clarification checks made up 10.2% of the texts, more than double that of any other session (see Figure 6). It is also worth noting that the rate of connected interaction reached 54% in Session 3, the highest rate of the five sessions. Session 2 had a connected interaction rate of 44% and the rate in Session 4 was 48%. This means that 54% of the texts produced in Session 3 were in response to texts produced by other participants, indicating that the participants paid more attention to one another's texts in Session 3 than in the other sessions.

Since negotiation of input is beneficial for SLA, understanding more about the interaction in Session 3 can lead to a better understanding of the language benefits of MMORPGs. The higher rate of interaction and negotiation in Session 3 can be attributed to the main tasks each individual player needed to accomplish. Until Session 3, the three participants had been given the same main tasks. Through a series

*Figure 6. Checking information percentages per game session*

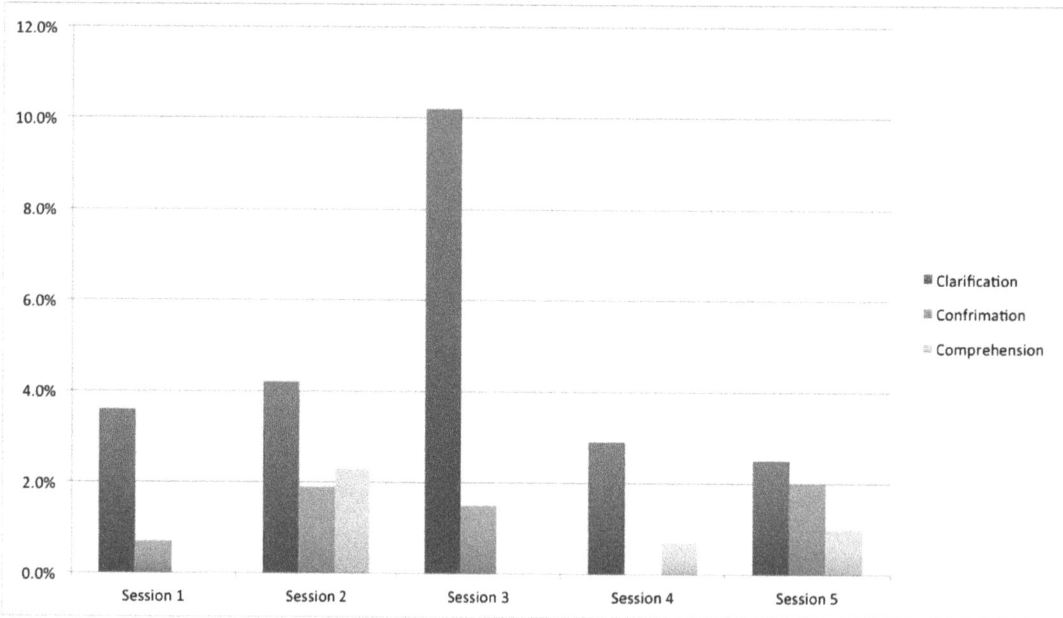


of clarification checks and requests for information, the participants discovered that they had different main tasks in Session 3, as shown in Example 6. Bolded texts were categorized as instances of clarification checks and italicized texts were requesting information.

Example 6:

1. **Pine:** *Do you get the task?*
2. **Thief: Which?**
3. **Pine:** Twilight of the wolf
4. **Mary:** Follow the green line
5. **Thief:** No
6. (Some texts omitted.)
7. **Thief:** *Can we just finish daily task?*
8. **Mary:** ***What do u need to do?***
9. (Some texts omitted.)
10. **Thief:** I found my mainly task.
11. **Thief:** But you guys cannot help me…maybe
12. **Pine:** What is that?
13. **Thief:** A Pup's illness
14. **Pine:** ***Where is that?***

Thief decides that he will do his task alone. When he tries to accomplish the task by himself, he fails because the task is too difficult to do alone. He then requests help from the other two players, and they come to help him. However, because the other two players do not have the same task, they cannot see the information related to the quest. This situation elicits a series of requests and checks in order to share task related information so that everyone knows what is required to complete Thief's task. Once Thief's task is finished, the group engages in another conversation and discovers that Thief's next main task is still different from Pine and Mary's current main task. They decide that, as a group, they will try to complete Mary's and Pine's task first and, then, later go back and try to complete Thief's task. This process requires another series of requests and checks. Thief cannot see the details of the other members' task just like the other two could not see Thief's task. When in-game tasks were not identical for the entire group, there were more instances of requesting and checking information. These in-game tasks are similar to information gap activities used in instructional settings because they require that players request information from others in order to successfully complete tasks.

To summarize, the results and discussion above aim to provide insight into the ways in which MMORPGs support SLA. The three general areas discussed were (1) output, input, and connected interaction, (2) form-focused feedback and modified output, and (3) negotiation of meaning. These three areas of SLA are prominent throughout the 12 hours of gameplay analyzed in this study. The analysis quantified the type and number of learning and communication strategies used by the participants in order to better understand the interaction that took place in these three areas of SLA. The findings add to previous research that indicates MMORPGs may have a positive impact on SLA and provide insight into the reasons.

## FUTURE RESEARCH DIRECTIONS

While it seems clear based on the data presented in this study that MMORPGs provide opportunities for L2 learners to interact and negotiate meaning in the target language, there are still gaps in the research and avenues for future inquiry on MMORPGs that have not been specifically addressed to date. Although the data from the current study show that *Guild Wars 2* provides opportunities for interaction and negotiation of input among English learners, it is important to remember that there were only three participants; consequently, it is not possible to generalize findings from the current study to other contexts. Studies with larger numbers of participants are needed. At the same time, it is important to remember that analyzing data for only three participants was a time-consuming and labor-intensive process, requiring hundreds of hours of data analysis. To engage in similar research with a larger N-size would require a level of support that is likely beyond the capabilities of a researcher-funded study.

The way that the current study was configured did not ask participants to engage with native speakers of English. In other words, the participants were not asked to communicate with players outside of their group. There were always native speakers of English playing the game around them, so it would be possible to create a research design in which data could be collected from interactions that involved native speakers and non-native speakers. It is unknown whether or not the participants in this study paid attention to anyone else's conversations because they did not have a strong need to talk to anyone outside of their group. As a group of three players, they were strong enough to complete many of the lower level tasks without much difficulty. A research study designed around a nonnative speaker of English in a group of native speakers of English playing an MMORPG could produce interesting results in terms of opportunities for negotiation of meaning.

In the current study, all three participants shared the same native language. If participants from different native language backgrounds could be found, it could be determined whether the types of strategies employed by the participants were culturally motivated or not. The culturally insular characteristic of the group in the current study likely contributed to the lack of attention they paid to conversations and interactions outside of the participant group. However, it is important to note that even though the participants shared a common L1, 99.2% of all the texts they produced were done so in English. A study that included participants who do not share an L1 would give greater insight into the role of form-focused feedback and modified output. It seems that modified output was produced from implicit form-focused feedback. Learners would be more likely to notice one another's grammar mistakes if they did not share an L1. The inclusion of learners from different L1s might lead to opportunities for more explicit feedback and perhaps more modified output. The limitation of a shared L1 among participants is common among studies involving MMORPGs and SLA, and Peterson (2016) points out that future research "would be of particular value if it involved diverse learner groups of varying L1 backgrounds and proficiency levels" (p. 1192).

Another avenue for future research would be a qualitative examination of the participants' perceptions of MMORPGs as a vehicle for English use (if not explicit learning). In addition to the qualitative data that were collected as part of the text analysis during game play in the current study, qualitative data were also collected using an initial written survey and follow-up face-to-face interviews. A reporting on the results of these data is beyond the scope of this chapter; however, three general observations from the qualitative perceptual data from the current study can be noted. First, it is very clear from a summary of the qualitative data that the participants enjoyed playing the game. Although this fact may not seem surprising because they all indicated they liked video games before the study began, what is interesting about this perception is that even though they were required to communicate in their L2 during game playing, this requirement did not seem to frustrate them. All of the participants perceived the game to be fun and looked forward to their game time together. Second, all three of the participants indicated that their favorite part of playing the game was working as a team to complete tasks. The social and collaborative nature of MMORPGs is one reason why they enjoyed the game as much as they did and why it was perceived as being fun, even though it was being played in the L2. Third, the participants indicated how much they enjoyed the process of leveling up their characters, acquiring new abilities and skills, and then testing out the new skills during the game. These data support the idea that learners enjoy participating in problem-solving tasks, and tasks that require the use of higher-order thinking skills, such as analyzing, synthesizing, and evaluating.

Finally, researchers interested in MMORPGs might investigate are studies that focus on oral rather than written communication. The research cited in this chapter had participants communicating via texts. Some recently released MMORPGs, especially those released on consoles, such as the PlayStation 4 and Xbox One, use voice chat to communicate with other players. The option for oral communication is needed because consoles use a controller rather than a keyboard, and without a keyboard it is impossible to type a message. Using a console MMORPG, such as *The Elder Scrolls Online*, could allow the collection of data relative to the potential benefits MMORPGs have for the development of L2 oral skills. This research is noticeably missing from the current literature.

## CONCLUSION

In this study, the texts that participants used while playing the MMORPG *Guild Wars 2* were categorized based on the use of learning and communication strategies. An analysis of the data found that the most common type of learning strategy employed was pooling information, which outnumbered the other learning strategies of commands, statements, suggestions, and modeling. Furthermore, the study found that MMORPGs do support opportunities for language learners to negotiate meaning in the form of player-produced input and environmental input. The most common types of communication strategies used while negotiating meaning were requesting information and checking information.

The quantitative data from categorized texts was used to analyze participant interaction in terms SLA. This study provides evidence for the fact that MMORPGs are beneficial to SLA because they provide opportunities for L2 learners to receive large amounts of input and produce large amounts of output as players are required to pool information by responding to one another's requests for information and working cooperatively to complete tasks. Output produced by one player is a meaningful source of contextual input for other players, which creates connected interaction between players. Participants' implicit focus on form can also lead to modified-output. Furthermore, players have the opportunity to negotiate both player-produced input and environmental input as a means to complete in-game tasks in a contextually rich social environment. Finally, players engage in cooperative problem solving that share many characteristics with language instructional activities that deemed beneficial for language learning.

The benefits that video games, and specifically MMORPGs, have for language learners show great potential. Learners can acquire both vocabulary and language forms through interaction with other players and through completing the in-game tasks. Anonymity can promote positive affect and lower the affective filter, thereby providing learners with a language-learning environment that is conducive to language experimentation. Interaction is especially advantageous for language learners who do not have access to face-to-face interactions with native speakers because of the social nature built into MMORPGS.

Video games that are designed specifically to improve SLA have been around for some time, as have MMORPGs that aim to create massive social communities. It is unknown what the future will bring in terms of advances in technology, particularly as these advances relate to L2 learning online technologies. In the future applied linguists and game developers might collaborate to create Massive Multi-learner Online Language Spaces (MMOLSs) that are just as engaging as MMORPGs but are designed specifically for SLA. What is known is that the development and uses of online technologies will continue to expand, making the language classroom of tomorrow and the opportunities for language learning quite different from what they are today. Educators need to be open to the possibilities that online technologies affords us, especially in terms of creating optional learning environments for L2 learners.

## REFERENCES

Allen, I. E., & Seaman, J. (2013). *Changing course: Ten years of tracking online education in the United States*. Retrieved from http://www.onlinelearningsurvey.com/reports/changingcourse.pdf

Beauvois, M. H., & Eledge, J. (1995). Personality types and megabytes: Student attitudes toward computer mediated communication (CMC) in the language classroom. *CALICO Journal*, *13*(2 & 3), 27–45.

Blake, R. J. (2011). Current trends in online language learning. *Annual Review of Applied Linguistics*, *31*, 19–35. doi:10.1017/S026719051100002X

Chamot, A. U., & O'Malley, M. (1992). The cognitive academic language learning approach: A bridge to the mainstream. In P. A. Richard-Amato & M. A. Snow (Eds.), *The multicultural classroom* (pp. 39–57). Boston, MA: Addison Wesley; doi:10.2307/3586733

Dudeney, G., & Hockly, N. (2012). ICT in ELT: How did we get here and where are we going? *ELT Journal*, *66*(4), 533–542. doi:10.1093/elt/ccs050

Gardner, R. C. (1985). *Social psychology and second language learning: The role of attitudes and motivation*. London: Edward Arnold.

Gass, S. M. (1997). *Input, interaction and the second language learner*. Mahwah, NJ: Lawrence Erlbaum.

Gass, S. M., & Varonis, E. M. (1994). Input, interaction, and second language production. *Studies in Second Language Acquisition*, *16*(03), 283–302. doi:10.1017/S0272263100013097

Kongmee, I., Strachan, R., Montgomery, C., & Pickard, A. (2011). *Using massively multiplayer online role playing games (MMORPGs) to support second language learning: Action research in the real and virtual world*. Retrieved from http://nrl.northumbria.ac.uk/279/1/kongmee%20iverg%20paper2.pdf

Krashen, S. (1982). *Principles and practice in second language acquisition*. Oxford, UK: Pergamon Press.

Lee, L. (2001). Online interaction: Negotiation of meaning and strategies used among learners of Spanish. *ReCALL*, *13*(02), 232–244. doi:10.1017/S0958344001000829a

Long, M. H. (1983). Linguistic and conversational adjustments to non-nativespeakers. *Studies in Second Language Acquisition*, *5*(2), 177–193. doi:10.1017/S0272263100004848

Long, M. H. (1996). The role of linguistic environment in second language acquisition. In W. C. Ritchie & T. K. Bhatia (Eds.), *Handbook of second language acquisition* (pp. 413–454). San Diego, CA: Academic Press; doi:10.1016/B978-012589042-7/50015-3

OECD. (2005). *E-learning in tertiary education: Where do we stand?* Paris, France: OECD.

Peirce, B. N. (1995). Social identity, investment, and language learning. *TESOL Quarterly*, *29*(1), 9–31. doi:10.2307/3587803

Peterson, M. (2010). Massively multiplayer online role-playing games as arenas for second language learning. *Computer Assisted Language Learning*, *23*(5), 429–439. doi:10.1080/09588221.2010.520673

Peterson, M. (2011). Digital gaming and second language development: Japanese learners interactions in a MMORPG. *Digital Culture & Education*, *3*(1), 56–73.

Peterson, M. (2012). Learner interaction in massively multiplayer online role playing game (MMORPG): A sociocultural discourse analysis. *ReCALL*, *24*(03), 361–380. doi:10.1017/S0958344012000195

Peterson, M. (2016). The use of massively multiplayer online role-playing games in CALL: An analysis of research. *Computer Assisted Language Learning*, *29*(7), 1181–1194. doi:10.1080/09588221.2016.1197949

Pica, T. (1994). Research on negotiation: What does it reveal about second-language learning conditions, processes, and outcomes. *Language Learning*, *44*(3), 493–527. doi:10.1111/j.1467-1770.1994.tb01115.x

Pica, T., Lincoln-Porter, F., Paninos, D., & Linneln, J. (1996). Language learners interaction: How does it address the input, output, and feedback needs of L2 learners? *TESOL Quarterly*, *30*(1), 59–84. doi:10.2307/3587607

Rankin, Y. A., McNeal, M., & Shute, M. W. (2008). User centered game design: Evaluating massive multiplayer online role playing games for second language acquisition. In *Sandbox Symposium*, (pp. 43-49). Los Angeles, CA: Association for Computing Machinery. doi:10.1145/1401843.1401851

Rubio, F., & Thoms, J. (Eds.). (2013). *Hybrid language teaching and learning: Exploring theoretical, pedagogical, and curricular issues*. Boston, MA: Heinle/Cengage Learning.

Scholz, K., & Schulze, M. (2017). Digital-gaming trajectories and second language development. *Language Learning & Technology*, *21*(1), 100–120.

Swain, M. (1985). Communicative competence: Some roles of comprehensible input and comprehensible output in its development. In S. Gass & C. Madden (Eds.), *Input in Second Language Acquisition* (pp. 235–256). New York, NY: Newbury House Publishers.

Swain, M. (2000). The output hypothesis and beyond: Mediating acquisition through collaborative dialogue. In J. Lantolf (Ed.), *Sociocultural theory and second language learning* (pp. 97–114). Oxford, UK: Oxford University Press.

Swain, M., & Lapkin, S. (1995). Problems in output and the cognitive processes they generate: A step towards second language learning. *Applied Linguistics*, *16*(3), 371–391. doi:10.1093/applin/16.3.371

Sykes, J. M., & Reinhardt, J. (2013). *Language at play: Digital games in second and foreign language teaching and learning*. Boston, MA: Pearson Education.

Sylvén, L. K., & Sundqvist, P. (2012). Gaming as extramural English L2 learning and L2 proficiency among young learners. *ReCALL*, *24*(03), 302–321. doi:10.1017/S095834401200016X

Thorne, S. L. (2008). Transcultural communication in open Internet environments and massively multiplayer online games. In S. Magnan (Ed.), *Mediating discourse online* (pp. 305–327). Amsterdam: Benjamins; doi:10.1075/aals.3.17tho

Varonis, E. M., & Gass, S. (1985). Non native/ non-native conversations: A model for negotiation of meaning. *Applied Linguistics*, *6*(1), 71–90. doi:10.1093/applin/6.1.71

Vygotsky, L. S. (1978). *Mind and society: The development of higher psychological processes*. Cambridge, MA: Harvard University Press.

## ADDITIONAL READING

Beatty, K. (2003). *Teaching and researching computer-assisted language learning*. Hong Kong, People's Republic of China: Longman.

Chapelle, C. (2003). *English language learning and technology: Lectures on teaching and research in the age of information and communication*. Amsterdam, The Netherlands: John Benjamins; doi:10.1075/lllt.7

Levy, M., & Stockwell, G. (2006). *CALL dimensions: Options and issues in computer-assisted language learning*. New York, NY: Lawrence Erlbaum Associates/Taylor & Francis.

Murray, D. E. (2000). Protean communication: The language of computer-mediated communication. *TESOL Quarterly*, *34*(3), 397–421. doi:10.2307/3587737

Price, S., & Rogers, Y. (2004). Lets get physical: The learning benefits of interacting in digitally augmented physical spaces. *Computers & Education*, *43*(1-2), 137–151. doi:10.1016/j.compedu.2003.12.009

Pujolă, J.-T. (2002). CALLing for help. Research in language learning strategies using help facilities in a web-based multimedia program. *ReCALL*, *14*(2), 235–262. doi:10.1017/S0958344002000423

## KEY TERMS AND DEFINITIONS

**Cooperative Learning:** A successful teaching strategy in which small teams, each with students of different levels of ability, use a variety of learning activities to improve their understanding of a subject.

**Interaction:** The act of talking or doing things with other people.

**L2 Interaction:** The manner in which information is exchanged in a second language during an interaction between parties.

**L2 Learning:** The process by which people learn a second language.

**Learning Strategies:** Students' self-generated thoughts, feelings, and actions, which are systematically oriented toward attainment of their goals.

**Negotiation of Meaning:** A process that language users go through to reach a clear understanding of each other.

**Online Gaming:** Playing of computer games over the Internet especially, games that enable two or more players to participate simultaneously from different locations.

**Online Language Learning:** The process and practice of acquiring a second or foreign language online.

**Video Games:** Games played by electronically manipulating images produced by a computer program on a television screen or other display screen.

# Chapter 15

# *¿Eres un Gamer?*

## Engaging Transnational Children in Game-Ecology Language and Identity Socialization Within the EFL Environment

**Steve Daniel Przymus**
*Texas Christian University, USA*

**Alejandro Romo Smith**
*University of Arizona, USA*

## ABSTRACT

*This chapter sheds light on the potential impact of CALL theory and practice on the language and identity socialization of transnational children when educators imagine and promote interaction beyond the classroom. The authors focus specifically on the educational trajectories of 1) children returnees, who were born in Mexico, at some point in their lives moved to the U.S., and then returned to Mexico and 2) international migrants, born and many attended school in the U.S., and then moved to Mexico as a result of repatriation and/or deportation (Zúñiga & Vivas-Romero, 2014). The authors advocate creating blended affinity spaces (Przymus, 2016) at schools where youth can meet and play digital role-playing games, discuss game-ecology literacy development within these spaces, detail the implementation of such spaces in schools, and share game screen shots, blog posts, and the perspectives of transnational students that support this kind of learning within the EFL environment.*

## INTRODUCTION

*We are all longing to go* home *to some place* we have never been—*a place half-remembered and half-envisioned we can only catch glimpses of from time to time.* Community. *Somewhere, there are people to whom we can* speak with passion *without having the words catch in our throats. Somewhere a circle of hands will open to* receive us, *eyes will light up as we enter, voices will celebrate with us whenever* we come into our own power. *Community means strength that joins* our strength *to do the work that needs*

DOI: 10.4018/978-1-5225-2933-0.ch015

*to be done. Arms to hold us when we falter. A circle of healing.* A circle of friends. *Someplace where we can be free (Starhawk, 1988, p. 92, emphasis added).*

Home, for the estimated 1.5 million transnational children caught in the historical circular migration pattern between the U.S. and Mexico border, can be, as Starhawk describes above, a half-remembered, half-envisioned place, that many have never seen, nor known. In the past decade, scholars have begun to bring to light the issues of these children's fractured schooling and traumatic experiences of trying to adapt to new countries, homes, and sociocultural practices that may be on the one hand in some ways connected to their heritage, but on the other hand vastly disconnected to their lived cultural and linguistic experiences (Borjian, Muñoz de Cote, van Dijk, & Houde, 2016; Medina & Menjívar, 2015; Zúñiga & Hamann, 2006, 2015; Zúñiga & Romero, 2014). The challenges facing youth swept up in reverse migration have also been highlighted beyond the academic literature as journalists have recently taken up this theme through stories in daily newspapers and radio news casts, such as the New York Times article by Cave (2012) "American children now struggling to adjust to life in Mexico," the article, "Deported to Mexico: A lost generation" by Lakhani (2015) in the Guardian, and a story on the PBS News Hour by Fred de Sam Lazaro (2016) "Young returnees start over in Mexico after growing up in the U.S."

The articles and stories in the media, referenced above, specifically document the experiences of 1. *children returnees,* or children who "were born in Mexico, eventually left to the U.S. (generally with their parents or at least one of them) and after some period of residency in the U.S., returned to Mexico" (Zúñiga & Vivas-Romero, 2014, p. 3) and 2. *international migrants*, who were born in the U.S., many attended school in the U.S., and then moved to Mexico as a result of repatriation and/or deportation (Zúñiga & Vivas-Romero, 2014). In the larger discussion on the educational attainment of transnational children traversing the U.S.-Mexico border, historically, studies have focused on the schooling and community adaptation of *1.5 generation migrants,* or an estimated 800,000 children who were born in Mexico, emigrated to the U.S., and have remained in the U.S. (Gonzales & Chávez, 2012; see also Zúñiga & Vivas-Romero, 2014). With exception to the articles and stories mentioned above, the narratives of reverse migration and the voices of children returnees and international migrants attending schools in Mexico have not been heard with the same volume. It can be estimated from the 2010 Mexican Population Census that 350,000 children returnees and 500,000 international migrants now reside in Mexico (Giorguli & Gutiérrez, 2011; Gonzales & Chávez, 2012; Zúñiga & Hamann, 2015). According to Zúñiga & Hamann's longitudinal survey studies, approximately 420,000 of these children have enrolled in Mexican schools, grades 1-9 alone, and that as many as 330,000 children were born in the United States (2015, p. 644; see also Zúñiga, 2012; Zúñiga & Hamann, 2006). As noted by Borjian et al., (2016), "With the exception of Zúñiga and Hamann (2006), transnational children's experiences in Mexico have, to a large extent, been over-looked" (p. 43).

In this chapter, it is our goal to not only continue to share the experiences of these youth, but to also draw connections to the research in the U.S. on 1.5 generation migrants that shows how increased opportunities for these youth to participate in school-based, out-of-classroom activities have helped them 1) reposition themselves in the eyes of their teachers and peers, 2) develop positive identities, and 3) have success at school (Przymus, 2015, 2016). In comparing the experience of 1.5 generation youth in the U.S. to the context of transnational children in Mexico, we may be able to learn from and detail how this same reconceptualization of learning could be theorized through CALL practice and specifically the promotion of game-ecology language and identity socialization through a peer-facilitated intervention that would create gaming communities of practice in Mexican schools. The title of our chapter, ¿Eres un Gamer?, translated as "Are you a Gamer?, is an example of what youth, like transnational children who can draw on features of multiple languages, might say to a peer in order to join such a community of practice. The overall goal of this article is a call to action for educators, specifically in Mexico, but on both sides of the border, to conceptualize and work towards the creation of spaces for such gaming communities of practice at schools. Valuing the identity of transnational children as gamers could have an impact on creating more equitable, social, and educational experiences for these youth.

In making these connections, we merge research on how individuals form identities over time within language socialization processes (Schieffelin & Ochs, 1986), through participation in communities of practice (Thorne, Black, & Sykes, 2009; Wenger, 1998), linked to interest-based peer activities (Canagarajah, 2007; Przymus, 2016, 2015), with research on gaming and affinity spaces (Cornillie, Thorne, & Desmet, 2012; Gee & Hays, 2012), in order to propose a concrete trajectory of bilingual language and identity formation for the thousands of transnational children in Mexican schools. Through bridging these theoretical traditions, we first explore the potential for interest-based extracurricular activities that value proficiency in English as an important skill for group membership, such as massively multiplayer online role-playing games (MMORPGs), as a context for transnational students' Spanish-English bilingual language socialization, academic success, and identity formation in Mexican schools. Then we propose and detail the implementation of *blended affinity spaces* at the English as a Foreign Language (EFL) setting in Mexican schools as a means for facilitating such interest-based participation opportunities for transnational students.

We begin by reviewing the relevant literature on communities of practice, interest-based language socialization, and affinity spaces, and suggest that some of the challenges facing transnational students in Mexican schools might be ameliorated through providing access to participation in school-supported gaming communities of practice. We continue by defining our understanding of game-ecology and gaming literacy, and provide concrete examples of these through screen shots of pre-game discourse on various gaming blogs, intra-game discourse from various MMORPGs, and of post-game discourse from a gaming blog. We show, through sharing former transnational children's voices, how game-ecology literacies can be cultivated in these peer, interest-based spaces, and how the cache of high proficiency in English can provide transnational children, many of whom have developed advanced proficiency in English as a result of living and attending school in the U.S., with an immediate valued role as a member in these gaming communities of practice. We conclude by referring to a similar peer, interest-based language socialization program model currently used by schools in the U.S., the ELL Ambassadors Program, as a guide for how to implement blended affinity spaces for game-ecology language and identity socialization to take place in Mexican schools.

## BACKGROUND

### Language Socialization, Communities of Practice, (Blended) Affinity Spaces, and Transnational Children in Mexican Schools

Community, for the almost 800,000 transnational children (children returnees and international migrants) living and attending schools in Mexico may not seem readily available nor familiar in their new educational contexts. Through classroom observations of and semi-structured interviews with transnational students in the Mexican state of Puebla, Galicia-Ramos (2016) found that transnational students often struggle with learning and showing knowledge in Spanish. The negative experiences that these youth can encounter in schools can range from feeling invisible in the sense that they are out-of-sight and out-of-mind of their former schools in the U.S. and not having their language and identity struggles addressed by their Mexican teachers who do not always know by looking at their appearance that they lack the linguistic and cultural background to be successful at schools, to not being allowed to enroll in schools all together until a new school-year cycle begins (Galicia-Ramos, 2016; Zúñiga & Vivas-Romero, 2014). "Mexican schools and teachers are not prepared to welcome transnational children" (Zúñiga & Vivas-Romero, 2014, p. 11; see also Sanchez-Garcia, Hamann, & Zuniga, 2012). Evidence from large survey data show that schools are "not responding to international migrant children's' needs" (Zúñiga & Vivas-Romero, 2014, p. 7). Inflexibility of Mexican school personnel to admit youth mid-year, causes many students to miss time in school (Zúñiga & Vivas-Romero, 2014). Ruptured educational trajectories from missing school and falling and being left behind in Mexican schools can lead to painful experiences, negative identity formation, and self-fulfilling prophecies of having "lost their capacity of being successful" (Zúñiga & Vivas-Romero, 2014, p. 10; see also Hamann & Zúñiga, 2011).

It must be a goal for all educators to mine the resources and interests of their students in order to discover what causes youth to speak with passion and what activities and in what contexts might this be facilitated. In researching contexts and programs that promote interest-based, out-of-classroom peer interaction for 1.5 generation migrants in U.S. schools, Przymus (2016) makes theoretical connections and points to previous and current work stating,

*Scholars have shown strong interest in the ways that language learners "do" and perform identities in their everyday lives (Bucholtz & Hall, 2005; Harklau, 2003; Kramsch, 1997)...to conceptualize the ways individuals form identities over time within language socialization processes (Schieffelin & Ochs, 1986; Zuengler & Cole, 2005), through participation in specific communities of practice (Eckert & McConnell-Ginet, 2003; McConnell-Ginet, 2003; Thorne, Black, & Sykes, 2009; Wenger, 1998) and in relation to imagined communities." (p. 266; see also Kanno & Norton, 2003; Norton, 2000, 2001)*

Zúñiga's extensive work in Mexico with transnational children, together with the scholars Vivas-Romero once and Hamann on multiple occasions, has shown that ruptured schooling, challenges with communicating in Spanish, and negative identity development can make participation and acceptance in face-to-face communities of practice difficult for these youth. We may find a beginning to addressing this challenge through the relevant Gee & Hayes (2012) description of affinity spaces. Affinity spaces are defined as virtual or physical locations where groups of people are drawn together because of a shared, strong interest or engagement in a common activity. Gee & Hayes (2012) draw a connection to affinity spaces, learning, and school by stating that:

*Humans do not learn anything in depth without passion and persistence. That is why, for most people, what they learn in school is short-lived unless they practice it in work or other settings after school. It is also why so many people, children and adults, learn more important things in their lives out of school than in it. (p. 145)*

The reality, however, is that all children, and especially students new to a context like children returnees in Mexico or immigrant and refugee students in the U.S., are ascribed identities and judged by how they do perform at schools. Too often they are judged by other youth and assessed by teachers based on the expected norms and "second space" Discourses of formalized institutions (Spanish in Mexico and English in the U.S.), and not by how they perform their "first space" semiotic activities of home and community, which for transnational students have been disrupted by moving away from former homes and communities of practice (Moje, Ciechanowski, Kramer, Ellis, Carrillo, & Collazo, 2014, p. 41). Conceptualizing computer assisted language learning (CALL) theory and practice to include spaces for game-ecology language and identity socialization, beyond the classroom, but still within the school walls, provides an opportunity for widening this narrow band of normalcy for success at school to include "third spaces" (Moje, et al., 2014, p. 41). In this conceptual chapter, we call for and detail the implementation of third spaces for the merging of "first space," plurilingual practices of Spanish and English that tap into the strengths and interests of transnational children, where they can speak with passion without the words getting caught in their throats and where they can come into their own power, with the "second space" Discourses needed to be successful at school. For 1.5 generation migrants or emergent bilinguals in U.S. schools, who find it hard to escape being labeled for their race, language, and social class and for transnational children in Mexican schools, whose limited academic Spanish and different sounding social Spanish language skills label them as different from the rest, these spaces can be very empowering (Przymus, 2015). "These communities of practice and affinity spaces allow language learners to challenge these labels" (Przymus, 2015, p. 505).

Traditional conceptions of affinity spaces, however, have mostly included non-educational arenas, such as youth connecting, many times alone at home, with like-minded youth from around the world online. However impactful these interactions are for language learning and identity exploration, they are still isolated interactions away from the peer and adult groups at the transnational students' new educational contexts, precisely where the need to reposition themselves with their desired and imagined identities exists and where educational and life success opportunities are often created and nurtured. Without finding a way to blend transnational students' non-educational arena strengths with schooling expectations, these youth may continue to be positioned negatively.

Strengths of transnational children, however, are not always celebrated in schools on either side of the border. Often positioned negatively in Mexican schools as not good Spanish speakers and with identities of having done something wrong, we propose here to shift the positioned identities of these youth by taking an asset approach of viewing their proficiency in English as the cultural and linguistic capital (Bourdieu, 2011) needed to become valuable members of digital role-playing game (DRPG) communities of practice and view their future participation in these communities of practice as a potential means for these students to re-write their identity narratives in their new schools and communities. Building off of previous work on interest-based, peer-language socialization programs in U.S. schools with 1.5 generation migrants, such as the ELL Ambassadors program (Przymus, 2016), we propose the creation of *blended affinity spaces* (Przymus, 2015) in Mexican schools, where youth are encouraged to meet and play massively multiplayer online role-playing games (MMORPGs), capitalizing on both the high motivation that many youth have in playing MMORPGS, such as World of Warcraft, and the great potential for Spanish/English language socialization and identity formation that can take place interacting in the game-ecology. In these blended affinity spaces there exists "a combination of access with the global community and also with peers at school who share the same gaming interests and who could act as…Spanish language (SL) ambassadors" (Przymus, 2015, p. 512). Below, we share the perspectives of four former transnational children (two currently living in Mexico and two living in the U.S.). Through their voices we hear stories of how they both learned Spanish talking with gamers in Mexico about playing games and were valued for their high proficiency in English as they taught others what words and phrases meant in the intra-game discourse and helped group members succeed through reading English and explaining game details in person and on gaming blog sites.

What can bring youth, such as gamers, together is their shared interest in the game, recognition that English is a lingua franca in many popular digital games, and that group members' ability to share resources, such as English proficiency, is important for achieving the group's goals (Canagarajah, 2007; House, 2003; Seidlhofer, 2004). Transnational students, who can sometimes not feel welcomed at their new schools, can become highly valued members of these blended affinity spaces for gaming because of the linguistic expertise that they can contribute to the group. In return, transnational children become socialized in the Spanish language, highly needed for success at school and for adjusting in their new communities, form friendships that are important for feeling emotionally connected at school, and can achieve academic success as a result of greater peer networking at schools (Przymus, 2016). Przymus (2016) shows a direct relationship between the beginning of immigrant and refugee youth' participation in the ELL Ambassadors Program with these youths' increased academic success in classes and ultimate high school graduation and university attendance. This reciprocity between expert and novice English users and gamers, important for the sustainability of a community of practice, may afford transnational children with opportunities for important membership roles in their new social and educational contexts in Mexico and in turn facilitate their success at school.

The social skills and strategies learned while interacting in these proposed blended affinity spaces are important for the language and identity socialization of transnational children in Mexican schools and well describe what we consider the literacies of the game-ecology. Below we share screen shots of the interface of popular MMORPGs and gaming community blog posts to demonstrate the ubiquitous use and internationally recognized value of English and the potential gaming literacy development at all stages of the game-ecology. We also bring in the voice of former transnational students in Mexico and in the U.S., who share their stories of Spanish language development in Mexico, identity formation as valued members of gaming communities of practice, and offer their perspectives on the potential impact of creating blended affinity spaces for game-ecology socialization at Mexican schools. These individuals are young adults whose lived experiences were of children returnees and transnational children, and whose perspectives on the potential impact of establishing peer-language/identity socialization spaces for gaming at Mexican schools provide an on the ground view and first hand account of how beneficial these spaces could be for transnational children. They provided thoughts via online anonymous survey responses and a semi-structured interview, and assented to participate in the research in compliance with the authors' institutional review board protocol. All game-ecology screen shots below were gathered by one of the authors, who is an active gamer in various affinity spaces and gaming communities of practice. All usernames that are visible on the chat and the head-up display (HUD) of the game in the Final Fantasy XIV screen cap have been vetted as adults and no usernames correlate with actual names in any way. Finally, all of the names on the screen caps from Reddit (a public access blog), the chat-box from Final Fantasy, and the public access blog, Discord, that show game-ecology discourse, have been blacked out.

## MAIN FOCUS OF THE CHAPTER

### Game-Ecology Literacies and the Valued Role of English

A massively multiplayer online role-playing game, or MMORPG, is a video game that takes place in a persistent state world with thousands, or even millions of players developing their characters in a role-playing environment. It is an environment where events are constantly occurring, regardless of whether or not the player is actively logged on. Whereas most games' objective is simply to complete the game, MMORPGs depend on gameplay that revolves around interactions between players or groups of players. Therefore, it can be said that an objective of MMORPGs is not to "complete the game" but rather to make meaningful interactions with real people within the game itself. While it has been well recognized in the literature that MMORPGS can be viewed as designed learning environments (Gee, 2007) which can be used for language learning (Sykes & Holden, 2011; Sykes & Reinhardt, 2013; Reinhardt, 2016) and have ushered in a new era of interconnectivity through the use of real-time communication and in-game collaboration (Cornillie et al., 2012; Gee & Hays, 2012), these games have also inadvertently created zones where people can physically meet and both practice and apply English or any other target language. According to a research proposal conducted by Engadget, both physical face-to-face and online, anonymous interaction, are key, because players are not just writing and speaking words, but being spoken to. Informal chat and online games in general, become a learning environment that can then be enhanced through face-to-face interactions and conversations about playing (The science of language, community, and MMORPGs, 2014). This is the game-ecology.

Tremendous amounts of language socialization happen in the game-ecology of online role-playing games such as World of Warcraft. Gaming literacy from the game-ecology includes 1) meta-game discourse, or the talk about playing, before, during, and after, either in person or online in chat groups and blog posts, and 2) the intra-game discourse of interacting with other players from around the world within the game interface (see screen shot examples of meta-game discourse and intra-game discourse below). In contrast to classroom learning, much learning happens within the game-ecology, without the individuals even realizing, through normal activities.

In searching for how to nurture the creation of a circle of friends for transnational children in Mexican schools, we once again think about the linguistic and cultural capital of these students who may possess high proficiency in English as a valued strength and skill needed for membership in gaming communities of practice. Most players agree that the use of English in MMORPG's increases the likelihood of communication particularly with international servers. This increase in international communication via English has in part led to the reduced use of local servers and in the case of some popular games, such as Final Fantasy XIV: A Realm Reborn (ARR), the complete discarding of these local servers (MMORPGs for Language Learning, n.d.). It becomes clear that using English increases collaboration and coordination and therefore encourages communication with an agreed language. A high level of English proficiency can provide youth with immediate roles of expertise in games with English as a lingua franca and indeed this is supported through the former transnational children's comments shared later in the chapter. Figure 1 is a screen shot that illustrates how ubiquitous English is as a lingua franca in some of the most popular MMORPGs.

*Figure 1. The prominence of English on the international servers of Final Fantasy XIV*

The following screen shots give the reader an idea of the pre-game-ecology of individuals promoting aspects of a game via blog posts in English. Figure 2 is a screen shot that shows a flyer, advertising the event Moonfire Faire that will take place in the future, within intra-game interaction.

Figure 3 is a screencap from a *Team Chat* blog called *Discord*. This is an example of a public post where a group of players put out an ad looking to find and recruit other MMORPG players for their guild and they specify what they are looking for. While Discord is a global app and anyone can post in any language, most of the examples you see are in Spanish, English and Japanese, with English being the predominant language used.

Going inside a game, Final Fantasy XIV: A Realm Reborn (FF:ARR), with Figures 4 and 5 below, we see examples of intra-game discourse and the potential of gaming literacy as many players are having casual conversations and exchanging game lingo all in English. Figure 4 is a chat box screencap of FF:ARR and is a good example of a blend of casual English and game lingo usage, such as "apparently im the only one who wants to fight titan tonight. this is the first time ive had to wait for a pug" and more academic English language, such as "Updating online status" and "of the 71 parties currently recruiting, all match your search conditions."

Figure 5 is another screencap from FF:ARR that strengthens the claim that English is a very powerful language to be able to use in MMORPGs, as it shows two strangers from completely different parts of the world having a casual conversation in English. Although the conversation is casual, it at times is

*Figure 2. Pre-game event advertisement (flyer) in English promoting future interaction within the intra-game game-ecology*

*Figure 3. Player recruitment conversation in English via a team chat blog called Discord*

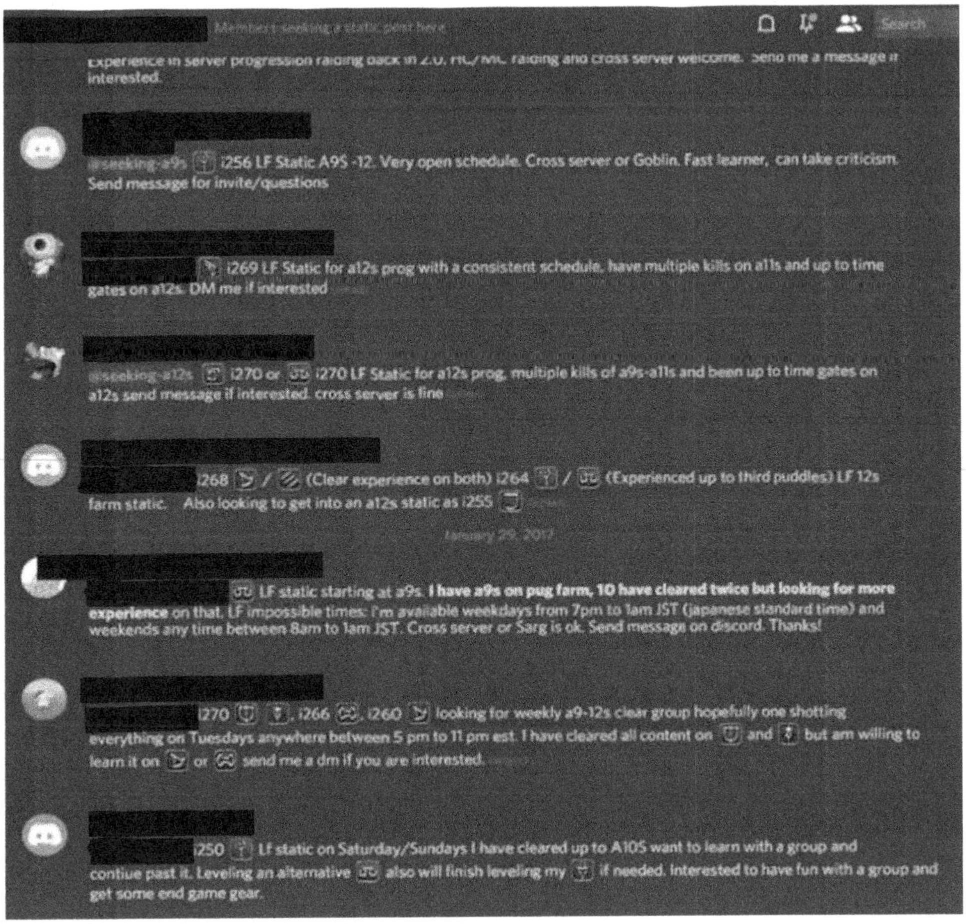

*Figure 4. Screen shot of a chat box conversation in English within the Final Fantasy game*

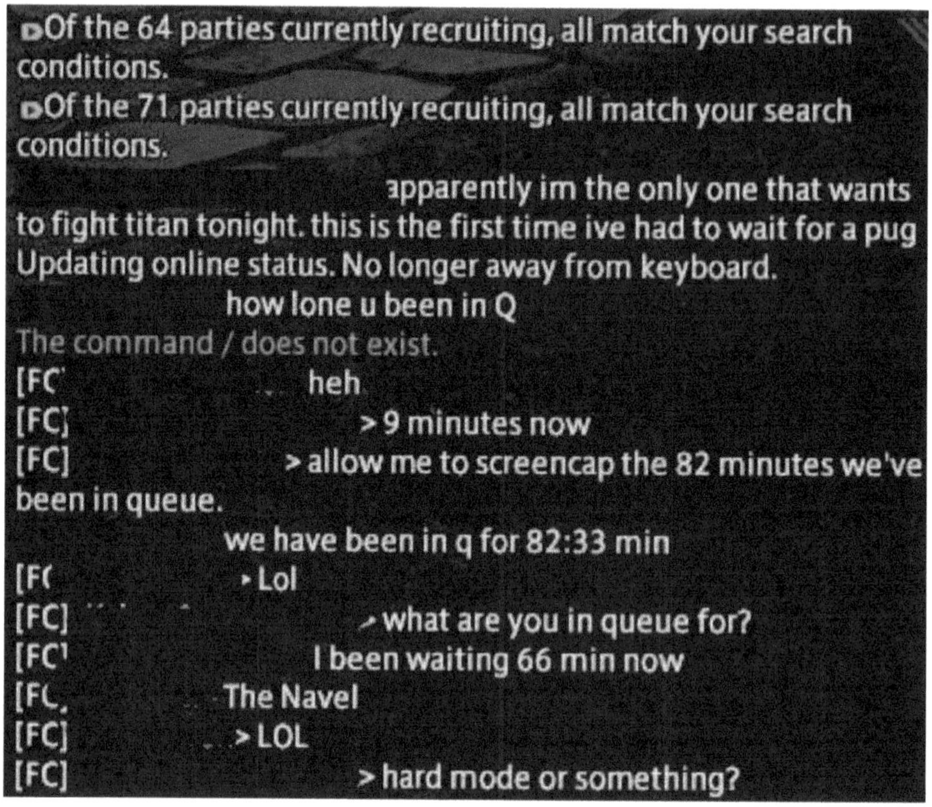


*Figure 5. Screen shot of intra-game discourse in English within Final Fantasy XIV*

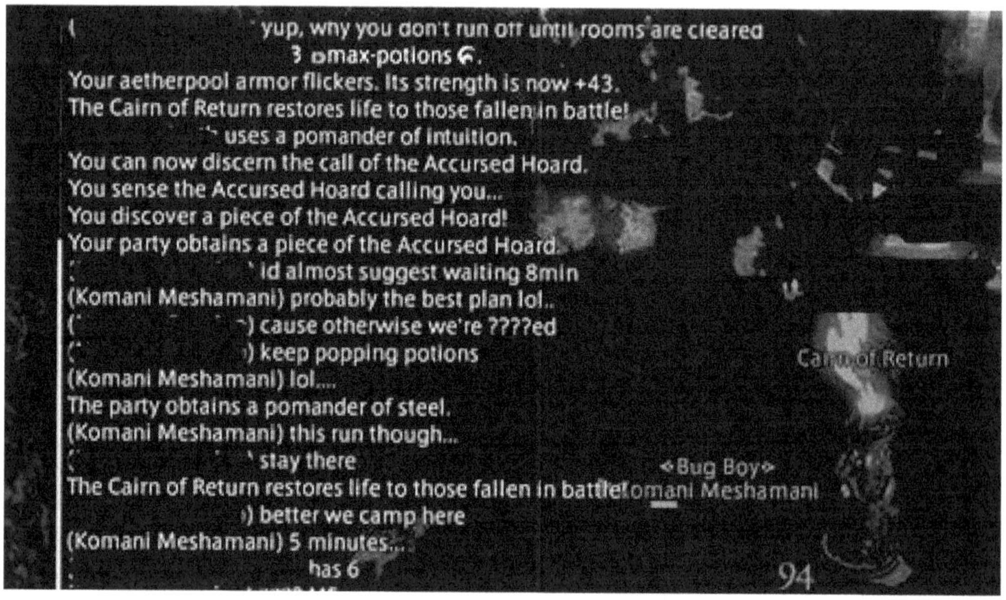

an interesting blend of narrative and expository writing, where one member is clearly giving directions, but it feels like a story. "You can now discern the call of the Accused Hoard. You sense the Accused Hoard calling you…You discover a piece of the Accused Hoard! and Your party obtains a piece of the Accused Hoard."

Finally, we can observe in Figure 6, a screen shot of how individuals communicate after playing via blog posts and website discussions about the impact of game-ecology interaction on language learning. Notice how the members compare learning in school with the kinds of learning that take place within the game-ecology. One member posts to have learned "a large vocabulary and a decent grasp of spelling and grammar from quests and such" and the next member responds that "Runescape taught me how to type faster than any computer software we had to do in school."

It is clear that MMORPGs can be both online and in-person communities of practice that provide many opportunities for language practice, language socialization, and desired identity formation.

We see examples in the above screen shot images of meta-game discourse or communicative interactions about playing and the intra-game discourse or the literacies that are developed while playing games through interacting with other players. For transnational children, the meta-game discourse is very important, as much of this could take place face-to-face in Spanish if opportunities for connecting these youth with other gamers at school were created. This could provide these youth with practice opportunities for improving their Spanish in a welcoming community, through opportunities to practice talking about something that they have a passion for, and as we will see in the following comments, the multimodal nature of gaming provides a highly context embedded situation for negotiating meaning in two languages. In the following section, voices of former transnational children are shared to lend support for the kinds of Spanish/English language socialization and development, identity formation, and crucial friendships that are formed through interacting in the game-ecology.

*Figure 6. Reddit blog post discussing English language learning via multiple MMORPGs*

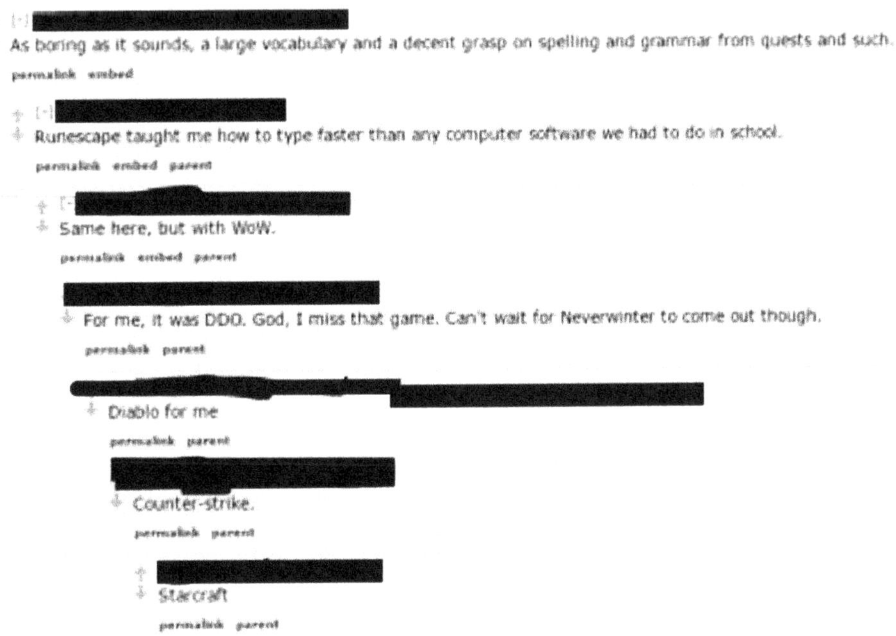

### "Uncovering a Hidden Treasure": Former Transnational Children's Perspectives on Learning through Gaming and the Potential of Blended Affinity Spaces in Mexican Schools

In our conversations with transnational youth about their experiences with gaming and interacting in gaming communities in Mexico, two overarching themes of responses and reactions emerged: 1) An obvious and contagious passion for gaming, sharing gaming stories, and appreciation for being asked to talk about gaming, flowed over youths' faces and 2) stories about friendship formation and complex bilingual communicative interactions, scaffolded by the multimodal context of games and the understood, accepted, and valued role of English in some of the most popular games, were bountiful.

#### Perspectives From the U.S. Side of the Boarder on Learning Through Gaming

During an interview with two 20-year-old, former transnational youth, currently living in the U.S. state of Texas, but with strong ties to extended family in Mexico, Cuauhtémoc and Zelda (these and all names below are pseudonyms) related accounts of playing World of Warcraft, Grand Theft Auto, Final Fantasy, Halo, and other console games with cousins and neighborhood kids at their grandma's house in Mexico and with strangers, who shared the affinity of playing these games, at gaming stores and cyber cafes. Zelda described an experience, noteworthy for the argument being made in this chapter regarding the bilingual language socialization potential of the game-ecology, of using Spanish to talk about playing games with other gamers in arcades and game stores in Zacatecas and San Luis, Mexico, but how she would switch to English while actually playing the games. She repeatedly mentioned that even though other gamers, who did not know English, were able to somehow understand most of the game play, her ability to read in English positioned her with the role of explaining what was going on in the game-interface. Zelda noted that this was especially true while playing with her cousins who would ask her a lot about what things meant in English. Cuauhtémoc offered that while playing with extended family and friends in Tamaulipas, México, he often tried to explain gaming tips and strategies first in Spanish, but when he got frustrated, switched to English. Cuauhtémoc reflected that in these moments he was surprised by how much the other gamers seemed to understand his English explanations and how he realized the advantage of knowing English in these gaming communities of practice.

When asked in what ways do gamers practice language before playing, while playing, and after playing (the game ecology), both Zelda and Cuauhtémoc shared examples of bilingual language socialization. Cuauhtémoc stated that he frequently joins the Latin American World of Warcraft server *Ragnaros* and commented that much of the chat is in Spanish, but game talk in English. He recalled moments of posting in English about the game and gamers responding to him in Spanish. Cuauhtémoc believes that he learns Spanish phrases playing in these bilingual servers, "like how to cast a spell, by observing and copying how other gamers talk about playing," and he is pretty sure that the others learn English from him. This idea of reciprocal sharing and learning can be understood within a communities of practice framework where each member contributes to the over all group's desire to accomplish goals. Zelda related a memory of playing the Legend of Zelda where she shared with other gamers, who were stuck in a game, the steps to "uncovering a hidden treasure and how to use a stone to get out of a dungeon." Zelda recalls how proud she was and how good this made her feel to be counted on to help the group.

## Perspectives From the Mexico Side of the Boarder on Learning and the Potential for Blended Affinity Spaces in Mexico

Panda, a 20-year-old male from the Mexican state of Sinaloa, responded in an anonymous online survey that he had lived and attended school in the U.S. for 11 years before returning to Mexico. Panda, an avid gamer who lived most of his school-age life in the U.S., reported that he would have loved to have had the opportunity to participate in gaming club groups at school when he moved to Mexico. He offered his perspective that having the opportunity to play MMORPGs at schools would help transnational children feel more comfortable, make friends with other gamers, and help students learn both Spanish and English, because it would "help students have more variety of ideas" for relating to others in their new contexts. A final perspective comes from a former child returnee who lived in the U.S. for 16 years before returning to Mexico. William, a 25-year-old from the Mexican state of Sinaloa, shared in the online survey that communicating with others in Spanish was the hardest part of returning to live in Mexico. William explained (rendered here as is from the survey), "i didn't know any spanish at all but my cousin did, so he ended up translated everything i said. but i understood most of the spanish that was being said to me. i just didnt know how to speak spanish at all." Drawing on his experience participating in school-based clubs when he lived in the U.S., William offered that creating spaces for gaming at school, or at least encouraged by school personnel, would be nice, such as the gaming club at his old school in the United States.

In the section that follows, we document how communities of practice, or groups of people who share a concern or passion for something they do and learn to do it better as they interact regularly (Wenger, 1998), can be encouraged at schools. We specifically look to solutions found in blended affinity spaces that have been created in U.S. schools for refugee and 1.5 generation migrants that promote interaction with mainstream peers who share similar interests and discuss the challenges that might arise from creating such spaces in Mexican schools.

# SOLUTIONS, CHALLENGES, AND RECOMMENDATIONS

## Creating Blended Affinity Spaces in Mexican Schools

In the context of schools in the U.S., it has been found that immigrant students often experience similar structural constraints and isolation as transnational students in Mexican schools and may self-eliminate from competing academically and attending university (Kanno & Varghese, 2010; Przymus, 2016). In working with elementary, middle, and high school students, Przymus has implemented a peer, interest-based language and identity socialization program with 1.5 generation and emergent bilinguals in three U.S. states, called the ELL Ambassadors program, where current members of school-based extracurricular activities reach out to immigrant and refugee students, new to schools, and invite them to become members of groups and clubs that match these students' interests, skills, and background knowledge (Przymus, 2016). Results across schools in each state have shown that English Language Learners (emergent bilinguals) that participate in extracurricular activities that match their personal interests are exposed to more meaningful second language (L2) input, have increased opportunities for communicative practice, demonstrate accelerated L2 development, form more culturally and linguistically diverse friendships, which can lead to lessening negative aspects of culture shock, and through forming an identity of affiliation in interest-based communities of practice, have expressed deeper feelings of belonging (Przymus, 2016). Furthermore, 1.5 generation migrant participants in the ELL Ambassadors program have shared perspectives that the above results from having participated in the program have contributed to their successful academic achievement at schools; a finding that has been supported by cross-referencing these students' complete academic records with the years that they participated in the ELL Ambassadors Program (Przymus, 2016).

What is proposed in this article does not require educators to create complex programs at schools, but rather to recognize on the one hand that transnational children face tremendous linguistic, cultural, and identity differences and challenges in their new schools, and on the other hand how these challenges and differences can be converted into positive assets when spaces for peer-interest-based interaction at school are allowed. Can educators envision the role of schools and the concrete steps in creating spaces for youth to meet, play games, and share with each other, as a way of meeting the needs of transnational children? We propose the idea that educators merely need to support this kind of interaction at school and do not need to structure, control, or greatly intervene in it.

Anticipated challenges of encouraging and implementing blended affinity spaces at schools in Mexico for youth to meet and play games, might include the high cost of gaming systems and lack of infrastructure, such as internet connectivity or even space for the gaming club to meet. Although a physical space at schools would be optimal, we advocate in this chapter that the simple gestures of teachers valuing the potential gaming identity of transnational children, the facilitating of introducing transnational children to other peers who are gamers, and the positive encouragement of forming gaming communities of practice, either at school or outside of school, could act to improve transnational students' experience in their new schools and communities. We can learn from Cuauhtémoc and Zelda's comments above regarding playing games in Mexico in cyber cafes or game rooms and at the neighbor's house who has a system, for informing decisions on where these spaces could be formed. We can still conceptualize these spaces as blended affinity spaces if they are made up of peers from the same school and encouraged by school personnel.

What follows are steps for implementing interest-based blended affinity spaces at schools or beyond school walls. Included in this section is a brief discussion about the nuanced consideration of educators not appropriating youth cultural practices and what educators have learned from creating peer-mentoring programs in U.S. schools regarding encouraging, creating, and nurturing the environment for interaction to take place, but leaving the actual interaction up to the agency of the youth themselves.

## Steps for Implementing Peer, Interest-Based Blended Affinity Spaces

By looking at the implementation of the ELL Ambassadors Program, we can begin to envision how a similar program might be implemented in Mexican schools for the creation of blended affinity spaces that afford transnational children opportunities to engage in game-ecology language and identity socialization with like-minded peers. It is our hope that the following steps for implementing the ELL Ambassadors Program may act as a road map for educators interested in creating similar programs in Mexican schools, such as gaming clubs.

**Step 1:** Investigate, inquire, and make an inventory of the interests of transnational students.

**Step 2:** Introduce these students to peers that share the same interests.

**Step 3:** Implement the blended affinity spaces by finding physical space for students to meet, play, and interact, and intervene, only if necessary, by encouraging peers to reach out to transnational students who have expressed interest in gaming. Brainstorm with interested members possible locations for the gaming club, outside of the school, if the school lacks the needed resources.

**Step 4:** Check with the group to see if they need anything and interview students about their perceptions regarding participating in the blended affinity spaces.

Previous studies analyzing the effectiveness of the ELL Ambassadors Program have taught us that this program's success is based on what Przymus has previously referred to in the literature as *horizontal intercultural interpersonal interaction (H3I)* (Przymus, 2015, 2016). This can be described as interaction where like-minded youth display agency to interact on their own, without top-down mandates from teachers, parents, or school administrators (vertical intercultural interpersonal interaction, V3I). H3I can be very well understood by observing youth who gather to talk about and play MMPORPGs. However voluntary this interaction among youth may be, initial support and encouragement by educators, as described in the steps of implementation above, may be needed. This is especially important for encouraging participation among transnational children, who may not be able to immediately communicate with like-minded youth in order to participate in these communities of practice. After this initial support and encouragement, however, it is our hope for many of these youth, that their English proficiency will provide them with a certain cache and potential expert-member role, as it did for the youth who shared their perspectives above, in these school-based gaming communities of practice.

H3I is an important concept if CALL theory and practice, specifically school-based gaming communities of practice, beyond the classroom are to take hold in schools on both sides of the U.S./Mexico border. If implemented top-down (V3I) by administrators and teachers, who attach learning outcomes to the interaction, these programs might be seen by youth as adults appropriating their cultural practices. It is our opinion that educators need to view language and identity socialization through game-ecology as interaction based on voluntary, peer-to-peer affiliation of shared interests. Of course, there is the potential that some teachers are gamers as well and might like to participate along side the students in these blended affinity spaces. A wonderful success story and concrete example of how a teacher/gamer established a local area network (LAN) League of Legends gaming club for students at a school in the U.S. state of Iowa can be found in the Additional Resources at the end of this chapter.

## FUTURE RESEARCH DIRECTIONS

We believe that emerging trends in computer assisted language learning for educating refugee youth, 1.5 generation students, and transnational students on both sides of the U.S./Mexico border will continue to include programs that search for ways to connect youth through interest-based, extracurricular activities, such as the ELL Ambassadors Program. These trends come at a moment of uncertainty for many families in the U.S. struggling with issues of legal status and their futures in the U.S. within the current political climate. Educators in Mexico may have reason to believe that many more children returnees will be arriving. A recent Washington Post article from January 27, 2017, spotlights this trend of reverse migration. According to the author, Max Bearak, citing data from the Pew Research center, since 2012 "the net flow of migration from Mexico, both legal and not, has actually decreased." With the potential of even more transnational children attempting to form new lives in new schools and communities, research on how to meet their needs will need to continue across all aspects of their schooling and lives.

Future research projects will need to go further in connecting the diverse, yet connected studies focusing on the lives and educational experiences of transnational children in Mexico, and we see extending CALL theory and practice to beyond the classroom, but within the school walls with blended affinity spaces for game-ecology language and identity socialization, as one concrete and important opportunity for accomplishing this future research demand. After establishing blended affinity spaces for gaming in Mexican schools, future research should assess the impact of this kind of educational intervention by measuring how much these spaces 1) offer group affiliation through shared interests, 2) provide a platform for English-speaking transnational children to be linguistic experts, and 3) expose these same youth to contextual, real use of the Spanish language, performed before, during, and after the gaming experience between participants.

## CONCLUSION

In this chapter, we 1) put forth the idea of gaming experience and high levels of English proficiency as assets of cultural and linguistic capital that youth, who have lived in the U.S. and now attend schools in Mexico, might be able to use to reposition themselves with their desired identities in their new communities and schools and 2) discussed the role of schools in creating blended affinity spaces for youth to meet, play games, and share with each other, as a way of meeting the needs of transnational children. We hope that through providing opportunities for interest-based language socialization (both English and Spanish) and identity formation, some youth may begin to feel more at home, more accepted, and may begin to create more hopeful perceptions of their futures. As shown in the screen shot examples above, English can be a lingua franca in some of the most popular MMORPGS. This has potential for providing transnational children, who have grown-up and attended school in the United States and have high proficiency in English, with a potential in-road into much needed acceptance into these gaming communities of practice at their new schools in Mexico. Indeed, this sentiment was supported earlier through sharing Panda and William's perspectives regarding their experiences of moving from the U.S. to Mexico, attending school in Mexico, and the potential of blended affinity spaces at schools in Mexico for promoting language learning, friendship formation, positive identity development, and feeling welcome in transnational children's new schools and homes. Cuauhtémoc and Zelda's comments also aid in visualizing how interactions within the game-ecology take place in Mexico and what kinds of language and identity development can come from these interactions.

This is a call to action for educators to tap into transnational children's linguistic and cultural capital through the intrinsic motivation to play MMORPGs, that many of these youth might have, in order to provide and encourage blended affinity spaces at schools for the kinds of interaction explored in this chapter. We urge educators on both sides of the U.S./Mexico border to implement programs that carve out third spaces, that blend first space interests and linguistic practices with second space Discourse of school success, to provide for the same kind of H3I described earlier. Through creating and nurturing these spaces, transnational students may begin the process of repositioning themselves from ascribed identities such as *pocho* or someone of Mexican heritage that has lived in the U.S. and lacks fluency in

Spanish, or someone who has done something wrong, or is invisible, to avowed identities as gamers and adolescents, who are trying, like all the rest, to figure out who they are and who they will become. It is our hope that somewhere along the way in that journey, transnational children get to ask or are asked if ¿Eres un Gamer? With this desire, we are advocating for the creation of school-based communities, or circles of friends, where youth are welcomed because of shared interests, where strengths are combined to accomplish common goals, and where youth find their words, both in Spanish and English, through speaking from and with passion.

## REFERENCES

Bearak, M. (2017, January). Even before Trump, more Mexicans were leaving the U.S. than arriving. *The Washington Post.* Retrieved March 4, 2017 from https://www.washingtonpost.com/news/worldviews/wp/2017/01/27/even-before-trump-more-mexicans-were-leaving-the-us-than-arriving/?utm_term=.254fe61b2707

Borjian, A., Muñoz de Cote, L. M., van Dijk, S., & Houde, P. (2016). Transnational Children in Mexico: Context of Migration and Adaptation. *Diaspora, Indigenous, and Minority Education*, *10*(1), 42–54. doi:10.1080/15595692.2015.1084920

Bourdieu, P. (2011). The forms of capital. In I. Szeman & T. Kaposy (Eds.), *Cultural theory: An anthology* (pp. 81–93). Madden, MA: Wiley-Blackwell.

Bucholtz, M., & Hall, K. (2005). Identity and interaction: A sociocultural linguistic approach. *Discourse Studies*, *7*(4–5), 585–614. doi:10.1177/1461445605054407

Canagarajah, S. (2007). Lingua franca English, multilingual communities, and language acquisition. *Modern Language Journal*, *91*(s1), 923–939. doi:10.1111/j.1540-4781.2007.00678.x

Cave, D. (2012). American children, now struggling to adjust to life in Mexico. *New York Times*, *19*(6).

Cornillie, F., Thorne, S. L., & Desmet, P. (2012). ReCALL special issue: Digital games for language learning: challenges and opportunities. *ReCALL*, *24*(03), 243–256. doi:10.1017/S0958344012000134

de Sam Lazaro, F. (Writer), & Woodruff, J. (Anchor & Executive Editor). (n.d.). Young returnees start over in Mexico after growing up in the U.S [TV Episode]. *PBS NewsHour.* Retrieved November 26, 2016 from http://disq.us/p/14hhiy8

Eckert, P., & McConnell-Ginet, S. (2003). *Language and gender*. Cambridge, UK: Cambridge University Press. doi:10.1017/CBO9780511791147

Galicia-Ramos, A. J. (2016, October). *Transnational students' influence on the Mexican EFL classroom.* Paper presented at the 2016 MEXTESOL Convention, Monterrey, Mexico.

Gee, J. (2007). *What Video Games Have to Teach Us about Learning and Literacy*. New York, NY: St Martin's Griffin.

Gee, J. P., & Hayes, E. (2012). Nurturing affinity spaces and game-based learning. In C. Steinkuehler, K. Squire, & S. Barab (Eds.), *Games, learning, and society: Learning and meaning in the digital age* (pp. 129–153). New York, NY: Cambridge University Press. doi:10.1017/CBO9781139031127.015

Giorguli, S. E., & Gutiérrez, E. (2011). Niños y jóvenes en el contexto de la migración internacional entre México y Estados Unidos. *Coyuntura Demográfica*, *1*, 21–25.

Gonzales, R. G., & Chávez, L. R. (2012). Awakening to a Nightmare. *Current Anthropology*, *53*(3), 255–281. doi:10.1086/665414

Hamann, E. T., & Zúñiga, V. (2011). Schooling, National Affinity (ies), and Transnational Students in Mexico. In C. Coe, R. R. Reynolds, D. A. Boehm, J. M. Hess, & H. Rae-Espinoza (Eds.), *Everyday ruptures: Children, youth, and migration in global perspective* (pp. 141–160). Nashville, TN: Vanderbilt University Press.

Harklau, L. (2003). Representational practices and multi-model communication in U.S. high schools: Implications for adolescent immigrants. In R. Bayley & S. R. Schecter (Eds.), *Language socialization in bilingual and multilingual societies* (pp. 83–97). Clevedon, UK: Multilingual Matters.

House, J. (2003). English as a lingua franca: A threat to multilingualism? *Journal of Sociolinguistics*, *7*(4), 556–578. doi:10.1111/j.1467-9841.2003.00242.x

Kanno, Y., & Norton, B. (2003). Imagined communities and educational possibilities: Introduction. *Journal of Language, Identity, and Education*, *2*(4), 241–249. doi:10.1207/S15327701JLIE0204_1

Kanno, Y., & Varghese, M. M. (2010). Immigrant and refugee ESL students challenges to accessing four-year college education: From language policy to educational policy. *Journal of Language, Identity, and Education*, *9*(5), 310–328. doi:10.1080/15348458.2010.517693

Kramsch, C. (1997). The privilege of the nonnative speaker. *PMLA. Publications of the Modern Language Association of America*, *112*(3), 359.

Lakhani, N. (2015). Deported to Mexico: A lost generation. *The Guardian*, *17*. Retrieved March 22, 2017 from https://www.theguardian.com/global/2015/may/17/deported-to-mexico-immigration-america

McConnell-Ginet, S. (2003). What's in a name? Social labeling and gender practices. In J. Holmes & M. Meyerhoff (Eds.), *The handbook of language and gender* (pp. 69–97). Oxford, UK: Blackwell. doi:10.1002/9780470756942.ch3

Medina, D., & Menjívar, C. (2015). The context of return migration: Challenges of mixed-status families in Mexicos schools. *Ethnic and Racial Studies*, *38*(12), 2123–2139. doi:10.1080/01419870.2015.1036091

MMORPGs for Language Learning. (n.d.). Retrieved December 16, 2015, from http://positivevideogaming.web.unc.edu/mmorpgs-for-language-learning/

Moje, E. B., Ciechanowski, K. M., Kramer, K., Ellis, L., Carrillo, R., & Collazo, T. (2004). Working toward third space in content area literacy: An examination of everyday funds of knowledge and discourse. *Reading Research Quarterly*, *39*(1), 38–70. doi:10.1598/RRQ.39.1.4

Norton, B. (2000). *Identity and language learning: Gender, ethnicity and educational change*. New York, NY: Longman.

Norton, B. (2001). Non-participation, imagined communities and the language classroom. In M. P. Breen (Ed.), *Learner contributions to language learning: New directions in research* (pp. 159–171). Essex, UK: Pearson Education.

Przymus, S. D. (2015). Imagining and moving beyond the ESL bubble: Observing changes in identity, power, and language acquisition through the ELL Ambassadors Program. In M. Lengeling & I. Pablo (Eds.), *Perspectives on Qualitative Research* (pp. 501–516). Guanajuato: Universidad de Guanajuato Press.

Przymus, S. D. (2016). Imagining and moving beyond the ESL bubble: Facilitating communities of practice through the ELL Ambassadors program. *Journal of Language, Identity, and Education*, *15*(5), 265–279. doi:10.1080/15348458.2016.1213133

Sanchez-Garcia, J., Hamann, E. T., & Zuniga, V. (2012). What the youngest transnational students have to say about their transition from US schools to Mexican ones. *Diaspora, Indigenous, and Minority Education*, *6*(3), 157–171. doi:10.1080/15595692.2012.691135

Schieffelin, B. B., & Ochs, E. (1986). Language socialization. *Annual Review of Anthropology*, *15*(1), 163–191. doi:10.1146/annurev.an.15.100186.001115

Seidlhofer, B. (2004). Research perspectives on teaching English as a lingua franca. *Annual Review of Applied Linguistics*, *24*, 209–239. doi:10.1017/S0267190504000145

Starhawk. (1988). *Dreaming the dark: Magic, sex, and politics*. Boston, MA: Beacon Press.

Sykes, J. M., & Holden, C. L. (2011). Communities: Exploring digital games and social networking. In N. Arnold & L. Ducate (Eds.), Present and future promises of CALL: From theory and research to new directions in language teaching (pp. 311–336). San Marcos, TX: Computer Assisted Language Instruction Consortium (CALICO).

The science of language, community, and MMORPGs. (2014). Retrieved December 16, 2015, from http://www.engadget.com/2014/10/13/the-science-of-language-community-and-mmorpgs/

Thorne, S. L., Black, R. W., & Sykes, J. M. (2009). Second language use, socialization, and learning in Internet interest communities and online gaming. *Modern Language Journal*, *93*(s1), 802–821. doi:10.1111/j.1540-4781.2009.00974.x

Wenger, E. (1998). *Communities of practice: Learning, meaning, and identity*. Cambridge, UK: Cambridge University Press. doi:10.1017/CBO9780511803932

Zuengler, J., & Cole, K. (2005). Language socialization and second language learning. In E. Hinkel (Ed.), *Handbook of research in second language teaching and learning* (pp. 301–316). Mahwah, NJ: Lawrence Erlbaum.

Zúñiga, V. (2012). Migration de retour. Un regard quantitatif sur les enfants arrivant au Mexique en provenance des États-Unis. *Hommes et migrations. Revue française de référence sur les dynamiques migratoires, 1296*, 88-98.

Zúñiga, V., & Hamann, E. T. (2006). Going home? Schooling in Mexico of transnational children. *CONfines (México), 4*, 41–57.

Zúñiga, V., & Hamann, E. T. (2015). Going to a home you have never been to: The return migration of Mexican and American-Mexican children. *Childrens Geographies, 13*(6), 643–655. doi:10.1080/14733285.2014.936364

Zúñiga, V., & Vivas Romero, M. (2014). Divided families, fractured schooling. In *Mexico: educational consequences of children exposition to international migration (No. 4)*. Centre d'Études Mexicaines et Centraméricaines.

## ADDITIONAL READING

Alvarez Gutiérrez, L. (2013). Costo Alto de Política Anti-imigrante Sobre la Familia y Educación 1: The Adverse Consequences of Anti-Latino Immigration Laws. *Theory into Practice, 52*(3), 169–179. doi:10.1080/00405841.2013.804308

Arnseth, H. C. (2006). Learning to play or playing to learn-A critical account of the models of communication informing educational research on computer gameplay. *Game Studies, 6*(1). Retrieved from http://gamestudies.org/0601/articles/arnseth

Castañeda, E. (2013). Living in limbo: Transnational households, remittances and development. *International Migration (Geneva, Switzerland), 51*(s1), e13–e35. https://www.researchgate.net/profile/Ernesto_Castaneda2/publication/264271378_Living_in_Limbo_Transnational_Households_Remittances_and_Development/links/568ed45708ae78cc05160edb.pdf RetrievedMarch42017 doi:10.1111/j.1468-2435.2012.00745.x

Des Moines High School League of Legends Club. (2014, April). *YouTube League of Legends Club promotional video.* Retrieved March 4, 2017 from https://youtu.be/oJim_W5z_9o

Des Moines High School League of Legends Club. (2014, May). *More than just a club.* You Tube video explaining the success of the club. Retrieved March 4, 2017 from https://youtu.be/eWysttc6aqw

Hazán, M. (2014). Understanding return migration to Mexico: Towards a comprehensive policy for the reintegration of returning migrants. *Center for US-Mexican Studies, University of California, San Diego, March, 5*. Retrieved March 4, 2017 from http://ccis.ucsd.edu/_files/wp193.pdf

Masferrer, C., & Roberts, B. R. (2016). The Changing Patterns of Return Migration from the USA to Mexico and Their Policy Implications. In D. L. Leal & N. P. Rodríguez (Eds.), *Migration in an Era of Restriction and Recession* (pp. 235–258). New York City, NY: Springer International Publishing. doi:10.1007/978-3-319-24445-7_12

Pablo, I. M., Rivas, L. R., Lengeling, M., & Crawford, T. (2015). Transnationals Becoming English Teachers in Mexico: Effects of Language Brokering and Identity Formation. *Gist: Education and Learning Research Journal*, *10*, 7–28.

Przymus, S. D. (2016, October). *¿Eres un Gamer? Encouraging game-ecology language socialization at schools.* Paper presented at the 2016 MEXTESOL Conference. Monterrey, MX. https://tcu.box.com/s/jinn80s3ftmsoxab2ndp6h4hxmrkcn0z

Przymus, S. D. (2016, December). *ELL Ambassadors Program: Overview and implementation guide.* (Unpublished professional development PowerPoint presentation). Professional development presented at the Fort Worth Independent School District middle/secondary language centers meeting. Fort Worth, TX. Retrieved from https://tcu.box.com/s/k8emoimchvahj3lq0jdual0x642lav16

Reinhardt, J. (2016, October). *Social media and digital gaming in the L2 classroom: Everyday agency, awareness, and autonomy.* Keynote address given at the 2016 ASOCOPI Conference. Bogotá, Colombia. https://t.co/uh8TVRTBBn

Román, B., & Zúñiga, V. (2014). Children returning from the US to Mexico: School sweet school? *Migraciones Internacionales, 7*(4), 277-286. Retrieved March 4, 2017 from http://citeseerx.ist.psu.edu/viewdoc/download?doi=10.1.1.927.672&rep=rep1&type=pdf

Sánchez, P., & Machado-Casas, M. (2009). At the intersection of transnationalism, Latina/o immigrants, and education. *High School Journal*, *92*(4), 3–15. doi:10.1353/hsj.0.0027

## KEY TERMS AND DEFINITIONS

**Blended Affinity Spaces:** Spaces, either face-to-face or virtual, where like-minded groups of individuals, that consist of a blended mix of peers from the same educational community and potentially peers from diverse and often anonymous contexts, interact to perform activities that fall within the individuals' similar affinities.

**Communities of Practice:** Groups of people who share a concern or passion for something they do and learn to do it better as they interact regularly and contribute to the over all group's desired and shared goals.

**Game Ecology:** The game ecology is made up meta-game discourse, or the talk about playing, before, during, and after, either in person or online in chat groups and blog posts, and the intra-game discourse of interacting with other players from around the world within the game interface.

**H3I:** H3I stands for horizontal intercultural interpersonal interaction and is where the motivation for and impetus of communicative interaction between culturally and linguistically diverse youth comes from the youth themselves, based on similar interests, and not as a forced action driven by their teachers, parents, or other adults.

**Language Socialization:** The process of learning how to use the language needed to become a contributing member in specific contexts and groups through the social interaction with members in those groups and contexts through time.

**MMPORPGs:** An online video game that takes place in a persistent state world with thousands, or even millions of players developing their characters in a role-playing environment.

**Transnational Children:** Children who have lived in numerous countries, distinguished in this chapter as either, 1) Children Returnees, who were born in Mexico, at some point in their lives moved to the U.S. and now have returned to Mexico due to repatriation and/or deportation, and 2) International Migrants, who were born in the U.S. and now live in Mexico due to repatriation and/or deportation.

**V3I:** V3I stands for vertical intercultural interpersonal interaction and characterizes communicative interaction between culturally and linguistically diverse youth as a result of top-down teacher, school personnel, parent, or other adult mandated action.

# Chapter 16
# Augmented Reality:
## A Brief Introduction, Its Potentials, and Implications in Language Education

**Nhu Le**
*University of South Florida, USA*

**Hanh Dinh**
*Murray State University, USA*

## ABSTRACT

*Rapid advancement in technology has altered the way language education is conceptualized and practiced. Technological tools, when effectively integrated with appropriate pedagogical foundations, can enhance the quality of teaching and learning experiences. Augmented reality (AR) has emerged as one of the latest technologies offering a new way to bridge virtual and reality worlds. Due to the widespread proliferation of digital technology, the implementation of AR on mobile devices such as smartphones and tablets has become a growing trend in educational settings. Regardless of the advantages that AR technology brings to language classrooms, there have been very few studies exploring the design, evaluation, and applications of AR for educational purposes. Therefore, this chapter aims to (a) introduce AR technology in learning environments, (b) embrace its potentials and foreseeable hindrances to language education, (c) discuss practical and applicable ways to use this merging technology effectively in the classroom, and (d) propose some issues for future research.*

## INTRODUCTION

Let us imagine two scenarios. In the first one, the young English language learners (ELLs) listen to the story, "The Enormous Turnip," told by their teacher and acted out with the puppets and props that the teacher had spent a great amount of time preparing. In the second scenario, the learners use their mobile devices to read the same story with pop-up virtual characters and theme music out of their textbook. After that, they go out to the playground to search for those characters' representations to learn more how to spell the words, pronounce them, and other information like their habitats and/or characteristics. They

DOI: 10.4018/978-1-5225-2933-0.ch016

also need to grow the turnip from the seed on their mobile device. When the turnip reaches its maximum size, the students then work in pairs dragging all the characters they have found together until the gigantic turnip is pulled out by the power of teamwork. Isn't it fascinating to have these ELLs interact with both real and synthetic environments as in the second scenario? Then, welcome to the world of Augmented Reality (AR) in language education!

AR is defined as a technology where virtual images are blended with real the world and real-time interaction is ensured (Azuma, 1997). The applications created by AR enable the usage of three-dimensional models (i.e., 3D objects, images, videos, and animations) both separately and simultaneously (Wang, Kim, Love, & Kang, 2013). Mobile AR technology has gained increased research attention since it has multiple benefits in language education. Not only does it allow real-time interaction, but it also provides learning through experience, which can boost users' attention and motivation (Barreira, Bessa, Pereira, Adao, Peres, & Magalhaes, 2012; Singhal, Bagga, Goyal, Saxena, 2012). Furthermore, several studies have investigated the effectiveness of AR as multimedia in optimizing students' performance (Cadavieco, Goulão & Costales, 2012; Liu & Tsai, 2013; Santos, Lübke, Taketomi, Yamamoto, Rodrigo, Sandor, & Kato, 2016). AR technology can also be combined with global positioning system (GPS)-enabled smart devices or quick response (QR) codes to create a unique, compelling and meaningful learning experience (Lara-Prieto, Bravo-Quirino, Rivera-Campa, & Gutiérrez-Arredondo, 2015). Students can get access to their smart phones, scan the codes, and reach the 3D demonstrations in front of their eyes.

Regardless of the advantages that AR technology can bring to language classrooms, there have been few research studies conducted exploring the design, evaluation, and applications of AR for educational purposes. Therefore, this chapter gives a brief introduction about AR technology, provides literature review of AR in pedagogy, discusses some challenges that AR technology is facing in educational contexts, and proposes practical applications for EFL/EFL teachers. The authors of this chapter hope to inspire educators to bring this emerging tool into their classroom in an intriguing and creative way.

## BACKGROUND

### What Is Augmented Reality (AR)?

Augmented Reality (AR) is commonly mistaken for Virtual Reality (VR). AR and VR are related, yet different in that VR *brings* the users to an immersive artificial world by putting on a VR headset or creating an avatar in the VR environment (Solak & Erdem, 2015), whereas AR allows the users to see the real world enhanced or augmented by the virtual objects (Azuma, 1997). For instance, the user puts on the VR goggles and is completely immersed into the synthetic world of the dinosaurs without sensing any presence of the real world (Figure 1).

On the contrary, Figure 2 shows that the AR app on the iPad still gives the user the sense of copresenting in both synthetic and real environments.

There are currently two developed forms of AR: (a) location-aware AR and (b) vision-based AR (Dunleavy & Dede, 2014; Pence, 2011). Location-aware AR allows users to track the distance from their current place to different ones by using a mobile device enabled with a Global Positioning System (GPS) feature. This form of AR is presented by multimedia (i.e., the combination of text, audio, image, animation, and/or 3D objects) to modify the navigation to the specific location. In Figure 3, for example,

*Figure 1. Experiencing the era of the dinosaurs with VR (Liszewski, 2015)*
*Source: Andrew Liszewski, 2015*

*Figure 2 Experiencing the dinosaurs era with AR (Augmented Reality, 2014)*
*Source: Augmented Reality, 2014*

*Figure 3. An example of location-aware AR (Dorogan, 2014)*
*Source: Daryna Dorogan, 2014*

the user experiences location-aware AR showing different directions to different places within estimated distances.

Vision-based AR, on the other hand, provides the multimedia when the user points the camera of the mobile device at the particular 2D object or Quick Response (QR) code, like the Statue of Liberty in Figure 4.

## AR and Its Theoretical Frameworks

Situated learning theory and constructivist learning theory are the two evident theoretical foundations for AR technology (Dunleavy & Dede, 2014; Keneman & Waller, 2016). Situated learning theory, which has been built up on sociocultural theory of Vygotsky (1978), asserts that learning in general and language acquisition in specific take place in a certain context and that mutual interactions among the participants, objects, and cultural aspects within that context can help boost the learning performance (Brown, Collins, & Duguid, 1989). AR creates a mixed-reality environment in which the users experience, interact, complete the learning task, solve the problem, and apply what they have learned to other similar situations, the ability technically referred to as *transfer* (Dede, 2008, 2009). According to Hendricks (2001), "situated cognition has a significant impact on immediate transfer" and location-based

*Figure 4. An example of vision-based AR (Dorogan, 2014)*
*Source: Daryna Dorogan, 2014*

materials can be used in order to provide authentic learning contexts, which not only enhances situated learning but also boosts students' motivation (as cited in Lakarnchua & Reinders, 2014, pp. 42-43). In their study, Lakarnchua and Reinders (2014) asked their students take part in two AR activities with the hope that these Thai students would have more opportunities to use English outside their classroom for real communicative purposes. In the first activity, the participants designed a campus tour in groups to introduce five popular sites within their university to future visitors. In the second activity, these groups took a tour of each other's sites to explore the experience as well as provide constructive feedback on the designs. For instance, the group that had created a tour of social sites would take a tour of academic sites designed by another group, and vice versa. The findings of the study show that not only did the AR activities increase the participants' enthusiasm and engagement but they also bring students out of the traditional classroom (Lakarnchua & Reinders, 2014).

Therefore, the Lakarnchua and Reinders (2014) study proposes an innovative way to handle criticism claiming that AR fails to attain far-reaching transfer because the learning setting is still limited within the four walls of the classroom. Yet, as illustrated with this study, AR technology, indeed, has a potential to *break* these walls and provide learners with simulated immersive interfaces for situated learning, thus, enhancing their transfer (Dunleavy & Dede, 2014; Gallagher & Sullivan, 2011). Even though research on the use of AR for language education is recent and limited, there have been several efforts to trial AR technology in various contexts. In addition to the study conducted in Thailand (Lakarnchua & Reinders, 2014), Holden and Sykes (2011) also developed an AR location-based game in which the users tried to solve a historical murder in a particular place in the US with the aid of local clues and teamwork. In Taiwanese context, Liu, Tan, and Chu (2010) designed a handheld augmented reality mobile English learning system (HELLO) that provided learners with reachable context-aware learning materials. In their study, the learners followed the guiding map on their phone screen to get to the learning zones and then use the QR app to decode the QR codes embedded in the objects at the zones. Similarly, Liu and Tsai (2013) had a small group of students take a short campus tour on which they could actually interact with the digital-information-tagged objects to learn about specific vocabulary and expressions. This interactive activity provided these undergraduates students majoring in English with not only a new authentic learning environment, but also sufficient linguistic knowledge to develop their academic writing skills. Additionally, a recent study by Richardson (2016) investigated the effectiveness of a similar AR game with the use of Aurasma mobile application in the language learning process for advanced level EFL learners. This research examined the learners moving around a city in Germany, utilizing the app in order to complete a series of challenging language tasks. His study affirmed that this type of AR technology proved to be user-friendly and effective in that the learners felt more motivated and engaged in the situated learning activities.

Constructivist/Interpretivist advocates, on the other hand, posit that the individuals along with their prior knowledge and sociocultural background play a more critical role than the context by itself (Dede, 2008; Vygotsky, 1978). In an AR environment, learners not only establish their personal interpretations of the immersive interfaces according to their own life experiences, but also interact with their virtual or real-life partners to negotiate the meaning of the multimedia presentations and construct new context-appropriate comprehension (Dunleavy & Dede, 2014). As noticed from the studies mentioned earlier, the students completed their AR-based tasks or activities in groups so that they could support one another through negotiation and peer-feedback (Holden & Sykes, 2011; Lakarnchua & Reinders, 2014). In the Barreira et al. (2012) study, elementary students worked in pairs to join the AR-based matching game called matching objects and words (MOW) together in order to learn words related to animals in different languages such as English, Spanish, and Portuguese. A comparison between a control group (i.e., a group of students who learned the words in a traditional way without the aid of AR) and an experimental group (i.e., those who learned the words with the aid of AR) indicated that the students in the latter group had better academic performances. Figure 5 shows children playing with MOW during their English class.

Another AR app to help the same group of learners learn body parts in and outside of the classroom is the mobile-based interactive learning environment (MOBILE) developed by Tan and Liu (2004). The findings of their study also suggested the students learned better with the assistance of AR technology in comparison with the traditional teaching method.

AR technology not only helps boost learners' language development, but it also enhances their cultural understanding and communication skills (Liu, Holden, & Zheng, 2016). In their study, an AR mobile game, *Guardians of the Mo'o* (who is a gecko or Lizard Goddess in Hawaiian culture) was created to provide the learners in Mãnoa, Hawai'i with a new engaging learning environment in which they could interact with both the virtual world (e.g., virtual drawings, notes, etc.) and the physical world (e.g., trees and artwork on the campus) to promote their active language learning by raising linguistic awareness and exchanging various cultural aspects. Based on their conversation analysis and multimodal analysis, Liu et al. (2016) found out that active learning took place through their collaborative negotiation and coordination among team gamers in order to solve problems together.

Hence, AR technology, when utilized meaningfully, binds tightly with situated learning theory and constructivist learning theory in that it creates an interactive learning environment in which learners can both make sense of the real world and apply what they have gained to the augmented one with the presence of the multimedia aiding as scaffolding, background knowledge activator, motivator, and facilitator (Dunleavy, Dede, & Mitchell, 2009; Klopfer & Squire, 2010).

*Figure 5. Children playing with MOW during their English class (Barreira et al., 2012)*
*Source: Barreira et al., 2012*

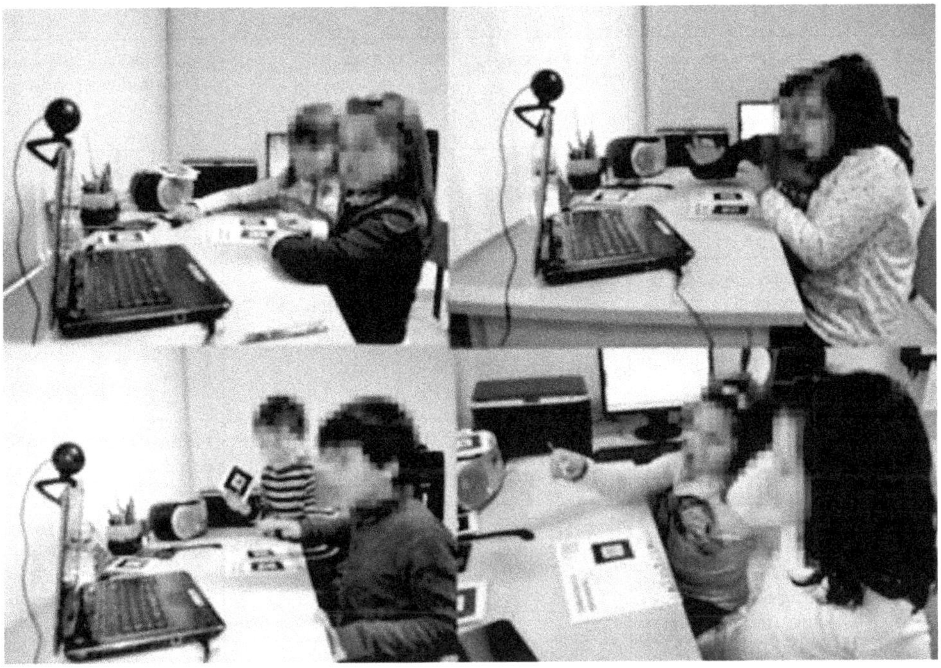

# AR EDUCATIONAL POTENTIALS AND CHALLENGES

## AR Educational Potentials

McKalin (2014), a writer of the *TechTimes*, highlights the gradual development of AR software as well as hardware devices to meet the demands of both language instructors and learners. Upon completing careful research on the use of AR in language education from several well-known databases (e.g., *Computers & Education, Research & Practice in Technology, Literacy Practice & Research, Modern English Teacher)* in the previous 10 years, we have found 17 inspiring peer-reviewed academic articles that share numerous innovative AR ideas and applications. The summary in table 1 shows three popular themes emerging from the use of AR technology in language teaching and learning: (1) AR-based reading books, (2) AR game-based learning environment, and (3) AR authoring tools. Table 1 lists a summary of AR usage in language classroom research.

## AR-Based Reading Books

Regular print books whose illustrations are made into 3D graphics are referred to as AR-based reading books. Figure 6 shows an example of the AR-based reading book based on the fable "*The Travelers and the Sea.*"

As the story begins "Two travelers were walking along the seashore," the AR app on the iPad recognizes the AR book and pops up the 3D virtual main characters and setting. Sometimes, the learners can even hear the sound of the waves and seagulls embedded to this AR-based reading book.

*Table 1. Summary of AR usage in language classroom*

| Author(s) (Year of Publication) | Topics | Methods | AR App/Tool | Findings |
|---|---|---|---|---|
| Liu, Tan, & Chu (2010) | QR code and augmented reality-supported mobile English learning system | Survey & case study | HELLO app<br>QR codes | University students showed high level of satisfaction when using the app to explore the learning environment outside classroom. |
| Holden & Sykes (2011) | Leveraging mobile games for place-based language learning | Design-based research (DBR) | Using the open-source software, MITAR and ARIS to create an AR mobile game, *Mentira* | The AR location-game based provided the participants with new engaging learning environment to enhance their HOTs and cultural understanding. |
| Barreira et al. (2012) | Augmented reality game to learn words in different languages: Case study: Learning English names of animals in elementary school. | Experimental study | AR based game: Matching Objects and Words (MOW) | Those Portuguese primary school students at 3rd grade in the experimental group performed better in vocab retention and tasks than those in the control group. |
| Billinghurst & Dünser (2012) | Using AR in the classroom | Practical research | AR books - MagicBook<br>CityViewAR<br>BuildAR | Mobile AR got students actively engaged both inside and outside the class |
| Mahadzir & Phung (2013) | The use of augmented reality pop-up book to increase motivation in English language learning for national primary school | Observation & semi structured interview | ZooBurst | Five elementary students (4 Malay & 1 Indian) perceived AR pop-up books as a motivational tool that helped enhance their learning engagement and language performance. |
| Liu, P-H. E., & Tsai, M-K. (2013) | Using augmented-reality-based mobile learning material in EFL English composition: An exploratory case study | Mixed method: student essays & reflections, questionnaire | Global positioning & AR technique | The AR learning activity provided five Taiwanese undergraduates with authentic environment as well as necessary linguistic knowledge and writing skills. |
| Solak & Cakir (2015) | Exploring the effect of materials designed with augmented reality on language learners' vocabulary learning | Descriptive research model | AR teaching materials | AR technology materials had positive impact on boosting Turkish undergraduate students' motivation towards vocabulary learning in classroom, and hence enhancing their academic performances. |
| Cheng & Tsai (2014)<br>Cheng & Tsai (2016) | AR picture book<br>Reading skill<br>Children-parent cognition | Qualitative - observation | AR picture book *"The Adventure of Yuyu: Yuyu Yang Artistic Journey"* published by National Chiao Tung University Press, Taiwan | Identified 4 behavioral patterns: parent as dominator, child as dominator, communicative child–parent pair, and low communicative child–parent pair |
| Chiang, Yang, & Hwang (2014) | Location-based AR environment Share knowledge in inquiry learning activities | Experimental study | JAVA for website<br>Oracle for database<br>Xcode for iPad | Comparing with the control inquiry-based mobile learning activity, the AR-based inquiry learning activity engaged students in more interactions for knowledge construction |
| Küçük, Yýlmaz, & Göktaþ (2014) | Using AR for Learning English | Casual comparative and correlational methods | AR reading book<br>AutoDesk Maya<br>Muvizu & Adobe Flash | Learning English by AR apps affected the achievement, cognitive load, and attitude of learners in positive ways |
| Pilton, S. (2014) | Practical ideas for how to use augmented reality in EFL | Practical research | Aurasma App | AR apps gave teachers more possibilities for taking classes outside. |
| Lakarnchua & Reinders (2014) | AR app as a tool for a class project | Action study<br>Qualitative research - interview | Wikitude to create virtual tour | AR-created activities boosted students' motivation, interest and enthusiasm |

*continued on next page*

*Table 1. Continued*

| Author(s) (Year of Publication) | Topics | Methods | AR App/Tool | Findings |
|---|---|---|---|---|
| Chen, Ho, & Lin (2015) | AR game-based learning environment | Pilot study | ARToolKit<br>Visual Studio C++<br>3D Max<br>Adobe Illustrator | Students were quite interested in the game-based system.<br>Modifications were needed. |
| Koutromanos, Sofos, & Avraamidou (2015) | The use of AR in games | Literature review | Designboom to create virtual graffiti<br>Zoo-AR<br>ZooBurst<br>SkyView<br>World Lens<br>Transparent Earth<br>Spacecraft 3D<br>Popar Toys | Pedagogical practices with AR took place in formal and informal contexts. |
| Kenema & Waller (2016) | Development of AR app to enhance the exhibition of animal bones | Practical research | Aurasma App<br>Digital Storytelling - Zoo Burst<br>ARIS (Augmented Reality and Interactive Storytelling) | AR changed the environment around students<br>AR allowed the students to construct their own engaging learning worlds |
| Santos, Lübke. Taketomi, Yamamoto, Rodrigo, Sandor, & Kato (2016) | Augmented reality as multimedia: the case for situated vocabulary learning | Experimental study | https://artoolkit.org/ | AR apps with good system usability led to better retention of words and improve student<br>attention and satisfaction |
| Liu, Holden, & Zheng (2016) | Analyzing students' language learning experience in an augmented reality mobile game: an exploration of an emergent learning environment | Conversation analysis & Multimodel analysis | Using the open-source platform ARIS to create an AR mobile game *Guardians of the Mo'o* | The game helped ESL learners enhance their linguistic development, communicative skills and cultural competence. |

*Figure 6. Example of AR-Based Reading Books (The Travelers and the Sea, 1919)*
*Source: The Travelers and the Sea, 1919*

Additional examples of this innovative AR book are the MagicBook (Billinghurst & Dunser, 2012), *The Adventure of Yuyu: Yuyu Yang Artistic Journey* published by National Chiao Tung University Press, Taiwan (Cheng & Tsai, 2014; 2016) and AR book designed by the combination of various tools such as Autodesk Maya, Muvizu and Adobe Flash software (Küçük, Yýlmaz, & Göktaþ, 2014). In Malaysia, Mahadzir and Phung (2013) developed a collection of AR pop-up books with ZooBurst (a user-friendly tool) and then had five primary students experience learning English with the aid of these books during recess time in the school library. One of the books taught the learners about animals and their sounds when the page popped up and showed different 3D images of familiar animals (e.g., cat, dog, horse, duck, etc.) and sound icons which the students could interact with to hear the real sound of these animals. Other books focused on English grammar topics and practice quizzes. The findings based on observation and semi-structured interviews showed that learners' interest and motivation was triggered as the learning activities met their needs, that is, to improve their English and introduced a new engaging way to learn the language. Thus, these young participants perceived AR pop-up books as a motivational tool that helped boost their attention, relevance, confidence, satisfaction level and academic performance as well (Mahadzir & Phung (2013).

These recent studies show that not only do the AR-based reading books engage students in active reading inside the class but also encourage them to practice reading outside the class with their peers and/or parents (Billinghurst & Dunser, 2012). Cheng and Tsai's research (2014, 2016) also supports the effectiveness of shared AR picture books between parents and their children. The parents in their research felt more motivated to read the AR books with their kids, which led to better learning in the child and instilled more positive attitudes in the children-parent relationship, which corresponds with the results of Küçük et al.'s (2014) scholarship.

## AR-Game Based Learning Environment

Another growing trend with AR use in language classrooms is the *edutainment* game based on AR technology, which can be both educational and entertaining. According to the literature review study on AR-game based learning environment by Koutromanos, Sofos, and Avraamidou (2015), numerous AR tools to design a game learning activity have been utilized in order to make use of the advantages that AR technology brings to the language classroom. Some of these tools include "FreshAiR" to develop an AR platform (Kamarainen et al, 2013 as cited in Koutromanos et al., 2015), "ARToolKitPlus 2.1.1" software for creating mobile AR game (Furio et al., 2013, as cited in Koutromanos et al., 2015), and "Open Scene Graph" (OSG) toolkit to design the tablet AR game, to name a few. Another pilot study on a new game about fishing was also conducted by Chen, Ho and Lin (2015) to evaluate its effectiveness in student engagement and learning. Data analysis from the survey and interview reveal positive results in that the participants expressed moderate interest in this game-based system (Chen et al., 2015). The game has been therefore modified based on the feedback and suggestions for a more successful and user-friendly AR game based learning platform.

Making use of available tools (e.g., open-source software MITAR and ARIS) that allow for the design of mobile games without extensive equipment or expertise, Holden and Sykes (2011) developed an AR location-based game, *Mentira*, in which the users tried to solve multiple historical murders in Los Griegos neighborhood, New Mexico with the aid of local clues and teamwork. The findings of the study indicated that this AR location-game provided the participants with a new engaging learning environment outside the four walls of traditional classroom. The AR game not only enhanced important skills in the 21st century, that is, their higher order thinking skills (HOTs) (e.g., knowledge application, collaboration, critical analysis, and product creation) and necessary IT skills, but also deepened their understanding of Spanish history and culture.

## AR Authoring Tools

One of the strengths of AR technology is that there are several AR authoring tools that are free, user friendly, and effective. By creating the AR products on their own learners will find learning more meaningful and develop their higher-order thinking skills. Thus, a simple authoring tool like *BuildAR* (www.buildar.org) can provide many learning opportunities by having the students use this app to design an interactive graphical interface without the need to be excellent at coding skills (Billinghurst & Dünser, 2012). In their paper, Billinghurst and Dünser (2012) combined BuildAR tool with free modeling software, *The Art of Illusion* (www.artofillusion.org), in order to create educational materials for elementary students. For instance, first and second graders learned how to use these tools to build AR scenes that helped them understand the lesson contents better. Thus process also provided students with an opportunity to develop their HOTs such as digital content creation and problem solving (Billinghurst & Dünser, 2012). Based on their real-life teaching experience with AR, Billinghurst and Dünser (2012) argue that "even young learners can create AR scenes and that creation process can be a powerful educational experience" (p. 59).

In addition, *Aurasma* is also an easy-to-use tool to create any AR code with already-made materials. The most recent study that made use of Aurasma was conducted by Richardson (2016). The advanced level EFL students in his study had a chance to use this app to complete a series of challenging language tasks in an AR game while they were walking around a city in Germany. The findings of this study indicated the potential effectiveness of location-aware AR mobile games in language education in that this user-friendly tool can boost learners' motivation and active engagement in learning activities. Figure 7 is a clear example of how the student can introduce others about Lake Helen in Florida; additional locations in this state can be added to an AR tour as well (Thompson, 2011). Figure 7. Illustrates the use of AR as an authoring tool.

## More AR Potentials

AR technology is paving its way to make an innovation in language teaching and learning. AR *cubes* first originated from the idea of bringing authentic materials to *chemistry* classroom by designing the Elements AR app for students to learn about various chemistry elements in a new engaging environment (Rouviere, 2012). In the web site elements4d.daqri.com, there are tutorials that show how to make these cubes and how students can use the app to scan the cubes to learn about certain element (e.g., hydro and oxygen) as well as about chemical reaction (e.g., when putting hydro cube and oxygen one together, they react and form water or H20). Figure 8 shows a ChineseCUBES sample.

Particularly, ChineseCUBES, a product designed with AR technology, is considered a novel way to start learning Chinese as it "fills a gap between having fun, self-exploration, learning and introducing the learner to the unique aspects of Chinese syntax and vocabulary/phrase formation" (Rouviere, 2012). As seen in Figure 8, there is a cube that shows a word 你 (phonetic script or Hanyu pinyin as *nǐ*, which means *you* in English) together with a cute little character that also pops up to speak the word. Learners can also learn new Chinese words, phrases and sentences by putting those AR cubes next to

*Figure 7. Example of AR Authoring Tool (Thompson, 2011)*
*Source: Thompson, K., 2011*

*Figure 8. ChineseCUBES Sample 1 (Rouviere, 2012)*
*Source: Rouviere, 2012*

one another. If combining random cubes together, the program will provide some suggestions for real words or phrases on the right side of the screen. Figure 9. provides real word phrases in ChineseCUBES

After the learner chooses a certain meaningful word or phrase, the bubbles will be connected together and he/she can select other functions such as *Speak*, *Translate*, or *Write* to practice the new input. The AR cube can be an innovative way to introduce and review vocabulary because it enhances memory cues and motivates students' exploration (Rouviere, 2012). For example, each side of the cube consists of a QR code, which represents a word. Learners will use their phones to scan the codes to see the word or its 3D illustration. With that usage, there is a lot of room for teachers to think of activities to present, review, or reinforce the vocabulary categorized by topics or themes. Another application of this 3D cube with QR codes is a storytelling activity in which the learners create their own stories using sequencing picture cues on six sides of the AR cube. This can be an engaging writing activity as the learners are able to interact with the cube and use it for learning. In addition, it enhances their higher-order thinking skills as they need to use their imagination and creativity to tell their own stories. Furthermore, students can learn about noun phrases or idiomatic expressions by combining the cubes together in the correct order. For instance, one cube has six sides teaching students about animals (e.g., dog, cat, fish, elephant, etc.). Another cube embeds different colors (e.g., black, brown, yellow, grey, etc.). When students put the two random cubes next to each other, they will learn new phrases such as *brown dog*, *black cat, grey elephant*, *black dog,* and so on. If the phrase does not make sense, for example, *purple elephant*, the cubes will not show any 3D illustration when being put together.

*Figure 9. ChineseCUBES 'Real Word' Phrases (Rouviere, 2012)*
*Source: Rouviere, 2012*

Another way to make use of AR cubes is that each cube introduces one idiomatic phrase (e.g., *raining cats and dogs*, *a piece of cake*, *kill one bird with two stones*, etc.). Side 1 of the cube shows its literal and figurative meanings. The second side has the audio showing how to say the phrase. The third one contains the video that provides authentic scenario when to use the phrase. Side 4 of the cube explains the origin of the idiom. Side 5 shows whether there is an equivalent with the learner's L1 as well as with other languages if applicable. The last side of the cube has a small quiz for the learner to practice the idiomatic phrase.

Moreover, AR technology can be a good tool to help learners gain cultural knowledge. For instance, each side of the cube has the name of popular countries/cities/places in the world together with the QR codes. When learners use the app on their phones to scan the code on the side, they will watch a short clip about the place, which could be followed by a short quiz to check their comprehension. Each student chooses one side to learn about the certain place, then they work in pairs or groups in order to talk about the main features of the place to other students. By doing this, they can share ideas together, enhance their cultural competence, and develop their collaborative skills as well. Language and culture are inextricably intertwined (Bayramova, 2016; Byram, 1989; Zhan, 2016); therefore, addressing culture is a critical aspect that teachers should embrace in foreign language education.

## AR Educational Challenges

The most challenging aspect of AR is that AR technology itself is still in the initiation stage. There are not a lot of AR apps or AR-connected devices available for teachers and students to apply in real-life classroom settings. AR technology is still considered as a funding research or pilot project at some particular schools or institutes. Another big challenge is that the cost for AR implementation is not low. It is also necessary to take into consideration the knowledge of AR that teachers currently possess. As AR is a recently emerging technology, conceivably not many educators know or hear about it. In addition, there is concern about the usability, convenience, and maintenance of the required technological devices to effectively operate AR.

It is worth mentioning that it may take some time for both teachers and researchers to agree on the effectiveness of AR, so that they can employ this technology to assist their students meet the standardized requirements in learning and assessment. Stimulating as the AR environment can be, at the same time it may be distracting and difficult to take control of. Thus, it is critical to highlight the need for further empirical and action research on pedagogical aspects of AR as García, Peña-López, Johnson, Smith, Levine, & Haywood (2010) emphasized:

*The possibilities that this technology can offer in higher education still remain to be discovered and depend on what we are able to imagine and devise as pedagogical applications rather than on the possibilities provided by the technology itself. (p. 29)*

Wu, Lee, Chang, & Liang (2013) also warn that AR technology can be cognitively overloaded for second language learners. Indeed, it will be difficult for them to navigate the new language input in such scenarios. Furthermore, it can be hard to control the embedded and complex environments if AR is applied (Wu et al., 2013). For instance, the teachers may find it challenging to control or scaffold each student's different language exposure because the instructions can be elaborate when they try to explain how to operate the devices and how to interact in a new environment. In other words, students can feel confused and overwhelmed by completing complicated multitasks as well as shifting their focus back and forth with the devices. Another concern is that the current available designs of AR content are still not flexible or diverse enough to suit the interests and demands of various students.

Regardless of those challenges, we look forward to the bright future in which teachers will be fully equipped with AR literacy, knowledge, and skills. They will also embrace the educational potentials of AR and therefore implement this technology in their language classrooms in a meaningful way. Beyond classroom boundaries, AR technology can break the four walls of the room and let the students experience learning in an authentic world augmented by virtual objects such as those in a game-based simulation environment.

## FUTURE RESEARCH DIRECTIONS

It is undeniable that AR poses many challenges for program designers, researchers, and teachers. However, AR is still in an early stage, and thus, the evidence of the effectiveness of AR is limited. Through years of empirical studies, the primary findings of the relationships between AR and learning outcomes are promising. While the design of the technology and the scale of AR research can certainly be more robust in the future, it will promise more hopeful, productive, and convincing results. Further detailed aspects of language learning should be investigated in the context of using AR in real classrooms. Specifically, some of the promising AR ideas in research could be: comparing different types of AR, developing AR-task based models, and combining AR and VR together for educational purposes.

## CONCLUSION

The educational potentials of AR technology are promising. Yet, an interesting question has been raised: Whether AR or VR is the future of language education. AR seems to receive more favor in that there are more AR-based apps and hardware devices on the current market and the fact that it does not completely separate the users from the authentic world. Nevertheless, AR and VR both have a chance to be successful in the future. Indeed, they can go hand in hand together to bridge the gaps in language classroom pedagogy and research, bring learners to new exciting learning environments, and maximize learning experiences and performances.

## REFERENCES

Augmented Reality. (2014). *Similarity and difference between augmented reality and virtual reality.* Retrieved November 22, 2016, from http://www.augmentedrealitytrends.com/augmented-reality/similarity-and-difference-between-ar-and-vr.html

Azuma, R. T. (1997). A survey of augmented reality. *Presence (Cambridge, Mass.)*, *6*(4), 355–385. doi:10.1162/pres.1997.6.4.355

Barreira, J., Bessa, M., Pereira, L. C., Adao, T., Peres, E., & Magalhaes, L. (2012). MOW: Augmented reality game to learn words in different languages: Case study on learning English names of animals in elementary school. *7th Iberian Conference on Information Systems and Technologies (CISTI)*, 1-6.

Bayramova, A. M. (2016). Interrelation of language and culture. *Theory & Practice in Language Studies*, *6*(10), 1940–1944. doi:10.17507/tpls.0610.07

Billinghurst, M., & Dunser, A. (2012). Augmented reality in the classroom. *Computer*, *45*(7), 56–63. doi:10.1109/MC.2012.111

Brown, J. S., Collins, A., & Duguid, P. (1989). Situated cognition and the culture of learning. *Educational Researcher*, *18*(1), 32–42. doi:10.3102/0013189X018001032

Byram, M. (1989). *Cultural studies in foreign language education*. Clevedon, UK: Multilingual Matters.

Cabero, J., & Barroso, J. (2016). The educational possibilities of Augmented Reality. *Journal of New Approaches in Educational Research*, *5*(1), 44–50. doi:10.7821/naer.2016.1.140

Cadavieco, J. F., Goulão, M. F., & Costales, A. F. (2012). Using augmented reality and m-learning to optimize students performance in higher education. *Procedia - Social And Behavioral Sciences, 46*, 2970-2977. doi:10.1016/j.sbspro.2012.05.599

Chen, C. H., Ho, C., & Lin, J. (2015). The development of an augmented reality game-based learning environment. *Procedia - Social And Behavioral Sciences, 174*, 216-220. doi:10.1016/j.sbspro.2015.01.649

Cheng, K. K., & Tsai, C. C. (2014). Children and parents reading of an augmented reality picture book: Analyses of behavioral patterns and cognitive attainment. *Computers & Education*, *72*, 302–312. doi:10.1016/j.compedu.2013.12.003

Cheng, K. K., & Tsai, C. C. (2016). The interaction of child-parent shared reading with an augmented reality (AR) picture book and parents' conceptions of AR learning. *British Journal of Educational Technology*, *47*(1), 203–222. doi:10.1111/bjet.12228

Chiang, T. H., Yang, S. J., & Hwang, G. (2014). Students online interactive patterns in augmented reality-based inquiry activities. *Computers & Education*, *78*, 97–108. doi:10.1016/j.compedu.2014.05.006

Dede, C. (2008). Theoretical perspectives influencing the use of information technology in teaching and learning. In J. Voogt & G. Knezek (Eds.), *International handbook of information technology in primary and secondary education* (pp. 43–62). New York, NY: Springer. doi:10.1007/978-0-387-73315-9_3

Dede, C. (2009). Immersive interfaces for engagement and learning. *Science*, *323*(5910), 66–69. doi:10.1126/science.1167311 PMID:19119219

Dorogan, D. (2014). *How to use location-based chat and AR in dating and social*. Retrieved November 22, 2016, from http://quickblox.com/blog/how-to-use-location-based-chat-and-ar-in-dating-and-social/

Dunleavy, M., & Dede, C. (2014). Augmented reality teaching and learning. In J. M. Spector, M. D. Merrill, J. Elen, & M. J. Bishop (Eds.), *Handbook of research on educational communications and technology* (4th ed.; pp. 735–745). New York, NY: Springer. doi:10.1007/978-1-4614-3185-5_59

Dunleavy, M., Dede, C., & Mitchell, R. (2009). Affordances and limitations of immersive participatory augmented reality simulations for teaching and learning. *Journal of Science Education and Technology, 18*(1), 7–22. doi:10.1007/s10956-008-9119-1

Gallagher, A. G., & Sullivan, G. C. (2011). *Fundamentals of surgical simulation: Principles and practice*. New York, NY: Springer.

García, I., Peña-López, I., Johnson, L., Smith, R., Levine, A., & Haywood, K. (2010). *Informe Horizon: Edición Iberoamericana 2010*. Austin, TX: The New Media Consortium.

Holden, C. L., & Sykes, J. M. (2011). Leveraging mobile games for place-based language learning. *International Journal of Game-Based Learning, 1*(2), 1–18. doi:10.4018/ijgbl.2011040101

Keneman, A., & Waller, R. (2016). Augmented reality in the classroom. *Literacy Practice & Research, 41*(3), 5–8.

Klopfer, E., & Squire, K. (2008). Environmental detectives—the development of an augmented reality platform for environmental simulations. *Educational Technology Research and Development, 56*(2), 203–228. doi:10.1007/s11423-007-9037-6

Koutromanos, G., Sofos, A., & Avraamidou, L. (2015). The use of augmented realty games: A review of the literature. *Educational Media International, 52*(4), 253–271. doi:10.1080/09523987.2015.1125988

Küçük, S., Yýlmaz, R. M., & Göktaþ, Y. (2014). Augmented reality for learning English: Achievement, attitude and cognitive load levels of students. *Education & Science, 39*(176), 393. doi:10.15390/EB.2014.3595

Lakarnchua, O., & Reinders, H. (2014). Implementing mobile language learning with an augmented reality activity. *Modern English Teacher, 23*(2), 42–50.

Lara-Prieto, V., Bravo-Quirino, E., Rivera-Campa, M. Á., & Gutiérrez-Arredondo, J. E. (2015). An innovative self-learning approach to 3D printing using multimedia and augmented reality on mobile devices. *Procedia Computer Science, 75*, 59-65. doi:10.1016/j.procs.2015.12.206

Liszewski, A. (2015). *Lucasfilm is making amazing Star Wars and Jurassic Park VR experiences.* Retrieved November 22, 2016, from http://gizmodo.com/fx-wizards-are-making-amazing-star-wars-and-jurassic-pa-1710872285

Liu, P.-H. E., & Tsai, M.-K. (2013). Using augmented-reality-based mobile learning material in EFL English composition: An exploratory case study. *British Journal of Educational Technology, 44*(1), E1–E4. doi:10.1111/j.1467-8535.2012.01302.x

Liu, T., Tan, T., & Chu, Y. (2010). QR code and augmented reality-supported mobile English learning system. *Lecture Notes in Computer Science, 5960*, 37–52. doi:10.1007/978-3-642-12349-8_3

Liu, T. Y. (2009). A context-aware ubiquitous learning environment for language listening and speaking. *Journal of Computer Assisted Learning, 25*(6), 515–527. doi:10.1111/j.1365-2729.2009.00329.x

Liu, Y., Holden, D., & Zheng, D. (2016). Analyzing students language learning experience in an augmented reality mobile game: An exploration of an emergent learning environment. *Procedia: Social and Behavioral Sciences*, *228*, 369–374. doi:10.1016/j.sbspro.2016.07.055

Mahadzir, N. N. N., & Phung, L. F. (2013). The use of augmented reality pop-up book to increase motivation in English language learning for national primary school. *IOSR Journal of Research & Method in Education*, *1*(1), 26–38.

McKalin, V. (2014). *Augmented Reality vs. Virtual Reality: What are the differences and similarities?*. Retrieved November 22, 2016, from http://www.techtimes.com/articles/5078/20140406/augmented-reality-vs-virtual-reality-what-are-the-differences-and-similarities.htm

Pence, H. E. (2011). Smartphones, smart objects, and augmented reality. *The Reference Librarian*, *52*(1-2), 136–145. doi:10.1080/02763877.2011.528281

Richardson, D. (2016). Exploring the potential of a location based augmented reality game for language learning. *International Journal of Game-Based Learning*, *6*(3), 34–49. doi:10.4018/IJGBL.2016070103

Rouviere, N. (2012, November 10). ChineseCUBES review: A novel way to start learning Chinese. *Confused Laowai*. Retrieved March 5, 2017, from http://confusedlaowai.com/2012/11/chinesecubes-review/

Santos, M., Lübke, A., Taketomi, T., Yamamoto, G., Rodrigo, M., Sandor, C., & Kato, H. (2016). Augmented reality as multimedia: The case for situated vocabulary learning. *Research & Practice in Technology Enhanced Learning*, *11*(1), 1. doi:10.1186/s41039-016-0028-2

Singhal, S., Bagga, S., Goyal, P., & Saxena, V. (2012). Augmented chemistry: Interactive education system. *International Journal of Computers and Applications*, *49*(15), 1–5. doi:10.5120/7700-1041

Solak, E., & Cakir, R. (2015). Exploring the effect of materials designed with augmented reality on language learners' vocabulary learning. *The Journal of Educators Online*, *13*(2), 50–72.

Solak, E., & Erdem, G. (2015). A content analysis of virtual reality studies in foreign language education. *Participatory Educational Research*, *2*(2), 21–26. doi:10.17275/per.15.spi.2.3

Squire, K. (2010). From information to experience: Place-based augmented reality games as a model for learning in a globally networked society. *Teachers College Record*, *112*(10), 2565–2602.

Tan, T., & Liu, T. (2004). The mobile-based interactive learning environment (MOBILE) and a case study for assisting elementary school English learning. *IEEE International Conference on Advanced Learning Technologies*, 530-534.

The Travelers and the Sea. (1919). *Aesopica: Aesop's fables in English, Latin and Greek* [image]. Retrieved November 22, 2016, from https://i.ytimg.com/vi/SL2ifIi_EwY/maxresdefault.jpg

Thompson, K. (2011). *6 shocking affordable sci-fi inventions*. Retrieved November 22, 2016, from http://www.cracked.com/article_19368_6-shockingly-affordable-sci-fi-inventions.html

Vygotsky, L. S. (1978). *Mind and society: The development of higher mental processes*. Cambridge, MA: Harvard University Press.

Wang, X., Kim, M. J., Love, P. E. D., & Kang, S. C. (2013). Augmented reality in built environment: Classification and implications for future research. *Automation in Construction*, *32*, 1–13. doi:10.1016/j.autcon.2012.11.021

Wu, H. K., Lee, S. W. Y., Chang, H. Y., & Liang, J. C. (2013). Current status, opportunities and challenges of augmented reality in education. *Computers & Education*, *62*, 41–49. doi:10.1016/j.compedu.2012.10.024

Zhan, C. (2016). The importance of culture factor in foreign language teaching. *Theory and Practice in Language Studies*, *6*(3), 581–586. doi:10.17507/tpls.0603.17

## ADDITIONAL READING

Chang, G., Morreale, P., & Medicherla, P. (2010). Applications of augmented reality systems in education. In D. Gibson & B. Dodge (Eds.), *Proceedings of Society for Information Technology & Teacher Education International Conference 2010* (pp. 1380-1385). Chesapeake, VA: AACE.

Liestol, G. (2011). *Learning through situated simulations: Exploring mobile augmented reality*. Retrieved March 29, 2017, from http://www.educause.edu/ecar

Rose, F. J., & Bhuvaneswari, R. (2014). Word recognition incorporating augmented reality for linguistic e-conversion. *Educational Media International*, *51*(1), 1–15.

Valle, R. (2014). *Teaching with augmented reality is here*. Retrieved March 29, 2017, from http://edtechreview.in/trendsinsights/insights/1503-teaching-with-augmented-reality-it-s-here

## KEY TERMS AND DEFINITIONS

**Augmented Reality:** An emerging technology that allows users to see virtual objects in the real world by using AR app.

**Constructivist Learning Theory:** A developing theory based on Vygotsky's Sociocultural theory, which posits that individual's background knowledge, history, and culture are more important than the context.

**GPS:** Global Positioning System, which is used to navigate specific locations.

**Location-Aware AR:** Allows users to track the distance from current location to different ones by GPS-enabled devices.

**QR Code:** Quick Response Code is a barcode to be scanned to show multimedia information.

**Situated Learning Theory:** A developing theory based on Vygotsky's Sociocultural theory, which emphasizes the positive impacts of social interactions on learning.

**Virtual Reality:** An emerging technology that allows users to be immersed in the virtual environment by wearing a VR goggles or headset.

**Vision-Based AR:** provides the multimedia when the user points the camera of the mobile device at the particular 2D object or QR code.

# Compilation of References


Abrams, Z. (2011). Interpersonal communication in intercultural CMC. In N. Arnold & L. Ducate (Eds.), *Present and future promises of CALL: From theory and research to new directions in language teaching* (pp. 61–92). San Marcos, TX: CALICO.

AbuSeileek, A., & Abualsha'r, A. (2014). Using peer computer-mediated corrective feedback to support EFL learners' writing. *Language Learning & Technology, 18*(1), 76-95. Retrieved from http://llt.msu.edu/issues/february2014/abuseileekabualshar.pdf

Achterhuis, H. (Ed.). (2001). American philosophy of technology: The empirical turn. Bloomington, IN: Indiana University Press.

Adair-Hauck, B., Willingham-McLain, L., & Youngs, B. E. (2000). Evaluating the integration of technology and second language learning. *CALICO Journal*, *17*(2), 269–306.

Adams, S. (2013). Needs met through role-playing games: A fantasy theme analysis of dungeons & dragons. *Kaleidoscope*, *16*, 69–86.

Agency for Quality Assurance in Romania. (2006). *External evaluation methodology, standards, reference standards and performance indicators*. Retrieved from http://www.aracis.ro/fileadmin/ARACIS/Proceduri/Methodology_for_External_Evaluation.pdf

Alabbad, A., Gitsaki, C., & White, P. (2015). CALL course design for second language learning: a case study of Arab EFL learners. In D. L. Pullen, C. Gitsaki, & M. Baguley (Eds.), *Technoliteracy, discourse, and social practice: Frameworks and applications in the digital age* (pp. 88–103). Hershey, PA: Information Science Reference.

Alatis, J. E. (1983). The application of instructional technology to language learning. *CALICO Journal*, *1*(1), 9–14.

Alderson, C. (1996). Do corpora have a role in language assessment? In J. Thomas & M. Short (Eds.), *Using corpora for language research* (pp. 248–259). London: Longman.

Alderson, J. C. (1990). Learner-centered testing through computers: Institutional issues in individual assessment. In J. de Jong & D. K. Stevenson (Eds.), *Individualizing the assessment of language abilities* (pp. 20–27). Clevedon, UK: Multilingual Matters.

Alderson, J. C., & Banerjee, J. (2001). Language testing and assessment (Part I). *Language Teaching*, *34*(4), 213–236. doi:10.1017/S0261444800014464

Al-Harbi, S. S., & Alshumaimeri, Y. A. (2016). The flipped classroom impact in grammar class on EFL Saudi secondary school students performances and attitudes. *English Language Teaching*, *9*(10), 60–80. doi:10.5539/elt.v9n10p60

Alimemaj, Z. (2010). YouTube, language learning, and teaching techniques. *AngloHigher Journal*, *2*(3), 10–12.

Al-Khatiri. (2015). Beyond the classroom walls: Edmodo in Saudi secondary school EFL instruction, attitudes and challenges. *English Language Teaching Journal, 8*(1), 189-204. doi:10.5539/elt.v8n1p189

Allen, I. E., & Seaman, J. (2010). *Learning on demand: Online education in the United States, 2009.* Babson Research Group. Retrieved from http://files.eric.ed.gov/fulltext/ED529931.pdf

Allen, I. E., & Seaman, J. (2013). *Changing course: Ten years of tracking online education in the United States.* Retrieved from http://www.onlinelearningsurvey.com/reports/changingcourse.pdf

Allen, I. E., Seaman, J., & Garret, R. (2007). *Blending in: The extent and promise of blended education in the United States.* Retrieved from https://www.onlinelearningsurvey.com/reports/blending-in.pdf

Alwehaibi, H. O. (2015). The impact of using YouTube in EFL classroom on enhancing EFL students content learning. *Journal of College Teaching & Learning, 12*(2), 121–126. doi:10.19030/tlc.v12i2.9182

Amer, M. (2014). Language learners usage of a mobile learning application for learning idioms and collocations. *CALICO Journal, 31*(3), 285–302. doi:10.11139/cj.31.3.285-302

Anwaruddin, S. M. (2013). Web 2.0 and language learners' motivation: An action research study. *Canadian Journal of Action Research, 14*(1), 51–68.

Anwaruddin, S. M. (2015a). ICTs in language and literacy education in Bangladesh: A critical review. *Current Issues in Education, 18*(1), 1–13.

Anwaruddin, S. M. (2015b). Teacher professional learning in online communities: Toward existentially reflective practice. *Reflective Practice: International and Multidisciplinary Perspectives, 16*(6), 806–820. doi:10.1080/14623943.2015.1095730

Anwaruddin, S. M. (2016). ICT and language teacher development in the global south: A new materialist discourse analysis. *Educational Studies, 52*(3), 260–278. doi:10.1080/00131946.2016.1169183

Appel, C., & Gilabert, R. (2006). Finding common ground in LSP: A computer-mediated communication project. In E. A. Macia, A. S. Cervera, & C. R. Ramos (Eds.), *Information technology in languages for specific purposes: Issues and prospects* (pp. 75–90). New York, NY: Springer. doi:10.1007/978-0-387-28624-2_5

Arkorful, V., & Abaidoo, N. (2014). The role of e-Learning, the advantages and disadvantages of its adoption in higher education. *International Journal of Education and Research, 2*(12), 397–410.

Arnaud, P. J., & Savignon, S. J. (1997). Rare words, complex lexical units and the advanced learner. In J. Coady & T. Huckin (Eds.), *Second language vocabulary acquisition* (pp. 157–173). Cambridge, UK: Cambridge University Press; doi:10.1017/CBO9781139524643.012

Arnold, N. (2013). The role of methods textbooks in providing early training for teaching with technology in the language classroom. *Foreign Language Annals, 42*(2), 230–245. doi:10.1111/flan.12020

Arnold, N., & Ducate, L. (2006). Future foreign language teachers' social and cognitive collaboration in an online environment. *Language Learning & Technology, 10*(1), 42–66.

Arnold, N., & Ducate, L. (Eds.). (2011). *Present and future promises of CALL: From theory and research to new directions in language teaching.* San Marcos, TX: CALICO Publications.

Arnold, N., Ducate, L., & Kost, C. (2012). Collaboration or cooperation? Analyzing group dynamics and revision processes in wikis. *CALICO Journal, 29*(3), 431–448. doi:10.11139/cj.29.3.431-448

Arnold, N., & Paulus, T. (2010). Using a social networking site for experiential learning: Appropriating, lurking, modeling and community building. *The Internet and Higher Education*, *13*(4), 188–196. doi:10.1016/j.iheduc.2010.04.002

Arnó-Macià, E. (2012). The role of technology in teaching languages for specific purposes courses. *Modern Language Journal*, *96*, 89–104. doi:10.1111/j.1540-4781.2012.01299.x

Ashouri, S., Arjmandi, M., & Rahimi, R. (2014). The impact of corpus-based collocation instruction on Iranian EFL learners' collocation learning. *Universal Journal of Educational Research*, *2*(6), 470–479.

Ashwell, T. (2000). Patterns of teacher response to student writing in a multiple-draft composition classroom: Is content feedback followed by form feedback the best method? *Journal of Second Language Writing*, *9*(3), 227–257. doi:10.1016/S1060-3743(00)00027-8

Augmented Reality. (2014). *Similarity and difference between augmented reality and virtual reality*. Retrieved November 22, 2016, from http://www.augmentedrealitytrends.com/augmented-reality/similarity-and-difference-between-ar-and-vr.html

Au, W. (2010). *Unequal by design: High-stakes testing and the standardization of inequality*. New York, NY: Routledge.

Aydin, Z., & Yildiz, S. (2014). Using wikis to promote collaborative EFL writing. *Language Learning & Technology*, *18*(1), 160–180. Retrieved from http://llt.msu.edu/issues/february2014/aydinyildiz.html

Azuma, R. T. (1997). A survey of augmented reality. *Presence (Cambridge, Mass.)*, *6*(4), 355–385. doi:10.1162/pres.1997.6.4.355

Bachman, L. (2007). What is the construct? The dialectic of abilities and contexts in defining constructs in language assessment. In J. Fox, M. Wesche, D. Bayliss, L. Cheng, C. E. Turner, & C. Doe (Eds.), *Language testing reconsidered* (pp. 41–71). Ottawa, Canada: University of Ottawa Press.

Bachman, L., & Palmer, A. (2010). *Language assessment in practice*. Oxford, UK: Oxford University Press.

Balkin, R. S., Buckner, D., Swartz, J., & Rao, S. (2005). Issues in classroom management in an interactive distance education course. *International Journal of Instructional Media*, *32*(4), 363–372.

Banados, E. (2006). A blended-learning pedagogical model for teaching and learning EFL successfully through an online interactive multimedia environment. *CALICO Journal*, *23*(3), 533–550.

Barblan, A. (2011). From the universities in Europe to the universities of Europe. In W. Rüegg (Ed.), A history of the university in Europe: Volume 4. Universities since 1945 (pp. 550-574). Cambridge, UK: Cambridge University Press.

Bardovi-Harlig, K., & Dörnyei, Z. (1998). Do language learners recognize pragmatic violations? Pragmatic versus grammatical awareness in instructed L2 learning. *TESOL Quarterly*, *32*(2), 233–259. doi:10.2307/3587583

Barkley, E. F. (2010). *Student engagement techniques: A handbook for college faculty*. San Francisco, CA: John Wiley & Sons, Inc.

Barootchi, N., & Keshavarz, M. H. (2002). Assessment of achievement through portfolios and teacher-made tests. *Educational Research*, *44*(3), 279–288. doi:10.1080/00131880210135313

Barreira, J., Bessa, M., Pereira, L. C., Adao, T., Peres, E., & Magalhaes, L. (2012). MOW: Augmented reality game to learn words in different languages: Case study on learning English names of animals in elementary school. *7th Iberian Conference on Information Systems and Technologies (CISTI)*, 1-6.

Barrett, H. C. (2007). Researching electronic portfolios and learner engagement: The REFLECT Initiative. *Journal of Adolescent & Adult Literacy*, *50*(6), 436–449. doi:10.1598/JAAL.50.6.2

Barrington, R. (2014). *Moodle Gradebook*. Birmingham, UK: Packt Publishing Ltd.

Barrot, J. S. (2016). Using Facebook-based e-portfolio in ESL writing classrooms: Impact and challenges. *Language, Culture and Curriculum*, *29*(3), 286–301. doi:10.1080/07908318.2016.1143481

Barton, D., & Potts, D. (2013). Language learning online as a social practice. *TESOL Quarterly*, *47*(4), 815–820. doi:10.1002/tesq.130

Baturay, M. H., & Daloğlu, A. (2010). E-portfolio assessment in an online English language course. *Computer Assisted Language Learning*, *23*(5), 413–428. doi:10.1080/09588221.2010.520671

Bauer-Ramazani, C., Graney, J. M., Marshall, H. W., & Sabieh, C. (2016). Flipped learning in TESOL: Definitions, approaches, and implementation. *TESOL Journal*, *7*(2), 429–437. doi:10.1002/tesj.250

Bayramova, A. M. (2016). Interrelation of language and culture. *Theory & Practice in Language Studies*, *6*(10), 1940–1944. doi:10.17507/tpls.0610.07

Bearak, M. (2017, January). Even before Trump, more Mexicans were leaving the U.S. than arriving. *The Washington Post*. Retrieved March 4, 2017 from https://www.washingtonpost.com/news/worldviews/wp/2017/01/27/even-before-trump-more-mexicans-were-leaving-the-us-than-arriving/?utm_term=.254fe61b2707

Beare, K. (2008). *YouTube in the classroom*. Retrieved from http://esl.about.eom/od/listeninglessonplans/a/youtube.html

Beauvois, M. H., & Eledge, J. (1995). Personality types and megabytes: Student attitudes toward computer mediated communication (CMC) in the language classroom. *CALICO Journal*, *13*(2 & 3), 27–45.

Beckers, J., Dolmans, D., & van Merrienboer, J. (2016). e-Portfolios enhancing students' self-directed learning: A systematic review of influencing factors. *Australasian Journal of Educational Technology*, *32*(2).

Beer, C., Clark, K., & Jones, D. (2010). Indicators of engagement. In *Proceedings of ASCILITE - Australian Society for Computers in Learning in Tertiary Education Annual Conference 2010* (pp. 75-86). Australasian Society for Computers in Learning in Tertiary Education.

Belz, J. (2002). Social dimensions of telecollaborative foreign language study. *Language Learning & Technology*, *6*(1), 60–81.

Benson, P. (2013). Teaching and research autonomy (2nd ed.). New York, NY: Routledge.

Bergmann, J., & Sams, A. (2012). *Flip your classroom: Reach every student in every class every day*. Alexandria, VA: ASCD.

Bergmann, J., & Sams, A. (2013). Flipping for mastery. *Educational Leadership*, *71*(4), 24–29.

Bergmann, J., & Sams, A. (2014). *Flipped learning: Gateway to student engagement*. Alexandria, VA: ISTE.

Berk, R. A. (2009). Multimedia teaching with video clips: TV, movies, YouTube, and mtvU in the college classroom. *International Journal of Technology in Teaching and Learning*, *5*(1), 1–21.

Bernard, J. (2010). Motivation in foreign language learning: The relationship between classroom activities, motivation, and outcomes in a university language-learning environment (Honors Thesis). Pittsburgh, PA: Carnegie Mellon University. Retrieved from http://repository.cmu.edu/cgi/viewcontent.cgi?article=1077&context=hsshonors

Berner, A., Boswell, W., & Kahan, N. (1996). Using the tape recorder to respond to student writing. In G. Rijlaarsdam, H. van der Bergh, & M. Couzijn (Eds.), *Effective Teaching and Learning of Writing* (pp. 339–357). Amsterdam: Amsterdam University Press.

Biber, D., & Conrad, S. (2001a). Multi-dimensional analysis and the study of register variation. In S. Conrad & D. Biber (Eds.), *Variation in English: Multidimensional Studies* (pp. 3–12). London: Longman.

Biber, D., & Conrad, S. (2001b). Quantitative corpus-based research: Much more than bean counting. *TESOL Quarterly*, *35*(2), 331–336. doi:10.2307/3587653

Biber, D., Conrad, S., & Cortes, V. (2004). If you look at…: Lexical bundles in university teaching and textbooks. *Applied Linguistics*, *25*(3), 371–405. doi:10.1093/applin/25.3.371

Bickerton, D. (1999). Authoring and the academic linguist: The challenge of MMCALL. In K. Cameron (Ed.), *CALL: Media, design and applications* (pp. 59–79). Lisse, The Netherlands: Swets & Zeitlinger.

Bickerton, D., Stenton, T., & Temmermann, M. (2001). Criteria for the evaluation of authoring tools in language education. In A. Chambers & G. Davies (Eds.), *ICT and language learning: A European perspective* (pp. 53–66). Lisse, The Netherlands: Swets & Zeitlinger.

Biesenbach-Lucas, S. (2003). Asynchronous discussion groups in teacher training classes: Perceptions of native and non-native students. *Journal of Asynchronous Learning Networks*, *7*(3), 24–46.

Bilgin, H. (2013). Students' CALLing: Blended learning for students. In B. Tomlinson & C. Whittaker (Eds.), *Blended learning in English language teaching: Course design and implementation* (pp. 207–211). London: British Council.

Billinghurst, M., & Dunser, A. (2012). Augmented reality in the classroom. *Computer*, *45*(7), 56–63. doi:10.1109/MC.2012.111

Bin, Z., Hu Xiang, C., & Jeaco, S. (2012). An investigation of the use of wikis in English language learning. *Canadian Journal of Applied Linguistics*, *35*(1), 99–116. https://doi.org/10.1515/cjal-2012-0008

Bitchener, J., & Knoch, U. (2008). The value of written corrective feedback for migrant and international students. *Language Teaching Research*, *12*(3), 409–431. doi:10.1177/1362168808089924

Bitchener, J., & Knoch, U. (2009). The value of a focused approach to written corrective feedback. *ELT Journal*, *63*(3), 204–211. doi:10.1093/elt/ccn043

Black, P., & Wiliam, D. (1998). Assessment and classroom learning. *Assessment in Education: Principles, Policy & Practice*, *5*(1), 7–74. doi:10.1080/0969595980050102

Blair, K. L., & Takayoshi, P. (1997). Reflections on reading and evaluating electronic portfolios. In K. B. Yancey & T. Weiser (Eds.), *Situating portfolios: Four perspectives* (pp. 357–369). Logan, UT: Utah State University Press.

Blake, R. (2000). Computer mediated communication: A window on L2 Spanish interlanguage. *Language Learning & Technology*, *4*(1), 120–136.

Blake, R. (2007). New trends in using technology in the language curriculum. *Annual Review of Applied Linguistics*, *27*, 76–97. doi:10.1017/S0267190508070049

Blake, R. J. (2011). Current trends in online language learning. *Annual Review of Applied Linguistics*, *31*, 19–35. doi:10.1017/S026719051100002X

Blake, R. J. (2013). *Brave new digital classroom: Technology and foreign language learning*. Washington, DC: Georgetown University Press.

Blommaert, J. (2010). *The sociolinguistics of globalization*. Cambridge, UK: Cambridge University Press. doi:10.1017/CBO9780511845307

Boers, F., Eyckmans, J., & Stengers, H. (2007). Presenting figurative idioms with a touch of etymology: More than mere mnemonics? *Language Teaching Research, 11*(1), 43–62. doi:10.1177/1362168806072460

Bogdan, R., & Biklen, S. K. (1998). *Qualitative research for education: An introduction to theory and methods* (3rd ed.). London: Allyn & Bacon.

Bonnel, W. (2008). Improving feedback to students in online courses. *Nursing Education Perspectives, 29*(5), 290–294. PMID:18834059

Borg, S. (2003). Teacher cognition in language teaching: A review of research on what language teachers think, know, believe, and do. *Language Teaching, 36*(2), 81–109. doi:10.1017/S0261444803001903

Borjian, A., Muñoz de Cote, L. M., van Dijk, S., & Houde, P. (2016). Transnational Children in Mexico: Context of Migration and Adaptation. *Diaspora, Indigenous, and Minority Education, 10*(1), 42–54. doi:10.1080/15595692.2015.1084920

Bortfeld, H. (2003). Comprehending idioms cross-linguistically. *Experimental Psychology, 50*(3), 217–230. doi:10.1026//1617-3169.50.3.217 PMID:12874990

Boswood, T., & Dwyer, R. (1995). From marking to feedback: Audio-taped response to student writing. *TESOL Journal, 5*(2), 20–23.

Bourdieu, P. (2011). The forms of capital. In I. Szeman & T. Kaposy (Eds.), *Cultural theory: An anthology* (pp. 81–93). Madden, MA: Wiley-Blackwell.

Boutonglang, D., & Flores, F. (2011). A study on integrating technology to engage 7th grades into an English as a foreign language (EFL) classroom in a rural secondary school, Thailand. *International Journal of Arts & Sciences, 4*(18), 195–206.

Bradley, L., Lindström, B., Rystedt, H., & Vigmo, S. (2010). Rationalities of collaboration for language learning in a wiki. *ReCALL, 22*(2), 247–265. doi:10.1017/S0958344010000108

Brinks Lockwood, R. (2014). *Flip it! Strategies for the ESL classroom.* Ann Arbor, MI: University of Michigan Press. doi:10.3998/mpub.7110704

Brook, J. (2011). The affordances of YouTube for language learning and teaching. *Hawaii Pacific University TESOL Working Paper Series, 9*(1-2), 37-56.

Brooks, K., & Thurston, L. P. (2010). English language learner academic engagement and instructional grouping configurations. *American Secondary Education, 39*(1), 45–60.

Brown, E. K. (2006). *Encyclopedia of language and linguistics* (2nd ed.). Boston, MA: Elsevier.

Brown, H. D., & Lee, H. (2015). *Teaching by principles: An interactive approach to language pedagogy.* White Plains, NY: Pearson Education.

Brown, J. S., Collins, A., & Duguid, P. (1989). Situated cognition and the culture of learning. *Educational Researcher, 18*(1), 32–42. doi:10.3102/0013189X018001032

Bucholtz, M., & Hall, K. (2005). Identity and interaction: A sociocultural linguistic approach. *Discourse Studies, 7*(4–5), 585–614. doi:10.1177/1461445605054407

Bulger, M. E., Mayer, R. E., Almeroth, K. C., & Blau, S. D. (2008). Measuring learner engagement in computer equipped college classrooms. *Journal of Educational Multimedia and Hypermedia, 17*(2), 129–143.

Burston, J. (2003). Proving IT works. *CALICO Journal, 20*(2), 219–226.

Butler-Pascoe, M. E. (2009). English for specific purposes (ESP), innovation, and technology. In T. Chiang, W. Chuang, & L. Li (Eds.), *English education and ESP* (pp. 1–15). Taipei, Taiwan: Shih Chien University.

Buzzetto-More, N. A. (2014). An examination of undergraduate student's perceptions and predilections of the use of YouTube in the teaching and learning process. *Interdisciplinary Journal of E-Learning and Learning Objects*, *10*, 17–32.

Byram, M. (1989). *Cultural studies in foreign language education*. Clevedon, UK: Multilingual Matters.

Byrd, P., & Reid, J. (1998). *Grammar in the composition classroom: Essays on teaching ESL for college-bound students*. Portsmouth, NH: Heinle & Heinle.

Cabero, J., & Barroso, J. (2016). The educational possibilities of Augmented Reality. *Journal of New Approaches in Educational Research*, *5*(1), 44–50. doi:10.7821/naer.2016.1.140

Cadavieco, J. F., Goulão, M. F., & Costales, A. F. (2012). Using augmented reality and m-learning to optimize students performance in higher education. *Procedia - Social And Behavioral Sciences, 46*, 2970-2977. doi:10.1016/j.sbspro.2012.05.599

Canagarajah, S. (2007). Lingua franca English, multilingual communities, and language acquisition. *Modern Language Journal*, *91*(s1), 923–939. doi:10.1111/j.1540-4781.2007.00678.x

Canale, M., & Swain, M. (1980). Theoretical bases of communicative approaches to second language teaching and testing. *Applied Linguistics*, *I*(1), 1–47. doi:10.1093/applin/I.1.1

Cardine, S. (2008). *Is Education Ready for YouTube?*. Retrieved from http://www.centerdigitaled.com/edtech/Is-Education-Ready-For-YouTube.html

Carr, P. (2013). *What makes technology change?*. Retrieved from https://impactofinformationsystemsonsociety.wordpress.com/2013/01/21/what-makes-technology-change/

Caspi, A., & Blau, I. (2008). Social presence in online discussion groups: Testing three conceptions and their relations to perceived learning. *Social Psychology of Education*, *11*(3), 323–346. doi:10.1007/s11218-008-9054-2

Cavanaugh, A. J., & Song, L. (2015). Audio feedback versus written feedback: Instructors' and students' perspectives. *Journal of Online Learning and Teaching*, *10*(1), 122–138.

Cave, D. (2012). American children, now struggling to adjust to life in Mexico. *New York Times, 19*(6).

Celce-Murcia, M. (1991). Discourse analysis and grammar instruction. *Annual Review of Applied Linguistics*, *11*, 135–151. doi:10.1017/S0267190500002002

Cervantes, S. E., & Olson, R. C. (2012). Face-to-face communication and instant messaging: Similarities and difference. In R. Chartrand, S. Crofts, & G. Brooks (Eds.), *The 2012 Pan-SIG Conference Proceedings* (pp. 43-48). Hiroshima, Japan: JALT.

Chalhoub-Deville, M. (2003). Second language interaction: Current perspectives and future trends. *Language Testing*, *20*(4), 369–383. doi:10.1191/0265532203lt264oa

Chamot, A. U., & O'Malley, M. (1992). The cognitive academic language learning approach: A bridge to the mainstream. In P. A. Richard-Amato & M. A. Snow (Eds.), *The multicultural classroom* (pp. 39–57). Boston, MA: Addison Wesley; doi:10.2307/3586733

Chang, C. C., Tseng, K. H., Liang, C. Y., & Liao, Y. M. (2013). Constructing and evaluating online goalsetting mechanisms in web-based portfolio assessment system for facilitating self-regulated learning. *Computers & Education*, *69*, 237–249. doi:10.1016/j.compedu.2013.07.016

Chao, Y. C. J., & Lo, H. C. (2009). Students perceptions of wiki-based collaborative writing for learners of English as a foreign language. *Interactive Learning Environments*, *19*(4), 395–411. doi:10.1080/10494820903298662

Chapelle, C. (1997). CALL in the year 2000: Still in search of research paradigms? *Language Learning & Technology*, *1*, 19–43.

Chapelle, C. (1998). Multimedia CALL: Lessons to be learned from research on instructed SLA. *Language Learning & Technology*, *2*(1), 22–34. Retrieved from http://llt.msu.edu/vol1num1/chapelle/default.html

Chapelle, C. (2003). *English language learning and technology: Lectures on teaching and research in the age of information and communication*. Amsterdam, The Netherlands: John Benjamins Publishing; doi:10.1075/lllt.7

Chapelle, C. (2008). Interactionist theory in CALL research. In M. Warschauer & R. Kern (Eds.), *Network-based language teaching: Concept ad practice* (pp. 53–64). Cambridge, UK: Cambridge University Press.

Chapelle, C. (2009). Computer-assisted teaching and testing. In M. H. Long & C. J. Doughty (Eds.), *The handbook of language teaching* (pp. 628–644). Oxford, UK: Blackwell Publishing. doi:10.1002/9781444315783.ch33

Chapelle, C. A. (2005). *Computer applications in second language acquisition: Foundations for teaching, testing, and research* (4th ed.). Cambridge, UK: Cambridge University Press; doi:10.1017/CBO9781139524681

Chapelle, C. A. (2005). Interactionist SLA theory in CALL research. In J. Egbert & G. Petrie (Eds.), *CALL research perspectives* (pp. 53–64). London: LEA Publication.

Chapelle, C. A. (2009). The relationship between SLA theory and CALL. *Modern Language Journal*, *93*(4), 742–754. doi:10.1111/j.1540-4781.2009.00970.x

Chapelle, C. A., & Heift, T. (2009). Individual learner differences in CALL: The field independence/dependence (FID) construct. *CALICO Journal*, *26*(2), 246–266.

Chapelle, C. A., & Jamieson, J. (2008). *Tips for teaching with CALL: Practical approaches to computer-assisted language learning*. White Plains, NY: Pearson Education.

Chapelle, C., & Douglas, D. (2006). *Assessing Language through Computer Technology*. Cambridge, UK: Cambridge University Press. doi:10.1017/CBO9780511733116

Chen, C. H., Ho, C., & Lin, J. (2015). The development of an augmented reality game-based learning environment. *Procedia - Social And Behavioral Sciences, 174*, 216-220. doi:10.1016/j.sbspro.2015.01.649

Cheng, K. K., & Tsai, C. C. (2014). Children and parents reading of an augmented reality picture book: Analyses of behavioral patterns and cognitive attainment. *Computers & Education*, *72*, 302–312. doi:10.1016/j.compedu.2013.12.003

Cheng, K. K., & Tsai, C. C. (2016). The interaction of child-parent shared reading with an augmented reality (AR) picture book and parents' conceptions of AR learning. *British Journal of Educational Technology*, *47*(1), 203–222. doi:10.1111/bjet.12228

Chenowith, N., & Ferdig, R. (2016). Editorial: What we learned about technology and teacher education in 2016. *Journal of Technology and Teacher Education*, *24*(4), 373–382.

Chen, P. S. D., Gonyea, R., & Kuh, G. (2008). Learning at a distance. *Journal of Online Education*, *4*(3). Retrieved from http://innovateonline.info/index.php?view=article&id=438&action=login

Chen, Y. (2013). The possibility of applying YouTube to motivate learning autonomy. *Journal of International Education Research*, *9*(3), 207–216.

Chen, Y. H., & Baker, P. (2010). Lexical bundles in L1 and L2 academic writing. *Language Learning & Technology, 14*(2), 30–49.

Chen, Y., & Lai, H. (2014). The influence of cultural universality and specificity on EFL learners comprehension of metaphor and metonymy. *International Journal of Applied Linguistics, 24*(3), 312–336. doi:10.1111/ijal.12021

Chiang, T. H., Yang, S. J., & Hwang, G. (2014). Students online interactive patterns in augmented reality-based inquiry activities. *Computers & Education, 78*, 97–108. doi:10.1016/j.compedu.2014.05.006

Cho, H., & Gomabon, R. (2017). Engaging urban youth in critical media literacy. In R. Gordon (Ed.), *Challenges associated with cross-cultural and at-risk student engagement* (pp. 149–170). Hershey, PA: IGI Global. doi:10.4018/978-1-5225-1894-5.ch008

Christiansen, M. S., & Bloch, J. (2016). "Papers are never finished, just abandoned": The role of written teacher comments in the revision process. *Journal of Response to Writing, 2*(1), 6–42.

Chun, C. W. (2012). The multimodalities of globalization: Teaching a YouTube video in an EAP classroom. *Research in the Teaching of English, 47*(2), 145–170.

Chun, D., Smith, B., & Kern, R. (2016). Technology in language use, language teaching, and language learning. *Modern Language Journal, 100*(1), 64–80. doi:10.1111/modl.12302

Ciftci, H., & Kocoglu, Z. (2012). Effects of peer e-feedback on Turkish EFL students writing performance. *Journal of Educational Computing Research, 46*(1), 61–84. doi:10.2190/EC.46.1.c

Cifuentes, L., & Shih, Y.-C. D. (2001). Teaching and learning online: A collaboration between United States and Taiwanese students. *Journal of Research on Technology in Education, 33*(4), 456–474.

Clark, C., Chow-Hoy, T., Herter, R., & Moss, P. (2001). Portfolios as sites of learning: Reconceptualizing the connections to motivation and engagement. *Journal of Literacy Research, 33*(2), 211–241. doi:10.1080/10862960109548110

Cmap Home. (2014). *Florida institute for human and machine cognition (IHMC) website*. Retrieved April 20, 2017, from http://cmap.ihmc.us/

Cobb, T. (2002). *Web Vocabprofile* [An adaptation of Heatley, Nation & Coxhead's (2002) *Range*]. Retrieved from http://www.lextutor.ca/vp/

Cockrum, T. (2015, June 11). *Curate or create content in a flipped classroom* [Web log post]. Retrieved from https://flipyourglassroom.com/2015/06/11/curate-or-create-content-in-a-flipped-classroom/

Cockrum, T. (2014). *Flipping your English class to reach all learners: Strategies and lesson plans*. New York, NY: Routledge.

Cohen, A. D., & Robbins, M. (1976). Toward assessing interlanguage performance: The relationship between selected errors, learners characteristics, and learners explanations. *Language Learning, 26*(1), 45–66. doi:10.1111/j.1467-1770.1976.tb00259.x

Cohen, L., Manion, L., & Morrison, K. (2011). *Research methods in education* (7th ed.). London: Routledge.

Coiro, J., Knobel, M., Lankshear, C., & Leu, D. J. (2008). Central issues in new literacies and new literacies research. In J. Coiro, M. Knobel, C. Lankshear, & D. J. Leu (Eds.), *Handbook of research on new literacies* (pp. 1–21). New York, NY: Taylor & Francis Group.

Cole, M. (2009). Using Wiki technology to support student engagement: Lessons from the trenches. *Computers & Education, 52*(1), 141–146. doi:10.1016/j.compedu.2008.07.003

Coleman, V. B. (1972). *A comparison between the relative effectiveness of marginal-interlinear-terminal commentary and of audio-taped commentary in responding to English composition* (Unpublished doctoral dissertation). University of Pittsburgh, Pittsburgh, PA.

Colpaert, J. (2006). Pedagogy-driven design for online language teaching and learning. *CALICO Journal, 23*(3), 477–497. Retrieved from http://www.jstor.org/stable/24156348

Conrad, S. (2009). Corpus-based research is too complicated to be useful for writing teachers. In J. Reid (Ed.), *Writing myths: Applying second language research to classroom teaching* (pp. 115–139). Ann Arbor, MI: University of Michigan Press.

Cope, B., & Kalantzis, M. (Eds.). (2000). *Multiliteracies: Literacy learning and the design of social futures.* New York, NY: Routledge.

Cornillie, F., Thorne, S. L., & Desmet, P. (2012). ReCALL special issue: Digital games for language learning: challenges and opportunities. *ReCALL, 24*(03), 243–256. doi:10.1017/S0958344012000134

Council of Europe, Committee of Ministers. (1998). *Of the committee of ministers to member states concerning modern languages* (Recommendation No. R (98) 6). Retrieved from http://cm.coe.int/ta/rec/1998/98r6.htm

Council of Europe. (2001). *Common European framework of reference for languages: Learning, teaching, assessment.* Cambridge, UK: Cambridge University Press.

Coxhead, A. (2000). A new academic word list. *TESOL Quarterly, 3*(4), 213–238. doi:10.2307/3587951

Coxhead, A., & Byrd, P. (2007). Preparing writing teachers to teach the vocabulary and grammar of academic prose. *Journal of Second Language Writing, 16*(3), 129–147. doi:10.1016/j.jslw.2007.07.002

Crawford-Ferre, H., & Wiest, L. (2012). Effective online instruction in higher education. *The Quarterly Review of Distance Education, 13*(1), 11–14.

Creswell, J. W. (2012). *Educational research: planning, conducting, evaluating quantitative and qualitative research* (4th ed.). Boston, MA: Pearson.

Cruz, J. Q. (2007). Video games and the ESL classroom. *The Internet TESL Journal, 13.* Retrieved from http://iteslj.org/Articles/Quijano-VideoGames.html

Cummins, P. W., & Davesne, C. (2009). Using electronic portfolios for second language assessment. *Modern Language Journal, 93*(1), 848–867. doi:10.1111/j.1540-4781.2009.00977.x

Dalgarno, B. (2001). Interpretations of constructivism and consequences for computer assisted learning. *British Journal of Educational Technology, 32*(2), 193–194. doi:10.1111/1467-8535.00189

Darling-Hammond, L. (2004). Standards, accountability, and school reform. *Teachers College Record, 106*(6), 1047–1085. doi:10.1111/j.1467-9620.2004.00372.x

Dashtestani, R. (2014). English as a foreign language teachers perspectives on implementating online instruction in the Iranian EFL context. *Research in Learning Technology, 22*(1), 1–15. doi:10.3402/rlt.v22.20142

Daud, N. M. (1992). Issues in CALL implementation and its implications on teacher training. *CALICO Journal, 10*(1), 69–78.

Davies, M. (2008) *The Corpus of Contemporary American English: 520 million words, 1990-present.* Retrieved from http://corpus.byu.edu/coca/

Davies, G. D. (1991). Expodisc: An interactive videodisc package for learners of Spanish. In H. Savolainen & J. Telenius (Eds.), *EUROCALL 91: Proceedings* (pp. 133–139). Helsinki, Finland: Helsinki School of Economics.

Davis, B., & Thiede, R. (2000). Writing into change: Style-shifting in asynchronous electronic discourses. In M. Warshauer & R. Kern (Eds.), *Netwok-based language teaching: concepts and practice* (pp. 87–120). Cambridge, UK: Cambridge University Press. doi:10.1017/CBO9781139524735.007

Davis, K. (2009). Agentive youth research: Towards individual, collective, and policy transformations. In T. G. Wiley, J. S. Lee, & R. Rumberger (Eds.), *The education of language minority immigrants in the USA* (pp. 202–239). London: Multilingual Matters.

Davison, C., & Leung, C. (2009). Current issues in English language teacher-based assessment. *TESOL Quarterly*, *43*(3), 393–415. doi:10.1002/j.1545-7249.2009.tb00242.x

de Oliveira, L. C., Maune, M., & Klassen, M. (2014). The Common Core State Standards in English language arts in the United States and teaching English language learners: Focus on writing. *L1-Educational Studies in Language and Literature*, *14*, 1–13. doi:10.17239/L1ESLL-2014.01.01

de Quincey, P. (1986). Stimulating activity: The role of computers in the language classroom. *CALICO Journal*, *4*(1), 55–66.

de Sam Lazaro, F. (Writer), & Woodruff, J. (Anchor & Executive Editor). (n.d.). Young returnees start over in Mexico after growing up in the U.S [TV Episode]. *PBS NewsHour.* Retrieved November 26, 2016 from http://disq.us/p/14hhiy8

De Wit, H., Hunter, F., Howard, L., & Egron-Polak, E. (2015). *Internationalisation of higher education.* Prepared for the European Parliament's Committee on Culture and Education. Policy department B: Structural and cohesion policies. doi:10.2861/444393

Deca, L., Egron-Polak, E., & Fiţ, C. R. (2015). Internationalisation of higher education in Romanian national and institutional contexts. In A. Curaj, L. Deca, E. Egron-Polak, & J. Salmi (Eds.), *Higher education reforms in Romania: Between the Bologna process and national challenges* (pp. 127–148). Dordrecht, The Netherlands: Springer International; doi:10.1007/978-3-319-08054-3_7

Dede, C. (2008). Theoretical perspectives influencing the use of information technology in teaching and learning. In J. Voogt & G. Knezek (Eds.), *International handbook of information technology in primary and secondary education* (pp. 43–62). New York, NY: Springer. doi:10.1007/978-0-387-73315-9_3

Dede, C. (2009). Immersive interfaces for engagement and learning. *Science*, *323*(5910), 66–69. doi:10.1126/science.1167311 PMID:19119219

Desmet, C. (2009). Teaching Shakespeare with YouTube. *English Journal*, *99*(1), 65–70.

Dewey, J. (1959). My pedagogic creed. In J. Dewey (Ed.), *Dewey on education* (pp. 19–32). New York, NY: Teachers College, Columbia University. (Original work published 1897)

Dickinson, L. (1987). *Self-instruction in language learning*. Cambridge, UK: Cambridge University Press.

Dizon, G. (2016). A comparative study of Facebook vs. paper-and-pencil writing to improve L2 writing skills. *Computer Assisted Language Learning*, *29*(8), 1249–1258. doi:10.1080/09588221.2016.1266369

Doman, E., & Webb, M. (2016). The flipped experience for Chinese university students studying English as a foreign language. *TESOL Journal*, *8*(1), 102–141. doi:10.1002/tesj.264

Donato, R. (2000). Sociocultural contributions to understanding the foreign and second language classroom. In J. P. Lantolf (Ed.), *Sociocultural theory and second language learning* (pp. 27–50). Oxford, UK: Oxford University Press.

Dong, Y. R. (2004). Dont keep them in the dark! Teaching metaphors to English language learners. *English Journal*, *93*(4), 29–35. doi:10.2307/4128977

Dörnyei, Z. (2007). Creating a motivating classroom environment. In J. Cummins & C. Davison (Eds.), *International handbook of English language teaching* (Vol. 2, pp. 719–731). New York, NY: Springer; doi:10.1007/978-0-387-46301-8_47

Dorogan, D. (2014). *How to use location-based chat and AR in dating and social*. Retrieved November 22, 2016, from http://quickblox.com/blog/how-to-use-location-based-chat-and-ar-in-dating-and-social/

Doughty, C. (2003). Instructed SLA: Constraints, compensation, enhancement. In C. Doughty & M. Long (Eds.), *The handbook of SLA* (pp. 256–310). London: Wiley Blackwell.

Doughty, C. J., & Long, M. H. (2003). Optimal psycholinguistic environments for distance foreign language learning. *Forum for International Studies*, *23*, 35–73.

Douglas, D. (2000). *Assessing language for specific purposes*. Cambridge, UK: Cambridge University Press.

Douglas, D. (2010). *Understanding language testing*. New York, NY: Routledge.

Douglas, D. (2013). ESP and assessment. In B. Paltridge & S. Starfield (Eds.), *The handbook of English for specific purposes* (pp. 367–384). Oxford, UK: Wiley-Blackwell.

Douglas, J., & Paton, C. (2013). The Cambridge CELTA course online. In B. Tomlinson & C. Whittaker (Eds.), *Blended learning in English language teaching: Course design and implementation* (pp. 111–123). London: British Council.

Ducate, L. C., Anderson, L. L., & Moreno, N. (2011). Wading through the world of wikis: An analysis of three wiki projects. *Foreign Language Annals*, *44*(3), 495–524. doi:10.1111/j.1944-9720.2011.01144.x

Ducate, L., & Arnold, N. (2011). Technology, CALL, and the net generation: Where are we headed from here? In N. Arnold & L. Ducate (Eds.), *Present and future promises of CALL: From theory and research to new directions in language teaching* (pp. 1–22). San Marcos, TX: CALICO.

Dudeney, G., & Hockly, N. (2012). ICT in ELT: How did we get here and where are we going? *ELT Journal*, *66*(4), 533–542. doi:10.1093/elt/ccs050

Dudley-Evans, T., & St John, M. J. (1998). *Developments in English for specific purposes: A multi-disciplinary approach*. Cambridge, UK: Cambridge University Press.

Du, H. S., Chu, S. K. W., Chan, R. C. H., & He, W. (2016). Collaborative writing with wikis: An empirical investigation. *Online Information Review*, *40*(3), 380–399. doi:10.1108/OIR-06-2015-0173

Dunleavy, J., & Milton, P. (2010). Student engagement for effective teaching and deep learning. *Education Canada*, *48*(5), 4–8.

Dunleavy, M., & Dede, C. (2014). Augmented reality teaching and learning. In J. M. Spector, M. D. Merrill, J. Elen, & M. J. Bishop (Eds.), *Handbook of research on educational communications and technology* (4th ed.; pp. 735–745). New York, NY: Springer. doi:10.1007/978-1-4614-3185-5_59

Dunleavy, M., Dede, C., & Mitchell, R. (2009). Affordances and limitations of immersive participatory augmented reality simulations for teaching and learning. *Journal of Science Education and Technology*, *18*(1), 7–22. doi:10.1007/s10956-008-9119-1

Dusek, V. (2006). *Philosophy of technology: An introduction*. Malden, MA: Blackwell.

Early, M., Kendrick, M., & Potts, D. (2015). Multimodality: Out from the margins of English language teaching. *TESOL Quarterly*, *49*(3), 447–460. doi:10.1002/tesq.246

Eckert, P., & McConnell-Ginet, S. (2003). *Language and gender.* Cambridge, UK: Cambridge University Press. doi:10.1017/CBO9780511791147

Egbert, J., & Hanson-Smith, E. (Eds.). (1999). Computers and pedagogy: CALL environments (Research, practice, and critical issues). Alexandria, VA: TESOL.

Egbert, J. (2005). *CALL essentials: Principles and practice in CALL classrooms.* Alexandria, VA: TESOL.

Egbert, J., Herman, D., & Lee, H. (2015). Flipped instruction in English language teacher education: A design-based study in a complex, open-ended learning environment. *The Electronic Journal for English as a Second Language*, *19*(2), 1–23.

Eick, C. J., & King, D. T. Jr. (2012). Nonscience majors' perceptions on the use of YouTube video to support learning in an integrated science lecture. *Journal of College Science Teaching*, *42*(1), 26–30.

Ellis, R. (1999). Theoretical perspective on interaction and language learning. In R. Ellis (Ed.), *Learning a second language through interaction* (pp. 3–32). Philadelphia, PA: John Benjamin; doi:10.1075/sibil.17.04ell

Ellis, R. (2009). A typology of written corrective feedback types. *ELT Journal*, *63*(2), 97–107. doi:10.1093/elt/ccn023

Engeström, Y. (1987). *Learning by expanding: An activity-theoretical approach to developmental research.* Helsinki, Finland: Orienta-Konsultit Oy.

Engeström, Y. (2001). Expansive learning at work: Toward an activity-theoretical perspective. *Journal of Education and Work*, *14*(1), 133–156. doi:10.1080/13639080020028747

England, L. (Ed.). (2012). *Online language teacher education: TESOL perspectives.* New York, NY: Routledge.

English in Action. (2015). *English in Action Teaching and Learning Materials.* Retrieved from http://www.eiabd.com/eia/

Erhel, S., & Jamet, E. (2013). Digital game-based learning: Impact of instructions and feedback on motivation and learning effectiveness. *Computers & Education*, *67*, 156–167. doi:10.1016/j.compedu.2013.02.019

Eurobarometer. (2014). *EU skills panorama. Analytical highlight. Focus on foreign languages.* Retrieved from http://skillspanorama.cedefop.europa.eu/en/analytical_highlights/focus-foreign-languages

European Commission. (2012). *Key data on teaching languages at school in Europe 2012.* Retrieved from https://webgate.ec.europa.eu/fpfis/mwikis/eurydice/index.php/Publications:Key_Data_on_Teaching_Languages_at_School_in_Europe_2012

European Commission. (2013). *European higher education in the world.* Communication from the Commission to the European Parliament, the Council, the European Economic and Social Committee and the Committee of the Regions. Retrieved from eur-lex.europa.eu/LexUriServ/LexUriServ.do?uri=COM:2013:0499:FIN:en:PDF

European Commission. (2014a). *Languages in Education and Training: Final Country Comparative Analysis.* Prepared by the TWG Languages in Education and Training with support by GHK. Retrieved from http://ec.europa.eu/dgs/education_culture

European Commission. (2014b). *Improving the effectiveness of language learning: CLIL and computer assisted language learning.* Retrieved from http://ec.europa.eu/dgs/education_culture

European Commission. (2015). *Study on comparability of language testing in Europe.* Prepared by Cambridge English Language Assessment. doi:10.2766/082033

European Commission. (n.d.). *Languages in education - Education and training*. Retrieved from http://ec.europa.eu/education/policy/multilingualism/languages-in-education_en

Farnsworth, M. B. (1974). The cassette tape recorder: A bonus or a bother in ESL composition correction. *TESOL Quarterly*, *8*(3), 285–291. doi:10.2307/3586172

Fathman, A. K., & Whalley, E. (1990). Teacher response to student writing: Focus on form versus content. In B. Kroll (Ed.), *Second language writing: Research insights for the classroom* (pp. 178–190). Cambridge, UK: Cambridge University Press. doi:10.1017/CBO9781139524551.016

Fazio, L. L. (2001). The effect of corrections and commentaries on the journal writing accuracy of minority- and majority- language students. *Journal of Second Language Writing*, *10*, 235–249.

Feenberg, A. (2012). *Making the gestalt switch*. Paper presented at the Society for Phenomenology and Existential Philosophy Conference, Rochester, NY. Retrieved from https://www.sfu.ca/~andrewf/Don_Ihde.pdf

Fernando, C. (1996). *Idioms and idiomaticity*. Oxford, UK: Oxford University Press.

Ferris, D. R. (2015). Inclusivity through community: Designing 11 response systems for "Mixed" academic writing courses. In M. Roberge, K. M. Losey, & M. Wald (Eds.), Teaching U.S.-educated multilingual writers: Pedagogical practices from and for the classroom (pp. 11–46). Ann Arbor, MI: The University of Michigan Press.

Ferris, D. R. (2003). *Response to student writing*. Mahwah, NJ: Lawrence Erlbaum.

Ferris, D. R. (2006). Does error feedback help student writers? New evidence on the short- and long-term effects of written error correction. In K. Hyland & F. Hyland (Eds.), *Feedback in second language writing: Contexts and issues* (pp. 81–104). New York, NY: Cambridge University Press. doi:10.1017/CBO9781139524742.007

Ferris, D. R., & Hedgcock, J. S. (1998). *Teaching ESL composition: Purpose, process and practice*. Mahwah, NJ: Lawrence Erlbaum Associates.

Ferris, D. R., & Roberts, B. (2001). Error feedback in L2 writing classes: How explicit does it need to be? *Journal of Second Language Writing*, *10*(3), 161–184. doi:10.1016/S1060-3743(01)00039-X

Fethi, K., & Marshall, H. W. (2017). Flipping movies for dynamic engagement. In J. Mehring & A. Leis (Eds.), *Innovations in flipped learning in the language classroom: Theories and practice*. New York, NY: Springer.

Fisher, J., Chouissa, C., Dugovicova, S., & Virkkunen-Fullenwider, A. (2011). *Guidelines for task-based university language testing*. Graz, Austria: European Centre for Modern Languages.

Flipped Learning Global Initiative. (n.d.). *The Flipped Learning Global Initiative*. Retrieved from http://flglobal.org

Flipped Learning Network. (2014). *The Four Pillars of F-L-I-P*. Retrieved from http://flippedlearning.org/definition-of-flipped-learning/

Flowerdew, L. (2003). A combined corpus and systemic-functional analysis of the problem-solution pattern in a student and professional corpus of technical writing. *TESOL Quarterly*, *37*(3), 489–511. doi:10.2307/3588401

Flowerdew, L. (2009). Applying corpus linguistics to pedagogy: A critical evaluation. *International Journal of Corpus Linguistics*, *14*(3), 393–417. doi:10.1075/ijcl.14.3.05flo

Folse, K. (2009). *Keys to teaching grammar to English language learners: A practical handbook*. Ann Arbor, MI: University of Michigan Press.

Folse, K. (2011). Applying L2 lexical research findings in ESL teaching. *TESOL Quarterly*, *45*(2), 362–369. doi:10.5054/tq.2010.254529

Foomani, E. M., & Hedayati, M. (2016). A seamless learning design for mobile assisted language learning: An Iranian context. *English Language Teaching*, *9*(5), 206–213. doi:10.5539/elt.v9n5p206

Fredricks, J. A., Blumfeld, P. C., & Paris, A. H. (2004). School engagement: Potential of the concept, state of the evidence. *Review of Educational Research*, *74*(1), 59–109. doi:10.3102/00346543074001059

Freiberg, J. (2001). Criteria-based assessment in senior high school English: Transcending the textual in search of the magical. In P. Freebody, S. Muspratt, & B. Dwyer (Eds.), *Difference, silence, and textual practice* (pp. 287–322). Cresskill, NJ: Hampton Press.

Gage, N., & Berliner, D. (1992). *Educational psychology* (5th ed.). Princeton, NJ: Houghton Mifflin Company.

Galicia-Ramos, A. J. (2016, October). *Transnational students' influence on the Mexican EFL classroom.* Paper presented at the 2016 MEXTESOL Convention, Monterrey, Mexico.

Gallagher, A. G., & Sullivan, G. C. (2011). *Fundamentals of surgical simulation: Principles and practice.* New York, NY: Springer.

Galvez, H. (2017). Flipped instruction for language learning. In J. P. Loucky & J. L. Ware (Eds.), *Flipped instruction methods and digital technologies in the language learning classroom* (pp. 91–107). Hershey, PA: IGI Global. doi:10.4018/978-1-5225-0824-3.ch004

García, I., Peña-López, I., Johnson, L., Smith, R., Levine, A., & Haywood, K. (2010). *Informe Horizon: Edición Iberoamericana 2010.* Austin, TX: The New Media Consortium.

García, O., & Sylvan, C. E. (2011). Pedagogies and practices in multilingual classrooms: Singularities in pluralities. *Modern Language Journal*, *95*(3), 385–400. doi:10.1111/j.1540-4781.2011.01208.x

Gardner, D., & Davies, M. (2007). Pointing out frequent phrasal verbs: A corpus-based analysis. *TESOL Quarterly*, *41*(2), 339–359. doi:10.1002/j.1545-7249.2007.tb00062.x

Gardner, R. C. (1985). *Social psychology and second language learning: The role of attitudes and motivation.* London: Edward Arnold.

Garrett, N. (2009). Computer-assisted language learning trends and issues revisited: Integrating innovation. *Modern Language Journal*, *93*, 719–740. doi:10.1111/j.1540-4781.2009.00969.x

Garrison, D. R., Anderson, T., & Archer, W. (2000). Critical inquiry in a text-based environment: Computer conferencing in higher education. *The Internet and Higher Education*, *2*(2-3), 1–19. doi:10.1016/S1096-7516(00)00016-6

Garrison, D. R., Anderson, T., & Archer, W. (2001). Critical thinking, cognitive presence, and computer conferencing in distance education. *American Journal of Distance Education*, *15*(1), 7–23. doi:10.1080/08923640109527071

Garrison, D. R., Anderson, T., & Archer, W. (2010). The first decade of the community of inquiry framework: A retrospective. *The Internet and Higher Education*, *13*(1–2), 5–9. doi:10.1016/j.iheduc.2009.10.003

Garrison, D. R., & Arbaugh, J. B. (2007). Researching the community of inquiry framework: Review, issues, and future directions. *The Internet and Higher Education*, *10*(3), 157–172. doi:10.1016/j.iheduc.2007.04.001

Gass, S. (1997). *Input, interaction, and the second language learner.* Mahwah, NJ: Lawrence Erlbaum Associates. doi:10.4324/9780203053560

Gass, S. M. (1997). *Input, interaction and the second language learner*. Mahwah, NJ: Lawrence Erlbaum.

Gass, S. M., Behney, J., & Plonsky, L. (2013). *Second language acquisition: An introductory course* (4th ed.). New York, NY: Routledge.

Gass, S. M., & Mackey, A. (2015). Input, interaction, and output in second language acquisition. In B. VanPatten & J. Williams (Eds.), *Theories in second language acquisition: An introduction* (pp. 180–206). New York, NY: Routledge.

Gass, S. M., & Varonis, E. M. (1994). Input, interaction, and second language production. *Studies in Second Language Acquisition*, *16*(03), 283–302. doi:10.1017/S0272263100013097

Gee, J. (2007). *What Video Games Have to Teach Us about Learning and Literacy*. New York, NY: St Martin's Griffin.

Gee, J. P., & Hayes, E. (2012). Nurturing affinity spaces and game-based learning. In C. Steinkuehler, K. Squire, & S. Barab (Eds.), *Games, learning, and society: Learning and meaning in the digital age* (pp. 129–153). New York, NY: Cambridge University Press. doi:10.1017/CBO9781139031127.015

Geertz, C. (1973). *The interpretation of cultures: Selected essays*. New York, NY: Basic Books.

Gergen, K. (2009). *An invitation to social construction* (2nd ed.). London: Sage Publications.

Gibbs, R. Jr. (2002). A new look at the literal meaning in understanding what is said and implicated. *Journal of Pragmatics*, *34*(4), 457–486. doi:10.1016/S0378-2166(01)00046-7

Gillions, M. (1987). Interactive video in schools: Modern languages project. In E. Brown (Ed.), *CALL Report 5* (pp. 28–30). London: Center for Information on Language Teaching and Research.

Giorguli, S. E., & Gutiérrez, E. (2011). Niños y jóvenes en el contexto de la migración internacional entre México y Estados Unidos. *Coyuntura Demográfica*, *1*, 21–25.

Godwin-Jones, R. (2007). Emerging technologies. Digital video update: YouTube, Flash, High-Definition. *Language Learning & Technology*, *11*(1), 16–21. Retrieved from http://llt.msu.edu/vol11num1/emerging/

Godwin-Jones, R. (2011). Emerging technologies: Mobile apps for language learning. *Language Learning & Technology*, *15*(2), 2 11.

Goertler, S. (2011). Blended and open/online learning: Adapting to a changing world of language teaching. In N. Arnold & L. Ducate (Eds.), *Present and future promises of CALL: From theory and research to new directions in language teaching* (pp. 471–502). San Marcos, TX: CALICO.

Goertler, S. (2012). Theoretical and empirical foundations for blended language learning. In F. Rubio & J. J. Thoms (Eds.), *Hybrid language teaching and learning: Exploring theoretical, pedagogical and curricular issues* (pp. 27–49). Boston, MA: Heinle/Cengage Learning.

Golonka, E. M., Bowles, A. R., Frank, V. M., Richardson, D. L., & Freynik, S. (2014). Technologies for foreign language learning: A review of technology types and their effectiveness. *Computer Assisted Language Learning*, *27*(1), 70–105. doi:10.1080/09588221.2012.700315

Gonzales, R. G., & Chávez, L. R. (2012). Awakening to a Nightmare. *Current Anthropology*, *53*(3), 255–281. doi:10.1086/665414

Gonzalez-Lloret, M. (2016). *A practical guide to integrating technology into task-based language teaching*. Washington, DC: Georgetown University Press.

Gonzalez-Lloret, M., & Ortega, L. (2014). *Technology-mediated TBLT: Researching technology and tasks*. Amsterdam, The Netherlands: John Benjamins Publishing Company. doi:10.1075/tblt.6

Goodfellow, R., Lea, M., Gonzales, E., & Mason, R. (2001). Opportunity and e-quality: Intercultural and linguistic issues in global online learning. *Distance Education*, *22*(1), 65–84. doi:10.1080/0158791010220105

Goodson, F. T. (2007). The electronic portfolio: Shaping an emerging genre. *Journal of Adolescent & Adult Literacy*, *50*(6), 432–434. doi:10.1598/JAAL.50.6.1

Granger, S. (2003). The international corpus of learner English: A new resource for foreign language learning and teaching and second language acquisition. *TESOL Quarterly*, *37*(3), 538–546. doi:10.2307/3588404

Granger, S. (2009). The contribution of learner corpora to second language acquisition and foreign language teaching. *Corpora and Language Teaching*, *33*, 13–32. doi:10.1075/scl.33.04gra

Grant, K., & Lee, V. (2014). Wrestling with issues of diversity in online courses. *Qualitative Report*, *19*(12), 1–25.

Greenberg, A., & Zanetis, J. (2012). *The impact of broadcast and streaming video in education*. Report Commissioned by Cisco Systems Inc. to Wainhouse Research LLC. Retrieved from http://www.cisco.com/web/strategy/docs/education/ciscovideowp.pdf

Hadjerrouit, S. (2013). A framework for assessing the pedagogical effectiveness of wiki-based collaborative writing: Results and implications. In E. Cohen & E. Boyd (Eds.), Proceedings of the Informing Science and Information Technology Education Conference 2013 (pp. 29–49). Informing Science Institute. Retrieved from https://www.learntechlib.org/p/114617

Hadjerrouit, S. (2014). Wiki as a collaborative writing tool in teacher education: Evaluation and suggestions for effective use. *Computers in Human Behavior*, *32*, 301–312. doi:10.1016/j.chb.2013.07.004

Hafner, C. A. (2015). Remix culture and English language teaching: The expression of learner voice in digital multimodal compositions. *TESOL Quarterly*, *49*(3), 486–509. doi:10.1002/tesq.238

Haines, K. J. (2015). Learning to identify and actualize affordances in a new tool. *Language Learning & Technology*, *19*(1), 165–180. Retrieved from http://llt.msu.edu/issues/february2015/haines.pdf

Hall, D., & Knox, J. (2009). Issues in the education of TESOL teachers by distance education. *Distance Education*, *30*(1), 63–85. doi:10.1080/01587910902845964

Hamann, E. T., & Zúñiga, V. (2011). Schooling, National Affinity (ies), and Transnational Students in Mexico. In C. Coe, R. R. Reynolds, D. A. Boehm, J. M. Hess, & H. Rae-Espinoza (Eds.), *Everyday ruptures: Children, youth, and migration in global perspective* (pp. 141–160). Nashville, TN: Vanderbilt University Press.

Hamilton, D. (2009). Blurred in translation: Reflections on pedagogy in public education. *Pedagogy, Culture & Society*, *17*(1), 5–16. doi:10.1080/14681360902742829

Hampel, R. (2003). Theoretical perspectives and new practices in audio-graphic conferencing for language learning. *ReCALL*, *15*(01), 21–36. doi:10.1017/S0958344003000314

Hampel, R. (2006). Rethinking task design for the digital age: A framework for language teaching and learning in a synchronous online environment. *ReCALL*, *18*(01), 105–121. doi:10.1017/S0958344006000711

Hanna, B., & de Nooy, J. (2003). A funny thing happened on the way to the forum: Electronic discussion and foreign language learning. *Language Learning & Technology*, *7*(1), 71–85.

Han, Y. J. (2015). Successfully flipping the ESL classroom for learner autonomy. *NYS TESOL Journal*, *2*(98), 98–109.

Harklau, L. (2003). Representational practices and multi-model communication in U.S. high schools: Implications for adolescent immigrants. In R. Bayley & S. R. Schecter (Eds.), *Language socialization in bilingual and multilingual societies* (pp. 83–97). Clevedon, UK: Multilingual Matters.

Harmer, J. (2007). *How to teach English*. London, UK: Longman.

Harrison, J., & Shi, H. (2016). English language learners in Higher Education: An exploratory conversation. *Journal of International Students*, *2*, 415–430.

Hasko, V. (2013). Capturing the dynamics of second language development via learner corpus research: A very long engagement. *Modern Language Journal*, *97*(S1), 1–10. doi:10.1111/j.1540-4781.2012.01425.x

Hatami, S. (2015). Teaching formulaic sequences in the ESL classroom. *TESOL Journal*, *6*(1), 112–129. doi:10.1002/tesj.143

Hatch, J. A. (2002). *Doing qualitative research in education settings*. Albany, NY: State University of New York Press.

Hattie, J., & Timperley, H. (2007). The power of feedback. *Review of Educational Research*, *77*(1), 81–112. doi:10.3102/003465430298487

Hawisher, G. E., & Selfe, C. L. (1997). Wedding the technologies of writing portfolios and computers. In K. B. Yancey & T. Weiser (Eds.), *Situating portfolios: Four perspectives* (pp. 305–321). Logan, UT: Utah State University Press.

Hayati, A., Jalilifar, A., & Mashhadi, A. (2013). Using short message service (SMS) to teach English idioms to EFL students. *British Journal of Educational Technology*, *44*(1), 66–81. doi:10.1111/j.1467-8535.2011.01260.x

Healey, D., Hanson-Smith, E., Hubbard, P., Ioannou-Georgiou, S., Kessler, G., & Ware, P. (2011). *TESOL technology standards: Description, implementation, integration*. Alexandria, VA: TESOL.

Heath, S. B. (1983). *Ways with words: Language, life, and work in communities and classrooms*. New York, NY: Cambridge University Press.

Heatley, A., Nation, I. S. P., & Coxhead, A. (2002). *Range and frequency programs*. Retrieved from http://www.victoria.ac.nz/lals/staff/paul-nation.aspx

Higgins, J., & Johns, T. (1984). *Computers in language learning*. London: Collins.

Hinkel, E. (2001). Matters of cohesion in L2 academic texts. *Applied Language Learning*, *12*(2), Ill-132.

Hinkel, E. (2011). What research on second language writing tells us and what it doesn't. In E. Hinkel (Ed.), *Handbook of research on second language teaching and learning* (Vol. 2, pp. 523–538). New York, NY: Routledge/Taylor & Francis.

Hinkel, E. (2013). Research findings on teaching grammar for academic writing. *English Teaching*, *68*(4), 3–21. doi:10.15858/engtea.68.4.201312.3

Hockly, N. (2015). Developments in online language learning. *ELT Journal*, *69*(3), 308–313. doi:10.1093/elt/ccv020

Holden, C. L., & Sykes, J. M. (2011). Leveraging mobile games for place-based language learning. *International Journal of Game-Based Learning*, *1*(2), 1–18. doi:10.4018/ijgbl.2011040101

Holmes, J. (1988). Doubt and certainty in ESL textbooks. *Applied Linguistics*, *9*(1), 21–44. doi:10.1093/applin/9.1.21

Holmes, T. (2016). PBLA: Moving toward sustainability. *TESL Canada Journal*, *32*(Special issue), 113–123. doi:10.18806/tesl.v32i0.1220

House, J. (2003). English as a lingua franca: A threat to multilingualism? *Journal of Sociolinguistics*, *7*(4), 556–578. doi:10.1111/j.1467-9841.2003.00242.x

Hsieh, J. S. C., Wu, W. V., & Marek, M. W. (2016). Using the flipped classroom to enhance EFL learning. *Computer Assisted Language Learning*, 1–25. doi:10.1080/09588221.2015.1111910

Hsu, C. K., Hwang, G. J., Chang, Y. T., & Chang, C. K. (2013). Effects of video caption modes on English listening comprehension and vocabulary acquisition using handheld devices. *Journal of Educational Technology & Society*, *16*(1), 403–414.

Hsu, H., Wang, S., & Comac, L. (2008). Using audioblogs to assist English-language learning: An investigation into student perception. *Computer Assisted Language Learning*, *21*(2), 181–198. doi:10.1080/09588220801943775

Huang, S. (2000). *A quantitative analysis of audiotaped and written feedback produced for students writing and student' perceptions of the two feedback methods*. ERIC Document Reproductive Service. (ED448604)

Hubbard, P. (2008). Twenty-five years of theory in the CALICO Journal. *CALICO Journal 25*(3), 387-399. Retrieved from https://www.calico.org/html/article_707.pdf

Hubbard, P. (2016). *An invitation to CALL: Foundations in computer-assisted language learning*. Retrieved from: http://www.stanford.edu/~efs/callcourse2/CALL6.htm

Hubbard, P. (2016). Unit 6-CALL theory and research. In *An invitation to CALL*. Retrieved from http://web.stanford.edu/~efs/callcourse2/CALL6.htm

Hubbard, P. (2004). Learner training for effective use of CALL. In S. Fotos & C. Browne (Eds.), *New perspectives on CALL for second language classrooms* (pp. 45–67). Mahwah, NJ: Lawrence Erlbaum.

Hubbard, P. (2008). CALL and the future of language teacher education. *CALICO Journal*, *25*(2), 175–188.

Hubbard, P. (2008). Twenty-five years of theory in the CALICO Journal. *CALICO Journal*, *25*(3), 387–399. doi:10.1007/978-94-009-8831-6

Hubbard, P. (2009a). Developing CALL theory: A new frontier. *Proceedings of the JALTCALL Conference*, 1-6.

Hubbard, P. (Ed.). (2009b). Computer assisted language learning: Vol. 1. *Critical concepts in linguistics*. London: Routledge.

Hubbard, P., & Levy, M. (2006). The scope of CALL education. In P. Hubbard & M. Levy (Eds.), *Teacher education in CALL* (pp. 3–20). Amsterdam, The Netherlands: John Benjamins. doi:10.1075/lllt.14.04hub

Hubbard, P., & Levy, M. (2016). Theory in computer-assisted language learning research and practice. In F. Farr & L. Murray (Eds.), *The Routledge handbook of language learning and technology* (pp. 24–38). New York, NY: Routledge.

Huh, K., & Hu, W.-C. (2005). Criteria for effective CALL research. In J. L. Egbert & G. M. Petrie (Eds.), *CALL research perspectives* (pp. 9–21). Mahwah, NJ: Lawrence Erlbaum.

Hung, H. (2015). Flipping the classroom for English language learners to foster active learning. *Computer Assisted Language Learning*, *28*(1), 81–96. doi:10.1080/09588221.2014.967701

Hung, H. (2017). Design-based research: Redesign of an English language course using a flipped classroom approach. *TESOL Quarterly*, *51*(1), 180–192. doi:10.1002/tesq.328

Hussey, K., & Katz, A. (2009). Perception of the use of metaphor by an interlocutor in discourse. *Metaphor and Symbol*, *24*(4), 203–236. doi:10.1080/10926480903310237

Hutchinson, T., & Waters, A. (1987). *English for specific purposes: A learning-centred approach*. Cambridge, UK: Cambridge University Press. doi:10.1017/CBO9780511733031

Hyland, K. (2005). Stance and engagement: A model of interaction in academic discourse. *Discourse Studies*, *7*(2), 173–192. doi:10.1177/1461445605050365

Hyland, K., & Hyland, F. (Eds.). (2006). *Feedback in second language writing: Contexts and issues*. New York, NY: Cambridge University Press. doi:10.1017/CBO9781139524742

Ice, P. (2008, April). *The impact of asynchronous audio feedback on teaching, social and cognitive presence*. Paper presented at the First International Conference of the Canadian Network for Innovation in Education, Banff, Alberta, Canada.

Ice, P., Curtis, R., Phillips, P., & Wells, J. (2007). Using asynchronous audio feedback to enhance teaching presence and students' sense of community. *Journal of Asynchronous Learning Networks*, *11*(2), 3–25.

Ice, P., Swan, K., Diaz, S., Kupczynski, L., & Swan-Dagen, A. (2010). An analysis of students perceptions of the value and efficacy of instructors auditory and text-based feedback modalities across multiple conceptual levels. *Journal of Educational Computing Research*, *43*(1), 113–134. doi:10.2190/EC.43.1.g

Ice, P., Swan, K., Kupczynski, L., & Richardson, J. (2008, June). The impact of asynchronous audio feedback on teaching and social presence: A survey of current research. *Proceedings of World Conference on Educational Multimedia, Hypermedia and Telecommunications*, 5646-5649.

ICT Home. (2017). *Use of ICT in support of language teaching and learning website*. Retrieved April 20, 2017, from http://ict-rev.ecml.at/

Ihde, D. (1990). *Technology and the lifeworld*. Bloomington, IN: Indiana University Press.

Inamorato dos Santos, A., Punie, Y., & Castaño-Muñoz, J. (2016). *Opening up education: A support framework for higher education institutions*. JRC Science for Policy Report, EUR 27938 EN. doi:10.2791/293408

Institute for International Education (IIE). (2015). Retrieved from http://www.iie.org/Services/Project-Atlas/United-States/International-Students-In-US#.WErZizvnvdk

Institute of International Education. (2016). *Open Doors 2016 "Fast Facts"*. Retrieved March 14, 2017, from http://www.iie.org/Research-and-Publications/Open-Doors

Jacot, M. T., Noren, J., & Berge, Z. L. (2014). The flipped classroom in training and development: Fad or the future? *Performance Improvement*, *53*(9), 23–28. doi:10.1002/pfi.21438

Jafari, A., & Kaufman, C. (Eds.). (2006). *Handbook of research on ePortfolios*. Hershey, PA: Idea Group. doi:10.4018/978-1-59140-890-1

Jaffar, A. A. (2012). YouTube: An emerging tool in anatomy education. *Anatomical Sciences Education*, *5*(3), 158–164. doi:10.1002/ase.1268 PMID:22383096

Jamaludin, R., & Osman, S. Z. M. (2014). The use of a flipped classroom to enhance engagement and promote active learning. *Journal of Education and Practice*, *5*(2), 124–131.

Jarvis, H. (2005). Technology and change in English language teaching. *The Asian EFL Journal Quarterly*, *7*(4), 213–227.

Jelfs, A., & Whitelock, D. (2000). The notion of presence in virtual environments: What makes the environment real. *British Journal of Educational Technology*, *31*(2), 145–153. doi:10.1111/1467-8535.00145

Jiang, M., & Ting, E. (2000). A study of factors influencing students' perceived learning in a web-based course environment. *International Journal of Educational Telecommunications*, *6*(4), 317–338.

Johanson, R. (1999). *Rethinking the red ink: Audio-feedback in the ESL writing classroom.* ERIC Document Reproductive Service. (ED 467865)

Johns, A. (1997). *Text, role, and context: Developing academic literacies.* Cambridge, UK: Cambridge University Press; doi:10.1017/CBO9781139524650

Johnson, N. (1987). Current uses of computers in ESOL instruction in the U.S. *CALICO Journal*, *5*(2), 71–77.

Johnston, N., & Karafotias, T. (2016). Flipping the classroom to meet the diverse learning needs of library and information studies (LIS) students. *Journal of Education for Library and Information Science*, *57*(3), 226–238. doi:10.12783/issn.2328-2967/57/3/1

Jordan, R. R. (1997). *English for academic purposes: A guide and resource book for teachers.* Cambridge, UK: Cambridge University Press. doi:10.1017/CBO9780511733062

Kachru, B. (1992). *The other tongue: English across cultures* (2nd ed.). Urbana, IL: University of Illinois Press.

Kamhi-Stein, L. (2000). Looking to the future of TESOL teacher education: Web-based bulletin board discussions in a method course. *TESOL Quarterly*, *34*(3), 423–455. doi:10.2307/3587738

Kanno, Y., & Norton, B. (2003). Imagined communities and educational possibilities: Introduction. *Journal of Language, Identity, and Education*, *2*(4), 241–249. doi:10.1207/S15327701JLIE0204_1

Kanno, Y., & Varghese, M. M. (2010). Immigrant and refugee ESL students challenges to accessing four-year college education: From language policy to educational policy. *Journal of Language, Identity, and Education*, *9*(5), 310–328. doi:10.1080/15348458.2010.517693

Kanuka, H., Liam, R., & Laflamme, E. (2007). The influence of instructional methods on the quality of online discussion. *British Journal of Educational Technology*, *38*(2), 260–271. doi:10.1111/j.1467-8535.2006.00620.x

Kear, K., Chetwynd, F., Williams, J., & Donelan, H. (2012). Web conferencing for synchronous online tutorials: Perspectives of tutors using a new medium. *Computers & Education*, *58*(3), 953–963. doi:10.1016/j.compedu.2011.10.015

Keneman, A., & Waller, R. (2016). Augmented reality in the classroom. *Literacy Practice & Research*, *41*(3), 5–8.

Kennedy, G. (1998). *An introduction to corpus linguistics.* London: Longman.

Kern, N. (2013). Blended learning: Podcasts for taxi drivers. In B. Tomlinson & C. Whittaker (Eds.), *Blended learning in English language teaching: Course design and implementation* (pp. 131–139). London: British Council.

Kern, N. (2013). Technology-integrated English for specific purposes lessons: Real-life language, tasks, and tools for professionals. In G. Motteram (Ed.), *Innovations in learning technologies for English language teaching* (pp. 87–115). London: British Council.

Kern, R. (2006). Perspectives on technology in learning and teaching languages. *TESOL Quarterly*, *40*(1), 183–210. doi:10.2307/40264516

Kern, R., & Warschauer, M. (2000). Theory and practice of network-based language teaching. In M. Warschauer & R. Kern (Eds.), *Network-based language teaching – Concepts and practice* (pp. 1–19). Cambridge, UK: Cambridge University Press. doi:10.1017/CBO9781139524735.003

Kessler, G. (2006). Assessing CALL teacher training: What are we doing and what could we do better? In P. Hubbard & M. Levy (Eds.), *Teacher education in CALL* (pp. 23–42). Amsterdam: John Benjamins. doi:10.1075/lllt.14.05kes

Kessler, G. (2007). Formal and informal CALL preparation and teacher attitude toward technology. *Computer Assisted Language Learning, 21*(3), 173–188. doi:10.1080/09588220701331394

Kessler, G. (2009). Student-initiated attention to form in wiki-based collaborative writing. *Language Learning & Technology, 13*(1), 79–95. Retrieved from http://llt.msu.edu/vol13num1/kessler.pdf

Kessler, G., & Bikowski, D. (2010). Developing collaborative autonomous learning abilities in computer mediated language learning: Attention to meaning among students in wiki space. *Computer Assisted Language Learning, 23*(1), 41–58. doi:10.1080/09588220903467335

Kessler, G., Bikowski, D., & Boggs, J. (2012). Collaborative writing among second language learners in academic web-based projects. *Language Learning & Technology, 16*(1), 91–109. Retrieved from http://llt.msu.edu/issues/february2012/kesslerbikowskiboggs.pdf

Kiernan, P. J., & Aizawa, K. (2004). Cell phones in task based learning: Are cell phones useful language learning tools? *ReCALL, 16*(01), 71–84. doi:10.1017/S0958344004000618

Kim, H.-J. (2014). The use of technology for learner autonomy in language classrooms. *ITBE Link, 42*(3). Retrieved from http://www.itbe.org/v_newsletters/article_23358209.htm

King, A. (1993). From sage on the stage to guide on the side. *College Teaching, 41*(1), 30–35. doi:10.1080/87567555.1993.9926781

Kirschner, P. A., van den Brink, H., & Meester, M. (1991). Audiotape feedback for essays in distance education. *Innovative Higher Education, 15*(2), 185–195. doi:10.1007/BF00898030

Klopfer, E., & Squire, K. (2008). Environmental detectives—the development of an augmented reality platform for environmental simulations. *Educational Technology Research and Development, 56*(2), 203–228. doi:10.1007/s11423-007-9037-6

Knobel, M., & Lankshear, C. (2014). Studying new literacies. *Journal of Adolescent & Adult Literacy, 58*(2), 97–101. doi:10.1002/jaal.314

Ko, C. J. (2012). A case study of language learners social presence in synchronous CMC. *ReCALL, 24*(01), 66–84. doi:10.1017/S0958344011000292

Kohn, A. (2000). Burnt at the high stakes. *Journal of Teacher Education, 51*(4), 315–327. doi:10.1177/0022487100051004007

Kon, C. K. (2002). *The influence on outcomes of ESL students' performance strategies on a CALL listening comprehension activity* (Unpublished master's thesis). Iowa State University, Ames, IA.

Kongmee, I., Strachan, R., Montgomery, C., & Pickard, A. (2011). *Using massively multiplayer online role playing games (MMORPGs) to support second language learning: Action research in the real and virtual world.* Retrieved from http://nrl.northumbria.ac.uk/279/1/kongmee%20iverg%20paper2.pdf

Kornum, L. (1993). Foreign language teaching and learning in a multimedia environment. *CALICO Journal, 10*(3), 65–76.

Kostka, I., & Voss, E. (2016). *Flipping the classroom to teach English for Academic Purposes.* Paper presented at the TESOL 2016 International Convention and English Language Expo, Baltimore, MD.

Kostka, I., & Brinks Lockwood, R. (2015). What's on the Internet for flipping English language instruction? *The Electronic Journal for English as a Second Language, 19*(2), 1–12.

Koukal, D. R. (2003). Review of the book American philosophy of technology: The empirical turn, edited by H. Achterhuis. Technology and Culture, 44(1), 225-226.

Kouritzin, S. G. (2002). The personal, practical, and professional rewards of teaching MA-TESOL courses online. *TESOL Quarterly*, *36*(4), 621–624. doi:10.2307/3588244

Koutromanos, G., Sofos, A., & Avraamidou, L. (2015). The use of augmented realty games: A review of the literature. *Educational Media International*, *52*(4), 253–271. doi:10.1080/09523987.2015.1125988

Kozan, K., & Richardson, J. C. (2014). Interrelationships between and among social, teaching, and cognitive presence. *The Internet and Higher Education*, *21*, 68–73. doi:10.1016/j.iheduc.2013.10.007

Kramsch, C. (1997). The privilege of the nonnative speaker. *PMLA. Publications of the Modern Language Association of America*, *112*(3), 359.

Kramsch, C., & Thorne, S. (2002). Foreign language learning as a global communicative practice. In D. Block & D. Cameron (Eds.), *Globalization and language teaching* (pp. 83–100). London, UK: Routledge.

Kramsch, C., & Thorne, S. (2002). Foreign language learning as global communicative practice. In D. Block & D. Cameron (Eds.), *Language learning and teaching in the age of globalization* (pp. 83–100). London, UK: Routledge.

Krashen, S. D. (1982). *Principles and practice in second language acquisition.* Oxford, UK: Pergamon.

Krause, K. L. (2005). *Understanding and promoting student engagement in university learning communities.* Paper presented at the Sharing Scholarship in Learning and Teaching: Engaging Students Conference, James Cook University (Townsville Campus), Queensland, Australia.

Kress, G. (2011). Discourse analysis and education: A multimodal social semiotic approach. In R. Rogers (Ed.), *An introduction to critical discourse analysis in education* (pp. 205–226). New York, NY: Routledge.

Küçük, S., Yýlmaz, R. M., & Göktaþ, Y. (2014). Augmented reality for learning English: Achievement, attitude and cognitive load levels of students. *Education & Science, 39*(176), 393. doi:10.15390/EB.2014.3595

Ku, D. T., Huang, Y.-H., & Hus, S.-C. (2015). The effects of GBL and learning styles on Chinese idiom by using TUI device. *Journal of Computer Assisted Learning*, *31*(6), 505–515. doi:10.1111/jcal.12085

Kuh, G. D. (2003). *What we're learning about student engagement from NSSE.* EBSCO Publishing.

Kuh, G. D. (2009). The national survey of student engagement: Conceptual and empirical foundations. *New Directions for Institutional Research, 2009*(141), 5–20. doi:10.1002/ir.283

Kumaravadivelu, B. (2006). *Understanding language teaching: From method to postmethod.* Mahwah, NJ: Lawrence Erlbaum.

Kuo, L. (2009). *The effects of YouTube listening/viewing activities on Taiwanese EFL learners' listening comprehension* (Doctoral dissertation). Available from ERIC Document Reproduction Service. (ED 535284)

Kuteeva, M. (2011). Wikis and academic writing: Changing the writer–reader relationship. *English for Specific Purposes*, *30*(1), 44–57. doi:10.1016/j.esp.2010.04.007

Kvashnina, O. S., & Martynko, E. A. (2016). Analyzing the potential of flipped classroom in ESL teaching. *International Journal of Emerging Technologies in Learning*, *11*(3), 71–73. doi:10.3991/ijet.v11i03.5309

Lage, M. J., Platt, G. J., & Treglia, M. (2000). Inverting the classroom: A gateway to creating an inclusive learning environment. *The Journal of Economic Education*, *31*(1), 30–43. doi:10.1080/00220480009596759

Lai, C., Lei, C., & Liu, Y. (2016). The nature of collaboration and perceived learning in wiki-based collaborative writing. *Australasian Journal of Educational Technology*, *32*(3), 80–95. doi:10.14742/ajet.2586

Laird, T. F., Shoup, R., & Kuh, G. D. (2005). Measuring deep approaches to learning using the National Survey of Student Engagement. *The Annual Meeting of the Association for Institutional Research*, 1-28.

Lakarnchua, O., & Reinders, H. (2014). Implementing mobile language learning with an augmented reality activity. *Modern English Teacher*, *23*(2), 42–50.

Lakhani, N. (2015). Deported to Mexico: A lost generation. *The Guardian, 17*. Retrieved March 22, 2017 from https://www.theguardian.com/global/2015/may/17/deported-to-mexico-immigration-america

Lalande, J. F. II. (1982). Reducing composition errors: An experiment. *Modern Language Journal*, *66*(2), 140–149. doi:10.1111/j.1540-4781.1982.tb06973.x

Lambert, J., & Fisher, J. (2013). Community of inquiry framework: Establishing community in an online course. *Journal of Interactive Learning Online*, *12*(1), 1–16.

Lam, R., & Lee, I. (2010). Balancing the dual functions of portfolio assessment. *ELT Journal*, *64*(1), 54–64. doi:10.1093/elt/ccp024

Lankshear, C., & Knobel, M. (2011). *New literacies: Everyday practices and classroom learning* (3rd ed.). Maidenhead, UK: Open University Press.

Lantolf, J., & Poehner, J. P. (2014). *Sociocultural theory and the pedagogical imperative in L2 education*. New York, NY: Routledge. doi:10.4324/9780203813850

Lara-Prieto, V., Bravo-Quirino, E., Rivera-Campa, M. Á., & Gutiérrez-Arredondo, J. E. (2015). An innovative self-learning approach to 3D printing using multimedia and augmented reality on mobile devices. *Procedia Computer Science, 75*, 59-65. doi:10.1016/j.procs.2015.12.206

Larsen-Freeman, D., & Anderson, M. (2011). *Techniques and principles in language teaching*. Oxford, UK: Oxford University Press.

Laufer, B., & Waldman, T. (2011). Verb-noun collocations in second language writing: A corpus analysis of learners English. *Language Learning*, *61*(2), 647–672. doi:10.1111/j.1467-9922.2010.00621.x

Lave, J., & Wenger, E. (1991). *Situated learning: Legitimate peripheral participation*. Cambridge, UK: Cambridge University Press. doi:10.1017/CBO9780511815355

Lawrence, G. (2014). A call for the human feel in today's increasingly blended world. *Contact - Refereed Proceedings of TESL Ontario Research Symposium, 40*(2), 128-141.

Lawrence, G. (2013). A working model for intercultural learning and engagement in collaborative online language learning environments. *Intercultural Education*, *24*(4), 303–314. doi:10.1080/14675986.2013.809247

Lawrence, G., Young, C., Owen, H., & Compton, C. (2009). Using wikis for collaborative writing and intercultural learning. In M. Dantas-Whitney & S. Rilling (Eds.), *Authenticity in the adult language classroom* (pp. 199–212). Alexandria, VA: TESOL.

Leech, G. (1998). Preface. In S. Granger (Ed.), *Learner English on computer*. London: Longman.

Lee, H., & Wang, P. (2013). Discussing the factors contributing to students involvement in an EFL collaborative wiki project. *ReCALL*, *25*(2), 233–249. doi:10.1017/S0958344013000025

Lee, L. (2001). Online interaction: Negotiation of meaning and strategies used among learners of Spanish. *ReCALL, 13*(02), 232–244. doi:10.1017/S0958344001000829a

Lee, L. (2016). Autonomous learning through task-based instruction in fully online language courses. *Language Learning & Technology, 20*(2), 81–97. Retrieved from http://llt.msu.edu/issues/june2016/lee.pdf

Lehman, R. (2006). The role of emotion in creating instructor and learner presence in the distance education experience. *Journal of Cognitive Affective Learning, 2*(2), 12–26.

Lehman, R. M., & Conceição, S. C. O. (2010). *Creating a sense of presence in online teaching*. San Francisco, CA: Jossey-Bass.

Leis, A., Tohei, A. A., & Cooke, S. (2015). The effects of flipped classrooms on English composition writing in an EFL environment. *International Journal of Computer-Assisted Language Learning and Teaching, 5*(4), 37–51. doi:10.4018/IJCALLT.2015100103

Leont'ev, A. N. (1978). *Activity, consciousness, and personality*. Englewood Cliffs, NJ: Prentice-Hall.

Lessard-Clouston, M. (2012). Word Lists for vocabulary learning and teaching. *CATESOL Journal, 24*(1), 287–304.

Levy, M. (1997). *CALL: Context and conceptualization*. Oxford, UK: Oxford University Press.

Levy, M., & Stockwell, G. (2006). *Call dimensions: Options and issued in computer assisted language learning*. New York, NY: Lawrence Erlbaum Associates. doi:10.4324/9780203708200

Levy, M., & Stockwell, G. (2006). *CALL dimensions: Options and issues in computer-assisted language learning*. Mahwah, NJ: Lawrence Erlbaum.

Lewis, R., Luk, R. W. P., & Ng, A. B. Y. (1998). Computer-assisted learning of Chinese idioms. *Journal of Computer Assisted Learning, 14*(1), 2–18. doi:10.1046/j.1365-2729.1998.1410002.x

Li, H., & Lin, Q. (2007). The role of revision and teacher feedback in a Chinese college context. *Asian EFL Journal, 9*(4), 230–239.

Li, M. (2013). Individual novices and collective experts: Collective scaffolding in wiki-based small group writing. *System, 41*(3), 752–769. doi:10.1016/j.system.2013.07.021

Li, M., & Zhu, W. (2013). Patterns of computer-mediated interaction in small writing groups using wikis. *Computer Assisted Language Learning, 26*(1), 61–82. doi:10.1080/09588221.2011.631142

Lincoln, Y. S., & Guba, E. G. (1985). *Naturalistic inquiry*. Beverly Hills, CA: Sage Publications.

Lin, H., & Kelsey, K. (2009). Building a networked environment in wikis: The evolving phases of collaborative learning in a wiki-book project. *Journal of Educational Computing Research, 40*(2), 145–169. doi:10.2190/EC.40.2.a

Lin, M. H., & Lee, J. (2015). Data-driven learning: Changing the teaching of grammar in EFL classes. *ELT Journal, 69*(3), 264–274. doi:10.1093/elt/ccv010

Liontas, J. I. (2002c). Context and idiom understanding in second languages. In S. H. Foster-Cohen, T. Ruthenberg, & M-L. Poschen (Eds.), *EUROSLA yearbook: Annual conference of the European second language association* (vol. 2, pp. 155-185). Philadelphia, PA: John Benjamins Publishing Company. doi:10.1075/eurosla.2.11lio

Liontas, J. I. (2002d). Reading between the lines: Detecting, decoding, and understanding idioms in second languages. In J. H. Sullivan (Ed.), Literacy and the second language learner: Vol. 1. Research in second language learning (pp. 177-216). Greenwich, CT: Information Age Publishing Inc.

Liontas, J. I. (2008). Toward a critical pedagogy of idiomaticity. *Indian Journal of Applied Linguistics, 34*(1-2), 11-30.

Liontas, J. I. (2001a). Reading and multimedia annotations: Going beyond bells and whistles, hot links and pop-up windows. *The IALL Journal of Language Learning Technologies*, *33*(1), 53–78.

Liontas, J. I. (2001b). That's all Greek to me! The comprehension and interpretation of Modern Greek phrasal idioms. *The Reading Matrix: An International Online Journal*, *1*(1), 1–32.

Liontas, J. I. (2002a). CALL media digital technology: Whither in the new millennium? *CALICO Journal*, *19*(2), 315–330.

Liontas, J. I. (2002b). Vivid phrasal idioms and the lexical-image continuum. *Issues in Applied Linguistics*, *13*(1), 71–109.

Liontas, J. I. (2002e). Transactional idiom analysis: Theory and practice. *Journal of Language and Linguistics*, *1*(1), 17–53.

Liontas, J. I. (2002f). Exploring second language learners notions of idiomaticity. *System: An International Journal of Educational Technology and Applied Linguistics*, *30*(3), 289–313. doi:10.1016/S0346-251X(02)00016-7

Liontas, J. I. (2003). Killing two birds with one stone: Understanding Spanish VP idioms in and out of context. *Hispania*, *86*(2), 289–301. doi:10.2307/20062862

Liontas, J. I. (2006). Artificial intelligence and idiomaticity. *The APAMALL Higher Education Journal*: *Language Learning & Technology*, *1*(1), 1–33.

Liontas, J. I. (2007). The eye never sees what the brain understands: Making sense of idioms in second languages. *Lingua et Linguistica*, *1*(2), 25–44.

Liontas, J. I. (2015a). Developing idiomatic competence in the ESOL classroom: A pragmatic account. *TESOL Journal*, *6*(4), 621–658. doi:10.1002/tesj.230

Liontas, J. I. (2015b). Straight from the horse's mouth: Idiomaticity revisited. In R. R. Heredia & A. B. Cieślicka (Eds.), *Bilingual figurative language processing* (pp. 301–340). New York, NY: Cambridge University Press; doi:10.1017/CBO9781139342100.016

Liontas, J. I. (2017in press). Let the games begin! Harnessing the power of gaming in second language education. In A. Faravani, H. R. Kargozari, M. Zeraatpishe, & M. Azarnoosh (Eds.), *Issues in SLA research: Syllabus designing and curriculum development*. Rotterdam, The Netherlands: SENSE Publishers B.V.

Liszewski, A. (2015). *Lucasfilm is making amazing Star Wars and Jurassic Park VR experiences*. Retrieved November 22, 2016, from http://gizmodo.com/fx-wizards-are-making-amazing-star-wars-and-jurassic-pa-1710872285

Little, D. (1991). *Learner autonomy 1: Definitions, issues and problems*. Dublin, Ireland: Authentik.

Little, D. (2005). The common European framework and the European language portfolio: Involving learners and their judgements in the assessment process. *Language Testing*, *22*(3), 321–336. doi:10.1191/0265532205lt311oa

Littlewood, W. (1999). Defining and developing autonomy in East Asian contexts. *Applied Linguistics*, *20*(1), 71–94. doi:10.1093/applin/20.1.71

Liu, D. (2003). The most frequently used spoken American English idioms: A corpus analysis and its implications. *TESOL Quarterly*, *37*(4), 671–700. doi:10.2307/3588217

Liu, D., & Jiang, P. (2009). Using a corpus-Based lexicogrammatical approach to grammar instruction in EFL and ESL contexts. *Modern Language Journal*, *93*(1), 61–78. doi:10.1111/j.1540-4781.2009.00828.x

Liu, P.-H. E., & Tsai, M.-K. (2013). Using augmented-reality-based mobile learning material in EFL English composition: An exploratory case study. *British Journal of Educational Technology*, *44*(1), E1–E4. doi:10.1111/j.1467-8535.2012.01302.x

Liu, T. Y. (2009). A context-aware ubiquitous learning environment for language listening and speaking. *Journal of Computer Assisted Learning*, *25*(6), 515–527. doi:10.1111/j.1365-2729.2009.00329.x

Liu, T., Tan, T., & Chu, Y. (2010). QR code and augmented reality-supported mobile English learning system. *Lecture Notes in Computer Science*, *5960*, 37–52. doi:10.1007/978-3-642-12349-8_3

Liu, X., Liu, S., Lee, S., & Magjuka, R. J. (2010). Cultural differences in online learning: Interna- tional student perceptions. *Journal of Educational Technology & Society*, *13*(3), 177–188.

Liu, Y., Holden, D., & Zheng, D. (2016). Analyzing students language learning experience in an augmented reality mobile game: An exploration of an emergent learning environment. *Procedia: Social and Behavioral Sciences*, *228*, 369–374. doi:10.1016/j.sbspro.2016.07.055

Logan, R. (2012). Using YouTube in perioperative nursing education. *AORN*, *95*(4), 474–481. doi:10.1016/j.aorn.2012.01.023 PMID:22464620

Lomicka, L., & Lord, G. (2009). Introduction to social networking, collaboration, and Web 2.0 tools. In L. Lomicka & G. Lord (Eds.), *The next generation: Social networking and online collaboration in foreign language learning* (pp. 1–11). San Marcos, TX: CALICO.

Long, M. H. (1983). Linguistic and conversational adjustments to non-nativespeakers. *Studies in Second Language Acquisition*, *5*(2), 177–193. doi:10.1017/S0272263100004848

Long, M. H. (1996). The role of linguistic environment in second language acquisition. In W. C. Ritchie & T. K. Bhatia (Eds.), *Handbook of second language acquisition* (pp. 413–468). San Diego, CA: Academic Press. doi:10.1016/B978-012589042-7/50015-3

Luke, C. L., & Britten, J. S. (2007). The expanding role of technology in foreign language teacher education programs. *CALICO Journal*, *24*(2), 253–267.

Lund, A. (2008). Wikis: A collective approach to language production. *ReCALL*, *20*(1), 35–54. doi:10.1017/S0958344008000414

Macaro, E., Handley, Z., & Walter, C. (2012). A systematic review of CALL in English as a second language: Focus on primary and secondary education. *Language Teaching, 45*(1), 1-43. https://doi.org/10.1017/S0261444811000395

Macis, M., & Schmitt, N. (2016). Not just 'small potatoes': Knowledge of the idiomatic meanings of collocations. *Language Teaching Research*, 1–20. doi:10.1177/1362168816645957

Magrath, W. (2001). A return to interactivity: The third wave in educational uses of information technology. *CALICO Journal*, *18*(2), 283–294.

Mahadzir, N. N. N., & Phung, L. F. (2013). The use of augmented reality pop-up book to increase motivation in English language learning for national primary school. *IOSR Journal of Research & Method in Education*, *1*(1), 26–38.

Majid, N. (2011). The Use of Information Technology in Teaching English: An Attemptto Develop Student-Centered Learning at Telkom Polytechnic. *Prosidingkonferensi Nasional ICT-M Politeknit Telkom (KNIP)*. Retrieved from http://openjournal.politekniktelkom.ac.id/

Malt, B. C., & Eiter, B. (2004). Even with a green card, you can be put out to pasture and still have to work: Non-native intuitions of the transparency of common English idioms. *Journal of Memory and Cognition*, *32*(6), 896–904. doi:10.3758/BF03196868 PMID:15673178

Manara, C. (2014). “That’s what worries me”: Tensions in English language education in today’s Indonesia. *International Journal of Innovation in English Language Teaching and Research*, *3*(1), 21–35.

Marshall, H. W. (2014). *Three reasons to flip your ESL classroom.* Retrieved from http://newsmanager.commpartners.com/tesolc/issues/2014-02-01/2.html

Marshall, H. W. (2016). *Flipping the online learning space.* Paper presented at FlipCon 2016, Allen, TX. Retrieved from http://www.tesl-ej.org/wordpress/issues/volume19/ej74/ej74int/

Marshall, H. W., & Kostka, I. (2017). *Flipped learning in TESOL: The first five years.* Paper presented at the TESOL 2017 International Convention and English Language Expo, Seattle, WA.

Martinez, R., & Murphy, V. A. (2011). Effect of frequency and idiomaticity on second language reading comprehension. *TESOL Quarterly*, *45*(2), 267–290. doi:10.5054/tq.2011.247708

Martinez, R., & Schmitt, N. (2012). A phrasal expressions list. *Applied Linguistics*, *33*(3), 299–320. doi:10.1093/applin/ams010

Masduqi, H. (2014). EFL reading in Indonesian universities: Perspectives and challenges in cultural contexts. *Journal of Teacher Education*, *3*(03), 385–397.

Mason, L. (2016). McLuhans challenge to critical media literacy: The City as Classroom textbook. *Curriculum Inquiry*, *46*(1), 79–97. doi:10.1080/03626784.2015.1113511

Mayora, C. A. (2009). Using YouTube to encourage authentic writing in EFL classrooms. *TESL Reporter*, *42*(1), 1–12.

Mazur, E. (1997). *Peer instruction.* Upper Saddle River, NJ: Prentice Hall.

McCarthy, M., & Carter, R. (1995). Spoken grammar: What is it and how can we teach it? *ELT Journal*, *49*(3), 207–218. doi:10.1093/elt/49.3.207

McConnell-Ginet, S. (2003). What’s in a name? Social labeling and gender practices. In J. Holmes & M. Meyerhoff (Eds.), *The handbook of language and gender* (pp. 69–97). Oxford, UK: Blackwell. doi:10.1002/9780470756942.ch3

McFarlane, K. (2009). *Using audio feedback for summative purposes.* Retrieved March 14, 2017, from http://www.keele.ac.uk/depts/aa/landt/projects/projectreports/talwt/A15-KathrynMcFarlane-TaLwTportfolio.pdf

McGrew, J. B. (1969). *An experiment to assess the effectiveness of the dictation machine as an aid to teachers in the evaluations and improvement of student compositions.* Report to Lincoln Public Schools, Lincoln, NE. ERIC Document Reproductive Service. (ED 034776)

McKalin, V. (2014). *Augmented Reality vs. Virtual Reality: What are the differences and similarities?.* Retrieved November 22, 2016, from http://www.techtimes.com/articles/5078/20140406/augmented-reality-vs-virtual-reality-what-are-the-differences-and-similarities.htm

Medina, D., & Menjívar, C. (2015). The context of return migration: Challenges of mixed-status families in Mexicos schools. *Ethnic and Racial Studies*, *38*(12), 2123–2139. doi:10.1080/01419870.2015.1036091

Mehring, J. G. (2015). *An exploratory study of the lived experiences of Japanese undergraduate EFL students in the flipped classroom* (Unpublished doctoral dissertation). Pepperdine University, Malibu, CA.

Mehring, J. G. (2016). Present research on the flipped classroom and potential tools for the ESL classroom. *Computers in the Schools*, *33*(1), 1–10. doi:10.1080/07380569.2016.1139912

Menken, K. (2008). *English learners left behind: Standardized testing as language policy*. Clevedon, UK: Multilingual Matters.

Merriam, S. B. (2009). *Qualitative research and case study applications in education*. San Francisco, CA: Jossey-Bass Publishers.

Meskill, C., & Ranglova, K. (2000). Curriculum innovation in TEFL: A study of technologies supporting socio-collaborative language learning in Bulgaria. In M. Warschauer & R. Kern (Eds.), *Network-based language teaching: Concepts and practice* (pp. 20–40). Cambridge, UK: Cambridge University press. doi:10.1017/CBO9781139524735.004

Mihăeş, L. (2016). The emergence of English as a medium of instruction and its impact on the English for specific purposes class. *Proceedings of the 8th international conference on education and new learning technologies*, 7169-7176. doi:10.21125/edulearn.2016.0563

Mihăeş, L., & Ionita, D. (2016). Task-based approach revisited: A guide of good practices for university English teaching and assessing (The University of Bucharest). *Proceedings of the 8th international conference on education and new learning technologies*, 6087-6094. doi:10.21125/edulearn.2016.0303

Miles, M. B., & Huberman, A. M. (1994). *Qualitative data analysis* (2nd ed.). Thousand Oaks, CA: Sage Publications.

Milman, N. (2012). The flipped classroom strategy: What is it and how can it be used? *Distance Learning*, *9*(3), 85–87.

MMORPGs for Language Learning. (n.d.). Retrieved December 16, 2015, from http://positivevideogaming.web.unc.edu/mmorpgs-for-language-learning/

Moje, E. B., Ciechanowski, K. M., Kramer, K., Ellis, L., Carrillo, R., & Collazo, T. (2004). Working toward third space in content area literacy: An examination of everyday funds of knowledge and discourse. *Reading Research Quarterly*, *39*(1), 38–70. doi:10.1598/RRQ.39.1.4

Moodle Statistics. (n.d.). Retrieved from https://moodle.net/stats/

Moore, G. E. (1977). Providing instructional feedback to students in education classes. West Lafayette, IN: Purdue University. ERIC Document Reproduction Service. (ED 173309)

Morgan, G. L. (2008). *Improving student engagement: Use of the interactive whiteboard as an instructional tool to improve engagement and behavior in the junior high school* (Unpublished doctoral dissertation). Liberty University, Lynchburg, VA.

Morgan, B. (2010). Fostering conceptual roles for change: Identity and agency in ESEA teacher preparation. *Kritika Kultura*, *15*, 34–55.

Morrell, E., Duenas, R., Garcia, V., & Lopez, J. (2013). *Critical media pedagogy: Teaching for achievement in city schools*. New York, NY: Teachers College Press.

Motteram, G. (2013). Introduction. In G. Motteram (Ed.), *Innovations in learning technologies for English language teaching* (pp. 5–14). London: British Council.

Mullen, T., Appel, C., & Shanklin, T. (2009). Skypebased tandem language learning and web 2.0. In M. Thomas (Ed.), *Handbook of research on web 2.0 and second language learning* (pp. 101–118). Hershey, PA: IGI Global; doi:10.4018/978-1-60566-190-2.ch006

Murray, D. (2013). A case for online English language teacher education. Monterey, CA: Trustees of the International Research Foundation.

Murray, D. E., & Christison, M. A. (2017). Going online: Affordances and limitations for teachers and teacher educators. In K. Hyland & L. Wong (Eds.), *Faces of English education: Students, teachers and pedagogy*. London: Continuum.

Murray, D. E., & Christison, M. A. (in press). Online language teacher education (OLTE): Participants' experiences and perspectives. *The International Research Foundation for English Language Education.*

Murray, G. L. (1999). Autonomy and language learning in a simulated environment. *System*, *27*(3), 295–308. doi:10.1016/S0346-251X(99)00026-3

Musallam, R. (2011). A pedagogy-first approach to the flipped classroom. *OnCUE*, *35*(1), 6–8.

Myers, C., & Jones, T. B. (1993). *Promoting active learning: Strategies for the college classroom.* San Francisco, CA: Jossey-Bass.

Nakamaru, S. (2012). Investment and return: Wiki engagement in a remedial ESL writing course. *Journal of Research on Technology in Education*, *44*(4), 273–291. doi:10.1080/15391523.2012.10782591

National Education Law no. 1/2011.

Nation, P. (2007). The four strands. *International Journal of Innovation in Language Learning and Teaching*, *1*(1), 2–13. doi:10.2167/illt039.0

Neill, D. M., & Medina, N. J. (1989). Standardized testing: Harmful to educational health. *Phi Delta Kappan*, *70*, 688–697.

Nemec, E. C., & Dintzner, M. (2016). Comparison of audio versus written feedback on writing assignments. *Currents in Pharmacy Teaching and Learning*, *8*(2), 155–159. doi:10.1016/j.cptl.2015.12.009

New London Group. (1996). A pedagogy of multiliteracies: Designing social futures. *Harvard Educational Review*, *66*(1), 60–92. doi:10.17763/haer.66.1.17370n67v22j160u

Nicolson, M., Murphy, L., & Southgate, M. (Eds.). (2011). *Language teaching in blended contexts.* Edinburgh, UK: Dunedin Academic Press.

Norton, B. (2000). *Identity and language learning: Gender, ethnicity and educational change.* New York, NY: Longman.

Norton, B. (2001). Non-participation, imagined communities and the language classroom. In M. P. Breen (Ed.), *Learner contributions to language learning: New directions in research* (pp. 159–171). Essex, UK: Pearson Education.

Norton, B., & Nunan, D. (2002). Teaching MA-TESOL courses online: Challenges and rewards. *TESOL Quarterly*, *36*(4), 617–621. doi:10.2307/3588243

Nunan, D. (1987). Communicative language teaching: Making it work. *ELT Journal*, *41*(2), 136–145. doi:10.1093/elt/41.2.136

Nunan, D. (1999). A foot in the world of ideas: Graduate study through the Internet. *Language Learning & Technology*, *3*(1), 52–74.

Nunan, D. (2004). *Task-Based Language Teaching.* Cambridge, UK: Cambridge University Press. doi:10.1017/CBO9780511667336

O'Dowd, R. (2007). *Online intercultural exchange: An introduction for language teachers.* Clevedon, UK: Multilingual Matters.

O'Flaherty, J., & Phillips, C. (2015). The use of flipped classrooms in higher education: A scoping review. *The Internet and Higher Education*, *25*, 85–95. doi:10.1016/j.iheduc.2015.02.002

O'Keeffe, A., McCarthy, M., & Carter, R. (2007). *From corpus to classroom: Language use and language teaching.* Cambridge, UK: Cambridge University Press. doi:10.1017/CBO9780511497650

OECD. (2005). *E-learning in tertiary education: Where do we stand?* Paris, France: OECD.

Ohta, A. S. (2000). Re-thinking interaction in SLA: Developmentally appropriate assistance in the zone of proximal development and the acquisition of L2 grammar. In J. P. Lantolf (Ed.), *Sociocultural theory and second language learning* (pp. 51–78). Oxford, UK: Oxford University Press.

Olesova, L. (2013). *Feedback in Online Course for Non-Native-English-Speaking Students.* Newcastle upon Tyne, UK: Cambridge Scholars Publishing.

Oliver, A., Osa, J. O., & Walker, T. M. (2012). Using instructional technologies to enhance teaching and learning for the 21st century pre K-12 students: The case of a professional education programs unit. *International Journal of Instructional Media, 39*(4), 283–295.

Oliver, M. (2011). Technological determinism in educational technology research: Some alternative ways of thinking about the relationship between learning and technology. *Journal of Computer Assisted Learning, 27*(5), 373–384. doi:10.1111/j.1365-2729.2011.00406.x

Omidian, T., Shahriari, H., & Ghonsooly, B. (2016). *Evaluating the pedagogic value of multi-word expressions based on EFL teachers' and advanced learners' value judgments. TESOL Journal.* doi:10.1002/tesj.284

Oomen-Early, J., Bold, M., Wiginton, K. L., Gallien, T. L., & Anderson, N. (2008). Using asynchronous audio communication (AAC) in the online classroom: A comparative study. *Journal of Online Learning and Teaching, 4*(3).

Ornberg Berglund, T. (2009). Multimodal student interaction online: An ecological perspective. *ReCALL, 21*(2), 186–205. doi:10.1017/S0958344009000184

Ortega, L. (2009). *Understanding second language acquisition.* London: Hodder Education.

Ortiz Navarrete, M., & Ferreira Cabrera, A. (2014). Proposing a wiki-based technique for collaborative essay writing. *Profile Issues in Teachers' Professional Development, 16*(2), 185–198. doi:10.15446/profile.v16n2.38877

Osman, M. E. (2005). Students' reaction to WebCT: Implications for designing online learning environments. *International Journal of Instructional Media, 32*(4), 353–362.

Oxford, R. L. (2001). Language learning styles and strategies. In M. Celce-Murcia (Ed.), *Teaching English as a second or foreign language* (pp. 359–366). Boston, MA: Heinle & Heinle.

Palmer, B. C., Shackelford, V. S., Miller, S. C., & Leclere, J. T. (2007). Bridging two worlds: Reading comprehension, figurative language instruction, and the English-language learner. *Journal of Adolescent & Adult Literacy, 50*(4), 258–267. doi:10.1598/JAAL.50.4.2

Papastergiou, M. (2009). Digital game-based learning in high school computer science education: Impact on educational effectiveness and student motivation. *Computers & Education, 52*(1), 1–12. doi:10.1016/j.compedu.2008.06.004

Patrie, K. (1989). The use of the tape recorder in an ESL composition programme. *TESL Canada Journal, 6*(2), 87–89. doi:10.18806/tesl.v6i2.554

Pawan, F., Wiechart, K., Warren, A., & Park, J. (2016). *Pedagogy and practice for online English language teacher education.* Alexanderia, VA: TESOL Press.

Peachey, N. (2013). A blended learning teacher development course for the development of blended learning in English language teaching. In B. Tomlinson & C. Whittaker (Eds.), *Blended learning in English language teaching: Course design and implementation* (pp. 65–73). London: British Council.

Peirce, B. N. (1995). Social identity, investment, and language learning. *TESOL Quarterly*, *29*(1), 9–31. doi:10.2307/3587803

Pence, H. E. (2011). Smartphones, smart objects, and augmented reality. *The Reference Librarian*, *52*(1-2), 136–145. doi:10.1080/02763877.2011.528281

Penttinen, E., Rossi, M., & Tuunainen, V. K. (2010). Mobile games: Analyzing the needs and values of the consumers. *Journal of Information Technology Theory and Application*, *11*(1), 2.

Perren, J., & Wurr, A. J. (2015). *Learning the language of global citizenship: Strengthening service-learning in TESOL.* Champaign, IL: Common Ground Publishing.

Peterson, M. (2010). Massively multiplayer online role-playing games as arenas for second language learning. *Computer Assisted Language Learning*, *23*(5), 429–439. doi:10.1080/09588221.2010.520673

Peterson, M. (2011). Digital gaming and second language development: Japanese learners interactions in a MMORPG. *Digital Culture & Education*, *3*(1), 56–73.

Peterson, M. (2012). Learner interaction in massively multiplayer online role playing game (MMORPG): A sociocultural discourse analysis. *ReCALL*, *24*(03), 361–380. doi:10.1017/S0958344012000195

Peterson, M. (2016). The use of massively multiplayer online role-playing games in CALL: An analysis of research. *Computer Assisted Language Learning*, *29*(7), 1181–1194. doi:10.1080/09588221.2016.1197949

Pica, T. (1994). Research on negotiation: What does it reveal about second-language learning conditions, processes, and outcomes. *Language Learning*, *44*(3), 493–527. doi:10.1111/j.1467-1770.1994.tb01115.x

Pica, T., Lincoln-Porter, F., Paninos, D., & Linneln, J. (1996). Language learners interaction: How does it address the input, output, and feedback needs of L2 learners? *TESOL Quarterly*, *30*(1), 59–84. doi:10.2307/3587607

Picciano, A. (2009). Blending with purpose: The multimodal model. *Journal of the Research Center for Educational Technology*, *5*(1), 4–14.

Pirahsteh, P. (2014). Computer-assisted language learning (CALL) on learning grammar by Iranian EFL learners. *Social and Behavioral Sciences*, *98*, 1422–1427.

Plass, J. L., Chun, D. M., Mayer, R. E., & Leutner, D. (1998). Supporting visual and verbal learning in a second-language multimedia learning environment. *Journal of Educational Psychology*, *90*(1), 25–36. doi:10.1037/0022-0663.90.1.25

Prensky, M. (2001). Digital natives, digital immigrants (Part 1). *On the Horizon*, *9*(5), 1–6. doi:10.1108/10748120110424816

Priestley, M., Biesta, G., & Robinson, S. (2015). *Teacher agency: An ecological approach.* London: Bloomsbury.

Priestley, M., Edwards, R., Priestley, A., & Miller, K. (2012). Teacher agency in curriculum making: Agents of change and spaces for manoeuvre. *Curriculum Inquiry*, *42*(2), 191–214. doi:10.1111/j.1467-873X.2012.00588.x

Prihatin, P. N. (2012). *The computer integration into EFL instruction in Indonesia: An analysis of two university instructors in integrating computer technology into EFL instruction to encourage students' language learning engagement* (Unpublished doctoral dissertation). Loyola University, Chicago, IL.

Przymus, S. D. (2015). Imagining and moving beyond the ESL bubble: Observing changes in identity, power, and language acquisition through the ELL Ambassadors Program. In M. Lengeling & I. Pablo (Eds.), *Perspectives on Qualitative Research* (pp. 501–516). Guanajuato: Universidad de Guanajuato Press.

Przymus, S. D. (2016). Challenging the monolingual paradigm in secondary dual-language instruction: Reducing language-as-problem with the 2–1-L2 model. *Bilingual Research Journal*, *39*(3-4), 279–295. doi:10.1080/15235882.2016.1220995

Przymus, S. D. (2016). Imagining and moving beyond the ESL bubble: Facilitating communities of practice through the ELL Ambassadors program. *Journal of Language, Identity, and Education*, *15*(5), 265–279. doi:10.1080/15348458.2016.1213133

Rahimi, M. (2009). The role of teachers corrective feedback in improving Iranian EFL learners writing accuracy over time: Is learners mother tongue relevant? *Reading and Writing*, *22*(2), 219–243. doi:10.1007/s11145-008-9139-5

Rankin, Y. A., McNeal, M., & Shute, M. W. (2008). User centered game design: Evaluating massive multiplayer online role playing games for second language acquisition. In *Sandbox Symposium*, (pp. 43-49). Los Angeles, CA: Association for Computing Machinery. doi:10.1145/1401843.1401851

Rea-Dickins, P. (2001). Mirror, mirror on the wall: Identifying processes of classroom assessment. *Language Testing*, *18*(4), 429–462. doi:10.1191/026553201682430120

Read, J. (2004). Research in teaching vocabulary. *Annual Review of Applied Linguistics*, *24*, 146–161. doi:10.1017/S0267190504000078

Reinders, H., & Hubbard, P. (2013). CALL and learner autonomy: Affordances and constraints. In M. Thomas, H. Reinders, & M. Warschauer (Eds.), *Contemporary computer assisted language learning* (pp. 359–375). London: Bloomsbury.

Reinders, H., & White, C. (2011). Learner autonomy and new learning environments. *Language Learning & Technology*, *15*(3), 1–3.

Reinhardt, J., & Sykes, J. M. (2014). Special issue commentary: Digital game activity in L2 teaching and learning. *Language Learning & Technology*, *18*(2), 2–8. Retrieved from http://llt.msu.edu/issues/june2014/commentary.pdf

Reppen, R., & Gordon, D. (2011). *Grammar and Beyond Level 2 Student's Book*. Cambridge, UK: Cambridge University Press.

Retinschi, S. (1979). *English for Intermediate and advanced students.* Bucuresti: Universitatea din Bucuresti.

Rian, J. P., Hinkelman, D., & McGarty, G. (2012). Integrating video assessment into an oral presentation course. In A. Stewart & N. Sonda (Eds.), *JALT 2011 Conference Proceedings* (pp. 416-425). Tokyo, Japan: JALT.

Richards, J. C. (2001). *Curriculum Development in Language Teaching*. Cambridge, UK: Cambridge University Press; doi:10.1017/CBO9780511667220

Richards, J. C., & Rodgers, T. S. (2001). *Approaches and methods in language teaching* (2nd ed.). Cambridge, UK: Cambridge University Press. doi:10.1017/CBO9780511667305

Richardson, D. (2016). Exploring the potential of a location based augmented reality game for language learning. *International Journal of Game-Based Learning*, *6*(3), 34–49. doi:10.4018/IJGBL.2016070103

Richardson, J., & Swan, K. (2003). An examination of social presence in online learning: Students' perceived learning and satisfaction. *Journal of Asynchronous Learning Networks*, *7*(1), 68–88. Retrieved from http://hdl.handle.net/2142/18713

Rilling, S., Dahlman, A., Dodson, S., Boyles, C., & Pazvant, O. (2005). Connecting CALL theory and practice in pre-service teacher education and beyond: Processes and products. *CALICO Journal*, *22*(2), 213–235.

Robb, T., Ross, S., & Shortreed, I. (1986). Salience of feedback on error and its effect on EFL writing quality. *TESOL Quarterly*, *20*(1), 83–95. doi:10.2307/3586390

Rodriguez-Buitrago, C. (2016). *Raising EFL teacher-researchers.* Paper presented at the 3rd Symposium on Innovative Pedagogical Project Implementations, Bogotá, Colombia.

Rogers, R. (Ed.). (2011). *An introduction to critical discourse analysis in education.* New York, NY: Routledge.

Römer, U., & Wulff, S. (2010). Applying corpus methods to written academic texts: Explorations of MICUSP. *Journal of Writing Research*, *2*(2), 99–127. doi:10.17239/jowr-2010.02.02.2

Romova, Z., & Andrew, M. (2011). Teaching and assessing academic writing via the portfolio: Benefits for learners of English as an additional language. *Assessing Writing*, *16*(2), 111–122. doi:10.1016/j.asw.2011.02.005

Rott, S., & Weber, E. D. (2013). Preparing students to use wiki software as a collaborative learning tool. *CALICO Journal*, *30*(2), 179–203. doi:10.11139/cj.30.2.179-203

Rouviere, N. (2012, November 10). ChineseCUBES review: A novel way to start learning Chinese. *Confused Laowai.* Retrieved March 5, 2017, from http://confusedlaowai.com/2012/11/chinesecubes-review/

Rubio, F., & Thoms, J. (Eds.). (2013). *Hybrid language teaching and learning: Exploring theoretical, pedagogical, and curricular issues.* Boston, MA: Heinle/Cengage Learning.

Rubio, F., & Thoms, J. J. (Eds.). (2012). *Hybrid language teaching and learning: Exploring theoretical, pedagogical and curricular issues.* Boston, MA: Heinle/Cengage Learning.

Ruiz, R. (1984). Orientations in language planning. *NABE Journal*, *8*(2), 15–34.

Sa'd, S. H. (2014). Implementing Internet-based EFL teaching in Iran: (Dis)advantages, obstacles, and challenges from EFL learners' viewpoint. *Journal of Language and Literature Education*, *10*, 24–40.

Saito, H. (1994). Teachers' practices and students' preferences for feedback on second language writing: A case study of adult ESL learners. *TESL Canada Journal/Revue TESL du Canada*, *11*(2), 46-68.

Saito, H. (2008). EFL classroom peer assessment: Training effects on rating and commenting. *Language Testing*, *25*(4), 553–581. doi:10.1177/0265532208094276

Salaberry, M. R. (1996). A theoretical foundation for the development of pedagogical tasks in computer mediated communication. *CALICO Journal*, *14*(1), 5–34.

Salmasi, M., Bonyadi, A., & Alavinia, P. (2015). CALL-assissted enhancement of gramatical accuracy: Iranian EFL learners studying in rural settings. *Theory and Practice in Language Studies*, *5*(4), 765–772. doi:10.17507/tpls.0504.12

Sanchez-Garcia, J., Hamann, E. T., & Zuniga, V. (2012). What the youngest transnational students have to say about their transition from US schools to Mexican ones. *Diaspora, Indigenous, and Minority Education*, *6*(3), 157–171. doi:10.1080/15595692.2012.691135

Santos, M., Lübke, A., Taketomi, T., Yamamoto, G., Rodrigo, M., Sandor, C., & Kato, H. (2016). Augmented reality as multimedia: The case for situated vocabulary learning. *Research & Practice in Technology Enhanced Learning*, *11*(1), 1. doi:10.1186/s41039-016-0028-2

Schachter, J. (1983). Nutritional needs of language learners. In M. Clarke & J. Handscombe (Eds.), On TESOL '82: Pacific Perspectives on Language Learning and Teaching (pp. 175-189). Washington, DC: TESOL.

Schauer, G. A. (2006). Pragmatic awareness in ESL and EFL contexts: Contrast and development. *Language Learning*, *56*(2), 269–318. doi:10.1111/j.0023-8333.2006.00348.x

Schieffelin, B. B., & Ochs, E. (1986). Language socialization. *Annual Review of Anthropology*, *15*(1), 163–191. doi:10.1146/annurev.an.15.100186.001115

Schneider, E. W., & Bennion, J. L. (1984). Veni, Vidi, Vici, via videodisc: A simulator for instructional courseware. In D. H. Wyatt (Ed.), *Computer assisted language instruction* (pp. 41–46). Oxford, UK: Pergamon Press.

Scholz, K., & Schulze, M. (2017). Digital-gaming trajectories and second language development. *Language Learning & Technology*, *21*(1), 100–120.

Schön, D. (1983). *The reflective practitioner: How professionals think in action*. New York, NY: Basic Books.

Schultz, J. M. (2000). Computers and collaborative writing in the foreign language curriculum. In M. Warschauer & R. Kern (Eds.), *Network-based language teaching: Concepts and practice* (pp. 20–40). Cambridge, UK: Cambridge University press. doi:10.1017/CBO9781139524735.008

Seidlhofer, B. (2004). Research perspectives on teaching English as a lingua franca. *Annual Review of Applied Linguistics*, *24*, 209–239. doi:10.1017/S0267190504000145

Selingo, J. J. (2015). *The view from the top: What presidents think about financial sustainability, student outcomes, and the future of higher education.* Washington, DC: The Chronicle of Higher Education, Inc.

Selwyn, N. (2008). From state-of-the-art to state-of-the-actual? Introduction to a special issue. *Technology, Pedagogy and Education*, *17*(2), 83–87. doi:10.1080/14759390802098573

Servon, L. J. (2008). *Bridging the digital divide: Technology, community and public policy*. Malden, MA: Blackwell Publishing.

Shafiee, S., Koosha, M., & Afghari, A. (2015). CALL, prewriting strategies, and EFL writing quantity. *English Language Teaching*, *8*(2), 170-177.

Shanahan, L. E. (2013). Composing kid-friendly multimodal text: When conversations, instruction, and signs come together. *Written Communication*, *30*(2), 194–227. doi:10.1177/0741088313480328

Shapiro, S., & Leopold, L. (2012). A critical role for role-playing pedagogy. *TESL Canada Journal*, *29*(2), 120. doi:10.18806/tesl.v29i2.1104

Shea, P., & Bidjerano, T. (2009). Community of inquiry as a theoretical framework to foster epistemic engagement and cognitive presence in online education. *Computers & Education*, *52*(3), 543–553. doi:10.1016/j.compedu.2008.10.007

Sheen, Y. (2007). The effect of focused written corrective feedback and language aptitude on ESL learners acquisition of articles. *TESOL Quarterly*, *41*(2), 255–283. doi:10.1002/j.1545-7249.2007.tb00059.x

Sheen, Y., Wright, D., & Moldawa, A. (2009). Differential effects of focused and unfocused written correction on the accurate use of grammatical forms by adult ESL learners. *System*, *37*(4), 556–569. doi:10.1016/j.system.2009.09.002

Shin, D., & Nation, P. (2008). Beyond single words: The most frequent collocations in spoken English. *ELT Journal*, *62*(4), 339–348. doi:10.1093/elt/ccm091

Shohamy, E. (2011). Assessing multilingual competencies: Adopting construct valid assessment policies. *Modern Language Journal*, *95*(3), 418–429. doi:10.1111/j.1540-4781.2011.01210.x

Short, J., Williams, E., & Christie, B. (1976). *The social psychology of telecommunications*. London, UK: John Wiley & Sons.

Simonsson, M., Kupczynski, L., Ice, P., & Pankake, A. (2009, April). *The impact of asynchronous audio feedback in the dissertation advising process*. Paper presented at the American Educational Research Association Annual Meeting, San Diego, CA.

Singhal, S., Bagga, S., Goyal, P., & Saxena, V. (2012). Augmented chemistry: Interactive education system. *International Journal of Computers and Applications*, *49*(15), 1–5. doi:10.5120/7700-1041

Sloan Consortium. (2005). *Growing by degrees: Online education in the United States, 2005*. Retrieved from http://sloanconsortium.org/sites/default/files/growing_by_degrees_1.pdf

Smaldino, S. E., Lowther, D. L., Mims, C., & Russell, J. D. (2015). *Instructional technology and media for learning*. Upper Saddle River, NJ: Pearson Education.

Smart, J. (2014). The role of guided induction in paper-based data-driven learning. *ReCALL*, *26*(2), 184–201. doi:10.1017/S0958344014000081

Smith, B. (2003). Computer-mediated negotiated interaction: An expended model. *Modern Language Journal*, *87*(1), 38–57. doi:10.1111/1540-4781.00177

Smith, B. (2016). *Technology in language learning: An overview*. New York, NY: Routledge.

Solak, E., & Cakir, R. (2015). Exploring the effect of materials designed with augmented reality on language learners' vocabulary learning. *The Journal of Educators Online*, *13*(2), 50–72.

Solak, E., & Erdem, G. (2015). A content analysis of virtual reality studies in foreign language education. *Participatory Educational Research*, *2*(2), 21–26. doi:10.17275/per.15.spi.2.3

Squire, K. (2010). From information to experience: Place-based augmented reality games as a model for learning in a globally networked society. *Teachers College Record*, *112*(10), 2565–2602.

Stanford, J. (2009). *Moodle 1.9 for second language teaching*. Birmingham, UK: Packt Publishing Ltd.

Starhawk. (1988). *Dreaming the dark: Magic, sex, and politics*. Boston, MA: Beacon Press.

Stern, L. A., & Solomon, A. (2006). Effective faculty feedback: The road less traveled. *Assessing Writing*, *11*(1), 22–41. doi:10.1016/j.asw.2005.12.001

Stickler, U., & Shi, L. (2016). TELL us about CALL: An introduction to the Virtual Special Issue (VSI) on the development of technology enhanced and computer assisted language learning published in the System Journal. *System*, *56*, 119–126. doi:10.1016/j.system.2015.12.004

Stoddart, A., Chan, J. Y., & Liu, G. (2016). Enhancing successful outcomes of wiki-based collaborative writing: A state-of-the art review of facilitation frameworks. *Interactive Learning Environments*, *24*(1), 142–157. doi:10.1080/10494820.2013.825810

Stoks, G. (1993). Integrating new technologies into the modern languages curriculum. *CALICO Journal*, *11*(1), 76–93.

Storch, N. (2002). Patterns of interaction in ESL pair work. *Language Learning*, *52*(1), 119–158. doi:10.1111/1467-9922.00179

Storch, N. (2011). Collaborative writing in L2 contexts: Processes, outcomes, and future directions. *Annual Review of Applied Linguistics*, *31*, 275–288. doi:10.1017/S0267190511000079

Strevens, P. (1988). ESP after twenty years: A re-appraisal. In M. Tickoo (Ed.), *ESP: State of the Art* (pp. 1–13). Singapore: SEAMEO Regional Centre.

Swain, M. (1985). Communicative competence: Some roles of comprehensible input and comprehensible output in its development. In S. Gass & C. Madden (Eds.), *Input in Second Language Acquisition* (pp. 235–256). New York, NY: Newbury House Publishers.

Swain, M. (2000). The output hypothesis and beyond: Mediating acquisition through collaborative dialogue. In J. Lantolf (Ed.), *Sociocultural theory and second language learning* (pp. 97–114). Oxford, UK: Oxford University Press.

Swain, M. (2006). Languaging, agency and collaboration in advanced second language learning. In H. Byrnes (Ed.), *Advanced language learning: The contribution of Halliday and Vygotsky* (pp. 95–108). London, UK: Continuum.

Swain, M., & Deters, P. (2007). New mainstream SLA theory: Expanded and enriched. *Modern Language Journal*, *91*(5), 820–836. doi:10.1111/j.1540-4781.2007.00671.x

Swain, M., & Lapkin, S. (1995). Problems in output and the cognitive processes they generate: A step towards second language learning. *Applied Linguistics*, *16*(3), 371–391. doi:10.1093/applin/16.3.371

Swales, J. M. (1988). *Episodes in ESP: A source and reference book on the development of English for Science and Technology*. New York, NY: Prentice-Hall.

Swan, K. (2002). Building learning communities in online courses: The importance of interaction. *Education Communication and Information*, *2*(1), 23–49. doi:10.1080/1463631022000005016

Swan, K. (2003). Learning effectiveness: What the research tells us. In J. Bourne & J. C. Moore (Eds.), *Elements of quality online education: Practice and direction* (pp. 13–45). Needham, MA: Sloan Consortium.

Swan, K., Garrison, D. R., & Richardson, J. C. (2009). A constructivist approach to online learning: The Community of Inquiry framework. In C. R. Payne (Ed.), *Information technology and constructivism in higher education: Progressive learning frameworks* (pp. 43–57). Hershey, PA: IGI Global. doi:10.4018/978-1-60566-654-9.ch004

Swan, K., & Shea, P. (2005). The development of virtual learning communities. In S. R. Hiltz & R. Goldman (Eds.), *Asynchronous Learning Networks: The Research Frontier* (pp. 239–260). New York, NY: Hampton Press.

Swan, K., Shea, P., Fredericksen, E., Pickett, A., Pelz, W., & Maher, G. (2000). Building knowledge building communities: Consistency, contact and communication in the virtual classroom. *Journal of Educational Computing Research*, *23*(4), 389–413. doi:10.2190/W4G6-HY52-57P1-PPNE

Swan, M. (1985). A critical look at the communicative approach. *ELT Journal*, *39*(2), 76–87. doi:10.1093/elt/39.2.76

Sykes, J. M., & Holden, C. L. (2011). Communities: Exploring digital games and social networking. In N. Arnold & L. Ducate (Eds.), Present and future promises of CALL: From theory and research to new directions in language teaching (pp. 311–336). San Marcos, TX: Computer Assisted Language Instruction Consortium (CALICO).

Sykes, J., & Reinhardt, J. (2012). *Language at play: Digital games in second and foreign language teaching and learning*. Boston, MA: Pearson Education.

Sylvén, L. K., & Sundqvist, P. (2012). Gaming as extramural English L2 learning and L2 proficiency among young learners. *ReCALL*, *24*(03), 302–321. doi:10.1017/S095834401200016X

Syncox, D. (2003). *The effects of audio-taped feedback on ESL graduate student writing*. Available from ProQuest Digital Dissertations Database. (AAT EC53307)

Tabatabaei, O. (2012). The effect of computer-assisted language learning (CALL) on learning idiomatic expressions: A case of Iranian EFL students. *Language, Culture, and Translation*, *1*(1), 119–137.

Talbert, R. (2016). *How much research has been done on flipped learning?* [Web log post]. Retrieved from http://rtalbert.org/blog/2016/how-much-research

Talebinezhad, M. R., & Abarghoui, M. A. (2013). The Iranian high school students attitude toward CALL and the use of CALL for EFL receptive skills. *Theory and Practice in Language Studies*, *3*(2), 329–337. doi:10.4304/tpls.3.2.329-337

Talmy, S. (2008). The cultural productions of the ESL student at Tradewinds High: Contingency, multidirectionality, and identity in L2 socialization. *Applied Linguistics*, *29*(4), 619–644. doi:10.1093/applin/amn011

Tamim, R. M. (2013). Teachers use of YouTube in the United Arab Emirates: An exploratory study. *Computers in the Schools*, *30*(4), 329–345. doi:10.1080/07380569.2013.844641

Tan, E., & Pearce, N. (2011). Open education videos in the classroom: Exploring the opportunities and barriers to the use of YouTube in teaching introductory sociology. *Research in Learning Technology*, *19*(sup1), 128–137. doi:10.3402/rlt.v19s1/7783

Tan, L., Wigglesworth, G., & Storch, N. (2010). Pair interaction and mode of communication: Comparing face-to-face and computer mediated communication. *Australian Review of Applied Linguistics*, *33*(3), 1–27. doi:10.2104/aral1027

Tanner, B. (1964). Teacher to disc to student. *English Journal*, *53*(5), 362–363. doi:10.2307/810191

Tan, T., & Liu, T. (2004). The mobile-based interactive learning environment (MOBILE) and a case study for assisting elementary school English learning. *IEEE International Conference on Advanced Learning Technologies*, 530-534.

Taylor, L., & Parsons, J. (2011). Improving student engagement. *Current Issues in Education*, *14*(1), 1–32.

The science of language, community, and MMORPGs. (2014). Retrieved December 16, 2015, from http://www.engadget.com/2014/10/13/the-science-of-language-community-and-mmorpgs/

The State of Hawaii. (2016). *Detailed languages spoken at home in the state of Hawaii.* Retrieved from http://files.hawaii.gov/dbedt/census/acs/Report/Detailed_Language_March2016.pdf

The Travelers and the Sea. (1919). *Aesopica: Aesop's fables in English, Latin and Greek* [image]. Retrieved November 22, 2016, from https://i.ytimg.com/vi/SL2ifIi_EwY/maxresdefault.jpg

Thomas, M., Reinders, H., & Warschauer, M. (Eds.). (2013). *Contemporary computer assisted language learning.* London: Bloomsbury.

Thompson, K. (2011). *6 shocking affordable sci-fi inventions.* Retrieved November 22, 2016, from http://www.cracked.com/article_19368_6-shockingly-affordable-sci-fi-inventions.html

Thoms, J. J. (2012). Analyzing linguistics outcomes of second language learners: Hybrid versus traditional course contexts. In F. Rubio & J. J. Thoms (Eds.), *Hybrid language learning and teaching: Exploring theoretical, pedagogical and curricular issues* (pp. 177–195). Boston, MA: Heinle/Cengage Learning.

Thonus, T. (2004). What are the differences? Tutor interactions with first- and second-language writers. *Journal of Second Language Writing*, *13*(3), 227–242. doi:10.1016/j.jslw.2004.04.012

Thorne, S. L. (2003). Artifacts and culture-of-use in intercultural communication. *Language Learning & Technology*, *7*(2), 38–67.

Thorne, S. L. (2008). Transcultural communication in open Internet environments and massively multiplayer online games. In S. Magnan (Ed.), *Mediating discourse online* (pp. 305–327). Amsterdam: Benjamins; doi:10.1075/aals.3.17tho

Thorne, S. L., Black, R. W., & Sykes, J. M. (2009). Second language use, socialization, and learning in Internet interest communities and online gaming. *Modern Language Journal*, *93*(s1), 802–821. doi:10.1111/j.1540-4781.2009.00974.x

Tour, E. (2015). Digital mindsets: Teachers' technology use in personal life and teaching. *Language Learning & Technology*, *19*(3), 124–139. Retrieved from http://llt.msu.edu/issues/october2015/tour.pdf

Trice, A. G. (2001). *Faculty perceptions of graduate international students: The benefits and challenges*. Paper presented at the 26th Annual Meeting of the Association for the Study of Higher Education, Richmond, VA. (ERIC Document Reproduction Service No. ED 457 816)

Trim, J. (1979). The integration of elements in multi-media language learning systems. In *The Use of Media in English Language Teaching* (pp. 8–14). London: The British Council Printing and Publishing Department.

Truscott, J. (1996). The case against grammar correction in L2 writing class. *Language Learning*, *46*(2), 327–369. doi:10.1111/j.1467-1770.1996.tb01238.x

Tsutsui, M. (2004). Multimedia as a means to enhance feedback. *Computer Assisted Language Learning*, *17*(3-4), 377–402. doi:10.1080/0958822042000319638

Turner, K. C. N. (2011). Rap universal: Using multimodal media production to develop ICT literacies. *Journal of Adolescent & Adult Literacy*, *54*(8), 613–623. doi:10.1598/JAAL.54.8.6

Tuzi, F. (2004). The impact of e-feedback on the revisions of L2 writers in an academic writing course. *Computers and Composition*, *21*(2), 217–235. doi:10.1016/j.compcom.2004.02.003

Tuzlukova, V., & Hall, A. (2017). A virtual professional development model: Bringing innovation to language teaching practice. *Journal of Teaching English for Specific and Academic Purposes*, *4*(3), 603–614.

U. S. Census. (2016). *Population demographics for Hawaii 2017 and 2016*. Retrieved from https://suburbanstats.org/population/how-many-people-live-in-hawaii

Valdés, G., & Figueroa, R. A. (1994). *Bilingualism and testing: A special case of bias*. Westport, CT: Ablex Publishing.

Valsiner, J., & van der Veer, R. (2000). *The Social Mind. Construction of the Idea*. Cambridge, UK: Cambridge University Press.

Van Lancker Sidtis, D. (2003). Auditory recognition of idioms by native and nonnative speakers of English: It takes one to know one. *Applied Linguistics*, *24*(1), 45–57. doi:10.1017/S0142716403000031

van Lier, L. (2004). The semiotics and ecology of language learning: Perception, voice, identity and democracy. *Utbuilding & Demokrati*, *3*, 79–103.

van Manen, M. (1983). Editorial. Invitation to Phenomenology + Pedagogy. *Phenomenology + Pedagogy*, *1*(1), i–ii.

van Manen, M. (2008). Pedagogical sensitivity and teachers practical knowing-in-action. *Peking University Educational Review*, *6*(1), 1–23.

Varonis, E. M., & Gass, S. (1985). Non-native/ non-native conversations: A model for negotiation of meaning. *Applied Linguistics*, *6*(1), 71–90. doi:10.1093/applin/6.1.71

Vasiljevic, Z. (2015). Teaching and learning idioms in L2: From theory to practice. *MEXTESOL Journal*, *39*(4), 1–24.

Vasudevan, L. M. (2006). Looking for angels: Knowing adolescents by engaging with their multimodal literacy practices. *Journal of Adolescent & Adult Literacy*, *50*(4), 252–256. doi:10.1598/JAAL.50.4.1

Verbeek, P.-P. (2001). Don Ihde: The technological lifeworld. In H. Achterhuis (Ed.), *American philosophy of technology: The empirical turn* (pp. 119–146). Bloomington, IN: Indiana University Press.

Verbeek, P.-P. (2006). Materializing morality: Design ethics and technological mediation. *Science, Technology & Human Values*, *31*(3), 361–380. doi:10.1177/0162243905285847

Verspoor, M., & Lowie, W. (2003). Making sense of polysemous words. *Language Learning*, *53*(3), 547–587. doi:10.1111/1467-9922.00234

Vespignani, F., Canal, P., Molinaro, N., Fonda, S., & Cacciari, C. (2010). Predictive mechanisms in idiom comprehension. *Journal of Cognitive Neuroscience*, *22*(8), 1682–1700. doi:10.1162/jocn.2009.21293 PMID:19580384

Vinogradova, P., Linville, H. A., & Bickel, B. (2011). Listen to my story and you will know me: Digital stories as student-centered collaborative projects. *TESOL Journal*, *2*(2), 173–202. doi:10.5054/tj.2011.250380

Vygotsky, L. S. (1978). *Mind and society: The development of higher mental processes.* Cambridge, MA: Harvard University Press.

Vygotsky, L. S. (1978). *Mind and society: The development of higher psychological processes.* Cambridge, MA: Harvard University Press.

Vygotsky, L. S. (1978). *Mind in society.* Cambridge, MA: Harvard University Press.

Vygotsky, L. S. (1978). *Mind in society: The development of higher psychological processes.* Cambridge, MA: Harvard University Press.

Vygotsky, L. S. (1997). The collected works of L.S. Vygotsky: Vol. 3. *Problems of the theory and history of psychology.* New York, NY: Plenum.

Walsh, C., Power, T., Khatoon, M., Biswas, S., Paul, A., Sarkar, B., & Griffiths, M. (2013). The trainer in your pocket: Mobile phones within a teacher continuing professional development program in Bangladesh. *Professional Development in Education*, *39*(2), 186–200. doi:10.1080/19415257.2013.766232

Wang, L. (2005). The advantages of using technology in second language education: Technology integration in foreign language teaching demonstrates the shift from a behavioral to a constructivist learning approach. *Technological Horizons in Education Journal*, *32*(10), 39–42.

Wang, S., & Vásquez, C. (2012). Web 2.0 and second language learning: What does the research tell us? *CALICO Journal*, *29*(3), 412–430. doi:10.11139/cj.29.3.412-430

Wang, X., Kim, M. J., Love, P. E. D., & Kang, S. C. (2013). Augmented reality in built environment: Classification and implications for future research. *Automation in Construction*, *32*, 1–13. doi:10.1016/j.autcon.2012.11.021

Wang, Y. (2014). Using wikis to facilitate interaction and collaboration among EFL learners: A social constructivist approach to language teaching. *System*, *42*, 383–390. doi:10.1016/j.system.2014.01.007

Wang, Y. (2015). Promoting collaborative writing through wikis: A new approach for advancing innovative and active learning in an ESP context. *Computer Assisted Language Learning*, *28*(6), 499–512. doi:10.1080/09588221.2014.881386

Ward, W. C., & Bennett, R. E. (Eds.). (2012). *Construction versus choice in cognitive measurement: Issues in constructed response, performance testing, and portfolio assessment*. New York, NY: Routledge.

Ware, P. (2005). "Missed" communication in online communication: Tensions in a German-American telecollaboration. *Language Learning & Technology*, *9*(2), 64–89.

Ware, P. D., & Warschauer, M. (2006). Electronic feedback and second language writing. In K. Hyland & F. Hyland (Eds.), *Feedback in second language writing: Contexts and issues* (pp. 105–122). Cambridge, UK: Cambridge University Press. doi:10.1017/CBO9781139524742.008

Ware, P., & Kessler, G. (2013). CALL and digital feedback. In M. T. Reinders & M. Warschauer (Eds.), *Computer-assisted language learning* (pp. 323–339). London, UK: Bloomsbury.

Warschauer, M. (1998). Researching technology in TESOL: Determinist, instrumental, and critical approaches. *TESOL Quarterly*, *32*(4), 757–761. doi:10.2307/3588010

Warschauer, M. (2000). Online learnings in a second language classroom. An ethnographic study. In M. Warschauer & R. Kern (Eds.), *Network-based language teaching: Concept ad practice* (pp. 41–58). Cambridge, UK: Cambridge University Press. doi:10.1017/CBO9781139524735.005

Warschauer, M. (2005). Foreword. In E. A. Macia, A. S. Cervera, & C. R. Ramos (Eds.), *Information technology in languages for specific purposes: Issues and prospects* (pp. xiii–xv). New York, NY: Springer; doi:10.1007/978-0-387-28624-2

Warschauer, M., & Healey, D. (1998). Computers and language learning: An overview. *Language Teaching*, *31*(2), 57–71. doi:10.1017/S0261444800012970

Watanabe, Y. (2008). Peer-peer interaction between L2 learners of different proficiency levels: Their interactions and reflections. *Canadian Modern Language Review*, *64*(4), 605–663. doi:10.3138/cmlr.64.4.605

Webb, M., & Doman, E. (2016). Does the flipped classroom lead to increased gains on learning outcomes in ESL/EFL contexts? *The CATESOL Journal*, *28*(1), 39–59.

Webb, M., Doman, E., & Pusey, K. (2014). Flipping a Chinese university EFL course: What students and teachers think of the model. *The Journal of Asia TEFL*, *11*(4), 53–87.

Weigle, S. (2002). *Assessing writing*. Cambridge, UK: Cambridge University Press; doi:10.1017/CBO9780511732997

Wenger, E. (2006). *Communities of practice: Learning, meaning, and identity*. Cambridge, UK: Cambridge University Press.

Wertsch, J. V. (1998). *Mind as action*. New York, NY: Oxford University Press.

White, C. (2014). The distance learning of foreign languages: A research agenda. *Language Teaching*, *47*(4), 538–553. doi:10.1017/S0261444814000196

Whittaker, C. (2013). A military blend. In B. Tomlinson & C. Whittaker (Eds.), *Blended learning in English language teaching: Course design and implementation* (pp. 175–183). London: British Council.

Wigglesworth, G., & Storch, N. (2012). What role for collaboration in writing and writing feedback. *Journal of Second Language Writing*, *21*(4), 364–374. doi:10.1016/j.jslw.2012.09.005

Wildner, S. (2000). Technology integration into preservice foreign language teacher education programs. *CALICO Journal*, *17*(2), 223–250.

Willis, J. R. (1996). *A framework for task-based learning*. Harlow, UK: Longman Publishing.

Wiseman, C. S., & Belknap, J. P. (2013). Wikis: A knowledge platform for collaborative learning in ESL reading. *TESOL Journal*, *4*(2), 360–369. doi:10.1002/tesj.83

Wong, L.-H., Chin, C.-K., Tan, C.-L., & Liu, M. (2010). Students' personal and social meaning making in a Chinese idiom mobile learning environment. *Journal of Educational Technology & Society*, *13*(4), 15–26.

Wong, L.-H., & Looi, C.-K. (2010). Vocabulary learning by mobile-assisted authentic content creation and social meaning-making: Two case studies. *Journal of Computer Assisted Learning*, *26*(5), 421–433. doi:10.1111/j.1365-2729.2010.00357.x

Woo, M. M., Chu, S. K. W., & Li, X. (2013). Peer-feedback and revision process in a wiki mediated collaborative writing. *Educational Technology Research and Development*, *61*(2), 279–309. doi:10.1007/s11423-012-9285-y

Wray, A. (2000). Formulaic sequences in second language teaching: Principle and practice. *Applied Linguistics*, *21*(4), 463–489. doi:10.1093/applin/21.4.463

Wray, A., & Perkins, M. R. (2000). The functions of formulaic language: An integrated model. *Language & Communication*, *20*(1), 1–28. doi:10.1016/S0271-5309(99)00015-4

Wu, H. K., Lee, S. W. Y., Chang, H. Y., & Liang, J. C. (2013). Current status, opportunities and challenges of augmented reality in education. *Computers & Education*, *62*, 41–49. doi:10.1016/j.compedu.2012.10.024

Xiao, R. Z. (2008). Theory-driven corpus research: Using corpora to inform aspect theory. In Corpus linguistics: An international handbook. Berlin, Germany: Mouton de Gruyter.

Yancey, K. (2009). Reflection and electronic portfolios: Inventing the self and reinventing the university. In D. Cambridge, B. Cambridge, & K. Yancey (Eds.), *Electronic portfolios 2.0* (pp. 5–16). Sterling, VA: Stylus.

Yang, C., & Xie, Y. (2013). Learning Chinese idioms through iPads. *Language Learning & Technology*, *17*(2), 12–23.

Yang, S.-H. (2016). Conceptualizing effective feedback practice through an online community of inquiry. *Computers & Education*, *94*, 162–177. doi:10.1016/j.compedu.2015.10.023

Yin, R. K. (2013). *Case study research: Design and methods* (5th ed.). Thousand Oaks, CA: Sage Publications.

Youngs, B., Ducate, L., & Arnold, N. (2011). Linking second language acquisition, CALL, and language pedagogy. In N. Arnold & L. Ducate (Eds.), *Present and future promises of CALL: From theory and research to new directions in language teaching* (pp. 23–60). San Marcos, TX: CALICO.

Yun, J. (2011). The effects of hypertext glosses on L2 vocabulary acquisition: A meta-analysis. *Computer Assisted Language Learning*, *24*(1), 39–58. doi:10.1080/09588221.2010.523285

Yu, S., & Lee, I. (2016). Peer feedback in second language writing (20052014). *Language Teaching*, *49*(4), 461–493. doi:10.1017/S0261444816000161

Zaini, A., & Mazdayanasna, G. (2015). The impact of computer-based instruction on the development of EFL learners writing skills. *Journal of Computer Assisted Learning*, *31*(6), 516–528. doi:10.1111/jcal.12100

Zainuddin, Z. (2017). First-year college students experiences in the EFL flipped classroom: A case study in Indonesia. *International Journal of Instruction*, *10*(1), 133–150. doi:10.12973/iji.2017.1019a

Zamel, V. (1985). Responding to student writing. *TESOL Quarterly*, *19*(1), 79–101. doi:10.2307/3586773

Zhan, C. (2016). The importance of culture factor in foreign language teaching. *Theory and Practice in Language Studies*, *6*(3), 581–586. doi:10.17507/tpls.0603.17

Zhang, Z., & Kenny, R. (2010). Learning in an online distance education course: Experiences of three international students. *The International Review of Research in Open and Distance Learning*, *11*(1). Retrieved March 14, 2017, from http://www.irrodl.org/index.php/irrodl/rt/printerFriendly/775/1481

Zhao, N., & McDougall, D. (2008). Cultural influences on Chinese students' asynchronous online learning in a Canadian university. *Journal of Distance Education*, *22*(2), 59–80.

Zhao, Y. (2003). Recent developments in technology and language learning: A literature review and meta-analysis. *CALICO Journal*, *21*(1), 7–27.

Zhou, A. (2009). What adult ESL learners say about improving grammar and vocabulary in their writing for academic purposes. *Language Awareness*, *18*(1), 31–46. doi:10.1080/09658410802307923

Zubizarreta, J. (2009). *The learning portfolio: Reflective practice for improving student learning*. San Francisco, CA: Jossey-Bass.

Zuengler, J., & Cole, K. (2005). Language socialization and second language learning. In E. Hinkel (Ed.), *Handbook of research in second language teaching and learning* (pp. 301–316). Mahwah, NJ: Lawrence Erlbaum.

Zuengler, J., & Miller, E. R. (2006). Cognitive and sociocultural perspectives: Two parallel SLA worlds? *TESOL Quarterly*, *40*(1), 35–58. doi:10.2307/40264510

Zúñiga, V. (2012). Migration de retour. Un regard quantitatif sur les enfants arrivant au Mexique en provenance des États-Unis. *Hommes et migrations. Revue française de référence sur les dynamiques migratoires, 1296*, 88-98.

Zúñiga, V., & Hamann, E. T. (2006). Going home? Schooling in Mexico of transnational children. *CONfines (México)*, *4*, 41–57.

Zúñiga, V., & Hamann, E. T. (2015). Going to a home you have never been to: The return migration of Mexican and American-Mexican children. *Childrens Geographies*, *13*(6), 643–655. doi:10.1080/14733285.2014.936364

Zúñiga, V., & Vivas Romero, M. (2014). Divided families, fractured schooling. In *Mexico: educational consequences of children exposition to international migration (No. 4)*. Centre d'Études Mexicaines et Centraméricaines.

# About the Contributors

**James Perren** is an associate professor in the TESOL Program at Alliant International University. James earned his Doctorate in Education in the Department of Curriculum, Instruction, and Technology in Education at Temple University (Philadelphia, Pennsylvania and Osaka, Japan). Dr. James Perren holds both BA: Spanish and an MA: TESOL Degrees from San José State University in California. His interdisciplinary scholarship has examined CALL in TESOL, service-learning in applied linguistics, materials development, teacher training, intercultural communication, and critical SLA theory. He has published an edited collection on service-learning in TESOL, refereed book chapters on CALL, peer-reviewed journal articles, contributions to TESOL publications, and TESOL affiliate newsletter articles.

**Ken Kelch** is associate professor and system-wide director of TESOL at Alliant International University. He received his doctorate in TESOL from Alliant and his master's degree from the University of Hawaii. He was instrumental in the development of an online TESOL master's program and a California K-12 teacher credential program in teaching English learners, of which he is also the director. His areas of specialization are curriculum development, research methods, and qualitative research, as well as supervising and guiding doctoral candidates through the dissertation process.

**Jin-suk Byun** is an assistant professor in the TESOL program at Alliant International University. He graduated with a Ph.D. in Linguistics with a focus on second language acquisition (SLA) from the University of Illinois at Urbana-Champaign after he received his two MA's in Teaching English as a Second Language (TESL) and in linguistics from the same university. He taught various groups of English Language Learners and Korean language learners as well as TESOL master and doctoral students. He also worked as an ESOL coordinator in a preservice teacher education program and developed various TESL/TEFL certificate and master programs. His research interests include input, interaction, output, and automaticity in SLA, and the development of TESOL/TEFL programs.

**Seth E. Cervantes** is an adjunct professor at the California School of Education, Alliant International University. He is also an English instructor at UC San Diego Extension, English Language Institute, and a graduate student in Alliant's TESOL doctorate program. He has taught in both EFL and ESL settings since 1999, and has been an editor of the Eurasia Border Review.

**Setareh Safavi** is pursuing a doctoral education in TESOL and has research interests in accent and pronuncation related pedagogy and research, identity and sociocutural theory, and the benefits of music in second language education.

* * *

**Sardar M. Anwaruddin** is a postdoctoral fellow in the Faculty of Education of St. Francis Xavier University in Nova Scotia, Canada. He is also an instructor at York University English Language Institute in Toronto, Canada.

**Hyesun Cho** is an associate professor of TESOL in the Department of Curriculum and Teaching at the University of Kansas. She has published research in Race, Ethnicity, and Education, Computers and Education, Curriculum Inquiry, Language and Education, and TESOL Journal. Her research interests include social identity, critical literacy, heritage language education, and multiliteracies.

**MaryAnn Christison** is a professor in the Department of Linguistics and the Urban Institute for Teacher Education at the University of Utah in Salt Lake City, Utah, USA. She has a long history as an English language teacher, teacher educator, and language program administrator, having been the founding Director of the International Center and the Teaching Second and Foreign Languages (TSFL) Program at Snow College for 20 years and having worked in both K-12 contexts and in adult education. For seven years, she served on the Board of Directors of TESOL international association, including a term as President in 1997-1998, and as a chair and co-chair for three TESOL conventions—1991 in New York City, 1995 in Long Beach, and 2002 in Salt Lake City. In 2012, she received the James E. Alatis Award from TESOL International Association for distinguished service to the profession, and in 2016 as part of TESOL's 50th anniversary, she was recognized with a "TESOL 50@50 Award," an award given to 50 TESOLers who have made a significant contribution to the TESOL profession through teaching, research, and leadership. She is on the Board of Trustees for The International Research Foundation (TIRF), serving as Chair of the Research Advisory Committee. Dr. Christison's current research interests include content and language integrated learning, language teacher education, OLTE, teacher cognition, leadership in language education, and language and the brain. She has published over 100 articles in refereed journals and chapters in books and is an author, co-author, and co-editor of more than 20 books. As a second language teacher educator, she has trained English language teachers in over 35 countries.

**Luciana C. de Oliveira**, Ph.D., is Chair and Associate Professor in the Department of Teaching and Learning at the University of Miami, Florida. Her research focuses on issues related to teaching English language learners (ELLs) at the K-12 level, including the role of language in learning the content areas, second language writing, and teacher preparation for ELLs. Her work has appeared in Teachers College Record, Journal of Teacher Education, Journal of English for Specific Purposes, English Education, Multicultural Education, The History Teacher, and other books and journals. She is the editor (with Tony Silva) of L2 Writing in Secondary Classrooms: Academic Issues, Student Experiences, and Teacher Education (Routledge, 2013) and Second Language Writing in Elementary Classrooms: Instructional Issues, Content-Area Writing and Teacher Education (Palgrave MacMillan, 2016) and has several other authored, co-authored, edited, and co-edited books.

**Hanh Dinh** is from Vietnam and is currently a PhD student in Curriculum and Instruction at the University of Albany. She is also a test-preparation and ESL instructor in Manhattan, New York. She has earned her Master Degree in TESOL (Teaching English to Speakers of Other Languages) at Murray State University. She earned a Bachelor's degree in TESOL and has been teaching English for more than 5 years in both Vietnam and America. Her interests focus on the blended curriculum development and the impact of technology on English teaching.

**Daniel Dixon** is an Academic Instructor at the University of Utah Asia Campus in South Korea. He teaches academic writing courses to undergraduate students. He completed his MA in Applied Linguistics at the University of Utah. In 2014, before coming to South Korea, he received a Fulbright ETA scholarship to teach in Brazil at the Universidade Federal de Mato Grosso.

**Tülay Dixon** is a faculty member at the University of Utah Asia Campus, where she teaches writing and rhetoric courses. Her research focuses on course and curriculum development, technology integrated language teaching, teaching of pragmatics, and corpus approaches in language and writing classes.

**Sally Durand** has a Master's degree in TESOL from the University of Illinois at Chicago where she is currently pursuing a doctorate in Literacy, Language and Culture. She has taught language learners for over 6 years in the USA (ESL) and abroad (EFL). Her research interests are in corpus linguistics, vocabulary acquisition and learning through multiple modalities.

**Monica Jackson** is an adjunct professor and doctoral student at Alliant International University. Her field of study is Teaching English to Speakers of Other Languages (TESOL). Her interest is in using innovative materials and engaging curriculum that will help build intrinsic motivation in English as a Second Language (ESL) students. Her hope is to create a long-lasting desire for learning.

**Kris Johnston** is an ESL teacher, teacher educator and a PhD candidate at York University. His focus is on web-based language learning and teaching, as well as the research and development of online educational technologies.

**Ilka Kostka**, PhD, is an assistant teaching professor in the American Classroom and Global Pathways Programs at Northeastern University where she teaches reading and writing courses to English language learners. Her areas of scholarly interest include second language academic writing, flipped learning, and technology. She is the managing editor of SLW News, the official newsletter of the Second Language Writing Interest Section of TESOL International Association, and serves on the Editorial Review Board of TESOL Journal.

**Geoff Lawrence** is a teacher educator, researcher and curriculum designer interested in exploring the potential of online, blended and classroom-based second language teaching and teacher education programs. His research examines online/blended language teaching methodology, teacher beliefs towards educational innovation, identity and intercultural learning in language and teacher education.

**Nhu Le** is from Vietnam and is currently a PhD student majoring in Technology in Education and Second Language Acquisition at University of South Florida. Her interests include CALL, MALL, Virtual Learning Environments (VLEs), Educational Open Resources (EORs) and Digital Literacy. She presented various research and pedagogical projects at national and international conferences including International TESOL, Kentucky TESOL, CamTESOL and Ho Chi Minh City TESOL.

**Soo Min Lee** is a doctoral student in TESOL at Alliant International University, and has experience in teaching both IEP and credit ESL. Her research interests mainly lie in teaching L2 reading & writing, corrective feedback, SLA, and identity of international speakers of English in the field of TESOL.

**John I. Liontas** is an associate professor of foreign languages, English for speakers of other languages (ESOL), and technology in education and second language acquisition (TESLA), and director and faculty of the TESLA doctoral program at the University of South Florida. He has over 30 years of K-16+ teaching experience and research in the United States and other countries. He has a long-standing interest in idiomaticity and in its application in the second and foreign language classroom. He is presently involved in the design and production of a multimedia computer software program for learning English idioms called It's All Greek to Me! Learning English Idioms in Context.

**Helaine W. Marshall**, Ph.D., is professor of education at LIU Hudson and director of language education programs. She teaches courses in linguistics, second language acquisition, TESOL methodology, and multicultural education in face-to-face, blended and online formats. Her research interests include culturally responsive teaching, nontraditional approaches to the teaching of grammar, and uses of instructional technology in language teaching, particularly the flipped learning approach. She is the author of two books with University of Michigan Press and numerous journal articles. Dr. Marshall serves on the boards of the NYS TESOL Journal and the Flipped Learning Network.

**Lorena Mihăeş** has taught English for Specific Purposes at the University of Bucharest since 2014. She holds a BA in English and French, an MA in Literary Translation, and a PhD in Philology, all from the same university, the Faculty of Foreign Languages and Literatures. Her PhD thesis dwells on narrative unreliability in the novels of Kazuo Ishiguro. A revised version of it was published in 2014 (Kazuo Ishiguro' Fiction. A Perspective on Narrative Unreliability). She has translated several fictional books from English for various publishing houses. Her interests include pragmatics, stylistics, cognitive studies, translation studies and, more recently, blended learning in higher education.

**Amirhossein Monfared** has taught in EFL/ESL settings for over 15 years. He has been a phonetics lecturer and his MATESOL thesis was on oral dialogue journals for teaching pronunciation. He was accepted in a TESOL doctoral program at Alliant University, California School of Education, in San Diego and graduated with an award for outstanding doctor of education in 2016. His area of research is instructed second language acquisition including isolated and integrated form-focused instruction and teachers' cognition. He is also interested in the utilization of technology for teaching all English skill areas. Dr. Monfared has developed curriculum and assessment for TESOL certificate program and presented at regional and state professional workshops as well as TESOL international convention and AAAL.

**Sri Rejeki Murtiningsih**, also known as Jackie, received her masters in education from Flinders University of South Australia. After receiving her Ph. D in education from the University of Oklahoma, Jackie started teaching in the English Education Department at Universitas Muhammadiyah Yogyakarta, Indonesia. Her research interests include teaching ESL/EFL reading and writing, reflective practice, and curriculum development.

**Larisa Olesova**, Ph.D., is an instructional designer and adjunct professor specializing in distance education at George Mason University. Her research focuses on the effectiveness of instructional strategies in online learning environments.

**Steve Daniel Przymus** is an Assistant Professor of Bilingual Education at Texas Christian University. Steve's experiences as a U.S. Peace Corps Volunteer, Fulbright Distinguished Awards in Teaching Grantee, and U.S. public school teacher have driven his passion for developing and promoting multimodal/multilingual pedagogies that recognize individuals' full semiotic repertoires and educational life histories.

**Fitria Rahmawati** currently teaches at English Education Department of Universitas Muhammadiyah Yogyakarta (UMY), Indonesia. Her teaching areas include Academic Reading and Writing, Reading and Writing for Career Development, Academic Presentation, Digital Technology in Education, and Research Methodology. Additionaly, her current research interests are Technology in Language Learning, Teaching Strategies and Media in Writing Skills, and Teaching Practice Implementation.

**Alejandro (Alex) Romo Smith** is a former English Language Learner, first in his family to graduate college (Bachelors Degree in Global Health with an emphasis in Public Health and Spanish from the University of Arizona), and an avid gamer and game platform designer. Alex currently lives in Japan and is an Assistant Language Teacher of English for the Japan Exchange and Teaching (JET) Program.

**Dong-shin Shin** is an assistant professor in the Literacy and Second Language Studies Program at the University of Cincinnati. She is working with K-12 teachers in graduate courses. Her research interests include digital literacies for L2 academic literacy development, computer-mediated communication, systemic functional linguistics, multimodal writing, and language teacher development. Her work has appeared in Language Learning & Technology, Language and Education, Computers and Composition, the CALICO Journal, Journal of International and Intercultural Communication, and The Urban Review among others.

# Index

# F



# G



# H



# I



# L



# M



# N



# O

## P



## Q



## R



## S



## T



## U



## V



## W



## Y



## Z

www.ingramcontent.com/pod-product-compliance
Lightning Source LLC
LaVergne TN
LVHW062120300926
849161LV00010B/2498